READING SAUSSURE

READING SAUSSURE

A critical commentary on
the *Cours de linguistique générale*

ROY HARRIS

Professor of General Linguistics
in the University of Oxford

Open  Court

La Salle, Illinois

Published by arrangement with Gerald Duckworth and Co., Ltd., London.

First printing 1987
Second printing 1991

Printed and bound in the United States of America.

Library of Congress Cataloging-in-Publication Data

Harris, Roy, 1931–
    Reading Saussure.

    Bibliography: p.
    Includes index.
    1. Saussure, Ferdinand de, 1857–1913. Cours de linguistique générale. 2. Linguistics. I. Title.
P121.S369H37   1987   410   87-11101
ISBN 0-8126-9049-4
ISBN 0-8126-9050-8 (pbk.)

Contents

Preface

... quoi que je n'aie pas de plus cher vœu que de ne pas avoir à m'occuper de la langue en général.

Cela finira malgré moi par un livre ...

... although I have no dearer wish than not to have to concern myself with language in general.

It will come to a book in the end, in spite of my reluctance ...

– F. de Saussure, letter to A. Meillet, 4.1.94.

History was to prove Saussure right. It produced, *malgré lui* and twenty-two years later, a book: the *Cours de linguistique générale*. Evidently, Saussure had not tried hard enough to prevent that reluctant consummation. His ultimate trump cards (premature decease; fragmentary notes; failure to leave a manuscript) were blandly overtrumped by his pupils and colleagues. It took them barely more than a couple of years to bring out the book that Saussure had managed to avoid writing for the previous twenty.

What Bally and Sechehaye published in 1916 can certainly be read. But *Reading Saussure* might perhaps be regarded as a controversial title for a study of a book which Saussure never wrote. In one sense, we can no more read the Saussure who was the founder of Saussurean linguistics than we can read the Socrates who was the founder of Socratic philosophy. Our access to Saussure's ideas through reading the *Cours de linguistique générale* is indeed comparable to our access to the ideas of Socrates through reading the Platonic dialogues. Inevitably, all we can read on the page is a second-hand account of what a particular thinker is represented as having said, or as likely to have meant. Saussure and Socrates are classic examples of our cultural reliance on written reports, and even on reports which take the form of imaginative reconstructions. Such reports are, for obvious reasons, wide open to the charge of 'misrepresentation'; but, ironically, the more influential the thinker the less relevant the charge of misrepresentation becomes.

It is a measure of their importance that the possibility of misrepresentation hardly matters in either Saussure's case or that of Socrates. Just as 'Socratic' ideas reached a far wider public through Plato's written reconstruction of them (however misguided) than could ever have been the case otherwise, so more people assimilated 'Saussurean' ideas by reading the *Cours* than ever attended Saussure's lectures or asked him questions about points of linguistic theory. (It may come as something of a shock today to realize that none of Saussure's three courses at Geneva was attended by more than a handful of students.) As readers, we have no option but to read the Saussure who is presented as the author of the *Cours*, unless we renounce all possibility of investigating the source of some of the most basic notions current in contemporary discussions of language. It is not that nothing readable at all survives from the hand of Saussure: but this does not differentiate the Socratic from the Saussurean problem. For there is no doubt that the formative influence was exercised not by Saussure in person but by the text which his editors published after his death.

A quarter of a century after the appearance of the *Cours*, one of its editors wrote:

> Even if Ferdinand de Saussure's *Cours de linguistique générale* were eventually to become entirely outdated, it would be destined to remain alive in the memory of linguistic science because of its powerful and productive influence at a certain point in the evolution of that science. (Sechehaye 1940:1)

A quarter of a century had given the editors ample time to realize that as far as most people were concerned 'reading Saussure' was to all intents and purposes reading their version of Saussure's teachings.

The question then is – and has been for many years – how to make sense of reading this Saussure who is the presumptive author of the *Cours*; not whether what we read is a correct or an incorrect account of 'what the real Saussure really meant'. For whatever that may have been is arguably irrecoverable anyway. As mere 'readers', we shall never know what Saussure actually 'said'. (But whether that puts us in a position of disadvantage or, on the contrary, of advantage as compared to his original hearers is debatable: for none of them heard it all.) At the very worst, the Saussure of the *Cours* is a literary – and literal – fabrication of his editors. So might Socrates, conceivably, be a fabrication of Plato's. But as far as modern linguistics is concerned, it would have been necessary, as Voltaire said of God, to invent him had he not existed. In the modern academic world a book demands an author. We cannot blame the editors of the *Cours* for supplying one. They – rightly – sensed that this mode of presentation would be infinitely more authoritative than any publication of the original students' notes.

Less wise than Plato, however, Saussure's editors – on their own initiative – raised the question of authenticity in the reader's mind. Will anyone, they publicly wondered, 'be able to distinguish between Saussure and our interpretation of Saussure?' ([11]) It is undoubtedly the silliest query executors of Saussure's linguistic testament could possibly have raised; particularly if the executors had already rejected the idea of quoting their source material *verbatim*, and were therefore offering the reader no alternative basis for forming a judgment. Plato was not given to silliness of this order (in part, doubtless, because it never fell to his intellectual lot to endure the nineteenth century).

More unfortunately still, a later generation of Saussureans belatedly took this question of authenticity seriously, and proposed to deal with it by comparing the published text of the *Cours* with the surviving manuscript notes. Textual Pelion was thus piled upon textual Ossa (to the dismay of linguistic historiographers and the delight of university examiners). To say this is not to deny the interest of knowing what Saussure's pupils made of his lectures. It is simply to acknowledge the irony of the fact that this approach to Saussurean linguistics validates at Saussure's expense the methods of philology versus the methods of semiology. That may be one way of 'reading Saussure'. But the present study proposes, on the contrary, a semiological reading of Saussure, as against a philological reading, wherever the two conflict.

For some scholars, it would seem, it is only a 'philological' approach to the text which has any value at all. At least one eminent commentator on Saussure has been charged outright with lacking the requisite *formation philologique* to undertake a competent exegesis of the *Cours* (Frei 1950). Evidently 'philological' standards are so high that very few would-be commentators can hope to escape whipping. The shortcomings of the present commentary in that respect will doubtless be judged to be severe, if not positively provocative. Why is the reader not constantly referred to what survives of Saussure's manuscript notes and to his students' notebooks in order to elucidate obscure or contentious points? One reply might be that those who are looking for that kind of philological apparatus already have it available in Engler's monumental critical edition: but that is not the relevant reason. The rejection of a 'philological' approach to the *Cours* in the present commentary is based on conviction that such an approach would be quite misleading. For anyone who is interested in the *Cours* as linguistic theory, the 'philological' questions that can be both asked and answered concerning the text are simply the wrong questions. Quite apart from the fact that it was the Saussure of the *Cours* and not the Saussure of the Geneva lectures who was responsible for the 'Copernican' revolution in linguistic thought, and quite apart from the fallacy that there is just one 'authentic' version of Saussure lurking somewhere behind the textual facade, waiting to be discovered, there are two considerations which combine to call in question whether a 'philological' study of the *Cours* can tell us anything of critical value. One is simply that it begs the question to suppose that the alleged 'sources' confirm or modify certain possible interpretations of the *Cours*: for the 'sources' stand in just as much need of interpretation as the *Cours* itself. The other consideration is that all the crucial theoretical problems are raised in the *Cours* in any case: the 'sources' do not add to that inventory. It is certainly interesting to have confirmation that Bally and Sechehaye did not in that crude sense 'miss anything out'; but it would be obviously rash to conclude that anything not in the 'sources' Bally and Sechehaye simply invented. In short, apart from failing to reveal omissions, the 'sources' leave us no wiser on any substantive critical issue. To suppose that subjecting them to a sufficiently rigorous 'philological' analysis would throw light on any point of theory is either to confuse theory with biography or else to demand of philology more than philology is capable of giving.

No attempt either is made in the following chapters to enter into the labyrinthine and unending controversy concerning 'influences' on Saussure, important as these issues may be for historians. Are the key concepts of the *Cours* to be viewed as deriving specifically from the work of Humboldt, or Paul, or Gabelentz, or Durkheim, or Whitney ...? Or were they, as Bloomfield brusquely claimed in his review of the book (Bloomfield 1923), just ideas which had been 'in the air' for a long time? There is a sense in which detailed answers to such questions could make a difference to one's reading of Saussure. But there is also a sense in which they need not matter a jot. Saussure, as it happens, provides an awkward test case for the claims of 'influential' historiography, inasmuch as the Saussurean influence on his successors was manifestly unrelated to the extent of their curiosity about the influence of Saussure's predecessors on Saussure. To acknowledge this is not to belittle the researches of historiographers. Nor is it to espouse an idealistic 'context-neutral' approach to reading the *Cours*. For it is always worth considering what is to be gained by comparing the ideas of one thinker with those of another working within the same (or some other) intellectual tradition. Saussure's case is no exception. It is, indeed, virtually impossible for intelligent readers not to place what they read within the context of some kind of 'history of ideas', however minimal. To that extent, the concept of historical contextualization is already implicit in the concept of reading. But the contextualization thus implied is of a quite different order from the historiographer's. The comparisons occasionally drawn between Saussurean ideas and those of other thinkers in the course of the present commentary are to be understood with this important distinction in mind. They are not intended as contributions to the history of linguistics.

It is therefore the reader's Saussure, the hypothetically reconstructable author of the *Cours*, who is the focus of attention and interpretation in the chapters that follow. This Saussure is neither complete fact nor complete fiction, neither an authority on the 'real' Saussure nor an authorial persona. Elusive as he may be, it is this author who drafted the Magna Carta of modern linguistics. He is also the author whom Bühler, Hjelmslev, Merleau-Ponty, Lévi-Strauss, Piaget and Derrida – to mention but a few – read: and their various readings of Saussure became part of the mainstream of twentieth-century thought.

Perhaps it will be objected that to proceed in this manner is to interpose 'between the image of Saussure and the man Saussure simply the ideological projection and the epistemological imperfections of two generations of linguists' (Calvet 1975: 54). The answer to this objection is that we have no alternative nowadays but to read Saussure through the academic spectacles provided by the subsequent history of Saussurean linguistics. The case is at least less desperate than that of Socrates, whom we read through the distorting lens of two thousand years of Western philosophy.

May it, alternatively, be objected that such an approach to reading Saussure simply conflates author and editors? This is not so. For a reader is still free to distinguish between the two roles whenever there is occasion to do so. The author is the presumptive source of ideas, terminology, arguments and examples: the editors are responsible for their arrangement and the construction of an articulated text. That distinction, contentious though it must inevitably be, is what makes possible the projection of different readings of Saussure, of which his editors have given us just theirs – albeit a consciously 'open' version. Only those readers who cling to the vain hope of uncovering some unique and 'authentic' version of Saussure will be unduly worried by the prospect. His editors clearly were not. Saussure, they tell us, was one of those thinkers for whom thinking is a constant process of intellectual renewal ([9]). They 'edited' Saussure in just that spirit; and that is one merit of their version which cannot be denied, however much later critics may carp. Sechehaye subsequently said of Saussure's lectures that Saussure thought aloud in front of his students, in order to make them think for themselves (Sechehaye 1940:2). Similarly, to read Saussure is to be invited to re-think Saussure, and it is precisely for this reason that Saussure on linguistic theory is far more worth reading today than many of his more 'advanced' successors.

Saussure had already become compulsory reading for linguists within five years of the publication of the *Cours*, which was widely reviewed (de Mauro 1972:366). What linguists read into Saussure is a different question. It was to become almost a commonplace of Saussurean exegesis to point out that even those who were originally most sympathetic and most directly influenced by Saussure (Meillet, for instance; de Mauro 1972:368) did not always seem to understand some of his basic ideas. That this should have been so, if it was so, is doubtless an indication of the difficulty which a generation brought up to accept the assumptions of nineteenth-century comparative and historical linguistics experienced in coming to terms with Saussurean structuralism. More eloquent still, perhaps, is what Jespersen says in 1922 in his much acclaimed book *Language, its Nature, Development and Origin.*

He lists the first edition of the *Cours* in his bibliography, but nevertheless begins by announcing: 'The distinctive feature of the science of language as conceived nowadays is its historical character' (Jespersen 1922:7). In the four chapters Jespersen gives to the 'History of Linguistic Science', Saussure is mentioned just once, and then simply in an alphabetical list of scholars who 'have dealt with the more general problems of linguistic change or linguistic theory' (Jespersen 1922:98). By 1925, however, Jespersen felt obliged to devote a substantial part of the opening chapter of his new book, *Mankind, Nation and Individual from a Linguistic Point of View*, to a criticism of Saussure's distinction between *langue* and *parole* (here misleadingly – but influentially – rendering those terms into English as 'language' and 'speech'). Why that distinction had been passed over in silence three years previously in *Language, its Nature, Development and Origin* Jespersen does not explain. It was not that in 1922 he had not yet read the *Cours*: for he had published a review of it in 1917.

Part of the answer is that Saussure the scholar had already established himself in the minds of his contemporaries in a quite different but less distinguished – and less threatening – role. As Calvet points out (Calvet 1975:16), the entry under *Saussure* in the 1923 edition of the *Larousse Universel* refers to his work of 'capital importance' on the primitive system of Indo-European vowels, but makes no mention at all of the *Cours de linguistique générale*. These attested cases of historical myopia go to reinforce the thesis that Saussure falls into that Shakespearian category of those who, retrospectively, 'have greatness thrust upon them'. This leads in turn to an academic reading of Saussure in which the author of the *Cours* was really a happy, orthodox historical comparativist, who suffered intermittently from an unfortunate neurosis about terminological distinctions. Or, to borrow Calvet's metaphor, Saussure appears as an intellectual Columbus who by accident discovered America while exploring in search of the Indies.

Another eloquent piece of evidence about academic readings of Saussure comes from Leonard Bloomfield's book *Language*, published a decade after Jespersen's. Here too Saussure is given a single passing mention (Bloomfield 1935:19) in an introductory chapter on the history of linguistics. At first sight, it might seem that, like Jespersen in 1922, Bloomfield had somehow failed to register the fact that the *Cours* was a major landmark in the development of the subject. This is not the case, however. Bloomfield too had published a previous review of the *Cours* (Bloomfield 1923). This review makes interesting reading. In it, Bloomfield begins by acknowledging Saussure's standing as the scholar who first faced the problems involved in constructing a comprehensive theory of language. Bloomfield says of Saussure, 'in lecturing on "general linguistics" he stood very nearly alone, for, strange as it may seem, the nineteenth century, which studied intensively the history of one family of languages, took little or no interest in general aspects of human speech.' Here, in effect, Bloomfield acknowledges Saussure as the founder of modern general linguistics, even though Bloomfield's earlier book *An Introduction to the Study of Language* had come out in 1914, thus preceding the original publication of the *Cours* by two years. Saussure, says Bloomfield, 'has here first mapped out the world in which historical Indo-European grammar (the great achievement of the past century) is merely a single province: he has given us the theoretical basis for a science of human speech.' But by the time he wrote *Language*, Bloomfield had changed his first estimate of Saussure's *Cours* and its significance.

The reason for the disparity between Bloomfield's eulogy of Saussure in 1923 and his virtual dismissal of Saussure ten years later is not difficult to explain. The Bloomfield of the 1923 review is Bloomfield in his pre-behaviourist period; and in his pre-behaviourist period Bloomfield was a follower of the psychologist Wundt. So the 1923 review gives us a reading of the *Cours* as viewed by an American Wundtian who was also a Germanic philologist of the traditional stamp (and a student of Amerindian languages as well). But ten years later Bloomfield had rejected Wundt in favour of Watson. His reading of Saussure had altered accordingly. Saussure was now read not as the adventurous founder of modern linguistics, but as a perpetuator of the endemic psychologism of late-nineteenth-century approaches to language. That later Bloomfieldian reading was to dictate the relationship between American and European versions of structuralism for the next quarter of a century.

A complementary but interestingly different Anglo-Saxon reading of Saussure is manifest in the objections to the *Cours* raised by Ogden and Richards (1923), Gardiner (1932) and Firth (1950). Nevertheless, although different individual positions might be taken whether in Europe or America, few theorists were prepared to deny that the distinctions drawn by Saussure provided the basis on which a modern science of language might be established. In this respect, Saussure eventually appeared to be less innovative and less controversial than had formerly been supposed. Thus whereas Firth in 1950 (Firth 1950:179) could still classify professional linguists into four groups ('Saussureans, anti-Saussureans, post-Saussureans, or non-Saussureans'), by 1957, the centenary year of Saussure's birth, a fellow professional linguist could make the bland pronouncement: 'We are all Saussureans now' (Spence 1957:15).

As the case-history of Bloomfield demonstrates, the question of 'reading Saussure' merges inextricably with that of reading readings of Saussure. For when Bloomfield wrote *Language* nothing of the readable Saussure had changed since 1916 (with the exception of trivial emendations to the 1922 edition). Furthermore, it would be a mistake to infer from the way in which Bloomfield's *Language* deliberately ignores Saussure that Saussurean ideas left no trace in American academic linguistics of the interwar period. Bloomfield himself admitted to

Jakobson that reading the *Cours* was one of the events which had most influenced him (de Mauro 1972:371). Editing a collection of papers spanning the period 1925-1956, Joos (1957:18) wrote: 'At least half of these authors had read the *Cours*. The others got it second-hand: in an atmosphere so saturated with those ideas, it has been impossible to escape that. The difference is hard to detect, and it is generally unsafe to accuse a contemporary linguist of not having read the *Cours* ...' In other words, by the late 1950s the experience of reading Saussure seemed to have been so thoroughly absorbed as to make a distinction between Saussureans and non-Saussureans meaningless.

However, as if to give the lie to the dictum that 'we are all Saussureans now', there appeared in the very same year of 1957 the first manifesto of a new school of transatlantic linguistics which apparently owed little if anything to Saussure, however directly or indirectly assimilated. This was A.N. Chomsky's *Syntactic Structures*. The new theory proposed to treat a language as 'a set (finite or infinite) of sentences, each finite in length and constructed out of a finite set of elements' (Chomsky 1957:13) – a definition which might well have made the author of the *Cours* turn in his authorial grave. The essential novelty of transformational-generative grammar, as proposed in *Syntactic Structures*, was the eminently unSaussurean notion of considering languages as mathematical systems, on a par with the formal systems of mathematical logic. In retrospect, that approach may well now appear to have been naive or misguided; but in 1957 – to some at least – it looked full of promise. So rapidly did the new school win adherents that it doubtless seemed to many by the late 1950s that the advent of transformational grammar meant that Saussurean ideas had at last exhausted their usefulness, and a radically different era of linguistic theorizing had dawned.

From its inception, transformational-generative linguistics was based on a distinctly second-hand – if not third-hand – idea. Already in the nineteenth century, Boole had mathematicized logic. Subsequently Frege re-mathematicized it, by generalizing function-theory instead of algebra. The formal linguistics of the twentieth century was destined to follow – surprise, surprise – an exactly parallel course. Saussure's thinking about language owed nothing to this 'mathematical' tradition whatsoever, and was in spirit opposed rather than congenial to any unification of logical and linguistic formalism.

All the more remarkable is the fact that in less than ten years from the publication of *Syntactic Structures* a significantly altered and much more Saussurean theory of language was being proclaimed under the same 'transformational-generative' banner. This new version of transformational-generative linguistics drew a fundamental distinction between linguistic 'competence' and linguistic 'performance': furthermore the distinction was acknowledged as echoing Saussure's classic dichotomy between *langue* and *parole* (Chomsky 1964:62, Chomsky

1965:4), and the 'generative grammar internalized by someone who has acquired a language' identified as the Saussurean *langue* (Chomsky 1964:52). It can hardly be dismissed as mere coincidence that the first English translation of the *Cours* was published in the U.S.A. in 1959, and that in the 1957 manifesto of transformationalism Saussure's name had not even appeared in a footnote. In other words, it took less than a decade (a mere hiccough in the history of linguistics) before we were 'all Saussureans again'. Needless to say, the recently discovered author of the *Cours* had to be castigated for failure to teach transformationalism *avant la lettre* (Chomsky 1964:59-60, Chomsky 1965:4); but, nevertheless, a reading of Saussure had evidently left its mark on the formulation of a doctrine which was to become as important in the linguistics of the 60s and 70s as Saussurean structuralism itself had been in the linguistics of the 20s and 30s.

* * *

'Well-known but little understood,' said Firth epigrammatically of the *Cours* (Firth 1950:179). It is not the purpose of the present study to document or evaluate the various readings of Saussure which have influenced, either positively or negatively, the course of twentieth-century linguistics to date. That, in any case, would be a task far beyond the scope of a single book. The project to hand is a much more modest one, and in one respect has quite the opposite aim: to seek out what in the *Cours* remains 'unread'.

It would be presumptuous to present this as the discovery of an 'alternative Saussure'. However, reading the 'unread' Saussure will involve, in the interpretation of various aspects of the work, an implied contrast between how the twentieth century in fact chose to read the *Cours* and how it might have been read. In many cases this may appear to be merely a difference of emphasis, or a difference in what is taken for granted and left unsaid. But such differences may have a cumulative value which in the end refocuses the whole. The spirit of such an enterprise is eminently Saussurean, for obvious reasons. Central to Saussure's thinking is the idea that every semiological fact is constituted by an imaginative juxtaposition of other unrealized possibilities. To explore such possibilities at points where it is of interest to do so is not so much to offer a reassessment of the *Cours* as part of the history of linguistics, but rather to reaffirm its potential for our understanding of language in the present.

Most of what remains 'unread' in Saussure is not in any way obscure or difficult to read. On the contrary, no exegetic excavation is required to dig it out: it already lies conspicuously on the surface of the text. But it lies there rather like some hidden object in a puzzle picture, which remains 'invisible' until we look at the picture in a certain way. Once the object is 'seen', it becomes clear that it was visible all the time. Its invisibility was simply due to the fact that our visual attention was concentrated on other things. So it is with our 'reading attention' in the *Cours*.

Reading the 'unread' Saussure will include bringing into visibility the hidden premises about language and linguistics – and there are not a few of these – which, although never explicitly acknowledged in the text as 'principles' or 'postulates', nevertheless play such a role in the work. To examine this theoretical infrastructure would itself justify writing a commentary on the *Cours*, even in the absence of any other motive.

Last but not least, reading the 'unread' Saussure will involve reading the book as a book, as distinct from reading it as a collection of theses about language, or as the palimpsest of a set of lectures. The present commentary is not intended to be an apologia for the book or for its editors. No one, however, who has taken the trouble to read the text with the attention that a commentary requires can fail to be struck by the fact that it commands the reader's respect on a level for which it is rarely given credit. The *Cours* is not merely an important scientific document. It is also a work of literature in the same sense as Plato's dialogues: an example of the art of imaginative exposition at its best.

The form of treatment adopted in the present study has been in part determined by this last consideration. Any literary work deserves to be read in the way it was intended to be read; that is to say as a consecutive text which unfolds 'syntagmatically', to use the appropriate Saussurean term. Hence the chapter-by-chapter analysis presented here in Part One. A commentary which did not respect this syntagmatic development would be particularly inappropriate in the case of the *Cours*; for its expository method relies heavily on a technique of presenting successive reformulations of major points, examined in gradually increasing detail and from slightly different angles. (Some of the 'internal contradictions' in the work which critics have detected can be traced to the use of this technique.) In any case, as Calvet pertinently remarks, 'to undertake, in the wake of the immense bibliography devoted to the *Cours de linguistique générale*, yet another account of the theses there put forward would today be an enterprise of no interest whatsoever' (Calvet 1975:13).

Calvet adds: 'Any reader can refer to the text itself ...' which is true enough but hardly sufficient. Most readers making a serious study of the *Cours* will also need to refer to notes of the kind to be expected from a good critical edition. The present commentary assumes that the reader will have access to the standard modern edition of the text (de Mauro 1972), and no attempt is made here to repeat the detailed factual information which that edition supplies. The page references to the *Cours* (given throughout in square brackets) are to the 1922 version of the text, the pagination of which is retained in de Mauro 1972. A chapter-by-chapter commentary of the kind here presented in Part One, however, inevitably has to leave on one side certain more general issues of interpretation which arise in connexion with the work as a whole. Such issues have been reserved for consideration in Part Two.

Recent commentary on Saussure seems to be obsessed with steering a middle course between the Scylla of adulation and the Charybdis of contempt. Commentators do not wish to be seen either as defending Saussure *contre vents et marées* (Engler 1974: 120): or as guilty of *la chicane de ceux qui ne veulent pas comprendre* (Martinet 1974: 225). Steering such a course may be a feat of admirable academic navigation. It has not been attempted here.

Hardly anyone nowadays tackles the *Cours* without having in advance some notion of what ideas it contains and why they are said to be important – in short, without having at least an elementary background in linguistics and knowing where Saussure stands in the history of the subject. That too is taken for granted throughout the following chapters, since it would have been naive to assume otherwise. The task of a commentator is neither to duplicate that of an editor nor to usurp that of a historiographer, but to construct and justify a reading of the text which makes sense. The richer the text, the more readings it will support. Any commentator who recognizes this has already dismissed the notion of the 'definitive' commentary as a will o' the wisp, and will be satisfied to have contributed in even a minor way to that continued renewal of thought which is the permanent legacy of every great text.

PART ONE

The Syntagmatics of the *Cours*

I believe it to be one of the most penetrating books I have ever read, but it is also one of the most obscure.

A.H. Gardiner

INTRODUCTION

CHAPTER I

A Brief Survey of the History of Linguistics

Saussure begins by offering the reader a five-act historical scenario. Act I comprises 'Grammar'. Grammar is characterized as a prescriptive discipline which aims solely at providing rules which distinguish between correct and incorrect forms. It is concerned with the study of language, but a study which is 'unscientific'. Act II is 'Philology'. Philology is said to aim primarily at establishing, interpreting and commenting on written texts. Act II makes an advance over Act I, in that it is, at least within certain limits, 'scientific'; but inasmuch as it is concerned mainly with written texts, fails to be a *linguistic* science. Act III is 'Comparative Philology' or 'Comparative Grammar'. This is both linguistic and also a science, but a very limited one, principally concerned with determining relationships between languages of the Indo-European family. Act IV in the scenario is 'linguistics proper' ([18]). This emerged from the nineteenth-century historical study of the Romance and Germanic languages. In its development the Neogrammarian school played a key role. Whereas the comparativists had failed to place the results of their investigations in the right historical perspective, the Neogrammarians succeeded; and whereas the comparativists misguidedly treated a language as if it were a natural organism, the Neogrammarians correctly saw it as a product of the collective mind of a community ([19]). In spite of this, however, the Neogrammarians left unresolved the fundamental problems of general linguistics. Finally, Act V concerns the foundation of a 'true' science of language: and it is on this fifth act that the *Cours* claims to raise the curtain.

It is worth noting at the outset the recurrent use of the terms *science* and *scientifique* throughout this first chapter (thirteen times in all). The reader is never told exactly what the requirements for a 'science' in Saussure's sense actually are. Certain inferences can nevertheless be drawn which tie in with later claims in the *Cours*. A principal requirement is evidently that a science must have identified its 'true object'. What this in turn means is not at all clear, but it is assumed from the start that linguistics has *son véritable et unique objet* ([13]). Furthermore, it was because the comparativists failed to identify this object that comparative philology did not succeed in becoming a *véritable science linguistique* ([16]). More remarkable still is the statement that Romance studies inaugurated by Diez brought linguistics nearer to this *véritable objet* ([18]). Evidently, then, a science (*la linguistique*) can exist which has not yet discovered its 'true object', but is somehow engaged in a historical process of working progressively towards it. How anyone knows when the 'true object' has at last been discovered Saussure does not explain. The 'true object' thus appears as a kind of intellectual holy grail which initiates will recognize when they see it, and whose eventual discovery makes sense of previous unsuccessful quests in search of it. Nothing could more clearly illustrate than these opening pages the late-nineteenth-century romanticism of science with which the *Cours* is deeply imbued.

As is typical of the period, the scientific romanticism of the *Cours* is an evolutionary romanticism. Each of the historical phases identified by Saussure marks a certain progress towards the ultimate scientific goal. Later is better and earlier is worse. At the opposite end of the historical scale from the 'true' science of language we find its implied antithesis: 'grammar' as developed originally by the Greeks and subsequently by the French. Although very diverse types of activity connected with language are approved in this chapter as 'scientific' – Wolf is credited with founding a 'scientific' philology, Bopp with creating an autonomous 'science' of comparativism – and although these scientific efforts are criticized on various counts, it is only the work of the grammarians which is condemned in this perspective as *dépourvue de toute vue scientifique et désinteressée sur la langue elle-même* ([13]).

This condemnation is of interest in several ways. The attitude towards traditional grammarians is not consistently hostile throughout the *Cours*. The concepts developed in traditional grammar are later said to provide the basis on which linguistics has to work ([153]). Traditional grammarians are even praised for having adopted a strictly synchronic approach to their subject ([118]). The twin sins of traditional grammar for Saussure are apparently that it is 'based on logic' and is prescriptive ([13]). The first of these two charges might certainly be levelled at Port Royal, but it is difficult to see in what sense the work of a Dionysius Thrax or a Priscian is based on logic. As for the second, Saussure conveniently overlooks the extent to which prescriptivism is also inherent in certain kinds of philological work (for instance, in editing texts) and remains latent in much nineteenth-century historical linguistics (lexicography in particular). Yet these endeavours, unlike traditional grammar, are given the Saussurean 'scientific' seal of approval.

Saussure never explains why a prescriptive linguistic discipline cannot be 'scientific' in his sense. What seems to lie behind his initial condemnation of grammar is its tacit identification as a kind of anti-science of language. It purports to teach linguistic truths for which there is no basis. More specifically, its prescriptivism is perhaps implicitly equated with propagating an erroneous linguistic theory. For anyone who holds, as Saussure does, not only that the linguistic sign is arbitrary but that this is a foundational principle of the 'true' science of language, it may be tempting to present the prescriptive grammarian as a Cratyline figure, committed to denying this principle and proclaiming that certain linguistic forms are 'naturally' right and others 'naturally' wrong. If so, then it would make sense from the viewpoint of evolutionary scientific romanticism to see the first step towards the 'true' science of language as being the abandonment of this deeply 'false' view.

Straight away, then, in this opening chapter – and even in its title – we meet the first of the hidden theoretical premises of the *Cours*. Usually these premises are 'hidden' by being disguised either as undisputed historical facts or as matters of commonsense observation. This initial premise is no exception. It is the premise that linguistics is a subject with an identifiable history. Since Saussure's day, that premise has not merely remained hidden but has become even more effectively concealed, buried ever deeper under layers of accumulated scholarship. Histories of linguistics unknown to Saussure have become standard works, and 'the history of linguistics' has been promoted to the status of a university subject, with specialized journals devoted to it. All this serves to obscure from the present-day reader the significance of the fact that Saussure declines to acknowledge that we are here dealing with a theoretical decision to treat linguistics in a certain way, and that neither history nor historians have any authority to impose that decision upon anyone. By just not admitting this, Saussure avoids the necessity of undertaking any theoretical defence of the decision. He can therefore simply omit the most difficult part of a prolegomena to any general inquiry into language. The Saussurean programme for linguistics is able to start *in medias res* by presenting a spurious certificate of authentication from the academic past.

The full piquancy of adopting this 'historical' approach to linguistics cannot be savoured except retrospectively. For it has to be compared with Saussure's attitude towards adopting a 'historical' approach to linguistic phenomena; and this does not emerge until later in the *Cours*. For the moment, the reader has to be content with noting the fact that the first question Saussure deals with is not 'What is language?' but 'What is linguistics?'. The tension between these two questions will be a persistent *leitmotiv* throughout the book. At times the former question appears to be dominant and at times the latter. But in the end neither is subordinated to the other: that, at least, is one way of reading the *Cours*.

Did academic linguists of Saussure's generation think of their subject with sufficient detachment to see how dubious its historical status was? Doubtless many did not, and would therefore have been all the less likely to treat Saussure's initial premiss as contentious. That in no way alters the role this premiss plays in the overall rationale of the *Cours*. In some respects it is rather surprising that the theoretical manoeuvre of the opening chapter has not been more clearly recognized as such; for it treats the history which it alleges to exist in such a conspicuously cavalier way as to attract adverse comment from later scholars who took the subject more seriously. Aarsleff's observation (1982:395 n.15) that 'Saussure's understanding of the history of linguistics is often not well informed' is a mild understatement. Saussure's 'history of linguistics' is grotesque. The significant point is that it does not matter for Saussure's purposes. What matters theoretically is that the subject has had *some* such history. Saussure nevertheless takes the opportunity of slanting his selected history in a way which will suit the pattern of exposition which immediately follows. Chapters I and II of the Introduction are essentially complementary, and serve to direct the reader's attention along certain lines.

Once the 'orientational' function of these two chapters is grasped, some of the details which might otherwise be puzzling can be explained. For example, it explains the omission of any reference to philosophical discussion of linguistic topics in Graeco-Roman antiquity, or to the modistic grammarians of the Middle Ages. It also explains why c.1870 is chosen as the date which marks the beginning of 'inquiry into the conditions governing the life of languages'; why Schleicher is selected as a target for criticism; and why the Neogrammarians emerge in such a favourable light, in spite of the fact that, as de Mauro points out, the Neogrammarians had been hostile to the *Mémoire sur le système primitif des voyelles dans les langues européennes* of 1879 (de Mauro 1972:413, n.37). The expository aim of this potted 'history' is to make clear what, in Saussurean terms, a 'science of language' *was not and could not be*. It is a chapter which deals with possible misconceptions of the subject, a kind of 'warning to the reader' about what not to expect from this particular 'course in general linguistics'.

To appreciate the possibility of this reading, it may be helpful to compare the opening pages of the *Cours* in the first instance to the opening pages of another general book on linguistics published forty years earlier (almost at the same time as the precocious *Mémoire sur le système primitif des voyelles*): Abel Hovelacque's *La linguistique*.

Hovelacque's book begins, in a vein remarkably similar to the *Cours*, by drawing a distinction between *linguistique* and *philologie*, pointing out that even scholars confuse the two, and taking the great French lexicographer Littré to task for the definitions of these terms given in the latter's monumentally authoritative *Dictionnaire*. Furthermore, the way in which Hovelacque defines philology (as distinct from linguistics) corresponds in certain respects exactly to the account given in the opening paragraphs of the *Cours*. On this point, clearly, nothing had changed much throughout the second half of the nineteenth century. The *Cours* merely accepted an intradisciplinary commonplace of the times (namely, that linguistics was not philology), even if it involved a distinction still obscure to the generality of academics. (The incomprehension of fellow academics remains today: 'But it's all to do with languages, isn't it?' End of discussion.) Hovelacque's opening chapter also contains the quasi-obligatory academic genuflexions to Sir William Jones, à propos of Sanskrit, and to Bopp for his inauguration of comparative philology. But there the similarity ends.

The way Hovelacque's opening chapter then proceeds is not at all along Saussurean lines. In Hovelacque we find no criticism of Bopp and the comparativist school. Worse still, we find that the authority cited on the crucial distinction between linguistics and philology is none other than the misguided Schleicher. For Hovelacque, Schleicher is 'the man of method' (*l'homme de la méthode* (Hovelacque 1877:6)): whereas others, including Wertheimer's successor at Geneva, thought him a complete mediocrity and pretentious to boot (de Mauro 1972: 412 n.32). Furthermore, Hovelacque praises Schleicher for precisely the reasons that Saussure attacks him. These are: Schleicher's view of languages as organisms, the concomitant assimilation of linguistics to botany, and the ranking of linguistics among the 'natural' (as opposed to the 'historical') sciences. Seen from this angle, the first chapter of the *Cours* reads almost like a deliberate rebuttal of Hovelacque's introduction to the subject.

Support for such an interpretation would be provided by the lukewarm remarks in this chapter ([16]) about Max Müller, Oxford's German-born first Professor of Comparative Philology, and chief propagandist for the subject in Victorian England. Already in the early 1860s Müller had loudly proclaimed the advent, at long last, of a 'science of language'. This new science, moreover, was in Müller's view one of the natural sciences, on a par with geology and botany (Müller 1864: 1):

... the language which we speak, and the languages that are and that have been spoken in every part of our globe since the first dawn of human life and human thought, supply materials capable of scientific treatment. We can collect them, we can classify them, we can reduce them to their constituent elements, and deduce from them some of the laws that determine their origin, govern their growth, necessitate their decay; we can treat them in fact, in exactly the same spirit in which the geologist treats his stones and petrifactions, – nay, in some respects, in the same spirit in which the astronomer treats the stars of heaven, or the botanist the flowers of the field.

It is difficult not to see in this passage a reflection of Schleicher's famous parallel likening the difference between linguistics and philology, on the one hand, to the difference between botany and horticulture on the other (Schleicher 1860: Intr.). This parallel Hovelacque cites with approval as explaining better than any other what linguistics aims to do.

A second comparison may be even more helpful. This is between the *Cours* and a general book on language published some twenty years later: Leonard Bloomfield's *Language*. The comparison is telling in this instance too, because Bloomfield's book – unlike Hovelacque's, but like the *Cours* – established a landmark in the subject.

We find in Chapter I of *Language* another variation on the strategy of using an introductory discussion of the 'history' of language studies in order to explain to the reader what linguistics is not (or should not be). Bloomfield's attack is directed in the first instance against the tradition of school 'grammar' and the accompanying 'preconceptions which are forced upon us by our popular-scholastic doctrine' (Bloomfield 1935:4), and more generally against any approach to linguistic analysis based on philosophical or psychological premisses. Thus he criticizes the ancient Greeks for taking it for granted 'that the structure of their language embodied the universal forms of human thought' (Bloomfield 1935:4) and for stating their grammatical observations 'in philosophical form'; while on the other hand praising the Sanskrit and Hindu grammarians for demonstrating that it is possible to present 'a complete and accurate description of a language, based not upon theory but upon observation' (Bloomfield 1935:11). He is particularly severe on the European medieval scholastic philosophers, whom the *Cours* never mentions. They, in his view, contributed much less than the ancients and mistakenly 'saw in classical Latin the logically normal form of human speech' (Bloomfield 1935:6). Nor has he anything but condemnation for the post-Renaissance attempts to write 'general grammars'; for these embody the same error of seeking to force language into the mould of logic. 'Philosophers, to this day, sometimes look for truths about the universe in what are really nothing but formal features of one or another language' (Bloomfield 1935:6). The Port Royal grammar of 1660 in particular, which received qualified praise from Saussure ([118]), Bloomfield singles out for criticism on this score. What eventually rescued the European tradition of language studies from this dismal plight, according to Bloomfield, was the discovery of Sanskrit. 'Hindu grammar taught Europeans how to analyze speech-forms' (Bloomfield 1935:12). The European comparativist school took it from there; and henceforward Bloomfield speaks only of 'progress', until he comes to the Neogrammarians. His exemplar-target here is Hermann Paul, whose 'standard work' (*Principien der Sprachgeschichte*, 1880) suffers from two 'great weaknesses'. One of these weaknesses is 'neglect of descriptive language study' and concentration on questions of linguistic change, a fault Paul shared with his contemporaries. 'The historical language students of the nineteenth century suffered under these limitations, but they seem not to have grasped the nature of the difficulty' (Bloomfield 1935:17). The other 'great weakness' of which Paul is guilty is 'his insistence upon "psychological" interpretations'. As a behaviourist, Bloomfield was utterly opposed to discussing language in terms of mental processes. 'The only evidence for these mental processes is the linguistic process; they add nothing to the discussion but only obscure it. In Paul's book and largely to the present day, linguistics betrays its descent from the philosophical speculations of the ancient Greeks' (Bloomfield 1935:17). Bloomfield's *Language*, like the *Cours*, lists many names on its roll-call of honours in nineteenth-century linguistics. One of the names mentioned is that of Saussure: but he is only one among several others (Böhtlingk, Müller and Finck) credited with having seen 'the natural relation between descriptive and historical studies' (Bloomfield 1935:18-19).

Thus comparison between the opening chapter of the *Cours* and of Bloomfield's book is particularly revealing. It alerts any intelligent reader of the *Cours* to the fact that what to look for is the balance of praise and blame; and, more important still, the reasons given for both praise and blame. Whether the judgments formulated are 'historically accurate' is a quite secondary – and almost irrelevant – matter. For example, while it is perfectly true, as Aarsleff points out (Aarsleff 1982: 395 n.15), that the *Cours* gives the Neogrammarians credit for a view which Bréal had expressed long before (i.e. that a language is the product of a 'collective mind'), the point to note in context is that, historically accurate or not, this attribution is part of the Saussurean case against the comparativists. It could hardly be so for Bloomfield, since behaviourism is no less suspicious of collective minds than of individual minds; perhaps even more suspicious. (In fact, Bloomfield has nothing but praise for the comparativists: they at least were not guilty of 'psychologism'.)

The reader who grasps that the 'history' of linguistics with which the *Cours* opens can be read simply as an account of 'what linguistics is not' will also see that the misconceptions attacked fall into two groups. The first group are the three 'popular' misconceptions: that linguistics is prescriptive (= 'grammar'), that linguistics is concerned with textual study (= 'philology'), and that linguistics is to be equated with the investigation of relationships between languages (= 'comparative philology'). The second group are the 'academic' misconceptions: that linguistics studies languages a-historically, and that linguistics studies languages as organisms. The second group is by far the more interesting, the two 'academic' misconceptions being presumably chosen for their complementarity. In other words, for many of Saussure's contemporaries it must have seemed that the choice for linguistics as an academic discipline lay, precisely, between treating languages as living organisms – and hence studying what Müller (in the passage cited above) called their 'origin', 'growth' and 'decay' – as opposed to treating languages as abstract systems with no 'life'. The latter alternative is particularly significant inasmuch as Saussurean synchronic linguistics itself is sometimes represented as taking an a-historical approach to languages. The point of criticizing comparativism for its a-historicity is thus an important one. It hinges on what has been called the 'radical historicity' of Saussure's view of languages (de Mauro 1972:448 n.146, Culler 1976:35). The comparativists come under attack from a Saussurean vantage-point because they simply disregard history altogether: their approach is a-historical because it is non-historical. Saussurean synchronic linguistics, on the other hand, is a-historical in a quite different way; namely, that it rejects a conflation of data pertaining to different historical states. But it is at the same time 'radically historical' in that it proposes an analysis based solely on data which are historically coherent in the sense of belonging to a single system. Such a system does indeed have a 'life', as far as Saussure is concerned; and in at least two quite different respects. First, it may last for hundreds or even thousands of years. Second, while it lasts it functions as an active generator of the consistency of speech (*parole*). Perhaps the essence of Saussure's 'radical historicity' might be crystallized in two aphorisms which the Saussure of the *Cours*, despite his apparent love of paradox, never formulated: 'There are no dead languages' and 'Languages live by resisting change'.

CHAPTER II

Data and Aims of Linguistics: Connexions with Related Sciences

Having first been told what linguistics is *not*, a reader of the *Cours* now presumably expects to be told what it *is*. If so, the expectation will be frustrated. A point which commentators have missed here is that the exposition adopted in the *Cours* exemplifies admirably – and presumably not coincidentally – the Saussurean concept of 'value' (*valeur*). Just as the identity of a Saussurean linguistic sign is determined by its place in a system of related but contrasting signs, so the identity of Saussurean linguistics is determined by its place in an academic system of related but contrasting disciplines (anthropology, sociology, psychology, etc.). Here we glimpse the possibility of a full Saussurean semiology of the forms of intellectual inquiry in society. What is significant is the avoidance in the *Cours* of any naively 'positive' definition of the kind commonly encountered in dictionaries and introductory textbooks, where the term *linguistics* itself is presented as the established name of a certain branch of study ('the study of language and languages', for example). Such a definition would have been incongruous to say the least, in view of Saussure's forthright and absolute condemnation of nomenclaturism ([97]f.). It is to the credit of the editors that they recognized the expository problem, and managed to deal with it in a way faithful to the principles of Saussurean structuralism. They saw that the implications of a Saussurean approach to languages forbade any simplistic definition of linguistics in terms of its subject matter. They also saw that, from a Saussurean viewpoint, the way linguistics is to be defined and the way languages are to be defined will be head and tail of the same coin.

To pursue the notion of a semiology of intellectual inquiry a little further, it may also strike the alert reader that the distinction drawn between the data (*matière*) of linguistics and its object (*objet*) is parallel to the distinction Saussure later draws for languages between substance and form. Linguistics accepts as raw material, the *Cours* tells us, 'all manifestations of human language', including written texts ([20]). But the form linguistics takes, the organization it imposes upon this raw material, is determined by the aims (*tâche*) of the discipline. Exactly the same data could in principle be treated in many different ways (of which philology, anthropology and other disciplines offer concrete examples). The aims of linguistics are thus of crucial importance; and at the same time raise an obvious question. How are *they* determined? For presumably a discipline's internal aims do not drop unbidden out of a clear blue academic sky. The answer is that Saussure's 'radical historicity' can be read as applying not merely to languages but also – and *in the first instance* – to linguistics itself.

That this answer is plausible can be immediately confirmed by considering the account now given ([20]) of what the specific disciplinary aims of linguistics are. They are just three in number. The first ('to describe all known languages and record their history') sounds like a fairly straightforward – albeit interminable – task of cataloguing and classifying linguistic data; in short, an enterprise of the kind already very familiar to the linguists of the nineteenth century. The second, however, ('to determine the forces operating permanently and universally in all languages, and to formulate general laws which account for all particular linguistic phenomena historically attested') is of an entirely different stamp. By no stretch of the academic imagination could this second aim be accomplished by processes of cataloguing and classification. But it is the third aim which gives the game away: 'to delimit and define linguistics itself.' Was not that the very question we started with? Indeed, it was. And the moment we realize this we also realize that what have been offered as the three aims of Saussurean linguistics are simply the result of applying to the study of linguistic phenomena a general paradigm from the philosophy of science. (For any science *S*, it falls to that science to describe the phenomena within its domain. Second, it falls to that science to explain the same phenomena as particular instances of the general laws of *S*. Third, the way *S* accomplishes these twin objectives defines *S* as a science.) The 'radical historicity' of Saussurean linguistics can be construed as residing precisely in the application of this paradigm as a paradigm dictated by the cultural context of the historical Saussure's day and age.

Thus the claim, on this reading, will be that the development of linguistics (in the early years of the twentieth century) has reached a turning point at which only two historical paths into the future are possible. Either it must establish itself as a unified science, or else it is doomed to fragmentation and will be absorbed piecemeal into other disciplines which deal in their own terms with various aspects of human linguistic activity. The question therefore is: how can linguistics meet the conditions required of a modern science? Saussure's proposed solution, all commentators agree, is to identify *la langue* as the object of linguistic study. This is presented initially in the *Cours* as a solution dictated by fundamental difficulties, which are seen as arising out of the very nature of linguistic phenomena.

CHAPTER III

The Object of Study

The first difficulty a theorist has to face ([23]) is that whereas other sciences study objects 'given in advance', in linguistics, on the contrary, 'it is the viewpoint adopted which creates the object'. The single example provided to illustrate this point, however, is in some respects an unhappy one. The reader is invited to consider the word *nu* in spoken French and to realize that there are various ways of considering it: (i) as a sound, (ii) as the expression of an idea, (iii) as corresponding to Latin *nūdum*, etc. The different viewpoints thus briefly identified make it appear, unfortunately, as if all that is being claimed here is that words may be studied in different ways and with different interests in mind by the phonetician, by the lexicographer, by the etymologist, and so on. And since no linguist of the late nineteenth century would ever have contested this, what was intended to illustrate a fundamental problem for linguistics collapses into a banality which fails completely to perform its intended function. On the contrary, linguistics seems in this respect to be in the same boat as many other disciplines. Medical science, for example, both allows and requires consideration of the human body from various points of view, depending on the interests of different specialists. But it would be odd to cite this as a reason for claiming that the human body constitutes a number of different objects, or for denying that the human body is 'given in advance' of the efforts of medical science to understand how it works.

Saussure's point can hardly be the academic banality which the laconically glossed example of *nu* makes it seem. For this the editors must take responsibility. In claiming that where language is concerned the point of view precedes the object, Saussure is saying something much more basic: that the phonetician, the lexicographer, the etymologist and their fellow specialists having *nothing to make statements about at all* unless what we hear as a certain sound and write as *nu* is first seen as having a certain linguistic status, namely as being the utterance of a particular French word. As Barthes (1964: 1.1.4) puts it: 'any speech, as soon as it is grasped as a process of communication, is *already* part of the language'. To which we might add that *until* it is thus grasped, it does not exist at all as a linguistic phenomenon. In this respect there is no parallel with the human body and medical science: that is to say, there is no question of physicians having first to 'see' a human body as a human body, or its parts as parts of a human body. Whereas, *mutatis mutandis*, that is precisely what is required in the linguistic case. If *nu* were not a word but a sneeze or grunt, the linguist would not be interested in it, even though it might sound no different: and if *nu* were not a French word but English or Japanese then both lexicographer and etymologist would be looking at quite a different linguistic unit. In short, there just is no linguistically relevant item *nu* which exists independently of the processes of linguistic identification. It is in this sense that the linguistic viewpoint creates the linguistic object. That is not, admittedly, the only possible way of taking Saussure's point: but it makes far more sense of the *Cours* than any other.

The second general difficulty ([23-6]) is that at no level of linguistic observation are simple autonomous units to be found. On the contrary, at all levels of linguistic observation the observer finds dualities. Furthermore, these dualities involve combinations of apparently quite disparate kinds. For example, the 'consonant *n*' is a duality involving on the one hand articulatory movements and on the other hand auditory impressions; the 'word *nu*' is a duality involving on the one hand an audible sound and on the other hand an inaudible meaning; and so on. There is never just a single dimension or a single criterion involved in identifying such units. How, in view of this diversity, will any uniform method of analysis be possible in linguistics at all? A discipline forced to choose between a variety of methodologically diverse approaches, which examine different aspects of the phenomena selected for study but are never brought together in any meaningful synthesis, will have no claim to be an independent science.

The foregoing difficulties will be resolved, and can only be resolved – the *Cours* tells us – if linguistics takes *la langue* as its object of study. Again, it is to be noted how the exposition adopted by the editors presents, in a typically Saussurean manner, the related conceptual framework into which the notion of *la langue* is required to fit, before making any attempt to enlighten the reader as to just what *la langue* is. In fact, the reader is never told exactly what *la langue* is at any point in the *Cours*: there is no definitive or final formulation. All we find are successive reformulations which bring out different contrasts between *la langue* and everything which *la langue* is not. The procedure is an object-lesson in Saussurean methodology, and in this sense the *Cours* itself is the great masterpiece of Saussurean linguistics.

Typically, the first statement made about *la langue* is negative: *la langue* is not to be equated with *le langage* ([25]). And the first paragraph of this much-quoted passage proceeds to concentrate not on *la langue* at all but on language in general, explaining why the very heterogeneity of language makes it impossible for us to place it in any one category of human phenomena. *La langue*, on the contrary, it claims, is 'both a self-contained whole and a principle of classification'. But how or why that might be the reader is not yet told. Instead the discussion veers off into dealing in advance with a possible objection to taking this as the *appropriate* principle of classification for purposes of linguistics. Again, the expository procedure adopted here is quite remarkable. Before any explanation is given of what was meant by claiming that *la langue* provides a 'principle of classification' for linguistics we find an account of why an alternative principle of classification will *not* do.

The objection brought up for consideration at this point is that the language faculty is one of humanity's basic natural endowments; whereas particular languages are simply sets of acquired social conventions established on the basis of this natural endowment. Should not linguistics, therefore, give priority to the natural endowment, rather than to the socially superimposed conventions (*la langue*)? The way this objection is dealt with in the *Cours* is revealing. First of all, argues Saussure, although it is true that all (normal) human beings can speak, it is not at all clear that the human vocal apparatus is naturally designed for speaking in the way human legs are designed for walking. Saussure rejects Whitney's view that humanity might just as easily have opted for a different medium (than speech) for linguistic expression; but nevertheless accepts the American linguist's insistence that the vocal nature of linguistic signs is a matter of secondary importance. In other words, what is natural to the human species is not spoken language, but rather the ability to construct and use systems of signs, whether spoken or not. Brief reference is made at this point to Broca's investigation of the localization of language in the brain. What Broca discovered, the *Cours* claims, is that the brain's control of speech is bound up inseparably with its control of other forms of communication, including writing; and consequently there is no separate physiological basis for treating speech as a distinct natural endowment. Finally, in any case, even if speech were a separate natural (i.e. physiological) endowment, it could not be exercised unless society provided a public instrument (*la langue*) for its exercise. The particular form this instrument takes will vary from one society to another: and here the distinction between *langage* and *langue* ties in with the Saussurean doctrine of the arbitrariness of the linguistic sign, to be developed later in the *Cours*.

But the question inevitably now arises as to whether the rational strategy for the scientific investigation of language ought not to take as its starting point this natural faculty of using signs, which Saussure recognizes as the *faculté linguistique par excellence* ([27]). The answer to this brings us to the next 'hidden premiss' of the *Cours*: more precisely, to two 'hidden premisses', which underlie Saussure's apparently unquestioning acceptance of the doctrine of the 'primacy of speech'. The first and more general of these premisses is that implicational relationships may hold between sign systems: that is to say, that one system may be semiologically dependent upon another. The second premiss is that what constitute from a lay point of view spoken and written forms of 'the same language' are examples of this relationship, the spoken system being semiologically presupposed by the written. Why Saussure needs these premisses becomes apparent not so much from the arguments he advances, but from the arguments he does not advance. What these missing arguments are must now be examined.

First, it should be noted that it is by no means clear that Saussure accepts the doctrine of the 'primacy of speech'; at least, not in the crude form in which it was usually presented in the nineteenth century. It would certainly be rash to infer too much simply from the fact that when the *Cours* refers to French, English, Greek, etc. as *langues* the reference is to the spoken language, even though in some cases the linguist may have access to the spoken form only indirectly through written records. What the *Cours* states quite unambiguously is that *écriture* and *langue* constitute two separate systems of signs, and that the former exists only to represent the latter ([45]). The conclusion from this is that writing is of interest to the linguist only insofar as it is amenable to treatment as a representation of *langue*: its other properties are strictly irrelevant. (Later theorists were to insist on this even more emphatically than Saussure. Bloomfield, for instance, stated bluntly: 'Writing is not language' (Bloomfield 1935:21).) So in practice Saussure proceeds *as if* accepting the 'primacy of speech' doctrine, but nevertheless stops short of offering any theoretical justification for it.

Given that the *Cours* is a work of linguistic theory, this reticence is striking. Was the assumption that the arguments were so obvious as not to be worth stating? This scarcely seems plausible, given the evident concern elsewhere in the *Cours* to reject popular misconceptions about the status of writing. In general, the *Cours* shows no evidence of reluctance to state the obvious, provided that the point is of sufficient importance. A more likely explanation of Saussure's reticence is that it corresponds to an unresolved problem of semiological theory, for which Saussure has no option but to assume a solution.

That this is the most probable reason for Saussure's silence emerges if we consider the usual arguments which linguists have offered in favour of the doctrine of the primacy of speech. These arguments have been summarized by Lyons (1972: 62-3) under four heads. (i) *Phylogenetic priority*. In all communities, the emergence of writing, if and when it occurs, is subsequent to the establishment of a spoken language. (ii) *Ontogenetic priority*. The normal child learns a spoken language first, and only later, if at all, a written language. (iii) *Functional priority.* A spoken language normally has a wider range of communicative functions than a written language. (iv) *Structural priority.* Writing systems are normally based on representation of units and combinations belonging to a corresponding spoken language. To these four basic considerations may be added: (v) *Learning priority.* 'It is entirely possible to learn a foreign language without knowing anything of the way it is written ... On the other hand, it is next to impossible to learn *only* to read and write a foreign language' (Moulton 1970:14).

These arguments were already available to linguists in the nineteenth century: the problem is that from a Saussurean point of view they are the wrong arguments. They are all 'external' linguistic arguments. That is to say, they are based on empirical generalizations of various kinds about human intellectual and cultural development. As such, they are in no sense 'principles of semiology'. Thus they are quite irrelevant, for example, to the semiological problem of whether in cases where spoken and written signs co-exist they may function as complementary components of a single system. No semiological principle is posited in the *Cours* which rules out *a priori* the existence of 'mixed' semiological systems. In fact, the section on semiology ([32-5]) nowhere lays down any specific criteria for the identification of a sign system.

What Saussure needs, ideally, is a semiological principle which will allow him to demonstrate, deductively, the dependence of writing on speech: and this will have to be a general principle which simultaneously determines the same relationship for any independent sign system S_1 and a dependent system S_2. This will presumably be part of a theory of implicational relations which allows the semiologist to say under what conditions any given sign system presupposes another given sign system. But all that, for Saussure, lies in the domain of the future science of semiology. He is simply forced to assume in advance the availability of the result which the *Cours* will take for granted. That is why the *Cours* very meticulously avoids the more obvious linguistic arguments for according priority to spoken language, and is careful to treat the relationship between spoken and written forms as a semiological relationship, not a historical or cultural one.

What would be quite unwarranted is to treat Saussure's reticence as obliviousness to the semiological problem. It had already been raised in the nineteenth century by scholars far less theoretically astute than the author of the *Cours*. Murray, for example, in the Preface to the first volume of the *Oxford English Dictionary*, accepts that in 'the natural order of language ... speech comes first, and writing is only its symbolization' but points out that a word like *gaseous* 'reverses the natural order' because it belongs essentially to writing. Such words do not have a spoken form in the same sense as the words of colloquial speech: 'for "pronunciation" anything passes muster which suffices to recall the written symbol in question; just as any reading of a mathematical formula passes muster, if it enables an auditor to write down the formula again' (Murray 1888: xi). Now what Murray regarded as a reversal of 'the natural order', and hence a problem for the lexicographer, would be for Saussure a reversal of semiological dependence, and hence a problem for the semiologist. That there will be problems of this order in semiology is evident from various remarks in the chapter which the *Cours* devotes to writing; in particular on *la tyrannie de la lettre* ([53]) and on the case of Chinese, where Saussure surprisingly concedes that writing constitutes *une seconde langue* ([48]). Even in this latter example, however, the word *seconde* implies a relationship of semiological dependence between two separate systems.

For Saussure's argument about the 'object' of linguistics, what matters is that writing is a separate system, albeit semiologically dependent on *la langue*. Since linguistics, conceived of as the science of *la langue*, does not even embrace the study of *l'écriture* except insofar as that may be necessary to establish evidence about *faits de langue*, it can hardly propose to undertake the more general study of the postulated human 'sign faculty' underlying *all* sign systems. That would be the province not of linguistics but of semiology. Thus there is no contradiction in Saussure's admitting that the human 'sign faculty' is our natural *faculté linguistique par excellence*, but at the same time maintaining that the study of this natural faculty does not fall within the scope of linguistics.

The importance of these arguments has gone virtually unnoticed in later Saussurean exegesis. They form an essential link between two superficially unrelated Saussurean theses; one about the relationship between speech and writing, and the other about the relationship between linguistics and semiology.

The way the case is argued appears at first sight to make a concession to the view that a science is – or should be – concerned with the investigation of natural phenomena. What Saussure is apparently concerned to defend is the proposition that linguistics, on the contrary, has to address itself first to the investigation of a cultural phenomenon (*la langue*) if it is to proceed to establish itself as a science. The arguments he deploys fall into two groups. On the one hand, there are arguments derived from our inability to identify immediately the 'natural' basis of human speech. On the other hand, there are arguments derived from the consideration that even if such a basis could be identified, what matters is the cultural implementation of our natural linguistic abilities, since they would otherwise lie fallow.

In order to clarify Saussure's position, let us suppose for a moment that human beings had a rather different vocal apparatus, which served no other purpose than speech (being physiologically independent of the organs for breathing, mastication, swallowing, etc.). Let us also suppose that Broca had discovered in the brain a localized control system specialized exclusively for the operation of this physiologically independent vocal apparatus. Let us even suppose that human beings were born with two sets of ears, one receiving just the output of the vocal apparatus and the other receiving any other audible signals. Finally, let us suppose that in pathological cases where there was any impairment of this articulatory-cum-auditory system, the patient in question was recognized as linguistically deficient: in other words, as having no alternative mode of linguistic expression or comprehension available. Thus, for example, impairment of the system would entail corresponding impairment of writing or reading. Let us, in short, take literally the much invoked metaphor of a 'language organ', and imagine that human beings clearly had such an organ – just as clearly as, for instance, they have eyes to see. Now what, in this hypothetical situation, would Saussure's stance be?

The answer has to be that the putative author of the *Cours* is then apparently faced with a choice. One alternative is that linguistics thereby becomes a science with two distinct branches: one branch, the psycho-physiological, studying the general workings of this hypothetical language organ, and the other branch, the cultural, studying its various products in different social and historical circumstances. The other alternative is that one of these two branches of study is relegated to the province of some other science, and the term *linguistics* is restricted to the other. Now what Saussure seems to urge is that, irrespective of terminology, a science of language can in no way ignore the centrality of languages as cultural phenomena. Furthermore, this centrality is logical rather than merely empirical. In other words, it would be so even if speech happened *not* to be the natural form of human linguistic expression. We cannot (logically) engage in linguistic activity at all unless there exist languages for us to use. And no language comes ready-made, supplied by Nature. No wonder Broca gets short shrift from Saussure. The case, in other words, is a subtly presented *reductio ad absurdum* of the notion that linguistics might be one of the natural sciences (a subdivision of neurophysiology, for instance). 'It is no absurdity to say that it is *la langue* which gives language what unity it has' ([27]).

To sum up, then, the Saussurean strategy for linguistics is based upon three propositions accepted without serious question: (i) that languages are systems of (non-natural) signs, (ii) that there are non-linguistic systems of signs, which human beings are capable of creating and using, and (iii) that linguistics is not concerned, except incidentally, with semiologically dependent systems, such as writing. Saussure at no point attempts to justify these three propositions in any detail; but all three are individually and collectively essential to his position.

Just how essential can be seen if we eliminate them one by one. A theorist who rejects (i) can have no common ground with Saussure, and must presumably find some alternative basis for linguistic analysis which either claims linguistic signs to be natural or else eliminates the need for a theory of the linguistic sign altogether. A theorist who rejects (ii), while accepting (i) and (iii), will be obliged to equate linguistics with semiology – a position clearly incompatible with Saussure's explicit distinction between the two. A theorist who rejects (iii) (that is, rejects the doctrine of the 'primacy of speech') but accepts (i) and (ii) presumably has two options open: either to maintain the 'primacy of writing', or else to treat spoken and written languages as autonomous and equipollent systems. The former option entails that pre-literate societies have to be treated as having no languages; and this is clearly quite unacceptable from a Saussurean point of view. The latter option leads straight to the paradox that in any given literate community there would be no linguistic relationship obtaining between the spoken and the written systems of signs. Thus, for example, it would from a linguistic point of view be merely fortuitous that written French and spoken French were both 'French', and that literate French people treat the two as systematically interrelated. This also is evidently unacceptable as far as Saussure is concerned. Finally, how about treating both spoken and written systems as alternative forms of the same *langue*? This possibility is also excluded for Saussure, who regards *la langue* as a system of bi-planar correlations, in which each unit on the plane of *signifiants* corresponds to just one unit on the plane of *signifiés*, and vice versa. Consequently writing and speech cannot belong to one and the same *langue*, since at least *two* sets of bi-planar correlations must be involved.

The Saussurean strategy for linguistics, it should be noted, and the arguments used in its support, although rejecting the availability of any natural basis for the classification of linguistic facts, in no way preclude the possibility that certain features of linguistic structure may be naturally determined (in the sense of being imposed by the nature of the general human 'sign faculty'). But since we do not know what, if any, these features are, we cannot make them the basis of classification for the purposes of a science of language.

* * *

The *Cours* has so far referred to *la langue* in very general terms as one (unidentified) part of language (*le langage*). The question which now inevitably arises in the reader's mind is, which part? Saussurean commentators have almost with one accord read the next section of the *Cours* as an immediate reply to this implicit question. Consequently, the remarks contained in §2 of Chapter III have been construed as supplying Saussure's basic definition of *la langue*. It is in the light of this supposed definition that all subsequent observations about *la langue* in later chapters have been interpreted. Likewise, it is in the light of this definition that various charges of inconsistency or incoherence in Saussure's views have ultimately been brought to court. What §2 offers, however, turns out to be merely the first in a series of progressive reformulations, in the course of which all the key technical distinctions of Saussurean linguistics will be introduced. The series begins with the distinction between *langue* and *parole*, and attempts first of all to situate that distinction in the context of a general model of communication.

The section begins by inviting the reader to consider a typical act of speech, in which two hypothetical interlocutors, A and B, are linked in what Saussure calls the 'speech circuit'. This circuit involves a chain of connexions between the brains, vocal organs and ears of the two persons in question. According to the 'speech circuit' account, what happens when, for example, A says something to B is that certain concepts in A's brain trigger or activate corresponding sound patterns in A's brain (*images acoustiques*) which in turn trigger certain movements in A's vocal apparatus, which in turn cause certain sound waves, which then eventually stimulate B's ears. This aural stimulation, being relayed to B's brain, triggers there the appropriate sound patterns, which in turn trigger the corresponding concepts. If B replies to A's utterance, an exactly similar chain of events will be set in motion in the opposite direction, going from B's brain to A's. Thus A might ask 'What time is it?' and B might reply 'Six o'clock'. That exchange, according to Saussure's model, would occupy just one complete lap of the speech circuit.

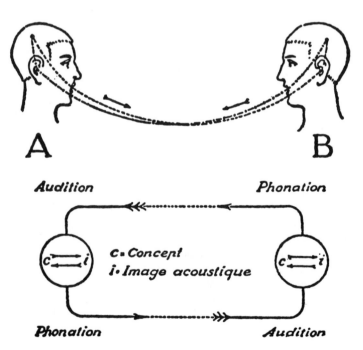

This simple picture seems at first sight clear enough: and to make assurance doubly sure, the text of the *Cours* includes an illustration with dotted lines and arrows tracing the hypothetical pathways connecting the two talking heads of A and B, and a diagram in which the speech circuit is shown laid out like the plan of a model railway.

The initial clarity of this picture is unfortunately blurred by various subsequent observations which may have misled Saussurean commentators. The first is the remark on p. [30] which appears to identify *la parole* with the 'executive' section of the circuit. The second is the remark on p.[31] claiming that *la langue* can be localized in that section of the circuit where sound patterns are associated with concepts; but this is followed immediately by the statement that *la langue* is the social part of language, and 'external to the individual' ([31]).

The impression created is that Saussure is trying to construe the distinction between *langue* and *parole* in a diversity of ways simultaneously. Hjelmslev (1942) argues that if *parole* is identified with execution it cannot also be identified with the individual – as distinct from the social – part of language. 'Every execution' objects Hjelmslev (1942:41) 'is not necessarily individual ... Everything which is individual is not necessarily an execution ...' This apparent inconsistency in Saussure leads Hjelmslev to set aside the distinction between *langue* and *parole* and replace it by a distinction between the abstract system of linguistic contrasts (*schéma* in Hjelmslev's terminology) and its social implementation (*usage*). Others have agreed that the various criteria which the *Cours* invokes in distinguishing *langue* from *parole* 'do not divide language in the same way and they thus leave much room for dispute' (Culler 1976:81). A useful survey of this 'room for dispute' and possible interpretations of Saussure's distinction is provided by Spence (1957, 1962), who finds that none is completely satisfactory and eventually concludes 'that scientific method in linguistics will be best served by the elimination from consideration of the duality between *langue* and *parole*' (Spence 1962:52). Since this distinction is usually taken to be the cornerstone of Saussure's theory, it is rather difficult to see what would remain of Saussurean linguistics without it.

Here, as in other instances, the editors of the *Cours* have been collared as whipping boys. 'The definition of the contrast *langue/parole* appears on p.38, whereas the problem of the *identity* of linguistic units is broached on p.249, and that of *valeur* on p.150. In other words, to reconstruct the Saussurean sequence of ideas, the reader must begin with Chapter 8 of Part Three (on 'Diachronic Units, Identities and Realities'), proceed to Chapters 3 and 4 of Part Two (on 'Identities, Realities, Values' and 'Linguistic Value'), thence to Chapter 1 of Part One ('Nature of the Linguistic Sign'), and eventually to Chapter 3 of the Introduction ('The Object of Study'), where the opposition between *langue* and *parole* should have been presented.' (Calvet 1975:20) If all this is necessary to understand Saussure's distinction, it is little wonder that reading Saussure has come to be regarded as requiring the expertise of a Talmudist.

Whether the text of the *Cours* actually contains all the inconsistencies of which Saussure or his editors are often accused is another matter. A careful reader will observe that the sentence in which *parole* is allegedly identified as 'execution' occurs in a passage comprising several paragraphs ([29-30]) devoted to explaining the origin of the 'social crystallization' which is necessary for the establishment of *la langue* in society. The relevant contrast here is between 'active' processes in the brain and 'passive' ones, and the term *exécutif* stands opposed to *réceptif*. Saussure's claim is that the individual plays no active part in this 'social crystallization' of *la langue*, but is merely the passive recipient of an accumulated fund of linguistic signs used in *la parole*. This proposition might, doubtless, be contested on various grounds: but what is more to the point is that it makes nonsense of Saussure's claim if he is also taken to be opposing *parole* to *langue* as execution to reception. What the *Cours* says here is that 'execution is never carried out by the collectivity' ([30]); but it might also have added, had it been relevant to the argument, 'and nor is reception either'. What John Smith hears, in that sense, is not heard by anyone else in the community; any more than what John Smith says is said by anyone else. There is no question of identifying what distinguishes execution from reception in the speech circuit with what distinguishes *parole* from *langue*. Execution and reception are both processes of *parole*, and once that is grasped the alleged incompatibility with the opposition of *parole* to *langue* as 'individual' to 'social' vanishes.

As regards the alleged inconsistency between treating *langue* as 'external' to the individual but nevertheless localizing it within one of the 'internal' sections of the speech circuit, any contradiction disappears once the point is taken that in order to function, according to Saussure, the processes of *parole* need access to *la langue*. Saussure's 'localization' of *langue* in the brain is the answer to the question of how and where this access occurs. Again the answer may perhaps be contested; but it does not contradict the notion that *la langue* is a social, supra-individual reality to claim that each person has an individual internal representation of it (any more than it would be contradictory to claim that each individual may reliably be guided by his or her own copy of the rules of a game in spite of the fact that the rules as such exist 'outside' the distributed set of copies, and indeed 'outside' any particular episodes of play).

The *Cours* is the first treatise on language to insist that speech communication is to be viewed as a 'circuit', and to attach any theoretical significance to the fact that the individuals linked by this circuit act in turn as initiators of spoken messages and as recipients of such messages. Later theorists sometimes used the Saussurean term *circuit de la parole* (e.g. Malmberg 1968) as if this emphasis on reciprocality were of no particular importance. However, the *Cours* is quite explicit on the matter: without two individuals capable of exchanging spoken messages, 'the circuit would not be complete' ([27]). Exactly what the implications of a 'circuit' are will be discussed at greater length below in connexion with Saussure's theory of communication (p.204ff.). Here it suffices to note three general points. First, by taking the speech-circuit model with its two talking heads as basic, Saussure makes it clear that *la langue* is a system which assumes face-to-face communication as the norm. This assumption reinforces the Saussurean distinction between *langue* and *écriture*: for writing is, archetypally, a system which makes the opposite assumption (that is, that the sender and recipient of the message are *not* in a face-to-face situation). Second, without the notion of a speech circuit there would be no explanatory force behind Saussure's account of how *la langue* accumulates as a collective *trésor* ([30]). Unless there were assumed to be an essential link in circuitry between the two capacities of speech-production and speech-comprehension, it would need a separate theory to explain why, for example, when A says 'Good morning' and B replies 'Good morning', either could recognize the other as having said 'the same thing'. But that recognition, for Saussure, is essential to *la langue* as a social institution. In other words, there would be no collective *trésor* at all if individuals were not able to recognize the circuit as being circuitous (namely, that B, by saying 'Good morning', is now 'returning' to A via the circuit the same verbal message as B heard A originally deliver). Without that minimal assumption, *la langue* in the Saussurean sense could not exist. Third, the Saussurean thesis of the duality of all linguistic phenomena ([24]) would collapse unless speech communication were essentially circuitous. Thus if it were possible to identify, for instance, the consonant *n* by articulatory criteria alone or by auditory criteria alone, then it would not be a *linguistic* phenomenon as such. This ties in with Saussure's later claims about the 'amorphousness' of sound ([64-5]). What makes this amorphous substance viable as a medium of communication is precisely that reciprocality which somehow enables participants in the speech circuit to recognize some of their own articulatory productions as equivalent to some of the auditory impressions they receive when listening to others. The 'mutual delimitation' ([65]) of minimum units of speech would otherwise be impossible.

* * *

The speech-circuit model deals with a specific subcategory of signs; namely, signs belonging to *la langue*. The following section of the chapter proceeds immediately to deal with the science of signs as a whole (*sémiologie*). At this point, attention shifts from the question 'What is *la langue*?' to focus once more on the question 'What is linguistics?'

Saussure's status as the founder of modern linguistics is unproblematic: but his status as founder of twentieth-century semiology is nothing if not paradoxical. On the one hand, this latter role seems to be undeniable if we are to judge by the number of subsequent semiological studies and works of semiological theory claiming Saussure directly or indirectly as their inspiration (Barthes 1964, Prieto 1966, Metz 1971, Toussaint 1978, Broadbent, Bunt and Jencks 1980, etc.). On the other hand, what the *Cours* says on the subject of semiology could hardly pass muster as a theoretical foundation for anything, for reasons which will be discussed below. Nevertheless, according to our currently received history of ideas, Saussure disputes with C.S. Peirce the palm for having established the possibility of a general 'science of signs'. Saussure's use of the term *sémiologie* is dated back to 1894 and Peirce's use of the term *semiotic* to 1897 (Lange-Seidl 1977: 13-14). As regards academic spadework for this new science, Peirce is acknowledged as having done more than Saussure: perhaps even too much. For to start by distinguishing, as Peirce did, no less than 59049 types of sign is arguably enough to strangle any science of signs at birth. Saussure at least did not do that.

Three passages in the *Cours* discuss questions concerning semiology. The longest of these constitutes §3 of the third chapter of the Introduction, immediately following the discussion of the speech circuit. Two later passages in the text add significant clarifications. One ([100-101]) is a paragraph contained in the important section dealing with the principle of the arbitrariness of the linguistic sign. The other is a brief remark ([149]) at the end of the chapter on '*Les entités concrètes de la langue*', where Saussure takes up the question originally raised on p.[33] as to what makes *la langue* a special type of semiological system. These three passages do not amount to more than a thousand words all told. An exiguous theoretical foundation if ever there was one; and, not surprisingly, one which has given rise to conflicting interpretations.

Eco claims that the essential difference between Saussurean semiology and Peircian semiotic is that the former is dependent on the concept of communication:

> the sign is implicitly regarded as a communicative device taking place between two human beings intentionally aiming to communicate or to express something. It is not by chance that all the examples of semiological systems given by Saussure are without any shade of doubt strictly conventionalized systems of artificial signs, such as military signals, rules of etiquette and visual alphabets. Those who share Saussure's notion of *sémiologie* distinguish sharply between intentional, artificial devices (which they call 'signs') and other natural or unintentional manifestations which do not, strictly speaking, deserve such a name. (Eco 1976: 15)

For Peirce, on the other hand, the subjects of semiosis are not human subjects but 'three abstract semiotic entities, the dialectic between which is not affected by concrete communicative behavior' (Eco 1976: 15). Prieto, however, draws a very similar distinction within Saussurean semiology itself, citing Buyssens as a representative of those Saussureans who treat semiology as dealing only with 'communication' and Barthes as a representative of those who treat semiology as dealing more generally with 'signification' (Prieto 1968: 93-4).

If Saussure's speech circuit is to be read as a theory of communication, that might appear at first sight to lend support to Eco's interpretation of the difference between Saussure's general science of signs and Peirce's. However, what Eco offers with the right hand is speedily removed by his left: for he concedes that his account of Peirce's semiotic 'could also fit Saussure's proposal'. Nevertheless, he claims that Peirce's account 'does not demand, as part of a sign's definition, the qualities of being intentionally emitted and artificially produced'. Hence Peirce's notion 'can also be applied to phenomena that do not have a human emitter, provided that they do have a human receiver, such being the case with meteorological symptoms or any other sort of index.' So Peirce's approach, unlike Saussure's, it would seem, does not 'reduce semiotics to a theory of communicational acts' (Eco 1976: 15-16). Thus whereas rings round the moon 'meaning' rain, or spots 'meaning' measles, would fall within the province of Peirce's general science of signs, they would be excluded from Saussure's.

Unfortunately, Eco's reading of Saussurean semiology is not supported by what the text of the *Cours* says. In the *Cours* we read of 'a science *which studies the role of signs as part of social life*' ([33]). It is difficult to see how this could exclude, for example, meteorological signs (particularly when weather forecasts are appended to daily news broadcasts as a regular feature of a communications system available in principle to every member of the linguistic community). It might even include the astrological signs taken as a basis for the so-called 'horoscopes' featured by popular newspapers and magazines. At the very least, it would have to include doctors' interpretations of their patients' symptoms. Unless we adopt a curiously narrow interpretation of which parts of life are 'social', presumably all three categories of sign – meteorological, astrological and medical – are 'part of social life'. Although there is no indication that Saussure was particularly interested in meteorological, astrological or medical signs, they are certainly not excluded from the province of semiology by what the *Cours* says. It is no doubt true that isobars are not signs until interpreted as significant; nor are conjunctions of heavenly bodies or spots on the skin. But, to repeat, all the *Cours* apparently demands is that this significance should play a role in *social* life. Consequently, if there is a distinction between Saussure's approach to a general science of signs and Peirce's, it can hardly be drawn at the point where Eco draws it.

Worse still, it seems to be a misreading of the *Cours* which is responsible for the suggestion that the Saussurean sign is defined by reference to communicative intentions. This is to confuse *faits de langue* with *faits de parole*. The communal institution (*la langue*) has no intentions. It merely provides linguistic resources to be utilized by individuals who *do* have communicative intentions. Nowhere in the *Cours* does intention enter into any definition of the sign, linguistic or otherwise.

Two points certainly remain unclear from Saussure's rather vague observations about semiology: just how general this general science of signs is to be, and exactly what signs, other than linguistic signs, fall within its province. But the fact that Saussure leaves these questions open is doubtless in part due to the consideration that, as in the case of linguistics ([20]), one of the tasks of semiology would be to determine its own limits and objectives as a science ([100]). All that can be inferred on the basis of the remarks in the *Cours* may be summarized as follows. 1. Semiology is envisaged as a human science and part of social psychology ([33]). Therefore it would exclude, for example, the study of animal communication. 2. Semiology is not restricted to the study of signs as opposed to the study of symbols ([100-101]). Nevertheless, one of its main tasks will be the analysis of the various human systems of signs which are, like the linguistic sign, arbitrary. 3. Linguistics will occupy a privileged position within semiology, by providing a model (*patron général*) for all semiological investigation ([101]).

Thus there is no doubt that Saussure's semiology falls far short of being a general science of signs in the sense later defined by semioticians like Charles Morris: it does not deal with 'signs in all their forms and manifestations, whether in animals or men, whether normal or pathological, whether linguistic or nonlinguistic, whether personal or social' (Morris 1964: 1). But it does correspond to at least one part of the science which Locke in the last chapter of the *Essay Concerning Human Understanding* baptizes with the Greek term *semeiōtikē*: 'the business whereof is to consider the nature of signs the mind makes use of for the understanding of things, or conveying its knowledge to others' (Locke 1706: 4.21.4). That correspondence certainly invites consideration: the two neologisms do not exhibit etymological parallels by coincidence. (Scholars doubt whether Saussure had ever studied Locke at first hand (de Mauro 1972: 381 n.11, Aarsleff 1982: 27): but the question is irrelevant to a reading of the *Cours*.) Furthermore, it makes sense not only of the privileged position assigned to linguistics, which a more general science of signs would have to reject, but also of Saussure's statement that the exact role of semiology is a matter for the psychologist. In other words, Saussure's general science of signs takes its place as part of an inquiry into what Locke described as 'the objects of our understanding' and a later generation of academics called 'cognition'. It deals specifically with those communally and communicationally developed instruments of the understanding which comprise the whole gamut of social signs.

This view of semiology nevertheless leaves certain problems unresolved; in particular, how to construe Saussure's notion of the privileged position accorded to linguistics as a semiological science. For Barthes, what Saussure had implicitly done was not establish linguistics as a branch of semiology at all, but rather establish semiology as an extension of linguistics; and Barthes proposed to redefine the relationship accordingly (Barthes 1964: 11). This 'reversal' of Saussurean priorities met with acrimonious criticism, and Barthes was accused of having 'perverted' Saussure's idea of semiology (Lange-Seidl 1977: 44 n.12). The case for and against Barthes' position is of less importance than the fact that the controversy itself highlights a genuine difficulty concerning Saussure's assumption of a special relationship between linguistics and semiology.

Even if, for the sake of argument, it were conceded that Saussurean linguistics would eventually fall into place as part of a more general science of social signs, it remains quite unclear why it should be a foregone conclusion that the more general science should take linguistics as its model. For this seems to presuppose in advance of any investigation that all sign systems human societies develop are structured along the same lines as *la langue*. The assumption already points ahead to a theoretical conflict. If there are sign systems to which the Saussurean analysis of *la langue* cannot be applied, linguistics must lose its priority as a model of investigation. Alternatively, any systems which resist the imposition of a linguistic model will be rejected as systems of signs. The conflict could only result in an exhibition of theoretical dexterity in accommodating the maximum number of social signs as analogues of the linguistic sign, and in controversy over membership of the general class of signs.

That is not all. An even more critical conundrum is posed by Saussure's conjecture ([149]) that what distinguishes *la langue* from all other semiological systems is the fact that its entities are not immediately 'given'. This suggestion ties in with the famous Saussurean dictum that where the study of language is concerned 'it is the viewpoint adopted which creates the object' ([23]). As Spang-Hanssen points out (1954: 103-4), there is another fundamental difficulty here. How can the notion that *la langue* is unique in this respect be reconciled with the idea that 'the language sign can to advantage be studied as a special example of arbitrary signs'? Or, more bluntly, how can one avoid the conclusion that 'the basis for a semiology in Saussure's sense' does not in reality exist? Spang-Hanssen goes on to suggest that post-Saussurean semiology can be analysed in terms of attempts to salvage whatever can be salvaged from this conceptual disaster. The possibilities are four in number:

(a)   that semiology is preserved as the designation for the study of language signs and other signs as far as these have common characteristics (e.g. as arbitrary signs as opposed to 'natural signs'). In this case linguistics does not become a part of semiology, but language can be studied from a semiological aspect.

(b)   that semiology covers only the study of signs with the same formal properties as the language sign.

(c)   that semiology covers only the study of arbitrary signs which are not language signs.

(d)   that the designation is rejected.

(Spang-Hanssen 1954: 104)

Spang-Hanssen points to a division among Saussure's successors, arguing that Buyssens (1943) opts for possibility (a), while Hjelmslev (1943) opts for (b).

Firth thought that the view that linguistics must find its place among the sciences as part of semiology was 'perhaps the most striking thing in the whole of de Saussure's great work' (Firth 1935: 17); and that reaction is an interesting one in view of the very many 'striking things' which the academic world found in the *Cours*. What seems to have impressed Firth was the implicit denial that the linguistic sign can be studied scientifically as something *sui generis*. Identifying linguistics as a branch of semiology, and claiming quite specifically that 'the laws which semiology will discover will be laws applicable in linguistics' ([33]), makes it quite clear that the linguistic sign is only one variety of a more general phenomenon. This insistence connects in an important way with Saussure's critique of the comparative and historical linguistics of the nineteenth century. The connexion, once grasped, explains better than anything else the rationale of Saussure's curiously inchoate appeal to a future science of semiology.

The cornerstone of nineteenth-century linguistics had been the study of sound change. At the same time, the study of sound change relied almost entirely on the historical evidence of written forms. This placed far too much emphasis on the 'wrong' things for Saussure's liking. The interpretation of ancient texts was the province of philology: while the sounds of speech were the province of the phonetician. Consequently, a linguistics which continued to place the study of written texts and of speech sounds in the forefront of its investigations would be reversing the order of priorities necessary to establish its own scientific autonomy. To re-orient linguistics in the right direction, however, it did not suffice to identify *la langue* as a synchronic system, or to separate synchronic from diachronic studies. For even if *la langue* were defined as a synchronic system of vocal signs, the risk of ending up with linguistics as a minor branch of physiology or acoustics remained.

The strategic dilemma was this. One obvious way of refocussing attention towards the study of linguistic structure and away from the study of speech sounds would have been to treat languages as abstract systems which could be expressed *either* in spoken *or* in written form. But this would merely promote the study of written texts again for a different reason, and perhaps run the even greater risk of rehabilitating the popular prejudice, virtually endemic in literate societies, of treating the written language as superior to the spoken. Nevertheless, a solution had to be found which would relegate study of the phonic side of language to its proper place. Saussure's way out is to treat the (vocal) linguistic sign as being on a par with other signs which are non-vocal, but which can nevertheless be assumed to be in some way comparable to the signs of *la langue*. Hence the postulation of a more general science of social signs, in which the linguistic sign is just *primus inter pares*. For there is otherwise no division of human communicational activities which will keep writing out of the picture as a natural and equal partner to speech. Semiology, then, is Saussure's answer to the twin problems posed by the status of writing and the status of sounds. Semiology demotes writing to the level of 'just another social sign system' (comparable to the Morse code, symbolic rites, etc.) at the same time as it demotes phonetics to the role of a merely ancillary discipline to linguistics. Two birds are killed with one theoretical stone.

Saussure therefore needs semiology for two reasons. First because, as argued earlier, he cannot do without the premiss that the relationship of *écriture* to *langue* is that of dependent to independent sign system. That already means drawing one post-dated cheque on his account at the semiological bank. But he will also need another, to cover his theoretical debts in treating the structure of *la langue* as independent of its phonic materialization. For that too cannot be demonstrated except on the assumption of certain semiological principles. Here we first encounter the most important hidden premiss of the *Cours* so far, which will turn out to play a crucial role in the fully developed Saussurean theory of *la langue*. This is the premiss that a sign system is adequately defined, from a semiological point of view, in terms of 'form' rather than 'substance' (which in practical terms means abstracting from the specific channel of communication involved). A linguistics which did not accept that premiss would be destined to be either a sub-science of phonetics or a sub-science of philology, or else some hybrid of the two. Semiology, for Saussure, is the way round the grim academic alternatives of leaping from the philological frying-pan into the fire of phonetics, or vice versa.

Critics of Saussure's strategy might well complain that this manoeuvre merely buys independence from philology and phonetics at the expense of mortgaging the future of linguistics to semiology. The Saussurean reply to this criticism would doubtless have been (i) that since semiology does not yet exist, this in practice means an independent status for linguistics, and (ii) that linguistics is in any case guaranteed in advance a privileged position within semiology which it lacks under the hegemony of any other science. That this latter guarantee is quite bogus matters far less for our reading of the *Cours* than the fact that it is offered. The offer shows perhaps more clearly than anything else exactly how the Saussurean answers to the questions 'What is *la langue*?' and 'What is linguistics?' are interdependent. For Saussure, since *la langue* is the 'object' of linguistics, the question of what we take *la langue* to be must merge with what we take – or want – linguistics to be.

CHAPTER IV

Linguistics of Language Structure and Linguistics of Speech

Having situated linguistics within a scientific hierarchy (by placing it under the superordinate, albeit hypothetical, science of semiology) the *Cours* proceeds in Chapter IV of the Introduction to distinguish between a linguistics of *la langue* and a linguistics of *la parole*. This serves to emphasize and supplement the rather sparse indications already given ([27-32]) concerning what belongs to *la langue* and what belongs to *la parole*. Again, the expository point is a subtle one: it is not until we come to consider how the study of language might in practice be conducted that certain intuited linguistic distinctions fall into place as part of a coherent whole. (Another exemplification of the Saussurean priority of 'viewpoint' over 'object'.)

For the first time it is made absolutely clear that the study of speech sounds does not fall within the linguistics of *la langue*. This is, in fact, merely spelling out what is already implicit in the way the relationship between linguistics and semiology has been described in the preceding chapter. Here, however, the statements are unequivocal. 'The vocal organs are as external to the language system as the electrical apparatus which is used to tap out the Morse code is external to that code' ([36]). And on the same page we find the first of the celebrated Saussurean linguistic analogies, comparing *la langue* to a symphony. The symphony has a reality 'which is independent of the way in which it is performed'. This analogy was later borrowed by American generativists in the 1960s to validate their own distinction between 'competence' and 'performance' (Katz and Postal 1964: ix). (Saussure's use of the musical comparison is particularly apt, since his point here is about the status of sound-production. The distinction between competence and performance, on the other hand, is a broader distinction, involving far more than phonetic or phonological considerations. The later use of the musical analogy thus offers an interesting example in the history of linguistics of a second-order metaphor: a metametaphor.)

Saussure's underlying rejection of the preoccupation with sound-change in nineteenth-century linguistics now comes out into the open. A quibble is voiced: 'One may perhaps object to regarding phonation as separate from the language system. What about the evidence provided by phonetic changes, coming from alterations in sounds as produced in speech?' ([36]). The objection is no sooner raised than dismissed with impressive finality. 'The language itself as a system of signs is affected only indirectly, through the change of interpretation which results' ([37]). The dismissal is indeed so summary that its full thrust is not obvious here. But that will be rectified later, in the section of the *Cours* which deals with diachronic linguistics. What Saussure is rejecting is a whole tradition of scholarship which assumed that linguistic evolution could in large measure be 'explained' by reference to sound changes, themselves 'explained' by reference to general physiological processes of articulation.

Linguistics, then, as the study of *langage* divides naturally into (i) a primary linguistics of *la langue, la langue* being 'social in its essence and independent of the individual', and (ii) a secondary linguistics of *la parole*, dealing with 'the individual part of language' ([37]). Several details about the way the distinction between *langue* and *parole* is now drawn may be noted. This reformulation is deliberately more specific than in the preceding chapter. For example, we find the phrase 'speech, including phonation' (*la parole y compris la phonation*). Why might there be any doubt as to whether phonation is included in *la parole*? Because previously the term *parole* had been used only with reference either to the circuit as a whole (*circuit de la parole*) or specifically to the 'executive' section of its psychological component ($c \rightarrow s$) ([30]). But the notion of execution is now being applied less restrictedly, and the entire process of phonation is described as 'the execution of sound patterns' ([36]). Furthermore, it is now clear that the processes of *parole* include also the transmission of sound waves; for the linguistics of *la parole* is described as a 'psycho-physical' study ([37]). (Perhaps a more exact, if clumsier, term would have been 'psycho-physio-physical': for there is no doubt that the intention is to include all three subdivisions of the circuit in *la parole*.)

Thus what previously might have seemed to be gaps, tensions or even contradictions in the exposition are now, at least temporarily, dealt with. *La parole* is 'individual' in the sense of being that part of *le langage* manifested in the processes of linguistic interchange between individuals. Its individuality requires a separate speech circuit which is in no sense part of *la langue*. *La langue* is 'social' in the sense of being that part of *le langage* which collectively subsumes any individual linguistic interchange, being utilized in and presupposed by it. Now that is a complex distinction, which cannot straightforwardly be given a definitional gloss in terms of cruder contrasts such as 'actual' vs.

'potential', or 'execution' vs. 'plan', or 'unique' vs. 'common', or 'token' vs. 'type', or 'extension' vs. 'intension'; *even though it remains true that such contrasts will be applicable to particular cases*. But the distinction between *langue* and *parole* is not itself reducible to any one or any combination of these contrasts, for reasons which the *Cours* now attempts to elucidate.

The elucidation takes a curious and arresting form ([38]). The reader is presented with two quasi-mathematical formulae. The formula representing *la langue* is:

$$1 + 1 + 1 + 1 \ldots = I$$

We then have another of Saussure's celebrated linguistic analogies as a gloss upon it: 'a totality of imprints in everyone's brain, rather like a dictionary of which each individual has an identical copy' ([38]). This seems to suggest that the Arabic figures on the left-hand side of the equation stand for particular copies which, however numerous, do not 'add up' to more than one lexicon (represented by the Roman figure on the right). Thus far it looks as if the two sides of the equation symbolize multiple 'tokens' (on the left) vs. a single 'type' (on the right). But this is then contrasted with the formula representing *la parole*:

$$1 + 1' + 1'' + 1''' \ldots$$

The semiology of this 'mathematical' contrast, although striking, has either escaped the attention of Saussurean scholars or else been misconstrued (as, for example, by Spence (1957: 19), who ignores the difference between Arabic and Roman numerals, and thus reduces the example to mathematical nonsense). The first point to note is that the second formula is not an equation. The second point to note is that the primes in the second formula are appended to Arabic numerals, each of which in the first formula stands for one person's representation of *la langue*. (It is ironical, given Saussure's views on writing, that the *Cours* here employs conventions of written symbolism to express linguistic distinctions for which *la langue* apparently has no structurally articulated counterparts.)

What these formulaic devices attempt to express is the fact that there is no direct correspondence between *faits de langue* and *faits de parole*. The correspondence is always mediated via individuals. Were it not for this crucial mediation, the relationship between *langue* and *parole* would be a simple relationship of abstraction. As it is, however, there is inevitably a double classification to be reckoned with (individual vs. social). In addition, the two classifications operate on different principles. Classification from the individual point of view treats speech acts in relation to each individual's linguistic experience ($1 + 1 + 1 + 1 \ldots$). Classification from a social point of view generalizes across indefinitely many speech acts and indefinitely many individuals, ignoring their particularities. This explains why the priority as between *faits de langue* and *faits de parole* can be seen in different perspectives. A child could not acquire a language except through first having experience of particular acts of speech: the language is already 'there' to be acquired, but it is initially there only in the indirect mode of a finite number of acts of speech produced by particular individuals with whom the child comes into contact. Historically, too, the establishment of a language as the language of a particular community presupposes a finite number of acts of speech by a certain number of individuals. On the other hand, as an established social fact the language is not just a finite sum total of *faits de parole* involving a specific number of individuals: it is the unity (I) which makes an indefinite number of acts of speech (1 + 1' + 1'' + 1''' ...) by an indefinite number of individuals (1+ 1 + 1 + 1 ...) manifestations of one and the same language.

CHAPTER V

Internal and External Elements of a Language

The opening sentence of Chapter IV of the Introduction makes the bold claim that by allocating to a science of *la langue* its essential role within the study of *le langage* 'we have at the same time mapped out linguistics in its entirety' ([36]). The reader may consequently be surprised to find that Chapter V does not proceed to elaborate this new Saussurean cartography by filling in the contours of a linguistics of *la langue* and a linguistics of *la parole*. Instead, it examines and apparently defends a more obvious division of language studies between 'internal' and 'external' matters. Under the latter, the *Cours* tells us, fall questions relating to: (i) 'the relations which may exist between the history of a language and the history of a race or civilization' ([40]), (ii) 'relations between languages and political history' ([40]), (iii) 'the literary development of a language' ([41]), and (iv) 'everything which relates to the geographical extension of languages and to their fragmentation into dialects' ([42]). In short, the whole range of historical, geographical and cultural factors which bear upon the life of the linguistic community.

The perplexing question which may immediately arise in the reader's mind is whether such matters can properly be the concern of linguistics at all, given the radical re-casting of the subject which Saussure has just proposed in Chapter IV. To add to the perplexity, there is the title of Chapter V: *Éléments internes et éléments externes de la langue*. For how can *la langue*, as described in Chapter IV, have 'external elements' at all?

It is possible to dismiss the latter puzzle simply by blaming Saussure's editors for an ineptly chosen chapter heading. One suggestion is that it should have read: *Eléments internes et éléments externes de la linguistique* (de Mauro 1972: 428 n.82). Even if we accept this emendation the first enigma remains, and is rendered even more enigmatic by two arguments put forward in the course of Chapter V.

1. Languages often borrow foreign words. But this does not mean that an examination of foreign sources is an essential part of the study of imported elements in the vocabulary of a language. For once a borrowed word takes its place in the linguistic system, it functions just like any other word: 'it exists only in virtue of its relation and opposition to words associated with it, just like any indigenous word' ([42]). 2. In certain cases, history can tell us nothing about the peoples who spoke certain languages or the circumstances under which these languages were spoken. 'But our ignorance in no way prevents us from studying their internal structure, or from understanding the developments they underwent' ([42]).

These two arguments by no means validate the treatment of 'external' topics as an essential or integral part of a science of linguistics. They are simply further arguments supporting the recognition of *la langue* as an autonomous object of study, and, specifically, the independence of a linguistics of *la langue*. Nothing could make the irrelevance of 'external' considerations to a linguistics of *la langue* more conspicuous than the analogy with the game of chess (the first of a number of chess analogies) on which Chapter V closes. Here we are told that the fact that chess came to Europe from Persia, or that chess pieces are made of ivory, are facts which are 'external'. Whereas the fact that there are only a certain number of chess pieces in a set is 'internal': for the number of pieces affects the 'grammar' of the game. Thus the criterion for distinguishing between 'external' and 'internal' factors is: 'Everything is internal which alters the system in any degree whatsoever' ([43]).

The formula that 'Everything is internal which alters the system in any degree whatsoever' is, however, in certain respects an unfortunate one. In the first place, it appears to state only a sufficient condition, whereas arguably the condition is intended to be both necessary and sufficient. Furthermore, in the form stated it lends itself to more than one interpretation. It might, for instance, be read as implying that everything which brings about a change in the system counts as an internal factor. But that could make the Roman Conquest, for example, an internal factor; which is a conclusion patently inconsistent with what was said about the linguistic role of 'major historical events' a page earlier. In the context of the chess analogy, we are presumably expected to read Saussure's formula as meaning: 'All (and only?) things which, if they were altered, would *ipso facto* alter the system, are internal'. Thus even though the migration of chess from Persia to Europe could have resulted in certain changes in the rules of the game, that would not count. For a game is not automatically altered by being exported from one country to another: and this would remain true even if, as a matter of historical fact, it happened that in all known cases the change from one country to another were accompanied by a change in the rules. Such changes would still be merely contingent; whereas to 'play chess' without pawns, for instance, *ipso facto* makes it a different game, irrespective of where it is played.

If Saussure's criterion is interpreted along these lines, that still leaves open the question of how to reconcile the distinction of Chapter V between internal and external linguistics with the distinction of Chapter IV between the linguistics of *la langue* and the linguistics of *la parole*. How exactly the two distinctions are related is not explained in the text: they are presented independently and we are left to draw our own conclusions. Why? It is perhaps difficult to avoid the suspicion that Saussure's editors themselves were not entirely clear about how the various parts of Saussure's programme fitted together. That suspicion might be reinforced if we happen to know that many years later Sechehaye published an article in which he rationalized the Saussurean programme as comprising three components: (i) a linguistics of *la langue*, (ii) a linguistics of *la parole*, and (iii) diachronic linguistics. According to Sechehaye, the second of these components is intended to play a mediating or linking role between the first and third (Sechehaye 1940: 7). But that simply leaves Saussure's 'external' linguistics nowhere. Two possible but awkward ways of construing this would be: either (a) that 'external linguistics', in spite of being so called, is just not a branch of linguistics at all, or (b) that somehow external linguistics is subsumed under or split among the three major branches. Sechehaye is silent on the matter: and the silence might be taken as echoing the original question the editors of the *Cours* appeared to leave unanswered.

There is, however, another way of making sense of this section of the *Cours*. Given that we have not yet been introduced to the distinction between synchronic and diachronic studies, which is later to play such an important part in Saussure's programme, it is possible simply to read both Chapters IV and V of the Introduction as jointly providing the foundation for that later distinction. On this view, the two chapters present not separate slices of the academic linguistic cake (that is, subdivisions of a programme for linguistics) but simply a demonstration of possible alternative ways of using one and the same conceptual knife. The knife in question is the concept of *la langue*. In other words, we here have a first gloss on the hitherto unexplicated claim of Chapter III that *la langue* provides a 'principle of classification' ([25]), and at the same time yet another reformulation of the distinction between *langue* and *parole*.

In support of this reading, it may be pointed out that the distinction between the two linguistics of Chapter IV is based on exactly the same principle as the distinction between the two linguistics of Chapter V. The linguistics of *la langue* appears to embrace just the same range of facts as internal linguistics does. In both cases we are concerned with what 'belongs to the system'. Does this mean, then, that 'external linguistics' is another designation for *linguistique de la parole*? On one level, the answer has to be 'yes': for at least two reasons. First, it is required by the internal logic of Saussure's own position. This treats *faits de langage* as divisible into just two classes: *faits de langue* and *faits de parole*. There is no third category of *faits de langage*, and hence no third 'branch' of linguistics. Second, every example Saussure gives of what falls under external linguistics constitutes in fact a particular grouping of certain *faits de parole*. Thus, to pursue the chess analogy, to say that chess came to Europe from Persia is simply a way of describing certain facts about where and when particular games of chess were played. To say that chess pieces are made of ivory is a way of describing certain other facts about games actually played. These are all matters which relate to the *parole* of the game of chess. And these are the examples Saussure gives of external factors. Had these games been played elsewhere and in a different chronological succession, or had they been played in countries where ivory was unknown, then historians of chess might be telling us that chess was imported into Persia from Europe and that chess pieces were traditionally made of tin. Saussure's point is that *faits de langue* are not of this order, any more than the rules of chess are generalizations about the past history of playing chess.

Why, then, confuse the issue by suggesting two terminologically different distinctions? The answer to this question takes us back once again to the Saussurean dictum about viewpoints creating objects. External linguistics may indeed be concerned in the final analysis with the same set of phenomena as a linguistics of *la parole*: that is to say, its ultimate *matière* may be the sum total of acts of speech. What distinguishes external linguistics, however, is the fact that its classifications are based on considerations drawn from history, geography, etc., and not on considerations drawn from an analysis of speech processes. On that level, the terminological contrasts of Chapters IV and V correspond to two different objects of study. But in both cases, it is *la langue* which emerges as the *fundamentum divisionis*.

CHAPTER VI

Representation of a Language by Writing

Writing is first of all mentioned in passing in Chapter III of the Introduction of the *Cours* and described in somewhat curious terms as the 'tangible form' of the *images acoustiques* of *la langue*. The limited number of elements in any *image acoustique*, we are told, can be represented by a corresponding number of written symbols. Writing is thus able to 'fix' linguistic signs in 'conventional images' ([32]). These considerations about the nature of writing are introduced as part of an argument designed to show that *la langue* is no less concrete than *la parole*, and that linguistic signs are not mere 'abstractions'. The evidence provided by writing is held to demonstrate this fact. For whereas writing can record every relevant element of a given linguistic sign, not even a camera could record in every detail the elements involved in the corresponding act of *parole* ([32]). As an argument this is not immediately convincing (to say the least) and it has been suggested that it originated with Saussure's editors. There is no evidence that it featured in the Geneva lectures (de Mauro 1972: 425 n.70). A more interesting question than its ultimate intellectual sponsorship, however, is how it would fit in with the Saussurean thesis about writing set out in Chapter VI of the Introduction. This question will be taken up below.

The next reference to writing in the *Cours* occurs in the section on semiology, where it is made evident that writing is to be distinguished from *la langue*, since writing is listed among various examples of comparable systems of 'signs expressing ideas' ([33]). From this it is already clear that from a Saussurean point of view written signs are signs in their own right, and do not owe this status to their connexion with speech. Whether or not this is because the term *écriture* is acknowledged as covering systems of musical and choreographic notation, together with other non-linguistic forms of recording, does not emerge at all clearly from the text at this point. For reasons which will be discussed shortly, it seems doubtful whether Saussure can afford many concessions to the broader interpretation of the concept of writing.

Ecriture in Chapter VI of the Introduction certainly refers specifically to graphic systems devised for linguistic purposes. The first section of this chapter reaffirms that writing is not part of the 'internal system' of *la langue*, but explains why the study of writing is nevertheless essential for the linguist. 'Languages are mostly known to us only through writing', and even in the case of our native language the written form constantly intrudes ([44]).

The opening sentence of §2 reaffirms more explicitly the point already made on p.[33]. *Langue* and *écriture* are 'two separate systems of signs'. Furthermore, the sole reason for the existence of the latter is to represent the former. More explicitly still: 'The object of study in linguistics is not a combination of the written word and the spoken word.' Linguistics is concerned only with the spoken word ([45]). This deliberate emphasis on separating writing from speech raises an interesting question: why is such conspicuous reiteration necessary? The point, after all, was by no means new. It had been a commonplace in nineteenth-century linguistics (Paul 1890: 660) and for a long time earlier. So it cannot be regarded as one of the novel theoretical moves associated particularly with Saussure.

If Saussurean scholars have been somewhat slow to probe this question that may be because they take at their face value the reasons the *Cours* gives for insisting on the non-linguistic status of writing. 'As much or even more importance is given to this representation of the vocal sign as to the vocal sign itself' ([45]). Popular misconceptions abound concerning the effect of writing on the development of the spoken language ([45-6]). Even distinguished linguistic scholars such as Bopp and Grimm failed to distinguish clearly between letters and sounds ([46]). The *Cours* suggests four factors accounting for the unwarranted 'prestige of writing': (i) the permanence and solidity of the 'graphic image', (ii) the greater clarity of visual images as compared with auditory images, (iii) the importance of the literary language in a literate society, and (iv) inconsistencies between pronunciation and spelling ([46-7]). But none of this rather superficial discussion goes any way towards justifying the theoretical claims which lie at the heart of Saussure's treatment of the relationship between writing and *la langue*. Instead, the chapter moves swiftly on to the rather dogmatic account of systems of writing in §3.

There are only two basic kinds of writing, according to the *Cours*. These are: (i) ideographic, and (ii) phonetic ([47]). The classic example of ideographic writing is Chinese, each word being written as a simple sign bearing no relation to pronunciation. Phonetic systems of writing, on the contrary, do relate to pronunciation. They are either syllabic or alphabetic, the latter representing 'the irreducible elements of speech'

([47]). The *Cours* admits that it is also possible to have 'mixed' systems of writing: that is to say, partly ideographic and partly phonetic ([47]). Having drawn up this simple classification of writing, Saussure says no more about ideographic and 'mixed' systems but proceeds to concentrate on phonetic systems, and more particularly still on the European alphabet. Such an alphabet in principle provides the means for a 'rational' representation of *la langue*: but in practice we find many discrepancies between spelling and pronunciation. In the following section, §4, Saussure examines the reasons for these discrepancies. They are: (i) that *la langue* evolves, while spelling remains fixed ([48]), (ii) that an alphabet designed for the representation of one language may be borrowed to represent another, for which it is less well adapted ([49-50]), and (iii) that etymological preoccupations may affect spelling ([50]). Finally, there are some discrepancies which are just bizarre and unexplained ([50]). The results of the discrepancies are detailed in §5, with examples from French, German, English and Greek. These examples show to what extent 'writing obscures our view of *la langue*' ([51]). Worse still, 'the tyranny of the written form' may even modify *la langue* itself, through the introduction of erroneous pronunciations modelled on spelling ([53]).

What is remarkable throughout the whole of Chapter VI is that nowhere in this relatively detailed discussion of writing is any attempt made to offer a serious argument in support of the two highly controversial theses which it presents. Both theses are based on the two 'hidden' premises already identified which postulate certain semiological relations between systems of signs. In this chapter it becomes abundantly clear why Saussure needs these premises. For he is committed to arguing not just that writing is a semiologically secondary system, derived from speech, but that *écriture* is actually a semiological 'representation' of *langue*. This thesis is closely connected with Saussure's earlier claim that it is possible to study the linguistic structure of those languages which are available to the linguist *only* through written sources. Why does he insist on this? Because otherwise he would be obliged to conclude that in the case of dead languages a study of *la langue* ('the social product stored in the brain' ([44]) is impossible in principle. In other words, most of the work done by the Indo-Europeanists of Saussure's own generation would have to be excluded from linguistics. The iconoclasm of the *Cours* is not as extreme as this: it implies merely that the Indo-Europeanists had inextricably confused synchronic and diachronic analysis, consequently failing to put either on a firm theoretical foundation.

Here Saussure is accepting and trying to deal with the theoretical consequences of the kind of Neogrammarian position taken by Paul, who had claimed that writing is not language, that 'it is in no way an equivalent for it' (Paul 1890: 663), and furthermore that as far as the linguist is concerned writing 'always needs to be rendered back into speech before it can be dealt with' (Paul 1890: 661). The weakness of the Neogrammarian position was that in practice the proclamation of conjectural 'sound laws', worked out *ad hoc* and mainly on the basis of textual evidence, was substituted for a general theory of the relationship between speech and writing. This, from a Saussurean point of view, was to put the cart before the horse. It is Saussure's doctrine of 'sound types', to be considered in the following chapter, which will explain in detail how a 'rendering back into speech' of written evidence is in principle possible. But such an explanation would be still-born without the theoretical underpinning provided by Saussure's thesis concerning the representational function of writing.

To appreciate how much hangs on this question of the relationship between writing and *la langue*, it suffices to examine what Saussure's position would be on any alternative assumption. Suppose, for example, the assumption were that writing represented solely *la parole*. Now according to the *Cours*, not even a camera can capture all the details of an act of *parole* ([32]). (If, as has been suggested, the remarks about writing on p.[32] are an editorial interpolation, it is nevertheless an interpolation which fulfils a valid and valuable role: for it at least provides an otherwise missing reason for distinguishing between the problem of representing *parole* and the problem of representing *langue*.) It would follow that writing, by definition, as an attempt to capture the facts of speech is an intrinsically imperfect form of representation. To determine in any particular case, therefore, how reliable a system of writing is, it would be necessary to compare it with the actual data of *parole*. But these data are precisely what the linguist does not have access to in the case of dead languages. Likewise, if it is supposed that writing is partly a representation of *langue* and partly a representation of *parole*, then without access to the data of *parole* it becomes impossible to determine which graphic features represent what. Finally, if it is supposed that writing represents neither *langue* nor *parole*, its value as evidence for the linguist is in any case reduced to nil. None of these options will suit the purposes of Saussure, who requires the assumption that certain forms of writing are in principle optimal representations of *la langue*, and the only practical problem is to detect and allow for those lapses from optimal representation which the passage of time and similar factors have brought about.

The second Saussurean thesis about writing is more specific; namely, that an 'ideal' alphabet would give the 'ideal' representation of the *image acoustique*, in the sense of a one-one correspondence between letters and the units of the *image acoustique*. Without this idealization, obviously, there is for Saussure little point in discussing the accuracy or inaccuracy of systems of alphabetic writing. On the Saussurean scale of values, alphabetic writing ranks above syllabic and ideographic systems, precisely because only alphabetic writing mirrors – or can in principle mirror – faithfully this aspect of the composition of the linguistic sign. An ideographic system could certainly provide separate symbols for the word 'cat' and the word 'dog': but it would not necessarily mirror anything at all about the *image acoustique* – not even whether these two words were identically pronounced or differently pronounced.

Saussurean commentators have failed to examine the tension between this specific thesis of 'alphabetic idealization' and the more general thesis that writing represents *la langue*. It may well be this tension which explains the rather summary treatment accorded in the *Cours* to the whole question of writing. The difficulty can be pinpointed by means of a hypothetical example. Suppose a language has two separate systems of writing, one ideographic and the other alphabetic. The ideographic system has different ideograms for the words 'cat' and 'dog'. However, these two words, let us suppose, are identically pronounced, and hence the alphabetic system does not distinguish between them. The example is not an unfair one, since Saussure goes so far as to say that in the case of Chinese, writing is 'a second *langue*' ([48]), and mentions that when confusion arises in conversation a Chinese may 'refer to the written form in order to explain what he means' ([48]). This concession itself is the Achilles' heel of Saussure's position on writing. For once it is admitted that writing may independently represent an idea or a thing without thereby representing any *image acoustique*, the general thesis that writing represents *la langue* is in tatters: and *a fortiori* the special thesis that alphabetic writing represents the *signifiant* of the linguistic sign.

There is one fleeting indication that the author of the *Cours* recognized the vulnerability of this Achilles' heel and endeavoured to protect it. In the remarks on ideographic writing we are told that the ideogram 'represents the entire word as a whole, and hence indirectly the idea expressed' ([47]). The fleeting indication is the word 'indirectly'. Saussure cannot allow the possibility that writing *directly* represents ideas. But he is caught here in a dilemma arising from his central doctrine that *la langue* is a simple bi-planar system, in which units on both planes are determined solely by bi-planar interrelations. Granted that an ideogram does not represent the *image acoustique* at all, there is no way in which it represents 'the entire word as a whole', and therefore no way in which it only 'indirectly' represents the idea expressed. One might just as well claim that at the same time the ideogram represents the *image acoustique* 'indirectly'. But that would be too obviously to beg the whole question of *what* it is that graphic symbols represent, and why an alphabetic system should be held to represent the *image acoustique* 'directly' (which presumably means, *inter alia*, a representation independent of *la parole*).

CHAPTER VII

Physiological Phonetics

The final topic treated in the Introduction to the *Cours* is phonetics. In view of what Saussure has said in the immediately preceding chapter concerning the relationship between writing and speech, his problem here is to steer a none-too-straightforward course between dismissing the study of articulatory processes *per se* as belonging to a linguistics of *la parole*, and admitting that without it the linguist would be in no position to interpret written sources as evidence bearing upon *la langue*. The compromise offered is that physiological phonetics is an 'auxiliary science' which sets linguistics free from reliance on the written word ([55]), and from the graphic illusions which would otherwise beset it ([56]). This compromise, at the same time as acknowledging that movements of the vocal apparatus are not part of *la langue* ([56]), makes it clear that *la langue* nevertheless relies on contrasts between the auditory impressions derived from phonation ([56]).

Critics have claimed to detect a contradiction between the views on phonetic transcription expressed in §2 of Chapter VII and the views on sound as the material substrate of *la langue* to be found in later passages in the *Cours*. This is because they have taken the principle of phonetic transcription enunciated on p.[57], which lays down the requirement that transcription should 'provide one symbol for each unit in the sequence of spoken sounds', to indicate Saussure's commitment to a belief in a 'natural' segmentation of *la chaîne parlée*. According to de Mauro (1972: 431-2 n.105):

> Saussure here seems to be convinced that it is possible to devise an 'unambiguous' phonetic transcription ... based on a prior analysis of the 'speech chain' into its successive 'elements', and the classification of these segments solely on the basis of phonetic criteria. This conviction would be well founded if, in contrast with what Saussure demonstrates elsewhere, physio-acoustic phenomena did have any capacity whatever or any reason whatsoever to group themselves into distinct classes, and if there were divisions of a physio-acoustic nature within phonic sequences ... But this is

a view contradicted primarily and absolutely by Saussure's pages on the intrinsically amorphous nature of phonic substance ([155f.]).

It is undeniable, as de Mauro goes on to point out, that the phonetician can produce a number of different classifications of speech sounds and a variety of segmentations of a given sound sequence, depending on the phonetic criteria selected as a basis for the analysis. In this sense, there are no unique or ultimate phonetic analyses given by Nature. What is questionable is whether Saussure ever implies that there are and, in particular, whether his pronouncements about phonetic transcription are in fact in conflict with his claims about the 'amorphousness' of sound. The Appendix which follows Chapter VII sets out a system of phonetic classification for speech: but there is no claim that it is the only possible classification. What is claimed for the system, rather, is that its principles provide a 'natural basis' ([63]) and a 'natural starting point' ([64]) for the linguist's study of speech sounds. The 'naturalness' resides in the fact that, unlike certain other phonetic systems, this is a system based jointly on articulatory and auditory criteria. Why is this 'natural'? Because, we are told, that is the principle on which human speech perception in fact works. 'We cannot tell articulatorily where one sound ends and another begins ... It is the sequence the ear hears that enables us immediately to detect when one sound is replaced by another ...' ([64]). Now Saussure offers no physiological or experimental evidence in support of this claim: but that is a different matter. What is quite clear is that the claim itself does not deny the possibility of more than one way of analysing and classifying phonetic data. His system is an amplification, in short, of the point made previously in Chapter III about the duality of linguistic phenomena. 'One cannot divorce what is heard from oral articulation. Nor, on the other hand, can one specify the relevant movements of the vocal organs without reference to the corresponding auditory impression' ([24]). This is where the 'amorphousness' of sound is given due recognition: it remains an undifferentiated continuum until subjected to the conjoint discriminations provided by the articulatory and auditory processes of speech. The discriminations have to be conjoint because, taken separately, an articulatory sequence is as 'unanalysable' as the corresponding auditory sequence ([64-5]).

A different question again is whether we should read Saussure as being committed to the proposition that in speech there is a basic, universal (language-neutral) differentiation of the amorphous phonetic continuum. Relevant to this are his remarks in praise of the primitive Greek alphabet. 'Each *son simple* is represented by one symbol, and conversely each symbol invariably corresponds to a *son simple*' ([64]). But this principle, 'which is both a necessary and a sufficient condition for good transcription' ([64]), was a principle 'not grasped by other nations, and consequently their alphabets do not analyse sound sequences into

constituent auditory units' ([65]). Saussure cites as deficient in this
respect the Cypriot syllabary and the Semitic system of representing
consonants only. It is certainly very easy to construe this comparison as
implying that the Greeks had discovered a fact of nature about human
speech which had eluded other literate civilizations. Is it possible, on the
other hand, to treat these remarks as pointing out merely that not all
literate peoples manage to analyse what would nowadays be called the
'phoneme system' of their own language? There are various reasons for
regarding such a reading as implausible. In the first place, the
observations about the Greek alphabet occur in a chapter devoted to
phonetics, which has already been quite unequivocally described as a
merely 'auxiliary' discipline, concerned with *faits de parole* as distinct
from *faits de langue*. For Saussure: 'It is true that if no *langue* existed the
movements of the vocal apparatus would be pointless. None the less,
these movements are not part of *la langue*, and an exhaustive analysis of
the processes of phonation required to produce every auditory impression
tells us nothing about *la langue*' ([56]). In the second place, nowhere in
this chapter (or elsewhere in the *Cours*) do we find a discussion of the
possibility that the same sound sequence might be analysed differently
by speakers of different languages – a *topos* nowadays reiterated *ad
nauseam* in introductory manuals. This is a point Saussure never makes
in spite of the fact that it is eminently 'Saussurean'.

A third consideration is the way Saussure defines the minimum unit of
speech as 'an aggregate of auditory impressions and articulatory
movements, comprising what is heard and what is spoken, one delimiting
the other' ([65]). More explicitly still, 'a combination such as *ta* will
always comprise two units, each occupying a certain temporal segment'
([66]). There is no mention at all of the possibility that *ta* in different
languages might be treated as comprising different units. Thus there
appears to be no room in Saussurean phonetics for the hypothetical
Cypriot who claims that *ta* is just one sound (because clearly the Cypriot
syllable is a single unit), or for the hypothetical Semite who claims that
ta is just one variety of the single consonant *t* (because clearly the
Semitic root is a combination of consonants). Both these claims would be
objectively 'wrong' for Saussure. In short, the Saussurean *linguistique de
la parole* envisages a universal set of 'irreducible' phonetic units or
'sound types', of which the number is limited. (This again fits in with
Saussure's evident wish to allow the possibility of engaging in an analysis
of *la langue* for dead languages accessible only through written sources.
Otherwise, no concession at all to nineteenth-century linguistics would
be possible. But if the number of 'sound types' is universal and limited,
and if writing systems are sufficiently advanced to 'represent' them, the
possibility remains open. All the linguist analysing Greek or Latin has to
do is decide which of the universal 'sound types' are represented by
which letters in the Greek and Latin alphabets. Since the inventory is

limited, an analysis should be possible, always provided that the available written evidence is internally consistent.)

Fourth, it would be an anachronism to attribute retrospectively to Saussure any more 'modern' view of the phoneme. His approach to identifying the minimal units of speech is what would nowadays be called 'physical', as opposed to either 'psychological' or 'functional' (Fudge 1970). Not only that, but Saussure's is a very primitive variety of 'physical' theory. It is not the more sophisticated 'family of related sounds' of Daniel Jones, but rather the crude 'physiological alphabet' concept of Max Müller. Saussure, indeed, would doubtless have approved Müller's contempt for 'too much nicety' in phonetics and his insistence that all the linguist needs is to acquire 'a clear conception of what has been well called the *Alphabet of Nature*'. Müller wrote (1864: 165-6):

> If we have clearly impressed on our mind the normal conditions of the organs of speech in the production of vowels and consonants, it will be easy to arrange the sounds of every new language under the categories once established on a broad basis. To do this, to arrange the alphabet of any given language according to the compartments planned by physiological research, is the office of the grammarian, not of the physiologist.

In a similar vein, Saussure sees no problem of 'discovery procedures' for the linguist in identifying the sound units of an unfamiliar language: 'after analysing a considerable number of sound sequences from a variety of languages, the linguist is able to recognise and classify the units involved' ([66]). Just a question of professional experience, it would seem.

Such expertise is possible only on the assumption that Nature has provided for the exercise of *la langue* an instrument of very limited capacity (namely, the human vocal apparatus) constructed in a way which can be studied independently of its utilisation by this or that particular linguistic community. Consequently, the problem of 'rendering back into speech' the evidence of writing is analogous to the problem confronting a musicologist who has to interpret various forms of musical notation, but knows in advance that the melodies in question were all designed to be played on a pipe of which the entire constructional details are independently available. The musicologist, given this problem, will doubtless proceed on the assumption that an 'ideal' musical notation is one which indicates as simply and unambiguously as possible the different fingering positions corresponding to the various notes which the pipe is capable of producing. In addition, it might perhaps be assumed that the more musically sophisticated the civilization the closer its musical notation will tend to approximate to an ideal one-one correspondence between symbol and finger position (always allowing for a small number of discrepancies to be explained by reference to particular historical and cultural circumstances). In this complex of musicological assumptions, nothing precludes the possibility that different musical communities may have developed quite different musical scales, even though the instrument used for musical *parole* is identical. The musical analogy just outlined is nowhere suggested in the pages of the *Cours*, but it makes good sense overall of the various pronouncements in the *Cours* about the relationships between linguistics, phonetics and writing.

Was Saussure perhaps a more 'advanced' musicologist than this simple analogy suggests? It is sometimes implied by Saussurean scholars that a kind of pre-Prague-School concept of the phoneme as a purely differential unit within a system of phonological oppositions (irrespective of its exact pronunciation) is already in germ in the precocious *Mémoire sur le système primitif des voyelles* of 1879. If this is so, then it is fair comment to add that in the thirty-odd years between the publication of the *Mémoire* and the publication of the *Cours* germination had still not occurred. For nowhere does the Saussure of the *Cours* supply what a present-day reader would regard as an explicit and unequivocal distinction between minimum units of phonetic analysis and minimum units of phonological analysis. What will be found instead are various remarks which might lead us nowadays to expect that Saussure is about to formulate the very definition of the phoneme we anticipate. But a search for such a definition itself in the pages of the *Cours* is a search in vain.

Is this a lacuna in the *Cours*? Does Saussure's linguistics actually need a 'structural' definition of the phoneme? It may doubtless be regarded as heretical by some Saussureans to suggest that it does not, and that therefore it is quite gratuitous to suspect Saussure of failure to realize and explicate the phonological possibilities inherent in his own structuralism. But that is because modern intellectual fashions favour theories which are completely self-contained, as distinct from being merely free of internal contradictions. It is perfectly possible, on the other hand, to read Saussure as allowing that a human *faculté de langage* which presides over the culturally determined patterns of bi-planar correlation between sounds and concepts will 'naturally' (that is, biologically) choose certain modes of physiological articulation, irrespective of the particular circumstances of cultural history. It will not fall within the province of linguistics to *explain*, but merely to grasp these modes of articulation. For theoretical purposes, consideration of the connexion between the cultural facts and the biological facts may be indefinitely postponed through insisting on a series of 'intermediate' levels. But by the same token, the connexion might just as well be recognized as soon as convenient. It makes no theoretical difference; and considerations of intellectual 'economy' favour the latter strategy. In any semiological study, as defined by Saussure, there will come a point at which the possibility of semiological contrasts is restricted by or coincides with a certain range of physiological possibilities, if semiology is a human science. (How does the motorist distinguish between a 'red' traffic light and a 'green' one?) But the precise level at which that restriction is encountered is irrelevant. Clearly, there will be more or less naive conceptualizations of the interface between the cultural and the biological, as well as more or less sophisticated ones. The author of the *Cours* may well nowadays sound as if he is offering a fairly naive version. The interesting point to observe is however we read the *Cours*, it is clear that we are intended to treat linguistics as an investigation which is – to adopt a convenient Irish formulation – 'practicable, if only in theory'. At the time the *Cours* was published, it would have been academically impolitic, to say the very least, to draw the dividing line between the theoretically practicable and the theoretically impracticable in such a way as to exclude from a scientific linguistics the study of the languages of antiquity. The Classics were still the backbone of European education. The possibility of a 'scientific' study of Greek and Latin could be made more plausible by reducing the gap between the cultural and the biological aspects of language than by widening it. It is no matter for surprise that in the *Cours* we find the gap as narrow as it is.

APPENDIX

Principles of Physiological Phonetics

Saussure's linguistics is certainly not a phonetically based linguistics. Bloomfield said contemptuously of the phonetics in the *Cours* that it was 'an abstraction from French and Swiss-German which will not stand even the test of an application to English' (Bloomfield 1923). A more important point to make might have been that Saussure's phonetics is not in any serious sense phonetics at all, but merely an attempt to justify an alphabetic conceptualization of the *image acoustique*. Saussure comes close to conceding this when he remarks at the very beginning of Chapter VII: 'If we try to dismiss the written form from our mind, and do away with any visual image altogether, we run the risk of being left with an amorphous object which is difficult to grasp. It is as if someone learning to swim had suddenly had his cork float taken away' ([55]). The Appendix to the Introduction provides an example of the kind of cork float which Saussurean linguistics still assumed to be available. Although it does not advertise itself as a transcription system, in fact that is what it is. Its details do not matter a great deal, and will therefore not be discussed at length here. For purposes of Saussurean theory, any number of alternative systems would have served the turn just as well. That is why the editors – rightly – relegated it to an appendix.

The specific system of phonetic analysis adopted is based in part on notes from an earlier course of lectures given in 1897 ([63]) supplemented by a descriptive framework borrowed from Jespersen ([67] n.2). Its minutiae are irrelevant to the main linguistic issues with which the *Cours* is concerned. Thus, for example, the adoption of a classification of sounds by aperture ([70]ff.), in preference to the more usual classification by point of articulation, has no theoretical significance whatsoever. Articulatory and auditory phonetics have in any case moved a long way since the turn of the century. The main thing which is relevant to a present-day reading of the *Cours* is how its treatment of phonetics affects the theoretical coherence of Saussure's position, and this has already been discussed in connexion with Chapter VII.

Only one or two further points need be added in the present context. The division of the subject into two parts, one comprising an inventory of individual 'sound types' and the other a 'combinatory phonetics' of the speech chain, is obviously significant in relation to Saussure's 'second principle' of linguistics: the linearity of the *signifiant* ([103]). It also has certain implications for his treatment of sound change, which needs to be able to count classes of sound types and positions in the speech chain as 'naturally' given (that is to say, determined by purely physiological criteria) in order to claim (i) that phonetic evolution operates quite independently of *signifiés* and of linguistic structure in general, and (ii) that the developments formulated as 'sound laws' are in fact isolated, one-off events with no systematic properties ([132-4]).

Although phonetics is for Saussure merely 'an ancillary science to linguistics' ([77]), he is willing to concede that in certain cases it can help the linguist solve genuinely linguistic problems: for example, the much debated question of Proto-Indo-European sonants ([79]). He also seems willing to concede that there may be phonological universals in language which are to be explained by reference to purely phonetic factors ([79]).

Finally, it may be worth noting that Saussure's recognition that languages are not free to adopt just *any* linear combination of sound types as a *signifiant* (because of articulatory restrictions: [78-9]) in no way infringes his doctrine of the arbitrariness of the sign ([100-2]). Arbitrariness is a question of the relationship between a particular *signifiant* and a particular *signifié*: it has nothing to do with the range of the possible inventory of *signifiants* available.

PART ONE
General Principles

CHAPTER I

Nature of the Linguistic Sign

By the end of the Introduction, Saussure has presented the reader with a preliminary conceptual framework within which to situate general questions about language and the study of language. The basis of this framework is a broad distinction between *faits de langue* and *faits de parole*. These two classes combine to make up the totality of *faits de langage*. Linguistics as a science, according to Saussure, deals with nothing else. It does not include, except incidentally, the study of writing or of other modes of linguistic expression than the spoken. It does not claim to deal with language as a specific human mental faculty (if indeed any such faculty exists). As between *faits de langue* and *faits de parole*, a science of language will give priority to the former. But nothing has so far been said in detail about what exactly *faits de langue* are or how they may be investigated, other than that they are facts of a social and supraindividual character, which are nevertheless implicated in the individual acts of speech which constitute the sum total of human linguistic activity. Having established this framework in outline, the *Cours* now proceeds to lay down what the title of Part I calls 'General Principles' ([97]). The first chapter of Part I considers the nature of the linguistic sign, and in particular its duality.

Later commentators on the Saussurean linguistic sign principally focussed their attention on one or other of the features which Saussure posits as its fundamental characteristics: 'arbitrariness' and 'linearity'. Just how these characteristics are best interpreted for purposes of Saussurean linguistics will be discussed below. The former in particular has been the subject of prolonged controversy, which still continues. (Toussaint 1983. A bibliography of this controversy down to 1964 is given in Engler 1962 and 1964.) Concentration on this much-debated issue has meant, unfortunately, that an even more basic problem about the Saussurean linguistic sign has been virtually ignored. It is this more basic problem, however, which ultimately gives rise to precisely the difficulties which critics have encountered in trying to give a satisfactory interpretation to the Saussurean notion of arbitrariness. This is the problem, quite simply, of identifying which elements Saussure claims are 'combined' in the duality of the linguistic sign, and making sense of how they are thus 'combined'. On these issues the picture which the *Cours* initially presents is simple and dramatic, rather than perspicuous.

The reader, by now accustomed to the style of presentation typical of the *Cours*, will not be surprised to find the opening paragraphs of the chapter ([97-8]) devoted to explaining what linguistic signs are not. Signs are not, we are told, dualities which comprise pairings of names with things named (for instance, the name *tree* with a botanical specimen or specimens). The sole feature of this 'nomenclaturist' misconception which Saussure concedes not to be erroneous is its dualism: that is, its recognition of the linguistic sign as a bi-partite unit ([98]). For Saussure too the linguistic sign is bi-partite; but apparently a bi-partite entity of quite a different kind from the nomenclaturist's sign.

Saussure's attack on nomenclaturism in the *Cours* has been compared, not unreasonably, to Wittgenstein's in the *Philosophical Investigations* (Wittgenstein 1958: §1ff.). It is certainly interesting that both Saussure and Wittgenstein use an attack on nomenclaturism as a way of introducing a view of language which is – or purports to be – entirely antithetical to the nomenclaturist position. It is all the more interesting in that Wittgenstein, as far as is known, had never read Saussure, and neither Wittgenstein nor Saussure was drawing upon any earlier antinomenclaturist tradition. Wittgenstein chose to attack specifically the 'Augustinian' picture of language (Baker and Hacker 1980), which is an ancient and prototypical example of nomenclaturism. But Saussure's target is less clearly defined: and Saussure's objections are not Wittgenstein's.

According to the *Cours*, the nomenclaturist theory of the linguistic sign is open to many objections, but only three of these are specified ([97]). First, nomenclaturism presupposes that ideas exist 'ready made' in advance of names. Second, it fails to make clear whether names are vocal or mental entities. Third, it implies that the link between name and thing is a 'simple' one, which is not the case. These objections are so cryptic that it is by no means easy to judge exactly what target they are aimed at. Is Saussure attacking the Biblical account of the origin of names? (There is a manuscript note which refers to the story of Adam in Genesis: de Mauro 1972: 439-40 n.129.) Or is he attacking some philosophically more sophisticated theory? All the *Cours* says is that, 'for some people' a language 'reduced to its essentials, is a nomenclature' ([97]).

More perplexing than the deliberate vagueness is this curious trio of indictments. For they do not, either individually or collectively, adequately identify the essentials of the thesis apparently under attack. Is it, for instance, an essential feature of nomenclaturism to leave open the question of whether names are vocal or mental? (Why, it might be asked, is this an important question anyway? Why cannot a name be both vocal and mental? Does one interpretation exclude the other?) Presumably a nomenclaturist who held, for whatever reason, that names are not vocal but mental would *ipso facto* not incur Saussure's criticism on that score. Is it essential for the nomenclaturist to hold that the relationship between name and thing is a 'simple' relationship? On the contrary, a commonly held nomenclaturist view going back via the medieval *modistae* to Aristotle (Harris 1980: 34ff.) maintained that names serve to signify things only indirectly, by way of concepts. Again, is the notion that ideas exist 'ready made' essential to the nomenclaturist? Is not the nomenclaturist's commitment rather to the proposition that things exist 'ready made'? Is it not the tree which the nomenclaturist regards as given by Nature, rather than our idea of what a tree is? In short, it seems possible to be a nomenclaturist and yet escape scot free on all three of Saussure's charges. The reader cannot fail to see that there is something very odd about this.

The oddity, as so often in the *Cours*, becomes less odd than at first sight appears if one bears in mind the probability that what is implicitly under attack here is not a philosophical thesis as such but the way nineteenth-century linguistics had made use of this thesis. The clue is provided for the attentive reader by the discrepancy between Saussure's claim that nomenclaturism pairs names with things and the immediately following objection that this involves supposing that 'ideas' are given in advance; whereas the objection one might expect is, rather, that it involves supposing that 'things' are given in advance.

Saussure's objection has to be read against an intellectual background where it was commonplace to claim that linguistics was 'scientific' precisely inasmuch as the linguist could 'prove' that, for example, French *arbre* was a direct descendant of Latin *arbor*. Part of the proof would be that *arbre* and *arbor* were both names of the 'same thing'. The framework of nineteenth-century linguistics had been built on etymologies which validated countless correlations such as that between *arbre* and *arbor* by tacit reference to the assumption that one could establish whether or not a word had changed its meaning by determining whether or not the thing it designated had remained the same. (This was not a necessary condition for etymological identity, nor even a sufficient condition; but conjointly with conformity to regular patterns of sound change it yielded a sufficient condition.) The point Saussure is making is that even if trees have not changed in any significant respect between Caesar's day and Napoleon's, and even if the thing designated by the word *arbor* is the same as the thing designated by the word *arbre*, this does not mean that there has been no change of meaning *unless we also assume that identity of things designated guarantees identity of ideas* (as Aristotle, for one, appears to have maintained, to judge by *De Interpretatione* I: '... the mental affections themselves, of which words are primarily signs, are the same for the whole of mankind ...'). Unless one accepts this Aristotelian assumption, which in effect guarantees that *arbor* and *arbre* 'mean the same' (granted the botanical invariance of trees) the semantic part of the linguist's etymological theory collapses. It lacks any way of proving that *arbor* and *arbre* have the same meaning. For identity of things referred to does not entail sameness of meaning (a point Frege had made in 1892, but which Saussure, who had almost certainly never read *Über Sinn und Bedeutung*, seems to have arrived at independently).

Once we see that Saussure's attack on nomenclaturism is an indirect attack on his linguistic predecessors (just as Wittgenstein's was an indirect attack on his philosophical predecessors), we also see that the three objections to nomenclaturism formally tabled in this chapter of the *Cours* are nothing other than counterparts to three claims which Saussure is committed to maintain against one widespread nineteenth-century view of the linguistic sign. The first of these is the most important, and is that the constitutive elements of the linguistic sign are not physical but mental. 'The linguistic sign links not a thing and a name, but a concept and a sound pattern' ([98]).

It is at this point ([99]) that the *Cours* proposes the introduction of the technical terms *signifiant* (= sound pattern), *signifié* (= concept) and *signe* (= *signifiant* + *signifié*) to avoid any potential misunderstanding arising from the way the word *signe* is commonly used. Ordinarily, says Saussure, the French word *signe* ('sign') designates solely the *image acoustique*. This is a surprising claim, which it seems difficult to justify. It takes far more metalinguistic subtlety than lay language-users have much time for to draw a careful distinction of the kind Saussure insists on between the 'sound' of a word in the sense of its *image acoustique* and the 'sound' of a word in the sense of the associated acoustic phenomena. In any case, the French word *signe*, like the English word *sign*, is much more generally employed in connexion with various forms of visual communication than to designate any mental correlate of the spoken word. More unfortunately still, having drawn this somewhat question-able distinction between the allegedly lay use of the term *signe* and its proposed technical use in linguistics, Saussure more than once in the *Cours* fails to follow his own terminological recommendation, and slips back into the 'non-technical' usage which he has previously rejected. (An example occurs in the very next chapter, p.[109].)

At this crucial point in the *Cours* where the new 'technical' concept of the linguistic sign is introduced the reader is given surprisingly little help towards understanding it. The only example offered is the Latin *arbor* ('tree'), and this is a particularly Delphic example. The diagrams ([99]) by means of which the *Cours* supposedly spells out the relationship between the *concept* and the *image acoustique* of *arbor* are especially problematic. The difficulty is that *arbor* can be interpreted in at least two ways; either lexemically or morphologically. That is to say, the written form *arbor* (Saussure never tells us how it is pronounced) can be taken to stand either for an item of Latin vocabulary (in the sense in which the conventional dictionary lists items of vocabulary) or, more specifically, for a particular word-form, the nominative singular in the paradigm of a certain Latin noun. These are two quite different linguistic units. Is this an example of false disingenuity which the reader is expected to see through? Does it deliberately blur the distinction between lexicology and grammar? Or does Saussure simply fail to recognize that the 'combination' of *signifiant* with *signifié* is not quite the simple bi-partite correlation which the diagrams suggest?

It is worth looking at the diagrams on p.[99] with these questions in mind, since this is a point on which the authenticity of the text of the *Cours* has been seriously questioned (de Mauro 1972: 441, n.132). It appears that the third diagram has been added by the editors, together with the arrows in all three diagrams.

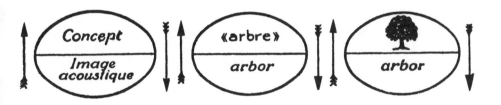

According to de Mauro (loc.cit.) we have here an example of how a minor editorial intervention may have quite serious consequences. The editors are also responsible for describing Latin *arbor* as a 'word' (*mot*), and for the observation that the two elements in a sign are 'intimately linked and each triggers the other'. The result, claims de Mauro, is that 'the reader has the impression that for Saussure the *signifiant* is the vocable, the *signifié* is the image of the object, and that each recalls the other, just as the nomenclaturist maintains. Thus we slide towards a concept which is the diametric opposite of Saussure's.'

How far is this criticism justified? One way of assessing it is to see how the reader would fare if the allegedly misleading additions were simply removed. This would leave the first two diagrams (without arrows), the status of *arbor* unexplained, and no comment on the connexion between the *image acoustique* and its corresponding *concept*. Now in certain respects this simple version makes interpretation easier; but in other respects more difficult. There is no longer any occasion for puzzling over the relationship between the second and third diagrams, because the third diagram has disappeared. On the other hand, the removal of the arrows and of the comment about the link between *image acoustique* and *concept* leaves something of a lacuna between this account of the linguistic sign and the account which the previously presented speech-circuit theory of *la parole* apparently demands, where concepts were said to trigger sound-patterns and vice versa ([28]). (These 'vertical' arrows come up for discussion again in the chapter on *La valeur linguistique* ([158ff.]), where they are distinguished from 'horizontal' arrows linking one sign to another.) Finally, and perhaps most importantly, in this simplified version the Latin example is identified as a linguistic unit solely by means of pairing an orthographic form (*arbor*) with a French translation ('arbre').

The net result is to shift the balance on p.[99] in favour of a lexemic interpretation of *arbor*; for *arbor* and *arbre* appear to stand to each other as lemma and gloss respectively in an imaginary bilingual dictionary or 'mental lexicon' somewhere in the speaker's brain. The function of the third diagram now becomes clear: in effect, it warns the reader *not* to construe the second diagram in this simplistic way. For in the third diagram the French translation *arbre* is replaced by a picture of a tree. In isolation, such a diagram would doubtless suggest a rather naive equation of concepts with pictorial mental images; but as an alternative to the second diagram in which the same concept is represented by a translation, it assumes a different significance. The conceptual component of the sign *arbor* is evidently to be understood as an abstract 'meaning' which can be mentally interpreted in various ways, both verbal and visual.

So far, then, it seems that in Saussure's technical sense the linguistic sign *arbor* is to be construed simply as a mental combination of a certain sound pattern with a certain meaning. At this stage the reader has been told nothing about the internal relationship of the *signifiant* to the *signifié*, and it is this omission which makes *arbor* an unfortunate example to have chosen. If *arbor* is to be construed as representing a morphological form rather than a lexeme, would one not expect its conceptual component to include not only the notion 'tree' but also the notions 'nominative' and 'singular'? The fact that these notions are missing altogether from the account of the *signifié* presented on p.[99] raises a legitimate doubt in the reader's mind as to whether grammatical notions count as concepts at all in Saussure's sense. In fact, they do: but this does not become clear until later in the *Cours*. (On the basis of what is said in §3 of Chapter III on *La linguistique statique et la linguistique évolutive* it will be retrospectively evident that the 'full' Saussurean analysis of *arbor* treats it as a combination of stem plus a 'zero' sign: but we are not given this more sophisticated analysis on p.[99], since the ground has not yet been prepared for it.)

The explanation for this rather unsatisfactory expository strategy is presumably as follows. At the point in the text where *arbor* is introduced to exemplify the Saussurean theory of the linguistic sign, the prime concern is seen as being to ensure that the reader does not unwittingly identify the two components of this bi-partite unit with the 'names' and 'things' recognized by the nomenclaturist (who here represents the erroneous view accepted in nineteenth-century linguistics). This is why a typically nomenclaturist example is taken (the 'name' *arbor*) and explicitly re-interpreted in a Saussurean manner. To this end, the third diagram giving a pictorial version of the *signifié* on p.[99] deliberately utilizes again the same 'tree picture' as originally appeared on p.[97] to illustrate the misguided nomenclaturist pairing of 'name' and 'thing'. The intention is doubtless to emphasize that the difference between the nomenclaturist theory of the sign and the Saussurean theory of the sign is *not* a difference over what a tree is (or, *mutatis mutandis*, any other 'thing'). What distinguishes the two theories on this particular issue is solely and simply that whereas the 'tree picture' in the nomenclaturist diagram stands for a tree, the corresponding 'tree picture' in the Saussurean version stands for a concept of a tree (which is not just an internal visual image, as the equivalence between the second and third diagrams shows).

In short, the text of the *Cours* here attempts (not altogether successfully) to disabuse the reader of two possible misconceptions simultaneously. One misconception is that the bone of contention between Saussure and the nomenclaturist has something to do with the extent to which speakers' linguistic concepts are a true reflection of things in the external world: on the contrary, it has nothing at all to do with that. The other misconception is that speakers' linguistic concepts are just private pictorial images of corresponding things in the external world. (Exactly what linguistic concepts are, however, will not be fully explained until the chapter on *La valeur linguistique*.)

The expository price paid for this decision to emphasize at the outset just the main parallels and contrasts between two possible archetypes of a theory of the linguistic sign (one archetypally 'wrong' and the other archetypally 'right') is expensive. For it leads directly to the various uncertainties and difficulties of interpretation noted above. This expense is only justified if we grasp that the main thrust of the *Cours* at this point is to dissociate itself from certain 'built in' assumptions about language which a university student of linguistics who had followed the

established curriculum of comparative and historical studies in the early
years of the present century might be expected to have acquired. The
picture such studies project is that the 'scientific' approach to language
reveals mankind's linguistic activity over the centuries as a slow but
continuous process of developing new sets of vocal labels for a basic
universe of 'things' antecedently given by Nature (and subject to only
marginal cultural additions, discoveries or reclassifications). This is what
Saussure calls the view of languages as 'nomenclatures'. Saussurean
linguistics proposes to reject this view entirely, except – and the sole
exception is an important one – insofar as it endorses the idea that
languages are bi-planar systems and the linguistic sign is bi-partite.

One reason why the exception is important is that later critics claimed
that this retention of a bi-planar analysis of language was Saussure's
great mistake. Instead of championing bi-partition, he should have opted
for tri-partition. Rather than insisting that the meaning of a word was in
the mind, and not in the external world, he should have recognized that
language involves a triangular relationship between, for example, (i) the
word *arbor*, (ii) the botanical tree, and (iii) the mental concept 'tree'.
This is the gist of the anti-Saussurean position first taken by Ogden and
Richards in their book *The Meaning of Meaning* (1923) and subsequently
endorsed by others. According to critics of this school, Saussure correctly
perceived the inadequacy of the old 'name-and-thing' model of the
linguistic sign, but wrongly supposed that the simple solution was to
transpose both terms of this duality into the mental sphere. (Hence an
image acoustique coupled with a *concept*.) Thus, far from solving the
problem of the linguistic sign, Saussure simply perpetuated an old error
in a new disguise.

'How great is the tyranny of language over those who propose to inquire
into its workings,' say Ogden and Richards, 'is well shown in the
speculations of the late F. de Saussure, a writer regarded by perhaps a
majority of French and Swiss students as having for the first time placed
linguistics upon a scientific basis' (Ogden and Richards 1923: 4). This
attack on Saussure is placed right at the beginning of *The Meaning of
Meaning*, thus ironically emulating the Saussurean strategy of beginning
with the demolition of a linguistic Aunt Sally. All Saussure succeeded in
accomplishing as a theorist, according to Ogden and Richards, was (by
his definition of *la langue*) 'inventing verbal entities outside the range of
possible investigation' (Ogden and Richards 1923: 5). The fatal and
irremediable flaw was that Saussure's theory of signs 'by neglecting
entirely the things for which signs stand, was from the beginning cut off
from any contact with scientific methods of verification' (Ogden and
Richards 1923: 6). It might perhaps be noted at this point that if Ogden
and Richards had been writing fifty years later they would doubtless
have levelled exactly the same criticism against those proponents of
generative linguistics who, like Saussure, make a theoretical virtue out of

'neglecting entirely the things for which signs stand'.

Saussure's fatal omission Ogden and Richards proposed to remedy by including a 'referent' in their celebrated triangular model of the sign (Ogden and Richards 1923: 11):

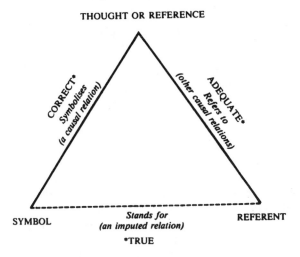

According to defenders of Saussure, on the other hand, any attempt to remedy the supposed omission from Saussure's theory of the linguistic sign, by 'adding' a third component, simply reveals a failure to understand Saussure's position (de Mauro 1972: 439 n.129). The conflict between these two attitudes towards the Saussurean view of the essential duality of linguistic signs is important for a reading of the *Cours*. How are we to construe Saussure's deliberate exclusion of the fact that the *prima facie* reason for the existence of the linguistic sign *arbor* is that speakers feel some social necessity or desirability for a word referring to trees (and, similarly, of other 'names' for 'things')?

There are very divisive issues involved here. Ullmann (dismissed by de Mauro (1972: 439 n.129) as a follower of Ogden and Richards) makes the point that there is nothing fundamentally new in the Ogden and Richards 'triangle': it is a reversion to the medieval scholastic dictum '*vox significat mediantibus conceptibus*' (Ullmann 1962: 56). Furthermore, in Ullmann's opinion the Ogden and Richards 'triangle' offers, from the point of view of the linguist, 'both too little and too much'. It offers too little because it 'seems to neglect the speaker's point of view' (Ullmann 1962: 37). On the other hand, it offers too much because 'the referent, the non-linguistic feature or event as such, clearly lies outside the linguist's province' (Ullmann 1962: 56). The reasons Ullmann gives for this exclusion, however, reveal his fundamental lack of sympathy with (or failure to comprehend) the Saussurean duality of the linguistic sign. Ullmann says: 'An object may remain unchanged and yet the meaning of its name may change for us if there is any alteration in our awareness of it, our knowledge about it, or our feelings towards it.' This Saussure would never have said. So Ullmann ends up by restricting the linguist's attention to a bi-partite relationship; but for reasons Saussure would not have endorsed.

That Saussure's analysis of the linguistic sign *arbor* (unlike the nomenclaturist's account) finds no place for the botanical 'thing' we call a tree is no reflection on the professional incompetence of linguists in botanical matters. There is, in principle, no reason why the linguist should not try to find out, if need be, everything the botanist knows about trees. Botanists, after all, are members of linguistic communities, no less than linguists. But from a Saussurean point of view the acquisition of endless information about trees is linguistically irrelevant. What matters as regards the meaning of the linguistic sign *arbor* is neither, on the one hand, the totality of what the Romans knew, believed or felt regarding trees; nor, on the other, which particular types of tree happened to grow in the Roman empire. What counts is how, conceptually, the Latin language used the sign *arbor* to contrast with other Latin linguistic signs. And this is essentially an 'internal' matter pertaining to the structure of Latin. It has to do only indirectly with the 'external' botanical facts, or with such knowledge of botany as the Romans possessed. Thus when Saussure's diagram offers *arbre* as a conceptual 'translation' of *arbor*, it implies neither that what the French mean by *arbre* the Romans meant by *arbor*, nor that botanical classifications have remained invariant for two thousand years; but merely – and more basically – that the relationship between the Latin *signifiant* and *signifié* in the case of *arbor* is of the same order as that between the French *signifiant* and *signifié* in the case of *arbre*.

*   *   *

The relationship between *signifiant* and *signifié*, the *Cours* tells us, is 'arbitrary'. This is not presented as a mere generalization, but as a 'principle': indeed, 'the first principle' of linguistics ([100]). It is necessary to insist on this point at the outset, if only for the reason that much subsequent criticism of the Saussurean concept of arbitrariness seems to be predicated on the misguided assumption that whether or not a sign is arbitrary is a matter to be resolved by simple observation of the facts (possibly with the tacit help of etymology). No one, says Saussure, disputes the arbitrariness of the linguistic sign ([100]). Perhaps some of his critics took this as a rash challenge which could easily be quashed by the simple expedient of proceeding to dispute it.

More serious is the fact that Saussure initially supports the thesis of arbitrariness by invoking examples and arguments which appear to be ultimately inconsistent with his own theory of the sign. Citing the fact that different languages have different terms for the same thing (French *bœuf*, German *Ochs*, [100]) is a blatantly nomenclaturist argument, particularly since the first section of this chapter has just been devoted to explaining why the internal *signifié* of a linguistic sign is not to be confused with the external thing which the sign may be the name of. On the face of it, therefore, interlinguistic disparity of nomenclature could not possibly be a relevant consideration for Saussure: or if it is, then it undermines his own case.

One explanation that has been offered for this apparent contradiction is that the editors of the *Cours* clumsily incorporated at this point an example originally given in an early lecture, before the introduction of the terms *signifiant* and *signifié* (de Mauro 1972: 443, n.137). Once again, this rescues Saussure at the expense of his editors, who are implicitly accused of overlooking a glaring inconsistency in the text. If we allow that the editors may have been a little less obtuse than this explanation would suggest, there is an alternative. It is that insistence on arbitrariness as a 'principle' of linguistics (and the word *principe* is used no less than five times on this page of the *Cours*) is to be understood as meaning that we are dealing with a truth which has to be recognized irrespective of one's own theoretical position. Thus we should take the *bœuf/Ochs* example as showing that even on a nomenclaturist view of the sign it has to be admitted that the connexion between the two parts of the sign is arbitrary. This gives point to the remark which immediately follows the example: that 'no one' (sc. not even a nomenclaturist) disputes the principle. Indeed, from a nomenclaturist point of view the principle is even more obvious than from a Saussurean point of view. But then, as Saussure goes on to observe, 'it is often easier to discover a truth than to assign it to its correct place'. The nomenclaturist, in other words, may well recognize that the bi-partite relationship is arbitrary, but fails to see what consequences for linguistics follow from this truth.

Similar considerations would explain why Saussure bothers to deal specifically with the straw 'counterexamples' of onomatopoeia and exclamations ([101-2]), which in fact do not endanger his own theoretical position in the least. The point is that these cases do not conflict with the principle of arbitrariness however interpreted. There may well be a natural connexion between the call of a cuckoo and the names of that bird in various languages. Likewise there may be a natural connexion between an exclamation and a cry of pain, fear, etc. But these connexions, far from supporting a 'naturalist' theory of the linguistic sign, serve as indirect evidence against such a theory by making all the more conspicuous the difficulty of explaining the general relationship between the two parts of *any* linguistic sign as determined non-arbitrarily. Onomatopoeic words and exclamations are not even for Saussure exceptions which prove the rule. The natural connexions to which they bear witness are contingent, not essential. There is no sense in which the cuckoo had to have a name which echoed its characteristic call, or exclamations had to mimic natural cries.

Thus far, then, the principle of arbitrariness is presented as acceptable and accepted, no matter which particular theory of the linguistic sign a linguist adopts. All this means is that there is simply no plausible basis for an alternative principle of non-arbitrariness, whether we are nomenclaturists, Saussureans, or adherents to any other theoretical approach. The agreement, in other words, is purely negative. But the question now arises: if we look at linguistic phenomena from a specifically Saussurean point of view, how is the notion of arbitrariness to be construed in positive terms? Where do the implications of arbitrariness begin to differ as between Saussurean and non-Saussurean theories of the sign?

Certain critics of Saussure evidently believed that for Saussure the notion 'arbitrary' simply stood opposed to the notion 'necessary': hence they attacked what they took the Saussurean position to be by asserting that even within the framework which Saussure himself proposed it had to be admitted that the connexion between *signifiant* and *signifié* was 'necessary'. Rebutting such criticisms, Bally (1940) saw that any attack along these lines simply misconstrues what the *Cours* says on the subject. If by 'necessary' is meant that language-users have no choice but to accept the connexion, or that the connexion is psychologically imperative, the *Cours* already concedes this ([101]). Clearly, linguistic arbitrariness for Saussure has nothing to do with *la parole*, and it is in retrospect astonishing that linguists could have read this into it. On the other hand, what the *Cours* says in no way runs at cross purposes to the logic which claims that there *must* be (necessarily) a certain connexion between a given *signifiant* and its *signifié* if it is to be accepted that the two are not independently definable. This, again, Saussure would readily concede. On such points as these the debate over the arbitrariness of the linguistic sign shows all the standard features of a *dialogue des sourds*.

Bally himself saw in Saussure's notion of arbitrariness (versus non-arbitrariness) nothing more than a version of the traditional Greek distinction between *phusei* and *thesei*, already drawn in Plato's *Cratylus* (Bally 1940: 202). This identification, however, was in turn seen as rather naive by other Saussurean commentators (de Mauro 1972: 442-3, n.137). Certainly it seems curious, if no more is meant by 'arbitrary' than is already covered by Greek *thesei*, that the *Cours* does not make the obvious reference to *Cratylus* or some other classical text, but instead gives credit to Whitney (of all people) for recognizing this feature of the linguistic sign ([110]). That would be rather like Russell congratulating Whitehead on recognizing seven as a prime number.

One reason why Saussure would not have been happy with the terms in which the debate between linguistic 'naturalists' and 'conventionalists' was formulated in the Western tradition is obvious enough. The conventionalists were fond of relying on the argument that words can be arbitrarily changed. An early example of this occurs already in *Cratylus* (384 D) where Hermogenes urges Socrates to accept that 'whatever name you give to a thing is its right name; and if you give up that name and change it for another, the later name is no less correct than the earlier, just as we change the names of our servants; for I think no name belongs to any particular thing by nature ...' With Hermogenes' conclusion Saussure would certainly have agreed; but equally certainly not for Hermogenes' reasons. Saussure is quite categorically opposed to the notion that an individual has the power to alter any linguistic sign as an element of *la langue* ([31],[101],[104 ff.]). He explicitly rejects the idea that arbitrariness has anything to do with individual whim. 'It must not be taken to imply that a signal depends on the free choice of the speaker' ([101]).

Less obvious, perhaps, is that for Saussure the linguistic sign does not depend on the communal choice of the collectivity either. This is why Whitney's concept of arbitrariness is singled out for mention. According to Saussure, Whitney (rightly) stressed the fact that the linguistic sign was arbitrary 'in order to emphasize that a language was nothing other than a social institution' ([110]). But for Saussure this concept of 'arbitrariness' is not radical enough. To link arbitrariness with the status of *la langue* as a social institution still suggests that what is 'arbitrary' stands simply opposed to what is naturally determined. In this weak sense of 'arbitrary' all social institutions, as cultural artifacts, are 'arbitrary'. Saussure wishes to go much further than this. He says that Whitney failed to see that the arbitrary character of *la langue* fundamentally distinguishes it 'from all other institutions' ([110]). This is a surprising and very important claim, and demands a criterion of linguistic arbitrariness which goes considerably beyond the weaker and more usual interpretations.

The essential difference for Saussure, it seems, lies in the fact that other social institutions (political, religious, legal, economic, etc.) deal with things which are already interconnected, directly or indirectly, in a variety of non-arbitrary ways. Hence these links in large measure determine in advance the structure of the institution. With *la langue*, however, this is not – *and could not be* – the case. The materials *la langue* operates with – sound and ideas – are not naturally connected at all (that is, externally to the connexions imposed by *la langue* itself). Features which may seem arbitrary in other social institutions are only so at a very superficial level. Saussure evidently thought this point so obvious as not to need illustration: but the kind of example he would doubtless have given is the apparent 'arbitrariness' of the market price of a commodity. It may seem arbitrary that a pound of potatoes should cost five pence (perhaps yesterday it cost less; perhaps another greengrocer charges six pence, etc.). But this superficial arbitrariness of the price is not comparable to the profound arbitrariness of the linguistic sign *soeur*. For in the case of *soeur*, (i) it would make no difference to the linguistic transaction (the act of *parole*) if the word for 'sister' were not *soeur* but *zoeur*, or *soeuf*, or *pataplu* ..., whereas it makes a fundamental difference to the commercial transaction whether the price of a pound of potatoes is five pence, or ten pence, or a thousand pounds. (For the commercial transaction hinges essentially on the possibility of implementing that equation between price and commodity.) Furthermore, (ii) although five pence may for various reasons seem a rather arbitrary price for that particular pound of potatoes, nevertheless the price structure operative in the greengrocery market as a whole is determined by economic factors which are far from arbitrary, and the price of potatoes is related more or less 'rationally' to other prices, both inside and outside the market. In the case of *soeur*, on the other hand, not only is there no linguistic 'reason' why the word for 'sister' should be *soeur* rather than *zoeur*, *soeuf*, etc., but its relations to other words are 'irrational' too, and the same is true for all French words. (Exceptions to this the *Cours* will later deal with under the head of *arbitraire relatif*.) So while it may seem that a particular price is arbitrary, it is not true that prices *as such* are arbitrary; but in the linguistic case, not only are particular words arbitrary, but words *as such* are arbitrary.

Soeur, therefore, is profoundly arbitrary both in that there is no reason 'external' to the social institution of *la langue* why the sound sequence *s-ö-r* should function as a *signifiant* at all; and also in that, given that it does so function, there is no 'internal' structural reason why it should function as the *signifiant* of the concept 'sister'. This 'double arbitrariness', as we might call it, Saussure sees as having no parallel in any other social institution. Other institutions are structured in ways which more or less directly reflect the 'external' social purposes which they serve and the material exigencies which they are called upon to deal with. Not so *la langue*.

Linguistic arbitrariness for Saussure, then, is not just a question of the rose by any other name smelling as sweet (true though that may be), nor just a question of the unexpected variety of ways different languages handle common features of human experience (true though that may be too). If that were all there were to arbitrariness, *la langue* would not differ along this dimension, except perhaps in degree, from other social institutions. But *la langue*, claims Saussure, is arbitrary in a unique way. The absence both of external and of internal constraints on the pairing of particular *signifiants* with particular *signifiés* means that for any given language the choice of actual signs (e.g. *soeur*) from among the range of possible signs (*zoeur*, *soeuf*, *pataplu* ...) is entirely unconstrained. This absolute freedom to vary 'arbitrarily' is the fundamental reason Saussure will adduce for the remarkable diversity of human languages and the no less remarkable susceptibility of languages to quite revolutionary structural changes. Other social institutions are not free to vary in this way because changes in their case (economic, legal, political, etc.) have immediate material consequences for the members of society. Thus although *la langue* is a social institution – and in certain respects the very archetype of a social institution – its arbitrariness gives it a structural autonomy vis à vis society which would be unthinkable (and incomprehensible) in the case of any other established social institution.

* * *

Saussure's second 'principle of linguistics', that of the linearity of the *signifiant*, has attracted considerably less comment and debate than the principle of arbitrariness, although the *Cours* tells us that both principles are equally important. The consequences of linearity are 'incalculable' and 'the whole mechanism of *la langue* depends upon it' ([103]). In view of this forthright statement, it is curious that Saussure's commentators have not inquired rather more closely into what the *Cours* means by 'linearity'. Perhaps they were disarmed by the casual remark that the principle of linearity 'is obvious, but it seems never to be stated, doubtless because it is considered too elementary' ([103]). This remark, at least, endorses the suggestion put forward above that what Saussure means by a 'principle' of linguistics is a truth about language so basic that all linguists must accept it in some form or other before they can even begin to agree or disagree about the right theoretical approach to the subject. On one level, the whole intellectual ingenuity of the *Cours* is devoted to showing how just two such principles, trivial or commonplace as they may appear, are all that are needed to provide the entire theoretical basis for a science of language (provided they are rightly interpreted).

Why these two principles in particular? (The *Cours* never claims that there are no other basic truths about language.) Godel (1964: 53) suggests that the first principle in effect provides Saussure's definition of the general term *signe* (since the term *symbole* ([101]) is reserved for communicational devices which incorporate a non-arbitrary element), while the second principle provides a corresponding definition of *signe linguistique*. Thus linguistic signs would be identified, on the basis of Saussure's two principles, as the class of signs having linear *signifiants*:

arbitrariness	−	+	+
linearity	+ −	+ −	+
	symbole	*signe*	*signe linguistique*

At the same time, this would automatically situate linguistics in its appropriate place within the wider discipline of semiology.

If this scheme correctly represented the definitional structure of Saussure's terminology, it would provide a very compelling answer to the question posed by Saussure's selection of 'principles', and also explain the order in which they are ranked. (The *Cours* never indicates why arbitrariness is the first principle, and linearity the second.) Unfortunately, although neat, this solution will not do. To correspond to Saussure's definitions, the second principle would have to appeal to something other than linearity. There is no specific claim in the *Cours* that only linguistic *signifiants* are linear, and to uphold this as a matter of definition would be to foist on Saussure a very odd concept of 'linearity'. But then, in spite of assurances in the *Cours* that this second principle is obvious and elementary, it is by no means clear exactly what Saussurean linearity entails.

Lepschy (1970:49) distinguishes two questions relating to linearity which the *Cours* leaves in obscurity. One is a question about linearity 'within' the *signifiant* and the other about linearity 'between' *signifiants*. As regards the former, the Saussurean principle of linearity has been criticized by those phonologists (Jakobson 1962: 419-20, 631-58) who construe Saussurean linearity as 'one-dimensional' in the sense of excluding simultaneous contrasts. This is equated with a failure on Saussure's part to recognize that phonemes are units composed of co-occurring distinctive features. (Thus although the *signifiant* of *sœur* comprises the linear sequence of sounds *s-ö-r*, each of these three units is itself a non-linear complex of specific phonetic features which combine to distinguish it from other units. Therefore at this level the principle of linearity is held to be invalid.) Against this charge, Saussure has been defended on the grounds that it involves anachronistically reading back into the *Cours* a post-Saussurean concept of the phoneme, and that in any case Saussure's principle of linearity applies to syntagmatic relations 'between' *signifiants*, not to the internal composition of the individual *signifiant* (de Mauro 1972: 447-8, n.145). It has also been argued in defence of Saussurean linearity that no phoneme combines distinctive features from the same dimension simultaneously (Ruwet 1963).

Here one suspects another Saussurean *dialogue des sourds*. The *Cours* nowhere rejects the notion of phonic complexity in the units of the speech chain, and the articulatory diagrams and tables given in the Appendix to the Introduction in substance already provide the basis for an elementary phonology of distinctive features. So it is quite gratuitous to interpret Saussure's principle of linearity as implicitly denying that the elements of *s-ö-r* are further analysable contrastively in phonetic or phonological terms. Nor, consequently, is there any need to leap to Saussure's defence by claiming that the principle of linearity was never intended to apply 'within' the *signifiant*. On the contrary, unless it does apply 'within' the *signifiant* the reader is hard put to it to make sense of the quite explicit terms in which the principle is introduced in the *Cours*. We are told that *le signifiant* (not *les signifiants*) occupies a certain temporal space (*une étendue*) which is measured in just one dimension: it is a line ([103]). Even more specifically, the elements (*éléments*) of these auditory *signifiants* 'are presented one after another; they form a chain' ([103]). Again, it is not a question of a sequence composed of *signifiants* as indivisible units but a sequence of elements of *signifiants*. This is quite simply a reiteration, in other words, of one of the basic points already made in the Appendix to the Introduction concerning the nature of the speech chain. Furthermore, the putative counterexample to the principle of linearity which Saussure raises and rejects in the final paragraph of this section is the phenomenon of syllabic stress. The example would scarcely make sense if linearity were only a principle which applied to the syntagmatic relationship between one *signifiant* and the next, but did not apply to the speech chain *in toto*.

Lepschy's second question, concerning linearity 'between' *signifiants*, simply falls if we take the principle of linearity as applying to the speech chain as a whole. (There were never two questions in the first place, but a single principle which has been doubly misunderstood.) In other words, if the speech chain itself is linearly structured then *a fortiori* syntagmatic sequences of *signifiants* are linearly structured, given that each *signifiant* is located in just one continuous linear segment of the speech chain. This is precisely what the *Cours* itself later assumes ([146ff.]), thus confirming the interpretation of the principle of linearity here proposed. On p.[170] we are told that words enter into relationships based on linearity, since the linearity of *la langue* precludes the possibility of pronouncing more than one thing at a time. Now this feature of relations between words could hardly be presented as one of the 'consequences' ([103]) of linearity if linearity itself were defined *ab initio* as a sequential relation between *signifiants*. One might then just as well dispense with linearity altogether and simply enunciate as a more general principle the impossibility of two or more signs occurring simultaneously. Why Saussure does *not* opt for this move brings us to the nub of the theoretical problem.

In what sense do *signifiants* enter into temporal or quasi-temporal relations? In what sense do the elements of a *signifiant* have such a relationship to one another? The *Cours* is quite adamant about the temporal character of linearity. *Le signifiant, étant de nature auditive, se déroule dans le temps seul et a les caractères qu'il emprunte au temps* ([103]). There is no indication that Saussure's reader is here expected to subscribe to a recondite metaphysics of time: it is time of the lay, common-or-garden, minutes-and-seconds variety that the *Cours* is talking about. So we cannot equate linearity with the more abstract concept of ordering. (There are many kinds of ordering other than temporal sequence.)

Various remarks in the laconic §3 of Chapter I may perhaps have misled commentators concerning the level at which Saussure envisages the *signifiant* as linear. One is the initial observation: the *signifiant* 'being auditory in nature' ... etc. This suggests that linearity somehow follows from the auditory character of the *signifiant*, or is intrinsic to the use of sound as a medium. (Saussure never mentions music; but most musicians would be surprised to be told that music, being auditory in nature, is confined to simply linear configurations.) Another potential source of confusion is the comparison in the next paragraph between auditory and visual signs. Again, one can easily read this as implying that the distinction between linearity and non-linearity is in some way related to the different modalities of sensory perception. This is particularly puzzling, since the comparison seems at first blush not to support very convincingly the thesis of auditory linearity. (Just as a visual signal may rely on the capacity of the human eye to distinguish, say, the simultaneous employment of vertical and horizontal contrast, may not an auditory signal likewise rely on the capacity of the human ear to discriminate the simultaneous utilization of pitch contrasts and amplitude contrasts?)

A third easily misinterpretable comment is the observation about syllabic stress, already referred to above. 'For example, if I stress a certain syllable, it may seem that I am presenting a number of significant features simultaneously. But that is an illusion. The syllable and its accentuation constitute a single act of phonation. There is no duality within this act, although there are various contrasts with what precedes and follows' ([103]). The reference to a 'single act of phonation' immediately seems to lend colour to the suspicion that there is some confusion here between the act of *parole* and the structure of the *signifiant*. For a single act of phonation entails nothing about the duality or otherwise of the linguistic elements thus given vocal expression. But critics who argue that Saussure is wrong because emphatic stress should be treated as a separate meaningful element (Henry 1970: 90-1) are missing the point here. It is open to Saussure to treat emphatic and non-emphatic pronunciations of the 'same word' as different *signifiants*, just as he treats liaison and non-liaison forms ([147]).

It is by no means necessary to interpret these various comments in the *Cours* as associating linearity exclusively with the fact that speech relies on sound. Saussure is here contrasting the linear nature of a spoken signal with the non-linear nature of alternative ways of conveying the same or a similar message: for instance, by means of ships' flags. In the case of speech, he argues, the distinction between stressed and unstressed syllables is not a matter of additional contrasts in a different dimension from linearity. A signal like a flag, on the other hand, will normally use more than one dimension of contrast simultaneously: for instance, contrasts in the size of particular configurational elements, their shape, number, relative position, colour, etc. There is no way all these contrasts can be construed as one-dimensional: whereas in the case of speech the single dimension of linearity will accommodate all the discriminations between structurally distinct elements which it is necessary to make. The phenomenon of stress will be construed not as an 'extra' element superadded simultaneously, but as a syntagmatic contrast between elements in linear succession. (Saussure never explains how to deal with intonation, but presumably it will have to be along the same lines, in order to conform to the principle of linearity.) Critics who have argued that the evidence of emphatic stress shows the *signifiant* to be not linear but 'bilinear' (Henry 1970: 91) have simply got it wrong. There is no double linearity (as there is, for example, in the case of choral music) because stresses in sequence do not contrast significantly with one another independently of the syllables thus stressed.

It might seem nevertheless that the trouble with Saussure's second principle is that it does confuse questions of *parole* with questions of *langue*. The messages transmitted via the speech circuit clearly take time to formulate and deliver. The sounds A utters are uttered as a temporal succession, and reach B's ear as a temporal succession of stimuli. But are not these facts of temporal transmission *faits de parole*? Everyone agrees, presumably, that if the message A sends to B includes the word *sœur* then it will be possible to measure (in milliseconds) exactly how long it took A to pronounce it, exactly how long the initial sibilant was, etc. But it does not follow from all this that the *signifiant* of the word *sœur* comprises a determinate number of consecutive phonological units, any more than the fact that it takes a certain length of time for a football to be kicked past a goalkeeper entails that the score (e.g. 'Blackpool 1: Manchester United 0') comprises a determinate sequence of sub-scores. (?'Blackpool ½: Manchester United 0'). Nor does it help matters to point out that since Blackpool cannot score two goals at once, the final score 'Blackpool 3: Manchester United 0' must mean that the Manchester United goalkeeper was beaten on three chronologically separate occasions. These occasions belong to the *parole* of a particular match, and its unfolding in time as a series of episodes of play.

Similarly, if A utters the sentence 'The cat sat on the mat', there is no doubt that the word *mat* will be uttered later than the word *cat*. But again this is a feature of an act of *parole*. It does not follow that it is automatically a feature of *langue*. A builder is obliged to construct a house by laying bricks in a certain temporal sequence because he cannot lay them all simultaneously. Nevertheless the spatial relations of the various parts of the completed house are what ultimately count, and not the chronological order in which the builder carried out the construction work. These analogies, however, perhaps suggest a plausible reason why linearity is more important in the case of speech than in the case of building or football. If we interchange the utterance of the words *cat* and *mat* a different sentence necessarily results. Likewise an internal change of the sequence of consonants and vowels in a word will produce either a different word or a non-word. In the case of the house, on the other hand, it will make no difference whether the kitchen was completed before the living room, or vice versa. Nor does it make any difference to the result of the football match in which order the goals were scored. Languages, in other words, make significant use of variations in word-order and in the syntagmatic succession of elements. Is this why Saussure selects linearity as the most basic feature of the *signifiant*?

It is at first very tempting to think that something like this must be the right answer. But further reflection leads one to doubt it. The fact that languages utilize the linearity of the *signifiant* contrastively in various ways is a contingent fact. It consequently cannot provide any ultimate justification for erecting linearity into a 'principle' of linguistics. From a Saussurean point of view, languages would still be languages even if free word-order were universal and words themselves were invariably monosyllables with a fixed structure which never contrasted in respect of the internal order of consonants or vowels. The rationale behind the Saussurean principle of linearity goes much deeper.

Trying to understand the principle of linearity takes us back to the question of what is meant by the Saussurean *image acoustique*: for originally we were given to understand that a *signifiant* is nothing else ([99]). We might even reformulate Saussure's second principle accordingly as that of *linéarité de l'image acoustique*. The term *image acoustique* itself is among the most enigmatic in the vocabulary of Saussurean linguistics. It perhaps suggests a combination of visual representation and acoustic content (cf. the application of the expression *visible speech* to sound spectrograms) as if the brain stores spectrograms rather than sounds. From the function of the *image acoustique* in the Saussurean speech circuit, however, it seems clear that its role is that of a 'mental representation' of some kind which is deemed to play a part both in the speaker's capacity to execute the appropriate motor programme required to utter the sounds desired *and* in the hearer's capacity to identify the auditory impressions received by the ear as those corresponding to a given concept. Now two questions which a sceptic might wish to ask immediately are: (i) why should there be any one 'mental representation' answering to this description? and (ii) even if there were, how could this mental representation occupy a temporal space, be measurable in just one dimension, etc.? In other words, what could possibly be meant by the claim that the mental representation (*image acoustique*) itself is linear (Henry 1970: 89)?

The first of these questions seems already to have occurred to Saussure's editors. Their unhappy footnote on the term *image acoustique* ([98]) bears witness to their anxieties on this score. They point out that language users presumably need a mental representation of muscular patterns of articulation as well as of auditory patterns (as the commentary on the original speech-circuit diagram ([28]) also concedes). Their explanation is that for Saussure the *image acoustique* is 'above all the natural representation of the word as *fait de langue virtuel*, independently of any actualization in speech. Hence the articulatory aspect of the word may be taken for granted, or relegated to a position of secondary importance in relation to its *image acoustique.*' This editorial comment unfortunately turns a mere lacuna into an outright incoherence. In the first place, there is no sense at all in our taking the *image acoustique* as a mental representation so abstract that it gives no information whatever about the actualization of the word in *la parole*: if that were so, there would be no point in calling such a representation an *image acoustique*. In the second place, if indeed the *image acoustique* does capture characteristic auditory properties of the spoken word, then it is more than just the representation of a *fait de langue virtuel* (for the same reason that if we represent the bishop in chess by an image which shows the characteristic shape of the bishop's mitre, we are doing something other than merely representing information about the role of the piece in the game: we are showing how it may be visually identified on the chess board). In the third place, if the *image acoustique* is something quite separate from the representation of an articulatory motor programme, it becomes impossible to see how it can fulfil the dual role assigned to it in the model of the speech circuit.

As regards the second question, it is difficult to refuse to admit the force of the objection. It can hardly be a 'mental representation' which has the property of linearity. Henry (1970: 89) cites in this connexion the way Saussure contrasts visual *signifiants* with auditory *signifiants* ([103]), but fails to point out that this comparison involves a tacit extension of the meaning of the term *signifiant*. (A flag, for example, can hardly be said to have an *image acoustique*.) So by the time Saussure's second principle is introduced, we are apparently dealing with a more generalized notion of the *signifiant*: it is now a mental representation including information of any sensory modality appropriate to the signalling system in question. That, however, does not dispose of the sceptic's point. Henry insists that the notion of a temporal chain is appropriate if referring to the sounds actualized in *la parole*; but inappropriate if referring to the *empreinte psychique* of *la langue*. Admittedly, he argues, the representation of *arbor* has to be a representation of *arbor* and not of *orarb*: in that sense, it must respect the order of constituent elements. But there is no question of temporal priorities in a representation which takes the form of an *aperception en bloc*, and he refers to certain types of motor aphasia which appear to involve precisely an inability to 'translate' information stored in non-linear form into the correct linear sequences (Henry 1970:89).

Whether the relevant modality is auditory, visual, or any other, the mental representation itself should not have attributed to it properties which are those of the items represented. (Whereas it makes perfectly good sense to say that Smith's idea of a triangle includes the information that triangles have three sides, it would be absurd to say that Smith's idea had three sides.) Now unless we read Saussure as indeed being guilty of this very confusion, there must be an alternative way of interpreting his second principle of linguistics.

The problem, in short, is to find a reading which simultaneously acquits Saussure both of the incoherence to which his editors' explanation of the *image acoustique* condemns him, and of the category mistake to which he is committed by a literal interpretation of the linearity of the *signifiant*. A solution of sorts is possible if we are willing to accept that for Saussure the key theoretical role of the *signifiant* is to integrate an account of the structure of the cognitive system (*la langue*) with a step-by-step account of the activity (*la parole*) through which the system is put to work. The combination implicit in this cognitive-cum-mechanical role means that to the *signifiant* are attributed whatever properties *both* these functions demand. Now linearity is totally irrelevant to the function of the *signifiant* as part of the cognitive system, but highly relevant to its mediation between system (*langue*) and activity (*parole*). In other words we can interpret Saussure's second principle as an elliptical way of saying: 'the semiology of linguistic systems demands that information about the significant ordering of certain features in *parole* be available for purposes both of encoding and of decoding the signal'. Whether this information is actually stored separately for auditory and articulatory operations, or how many distinct forms of 'mental representation' are involved, is no concern of Saussure's whatsoever. He merely simplifies by subsuming all this under a characterization of the *image acoustique*.

Thus Saussure's two principles correspond to two quite different ways of looking at *la langue*: in one case as supplying the system needed for a unique form of cognition, and in the other case as supplying the mechanism needed for a unique form of activity. From the cognitive point of view, the structure of *la langue* is seen as pairing sounds with concepts in a way which owes nothing to any independent connexions between sounds and things in the external world: hence the principle of arbitrariness. From the viewpoint which sees language as an activity, on the other hand, the way *la langue* is put to work is seen as reflecting the fact that all human activities in the external world take place in time: hence the principle of linearity. But from this latter point of view it is quite irrelevant whether the linguistic sign is arbitrary or not: the mechanism of *la parole* would operate in just the same way in any case. Saussure's two principles, in other words, provide yet another illustration of how the viewpoint selected creates the linguistic object.

By formulating the antithesis between these two principles – one denying and the other admitting an involvement of linguistic structure with the structure of the external world – the *Cours* makes the most profound revolution in grammatical theory since Port Royal. Whether Saussure correctly identified this involvement and its linguistic consequences is a different question, and a full answer to it would necessarily go far beyond the scope of a commentary on the *Cours*. It suffices here to note that Saussure's theory of language does assume that it is precisely the extent and modality of this involvement, as expressed in his two principles, which determine how language functions.

This high-level philosophical antithesis is not the whole story, however. There is a more practical academic reason why a single Saussurean principle of linguistics will not suffice, and why not *any* two principles will do either. The criterion of arbitrariness alone provides the linguist with no basis for a method of identifying and classifying linguistic signs, since in itself it does not distinguish signs from sequences of signs. Nor would the distributional principle that linguistic signs cannot co-occur help in this respect, basic though it may be. Something further is needed if linguistics is to have an analytic method. It is a mark of Saussure's brilliance as a theorist that he reduces this 'something further' to a single principle to complement his principle of arbitrariness (which he will need in any case, since without it linguistics could hardly be an autonomous discipline). To call this principle 'linearity', however, was arguably an unhappy choice of terminology. Arguably too, the explanation which treats linearity as being in some sense a 'temporal' feature of linguistic structure is quite specious. Speech is certainly an activity which has a temporal dimension: but no more so and no less so than every other human activity. The idea of time as a single continuous 'line' being drawn at uniform speed in the same direction is itself a sophisticated concept which relies on a spatial metaphor. It is also at odds with other and possibly less restrictive ways of conceptualizing time (Henry 1970: 80).

On the other hand, speech is by no means the only human activity to exhibit properties of the kind which Saussure wishes to attribute to the *signifiant*. These properties are the basic properties of single catenary articulation: for this is what Saussurean linearity essentially amounts to. No other types or features of linearity are taken into consideration in the theoretical use Saussure makes of the *signifiant*. The most revealing remark about linearity in the whole of the *Cours* is that the linearity of the spoken word becomes manifest when speech is set down in writing and 'a spatial line of graphic signs is substituted for a succession of sounds in time' ([103]). In other words, spoken language is articulated as a single, linked succession of discrete elements: it constitutes a chain. If this is assumed to be the case, then by combining both Saussurean principles linguistics is immediately provided with a method of analysis, which will consist basically of segmenting any given catenary sequence by determining which arbitrary sets of consecutive elements in that sequence could constitute single *signifiants* and which could not. (This is in fact the method later described in detail on pp.[146 ff.].)

It now becomes apparent that what underlies both of Saussure's principles is another – and perhaps the most fundamental – 'hidden premiss' of Saussurean linguistics. It is the premiss that the spoken word is 'invisibly' organized on exactly the same lines as the 'visible' organization of the written word. This premiss in turn relies on a particular theory about writing (namely, the theory that the alphabetic system provides not merely a flexible convention for writing but a 'true' description of the constitution of the spoken word). Once this is tacitly accepted, all that is required is a plausible inventory of universal phonic units corresponding to alphabetic letters. (The *Cours* has already supplied these fixed 'sound types' in the first chapter of the Appendix to the Introduction.) It then becomes unnecessary to give any further argument for linearity. By the same token, it becomes superfluous to offer any further case for arbitrariness. For just as a random string of letters is not meaningful unless it 'spells' a word, so 'sound types', which are *ex hypothesi* meaningless, do not concatenate into meaningful sequences other than those for which *la langue* provides a *signifié*. What was initially meaningless cannot by a mere chaining process, in itself equally meaningless, become automatically meaningful. Thus both arbitrariness and linearity spring conceptually from a single source. It is a source which subtly infuses Saussurean linguistics, in spite of lip-service paid to the primacy of speech, with all the latent scriptism of a pedagogic tradition in which writing was taken as the model to which language must – or should – conform.

CHAPTER II

Invariability and Variability
of the Sign

The chapter which the *Cours* devotes to '*Immutabilité et mutabilité du signe*' ([104-13]) is more often skipped than studied carefully. This may well be because it is seen as functioning merely as a bridge between the opening chapter of Part I, which explains the initial Saussurean conception of the linguistic sign, and the discussion of the distinction between synchronic and diachronic linguistics, which is about to be broached in Chapter III. Consequently, de Mauro suggests, the attention of Saussurean scholars has been diverted from it because they have been 'hypnotised' (de Mauro 1972: 448 n. 146) by the apparently far greater theoretical import of what immediately precedes and what immediately follows. To this one might add that it is a chapter which contains a curious mixture of points which sound as if they are labouring the obvious and points which sound rather too cleverly contrived. Neither variety brings out the best in a reader. The first impression is that a rather dull but necessary lecture for undergraduates has been livened up by throwing in a few academic rhetorical flourishes.

The formal structure of the chapter is also deceptively banal. The first half deals with factors which tend to maintain a linguistic *status quo*, while the second half deals with factors which tend to promote change. But the underlying argument by no means corresponds to this simple bi-partition: it is marshalled in a rather complicated way which obliges the reader to leap back and forth from one section to the other in order to follow it. The organization of the chapter is consequently unsatisfactory. Clearly, the overall plan of the *Cours* demands that, having thus far examined the linguistic sign purely from the point of view of its constitution and internal structure, there should now be some general discussion of the linguistic sign in relation to the linguistic community. This is needed to pave the way for the next theoretical move, which will be the absolute separation of synchronic from diachronic relations. Too much is sacrificed, however, to this transitional purpose. The thematic division between stability in the first part and change in the second part of the chapter is evidently intended to foreshadow the coming dichotomy between synchronic and diachronic. But however neat or aesthetically pleasing this may be, in the end it unnecessarily obscures an important part of the rationale behind that dichotomy.

Neglect of the main points this chapter makes is one of the main reasons, according to de Mauro, for the prevalence of a false view of Saussure. The author of the *Cours* is erroneously cast in the role of apologist for an abstract, 'anti-historical' linguistics, which would treat languages as static systems cut off both from their own past and from their social conditions of existence in the present. Such a view is refuted decisively, in de Mauro's opinion, by the evidence of this one chapter, which demonstrates Saussure's 'profound awareness of the historical necessity of the sign' and of the 'radical historicity of linguistic systems' (de Mauro 1972: 448, n.146).

True as all this may be, there is a risk that by over-reacting against sheer ignorance or subsequent distortions of Saussure's ideas it may retrospectively put the emphasis in the wrong place. The chapter is about language in a historical perspective: that much no one would deny. It is unlikely, however, that any linguist would devote a whole chapter of a book to establishing credentials which no contemporary reader would dream of questioning in the first place. Saussure's objective is a different one. The chapter makes more sense if we read it not as an endeavour to validate the historicity of the linguistic sign (which Saussure's contemporaries would have taken for granted without any prompting from Saussure) but as an attempt to show how very problematic – contrary to contemporary assumptions – that notion is. It is no coincidence that the problems of historicity which Saussure merely raises here, hinting at them rather than laying them out in full detail, are precisely the problems to which Saussure's fully developed theory of language will provide quite novel answers. Therefore it is worth while trying to reconstruct Saussure's argument in a more direct form, as it might have appeared if the bi-partite structure of this chapter, adopted for extraneous expository reasons, had been abandoned. In outline, Saussure's case might then have been put as follows.

Historicity manifests itself potentially in two ways: (i) stability over time, or (ii) change over time. At first sight, the linguistic sign appears to qualify under both criteria, since Indo-European historical linguistics apparently provides us with many examples of words remaining unchanged for long periods, but also with many examples of words undergoing change. In both cases, however, a careful examination of the question reveals unsuspected difficulties.

If the linguistic sign is arbitrary, and if languages are social institutions, it would seem to follow that a linguistic sign ought to be alterable at will. But, on the one hand, no individual has any power to alter either *signifiant* or *signifié*. On the other hand, in cases where it appears that a linguistic sign has altered (Latin *necare* 'to kill' > French *noyer* 'to drown' [109]) it can hardly be claimed that the linguistic community made a collective decision to alter it. Should we conclude, therefore, that history shows that the linguistic sign is not arbitrary after all? Or perhaps that languages are not, after all, social institutions?

Evidently, the *Cours* is committed both to the proposition that the linguistic sign is arbitrary and also to the proposition that *la langue* is a social institution. The latter proposition, however, is left in considerably deeper obscurity than the former. What exactly is meant by an institution? Nowhere in the *Cours* does Saussure define the term. The three examples of other institutions cited in this chapter on p.[110] ('customs', 'laws' and 'clothes') are not particularly helpful. However, there is a reference on the same page to Whitney and to Whitney's insistence on the arbitrary character of linguistic signs in order to 'emphasize that a language is nothing other than a social institution'. It would seem reasonable, therefore, to take as a point of departure Whitney's general definition of an institution as 'the work of those whose wants it subserves' (Whitney 1867: 48). However, the passage in which Whitney proposes this definition goes on to say of the institution of language:

> it is in their [sc. those whose wants it subserves] sole keeping and control; it has been adapted by them to their circumstances and wants, and is still everywhere undergoing at their hands such adaptation; every separate item of which it is composed is, in its present form ... the product of a series of changes, effected by the will and consent of men ...

'Every separate item' presumably includes, for Whitney, every single linguistic sign. Now this is a proposition which Saussure is loath to accept, as is made clear at the very beginning of §1 of this chapter. For Saussure, the community has no more power to alter a relationship between *signifiant* and *signifié* than the individual has. It cannot 'exercise its authority to change even a single word. The community, as much as the individual, is bound to its language' ([104]). Linguistic change is not a question of successive generations altering the linguistic contract, for there is no linguistic contract to be altered: a language is imposed on its speakers, not agreed to by them. History itself, for Saussure, shows this to be the case. 'At any given period, however far back in time we go, a language is always an inheritance from the past' ([105]).

This in turn, however, merely generates a new puzzle, which is the opposite of the first one. For if the connexion between a given *signifiant* and a given *signifié* is arbitrary, and speakers have no power to change it either individually or collectively, why, once established, does it not remain unchanged? Why did not the verb *necare* 'to kill' remain as it was? Alternatively, if we admit both (i) that the verb *necare* did as a matter of historical fact change (to French *noyer*), and (ii) that this change was not 'by the will and consent of men', have we not seriously undermined the thesis that the linguistic sign is arbitrary? (For it would seem that there must be forces at work controlling the linguistic sign which are 'natural', or at least not within institutionalized jurisdiction.) Thus, whichever way we look at the matter, history seems to make a mockery of the most basic premises it is reasonable to lay down concerning human language.

The problem, then, is how to reconcile the facts which history tells us about various languages with the theoretical assumptions of the arbitrariness and the institutionality of the linguistic sign. Saussure's response is twofold. It involves questioning (i) whether it is correct to assume that because *la langue* is a social institution it functions in the same way as other social institutions, and (ii) whether the notion of historicity is properly applicable to the individual linguistic sign. These two questions are interwoven throughout the discussion presented in Chapter II, but for present purposes it will be clearer to deal with them separately.

Whereas Whitney tends to equate linguistic arbitrariness with institutionality, or more exactly, to see arbitrariness as a consequence of institutionality, for Saussure this misses a crucial point. Whitney, says Saussure, 'did not go far enough' ([110]). Whitney failed to see that historical continuity and historical change present problems for a theory of the linguistic sign which have no parallel in the case of other social institutions. For other institutions 'are all based in varying degrees on natural connexions between things' and 'exhibit a necessary conformity between ends and means' ([110]). (Saussure's example here is that the clothes we wear, although 'arbitrary' in many respects, nonetheless exhibit a fundamental conformity to the natural configurations of the human body.) An institution bound by no necessary conformities whatsoever is in a unique and curious position. As an institution it combines simultaneously extremes of intrinsic stability and intrinsic instability. Since the connexion between a *signifiant* and *signifié* is arbitrary, that is the best of all reasons why it should remain stable: for nothing can be gained by altering it. At the same time, an arbitrary connexion is more vulnerable to change than any other. For there is nothing to be gained by keeping it either: any other sign would do just as well. A language is thus an institution which is 'intrinsically defenceless' ([110]) against change. This is true even of artificially created languages like Esperanto ([111]).

Saussure is arguing, then, that *la langue* is the unique case of a social institution in which the nature of the institution itself, being based on an arbitrary relationship, is equally conducive to variance as to invariance.

(This will clearly have two practical implications for linguistics which are not pursued in this chapter. One will be that why a linguistic sign remains unchanged over time needs just as much explaining as why it changes. The other is that the particular reasons for both stability and change become, in individual instances, extremely elusive. For in the end no one can demonstrate, because of the arbitrary nature of the linguistic sign, that it matters one way or another what the fate of any particular sign is. Historical reasoning which involves tracing chains of cause and effect consequently becomes even less straightforward in the case of *la langue* than in the case of social institutions based on natural relations.)

Now the nature of the difficulty is not just practical but, beyond a certain point, conceptual. It calls in question the whole lay concept of 'history', which is not geared to dealing with arbitrary relationships. The lay concept demands a contrast between invariance and change over time: without that, historicity becomes meaningless. But arbitrary relationships have precisely the characteristic that, within their given domain, substituting y for x makes no difference: the result is equivalent in all relevant respects to leaving x as it was. That is just what arbitrariness means. There is thus a profound conflict between arbitrariness and historicity. Arbitrariness demands at some level an equivalence between change and *status quo*, whereas historicity constantly demands an opposition.

If we read Saussure's argument in this way, it is evident that on one level the linguistic sign, being arbitrary, remains untouched and untouchable by history. Its historicity – if the term is appropriate – is of a quite different order from the historicity which pertains to other social institutions. That would also explain why in the second half of this chapter Saussure takes such meticulous pains to avoid using terms like 'change' and 'alteration' of the linguistic sign itself, but prefers instead the cumbersome circumlocution 'a shift in the relationship between *signifié* and *signifiant*' ([109]). The implication of this, evidently, is that historical factors in the lay sense may affect *signifié* or *signifiant* (or both separately): but not the sign as such. Changes in the pronunciation or in the meaning of words occur for various reasons totally unconnected with the relationship which binds any particular pronunciation to any particular meaning. That relationship, having itself no physical correlate in the world of historical time, is something on which historical forces are powerless to act. But they do act on linguistic communities. Thus it is the role of the linguistic community to provide the anchorage which links a system of arbitrary signs to the operation of historical processes. This is the significance of the diagram on p.[112]:

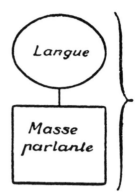

The sole unit of historical significance in linguistics is not the language alone but the language plus the linguistic community.

Even more important, as will become apparent later, is the emended diagram on p.[113], which adds the arrow of time to the bond between the community and its language. 'When this is taken into account, the language is no longer free from constraints, because the passage of time allows social forces to be brought to bear upon it' ([113]).

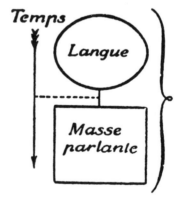

La langue, then, is the unique case of a social institution based on a relationship which simultaneously promotes stability (by making variation pointless) and facilitates change (by offering no resistance). That this single feature of the linguistic sign should give rise to two apparently conflicting tendencies might at first sight appear mysterious: but that is because the tendencies conflict only when seen in the perspective of history. What is an opposition in historical terms may be an equivalence in a semiological perspective. Thus, paradoxical though it may seem, 'variability and invariability are both, in a sense, characteristic of the linguistic sign' ([109]).

This conclusion evidently worried Saussure's editors enough for them to add a footnote of their own defending Saussure's assignment of these seemingly contradictory characteristics to the linguistic sign, and reassuring the reader that it is 'intended simply to emphasize the fact that a language changes even though its speakers are incapable of changing it' ([108] n.1). But this is merely to reiterate rather lamely what has already been said in the first part of the chapter. There is a further and much sharper point to Saussure's oxymoron which the editors' apologetic gloss misses entirely. The notion of linguistic change as it applies to *individual signs* also implies absence of change. In other words, change is conceived of as continuity, not as discontinuity. And this in turn presupposes what Saussure calls 'the survival of earlier material' ([109]) in the sign. (Three examples are provided on pp.[109-110]: Latin *necāre*, German *dritteil*, and Anglo-Saxon *fōti*.) Now if 'survival of earlier material' is a *sine qua non*, as it would appear to be, (for otherwise the lay concept of history would recognize an instance not of change but of complete disappearance) then it seems that the sign must be a linguistic unit conceived of as able to remain 'the same' in certain respects at the same time as becoming 'not the same' in others. Hence simultaneous variability and invariability must be a property of the linguistic sign as such.

This may at first sound like a hackneyed reworking of some ancient Greek paradox. As usual with Saussure, however, the target is not a philosophical but a linguistic theory: in this case, the entirely inadequate theory of linguistic change projected by the work of the comparative and historical philologists. It has been said of Whitney, for example, that 'his notion of historical processes, and hence methods of investigating them, depends on individual items in a language, at all structural levels, rather than on some a priori notion of structure' (Silverstein 1971: xv). But much the same could be said of a whole era of linguistic scholarship. When Whitney writes (1867: 54-5):

> Language is made up of signs for thought, which, though in one sense parts of a whole, are in another and more essential sense isolated and independent entities. Each is produced for its own purpose; each is separately exposed to the changes and vicissitudes of linguistic life, is modified, recombined, or dropped, according to its own uses and capacities.

he is expressing a doctrine of linguistic change which was to be taken to its logical conclusion by others and summed up in Gilliéron's famous anti-structuralist aphorism: *chaque mot a son histoire* ('every word has its own history'). The nineteenth century had seen nothing problematic at all in the notion of a word 'surviving' over the centuries, irrespective of its incorporation at different times into different linguistic systems (as if one were dealing with the historical continuity of a physical object, or some analogue thereof). Why this will not do is a question Saussure will return to again in his discussion of panchronicity ([134-5]). How to replace this inadequate notion by a more satisfactory concept of historical continuity in language is a problem which will occupy much of the remainder of the *Cours*. Its ultimate solution will involve the fully-fledged structuralist theory of *valeurs linguistiques*. A first step will be the establishment of the dichotomy between synchronic and diachronic relations, to which the *Cours* now turns.

CHAPTER III

Static Linguistics and Evolutionary Linguistics

The programmatic conclusion towards which this chapter steadily progresses throughout its nine sections is stated unequivocally in the two final sentences ([140]):

> *Synchronic linguistics* will be concerned with logical and psychological connexions between coexisting items constituting a system, as perceived by the same collective consciousness.
> *Diachronic linguistics* on the other hand will be concerned with sequences of items not perceived by the same collective consciousness, which replace one another without themselves constituting a system.

It is interesting to examine the strategy Saussure deploys in order to lead up to this conclusion, but at the outset it may be useful simply to contrast the position which this conclusion represents with the kind of position against which Saussure is implicitly arguing.

Hermann Paul, for example, in his *Principien der Sprachgeschichte* had distinguished between descriptive grammar (which at first sight corresponds to Saussure's 'synchronic') and historical grammar (which at first sight corresponds to Saussure's 'diachronic'), but maintained nevertheless that this did not demand a difference of perspective within linguistics. For Paul, in the scientific study of language only a historical perspective is valid.

> What is explained as an unhistorical and still scientific observation of language is at bottom nothing but one incompletely historical, through defects partly of the observer, partly of the material to be observed. (Paul 1890: xlvi-xlvii)

Paul held that it was impossible to describe scientifically even one state of a single dialect without tacitly relating forms to one another on a historical basis.

If we compare, for example, the different significations of a word with each other, we attempt to establish which of these is the fundamental one, or to what fundamental signification, now obsolete, they point. If, however, we define a fundamental signification from which the others are derived, we lay down a historical fact. Indeed, we cannot even assert that related forms are derived from a common basis without becoming historical. (Paul 1890: xlviii)

Paul concludes:

And so I cannot conceive how anyone can reflect with any advantage on a language without tracing to some extent the way in which it has historically developed. (Paul 1890: xlviii)

This is as good an example as one can find of a position which is diametrically opposed to Saussure's.

For Saussure, Paul's single 'historical' point of view which embraces states as well as changes (Paul 1890: 8) is theoretically incoherent. It fails to recognize that relations between co-existing linguistic items are logically and psychologically of a quite different order from relations between chronologically successive linguistic items. This difference, apparently so simple in principle, nevertheless turns out to involve unexpected difficulties. Chapter III shows Saussure attempting to grapple with some of them, in the context of working towards the statement of a rational 'scientific' programme for linguistics.

The first step in §1 prior to the introduction of the terms *synchronique* and *diachronique* is the observation that all 'sciences which involve the study of values' (*valeurs*) are obliged to distinguish between an 'axis of simultaneity' and an orthogonal 'axis of succession' ([115]). This is the first mention of a technical term (*valeur*) which will assume a key position in Saussure's fully elaborated linguistic theory. What exactly values are in this sense is not yet explained, but already Saussure proclaims in advance that '*la langue* is a system of pure values, determined by nothing else apart from the temporary state of its constituent elements' ([116]). The system of values is thus allocated unequivocally to the axis of simultaneity, which concerns 'relations from which the passage of time is entirely excluded' ([115]).

Even in this respect, however, Saussure claims that *la langue* is not quite like any other system of values. Since the linguistic sign is arbitrary, the separation between the axis of simultaneity and the axis of succession is more absolute than in other cases.

Insofar as a value, in one of its aspects, is founded upon natural connexions between things (as, for example, in economics the value of a piece of land depends upon the income derivable from it), it is possible up to a point to trace this value through time, bearing in mind that it depends at any one time upon the relevant system of contemporary values. However, its connexion with things inevitably supplies it with a natural basis, and hence any assessment of it is never entirely arbitrary. There are limits upon the range of variability. But, as we have already seen, in linguistics these natural connexions have no place. ([116])

For the reader, this caveat about the special status of linguistic values, although it ties in with the point made in the preceding chapter that *la langue* is unique as a social institution in virtue of being based entirely on non-natural connexions, cannot fail to make the notion of *valeurs* initially all the more perplexing. If it is possible to trace changes in the value of a piece of land over the years, why is it not possible to trace changes in the meaning of a word over the years? On the other hand, if indeed this is not possible in the case of language, why does the axis of simultaneity intersect at all with the axis of succession (as shown in the diagram on p.[115])? For intersection presumably implies that at least one item may be situated on both axes.

Instead of answering such queries immediately, §1 leaves them pending and proceeds to a discussion of terminology. 'Historical linguistics' is rejected in favour of 'evolutionary linguistics' or, better still, 'diachronic linguistics'; while 'static linguistics' and 'synchronic linguistics' are proposed as designations of the science of 'linguistic states' (*états de langue*). In view of Saussure's explicit refusal to accept the implications of the usual term 'historical linguistics', it is quite remarkable how readily later commentators assumed that this was at bottom merely a terminological quibble, and that Saussurean diachronic linguistics was just historical linguistics under a new academic title. Bloomfield (1923) even went as far as to gloss Saussure's term *linguistique diachronique* as 'historical linguistics' and identified its subject matter as being sound changes and analogical changes 'such as are recorded in our historical grammars'. Evidently a case of *plus ça change*.

Bloomfield was by no means an exception. His profound incomprehension of Saussure's distinction between synchronic and diachronic relations demonstrates strikingly just how difficult it was in the 1920s for an eminent linguist trained in the traditional philological approach to his subject to realise that Saussure was not just re-affirming (in a novel terminology, to be sure) the assumptions which had for so long underwritten the discipline of language studies. For Bloomfield, evidently, Saussure was saying nothing very different from what Hermann Paul had already said some thirty years earlier when distinguishing between descriptive grammar and historical grammar. Saussure's disclaimers are simply ignored and his reasons for rejecting the equation 'diachronic = historical' are not challenged but passed over in silence. It is all the more important to appreciate what these reasons are.

The first reason given ([116-17]) is that the terms 'history' and 'historical' not only fail to mark the distinction Saussure intends to draw by opposing 'synchronic' to 'diachronic', but actually conflate that distinction. For 'history', as commonly understood, includes not only facts pertaining to states but also facts pertaining to evolutions. The typical error of 'historical linguistics' for Saussure was a failure to distinguish these two orders of facts, and consequently a pervasive tendency to describe linguistic states in evolutionary terms and linguistic developments in static terms.

The second reason, however, is the more important: that juxtaposing descriptions of successive *états de langue* is not a way of studying languages along the temporal axis. In order to study linguistic phenomena along this axis of succession, 'it would be necessary to consider separately the factors of transition involved in passing from one linguistic state to the next' ([117]). This is exactly what Saussure's predecessors had failed to do. The same point will be reiterated even more forcefully in the *Cours* at the beginning of Chapter VII of Part II, where we find the blunt, uncompromising statement that in Saussure's view there is no such thing as 'historical grammar' ([185]). Now since the crowning achievement of language studies in the nineteenth century had been working out the details of the 'historical grammar' of the various Indo-European languages, and since, as Bloomfield (1923) put it,

> Outside of the field of historical grammar, linguistics has worked only in the way of a desperate attempt to give a psychologistic interpretation to the facts of language, and in the way of phonetics, an endless and aimless listing of the sound-articulations of speech.

it is small wonder that an outright rejection of historical grammar might have seemed so blasphemous to linguists of Bloomfield's generation that they could hardly bring themselves to believe that this was the message of Saussurean linguistics.

Seeking to avoid this heretical conclusion at all costs, they doubtless misread the rider which immediately follows the dismissal of 'historical grammar' ('What is called 'historical grammar' is in reality simply diachronic linguistics' [185]) as affirming an equation between diachrony and history. Nothing could make more complete nonsense of Saussure's earlier refusal to accept that equation on pp.[116-17]. The point of the remark on p.[185], as its context makes clear, is to deny that there is any grammar over and above synchronic grammar: the changes between one grammatical system and its successor or successors in time are not themselves part of grammar. To put the point in terms of Saussure's chess analogy, any move which changes one state of the board into another state of the board belongs to neither state ([126]). For Saussure, 'diachronic grammar' would be a contradiction in terms. What, in his view, distinguishes so-called 'historical grammar' from 'descriptive grammar' is that the former mistakenly incorporates facts which rightly belong to diachronic linguistics.

In §2 of Chapter III Saussure develops this critique of 'historical linguistics' further. 'Historical linguistics' fails to describe *la langue* as it exists here and now for the language user, who neither knows nor needs to know anything about the past history of elements in a present *état de langue*; and it is in any case unscientific because it adopts no single, consistent point of view. 'It would be absurd to try to draw a panorama of the Alps as seen from a number of peaks in the Jura simultaneously' ([117]). But this is the kind of enterprise historical linguistics engages in. Furthermore, exclusive concentration on linguistic changes results in an atomistic approach in which *états de langue*, insofar as they are recognized at all, 'are considered only in fragments and very imperfectly' ([118]). In these respects nineteenth-century 'historical linguistics' is inferior to traditional grammar which, for all its shortcomings, adopted a 'strictly synchronic' programme ([118]). 'Having paid too much attention to history, linguistics will go back now to the static viewpoint of traditional grammar, but in a new spirit and with different methods' ([119]).

In §3 the reader is presented with analyses of a number of examples of linguistic change (French *décrépit*, Germanic noun plurals, French word stress, Slavic case distinctions) in order to illustrate that the contrast between synchronic and diachronic points of view 'is absolute and admits no compromise' ([119]). Although there may be an intimate connexion between diachronic process and resultant synchronic system, the two remain independent. 'The reason for a diachronic development lies in the development itself. The particular synchronic consequences which may ensue have nothing to do with it' ([121]). 'The language system as such is never directly altered. It is in itself unchangeable' ([121]). Diachronic changes affect individual elements of a system only. 'It is as if one of the planets circling the sun underwent a change of dimensions and weight: this isolated event would have general consequences for the whole solar system, and disturb its equilibrium' ([121]). This analogy alone perhaps sums up better than anything else Saussure's objections to 'historical linguistics'. By treating languages as continuously evolving 'historical' systems, it is intrinsically incapable of distinguishing between changes and their consequences. As a result, it achieves no level of explanation at all. To pursue Saussure's analogy, there will be neither an explanation of what happened to the planet, nor an explanation of what happened to the solar system (in both cases because what happened to the planet will be 'historically' indistinguishable from what happened to the system, the one being treated as part of the other).

By this point in the chapter it is already clear that one of the theoretical consequences of drawing an absolute distinction between synchronic and diachronic relations is that linguistics will require a concept of 'system'. For diachronically related items do not belong to any system, whereas synchronically related items do. But how exactly is the concept of a synchronic system to be construed? It is here that the theoretical difficulties attendant upon the apparently simple differentiation of synchronic from diachronic relations begin to emerge.

In §4 three analogies are suggested. The first compares the difference between diachrony and synchrony to the difference between a three-dimensional object and its two-dimensional projection. 'Studying objects, that is to say diachronic events, will give us no insight into synchronic states, any more than we can hope to understand geometrical projections simply by studying, however thoroughly, different kinds of object' ([125]). The second analogy compares the difference between diachrony and synchrony to the difference between a longitudinal section of the stem of a plant and a cross-cut of the same stem. 'The longitudinal section shows us the fibres themselves which make up the plant, while the transversal section shows us their arrangements on one particular level. But the transversal section is distinct from the longitudinal section, for it shows us certain relations between the fibres which are not apparent at all from any longitudinal section' ([125]). The third analogy is the celebrated comparison with chess. The difference between diachrony and synchrony is compared with the difference between the sequence of moves in a game of chess and the successive states of the board which result therefrom.

The appositeness of the chess analogy for Saussure is evidently that it emphasizes more clearly than either of the two preceding analogies the autonomous systematicity of the *état de langue*. 'In a game of chess, any given state of the board is totally independent of any previous state of the board. It does not matter at all whether the state in question has been reached by one sequence of moves or another sequence. Anyone who has followed the whole game has not the least advantage over a passer-by who happens to look at the game at that particular moment. In order to describe the position on the board, it is quite useless to refer to what happened ten seconds ago. All this applies equally to a language, and confirms the radical distinction between diachronic and synchronic' ([126-7]). As Saussure acknowledges, 'in chess, the player *intends* to make his moves and to have some effect upon the system. In a language, on the contrary, there is no premeditation. Its pieces are moved, or rather modified, spontaneously and fortuitously' ([127]). This, claims Saussure, is the only respect in which the comparison is defective. But this is not quite true. The analogy also limps in various other respects. In the first place, there is an equivocation between states of the board and states of the game. Except in the context of a game, there is no 'state of the board'. But the state of the game is not defined solely by the state of the board. The state of the game is as much a question of missing pieces as of the relative positions of the chessmen present on the board. The passer-by of

Saussure's example will 'read' the state of the game in the light of the knowledge that there is a characteristic structure to the development of games of chess: and this, presumably, it is not in Saussure's interest to concede in the case of languages. In any case, the state of the game is not to be identified with the state of the board alone. Saussure's passer-by will also need to know at least one piece of information which cannot be inferred from the state of the board; namely, whose move it is next. Again, there is no linguistic analogue. In the second place, a move in a game of chess *by definition* alters the state of the board. This is quite independent of any *intention* on the part of the player. But it is far from clear that anything analogous holds in the linguistic case; for Saussure will hardly wish to concede that synchronic states and diachronic changes are defined interdependently. Thus, for example, a consonant change which resulted in no new homophonies or grammatical syncretisms would leave the number of linguistic signs 'in play', their values and their synchronic relations unaltered. It would be like altering the shape of certain pieces on the board in some identical and trivial way which still left them distinguishable from other pieces without affecting the position of any one of them. But in chess that would not count as a move. In the third place, possible states of the board and possible moves are alike governed by the rules of chess, which exist independently of the course of any particular game. It is the rules, ultimately, and not the state of the board, which determine the values involved. Saussure does not see this as a defect in his analogy, because he claims that such rules 'fixed once and for all, also exist in the linguistic case: they are the unchanging principles of semiology' ([126]). Later, on p.[135], a slightly different line is taken, and the constancy of phonetic change (which could hardly be a 'principle of semiology') is instanced as a general linguistic law. But none of this will save the analogy. No unchanging principles governing games in general, or even board games in particular, determine the rules of chess. With the same board and the same pieces, it would be possible to devise many other games than the one we call 'chess'.

It is this third disanalogy which is in the end more devastating than any other for Saussure's comparison between *la langue* and chess. For it affords no way of delimiting the system which identifies a given *état de langue* along the axis of simultaneity other than by reference to rules which would simultaneously delimit all possible *états de langue* which might precede or follow. This is a problem for Saussure because, as §7 will subsequently make clear, he is committed to denying the validity of any 'panchronic' point of view where *la langue* is concerned. The upshot is that although the comparison with chess in this chapter carries the whole burden of clarifying Saussure's concept of a linguistic 'system', in the final analysis it does so at the expense of apparently posing a quite intractable problem for the linguist, who is left to find some way of describing the state of the game before knowing what the rules are.

Nothing in §5 makes this problem seem any less intractable. On the contrary, it becomes even more so with the important qualifications to the concept of synchrony which this section introduces. Synchronic and diachronic studies, we are told, are not on an equal footing. The former take precedence over the latter. Indeed, the linguist who takes a diachronic point of view 'is no longer examining *la langue*, but a series of events which modify it' ([128]). The methods of synchronic and diachronic linguistics will differ in two major respects. First, there is a difference in perspectives, and hence in methods. 'Synchrony has only one perspective, that of the language users; and its whole method consists of collecting evidence from them' ([128]). Diachronic linguistics, on the other hand, has two perspectives. 'One will be *prospective*, following the course of time, and the other *retrospective*, going in the opposite direction' ([128]). In the second place, diachronic linguistics does not need to confine itself to the study of sequences of items belonging to the same language: it may, for example, trace sequences of forms going back from French to Latin and to Proto-Indo-European. Synchronic studies, by contrast, cannot cross linguistic boundaries in this way. Furthermore, 'the object of synchronic study does not comprise everything which is simultaneous, but only the set of facts corresponding to any particular language. In this it will take into account where necessary a division into dialects and subdialects. The term *synchronic*, in fact, is not sufficiently precise. *Idiosynchronic* would be a better term ...' ([128]).

Here we have two quite crucial modifications to the concept of synchrony: so crucial that in certain respects they force a new interpretation of the original distinction between the synchronic and the diachronic. Hitherto the proposed basis of that distinction has been purely temporal: hence the actual terms *synchronic* and *diachronic*. Now, however, there is a retreat from temporality. Diachronic studies will include, in appropriate cases, the comparison of coeval signs (French *est*, German *ist*): for 'in order to justify comparing two forms, it is sufficient that there should be some historical connexion between them, however indirect' ([129]). So the scope of diachronic studies expands to include not merely historical sequentiality but historical relatedness, irrespective of sequentiality. At the same time, the scope of synchronic studies is restricted. It does not embrace everything which is simultaneous, but only signs which belong to the same linguistic system (whether language, dialect or sub-dialect). Thus, terminologically, it hardly suffices to replace *synchronic* by *idiosynchronic*, as Saussure proposes. What is needed in order to do terminological justice to this new contrast would be to drop the pair *synchronic* and *diachronic* altogether and replace them by the pair *idiosystemic* and *phylogenetic*. In spite of signs of hesitation, the *Cours* clings nevertheless to *synchronic* and *diachronic*: and in so doing lays itself open to a serious charge of inviting potential confusion.

More serious still as a theoretical issue, however, is the consequence of this shift away from the original contrast of axes ('simultaneity' vs. 'succession'). It complicates beyond measure the question of delimiting the 'linguistic system', and at the same time promotes this question to a position of central importance for the now misnamed study of 'synchrony'. For patently it will be no less grave an error to conflate facts pertaining to co-existing but separate idiosynchronic systems than to conflate facts pertaining to diachronically successive systems. Mistaking one such system for a co-existing one emerges as the synchronic counterpart to the historical mistake of failing to distinguish one *état de langue* from its predecessor. This shift from the synchronic to the idiosynchronic forces Saussure to face up to a new problem for linguistic theory.

By what criteria are idiosynchronic relations to be recognized? The *Cours* offers only one answer: by the criteria which make the linguistic system a social reality for its users. It now becomes apparent why in the preceding chapter Saussure had insisted that 'in order to have a language there must be a *community of speakers*' ([112]). This is not quite the banal platitude it at first appears to be. It is, in fact, a theoretical requirement for treating any *état de langue* as an objectively identifiable system. Otherwise, it would be open to the individual investigator to adopt whatever criteria seemed subjectively appropriate, and this would be no basis for establishing the status of linguistics as a science. The theoretical role of the linguistic community, therefore, is to provide the guarantee that the idiosynchronic system is not merely an abstraction invented by the linguist.

By what criteria, then, does the linguistic community recognize idiosynchronic relations? That, presumably, is for the linguist to find out. But how does the linguist identify the members of the linguistic community? Doubtless by their collective use of the same linguistic system. It is at this point that Saussure, in effect, draws the boundary of linguistic theory. The idea of idiosynchrony would be vacuous if not supported by reference to the collective consciousness: but the idea of a collective consciousness is not further explicated in the *Cours*. Probing it simply leads us straight back to the idiosynchronic system. It is thus the interlocking of these two ideas which will provide the theoretical keystone for the conceptual framework of Saussurean linguistics.

Already, however, the analogical explanation of systematicity has opened up certain awkward questions for a linguistics which proposes to treat synchronic and diachronic relations independently. The chapter now turns to deal provisionally with these. The most important is the question already hinted at in the analogy between *la langue* and the game of chess: the question of linguistic 'laws'. The question is awkward for Saussure because the chess analogy inevitably suggests a rather different programme for linguistics than the one Saussure proposes to offer. Consequently he now has to retract or at least limit the possible implications of that analogy. It is a task which proves unexpectedly difficult, and he makes rather heavy weather of it.

In §6, Saussure distinguishes between possible synchronic laws and possible diachronic laws, and gives examples of each. All, as it happens, concern phonetic facts, and all the illustrations are from Latin or Greek; but the implications are clearly meant to have general applicability. More important than the examples, however, is the premiss of Saussure's argument: 'any social law has two fundamental characteristics: it is *imperative* and it is *general*' ([130]). The term 'law' is here to be understood 'in its legal sense' ([134]). The question, according to Saussure, is simply whether so-called linguistic 'laws' of the synchronic or the diachronic type satisfy these two conditions.

Synchronic 'laws' do not satisfy the conditions, Saussure argues, because they are 'general, but not imperative' ([131]). By denying their 'imperative' character is meant not that speakers are not obliged to conform, but that '*in the language* there is nothing which guarantees the maintenance of regularity on any given point' ([131]). What Saussure means by a synchronic 'law' is, in fact, a generalization which holds for a given *état de langue*: for instance, the law determining which syllable in a Latin word bears the primary stress (this being regularly predictable on the basis of the number of syllables, length of the vowels, etc.). That this Latin stress law was not 'imperative' Saussure regards as proved by the fact that it altered in the course of time. No such pattern, however well established, is immune from change. Saussure's conclusion is that so-called synchronic 'laws' are not laws at all.

A parallel conclusion is reached concerning diachronic 'laws' also, on the ground that they fail to satisfy the second of the two conditions. Although imperative, they are not general. 'One speaks of a law only when a set of facts is governed by the same rule. In spite of appearances to the contrary, diachronic events are always accidental and particular in nature' ([131]). Saussure goes to some lengths to justify this latter claim. He takes it as obviously true in the case of semantic change: the fact that the French word *poutre*, meaning 'mare', eventually came to mean 'beam, rafter' is an isolated fact, to be explained by factors which affect no other item of French vocabulary. In cases of morphological and syntactic evolution, however, there might seem to be examples of general changes: for instance, the disappearance at a certain period of Old French nominative forms. But Saussure rejects this counterexample on the ground that in the more or less simultaneous disappearance of so many forms we see 'merely multiple examples of a single isolated fact', namely the disappearance of the Old French nominative case. This 'only appears to be a law because it is actualised in a system' ([132]). The same applies to so-called 'phonetic laws'. These affect many words simultaneously: but this is because the words in question all contain the particular sound which undergoes the change. Thus 'however many cases confirm a phonetic law, all the facts it covers are simply manifestations of a single particular fact' ([133]).

According to Saussure, then, neither synchronic 'laws' nor diachronic 'laws' are laws at all, although for different reasons in the two cases. What is the reader to make of this? It is certainly among the least convincing passages in the *Cours*. In the first place, Saussure's premiss that all social laws are both imperative and general is ill suited to his argument. If 'imperative' is glossed by saying, as Saussure does, that such a law 'demands compliance', this must mean that individuals subject to a social law have no option but to accept it. Failure to comply will entail sanctions or potential sanctions of some kind. In the linguistic case, however, Saussure denies that this is what is meant, and points out that 'laws' such as those determining word stress are subject to change. In that sense, synchronic 'laws' do not have to be kept. But this is to give a different sense to the term 'imperative' and, worse still, a sense in which few if any social laws are imperative either. Nor is it clear that diachronic laws are 'imperative' in one or other of these two senses, although Saussure claims that they are. The condition that social laws must be 'general' is scarcely any more satisfactory, since Saussure explicates 'generality' as 'covering all cases, within certain limits of time and place' ([130]). But in this sense of 'generality', a social law is on no different footing from any linguistic law which can be shown to 'cover all cases, within certain limits of time and place'. The dismissal of diachronic laws on this ground is thus question-begging. Saussure here needs either a different reason for refusing to accept diachronic laws, or else a stronger criterion of 'generality'.

Saussure's particular counterarguments dealing with morphological and phonetic change involve what amounts to special pleading. To count the disappearance of many Old French nominative forms as a single diachronic fact – namely, the disappearance of the nominative case itself – comes oddly from a theorist who elsewhere argues not only that the linguistic system as such is unchangeable ([121]) but also that grammatical cases are 'abstract entities' based on relationships between signs ([190]). For if the disappearance of a whole grammatical case (as distinct from the disappearance of the various individual forms) is not an example of diachronic change in a grammatical system, it is difficult to see what conceivably could be. Hence either Saussure's generalization that linguistic changes never directly affect the system as such must have exceptions; or else it acquires the status of an axiom. Either way, there are theoretical problems which the *Cours* makes no attempt to deal with. Again, if grammatical cases are abstract entities, their existence or non-existence must depend on the presence or absence in the system of contrasts between many individual signs which mark the grammatical distinction in question. For in Saussurean linguistics, it is the individual sign which is the basic 'concrete entity' of *la langue*. Nowhere does the *Cours* lay the ground for claiming that it is possible for whole sets of independent 'concrete entities' to be abolished at one stroke because of a single 'abstract' change at some higher level of linguistic organization. This would run counter to the whole Saussurean concept of linguistic articulation and to the doctrine of *valeurs*.

To appreciate the point, it is essential for the reader to realize (although the text of the *Cours* never makes this clear) that the Old French system included a variety of declensional types, of which at least the following six are usually recognized.

	Singular	Plural
Nominative	*murs*	*mur*
Oblique	*mur*	*murs*
Nominative	*pere*	*pere*
Oblique	*pere*	*peres*
Nominative	*porte*	*portes*
Oblique	*porte*	*portes*
Nominative	*flor(s)*	*flors*
Oblique	*flor*	*flors*
Nominative	*cuens*	*comte*
Oblique	*comte*	*comtes*
Nominative	*cors*	*cors*
Oblique	*cors*	*cors*

In other words, this is not one of those examples where the maintenance of a grammatical distinction depends on a single consonantal or vocalic contrast, and where consequently a single sound change affecting the consonant or vowel in question may obliterate the distinction. If in Kalaba all noun plurals are distinguished from their singulars solely by the addition of the suffix -*a*, it follows that if final vowels fall at some stage in the history of the Kalaba language, henceforth singular forms and plural forms will be phonetically identical. Such a change Saussure would not describe as the 'disappearance of the Kalaba plural': far from it, for that would be the kind of mistake made in 'historical grammar' by failing to distinguish between changes and consequences of changes. The fact that the later *état de langue* in Kalaba has no distinction between singular nouns and plural nouns would be a synchronic consequence of a phonetic change having nothing to do with Kalaba grammar.

How, then, are we to make sense of Saussure's claim that in Old French it was the nominative case which disappeared (as distinct from any particular sound or affix)? The implication seems to be that for Saussure 'nominative case' was a *signifié* in Old French, which happened to be shared by a large number of *signifiants*. Furthermore, it seems we must understand that just as a sign may drop out of the language because, by reason of phonetic change, its *signifiant* disappears (as in the hypothetical case of Kalaba final *-a*), so there are cases in which a sign may drop out of the language because its *signifié*, for reasons of semantic change, disappears. What happened to the Old French nominatives would then fall under this latter head. Saussure, in short, appears to envisage a parallel between the operations of phonetic change and the operations of semantic change, which could result in similar synchronic consequences for a later *état de langue*. An earlier grammatical distinction might be lost for either of two quite distinct reasons: (i) because phonetic change 'accidentally' obliterated the relevant differences between forms, or (ii) because semantic change obliterated the relevant conceptual differences.

The trouble with this, as an interpretation of Saussure's use of the Old French example, is that it makes the theoretical difficulty for Saussure even more acute. In the first place, the facts do not warrant a claim that the nominative case *as such* disappeared from Old French. For if 'nominative case' is a semantic concept, then it is possible to argue that (i) it still survived, but was expressed in a different form (by contrasts of word order, instead of by nominal flexions), and (ii) it survived in the pronoun system, which still distinguishes morphologically between nominatives (*je, tu, il,* etc.) and obliques (*me, te, le,* etc.). In the second place, processes of semantic change are manifestly not like processes of phonetic change in any case. There is a world of difference between, say, the 'disappearance' of a final vowel (which may or may not be of morphological significance) and the 'disappearance' of a concept (that is, of a Saussurean *signifié*).

While it seems reasonable in certain circumstances to invoke the disappearance of one *signifié* to explain the fate of an individual sign (because a linguistic community no longer needs a word for something it ceases to have occasion to talk about) it is far from clear that it makes sense at all to invoke the disappearance of one *signifié* to explain the disappearance of a whole series of different phonological forms. What would the sociolinguistic mechanism for such a change be? It clearly could not be parallel to, say, the process by which gradually phasing out the manufacture of thimbles might eventually lead to an *état de langue* in English which had no word *thimble*. That is perfectly comprehensible. One can even imagine that the obsolescence of certain types of activity or craft (for instance, sewing) might lead to the obsolescence of a whole vocabulary associated with it (*thimble, needle, stitch*, etc.). But that is not quite the same as suggesting that the forms of the words *thimble, needle, stitch*, etc. would automatically be eliminated in a linguistic community which did not have the concept of sewing. For that presupposes that the meanings of the words *thimble, needle, stitch*, etc. are all necessarily defined by reference to sewing. Now the *Cours* offers very little in the way of specific proposals about topics in semantics: but what it does say does not suggest that Saussure's theory of the linguistic sign is committed in advance to some form of componential semantics. Consequently the *signifié* 'thimble' could well survive in the absence of the *signifié* 'sew', and the *signifiant* [θimbl] could well survive too. Saussure here fails to reckon with a fundamental asymmetry between attributing the loss of a semantic distinction to sound change and attributing the loss of a formal distinction to semantic change.

Saussure's argument concerning sound change itself is no less deeply flawed. One of his own examples (the fall of final stops: **gunaik→gúnai, *epheret→éphere, *epheront→épheron*) will suffice to illustrate why. If such a change affects a number of sounds ([k], [t], etc.) which, according to Saussurean phonetics, belong to different 'sound types', and if the sounds in question are all and only those meeting certain specifiable conditions (final stops), it must be self-contradictory to claim that the change is not 'general' under the definition of generality which Saussure demands for social laws. Such a change is, in fact, exactly parallel to the introduction of a new social law which affects all and only members of a certain specified class or inhabitants of a certain specified area. It is not a question of rejecting Saussure's claim that 'words themselves are not directly subject to phonetic change' ([133]). Even if true, this is quite irrelevant to the argument: for social laws are not (usually) instituted for specific individuals either. Jones and Smith may not be 'directly subject' to changes in legislation, in that the law does not name them specifically or single them out for special treatment: but they are subject to it nevertheless if they qualify under whatever general provisions the new legislation makes, and irrespective of whether they are or are not the only members of society who happen to qualify. *Mutatis mutandis*, the same applies to words. The fact that the fall of final stops is a sound change which leaves untouched words which did not have final stops in the first place is no reason for denying its 'generality'. The case would be quite different if a random selection of words with final stops were subject to the change. But in that case, *pace* Saussure, there *would* be an argument for saying that certain words only were 'directly subject' to the change in question.

It is difficult not to conclude that §6 is a tactical mistake from beginning to end. It takes back clumsily the very explanation the chess analogy offered just previously. For if linguistic 'laws' are not really 'law-like' after all in the way the rules of chess are, or in the way social laws in general are, then the original analogy was worthless. We are left with *états de langue* which are *not* like states of the chess board, since the patterns they conform to lack the force of laws. This certainly explains why it is no part of the Saussurean programme for linguistics to concern itself with the establishment of a set of general linguistic laws which, like the rules of chess, simultaneously explain both states and changes, and their interrelations, in all conceivable cases. But the price paid for this retraction is a heavy one. For we are once again left without an explanation of what is meant by the systematicity of an *état de langue*.

Although §6 is a tactical blunder, it is not a strategic catastrophe. Saussure's theoretical position is perfectly defensible if the defence is managed less clumsily. What Saussure ought to have argued may be summarized as follows. 1. There are no synchronic laws. For although *la langue* is a social institution, there is nothing corresponding to a legal system which exists precisely *in order to* impose certain patterns of behaviour in the community. 2. There are no diachronic laws either. For *la langue* is not like those social institutions in which the transition from a prior state to a subsequent state is regulated. *La langue* has nothing corresponding to social 'laws of inheritance', or to the rules for moves in chess, which regulate the transition from one state of the board to the next. 3. Apparent counterexamples to the absence of synchronic laws are illusions arising from the regularities observable in *parole*. 4. Apparent counterexamples to the absence of diachronic laws are illusions arising from the fact that, retrospectively, series of unconnected changes give the appearance of a reorganization of the system. Thus the so-called 'disappearance of the Old French nominative case' is a diachronic misdescription or oversimplification of a whole series of separate events affecting particular forms or sub-groups of forms. With a defence conducted along these lines, Saussure's rejection of both synchronic and diachronic laws would be more secure.

Next, an alternative possibility is explored. Why cannot a science of language establish panchronic laws which relate to languages as the laws of nature relate to events in the physical world? Because, §7 argues, although it is possible to generalize about universal features of language (for example, that phonetic changes constantly occur), where specific linguistic facts are concerned 'there is no panchronic point of view' ([135]). Any concrete fact amenable to panchronic explanation could not be part of *la langue*. For example, the French word *chose* may be distinguished synchronically from other words belonging to the same *état de langue*, and diachronically from words in earlier *états de langue* (for instance, from Latin *causa*, from which it is etymologically derived). But there is no independent panchronic means of identifying it. The sounds *šọz* may be considered panchronically in themselves: but the sounds as such do not constitute the word *chose*. 'The panchronic point of view never gets to grips with specific facts of *la langue*' ([195]). This is, obviously, another Saussurean reformulation of the charge already brought against 'historical linguistics': we cannot study 'the word' (whether it be *chose* or any other) as a continuously evolving entity with a life-span of two thousand years: for the simple reason that no such entity exists. All we can do is examine a number of different synchronic entities which do exist, and the separate diachronic changes which connect them. The 'panchronic' error, in other words, is another version of the 'historical' error. It is a mistake to imagine that there could be some more general perspective on language which would take in both synchronic and diachronic facts simultaneously.

§8 proceeds to give various exemplifications of the error, in the form of conflations between synchronic and diachronic facts. For years, says Saussure, 'linguistics has muddled them up without even noticing the muddle' ([137]). By unscrambling this muddle, one can arrive at a 'rational' programme for linguistic studies, which the table in §9 ([139]) summarizes;

$$
\text{Langage} \left\{ \begin{array}{l} \text{Langue} \left\{ \begin{array}{l} \text{Synchronie} \\ \text{Diachronie} \end{array} \right. \\ \text{Parole} \end{array} \right.
$$

As an essay in general linguistic theory, Chapter III can hardly be counted an unqualified success. It is a patchwork of examples and partial analogies, tacked together by rather tenuous threads of reasoning. But this patchwork quality itself demonstrates how unexpectedly difficult it is to argue for the apparently simple thesis which Saussure advances. It shows that it is one thing to grasp that the linguistic relationship between French *chose* and Latin *causa* must be of a quite different order from the linguistic relationship between French *chose* and French *chien*, but quite a different thing to supply a satisfactory theoretical framework which accommodates that difference. What emerges above all is that the programmatic separation of these two orders of relationship requires a concept of linguistic systematicity which it is far from easy to explicate when the signs involved are defined in terms of an arbitrary connexion between form and meaning. It is this major task of explication which is now to be tackled in Part II of the *Cours*.

PART TWO
Synchronic Linguistics

CHAPTER I
General Observations

The aim of general synchronic linguistics is announced straight away as being 'to establish the fundamental principles of any idiosynchronic system, the facts which constitute any *état de langue*' ([141]), and this will include not only the properties of the sign already discussed in Part I, but everything usually called 'general grammar' ([141]). This opening formulation raises the question of what the precise relation is between idiosynchronic system and *état de langue*. If the preceding chapter of the *Cours* had given the impression that there was little if any difference between the two, this equation is immediately called in question by what now follows.

The reader is told that (notwithstanding the analogy drawn in the previous chapter with a cross-cut through the stem of a plant) an *état de langue* is not to be thought of as what is revealed by a single slice through the evolutionary development of a language at a particular point in time. An *état de langue*, rather, is itself a phase in that development. It occupies 'a period of time of varying length, during which the sum total of changes occurring is minimal. It may be ten years, a generation, a century, or even longer' ([142]).

This second major revision of the opposition between synchrony and diachrony – for that is what it amounts to – is introduced almost casually, and accompanied by only the sparsest of explanations. The reader is simply referred to the historian's distinction between 'epochs' and 'periods', the former conceptualized as points in time, and the latter as lengths of time. 'None the less, a historian speaks of the "Antonine epoch" or the "Crusading epoch" when he is taking into consideration a set of features which remained constant over the period in question. One could likewise say that static linguistics is also in this sense concerned with epochs; but the term *state* is preferable' ([142]).

The implications of this revised concept of an *état de langue* are far-reaching. It should be noted first of all that herewith Saussure reverts again to time as the relevant dimension for defining a linguistic distinction, but now uses that dimension in a different defining role. In Part I, time had been treated (i) as the 'abstract' dimension validating the opposition between two different sets of relations (along the axes of simultaneity and succession), and (ii) as the 'real world' dimension providing the empirical basis for the action of social forces upon *la langue*. Now we have something different. The new viewpoint combines the two earlier treatments of time and supersedes them. In this third conceptualization of synchronic and diachronic relations, the sub-ordination of diachrony to synchrony is definitive. For now an *état de langue* is identified by its invariance over time: 'an absolute state is defined by lack of change' ([142]). Since diachronic studies by definition do not embrace the analysis of *états de langue*, this apparently excludes from the purview of diachronic linguistics any period in the history of a language during which no change occurs. Diachronic studies, conse-quently, are restricted to dealing with such periods of linguistic history as intervene between periods of stability. The text of the *Cours* seems to leave little room for doubt about this. 'Of two contemporary languages, one may evolve considerably and the other hardly at all over the same period. In the latter case, any study will necessarily be synchronic, but in the former case diachronic' ([142]). So now we have time itself, as the linguistic axis of succession, divided into successions of stability and change; while 'synchronic' and 'diachronic' become opposed modalities of investigation relative to the successive segmentations of this axis. Given the new concept of an *état de langue*, there will apparently be a simple one-one correspondence between period and modality of investigation; for each progressive transition along the temporal axis must be either a transition from stability to change or else a transition from change to stability.

The difference between this new temporal framework and the old one corresponds to the difference between the simple diagram of the two intersecting axes on p.[115] of the *Cours* and something more like the diagram shown opposite (p.105).

The new framework, it will be apparent, represents an elaboration of the chess analogy at the expense of the plant analogy. Intersection between horizontal and vertical axes is no longer a single momentary 'time-slice' revealing two exactly matching surfaces on the cross-cut, but a sectional excision laying bare non-identical patterns at either end. This corresponds exactly to the sequence of events in the game of chess. Any state of the board will remain unchanged for a variable length of time – as long as it may take between one move and the next. Once a move is

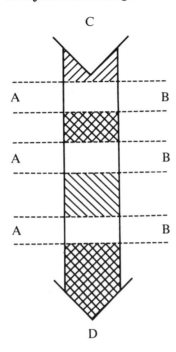

made, that puts an end to the preceding static period: the pattern on the board will no longer be the same as before. Each state of the board in turn is separated from the next by an interval, which may also be of greater or less duration, during which a change in the pattern of pieces is effected. Thus the game proceeds by regular alternations between states and changes. This is the model of linguistic development to be explored throughout Parts II and III of the *Cours*.

At this point in the text, one or two problems arising from the new framework are briefly mentioned. One is that of 'demarcation in time' ([143]). That is to say, there will be a problem in defining the chronological limits of a given *état de langue*. This problem is temporarily dismissed, however, by pointing out that since an exactly similar geographical problem arises over demarcation in space, the notion of an *état de langue* 'can only be an approximation' ([143]).

Ill prepared as the reader may have been for the first surprise about synchrony which the chapter held in store, this second one comes as an even greater shock. For now it appears that an *état de langue* is not only a period, but something much more enigmatic: a period with a geographical area. Saussurean commentators on the whole have displayed quite remarkable phlegm in dealing with this *prima facie* evidence of conceptual confusion. One would have expected it at least to provoke a footnote or two. Perhaps the explanation is that the coupling of the problem of chronological demarcation with that of geographical demarcation was taken by most readers simply as an elliptical way of saying that the question 'Exactly *when* was language X spoken?' can no more be answered precisely than 'Exactly *where* was language X spoken?' If so, this bears witness to a very superficial reading of the *Cours*. The text is quite specific. It speaks in both cases of 'the same problem', and of the difficulty it presents for 'the definition of an *état de langue*' ([143]). It is the first recognition in the *Cours* that a dimension *other than* time is relevant to linguistic theory.

The *Cours* does not take up the question again until Part IV on 'Geographical Linguistics'. However, it is worth pointing out briefly at this juncture in what sense the issue of geographical demarcation is relevant. The notion of an *état de langue* as something which has both a chronological and a geographical extension begins to make sense if we see it as the result of projecting the concept of an idiosynchronic system on to the plane of *la parole*. Here we encounter another of the hidden premises of Saussurean linguistics. It is: that the mechanism of diachronic continuity is contact between individual speakers. Already the reader was forewarned of this on p.[138]: 'everything which is diachronic in *la langue* is only so through *la parole*'. But there the context of the observation appeared to limit its scope to the question of explaining how linguistic change comes about through trial and error initiated by individuals. In fact, the remark has a much wider significance, which now emerges. Since each individual act of *parole* occurs in a spatio-temporally situated context, it follows that diachrony has spatial as well as temporal implications. Specifically, contact between individuals is what ensures diachronic succession: and this contact must take place *somewhere*. The world of Saussurean linguistics is a world of face-to-face interaction. Writing is overtly excluded by definition, and the possibility of transmitting the spoken word by telephone, radio or tape-recording is tacitly excluded as 'unnatural'. It is essentially a world which antedates the most recent of the technological revolutions in human communication, and the ensuing theoretical problems which arise concerning the location of communicative acts can consequently be ignored. Thus for Saussure there is no question of diachronic continuity without a chain of contact through *la parole* which is spatially identifiable. If two phylogenetically and geographically remote language-families were somehow to evolve identical dialects, that would be for Saussure a remarkable coincidence: but nothing which called for any kind of explanation in terms of linguistic theory.

Thus the problem of the geographical demarcation of the use of an idiosynchronic system and the problem of its temporal demarcation are quite literally, from a Saussurean point of view, *the same problem*. Why is this? The answer is that it must necessarily be so once the concept of an idiosynchronic system is mapped on to the facts of Saussurean *parole*, which is just what the new model of an *état de langue* accomplishes. More important for what follows is that this dual problem is now to be treated as of a merely practical rather than of a theoretical order. This is evident from the description of a linguistic state as a period 'during which the sum total of changes occurring is minimal' ([142]); from the recommendation that 'unimportant changes' be ignored, just as mathematicians 'ignore very small fractions for certain purposes, such as logarithmic calculation' ([142]); and from the appeal to a general scientific practice of 'conventional simplification of the data' ([143]). Whether this relegation of demarcational problems to the domain of the practical can ultimately be sustained is a quite different matter. Saussure's account of synchronic theory throughout the rest of Part II simply assumes that 'for all practical purposes' the linguist has managed to identify an epoch of linguistic history amenable to synchronic analysis, even if the exact demarcation of the relevant *état de langue* is still uncertain. The demarcation, indeed, is bound to remain uncertain until analysis has revealed the details of the idiosynchronic system on which that *état de langue* is based.

Also uncertain in the light of this new Saussurean interpretation of synchrony is what happens to the linguistic community in between periods of stability. Does it have no *langue*? By what means does communication continue, given that the previously established system has broken down and a new system has not yet replaced it? And if linguistic communication nevertheless does continue in the interim, what becomes of the original hypothesis that the sole linguistic reality for the speakers is an *état de langue*? Do they somehow carry on in the mistaken belief that they are still using the old system, without noticing that in fact its distinctions have collapsed? If so, are they already using a new system unwittingly, or using no system at all? Questions of this order inevitably arise once the concept of synchrony is no longer construed in terms of the very simple model provided by the two axes of simultaneity and succession. The conflicting demands of temporality and systematicity here, as elsewhere in the *Cours*, generate problems which are never satisfactorily resolved.

CHAPTER II

Concrete Entities of a Language

How is the linguist to identify the linguistic signs belonging to any idiosynchronic system? Saussure takes this question first for the obvious reason that unless an answer is available synchronic analysis cannot even begin. No system can be identified independently of its constituent signs, and to identify the constituent signs is *eo ipso* to engage in analysis of the system.

The reader is reminded in §1 of this chapter that in linguistics the 'concrete entity' is the linguistic sign, and that linguistic signs exist only in virtue of an association between *signifiant* and *signifié*. Consequently the linguist cannot proceed by trying to analyse sounds and meanings separately. The only viable method of procedure is to segment the continuous phonetic chain presented by each utterance into sections, each of which corresponds to a *signifié* in the spoken message. This method is represented schematically by the following diagram on p.[146]:

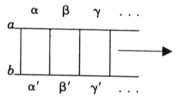

'Correct delimitation of signs requires that the divisions established in the sound sequence (α', β', γ' ...) match the divisions in the sequence of concepts (α, β, γ ...)' ([146]).

Only one example of this method is given: *sižlaprã* may be analysed either as *si-ž-la-prã* (= *si je la prends*, 'if I take it/her') or as *si-ž-l-aprã* (= *si je l'apprends*, 'if I learn it'), but in no other way, since no other segmentation of the sound sequence makes sense of the meaning. 'To check the results of this analysis and make sure that one has picked out the units, it is necessary to compare series of phrases in which the same unit occurs, and be able in each case to separate the unit in question from its context in a way corroborated by the sense' ([146-7]). In the two phrases *lafǫrsdüvā* (= *la force du vent*) and *abudfǫrs* (= *à bout de force*), 'the same concept coincides with the same sound-segment *fǫrs* in both cases: thus it is clearly a linguistic unit' ([147]). But in *ilməfǫrsaparlę* (= *il me force à parler*), '*fǫrs* has a quite different meaning: so it is a different unit' ([147]).

The implications of this method of analysis are examined in §3. The most obvious is that the Saussurean 'concrete entity' or 'concrete unit' does not correspond to the traditional unit 'word'. For instance, the singular *cheval* ('horse') and its plural *chevaux* ('horses') will count as two separate concrete units, although they are traditionally treated as forms of a single word. Similarly the two possible pronunciations of the French word for 'month' (*mwa* and, in liaison with a following vowel, *mwaz*) count for Saussure as the *significants* of two different signs. Suffixes, prefixes and stems with clearly identifiable meanings will also qualify as concrete units, although they are not recognized traditionally as separate words. On the other hand, there are certain concrete units (compounds, fixed phrases) which are larger than single words.

Saussure does not deny that in many cases it is quite difficult to analyse sound sequences in this way and to determine which units are present: 'delimiting them is such a tricky problem that one is led to ask whether they are really there' ([149]). But this is seen as one of the features which distinguishes languages from all other semiological institutions. 'A language thus has this curious and striking feature. It has no immediately perceptible entities' ([149]).

In this chapter, the hidden premiss that the 'invisible' articulation of *la langue* will turn out to correspond to the 'visible' articulation of writing again comes to the surface; and this time not merely at the level of phonology. It is significant, for instance, that Saussure fails to discuss whether his first segmentation of *sižlaprã* requires a further division between *l* and *a*. His analysis stops short, in other words, when it reaches a unit which answers to the usual orthographic form of the pronoun *la*. The assumption, evidently, is that this pronoun form corresponds to a single concept (although no attempt is made to state what this concept is). But since in French *la* stands in contrast to *le* (*si je la prends* vs. *si je le prends*), it is a perfectly reasonable question to ask whether these units cannot be broken down further. One possible analysis would be that *l* signals the pronominal person (third person, in traditional grammatical terms) while the vowel signals the gender (feminine in the case of *la*, masculine in the case of *le*). This analysis would be supported by Saussure's own second segmentation, where the consonant *l* alone represents a third person pronoun of indeterminate gender. The text of the *Cours* leaves the reader uncertain as to whether this possibility simply did not occur to Saussure, or whether he had reasons for rejecting it.

It seems fairly clear that there are a number of other hidden premisses lying behind Saussure's treatment of examples in this chapter. They appear to relate on the one hand to the native speaker's knowledge of *la langue*, and on the other hand to the organization of units within *la langue*. However, it is no easy matter to determine exactly what the content and theoretical status of these premisses is, for reasons which will emerge in the discussion below.

Basically, Saussure seems to assume that the native speaker is normally able to make a correct identification of features of linguistic structure, by some simple process of introspection and reflection. The theoretical significance of this assumption it would be difficult to exaggerate. Only its unquestioned acceptance will justify Saussure's lack of concern with providing any systematic 'discovery procedure' for the identification of linguistic signs. There may be difficulties over marginal cases but not, it would seem, over most. He is evidently confident that his treatment of *sižlaprã* will strike any French native speaker as totally uncontentious, and that there is no need to present evidence in support of the two analyses proposed. His denial that any other segmentations of the sequence make sense is quite categoric. Thus it would seem that the intelligent native speaker has only to reflect upon the matter for a moment in order to arrive at exactly the same conclusion as the linguistic theorist. Likewise, Saussure appears to take it for granted that it will be intuitively obvious to the native speaker, on reflection, that *mwaz* must be a quite separate linguistic sign from *mwa*, that *fɔrs* has a quite different meaning in *la force du vent* and *il me force à parler*, and so on.

Particularly revealing is the case of *mwaz* (as in *un mois après*) vs. *mwa* (as in *le mois de décembre*). Saussure does not discuss the possibility of treating *mwaz* and *mwa* as alternate forms of the same *signifiant*; nor the possibility of analysing *mwaz* into *mwa* + *z*, where *z* is simply a structural unit devoid of meaning. The implied rejection of the latter possibility raises a rather crucial question: for one can see two possible ways of rationalizing it.

The case might rest on the psychological claim that native speakers of French do not as a matter of fact recognize that *mwaz* segments into two elements, the first of which means 'month' and the second of which is meaningless; but, on the contrary, recognize *mwaz* as a single unit meaning 'month'. Alternatively, the case might rest on the methodological contention that the linguistic analyst cannot proceed on the assumption that there may be a 'residue' on the plane of expression which is semantically unaccounted for. The difference between these two positions is important. The former case rests on an alleged fact about a particular generation or generations of speakers of French, and will have no general consequences. The latter case amounts to postulating a linguistic universal. The hidden premiss would then be that in *la langue* there are no semantic zero-elements. (Whereas, by contrast, Saussure evidently sees nothing odd about *phonic* zero-elements, as has earlier been made clear on p.[124].) The premiss, in other words, is that there is an asymmetry in the composition of the linguistic sign, which allows a *signifié* to have a zero *signifiant*, but does not allow a *signifiant* to have a zero *signifié*.

Such a premiss in effect introduces an important but unannounced limitation on the principle of arbitrariness. This limitation will clearly have far-reaching consequences for the linguist's programme of analysis. For the assumption will be that linguistic structure does not permit the arbitrary introduction of meaningless elements in order to satisfy rules which pertain solely to the plane of expression. On the other hand, if semantic zero-elements are theoretically permissible, then it becomes a merely contingent fact that there is no such element in *mwaz*. This is not merely a puzzle about the linguistic status of liaison consonants in French: on the contrary, it has quite general implications for linguistic analysis, and in particular the relevance of native speakers' awareness of linguistic structure.

In one case, the analyst must presumably try to devise a reliable way of discovering whether native speakers recognize certain sounds as independent structural units, albeit meaningless ones. In the other case, it makes no difference whether they do or not. Saussure never suggests any test that linguists might carry out to determine whether a sequence like *mwaz* is analysable into *mwa + z*, even though he admits that the delimitation of linguistic units may pose problems ([148-9]). The only check he proposes on analyses flowing from the immediate deliverances of intuition is quite clearly regressive ([146-7]): it consists of finding further examples of the 'same linguistic unit' in other contexts. The problem with this method of verification is that exactly the same uncertainty then arises at one remove. It will not solve the analyst's query to switch attention from *mwaz* in *un mois après* to *mwaz* in *deux mois après*. The question, precisely, is how to recognize the presence of the 'same linguistic unit' in either. (The most lucid discussion of this and related problems in Saussurean analysis is that of Love 1984.)

Further hidden premisses appear to lie behind the diagram on p.[146] and the requirement for 'correct analysis' that divisions in the sound sequence (α', β', γ' ...) match divisions in the sequence of concepts (α, β, γ ...). One such premiss is what might be called the premiss of 'linear cohesion': the assumption that the *signifiant* is a linear unit which is 'uninterruptable'. In other words, there will be no cases in which a single *signifié* is represented on the plane of expression by *two* discrete segments of the speech chain. This premiss of linear cohesion in effect rules out any possibility of the following schema of analysis:

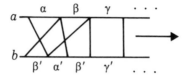

Why this should be impossible Saussure never explains. The lacuna may seem curious: for various examples given elsewhere in the *Cours* might suggest that recognizing the 'infixing' of one *signifiant* into another would be a plausible way of analysing the morphological structure of certain types of form. It is common in the Germanic languages, for example, to find morphological patterns in which vocalic variation with a fixed consonantal frame indicates a difference of tense, number, etc. (Saussure cites cases such as German *geben* vs. *gibt, schelten* vs. *schilt,* etc. in discussing the phenomenon of 'alternation' on pp.[217-20].) Similar patterning is even more prominent and regular in the Semitic system of consonantal roots (mentioned by Saussure on p.[256]).

The upshot of adopting the premiss of linear cohesion may be illustrated by reference to a simple English example: the plural forms *cats* and *mice.* On the basis of the premiss of linear cohesion, Saussurean analysis would treat *cats* as a combination of two *signifiants* but refuse to treat *mice* likewise. It will reject the possibility of treating the vowel of *mice* as a linguistic sign marking the plural, even though that is clearly what distinguishes *mice* from the corresponding singular *mouse* (just as the final *s* of *cats* is what distinguishes that from the corresponding singular *cat*). For this analysis of *mice* would entail treating the *signifié* 'mouse' as in this case having a *signifiant* split into the two linearly discrete elements [m] and [s]. The same example will also serve to illustrate a third possible hidden premiss, the premiss of 'representational discreteness'. This premiss would rule out the possibility of analytic schemata such as:

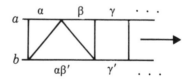

In other words, it rejects the possibility of treating a single *signifiant* as simultaneously functioning as the *signifiant* for two separate *signifiés.* The English plural *mice,* therefore, is not to be analysed as a form which simultaneously functions as the *signifiant* for both the *signifié* 'mouse' and the *signifié* 'plural'. The *signifié* of the form *mice,* accordingly, will be a single concept which in some way (not further elucidated) uniquely combines just the notions of plurality and mousehood. We have to treat it as unparadoxical, therefore, that *mice* means just 'mice', whereas *cats* does not mean 'cats' (but rather 'cat' plus 'more than one').

Between them, the premisses of linear cohesion and discrete representation yield a picture of linguistic structure which is clearly atomistic. That is to say, the *entités concrètes* of a language will emerge as units which never fuse or merge with one another, and cannot be split. These atomic units do not change their form or their behaviour when combined together, but retain their individual identities under all circumstances. The attractions of such a picture are not to be underestimated. It is precisely their atomistic invariance which will make the identification of such linguistic units possible; and this can hardly be a negligible consideration if the central task of linguistic analysis is indeed to identify them.

It will by now be clear what the problem is about the theoretical status of the hidden premisses on which this chapter of the *Cours* seems to be based. Saussure never says whether we are dealing here with psycholinguistic universals or just with methodological postulates. If the latter, he fails to explain whether these are the *only* postulates on which linguistic analysis might proceed, or merely one possible set. (He neither argues the case that no other postulates will do, nor justifies them as preferable to possible alternatives.) If the former, what the *Cours* conspicuously lacks is any rationale for treating these premisses as deriving from general 'laws' of the kind mentioned in Chapter II of the Introduction, or from higher-order principles of semiology either. The only glimmers of light which the text of the *Cours* sheds on this problem come much later – and almost incidentally – in the section devoted to Diachronic Linguistics: even then, they are no more than glimmers.

Whatever the answer, Saussure is clearly committed to an analytic methodology which poses at least two major questions concerning the analytic criteria for dealing with idiosynchronic systems. (1) By what criteria are *signifiés* to be identified? (2) By what criteria are *signifiés* to be located? The latter question is a question of 'location' by reference to the speech chain: for this is what the analyst's segmentation of examples such as *sižlaprã* involves. (Which segments of the sound sequence are the segments to which the *signifiés* α, β and γ correspond? The former question in practice resolves into two complementary questions: (1a) What are the meanings of the segments α', β', γ' (if they have any)? (1b) Are the meanings of α', β', γ' in this example the same as the meanings of the same phonic segments occurring elsewhere? These are the questions which have to be answerable if the atomic structure of discourse is to yield its secrets to the Saussurean analyst.

CHAPTER III

Identities, Realities, Values

Already in Chapter II the reader has been given various hints that matching up *signifiants* with their corresponding *signifiés* may be no straightforward matter. In Chapter III the nature of the difficulty is examined in greater depth. Saussure first emphasizes the point that in synchronic linguistics everything depends on the identification of linguistic units. This is not just a minor methodological issue: 'the fundamental concepts of static linguistics are directly based upon, or even merge with, the concept of a linguistic unit' ([150]). The whole of Chapter III is devoted to the demonstration of this proposition. The problem of linguistic units is broken down into three questions: A. What is a synchronic *identity*? B. What is a synchronic *reality*? C. What is a synchronic *value*?

The problem of synchronic identities is presented by Saussure as arising because occurrences of the same linguistic unit do not necessarily preclude either phonetic or semantic differences between one instantiation and the next. 'For example, we may hear in the course of a lecture several repetitions of the word *Messieurs!* We feel that in each case it is the same expression: and yet there are variations of delivery and intonation which give rise in the several instances to very noticeable phonic differences – differences as marked as those which in other cases serve to differentiate one word from another ... Furthermore, this feeling of identity persists in spite of the fact that from a semantic point of view too there is no absolute reduplication from one *Messieurs!* to the next' ([150-1]). The problem of identifying this 'sameness' is the same problem as that of defining the linguistic unit *messieurs*. A second example Saussure gives is that of the difference between the use of the verb *adopter* in *adopter une mode* ('to adopt a fashion') and *adopter un enfant* ('to adopt a child'), and between the use of the noun *fleur* in *la fleur du pommier* ('the flower of the apple-tree') and *la fleur de la noblesse* ('the flower of the nobility'). 'A word can express quite different ideas without seriously compromising its own identity' ([151]).

What kind of identity, then, is synchronic identity? Saussure proceeds to draw a distinction between formal or functional identity on the one hand, and material identity on the other. An example of formal or functional identity is the identity of the 8.45 train from Geneva to Paris ([151]), which is 'the same train' on different days in spite of the fact that locomotive, carriages and staff may be different. Another is the identity of a street, which survives demolition and reconstruction of its buildings ([151]). An example of material identity is that of a man's suit ([151]), which belongs to a particular individual, and will still be 'his' suit even if stolen. Linguistic identity, says Saussure, 'is not the kind of identity the suit has, but the kind of identity the train and the street have' ([152]). It is the task of the linguist to discover, in the case of linguistic units, on what factors this formal or functional identity is based.

Saussure's linguistic and non-linguistic examples here both call for comment. The linguistic examples cover two very different types of question. In the case of *Messieurs!* it is a question of the criteria for counting different utterances as utterances of the same word. In the case of *adopter* and *fleur* it is a question of the criteria for counting different usages as usages of the same word. The former problem is one nowadays commonly described in the terminology coined by C.S. Peirce (1931-58: 4.537, 2.245) as the problem of 'type-token' relations (Lyons 1977: 13ff; Hutton 1986). The latter problem is one of distinguishing between polysemy and homonymy (Ullmann 1962: 178ff.).

The distinction between linguistic types and linguistic tokens is classically exemplified by pointing out that a sentence such as *The cat sat on the mat* comprises in one sense six words, but in another sense only five, since the definite article occurs twice. In the sense in which only five words occur (which is the sense in which a dictionary lists words) the words are types. But in the sense in which six words occur (which is the sense a printer is interested in when calculating the length of a text) the words are tokens. Thus Saussure's lecturer will have uttered various non-identical tokens of the linguistic type *Messieurs!* The distinction between polysemy and homonymy, on the other hand, is usually construed as a matter of distinguishing between cases (i) in which the same word ('type') may be used in different senses, and cases (ii) in which two different words ('types') happen to be identically pronounced (or spelled). Thus the various related senses of the English noun *board* ('thin plank', 'tablet', 'table', 'food served at the table', etc.) would exemplify a typical case of polysemy; whereas the fact that the English word for an aquatic mammal of the Phocidae family and the English word for a piece of wax affixed to a letter are both pronounced and written identically (*seal*) would provide a typical case of homonymy (Ullmann 1962: 159). The difference between (i) and (ii) is problematic because, as Ullmann puts it, 'it is difficult to say in particular cases where polysemy ends and where homonymy begins' (Ullmann 1962: 178).

A preliminary query which therefore arises for the reader of the *Cours* is: does Saussure fail to see the difference between the type-token question and the polysemy-homonymy question? If we assume the answer to this to be 'yes', our estimate of Saussure's perspicacity as a linguistic theorist must be very low. But if we assume the answer to be 'no', then it presumably follows that Saussure here *deliberately* assimilates the two questions. The implications of this assimilation are worth thinking about. In the case of polysemy and homonymy it is notorious that individuals may differ as to whether they recognize 'the same word' in two divergent usages, even though they do not disagree as to the usages in question. Thus one important difference between the two problems of word-identity is that an appeal to speakers' intentions will not automatically yield comparable results. The lecturer who produces various pronunciations of *Messieurs!* presumably does intend to utter 'the same word' each time; whereas this will not necessarily be the case with different occurrences of *adopter* in the same lecture. By bringing together the type-token problem and the polysemy-homonymy problem, Saussure makes it clear that the criteria of synchronic identity which the linguist needs must simultaneously supply solutions to *both* problems, and that these criteria are *not* to be sought by reference to intentions or interpretations relating to particular speech acts on particular occasions. (These, for Saussure, would be factors belonging to the domain of *parole*, not of *langue*.)

This interpretation is borne out by the non-linguistic examples which follow. The 8.45 from Geneva to Paris corresponds to the word *messieurs*, which remains 'the same' in spite of the lecturer's variations of delivery. The passengers who travel regularly on the 8.45 doubtless intend to catch 'the same train' each time. But it is neither the invariance of the passengers' intentions, nor their possible failure to realize that the locomotive and coaches are different on different journeys, which either constitute or guarantee the identity of the train.

The case of the street demolished and rebuilt is a less happily chosen analogy. It runs the risk of suggesting that the 'sameness' here is one of diachronic continuity; but that would hardly be apposite as a Saussurean illustration of synchronic identity. The point here must be that, as in linguistic instances of polysemy and homonymy, recognizing or failing to recognize the buildings (because in fact they have changed) is irrelevant to the question of whether or not it is 'the same street'. Both 'the train' and 'the street' are, significantly, examples of social constructs. The identity of social constructs, for Saussure, remains unaffected both by material differences and by individuals' perception of – or failure to perceive – such differences.

The chapter next asks: 'What is a synchronic reality?' The question itself is significant: for it recognizes that systematic analysis alone is no guarantee that the realities of linguistic structure will be revealed. For

Saussure it remains an open question to what extent a systematic classification such as the traditional 'parts of speech' yields an inventory of the units of *la langue*: 'its division of words into nouns, verbs, adjectives, etc. does not correspond to any undeniable linguistic reality' ([152]). An even more telling example which Saussure might have chosen to make his point would have been the presentation adopted in the conventional dictionary. What the lexicographer provides, in effect, is an exhaustive inventory of lexemes, based on the principle of alphabetical order. Insofar as alphabetic spelling corresponds to the phonological structure of the words inventoried, this classification might claim to have a scientific basis. However, the principle of alphabetical order itself is completely extraneous to *la langue*; and, in any case, the relationships between words which derive from the order of constituent sounds are relationships of no linguistic significance whatever. In other words, systematic classifications, even when based on features of the linguistic units themselves, do not necessarily bring to light structural synchronic realities.

Finally comes the question: 'What is a synchronic value?' This will be discussed at greater length in Chapter IV. By way of giving a preliminary answer, Saussure reverts to the favourite analogy of chess, and compares the linguistic unit to a chess piece. The material properties of the individual chess piece do not matter: it can be replaced on the board by any other object, provided the substitute object is assigned the same value as the piece it replaces. *Mutatis mutandis*, the same applies to linguistic units. 'That is why in the final analysis the notion of value covers units, concrete entities and realities' ([154]).

CHAPTER IV

Linguistic Value

In the chapter on *La valeur linguistique* the question 'What is *la langue*?' returns once again to the centre of the discussion. It is without doubt the most important of the chapters on synchronic linguistics; and hence, arguably, the most important single chapter in the whole of the *Cours*. It attempts to resolve, although admittedly at a very general level and in a figurative rather than a practical way, the basic problem concerning *what* it is that synchronic analysis should be trying to analyse. It also includes some of the most celebrated of Saussure's analogies, and two of the most frequently cited of Saussure's epigrams: *dans la langue il n'y a que des différences* ([166]) and *la langue est une forme et non une substance* ([169]). These two dicta are often regarded, and not unreasonably, as summarizing the essentials of Saussure's linguistic teaching.

The notion of *valeur* is presented as the conceptual key to Saussure's solution of the problems of synchronic linguistics. But what exactly are linguistic *valeurs*? The chapter offers two remarkably contrasted approaches to defining the notion. One takes as its starting point the distinction between 'form' and 'substance', and attempts to explain *valeurs* as configurations of form. This approach relies for its exposition principally upon various versions of a geometrical metaphor; that of a 'plane' or 'surface'. The other approach attempts to explain *valeurs* in quasi-economic terms and relies principally on the metaphor of 'currency' or 'coinage'. To what extent these quite different approaches are successful will be discussed below.

The dichotomy between 'form' and 'substance' has a long history in European philosophy, of which the reader of the *Cours* is presumably expected to be aware. (Otherwise it would be baffling to know why those terms were chosen in order to express the ultimate linguistic truth that *la langue est une forme et non une substance*, neglect of which is responsible, according to Saussure, for 'all our mistakes of terminology, all our incorrect ways of designating things belonging to *la langue*'

([169]).) To be aware of that history, moreover, is to realize that Saussure's way of expressing that truth is itself an academic figure of speech. His version of the distinction between form and substance is not any of the classic philosophical versions; but there are parallels which are not fortuitous. It is a philosophical commonplace that form does not inhere in substance, even though it is embodied in substance. A chair does not exist apart from the wood, leather, etc. of which it is made; but those substantial components have to exist in a certain form in order to constitute a chair. It is the form which makes the chair a chair, and thereby distinguishes it from pieces of furniture which are not chairs. Analogously for Saussure, it is not the sound we articulate or the thought in our mind, or both, which make our utterance an utterance of the word *chaise*; but the way our utterance has a form determined by the synchronic system of values which we call 'the French language'.

Saussure's doctrine of form and substance is in certain respects quite unmysterious. At an elementary level, it can be read simply as a warning against confusing linguistic analysis (as formal analysis of *la langue*) with the study of 'substantially' related matters. Among these is phonetics. On this issue, §3 of the chapter is quite emphatic. 'It is impossible that sound, as a material element, should in itself be part of *la langue*' ([164]). Even more explicitly, the *signifiant* is 'not in essence phonetic'. It is not constituted by its *substance matérielle* but solely by the differences which distinguish it from other *signifiants* ([164]). Again, 'speech sounds are first and foremost entities which are contrastive, relative and negative' ([164]). A parallel caution is issued against confusing the *signifié* with an idea in the mind. Thus although the French word *mouton* and the English word *sheep* may 'have the same meaning' (by which Saussure presumably means that both may on appropriate occasions be used to express the same idea), their *valeurs* do not coincide, since in English *sheep* stands in contrast to *mutton*, whereas in French *mouton* covers both the animal (cf. *sheep*) and the meat of the animal (cf. *mutton*) ([160]). Thus far, Saussure is saying no more, *mutatis mutandis*, than many a philosopher might have said to the effect that a study of forms is not to be confused with a study of their material manifestations.

Where Saussure's distinction between linguistic form and substance takes on a metaphysics every bit as enigmatic as Plato's or Aristotle's is in the account Saussure gives of the dimension in which formal configurations are articulated. This dimension is described as a surface or, more exactly, an interface between the two substances of sound and thought. The meeting of these two substances is described as being like the contact between air and water: 'changes in atmospheric pressure break up the surface of the water into a series of divisions, i.e. waves. The correlation between thought and sound, and the union of the two, is like that' ([156]). Prior to this contact, Saussure claims, both planes are featureless and unstructured. The structure which results from their contact is *la langue*. The contact automatically gives rise to two 'planes' whose smooth expanses and corrugations match exactly: the atmospheric plane and the aquatic plane in the case of air and water, the conceptual plane and the phonetic plane in the case of language.

Puzzling as this metaphysics of 'contact' between thought and sound is, its evident purpose is to stress two ideas. One is that *la langue* does not belong to a third layer of substance. The other idea is that of the absolute interdependence and complementarity of the two 'faces' of the linguistic sign, *signifiant* and *signifié*. The relationship between them, in fact, is such that it makes no sense to think of separating the two. This idea is reinforced by a second 'surface' analogy: that of the recto and verso of a sheet of paper. 'Thought is one side of the sheet and sound the reverse side. Just as it is impossible to take a pair of scissors and cut one side of paper without at the same time cutting the other, so it is impossible in a language to isolate sound from thought or thought from sound' ([157]). Any attempt to separate the two will lead to 'pure psychology' or 'pure phonetics', not linguistics. In this version of the metaphor, the paper is 'substance' and the shape cut out is 'form'.

Valeurs, then, in terms of the 'surface' metaphor, are the formal thought-sound configurations which constitute *la langue*. They are the linguistic counterparts of the 'waves' at the interface where air makes contact with water, and the 'shapes' cut out by scissors in the sheet of paper. Saussure's dichotomy of form and substance has by this stage lost all connexion with its parent philosophical model (where it makes no sense at all to envisage form as the product of contact between different substances). As if to rescue the notion of *valeur* from this bleak metaphysical limbo, §2 proceeds to give a much more down-to-earth account, based on comparison with the more familiar notion of economic value.

Saussure's economic analogy assimilates the act of speech to a commercial transaction, and words to coins. For Saussure the *valeur* of a linguistic unit is like the value of a coin. The reader is told that in order to determine what a five-franc coin is worth, it is necessary to know two things: '(1) that the coin can be exchanged for a certain quantity of something different, e.g. bread, and (2) that its value can be compared with another value in the same system, e.g. that of a one-franc coin, or of a coin belonging to another system (e.g. a dollar).' Two such requirements are then identified in the linguistic case also. 'Similarly, a word can be substituted for something dissimilar: an idea. At the same time it can be compared to something of like nature: another word.' From this the reader is invited to draw the conclusion that the *valeur* of a word is 'not determined merely by that concept or meaning for which it is a token. It must also be assessed against comparable values, by contrasts with other words' ([160]). As in the case of the coin, then, the value is nothing concrete or tangible, but something determined by functional equivalences and differences within a system of exchange.

Whatever problems the reader may have with this account, they are at least of a different order from those encountered along the hypothetical interface between shapeless masses of sound and thought. In their own way, however, they are no less intractable. In the first place, Saussure's economic comparison simply does not work unless we are prepared to ignore the difference between coins as the objects actually exchanged in commercial transactions and coins as units in a system of currency: in other words, precisely the distinction which corresponds in the linguistic case to that between items of *parole* and items of *langue*. For whereas a five-franc coin in the former sense can be exchanged in a shop for five one-franc coins, or else for a certain quantity of – for example – bread, there is no sense at all in which 'the French five-franc coin' can be exchanged for either, whether in a baker's shop or anywhere else. This disanalogy is disastrous for Saussure's case, since what needs explication is the linguistic counterpart of the value of 'the French five-franc coin' (in other words, the unit of currency), and *not* the value of the coin in the shop. The value of the latter is simply whatever it will buy in that particular shop; or, alternatively, its various cash equivalents in small change from the till.

Worse still, there is no sense in which the Frenchman who utters the word *chaise* gets in exchange the idea of a chair (or an actual chair either). Linguistic transactions are in this respect not at all like commercial transactions. On the contrary the Frenchman who utters the word *chaise* is thereby not *receiving* anything, but *giving* his interlocutor certain information (which the interlocutor may or may not have asked for, and may or may not respond to by giving certain information in turn). If shops operated on this principle, it would revolutionize the world of commerce. However, even if we set these difficulties on one side, there remains a more important respect in which Saussure's analogy is contentious.

As Aarsleff notes (Aarsleff 1967: 233-4 fn.; 1982: 307-8), the application of the currency metaphor to language has a long history in the Western tradition, going back at least as far as Quintilian. Less remotely, where Saussure is concerned, the notion of linguistic value and its link with the economic concept of exchange is to be found in the work of Saussure's predecessor at the Ecole des Hautes Etudes, Michel Bréal. Bréal said that we treat words as bankers do securities, 'as if they were the coin itself, because they know that at a given moment they could exchange them for the coin' (Aarsleff 1982: 307-8). Saussure's use of the metaphor, however, differs from Bréal's, and in one crucial respect. The currency metaphor lends itself to two interpretations. For Saussure's purposes, it is quite essential to exclude the notion that the substance of which the coin is made is itself of value. A striking example of the alternative interpretation, which treats the coin itself as a piece of valuable metal, is provided earlier in the nineteenth century by its use in Bonald's *Législation primitive* (Bonald 1802: I, 99; Aarsleff 1967: 233-4 fn.). Bonald said of speech that it was 'to the commerce of thoughts what money is to the commerce of goods, a real expression of values, because it is of value itself.' What Bonald was attacking was the idea that speech is based upon conventional signs. That, he argued, would equate speech merely with the use of 'paper money': words would then be signs 'without value'. Bonald, who believed in the divine origin of language, goes on to say that paper can be made to designate anything we like, 'but it expresses nothing, except inasmuch as it can be cashed at will for money, which is the real expression of all values'. In other words, for Bonald we are confusing designation with expression if we think that words are just exchange counters. For Saussure, on the other hand, that is exactly what they are and no more.

Here we see, then, a conflict between two versions of the currency metaphor. In Bonald's terms, Saussure would be a theorist who believes that all money is paper money: or rather, a theorist who denies that there is any difference between paper money and gold coins. Precisely what a Saussurean economist could not accept would be the idea that a gold coin has an intrinsic value whereas a note has not, because it is 'only paper'. For it is of the essence of Saussurean structuralism that *valeur* derives not from the sign itself, but from the place which the sign occupies in the total system. It is indeed the system of values which determines the signs, and not the signs which come together to form a system.

Why does Saussure offer these two quite different analogical approaches to the definition of *valeur*? Readers interested in this question will not have failed to note that the dual approach is no unnecessary reduplication of labour. The two analogies do not cover exactly the same ground. In particular, the 'surface' analogy sits more comfortably with the Saussurean principle of arbitrariness, and to this the text of the *Cours* draws our attention. ('These observations clarify our earlier remarks about the arbitrary nature of the linguistic sign. Not only are the two areas which are linguistically linked vague and amorphous in themselves, but the process which selects one particular sound-sequence to correspond to one particular idea is entirely arbitrary' [157].) What this leaves unelucidated, however, is the sense in which values constitute a *system*; and it is here that the 'commercial' analogy offers a more attractive and readily understandable model.

This brings us back again, via a somewhat different route, to the dichotomy between 'form' and 'substance'. For Saussure, evidently, to suppose that the linguist is concerned with the analysis of linguistic signs as 'substance' would be like supposing that the economist is concerned with the study of coins. But granted that *valeurs* belong to the domain of form, we have now been given two rather different accounts of what 'form' is. The 'interface' analogy presupposes a state of affairs in which two intrinsically unstructured media (thought and sound) are brought into contact, and from this contact a system of values (*la langue*) somehow emerges. The 'commercial' analogy, on the contrary, presupposes a state of affairs in which two independently structured systems (commodities on the one hand and currency on the other) are brought into correlation, and the system of values (*la langue*) emerges from this correlation. Now either of these conceptualizations of a system of values may be independently comprehensible. What is quite incomprehensible, on the other hand, is how both could be combined. Is this simply an unfortunate clash of metaphors? That is one possibility. However, as will be argued below, there are also reasons for thinking that this clash of metaphors represents an unresolved contradiction in the Saussurean view of language.

CHAPTER V

Syntagmatic Relations and Associative Relations

Chapter V now distinguishes between two different orders of values. One order of values derives from relations into which signs enter as items linearly concatenated in discourse. Such concatenations are termed *syntagmas* by Saussure, and the corresponding relationships are 'syntagmatic' relationships. By occupying a linear place in a syntagma, 'any unit acquires its value simply in opposition to what precedes, or to what follows, or to both' ([171]). The other order of values is derived from the way signs are associated with one another in the memory, independently of the arrangements in which they occur in discourse. These connexions are 'associative relations'. The distinction between the two types of relation is assumed by Saussure to be absolute. 'Syntagmatic relations hold *in praesentia*. They hold between two or more terms co-present in a sequence. Associative relations, on the contrary, hold *in absentia*. They hold between terms constituting a mnemonic group' ([171]).

The first question which may arise in the reader's mind is whether the distinction between these two orders of values is as clear as the *Cours* seems to assume. For one obvious connexion which would lead to signs being associated in the memory is the connexion which derives from frequent occurrence in the same or similar syntagmas. In other words, Saussure seems to leave out of account the kind of relationship between words which Firth later christened 'collocation' (Firth 1951: 194ff.). Saussure's notion of associative relations does not cover this, for although according to §3 of this chapter the mind 'creates as many associative series as there are different relations' ([173]), the relations mentioned break down into similarities between *signifiants* and similarities between *signifiés* (or both). The kind of diagram provided on p.[175] for the associative series which contribute to the value of the word *enseignement* will hardly accommodate the kind of association which Firth identifies as linking the English word *time* with *saved, spent, wasted, frittered away, presses, flies* and *no*.

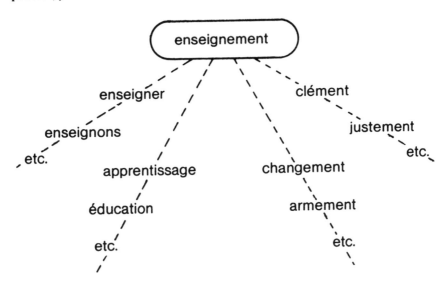

This flaw in Saussure's account is all the more glaring in that the *Cours* makes the point specifically on p.[173] that the establishment of linguistic 'types' depends on whether or not the relevant 'tokens' are to be found in sufficient abundance. In the discussion of syntagmas, the reader is told: 'Since there is nothing abstract in *la langue*, such types will not exist unless sufficiently numerous examples do indeed occur' ([173]). The 'occurrence' here referred to must be occurrence in *parole*: for in Saussurean terms there is no other domain of occurrence available. Once we accept this, however, there seems no reason to exclude the possibility that, say, the single word *fleece* may, in virtue of its occurrence in a well-known nursery rhyme, bring to mind the syntagma *Mary had a little lamb*.

Leaving on one side for the moment the issue of distinguishing Saussure's two orders of values, let us first consider the order of values deriving from syntagmatic relations. The disappointingly sparse remarks about syntagmatic relations in §§1-2, and the few examples given, leave a number of questions unanswered. First and foremost among these is: what exactly *is* a syntagmatic relation? In particular, is a syntagmatic relation defined solely and simply in terms of linearity? What the *Cours* says is that these relations are 'based on the linear character' of *la langue* ([170]); but what exactly that means is not altogether perspicuous. If syntagmatic relations are simply linear relations under another name, it seems doubtful whether they can be regarded as linguistic relations at all. If, for example, we take a syntagma consisting of 'noun + verb + adverb' occurring in that order, the *linear* relation between noun and verb will be exactly the same as the *linear* relation between verb and adverb: namely, a relation of immediate consecution in the chain. However, it is difficult to think of an example where the linguistic relation between noun and verb could plausibly be regarded as on a par, in the same syntagma, with the linguistic relation between verb and adverb. By contrast, it is very easy to think of examples in which such linguistic relations appear to be quite independent of linearity: *He arrived yesterday* vs. *Yesterday he arrived.* That is *prima facie* awkward for Saussure, since if the syntagmatic relationship is simply the *grammatical* relationship under another name, then syntagmatics *per se* has no basis in linearity. The linear order of units is only one possible means a language may utilize in order to signal grammatical relations.

A second question concerning syntagmatic relations is the question of exactly what is syntagmatically related to what. Given any syntagma (for example, the English syntagma *some unusually tall trees*), we may ask which of the constituent linguistic units is syntagmatically related to any of the others. Let us suppose, for purposes of this particular example, that a Saussurean analysis would recognize the following segmentations: (i) *unusually = un + usual + ly*, and (ii) *trees = tree + s.* The units *some* and *tall*, we will assume, are indivisible. On the basis of these assumptions, we may now ask such questions as the following. To which units is *some* syntagmatically related? Is *un* syntagmatically related to *tree*? Is *ly* syntagmatically related to *s*? Do any of the syntagmatic relations hold between a single unit and a combination of units, or are they all relations between single units?

On the last question the *Cours* gives some guidance. The reader is informed on p.[172] that 'it is not sufficient to consider merely the relation between the parts of a syntagma'. Thus in *contre tous* ('against all') and in *contremaître* ('overseer') account must be taken of the relation between the whole and the parts. The trouble is that this precept is easy enough to follow when a syntagma is clearly bi-partite, as in Saussure's two examples. It is more obscure in cases where a syntagma is complex; because the question which then arises is the question of how exactly the 'whole' in question divides into 'parts'. In the example *some unusually tall trees*, for instance, it is unclear whether the word *unusually* divides into *un + usually*, or into *unusual + ly*, or into *un + usual + ly*, or into all of these but in separate stages; and the question then focuses on which sequence the stages are to be taken in. Problems of this order Saussure never discusses, but they were extensively discussed by his transatlantic successors under the head of 'immediate constituency' (Bloomfield 1935:209f.). That discussion, however, did little to resolve the original question about syntagmatic relations. For problems of 'immediate constituent analysis' were discussed by

Bloomfield and others on the assumption that grammatical relations were in principle independent of linearity.

Comparable questions arise in respect of associative relations. If associative relations are simply, as the term suggests, relations of psychological association, it is legitimate to ask whether they are *eo ipso* linguistic relations at all. For presumably many terms may be associated in the mind for reasons other than linguistic reasons. But if this is so, then the need arises for a linguistic analyst to be able to distinguish between mnemonic groupings which have a linguistic basis and mnemonic groupings which do not. How to draw such a distinction is by no means obvious. Is the group *president-White House-Reagan* a group which generates values in the Saussurean sense? If not, how does one recognize the mnemonic groups which do?

Nowhere is the linguist who has already managed to analyse *sižlaprã* into constituent segments told explicitly how to proceed with the task of determining the *valeur* of each segment. This, nevertheless, is presumably the major part of the descriptive enterprise. If the analysis involves, as Saussure seems to imply, identifying all the relevant associative and syntagmatic relations, the task of describing even the single syntagma *sižlaprã* immediately assumes monumental proportions. One cannot, as Saussure has already made clear, 'suppose that a start could be made with individual signs, and a system constructed by putting them together' ([158]). On the contrary, in order to identify which sign in the system *prã* represents in *sižlaprã* it is presumably necessary to consider all those relationships *in absentia* and *in praesentia* which determine it. That will involve specifying which potentially available French forms *prã* displaces in this syntagma; and the number will clearly be very large indeed. It must be noted that there is no Saussurean short-cut via the use of traditional grammatical classifications ('verb', 'first person', 'present tense', 'singular', 'transitive', etc.), since from a Saussurean point of view the meaning of classificatory terms has first to be established by reference to the particular system of *valeurs* obtaining in the language in question. Nor, for the same reason, is there a ready-made system of semantic classifications available to specify the meaning of *prã*. Specifying that meaning will presumably involve considering how it alters if the syntagmatic context alters. For instance, by adding *avec moi* ('with me') or *demain* ('tomorrow') the range of interpretations is narrowed considerably from those available for *sižlaprã* in isolation. In short, the apparently simple task of giving an analysis of *sižlaprã* will turn out to be ultimately coextensive with the task of analysing very large areas of the grammatical structure of French. This must necessarily be so if, as Saussure consistently maintains, *la langue* is a system in which the parts do not exist independently of the whole.

CHAPTER VI

The Language Mechanism

The misgivings which the reader may have felt in Chapter V will no doubt surface again in Chapter VI. Here we are told straight away (as if it had been already established) that 'the whole set of phonetic and conceptual differences which constitute *la langue* are thus the product of two kinds of comparison, associative and syntagmatic' ([176]). (But are there, one asks, just *two* kinds of comparison involved? And if so, are the comparisons rightly contrasted as 'linear' vs. 'mnemonic'?) Misgivings of this order will not merely recur but be reinforced, and the concomitant analytic problems rendered even more acute. For it is not sufficient, apparently, to analyse *désireux* into two independent segments: stem *désir* + affix *eux*. The *valeur* of *désireux* is not a mere 'addition' of the *valeurs* of these two component units. It is a 'product' (*désir* × *eux*). 'The whole depends on the parts, and the parts depend on the whole. That is why the syntagmatic relation between part and whole is just as important as the syntagmatic relation between one part and another' ([177]).

If this is true of *désireux*, one supposes that it must also be true of any syntagma in which *désireux* itself occurs as a unit. For *désireux* cannot be the only combination in which the two units *désir* and *eux* occur. (If it were, it would not be recognized as a syntagma.) This expectation is corroborated explicitly on p.[177]. We are dealing here, the *Cours* tells us, with a 'general principle'. 'There are always larger units, composed of smaller units, with a relation of interdependence holding between both.'

Taken at face value, this must mean that Saussurean syntagmatics recognizes no maximum unit. This, again, is a theoretical position which appears to have quite alarming consequences for any Saussurean linguist attempting an enterprise of structural description. If, for example, the first line of Vergil's *Aeneid* stands in a relation of syntagmatic interdependence with all the following lines, that itself is problematic enough; for it means that a linguistic analysis of the first line will have to wait upon an analysis of the whole poem. But if there is no guarantee of being able to treat the whole poem as a maximum syntagmatic unit either (it being a mere accident of *parole* that Vergil did not incorporate it into an even longer Latin epic), then a syntagmatic analysis of *Arma virumque cano* becomes a research project which will require the services either of an endless supply of linguists, or at least of one or two blessed with indefinite longevity.

The only way Saussurean syntagmatics could have extricated its would-be practitioners from this predicament would have been by proposing – as a minimum – criteria by which *sižlaprã*, or any other sequence, might be recognized as incorporating consecutive signs or groups of signs between which there is *no* syntagmatic connexion. (Then it would be a purely contingent question as to whether in the *Aeneid*, as a matter of fact, it is possible to detect such internal syntagmatic boundaries or not.) However, as Martinet points out (Martinet 1974: 225-6), one thing the *Cours* fails to offer – and presumably deliberately – is any test for delimiting the syntagma by reference to linear succession, *even though* syntagmatic relations are said to be based on linearity. The theoretical implications of this reticence will be discussed at greater length below (p.233ff.).

The 'mechanism' of *la langue* to which the title of this chapter alludes is described more fully in §2. It consists of the simultaneous functioning in *la parole* of the 'dual system' of values, syntagmatic and associative. 'Our memory holds in store all the various complex types of syntagma, of every kind and length ... When someone says *marchons!*, he thinks unconsciously of various associative groups, at whose common intersection appears the syntagma *marchons!* This syntagma belongs to one series which includes *marche!*, *marchez!*, and *marchons!* stands in opposition to both as a form selected from this group. At the same time, it belongs to another series which includes *montons!*, *mangeons!*, etc., and represents a selection from this group as well. If the forms *marche!* and *marchez!* were to disappear from the language, leaving *marchons!* in isolation, certain oppositions would automatically collapse and *ipso facto* the value of *marchons!* would be different' ([179]).

The same must presumably hold for the lexical contrast between *marchons!* and *montons!*. Thus if there were no French verb *monter*, the value of *marchons!* would be different in yet another respect. This reinforces the conclusion the reader will already have drawn from the preceding chapter that even to identify the values of elements in a single syntagma demands a Saussurean descriptive enterprise of considerable magnitude, since the *mécanisme de la langue* makes it impossible to specify values in any other way than contrastively. Once again we are brought to face the descriptive consequences of the fact that *dans la langue il n'y a que des différences*.

The *Cours* then goes on to announce an important generalization. The mechanism just described operates at *all* levels of analysis. It applies not only 'to syntagmas and sentences of all types, even the most complex' ([179]) but also to phonetic units in the speech chain. 'If we take a hypothetical sequence like *anma*, the sound *m* is in syntagmatic opposition with the preceding and following sounds, and also in associative opposition with all the sounds the mind can suggest, as shown:' ([180])

$$a\ n\ m\ a$$
$$v$$
$$d$$

This generalization about the way the 'mechanism' of *la langue* operates has extensive implications, both theoretical and psycholinguistic. The psycholinguistic implications seem to be that for Saussure any utterance is to be viewed as the product of a simultaneous series of (unconscious?) choices by the speaker on a hierarchy of different levels. Presumably these choices cannot be independent of one another since some will determine others, although exactly what relations of dependence obtain in the 'mechanism' Saussure does not venture to state. The lowest level in the hierarchy is presented as being that of the choice of individual phonetic segments *a, n, m*, etc. Since the selection of any given phonetic segment (say *m*) can itself be treated as involving a selection of phonetic features – nasality, bilabiality, etc. – one may ask why there is not an even lower level of choice. The reason is not explicitly stated in the *Cours*, but seems to be that the level of discrete segments in the speech chain is the lowest level at which the utterance can be regarded as the product of a series of *single* syntagmatic selections from a succession of associative series presenting other possibilities. In other words, analysed in terms of distinctive features, the selection of *m* would have to be regarded not as a single choice, but a simultaneous multiple selection of the features of nasality, bilabiality, etc. from a total set of features. Since the individual choices involved at this level have no separate *linear* representation, they cannot be regarded as involving the operation of the 'language mechanism' as such (i.e. the 'dual system' of values). To put the point another way, for Saussure a phonetic choice such as 'nasal vs. oral' has no syntagmatic status. It is merely an 'abstraction' from the comparison of members of an associative series available at a certain point in the speech chain. In short, this is where the teeth of Saussure's principle of linearity bite at the level of identification of *signifiants*. Variations in pronunciation will be non-linguistic variations (that is, belong to *parole* and not to *langue*) if they do not implement different syntagmatic choices. This is what explains (as the *Cours* has already pointed out on pp.[164-5]) the tolerance of wide variations in pronunciation, such as those characteristic of French *r*.

So far, so good. The rest of the course is not such plain sailing. For if

Saussure is to apply to syntagmatic choices of segments in the speech chain (*a, n, m* ... etc.) the same rationale as applied to *marchons!*, he must presumably argue that the value of *m* in *anma* would be different if the associative oppositions were different (say *f, t,* as distinct from *v, d*). In other words, a necessary condition of linguistic identity for two occurrences of 'the same' *m* is that the same associative oppositions obtain. An *m* which is syntagmatically selected from the series *m, v, d* will not be the same as an *m* selected from the series *m, f, t.* Phonetic identity, therefore, does not guarantee linguistic identity. This is perfectly consistent with Saussure's claim that the *signifiant* is 'not in essence phonetic' ([164]): consequently, there is no paradox for Saussure in admitting the possibility that a language might be structured in such a way that one phonetic segment (say *m*) represented a variety of different units in the identification of *signifiants*. Here we see the opening up of a gap which was later widened by Saussure's successors into an axiomatic separation of phonetic analyses from phonemic analyses.

What happens, however, if simultaneously we apply the parallel rationale to the syntagmatic order of values in the case of *anma*? Or, for that matter, to *marchons!*? It must still be the case, presumably, that mere phonetic identity is no guarantee of linguistic identity; so if we take at face value Saussure's pronouncements about 'syntagmatic interdependences' ([176]) and treat every unit as acquiring its syntagmatic *valeur* simply 'in opposition to what precedes, or to what follows, or to both' ([171]), then there is no way to avoid the conclusion that the *m* of *anma* cannot be linguistically 'the same' as the *m* of, say, *amna;* for the syntagmatic oppositions are different, irrespective of the associative oppositions. On precisely the same reasoning, the final vowel of *marchons!* cannot represent 'the same' linguistic sign as the final vowel of *montons!* or of *mangeons!*

Why, it may be asked, should this conclusion in any way be a theoretical embarrassment to Saussure? The answer is that it need not be, if Saussure were willing to accept the principle that the operation of the *mécanisme de la langue* ensures that different linguistic contexts automatically entail different linguistic units. But that, clearly, is *not* one of the propositions which feature on the Saussurean programme for linguistics. On the contrary, the whole thrust of the Saussurean endeavour in linguistic theory is to establish that there *are* linguistic invariants identifiable across variations of context, that knowledge of these invariants is what makes it possible for members of a linguistic community to communicate with one another, and, finally, that these invariants are objectively available for 'scientific' description by the impartial observer (that is, the linguistic analyst).

A shadow of this theoretical embarrassment falls athwart the next section of the chapter, devoted to the distinction between 'absolute' and 'relative' arbitrariness. The terminology suggests a belated admission that the linguistic sign is after all not as arbitrary as Saussure's 'first principle' of linguistics would have us believe. *La langue*, Saussure tells us, 'is founded upon the irrational principle that the sign is arbitrary' ([182]). However, if this principle were applied without restriction, it would result, in 'utter chaos' ([182]). The mechanism of *la langue*, therefore, has to be viewed as 'a way of imposing a limitation on what is arbitrary' ([183]). 'There exists no language in which nothing at all is motivated. Even to conceive of such a language is impossible by definition' ([183]). Here Saussurean synchronic theory lies agonizing on a bed of nails of its own manufacture. Having accepted arbitrariness as a 'first principle', Saussure is at a loss to explain why this principle apparently fails to capture the most significant and characteristic properties of linguistic structure.

Saussure's problem here is that he has confused questions of arbitrariness with questions of systematicity. The confusion is evident in his own discussion ([181]) of the difference between *dix-neuf* ('nineteen') and *vingt* ('twenty'). According to Saussure, *vingt* is an example of a word which is absolutely arbitrary or 'unmotivated', while *dix-neuf* is only relatively so. This is presumably because although the elements *dix* ('ten') and *neuf* ('nine') are themselves arbitrary, their combination in *dix-neuf* is seen as corresponding 'rationally' to the meaning 'nineteen' (nineteen being the sum of ten and nine). To contrast *vingt* with *dix-neuf* on these grounds, however, is simply a muddle. For while it is true that *dix-neuf* goes with *dix, neuf, dix-huit, soixante-dix*, etc., it is also true that *vingt* goes with *vingt-deux, vingt-trois, quatre vingts*, etc.; and, on the other hand, it is no less arbitrary that *dix-neuf* should mean 'nineteen' (rather than 'ninety' or 'one hundred and nine') than that *vingt* should mean 'twenty'. Someone learning French has to learn that the word for 'nineteen' is *dix-neuf* (not *neuf-dix* or *neuze*), and this is on all fours with having to learn that the word for 'twenty' is *vingt* (not *dix-dix* or *deuzante*).

The muddle may not be unconnected with the fact that Saussurean linguistics gives no recognition to the tendency for systematicity (which Saussure misleadingly calls the *arbitraire relatif*) increasingly to dominate linguistic structure as one proceeds from smaller to larger syntagmatic combinations. It is on the whole more likely that a regularity of sentence construction will have no exceptions than that a declensional or conjugational regularity will have none, or a pattern of word formation. It may come as a surprise to the learner of French to find that the future tense of *voir* is *verrai*, but nothing like as much of a shock as it would be to find that although *Pierre voit Jean* meant 'Pierre sees Jean' and *Pierre voit André* meant 'Pierre sees André' the French for 'André sees Jean' was *Jean voit André*. Why this should be so Saussure never explains, and possibly his failure to do so arises from his confusion of systematicity with reduced arbitrariness. (The order 'subject-verb-object' is – in Saussure's sense – no less arbitrary than the order 'object-verb-subject'.)

To put the point in terms of one of Saussure's favourite analogies, it is important to see that the identity of shape between all pawns in a chess set belongs to a quite different order of facts from the fact that the particular shape in question is what it is. The systematicity in the design of the chess set has nothing at all to do with whether or not the shape of the pawn is arbitrary. These are not two 'degrees' of the same relationship, as the terms *arbitraire absolu* and *arbitraire relatif* unfortunately imply. Or, to switch to another of Saussure's analogies, the fact that the price of a loaf of bread is arbitrarily fixed at five francs does not mean that charging two and a half francs for half a loaf is only relatively arbitrary. This is simply a gross *non sequitur*. Both prices are equally arbitrary, and that arbitrariness has nothing to do with the systematicity which relates them. To concede as much in the case of language, however, would be tantamount to calling in question whether it makes sense to treat arbitrariness as the 'first principle' of linguistics. Saussure's distinction between *arbitraire absolu* and *arbitraire relatif* is a fudge, which serves the primary purpose of maintaining the 'first principle' at all costs.

CHAPTER VII

Grammar and its Subdivisions

Chapter VII embarks on a brief but trenchant criticism of misconceptions associated with the traditional notion of grammar. The first of these is a failure to see that grammatical relations cannot link items across linguistic systems. In other words, 'there is no such thing as "historical grammar" ' ([185]). What is commonly called thus is, for Saussure, simply diachronic linguistics. This conclusion is, clearly enough, simply a corollary of the Saussurean concept of a system of *valeurs*. Since French sentences and Latin sentences derive from different systems of *valeurs*, there is no way a grammatical relation could obtain between any item or feature of a French sentence and any item or feature of a Latin sentence.

Granted, however, that grammar is a matter of synchronic relations, the traditional subdivisions into morphology and syntax, together with the traditional exclusion of matters pertaining to vocabulary, are all highly questionable from a Saussurean point of view. The distinction between morphology and syntax is 'illusory' ([186]), since 'forms and functions are interdependent' ([186]). Similarly, the distinction between grammar and lexicology draws a distinction where none may exist: Latin *fio* ('I become') contrasts with *facio* ('I make') in just the same way as the passive form *dicor* ('I am said') with its active *dico* ('I say'). Thus it is clear that in a given language lexicological and syntactic devices may overlap. Grammar, Saussure concludes, 'needs a different basis, and a better one' ([187]).

It will come as no surprise to the reader that the better basis which Saussure proposes is a systematization based on the distinction between syntagmatic relations and associative relations. 'Everything in a given linguistic state should be explicable by reference to a theory of syntagmas and a theory of associations' ([188]). This will 'organize the whole subject-matter of grammar on its two natural axes' ([188]).

Brief as this chapter is, it sums up what for Saussure was one of the basic mistakes of nineteenth-century linguistics: that putting the adjective 'historical' in front of the traditional metalinguistic terms would automatically transpose a set of distinctions which had been originally drawn for pedagogic purposes into a valid, 'scientific' conceptual framework for the study of language.

CHAPTER VIII

Abstract Entities in Grammar

It is not until this final chapter in the section on Synchronic Linguistics that Saussure first makes explicit the proposal that synchronic linguistic analysis is ultimately to be judged by its correspondence with a psychological reality. 'One may say that the sum total of deliberate, systematic classifications set up by a grammarian studying a given state a-historically must coincide with the sum total of associations, conscious or unconscious, operative in speech' ([189]). Earlier Saussure had expressed misgivings about the correspondence between grammarians' classifications and linguistic realities ([153]), and here these misgivings are repeated. Saussure does not deny the reality of grammatical categories, parts of speech, etc. Such things 'exist in the language, but as abstract entities. It is difficult to study them, because one can never be sure whether the awareness of speakers of the language always goes as far as the grammarians' analyses' ([190]).

Worse still, the only detailed example which the *Cours* gives of the correspondence between an *entité abstraite* and a traditional grammatical classification, that of the Latin genitive, is not merely in itself a particularly awkward example from Saussure's point of view, but calls in question the whole rationale of including abstract entities in synchronic analysis. The case is badly argued to boot. What the *Cours* says is that although the three Latin genitive endings *-ī*, *-is* and *-ārum* afford no phonetic basis for constituting an associative series, they are nevertheless linked in the mind in virtue of an 'awareness of their common value'. Unfortunately, just the thing which *-ī*, *-is* and *-ārum* do *not* have is the same *valeur* in the Saussurean sense; for they stand in opposition in their respective paradigms to quite different sets of endings. So Saussure's claim that their 'common value' is 'sufficient to set up an association, in the absence of any material support' – and thus account for how 'the notion of "genitive", as such, takes its place in the language' as an abstract entity – is quite unfounded. Furthermore, the endings *-ī*, *-is* and *-ārum* do not even share a *signifié* in common (two of them being singular endings and one a plural). So it is actually far from clear on the basis of these considerations that Saussurean synchronic analysis offers any support for the recognition of the Latin genitive as an *entité abstraite*. On the contrary, the reader might have expected Saussure to cite this as an example where a traditional grammatical classification did *not* correspond to any real associative series in *la langue*.

However, even if the example were allowed to stand as valid, it would be quite unclear what purpose is served by recognizing 'Genitive' as a separate *entité abstraite* in Latin. For the various individual facts about the endings *-ī, -is, -ārum*, etc. will need to be stated separately in any case, each of these presumably being an independent *entité concrète* of the Latin language. What *else* there is to state over and above all this in a synchronic description is something of a mystery. In other words, we come face to face with a descriptive dilemma: *either* there is nothing more to say about the entity 'Genitive' other than what will already have been said about the entities *-ī, -is, -ārum*, etc., in which case the entity 'Genitive' is redundant, *or* there is more to say, in which case 'Genitive' cannot be an abstract entity after all (that is, it must be present in the *mécanisme de la langue* in some form which is not exhausted by its manifestations in the endings *-ī, -is, -ārum*.) Traditional grammar encounters no such dilemma, since for traditional purposes the classification 'Genitive' simply enables the grammarian to make generalizations about a whole class of Latin endings. Saussure, on the other hand, has specifically raised the question of how to determine when such classifications as this do and do not correspond to realities in *la langue*. So the one simple justification which synchronic analysis cannot accept is the straightforward grammarian's justification of descriptive utility.

Mutatis mutandis, what applies to the Latin 'Genitive' will apply to any putative candidate for recognition as an *entité abstraite*. Saussure is quite adamant that 'it would be a mistake to believe in the existence of an incorporeal syntax' ([191]). So it might be. But if we reject the notion of an incorporeal syntax, the role for abstract entities to play in *la langue* becomes immediately problematic, appearing to resolve itself always into a mere duplication of the role already played by particular concrete entities in particular cases. It is difficult to avoid the conclusion that Chapter VIII constitutes a major error of theoretical strategy on Saussure's part. The 'upper limit' for synchronic analysis of *la langue* would have been more satisfactorily drawn at a point corresponding symmetrically to its 'lower limit', which for Saussure, as has been made clear in Chapter VI, is the point determined by the limitations on single choices in the speech chain imposed by the phonological structure of the language. At the level of signs and sign combinations, the corresponding point has already been defined – even though evasively – by Saussure; it is the syntagma 'constructed on a regular pattern' ([173]). In other words, it is the point at which the sequence of syntagmatic combinations is not a choice freely determined by the individual speaker, but a choice imposed upon the speaker by *la langue*. However difficult a precise determination of that boundary might prove, it would supply a theoretically more elegant solution for Saussure than belatedly opening up the Pandora's box of *entités abstraites*. A wiser Saussure – or perhaps wiser editors – would have kept that lid firmly closed.

PART THREE
Diachronic Linguistics

CHAPTER I

General Observations

Saussure's discussion of diachronic linguistics begins by reiterating the conclusion already stated at the end of Part One concerning the scope of the subject. Unlike synchronic linguistics, it will study relations between 'successive terms substituted one for another over a period of time'. The formulation given on p.[193] makes an interesting comparison with that presented on p.[140]. The later statement drops the reference to 'systems' and to the 'collective consciousness'. It retains, however, the notion of 'substitution'.

This notion is clearly the keystone of diachronic linguistics. It raises a number of theoretical questions which are not at all obvious as long as attention remains focussed upon specific examples of linguistic change. The reader might perhaps have expected that the heading *Généralités* would have provided just the peg on which to hang a theoretical discussion of diachronic substitution in general. But neither here nor anywhere else in the *Cours* is a definition of the relation given. The lacuna is significant: just how significant will not emerge until later. Saussure initially appears to take for granted (i) that there exists a relationship of diachronic substitution, and (ii) that instances of this relationship are recognizable from the observational vantage point of historical linguistics.

Instead of plunging straight away into an examination of these assumptions, Chapter I offers a few rather banal Heracleitean maxims (to the effect that languages are constantly in a process of change, in spite of the appearance of stability which may be conveyed by a literary language ([193-4])), and a brief typological prospectus which predictably includes sound changes, changes of meaning and changes of grammar. However, the prospectus is accompanied by warnings against confusing the study of a change with the study of its consequences ([195]), and even vaguer warnings about the problems which arise because the evolution of one particular item 'splits up into a number of separate things' ([196]). This is as near as the chapter comes to acknowledging that there may be any general theoretical problem about the notion of diachronic substitution lying in wait.

CHAPTER II

Sound Changes

Without further ado, the *Cours* embarks on the topic of sound change. The examples it cites hold no surprises for a student of Indo-European comparative philology: that is part of the expository strategy. Where Saussure scores points is by showing that these familiar examples are misunderstood unless recast in terms of the Saussurean dichotomy between synchrony and diachrony. Thus Verner's law, for instance, is mis-stated in the form 'in Germanic *þ* in non-initial position became *d* if followed by the stress' because that formulation obscures (i) the fact that *þ* tended to voice in medial position, and (ii) that the cases in which this tendency was checked are cases in which the stress fell on the preceding vowel. So, as Saussure says, diachronically 'everything is the other way round' ([200-1]). This is the classic case of a misrepresentation which results from confusing the synchronic and diachronic perspectives. The condemned formulation of Verner's law conflates a synchronic result (the eventual voiced-voiceless distribution) with a diachronic process (the voicing).

More contentious is Saussure's general proposal to replace the traditional distinction between 'absolute' and 'conditioned' sound changes by a distinction between 'spontaneous' and 'combinative' changes. It is difficult to see that this is more than a terminological quibble. 'If a sound change is combinative', argues Saussure, 'it is always conditioned. But if it is spontaneous, it is not necessarily unconditioned' ([200]). The reason given for saying this is that a sound change may be conditioned negatively by the *absence* of certain factors relevant to change. But this is logic which simply amounts to defining all change as conditioned, including cases of 'zero change'. No more convincing is Saussure's account of 'spontaneous' phonetic developments. These, which include cases of zero change, are assumed to be produced by some 'internal cause' in the sound itself. What that internal cause was in any particular case we may have no means of knowing. So, for example, the development of Latin *qu* from Indo-European k_2, except when followed by o or u, Saussure claims was spontaneous, i.e. due to some internal cause in k_2; but this internal cause was presumably prevented from operating by the presence of following o or u. Since the internal cause remains unidentified, the mechanism of its alleged inhibition by certain following vowels must likewise remain unidentified. But then one wonders what has been explained by postulating an 'internal cause' in the first place.

Some aspects of what must nowadays strike the reader as gaps or deficiencies in Saussure's historical phonetics are not so much due to Saussure's own shortcomings as to the 'state of the art' in his day. Saussure's generation had never seen a sound spectrogram, and the sociolinguistic study of speech variation was in its infancy. The entire approach to sound change in the *Cours* reflects the preoccupations of an era in which the principal evidence on which such discussions were based was the orthographic evidence supplied by changes in spelling over time, attested in the documentary legacy of earlier centuries. That having been said, however, it is none the less true that Saussure's treatment of sound change seems conservative, and marked by the kind of rigidity often associated with the Neogrammarians. He evinces no inclination to challenge the doctrine that sound changes are 'exceptionless'. He insists again, as earlier in the *Cours* ([132]), that sound changes are particular, isolated events: they affect sounds as such, not words ([198]). He never suggests that the unit of change in some cases might be the cluster or the syllable, rather than the individual consonant or vowel. To this extent, his historical phonetics is entirely 'alphabetic'. (That does not preclude, however, a carpet-pulling suggestion later in Part III that perhaps we do not understand what the units of diachronic development are.)

Saussure does not even consider here the possibility that the historical fate of a particular sound might depend in part on its morphological function, even though this is just the kind of point a structuralist might perhaps be expected to make. But the reason for Saussure's reluctance to admit this is not difficult to see. To concede that a sound might be treated differently over time in different words, depending on whether it had a morphological function or not, would be tantamount to granting in some sense the reality of 'historical grammar'; and this Saussure is at pains to deny. His position is that grammatical units and relations have no history, in the sense that they cannot be passed on intact from one synchronic system to its successor. To allow morphological function as a possible conditioning factor in historical phonetics would for Saussure be a denial of the basic dichotomy between synchrony and diachrony.

Similarly, when the discussion moves on to general reasons ([202-8]) for the phenomenon of sound change (as distinct from particular types of change), Saussure goes through all the factors commonly adduced (race, climate, the 'law of least effort', conditions of learning, political circumstances, substratum influences, fashion), but conspicuously fails to add to this traditional list the one contribution which might have been expected from the founder of linguistic structuralism. He does not, in other words, argue that the structure of the linguistic system itself may promote or inhibit sound change. (This contribution to the subject was posthumously made on his behalf by others.)

The point of interest here is that the Saussure of the *Cours* is clearly willing to admit that the structure of the system may affect certain features of pronunciation (as is evident from the explanation ([165]) of the latitude of articulation allowed for French *r*). But features of pronunciation in this sense are features of *parole*. The step Saussure never takes is the step the Prague school phonologists later took, which involves extending the same way of thinking to sound change itself.

Again, there is for Saussure a major theoretical obstacle. Structural explanations of change have to assume that 'the system' as such evolves. The reason why this is unacceptable is that it automatically bridges the basic dichotomy between synchronic and diachronic. Hence the Saussurean preference for siding on this issue with the Neogrammarians and upholding the doctrine that sound changes operate 'blindly'. (The word *aveugle* is used on p.[209] in a context which leaves no doubt about its theoretical implications.) This is another example of the way in which the Saussurean demands of theoretical consistency to some extent block the explanatory potential of the theory itself.

The 'blindness' of sound change is in turn explained by reference to the arbitrary nature of the linguistic sign ([208]). That is why the effect of a sound change is 'unrestricted and incalculable' ([209]). If it were otherwise, then again 'sound change would merge with synchronic fact, and that is intrinsically impossible' ([209]). The reader will note that by this point in the *Cours* theoretical difficulties have become intrinsic impossibilities.

CHAPTER III

Grammatical Consequences of Phonetic Evolution

Chapter III occupies a particularly important place in the Saussurean argument, since it is by now apparent that a dichotomy between synchronic and diachronic has as one of its major corollaries the necessity of a clear differentiation between (i) a sound change and (ii) its grammatical (i.e. synchronic) consequences. If this differentiation should prove difficult or problematic in many cases, then much of the support for the basic dichotomy would be lost, and the whole edifice of Saussurean theory immeasurably weakened. A great deal therefore depends on the examples which this chapter supplies. There are several dozen of them, and the great majority are taken from French and German. This is no coincidence, since everything here assumes that the reader will accept the examples as intuitively plausible. The *Cours* simply presents them, offering virtually no evidence to show that they actually corroborate Saussure's case.

The main consequences of sound change, according to this chapter, are the disruption of grammatical links between signs ([211-12]), the obliteration of word-composition ([212-13]) and the establishment of alternations ([215] ff.). The case is flawed, unfortunately, by pervasive equivocation over the notion of 'consequence' itself, which is never clarified. The reader is treated like someone willing to suppose that if an earthquake occasioning widespread damage is followed by the implementation of an extensive rebuilding programme, that shows the rebuilding to be a consequence of the earthquake. There is no awareness that the establishment of a consequential relation might involve rather more than comparing a prior state of affairs with a subsequent state of affairs and then, in effect, inviting everyone to infer a consequential relation between them. Rather, the assumption seems to be that a consequential relation can be simply *exhibited* by juxtaposing the two states of affairs thus allegedly connected. What this amounts to is a licence to use the notion 'consequence' in virtually any instance where there is a diachronic connexion.

The difficulty here is that a theorist in Saussure's position cannot afford the luxury of using the notion 'consequence' in quite this generous way, since the account of associative relations already offered in Part Two makes it clear that in *la langue* there are no necessary phonetic conditions for the establishment of an associative series. The only phonetic conditions are sufficient conditions ([174]). In other words, the *Cours* has already supplied the reason for concluding that associative series are in principle immune from disruption by phonetic change unless phonetic change actually obliterates the distinctions between the *signifiants* in question. But this is certainly not the case in the examples cited here in §§1-2.

Thus, for example, it is question-begging to claim ([212]) that the Latin contrast between a Nominative *comes* and an Accusative *comitem* 'becomes' (*devient*) in Old French, as the result of sound change, a contrast between *cuens* (Nominative) and *comte* (Oblique), and thus *le rapport normal qui existait entre deux formes fléchies d'un même mot* ([212]) was broken. Had any comparative philologist said this, Saussure would have been the first to complain about the conflation of synchronic and diachronic perspectives. For according to Saussure ([134]f.) there is no 'panchronic' point of view from which it would be possible to identify a *rapport normal* between inflected forms of 'the same word'. Furthermore, to compare the Latin case system (of six possible oppositions) to the Old French case system (of only two) is an exercise which students convinced by Parts One and Two of the *Cours* ought by now to reject out of hand; for the *valeurs* are clearly not comparable. Nor does the *Cours* offer any evidence that in the twelfth century those who spoke, wrote or read Old French had any difficulty at all in recognizing *cuens* as the 'Nominative Singular' of *comte* (whatever in psycholinguistic terms that might involve). In short, what the example tacitly appeals to is the fact that 'we' (i.e. twentieth-century students of Old French) find *cuens* an 'unpredictable' Nominative Singular form, given 'our' expectations about relationships between Nominatives, Obliques, etc.

It is likewise question-begging to cite the French example *brebis* vs. *berger* as an instance of the obliteration of word-composition, by comparing it with Latin *vervex* vs. *vervecarius*. 'This separation,' says Saussure, 'naturally has an effect upon the value of the terms: hence in some local patois *berger* becomes specialized to mean "oxherd" ' ([211]). Here at least there is an attempt to back up the claim that a connexion between *brebis* and *berger* is lacking, by citing a semantic development in French patois. The trouble is that it assumes in advance what needed to be demonstrated; namely, that the semantic specialization is a consequence of the failure to connect *berger* and *brebis*. The fact that no such specialization has occurred in other French dialects, or in the literary language, evidently does not count for Saussure as significant. What damages Saussure's case in this and similar instances is that the *Cours* dodges the question of whether associative relations are relations of which the speakers are aware or not. It avoids discussing whether it might be possible for some members of a linguistic community consciously to recognize relationships which other members failed to recognize, and whether this would make any difference to their respective systems of *valeurs*. As a result, it is never quite clear what statements about the consequences of sound change mean in psycholinguistic terms. If the assumption is that speakers can operate grammatical systems of which they are not consciously aware *at all*, then it becomes difficult to see how it would be possible to prove that *brebis* and *berger* are *not* treated as derivationally connected. For at some inaccessible level of 'mental representation' they might be. So there is the possibility that the claim that sound change disrupted the grammatical relations might be quite simply wrong. If, on the other hand, the claim is that speakers of French do not consciously recognize in the relationship between *brebis* and *berger* the same relationship which obtains between *vervex* and *vervecarius*, the reply to that is presumably – as Saussure has given ample reason for maintaining – that this would be by definition out of the question. Even if speakers of French know Latin, the two grammatical systems are not linguistically comparable. This leaves the problem of establishing consequential relations between sound change and grammatical system in a theoretical deadlock. Saussure can hardly afford to accept the proposition that *any* sound change, since it must affect *some* associative series, thereby automatically disrupts *some* grammatical relation to *some* extent. For then indeed his attempt to drive a wedge between diachronic and synchronic facts would be on a hiding to nothing. The terms 'sound change' and 'grammatical change' would become interdefinable and it would be possible in theory to have a synchronic system which could be defined by reference to its immediate predecessor plus one sound change. Diachronic description would thus become simply an alternative way of stating facts about a succession of synchronic states.

A section of particular interest in this chapter is the one devoted to arguing that there are no phonetic doublets ([214-15]). Why, the reader may ask, does Saussure bother to argue that? Again, the answer is that otherwise (i.e. if there *are* phonetic doublets) the separation of synchrony from diachrony is palpably threatened. For if an *état de langue* includes phonetic doublets, this amounts to conceding that it may be impossible to determine whether a sound change has taken place or not. (That is to say, the 'earlier' form and the 'later' form coexist.) So again the diachronic fact merges with the synchronic fact. A way of dealing with all conceivable counterexamples is here proposed: namely, to dismiss them as 'borrowings' from a different system. Thus even if speakers manifestly alternate between two different pronunciations of a given word, this can always be explained by treating one of the pronunciations as a borrowing from a neighbouring dialect. Here emerges the theoretical significance of the proviso laid down much earlier in the *Cours* ([128]) that the distinction between idiosynchronic systems must be applied not only to languages but to dialects and subdialects. (Otherwise the 'borrowing' explanation would not hold water.)

CHAPTER IV

Analogy

Analogy for Saussure is the force which 'counterbalances' ([221]) the disruptive effects of sound change in the linguistic system. An analogical form is one 'made in the image of one or more other forms in accordance with a fixed rule' ([221]). Analogy 'works in favour of regularity and tends to unify formational and flexional processes' ([222]), but does not always succeed in eliminating irregularities. Thus it is sometimes 'capricious'; since 'it is impossible to say in advance how far imitation of a model would extend, or which patterns are destined to provoke it' ([222]). By emphasizing the 'capricious' nature of analogy, Saussure makes it clear that both the major forces operative in linguistic evolution (sound change and analogy) produce unpredictable results.

§2 of the chapter is devoted to the proposition that 'analogies are not changes'. According to Saussure, the 'illusion of analogical change' ([226]) is created simply by the fact that over a period of time a new form ousts an old form. Thus the old Latin nominative *honōs* was eventually replaced by *honor*, analogically formed on the basis of *honōrem, orator, oratōrem*, etc. Consequently, claims Saussure, it is a mistake to say that in Latin *honōs* 'changed' to *honor*: *honōs* did not change (it simply disappeared), while *honor* was not a changed form of anything but a new creation. What is the reader to make of this curiously strained reasoning?

The argument depends, clearly, on another terminological manoeuvre: in effect, the term 'change' is tacitly equated with 'phonetic change'. Once that is accepted, then it follows that any development which is not a phonetic change is not a change *tout court*. Hence there are no analogical changes. But why go to the trouble of such terminological contortion at all? The explanation is once again to be sought in the theoretical rigidity of the way the *Cours* applies the separation of synchronic from diachronic facts. It appears to take for granted that to admit the possibility of 'analogical change' would be tantamount to conceding that the morphological system itself evolves. This is Saussurean heresy, since it would mean that systematicity extends over time from one synchronic state to the next. Such 'changes', therefore, have to be dismissed as illusory (unlike phonetic changes, which can be allowed to count as 'real' because they merely disrupt existing systems).

In §3, it becomes even more evident that Saussure will simply refuse to admit that analogy could in any way be a diachronic phenomenon, even if this means redefining the concept 'change'. For analogy is needed as the mainspring of the Saussurean mechanism of grammar. It is what holds the parts of the system together. Analogy involves 'awareness and grasp of relations between forms' ([226]). By insisting on the exclusion of analogy from diachronic processes, Saussure is now in a position to tie up in a theoretically elegant way one loose end which has so far been left dangling in his account of linguistic evolution: how does the dichotomy between synchronic and diachronic relate to the no less important dichotomy between *langue* and *parole*? The answer has already been hinted at much earlier: *tout ce qui est diachronique dans la langue ne l'est que par la parole* ([138]). But only now does it become clear exactly how that interconnexion works. Analogy, which involves 'awareness and grasp of relations between forms', is a psychological function of the individual. Hence it is the individual who alone can create new forms ([227]). Whether the individual's analogical innovations will gain eventual acceptance in *la langue* is a separate matter: some may but others may not. Thus *parole* provides, as it were, a pool of individual analogical creations from which *la langue* may then choose.

Here the *Cours* is meticulously careful to distinguish two factors in the process of analogical creation: '(1) grasping the relation which connects the sponsoring forms, and (2) the result suggested by this comparison, i.e. the form improvised by the speaker to express his thought' ([227]). The latter alone, we are told, belongs to *parole*. Why insist on this? The reason is doubtless that without this distinction the explanation of the role of the individual runs the risk of suggesting that the grammatical system itself is a psychological creation of the individual. In other words, it cannot be admitted that the individual is free to imagine grammatical relations which just do not exist. *La langue* has to be a supra-individual reality. Hence stage (1) in the analogical process has to be removed from the domain of *parole*.

What this leaves unexplained is the sense in which, according to the definition given earlier in the chapter, analogical forms are made 'in accordance with a fixed rule' ([221]). Individual speakers, presumably, do not have the authority to invent fixed rules. But if the fixed rules are already part of *la langue*, that appears to make the individual's role in analogical creation superfluous. (For then all individuals will follow the fixed rule, and the analogical form will be automatically part of *la langue*.) Furthermore, a corollary of the fixed rule will presumably be that different individuals are not free to create different analogical innovations (given the same set of sponsoring forms). But if that is the case, then the reader begins to wonder in what sense the individual was ever free to create the analogical form in the first place. The chapter see-saws, as if the author feared that his explanation of analogy might perhaps be read as attributing *too much* freedom of linguistic action to the individual, and felt it necessary to reassert the restrictions imposed on that freedom by the collective institution.

This impression may be reinforced by Saussure's observations about the extent to which analogical possibilities are already inherent in *la langue* before the 'appearance' ([227]) of any new form. 'The continual activity of language (*langage*) in analysing the units already provided contains in itself not only all possibilities of speaking in conformity with usage, but also all possibilities of analogical formation' ([227]). This statement, which has attracted little attention from commentators, is one of the most theoretically crucial in the whole of the *Cours*. It explicitly assimilates the language-user's capacity for analogical innovation to the capacity for producing the ordinary syntagmatic structures of discourse. In other words, both are seen as creative procedures, which go beyond mere repetition or imitation, even though the patterns on which the creativity is based are already laid down in the language. The source of both is described as being *l'activité continuelle du langage*, a phrase not previously encountered in the text of the *Cours*. What does it mean? The activity envisaged is an analytic activity, since it involves the decomposition of linguistic units. It is evidently the activity of that *faculté de constituer une langue* ([26]) which Saussure claims to be one of the natural human faculties.

The chapter goes on to suggest ([228]) that in every language there is a distinction to be drawn between analogically 'productive' forms and analogically 'sterile' forms. The 'sterile' forms turn out to be those which are unanalysable (e.g. *magasin* 'shop', *arbre* 'tree', *racine* 'root'). This distinction between sterile and productive forms is explicitly linked to the distinction previously drawn between 'lexicological' and 'grammatical' languages ([183]). Chinese, on this scale, turns out to be an archetypically lexicological language, since most of its words are monosyllabic and (therefore?) unsegmentable ([228]). Esperanto, on the other hand, turns out to be maximally grammatical ([228]). Saussure is here revamping a well-known nineteenth-century typology of languages. This typology (Robins 1980: 250ff.) recognized a classification of languages into (i) isolating (or 'analytic'), (ii) agglutinative, and (iii) fusional (or 'inflecting'). What Saussure proposes, in effect, is a reinterpretation of this tripartite classification by collapsing the latter two categories, on the ground that in both of them the *arbitraire relatif* is favoured over the *arbitraire absolu*. However, to distinguish between 'sterile' and 'productive' forms is a particularly unhappy distinction to draw for a theorist who takes Saussure's view of linguistic structure. Sterility or productivity, for a Saussurean, can hardly reside in individual forms. What matters, as the preceding discussion of analogy in the *Cours* has made abundantly clear, is not the individual forms but the patterns of relationship between them. Why, then, is analogical potential or lack of potential attributed to the forms themselves? In the context of this chapter of the *Cours*, the answer seems to be that this is another way of emphasizing the point that the role of the individual in analogical creation is limited to actualizing a potential already present and embodied in the material supplied by *la langue*.

Finally, taking up the explanation of analogy in terms of proportions of the form $a : b = c : x$, Saussure suggests that this can be interpreted in two different ways, each of which reflects the 'predominant tendency' in different languages. One interpretation is typical of the descriptive methods of the Hindu grammarians, and the other of European grammarians. The former involves analysis and recombination of the elements present in the forms a, b and c of the proportion. The latter takes recognition of the proportionality itself to be a sufficient explanation for the generation of the missing x. 'In that way,' Saussure says, 'there is no need to credit the speaker with a complicated operation too much like the conscious analysis of the grammarian' ([229]). The observation is revealing. It shows that Saussure, who favours the 'analytic' interpretation of the proportion, evidently does not see attributing complicated analyses to individual language-users as something to be avoided. This ties in with the remarks on p.[189], where an equation is posited between the conscious classifications of the grammarian and the 'conscious or unconscious' associative series in the mind of the language-user. It appears, then, that a speaker is normally able, according to Saussure, to produce analogical forms without recognizing, understanding or reflecting upon the operations involved. Unfortunately, if this is so it leaves Saussure vulnerable to the objection that he has failed to show – and indeed cannot show, by his own account – that the proportional explanation provides the correct explanation of analogy in the first place; and still less can he show that the 'analytic' interpretation of the proportion is the correct one. Nevertheless, making the work of producing analogical forms in *parole* unconscious is another way of diminishing the contribution which the individual makes and of reaffirming the importance of the contribution made by *la langue*.

This chapter on analogy, therefore, shows Saussure grappling with the problem of attributing too much or too little to the individual. Both extremes are uncongenial to Saussurean theory. If the individual is allowed too much analogical freedom, this threatens the whole concept of *la langue* 'as a collective institution. On the other hand, if individual freedom is too narrowly circumscribed, this not only makes it appear (as on p.[227]) that individuals can only choose to initiate historical innovations which have already been determined in advance by *la langue*, but even calls in question whether a language ever changes at all (as distinct from implementing at various times various possible – but already inbuilt – potentialities). Why are these extremes uncongenial from a Saussurean point of view? Because in one case *langue* merges with *parole*, and in the other case synchrony merges with diachrony.

CHAPTER V

Analogy and Evolution

The beginning of Chapter V clears up one point which might have been left in doubt in the reader's mind from the discussion of analogy which the *Cours* has presented in the immediately preceding pages. This concerns the difference between the first appearance of an analogical form and its subsequent generalization. The two phenomena, for Saussure, evidently have quite different explanations. The former is due to the operations of a mental process involving proportionality (as described on p. [225]ff.). The latter, however, is due simply to imitation. An initial improvisation by one individual is imitated by others until it becomes accepted usage ([231]).

This throws a certain amount of light on the earlier definition of analogy ([221]) which referred to formation 'according to a fixed rule'. It now becomes apparent that this was *not* intended to suggest spontaneous implementation of some existing rule of analogical formation throughout the membership of a given linguistic community. In other words, the generalization of a successful analogy and its establishment in *la langue* here emerges clearly as a contingent – i.e. historical – process, and furthermore one in which 'external' linguistic factors (in the sense defined on p.[40]ff.) must play a key role. For the chances of the successful spread of an analogical form will presumably depend on the communicational contacts between its original improviser and its potential imitators, together with the sociolinguistic implications of these contacts. What might determine the diffusion of an analogical innovation, however, Saussure discusses only later, and then in very general terms, in Part IV of the *Cours*. The fate of an analogical innovation is not distinguished in any special way from the fate of other innovations. To this extent, there might appear to be a sizeable gap in the Saussurean account of analogy as it affects linguistic evolution.

In spite of this lacuna, Chapter V represents a theoretical triumph for Saussurean linguistics. For it exposes one of the major deficiencies of nineteenth-century historical linguistics and offers a solution. The deficiency in question resides in the fact that nineteenth-century historical linguistics had tacitly equated the study of linguistic evolution with the study of linguistic *change*. Linguistic *stability* was in practice ignored, and no explanation offered other than in terms of 'external' factors (political conditions, geographical isolation, the influence of education, etc.). Saussure, on the other hand, emerges from the *Cours* as a theorist who is fully aware that absence of change stands in as much need of theoretical explanation as change. It is all the more incumbent upon him to provide such an explanation as a theorist who proclaims that the linguistic sign is arbitrary (and hence intrinsically open to change, as already conceded on pp. [110-11]).

The brilliance of the Saussurean solution is that it is able to explain *both* change *and* absence of change by appeal to the same factor. Analogy, which is responsible for the appearance of new forms, is at the same time responsible for the conservation of old ones. 'Forms are kept because they are ceaselessly remade analogically' ([236]). This is the other – and less obvious – result of the same *activité continuelle du langage* which the human linguistic faculty sponsors.

CHAPTER VI

Popular Etymology

In spite of its title, this chapter offers no detailed account of popular etymology. Its sole purpose is to argue that popular etymology is not the same thing as analogy. The interesting question, again, is why there is any need to argue this: for in practice, as the *Cours* admits ([283]), the results are often similar. Commentators have pointed out that Saussure's editors subsequently toned down the dismissal of popular etymology by removing the description of it as a 'pathological phenomenon' from the text of the second (1922) edition (Ullman 1962: 103; de Mauro 1972: 473 n.286). It has been suggested that the great interest shown by linguists in the study of popular etymology made its condemnation as 'pathological' unacceptable: but the possible reasons for the editors' belated censorship of the term are not what is at issue here.

Popular etymology is an awkward nut for Saussurean linguistics to crack for two reasons. One is that it appears to be, as Vendryes later put it, *une réaction contre l'arbitraire du signe* (Vendryes 1952: 6); and since examples are widespread and well attested, their existence might be taken as undermining Saussure's 'first principle' of linguistics. When the *Cours* dealt with possible objections to that principle ([101-23]), however, popular etymology was not among them. Nor in this chapter is popular etymology defended as another manifestation of the effort to replace *l'arbitraire absolu* by *l'arbitraire relatif*. The problem is that although popular etymologies, as Saussure concedes, look like attempts to 'make sense' of words which are unfamiliar or poorly understood, the resultant innovations sometimes make just as little sense as the original forms, or even less. Seen as rationalizations of the arbitrary, popular etymologies in many cases appear to be either incomplete or misguided rationalizations. So it is difficult in such cases for a theorist who takes Saussure's position to explain (i) why the original arbitrary sign gave rise to any problem in the first place, (ii) why manifest failures to rationalize it satisfactorily should ever gain acceptance into *la langue*, (iii) what prevented 'better' attempts at rationalization (given that, in view of the arbitrary nature of the linguistic sign, nothing circumscribes in advance the extent to which parts of the original *significant* may be altered), and (iv) why popular etymology is not even more widespread (that is, why no attempts have been made to re-interpret many comparable forms which strike one as obvious candidates for rationalization). These difficulties suggest that there may be analytic and associative processes at work in language which Saussurean linguistics is in principle unable to account for. Somehow, therefore, Saussure needs a way of playing down the significance of popular etymology as a linguistic phenomenon.

The second reason why popular etymology is particularly irksome for Saussure is that on the surface it appears to involve exactly the same associative operations as analogy; and analogy, as the preceding chapters have made clear, occupies a very important position in Saussurean explanations of how language works. It is difficult, consequently, to dismiss or simply to ignore popular etymology. That would call in question the adequacy of his basic account of analogy. Therefore he chooses to argue instead that, in spite of certain similarities, analogy and popular etymology are fundamentally different. His analysis of the difference, however, relies heavily on dubious psychologizing. (The subsequently suppressed term 'pathological' suggests a hint of desperation in the attempt.) Saussure tries to claim that, unlike analogy, popular etymology does not involve creative analysis. It is a kind of mistake or 'distortion' ([240]), due to ignorance. Unlike analogy, it does not belong to 'the normal functioning of a language' ([241]). It always involves dimly 'remembering' the old form, whereas analogy involves 'forgetting' it. Given Saussure's earlier hesitations about the conscious or unconscious nature of associative relations, none of this carries much argumentative weight.

Why not, then, opt for admitting that popular etymology and analogy are basically the same, and treating popular etymologies as simply one type of result produced by the working of analogy? Because that would lead straight away to a paradox about *la langue*; namely, that part of the normal functioning of the *mécanisme de la langue* is to produce, in addition to regular, complete and symmetrical patterns, other re-analyses of linguistic structure which are irregular, fragmentary and poorly motivated. This would immediately make Saussure's triumph of the previous chapter hollow: for then analogy could no longer be given as the simultaneous explanation for the introduction of new regularities and the maintenance of old regularities. Even less could it be adduced to explain in addition the production of syntagmatically regular combinations in ordinary discourse. (For it might equally well produce irregular ones.) Come what may, therefore, popular etymology has to be banished as some kind of freak or deviation not belonging to the normal 'healthy' functioning of the *activité continuelle du langage*.

Unfortunately, the attempt to avoid one paradox leads straight into another. For if popular etymologies are indeed 'mistakes' perpetrated by ignorant language-users who are unfamiliar with certain forms in *la langue*, it becomes extremely difficult to explain how these mistakes ever gain acceptance in *la langue*, except on the assumption that most of its users are just as ignorant as the individual who perpetrated the original 'mistake'. The reader is then left with a theoretically puzzling picture of linguistic communities whose members do not know their own native language. The gap in Saussurean theory which begins to show here will be considered in detail later: it concerns Saussure's failure to reconcile Durkheimian and non-Durkheimian concepts of the collectivity.

CHAPTER VII

Agglutination

Agglutination presents another problem which is no less fraught for Saussurean linguistics than that of popular etymology. For agglutination, looked at from the point of view of its diachronic results, appears to be the antithesis of analogy. In other words, it innovates by obliterating existing distinctions, whereas analogy preserves and reinforces them. How can these two contradictory tendencies both be explained as due to the working of the same *mécanisme de la langue*? One is self-preserving but the other self-destructive.

It would doubtless have been possible for Saussure to argue that, as in the case of popular etymologies, agglutinations are simply the product of ignorance on the part of language-users who fail to grasp the structure of the forms they are using. But, given that he has just been forced to use that explanation to deal with popular etymology, perhaps a second appeal to the incompetence of native speakers would have sounded like one appeal too many. Instead, the *Cours* puts a bold face on things and claims that agglutination is a 'mechanical' syntagmatic process which amalgamates the meanings of the forms involved.

The explanation limps both on its semantic leg and on its phonetic leg. It limps on its semantic leg because in the examples of agglutination which are offered for the reader's consideration it is often quite unclear in what sense the meaning of the agglutinated form could possibly be the result of applying 'the concept as a whole to the sequence of signs as a whole' ([243]). Thus, for instance, the agglutination which produced French *encore* ([243]) from Latin *hanc horam* ('this hour') results in a unit with a new meaning which can hardly be explained just as a failure to distinguish the two separate elements in the original combination of *signifiés*. Furthermore, Saussure's suggestion that this is due to the fact that when a compound concept is expressed by a very familiar sequence of significant units 'the mind takes a short cut' ([243]) is a metaphor that scarcely makes sense in the context. (It is reminiscent of crude attempts to explain linguistic change as due to 'laziness' on the part of language-users.) There is no 'short-cut' for the mind to take in these cases if the intention is indeed to express the compound concept. And in any case it is difficult to see what 'short-cutting' the analysis of a compound concept like 'this hour' could mean.

The explanation limps no less badly on its phonetic leg. Saussure claims it would be a mistake to suppose that phonetic merging precedes and causes semantic merging. On the contrary, he argues, it is the other way round: it is the perception of a 'single idea' in two sequential elements which leads to their phonetic coalescence into a single word ([243]). But this is quite unconvincing in view of the frequency of agglutinations where phonetic merging still leaves two quite distinguishable elements and no accompanying 'amalgamation' of the concepts. The form *I'm* is no less analysable than *I am*, and *don't* no less analysable than *do not*, in spite of the phonetic consequences for the morphological units involved. Perhaps it might be argued that Saussure would have to reject these as examples of agglutination, on the ground that two elements are still recognizable, regardless of the phonetic coalescence uniting them into a syntagmatically inseparable combination. If so, it is hard to see how standard cases like *possum* from *potis* + *sum* ([244]), or *ferai* from *facere* + *habeo* ([245]fn.) could be allowed to count as examples of agglutination either. Since we are not told how the analyst is to recognize the difference between a single idea and a combination of two ideas, just as we are not told what the criteria are for distinguishing between an agglutinated syntagma and a non-agglutinated syntagma, it is difficult to pursue the question much further.

Even if this omission leaves the Saussurean concept of agglutination somewhat obscure in certain respects, what emerges clearly enough is a reluctance to accept the view that agglutination is determined or even triggered by changes in the pronunciation of two forms when they become syntagmatically linked. It is interesting to ask what the reason is for this reluctance. The answer is bound up with another enigmatic feature of this chapter: its insistence that agglutination is 'mechanical'. The mechanical nature of agglutination, we are told, sets it apart from analogy, which is now – for the first time – described as a linguistic 'procedure', as distinct from a linguistic 'process'. The difference between the two is that a procedure 'implies will and intention' ([242]). Thus whereas agglutination is 'totally involuntary', analogy on the contrary 'presupposes analyses and combinations', and is 'an activity of the intelligence' ([244]).

Now at first sight the notion that agglutination is mechanical appears to favour the explanation that the phenomenon results from purely phonetic factors which operate when two *signifiants* are habitually linked in syntagmatic combination. But, as noted above, this is evidently *not* the explanation Saussure proposes. The distinction now drawn between procedures and processes has a quite different theoretical objective. It is to deal with a problem which is consequential upon the new role assigned to analogy in the last chapter but one. This is the problem of explaining why it is that the conservative force of analogy, to which the *Cours* has just given the major theoretical role of guaranteeing the maintenance of regular forms, is apparently powerless to prevent agglutination from obliterating distinctions between signs already established in *la langue*. In short, we are dealing here with a possible objection to the idea that analogy is capable of fulfilling the conservational function allotted to it.

The objection is potentially a serious one, and it is important to see how the distinction between procedures and processes is designed to take care of it. Unfortunately, the *Cours* draws this distinction in terms which could easily give rise to misunderstandings. Three chapters previously the reader has been offered an account of analogy which fairly clearly implies that in many cases its workings do not take place at the level of conscious awareness on the part of the individual speakers. Yet now we are told that analogy is 'procedural' in nature, and linguistic procedures are defined as involving the intervention of the will and the intelligence. From that it might seem that the operations of analogy must fall under *parole*, which was early on in the *Cours* characterized as the domain of acts of 'the will and the intelligence' ([30]). And it might seem even more difficult to reconcile that assignment with having been told specifically on p.[227] that the initial improvisation of a new form is the only part of analogy which belongs to *parole*. In short, the reader may well feel that in the text of the *Cours* there is by now an internally generated muddle over whether analogy belongs to *langue* or to *parole*, and, specifically, to what extent it involves intentionality on the part of the language users.

It is difficult to exonerate Saussure or his editors entirely from blame on this score. What the *Cours* tells us could hardly be more vague. However, the reading which seems to make best theoretical sense of the distinction between linguistic processes and linguistic procedures is as follows. Processes and procedures do not belong to *parole* at all or to diachrony, even though it is in *parole* and in diachrony that their joint results become manifest. Process and procedure are two basic types of operation in the *activité continuelle du langage* which ceaselessly shapes *la langue* in the minds of its speakers (or perhaps in the collective mind of the community, if we construe Saussurean metaphysics in that way). Procedures are the creative analytic operations. Processes are merely mental handling operations. Procedures are responsible for the systematicity of *la langue*. Processes simply arrange the items and implement the patterns systematically created by procedures. (Hence the claim that agglutination is exclusively a syntagmatic phenomenon, and involves no associative relations ([244]).) However, processes may sometimes have marginal repercussions on the organization of *la langue*, for reasons which are purely internal to the handling operations required by the *activité continuelle*. Such a case is agglutination, in which the relevant factor is simply that it is operationally easier to amalgamate two units which are constantly being syntagmatically combined and treat them as if they were a single unit of *la langue*. Thus it is not that analogy is powerless to prevent agglutination, but that agglutination results from the constant processual implementation of those very syntagmatic relations which analogic procedures have established. In short, the appearance that agglutination counteracts or overrules analogy is another diachronic illusion (on a par with the diachronic illusion that there are analogical changes).

The above interpretation of the Saussurean distinction between processes and procedures, although speculative, has two merits. One is that what the *Cours* says about analogy can at least be construed as internally consistent. (Whether it is convincing is another matter.) The other is that in this particular chapter it ties in with the rejection of the view that agglutination, although a mechanical phenomenon, is not explicable by reference to phonetic factors.

To summarize, the underlying rationale seems to be this. If phonetic coalescence were a cause rather than a consequence of agglutination, and if no distinction were drawn between processes and procedures, this would leave Saussurean linguistics lacking an available explanation not only for (i) why a new sign should be 'spontaneously' generated simply as the result of the syntagmatic proximity of two *signifiants*, but also for (ii) why, given that the linguistic sign is arbitrary, phonetic merging should in any case lead to semantic merging, and (iii) how it is possible for agglutination to obliterate boundaries between signs, given that these boundaries reflect already established associative series in *la langue*.

Again, a chapter on a purportedly diachronic phenomenon turns out to be devoted principally to defending the implications of Saussurean synchronic theory.

CHAPTER VIII

Diachronic Units,
Identities and Realities

The final chapter of Part III at last turns to the question which, arguably, ought to have been discussed at the outset. By now, the reason for the delay is apparent. Without the important synchronic caveats which have just been announced, it would be impossible to give a complete Saussurean analysis of the problems of diachronic substitution. Without these caveats, moreover, it would be legitimate to read into the second paragraph on p.[248] a complete retraction of almost everything that the *Cours* has hitherto argued about the irreducible difference between synchronic and diachronic facts. (It is one of the besetting sins of Saussurean exegesis to juxtapose quotations cited out of context, and from different sources. Doubtless the whole botched textual history of the *Cours* made that in one sense inevitable. But inevitability is never a substitute for justification.)

What the reader is told on p.[248] is that an alteration in the linguistic sign is a shift in the relation between *signifiant* and *signifié*. 'This definition applies not only to changes in individual items, but to the evolution of the whole system. Diachronic development in its entirety is just that.' *Eppur si muove*? Is historical grammar a reality after all? Not so. It would be a mistake to look here for any last-minute recantation of the Saussurean faith that the linguistic system itself is *immuable* ([121]). As a conclusion to this section of the *Cours* devoted to Diachronic Linguistics, such a recantation would certainly be the most seat-raising second-act curtain of all. Nor would one wish to deny that whoever drafted those particular lines of the script on p.[248] had a keen sense of academic drama. (Otherwise they would fall flat.) The dramatic point, however, is precisely that now at last the reader is in a position to see how the apparent evolution of the *system* is a diachronic illusion. That illusion is all of a piece with the illusion that analogical innovations are changes. The truth is that the system does not evolve over time, and cannot evolve. The illusion is created by a succession of relations between *signifiants* and *signifiés* which retrospectively look as if the whole language were moving in a certain direction. Time plays a role, in brief: but its role is in the eye of the beholder. Here we eventually come to the full interpretation of that Sibylline diagram on p.[113], which represented the language and the community as static units, linked nevertheless by a chronological arrow. Simultaneously, we come to yet another application of the Saussurean dictum that the point of view creates the linguistic object.

Saussure's editors have been criticized for their strategic decision to postpone until this point the presentation of the connexion which Saussurean theory postulates between synchronic and diachronic identities (de Mauro 1972: 473,n.288), although it was announced as early as p.[150]. Any impartial academic inquiry into the alternatives must no doubt rule in favour of the editors. They saw that it would be merely confusing to incorporate into the section on Synchronic Linguistics a general discussion of problems of identity, before the reader had even been introduced to the full implications of the Saussurean dichotomy between synchrony and diachrony. That having been said, the fuss would be over nothing if it now emerged that the connexion was in any case uncontroversial.

Far from being uncontroversial, it raises the dire question of the extent to which diachronic linguistics is possible at all. This is the unexpected sting in the tail of Chapter VIII. 'Only the solution of the problem of the diachronic unit will enable us to penetrate beyond the superficial appearance of linguistic evolution and grasp its essence. Here, as in synchrony, understanding what the units are is indispensable in order to distinguish illusion from reality' ([248-9]). Do we, then, understand what the diachronic units are? Saussure, evidently, does not claim to. If we do, then we are cleverer than the author of the *Cours*. But he warns us against imagining that we have discovered the diachronic units merely by extrapolating from our identification of synchronic units. There are doubtless many kinds of diachronic change. 'The units identified for these purposes will not necessarily correspond to the units recognized in the synchronic domain' ([248]). On the contrary, one thing we can be fairly sure of is that 'the notion of a unit cannot be the same for both synchronic and diachronic studies' ([248]).

The same doubts are immediately confirmed by the dismissal on p.[249] of the facile claim of the historical philologist to be able to recognize diachronic identities simply by tracing the development of the individual sound changes from Latin *calidum* to French *chaud*, Latin *mare* to French *mer*, etc. This, argues Saussure, is to stand the problem on its head: for the basis for determining the historical continuity of individual sounds is precisely the assumption that the pairs *calidum* and *chaud, mare* and *mer*, etc. are indeed in diachronic correspondence.

How then can we break out of the circle? Saussure's enigmatic reply is stated with tantalising brevity on the very last page. Diachronic identities are extrapolations from series of synchronic identities 'without the link between them ever being broken by successive sound changes'. Hence the question of identifying diachronically Latin *calidum* with French *chaud* is directly related to the problem of identifying repetitions of the word *Messieurs!* in the same speech. The diachronic problem is simply 'an extension and complication' ([250]) of the synchronic problem. Unfortunately, the synchronic problem has itself been left unresolved on p.[152].

It is small wonder that historical linguists of Saussure's day preferred not to pursue the final implications of Chapter VIII. They might have found themselves inescapably cut off from a whole tradition of linguistic studies. Nowadays, however, considerations of that order are hardly relevant for a reader who is simply trying to make sense of the theoretical position which the *Cours* presents. For such a reader the question is what is meant by the claim that the problem of diachronic identity is simply an 'extension and complication' of the problem of synchronic identity.

It is difficult to shrug off the nagging suspicion that the very way in which the connexion between these two problems is raised betrays a deep Saussurean conflation between questions of *identity* and questions of *identification*. If we go back to the examples the *Cours* provides when discussing synchronic identity ([151-2]), it might appear that initially Saussure distinguishes between the *objective* question of whether a suit on a market stall is (or is not) my suit which had been stolen, and the *subjective* question of whether I identify the suit in question as mine. These appear to be two quite different issues: success or failure in identification does not, in principle, affect identity. Perhaps, after all, the suit I now claim as mine is not the one which was stolen: in which case I have confused two *non-identical* objects. (When the confusion is between one person and another person, such mistakes are commonly called cases of 'mistaken identity', but perhaps it would be less misleading if they were called cases of 'mistaken identification'.) Identity, in brief, is here not a matter of opinion or mere mortal judgment (unlike identification): either the suit is in fact mine or it isn't. Identity does not depend on how convinced I am that the suit is mine; nor on how good the evidence is for my identification. Questions of identification are quite different. How we identify things belongs to that area of psychology which deals with recognition, memory, attention, etc. Such questions, unlike questions of identity, are essentially *subjective*.

In the chapter on synchronic identities the reader was told that linguistic identity is *not* like the identity of the suit ([152]), but like the identity of the 8.45 train from Geneva to Paris, or the identity of the street demolished and rebuilt. In these latter examples, clearly, identity does *not* depend on the same material continuity: it is a formal or functional identity. But what exactly constitutes a formal or functional identity was left hanging in the air: metaphors were supplied in place of a definition. It is the chapter discussing diachronic identities which now brings the reader's attention back to those previously uninterpreted metaphors. For here we seem to be told that diachronic identity *is* indeed a matter of continuity (of the Latin word *calidum* with the French word *chaud*, etc.), but not of *phonetic* continuity. This is the point of the insistence on p.[249] that the identity '*chaud = calidum*' cannot be explicated purely and simply in terms of regular sound changes (even though they hold, as it happens).

All this is certainly puzzling, to say the least. For if the laws of sound change do not guarantee diachronic identity, what does? One possible answer is already dismissed when we recall that for Saussure there is no such thing as *panchronic* identity ([134-5]). The puzzle deepens further with the remarks on pp.[249-50] to the effect that the French dialect differences between *se fâcher* and *se fôcher* are simply divergent developments of a single form. But at the same time, if the two French dialects represent different idiosynchronic systems, there is no way *se fâcher* and *se fôcher* can be synchronically identical. Furthermore, in the same breath ([250]) the *Cours* tells its readers that the French negative *pas* is identical with the French noun *pas* (but without distinguishing between synchronic identity and diachronic identity).

Culler (1976: 39) interprets Saussure as saying that in the passage from Latin *calidum* to French *chaud* the succession of phonetic changes (*calidum* to *calidu*, *calidu* to *caldu*, *caldu* to *cald*, etc.) is linked by the synchronic identity, at some stage, of each of the successive pairs of different phonetic forms. However, as Love has pointed out, this leaves unresolved the problem of how to justify the identification of 'the *calidu* that occurs as a *messieurs*-type variant of *calidum* at stage one with the *calidu* that occurs as a *messieurs*-type variant of *caldu* at stage two'. Love concludes: 'The logic of the concept of an idiosynchronic language-state leaves one with just two ways to jump: either all the historical variants of a given form belong theoretically to the same *état de langue*, or there are uncountably many *états de langue* and no such thing as a diachronic identity. Culler's attempt to occupy a halfway house between these positions only serves to reveal the conceptual discontinuity between the notions of synchrony and diachrony, as expounded by Saussure'. (Love 1984: 228).

Is there any reading of Chapter VIII that can unscramble this tangle of confusions? It would take both a bold and an ingenious reader to maintain that there is. On the face of it, the reasons why a hearer might *identify* two utterances in a speech as utterances of the 'same word' (*messieurs*) have little to do with (a) whether the first utterance is auditorily or meaningfully indistinguishable from the second, or (b) whether a historian might claim that the French word *messieurs* is identical with some Latin word or expression (e.g. *meos seniores*). What might seem to bridge the gap is that an etymologist might identify a certain Latin form as the etymon of a certain French form (by saying 'It's the same word'), and two speakers of French might also (by saying 'It's the same word') identify one occurrence of *Messieurs!* with another occurrence. But all that shows – sceptics will doubtless claim – is that Saussure plays fast and loose (for his own purposes) with the concepts of linguistic identity and linguistic identification, or juggles with different metalinguistic interpretations of the term *same*.

Committed defenders of Saussure will doubtless reply that when it comes to questions of language, the distinction between identity and identification immediately becomes less clear cut and more contentious. This is because linguistic units do not, like garments or people or buildings, have an identity which can be defined in terms of spatio-temporal continuity. On the contrary, whether we are dealing with the same linguistic unit or two different linguistic units seems to be far more dependent on identification. This is due to the nature of language. What matters ultimately for linguistic comprehension is that the hearer correctly *identify* what the speaker has said. Hence the temptation to treat the identity of a linguistic unit as residing purely and simply in its identifiability across all the many instances of its occurrence in discourse. Provided that identifiability is guaranteed, it seems superfluous – and even nonsensical – to look for any *further* criteria of linguistic identity. So any contrast between the objectivity of identity and the subjectivity of identification, which holds good generally for our dealings with the physical world, immediately becomes blurred in the case of language.

Appendices to
Parts Two and Three

[NB. The erroneous title of this section survives from an earlier plan of the *Cours*, in which Part I was to have comprised material on writing and on phonetics, eventually incorporated into the Introduction. The editors evidently failed to notice that in consequence *Appendices aux troisième et quatrième parties* should have been altered to read *Appendices aux seconde et troisième parties.*]

Saussure's new distinction between 'subjective' and 'objective' analysis (Appendix A) raises two points of interest. Its connexion with *la distinction radicale du diachronique et du synchronique* ([252]) is not disguised. As earlier discussion in the *Cours* has already made clear, the distinction between synchrony and diachrony would have no basis were it not that the native speakers' view of their language and the historian's view of it will in certain respects inevitably and fundamentally differ. Nevertheless, to introduce the terms 'subjective' and 'objective' implies a relationship between these contrasting viewpoints for which no theoretical foundation has so far been laid in the *Cours*. For while it is clear in what sense the synchronic point of view may be called *subjectif* (namely, that it derives from the *sujet parlant* ([251])), that does not automatically validate the historian's point of view as an 'objective' one.

The reader is presumably expected to recall that on p.[189] an (ideal) equation was posited between the classifications proposed by the synchronic descriptive grammarian and the 'conscious or unconscious' associative series operative in *parole*. Now that equation already yields a sense in which the (ideal) synchronic description is or may be judged 'objective' (depending on whether or not its classifications do or do not correspond to the associative series of the native speaker). But nothing similar has so far been proposed to yield a sense in which the (ideal) diachronic description would be comparably 'objective'. History, in short, has so far been left to the eye of the historian (which is notoriously liable to take a view as 'subjective' as any).

It is only if we bear this in mind that the full significance of the ensuing attack on the Neogrammarians on p.[253] can be appreciated. At first sight, it looks like a case of pot calling the kettle black. For the *Cours* has already conceded on p.[153] that the linguist is condemned to working with concepts originally introduced by grammarians. So why should the Neogrammarian school in particular come under fire for 'remaining encumbered with a scientific apparatus which it could not dispense with after all' ([253])? Is not this precisely the charge which might be levelled at the author of the *Cours*? For does he not too speak constantly of 'words', 'roots', 'suffixes', 'nouns', 'verbs', and so on, even while proclaiming in the same breath that the validity of these terms is dubious?

The interesting point is that the Neogrammarians are *not* condemned just for retaining an inadequate descriptive terminology (or who should escape whipping?); *nor* for failing to acknowledge its descriptive inadequacies; but for attempting to justify it nevertheless on the grounds of 'convenience of exposition' ([253]). In short, they threw out the historical baby with the analytic bathwater.

This is an accusation which discloses more about the assumptions underpinning Saussurean diachrony than anything that has been explicitly admitted thus far in Part III. For the position here attributed to the Neogrammarians (whether justifiably so or not makes no difference) is that they simply wash their hands of the terminological question by making no claims for their descriptive framework *other than* convenience of exposition. Saussure, it will be noted, does not deny them that advantage. Nor are the Neogrammarians here attacked on the more general intellectual ground that to claim that a descriptive framework is justified on grounds of convenience of exposition alone must be either incoherent or disingenuous. The sins of the Neogrammarians on this score are, for Saussure, of a different order.

The first sin is that their terminological handwashing sets a bad academic example. In other words, linguistics could not possibly be a science ever if all its practitioners adopted this attitude. Specifically, synchronic linguistics could claim no analytic superiority over the practical pedagogic linguistics of the traditional grammarian. (For whatever is 'convenient' in terms of exposition is then automatically justified, and linguistics becomes one of the systematic sophistries of education.) The Saussurean inquiry into setting the study of language on a scientific basis is by implication condemned to futility if all the justification its conceptual frameworks ever need is 'convenience of exposition', and any 'pure abstraction of the mind' ([253]) which serves this purpose is *eo ipso* validated. So the Neogrammarians have to be punished on this count *pour encourager les autres*, if for no other reason.

The second Neogrammarian sin is different. It is the sin of historical agnosticism. By renouncing the task of devising an appropriate diachronic terminology, the Neogrammarians have in effect renounced the task of discovering the operative units of diachronic change. They rest content with being able to state the resultant diachronic correspondences in conveniently simple terms. For Saussure this will not do, *even if* the summarizing statements are unobjectionable. In other words, the hidden premiss underlying Saussurean diachrony is that history is 'real'; and this historical realism is what informs the choice of the term 'objective' to describe the kind of analysis which the linguistic historian *should be* engaged in. This is the other reason why the Neogrammarians cannot be allowed to get away with saying that their descriptive units are 'pure abstractions'.

The path to theoretical salvation which the *Cours* offers Neogrammarian heretics is a straight and narrow one. It is to embrace the belief that 'objective analysis, being linked internally to subjective analysis of the living language, has a legitimate and clearly defined place in linguistic method' ([253]). A more aggressive way of pronouncing the same punitive sentence would have been to say that *unless* objective analysis can be shown to be internally linked to subjective analysis, it has no legitimate place in linguistics. What exactly the nature of this crucial 'internal link' is the *Cours* never explains. All we can infer is that it does *not* validate an automatic correspondence between synchronic and diachronic units, since there is none ([248]): and that seems to leave internal linkage as a simple but fundamental article of Saussurean faith.

Faith, in this particular instance, is hardly fortified by the discussion of Greek stems and affixes which immediately follows (Appendix B), and purports to demonstrate that 'one cannot establish a method or formulate definitions except by approaching the task synchronically' ([253]). What in fact it bears witness to is a failure to distinguish between certain synchronic relationships which were subsequently recognized by Saussure's successors. Thus, for instance, on p.[254] Greek *zeug-* is held to have been an 'irreducible', 'second-grade' stem. Its irreducibility is unquestionable because 'by comparing related forms it is impossible to take its segmentation any further' ([255]). What this means in practical terms is that it is the twentieth-century linguist who is unable to take the process of segmentation any further. What it proves about the subjective analysis of those who spoke ancient Greek, however, is another matter. The discussion on pp.[254-5] concedes that this 'irreducible' Greek stem *zeug-* had what are called 'variants' (*zeuk-*, *zug-*), but does not allow the existence of these variants to cast doubt on the basic assumption that segmentation is the only valid procedure by which we can establish 'subjective' units for Plato, Aristotle and their contemporaries. In other words, Saussure here attributes to native speakers of ancient Greek a grammatical mentality corresponding to what post-Saussurean linguists later called the 'item-and-arrangement' model (Hockett 1954). It must be debatable whether that gratuitous historical attribution is preferable to a historical agnosticism which would make no bolder claim about Greek than that it is 'descriptively convenient' to treat *zeug-* as an unanalysable stem. The more modest claim at least does not suggest any diachronic *ivresse des grandes profondeurs*.

The reader's confidence in the method of analysis advocated here does not increase as the discussion proceeds. By p.[257], a *suffix* is defined as 'the element added to the root in order to form a stem (e.g. *zeug-mat-*), or to one stem in order to form a second-grade stem (e.g. *zeugmat-io*)'. But on p.[254], *zeug-* itself was already described as a 'second-grade' stem. Evidently, we have a conflation between (i) the relationship which links a root to the word forms based on that root, and (ii) the relationship which links the stem of any given word form to its ending. The trouble is the difficulty of treating both types of relationship as *linear* relationships. In short, this is just the kind of example which ought to have led to a rethink about the wisdom of adopting linearity as a 'second principle' of Saussurean linguistics. But evidently it did not.

Finally, etymology (Appendix C) is brought into the methodological picture. This is the unkindest cut of all to the Neogrammarians, whose achievements stand or fall by the reliability of their etymological evidence. But etymology, for Saussure, is a linguistic jack-of-all-trades. 'To achieve its aims, etymology makes use of all the means which linguistics makes available, but does not scrutinize the nature of the processes it is obliged to engage in' ([260]). In other words, it is endemically tainted with the failure to distinguish between synchronic and diachronic relations. This polemic completes the case against etymology already foreshadowed on p.[249], where it was argued that diachronic identity of forms could not be established on the basis of sound change, under pain of circularity: for the establishment of valid etymologies is itself a prerequisite for the recognition of any sound change.

PART FOUR
Geographical Linguistics

CHAPTER I

On the Diversity of Languages

Part IV is the only section of the *Cours* devoted to 'external linguistics' ([262]), apart from general comments on the subject in Chapter V of the Introduction, and a brief discussion of a rather random selection of topics in Part V. Why does linguistic geography command the lion's share of attention when other aspects of external linguistics find no mention in the *Cours* at all? (No mention is ever made for instance, of social diversity, which is no less conspicuous than geographical diversity.) Two reasons might be suggested. The first is that the latter part of the nineteenth century and the early years of the twentieth had seen the growth of European dialectology and the compilation of dialect atlases emerging as one of the major fields of empirical research in linguistics. To have ignored linguistic geography, therefore, would have run the risk of suggesting that the *Cours* represented a brand of armchair theorizing quite out of touch with contemporary developments in language studies. The second reason is that linguistic geography happens to be a field in which the relevance of certain Saussurean principles can be easily demonstrated. Indeed, it is conspicuous that this chapter of the *Cours* selects only those topics which afford this possibility of demonstration. Other less tractable problems of dialectology are simply ignored.

At the same time, in Part IV no opportunity is lost of emphasizing that linguistic geography is 'external' and the nature of its subject matter precludes it from any systematic scientific treatment within the linguistics of *la langue*. Throughout, Saussure points out the haphazard character of the phenomena which linguistic geography studies: the unpredictability of direction of change ([272]), of areas of diffusion ([274]), of dialect boundaries ([277-8]), of language boundaries

([278-80]), and in general of the interaction between the forces of parochialism and intercourse ([284]). The cumulative effect of this is to suggest that the methods of linguistic geography, far from throwing much light on *la langue* or on the structure of linguistic communities, on the contrary bring to light much which stands in need of explanation.

The only reference to the possibility that 'external' linguistics might be able to make some positive contribution to 'internal' linguistics occurs on p.[263], and there it is not linguistic geography as such but comparison between languages and their histories which holds out the prospect of revealing 'certain constant phonetic and psychological facts which circumscribe the establishment of any language'. According to Saussure, 'it is the discovery of these constant factors which is the main aim of any comparison between languages unrelated to one another' ([263]). Evidently these purely linguistic universals are of less importance for Saussure than the more general semiological universals referred to earlier in the *Cours*. That may be why there is no attempt to pursue the difficulty of establishing whether two languages are ultimately related or not. Saussure speaks simply of cases where 'no relationship is recognizable or demonstrable'. Since he concedes that even if all languages were phylogenetically related, the relationship 'would not be provable, because too many changes have taken place' ([263]), it presumably remains in doubt what value to attach to the eventual evidence of comparative studies on this score.

Comparison in general raises a theoretical problem about which the *Cours* is noticeably reticent, although it recurs at various points throughout Part IV. On p.[263] the reader is told that comparison 'is always possible and useful', that it can be made 'of grammatical systems and of general ways of expressing ideas, as well as of sound systems' and also of diachronic as well as synchronic facts. However, whether linguistic comparison is possible on a systematic or scientific basis Saussure does not say. Nor, if it *is* possible, is the appropriate scientific methodology described here. Whether, therefore, comparison requires a different linguistic 'point of view', neither that of subjective nor that of objective analysis, is a question apparently left open. The implication seems to be that comparison itself belongs to 'external' linguistics, and consequently its basis may vary according to the particular external factors involved. (It is far from clear, nevertheless, that this move lets 'internal' linguistics off the hook altogether, since the question of diachronic substitution, left unresolved at the end of Part III, presumably presupposes the possibility of comparison between diachronically connected *états de langue*. Without that possibility it is difficult to see that any statement to the effect that certain forms replace others over a period of time would be admissible in linguistics.)

CHAPTER II

Geographical Diversity: Its Complexity

The reader might be forgiven for supposing that the title of this chapter was chosen with tongue in cheek. Not only are the 'complications' discussed remarkably uncomplicated, but they are also dismissed with lightning speed. Chapter II in fact provides an unwitting demonstration of how narrowly ethnocentric the Saussurean approach to problems of external linguistics can be. The hidden premiss – only half-hidden, or in places barely concealed – underlying Saussure's whole treatment of linguistic geography is that the kind of linguistic distribution shown by the large-scale linguistic atlases of modern Europe represents a universal norm. The 'ideal' form of geographical diversity, we are told, is that in which 'different areas correspond to different languages' ([265]). Clearly, that happens to be the form to which the European linguistic situation closely approximates; but why it should be 'ideal' and other situations treated as deviations from it the *Cours* does not explain.

The first major consequence of this premiss is that bilingual situations are by implication counted as abnormal or marginal (even though on a world scale bilingualism predominates over monolingualism), while linguistic phenomena such as pidginization and creolization are not even mentioned at all in connexion with linguistic variation. The only kind of bilingualism in which any interest is shown here is the bilingualism which results from the superimposition of a literary language on a local dialect of the same language (which, again, happens to be a typical phenomenon of post-Renaissance European culture). Otherwise, the type of contact between linguistic communities envisaged is simply their separate coexistence within a given country or area.

In a quite breathtaking dismissal of 'non-ideal' linguistic facts, Saussure concedes that although certain types of departure from the monoglot situation occur so frequently 'that they might seem to be normal in the history of languages', it is necessary to set them aside because they 'obscure a clear view of natural geographical diversity' ([269]). 'This schematic simplification may seem to distort reality; but the natural state of affairs must first be studied in its own right' ([269]). The short answer to Saussure on this is that the schematic simplification proposed does not merely 'seem to distort' but actually does distort reality. What Saussurean linguistics here unaccountably takes to be 'the natural state of affairs' is simply a theoretical abstraction which isolates just those factors which it is convenient for the theorist to deal with by means of the techniques of linguistic geography.

CHAPTER III

Causes of Geographical Diversity

Having invented an 'ideal' type of geographical diversity, the *Cours* immediately proceeds to offer its ideal explanation, or rather to highlight one feature of an ideal explanation. The essential feature turns out to be that, contrary to appearances, geographical diversity has little to do with space, but everything to do with time. 'Geographical diversity has to be translated into temporal diversity' ([271]). Furthermore, 'the instability of the language depends on time alone. Geographical diversity is thus a secondary aspect of the general phenomenon' ([272]).

At first sight it is by no means clear exactly what Saussure is driving at here. Earlier in the *Cours* we have already been told that 'time changes everything', that 'there is no reason why *la langue* should be exempt from this universal law' ([112]), and that 'languages are always changing, however minimally' ([142]). These considerations hardly establish time as a *cause* of change. It would be naive to treat the statement that 'time changes everything' on a par with, say, 'compression changes density'. Time is not an external force causing changes but a dimension in which changes occur. Likewise, space is a dimension. But we all knew that anyway, a reader may reasonably object. So why is Saussure apparently so keen to make the point that it is time not space which changes languages? And exactly what point is it?

As so often in the *Cours*, in order to understand the line Saussure takes on a particular issue, it is essential to identify the theoretical error which is implicitly under attack. Here the clue is given by cryptic warning at the end of §1. 'The unity of related languages is to be traced only through time. Unless the student of comparative linguistics realizes this, all kinds of misconceptions lie in wait for him' ([272]). In short, the reader needs here to refer back to the temporal arrow in the diagram on p.[113], and even further back to the remarks about the failure of Bopp to found a 'true science of linguistics' ([16]). What Saussure is saying, with the indirectness which passes for academic *politesse*, is that the currently fashionable study of linguistic geography can no more offer a scientific basis for linguistics than Bopp could: *and for the same reason.* The reason is that it divorces the comparison of linguistic data from chronology.

This in turn throws light on Saussure's reticence about the theory of comparisons, already noted above. For Saussure, a linguistic atlas of the kind Gilliéron produced was simply the product of comparing the results obtained by sending round investigators with questionnaires at an arbitrarily chosen point in time. What is in principle inadequate about this has already been spelled out in the *Cours* on p.[128]; 'The object of synchronic study does not comprise everything which is simultaneous'. In other words, sending out a linguistic questionnaire to many speakers on January 1st 1900 in no way guarantees that the replies will somehow dovetail to present a picture of a synchronic system. Thus Gilliéron's approach exemplifies for Saussure an antipodean inversion of Bopp's mistake (Bopp having supposed that linguistic data could be compared *irrespective of* their coming from widely different chronological periods). The target of Saussure's attack is in both cases the same: it is a misconception of the temporality of languages.

Comparison cannot, for Saussure, be valid if it is based on this kind of misconception. The linguistic geographer's mistake here is perhaps even worse than Bopp's. For when Bopp compared a Latin form with a Sanskrit form, he did not suppose that their comparability was assured by their historical contemporaneity. On the other hand, when the linguistic geographer compares a form recorded at one locality in his survey with a form recorded at another locality he may well make precisely that assumption. (Here Saussure raises a problem for which twentieth-century sociolinguistics has yet to provide a convincing solution.)

Furthermore, it appears that geographical comparison of the type Gilliéron undertook must rely to some extent on the kind of nomenclaturism already roundly condemned in the opening pages of Part I ([97-8]). For example, a typical item of geographical linguistic comparative data ([275]) is that whereas at Douvaine the word for 'two' is *daue*, a few kilometres away it is *due*. This comparison, however, presupposes that there is a given numerical concept ('two'), and that both dialects independently have a word for it. The comparison leaves itself open to precisely the same order of objections as were earlier levelled against equating a French plural with a Sanskrit plural ([161]). For it remains to be demonstrated whether the numerical system at Douvaine is 'the same as' the numerical system at a village a few kilometres away. The fact that it is only a few kilometres away does not warrant dismissing the question as unimportant: this is the other cutting edge of Saussure's claim that in linguistic geography the distances involved are irrelevant ([271]). Exactly the same question would arise if the dialect with the form *due* happened to be spoken in Cambodia instead of at the foot of the Salève.

So there is for Saussure a sense in which all geographical developments are secondary and merely circumstantial, whereas historical change is primary. Once this underlying train of thought in Chapter III is grasped, it leads on to the otherwise startling conclusions that naturally there are no dialect boundaries (§3) and no language boundaries either (§4). How could there be? For geography plays no role whatever in the determination of an idiosynchronic system. Thus when geographical comparison appears to reveal a sharp territorial division between one language or dialect and its neighbour, what in fact it brings to light is simply the result of the obliteration in that locality of any intermediate varieties which would bridge the gap. Such 'boundaries' are 'the outcome of circumstances which have militated against the survival of gradual, imperceptible transitions' ([279]).

CHAPTER IV

Propagation of Linguistic Waves

Chapter IV shows the *Cours* at its most inscrutable. Its tone is blandly pedagogic and its examples very simple; but the lesson it presents can easily be read in the light of what has been said in previous sections of the *Cours* as a demonstration of the explanatory poverty of linguistic geography. Straight away, the linguistic geographer is presented as treating the propagation of linguistic features as if they were 'subject to the same laws as any other habit, such as fashion' ([281]). But presumably we are expected to read this in the light of the earlier highly critical remarks on p.[208] concerning the inadequacy of attempts to explain sound change as analogous to changes in fashion. In fact the general point made on p.[208] is exemplified quite specifically in this chapter in connexion with the change of *t* to *ts*. Saussure here emphasizes the importance of distinguishing 'carefully between areas of innovation, where a sound evolves solely along a temporal axis, and areas of propagation ... When a *ts* originating elsewhere is substituted for a *t*, that is not modification of a traditional prototype but imitation of a neighbouring dialect, regardless of the prototype' ([283]). Now it is clear that the linguistic atlas not only fails to indicate that distinction, but actually obscures it. Not unless we can compare a succession of linguistic maps for successive periods does it become possible to detect the likely area of innovation. In other words, diachronic information is necessary in order to interpret geographical information; and this connects up with the thesis of the preceding chapter that 'geographical diversity has to be translated into temporal diversity' ([271]).

The whole discussion of intercourse and parochialism as the forces responsible for geographical differentiation implicitly echoes the question left unanswered earlier; that of 'identifying the starting point of the imitative process' ([208]). The problem is rendered more rather than less crucial by §2, which argues that in any case intercourse and parochialism are simply positive and negative aspects of the same force. Nowhere, it appears, does linguistic geography bring to light specifically linguistic factors which explain the imitative process: on the contrary, only appeal to the vagaries of this unknown process and its mysterious mode of operation will explain the unpredictable peculiarities of geographical variation.

Furthermore, inasmuch as this is simply a general call to psychology for help (as in the case of changes in fashion), it would seem that linguistic geography even fails to bring to light any respects in which the diffusion of linguistic innovations differs from the diffusion of any other kind of 'habit' ([281]). Nor are distinctions drawn between the diffusion, say, of phonetic innovations and the diffusion of morphological features. All this highlights the extent to which linguistic geography is concerned with matters of an 'external' nature. Once again, the kind of point one might have expected the founder of linguistic structuralism to make about the spread of linguistic innovations is conspicuous by its absence. There is no suggestion, for instance, that the diffusion of feature a might facilitate the diffusion of feature b if the two were structurally related in some way; or that the motivation for 'imitation' by Dialect X of a feature in Dialect Y might have something to do with the internal structure of Dialect X at the time of borrowing.

Why are there no hints in this direction? The answer takes us back again to the Saussurean reluctance to supply structural explanations for sound change. The two cases, in fact, are exactly parallel. The *Cours* treats the geographical transmission of linguistic features in just the same way as the diachronic transmission of sound changes: that is, treats them as isolated one-off 'intrusions' into an otherwise static system. In both cases, the reason is the same: to admit any connexion between two or more such transmissional events would be tantamount to admitting that systems (or parts of systems) are themselves mobile. That in turn would mean denying, in one case, the independence of synchrony from diachrony, and in the other case the independence of co-existing *états de langue*. In terms of Saussurean theory, there is in principle no difference between the separateness of two systems in time and the separateness of two systems in space. So there can be no difference either in how features manage to be 'transferred' from one system to another. Just as Saussure denies the possibility of 'historical grammar', so he must also, for consistency's sake, deny the possibility of 'geographical grammar'.

This in turn explains the emphasis on the fact that linguistic geography falls into the domain of external linguistics. Otherwise the geographically 'visible' transitional gradations from one area to the next would call in question the very notion of a Saussurean *état de langue* as a homogeneous system. At the same time, as in the diachronic case, any *prima facie* evidence of grammar extending across *états* can be dismissed as another (this time 'geographical') illusion.

This ties in with the obvious parallel which there is for Saussure between the unpredictability of sound change and the unpredictability of geographical diffusion. Both are potentially disruptive for already established linguistic structures in the same way that meteorites from outer space are potentially disruptive for physical structures. The damage caused may necessitate extensive reconstruction. But that need cannot be assessed until the damage has actually occurred. That is why for Saussure it would make no sense to devote one chapter of the *Cours* to disruptions typically caused by geographical contact and a separate chapter to disruptions typically caused by evolution over time. These, within the Saussurean framework, are inseparable: for geographical variation simply *is* variation over time projected on to a map.

PART FIVE

Questions of Retrospective Linguistics Conclusion

CHAPTER I

The Two Perspectives of Diachronic Linguistics

Part V of the *Cours* is by any standards a disappointing conclusion to a boldly innovative book. It neither pursues the theoretical implications of what has gone before, nor even recapitulates the main Saussurean themes. The editors seem to have treated it as a ragbag into which they could put any material not, for one reason or another, incorporated into the main body of the text. The decision to treat this residue as constituting Part V, rather than as a simple Appendix (in the same way as pp.[251-60]) is puzzling; but no less puzzling than why the material in question had not already been incorporated into earlier chapters.

The discussion of the two perspectives of diachronic linguistics rightly belongs in Part III, and it is difficult to see any reason for not having included it at that point, particularly since the topic was broached as early as p.[128], and the terms 'prospective' and 'retrospective' already introduced there. Perhaps it might be argued on behalf of the editors that the choice which a linguist has to make between 'setting out the history of a language in detail following the chronological sequence' and the alternative of 'proceeding retrospectively against the chronological sequence of events' ([292]) is merely a second-order question of convenience and practicality, and is therefore rightly kept separate from the basic problems of diachronic linguistics treated in Part III. Nevertheless, the chapter also has theoretical implications, in view of Saussure's claim that in linguistics 'it is the viewpoint adopted which creates the object' ([23]).

The prospective and retrospective viewpoints in diachronic linguistics do not converge to create a single object. They create two different objects. This is clearly shown by the examples given on p.[294]. A prospective set of statements about what happened to Latin vowels in French cannot automatically be converted by a 'reversal' of viewpoint into an equivalent retrospective set of statements about the sources of French vowels in Latin. 'A study of sound changes will present a very different picture depending on which perspective is adopted' ([293-4]). A 'very different' picture is not just the same picture seen from the diametrically opposite point of view. This emerges even more clearly from Saussure's morphological examples. The fact that such disparate French forms as *aimé, fini, clos*, etc. have in common that they represent the ultimate development of descendants of forms originally containing the Proto-Indo-European suffix *-to-* has no place in the retrospective history of French at all. The 'development of *-to-* in French' is a 'fact' or set of 'facts' created solely by taking Proto-Indo-European as a point of departure and adopting a prospective viewpoint (which in this case includes deciding to treat the history of *-to-* as prolonged indefinitely into the future by means of any forms which continue forms themselves continuing forms which originally contained *-to-*). Thus *-to-* continues to have a prospective history long after it has disappeared, and will continue to do so long into the future. This history corresponds to no linguistic reality *either* for speakers of French themselves *or* for someone writing a retrospective history of the French language (which does not go back beyond Latin, when *-to-* had already ceased to exist).

This is also the lesson to be drawn from the comparison with geology ([293]), the point of which the editors seem to have missed entirely. In geology, the adoption of a prospective or retrospective viewpoint makes no difference, because either yields an account of the history of the earth's crust with the same factual content. In linguistics this is not the case, because where languages are concerned the facts are not, like the facts of geology, given in advance.

CHAPTER II

Earliest Languages and Prototypes

Chapter II returns to the theme of comparison. The first paragraph takes up again the criticism of Bopp and the comparativists. The objection is that linguistic comparison is not only worthless but potentially misleading when divorced from history. Thus quite different pictures emerge from comparing the Indo-European languages (i) on the assumption that all are descended from an unattested common ancestor, and (ii) on the (mistaken) assumption that Sanskrit was the parent of the others. This spells out in greater detail an objection voiced as early as the first chapter of the *Cours*, where the comparativists were taxed with not having grasped the fact that comparison alone offers no basis for drawing conclusions ([16-17]).

The chapter goes on to attack the 'muddled notion of antiquity' which results from conflating the question of the date of the earliest written records of a language with the question of the archaism of the forms it preserves. The connexion between this and the first paragraph of the chapter, apart from the fact that both errors were committed by the same scholars studying Sanskrit, is presumably that both can be seen as variants of the same basic failure in linguistics to ask what can legitimately be compared with what.

CHAPTER III

Reconstructions

Although the title of Chapter III and its position in the text suggest that it should be read simply as a further amplification of points relating to the methodology of retrospective linguistics, the points in question turn out to be not merely of some theoretical significance, but theoretically controversial into the bargain.

The question at issue in §1 is the theoretical status of the items which result from those comparisons which are not merely the 'sterile' ([299]) comparisons of comparative philology previously condemned. In other words, by placing comparison in an appropriate 'chronological perspective' ([299]), is it possible to arrive at reconstructed forms which have some degree of scientific value; and if so, what exactly is it? These pages, among the most fascinating in the *Cours*, show Saussure grappling once again with the problem of historical 'reality'.

Now the vacillations are more agonized and protracted than before. Already committed to the thesis that in linguistics the viewpoint creates the object, Saussure is desperately reluctant nevertheless to concede that the objects reconstructed are merely 'abstractions' which reflect the methods and assumptions of the linguist. For that is precisely the objection to the 'sterile' linguistic comparison already dismissed as worthless. On the other hand, how can the linguist *qua* scientist reasonably claim that hypotheses about the forms of languages long since extinct and never recorded at all have exactly the same status as descriptions of *états de langue* manifested in the observable *parole* of living speakers?

In this chapter, Saussure hops uncomfortably from one foot to the other. In §1 it is conceded that to say that, for instance, the Proto-Indo-European word for 'horse' was *akvas* is simply a summation of a certain set of hypotheses. 'The aim of reconstruction is thus not to restore a form for its own sake, which would be in any case rather ridiculous, but to crystallize and condense a series of conclusions which are held to be correct in the light of the evidence currently available. In a word, it records the progress made to date in our science' ([301]). On this 'nominalist' view, *akvas* designates nothing at all: it merely expresses in an abstract form certain opinions held by modern scholars. So the statement that the Proto-Indo-European word for 'horse' was *akvas* has, apart from a certain formal symmetry, virtually nothing in common with the statement that the French word for 'horse' is *cheval*. For the latter, presumably, is not a hypothesis of any kind, but an observational statement of fact.

Saussure's dilemma is that as a theorist he cannot afford to admit that, in spite of its form, the statement that the Proto-Indo-European word for 'horse' was *akvas* – whether accurate or not – is not a synchronic statement, but merely a disguised reformulation of several separate diachronic statements. For that would be tantamount to saying that no synchronic analysis of dead languages is possible; or, at the very least, to blurring in those cases the very distinction between synchronic and diachronic studies which he is committed to maintaining as absolute.

Blatant nominalism will in any case not satisfy the historical realist whom the reader has already recognized as the author of the earlier chapters on diachronic linguistics. It comes as no surprise, therefore, to find that in §2 a rather different tune is being sung. In this section, the question is presented as being to what extent a 'degree of certainty' can be attached to the reconstructed forms which summarize sets of hypotheses. Presumably a reconstruction of which the elements are only 50 per cent certain ranks lower than a reconstruction of which the elements are 75 per cent certain. In other words, the degree of certainty to be assigned to *akvas* is a total arrived at by adding up the certainty attached to the separate hypotheses underlying the five phonetic units involved. Even if each hypothesis were wrong, Saussure appears to take the view that it would at least be certain that there were only five units to be right or wrong about ([303]). So even if *akvas* as a set of individual hypotheses incorporated mistakes on every single count (i.e. even if the Proto-Indo-Europeans actually called a horse *igfoz*) nevertheless the reconstruction *akvas* itself could still be awarded a degree of certainty *qua* synchronic statement.

As an attempt to have the best of both worlds, this is brave but bungled. In the first place, introducing the notion of 'degree of certainty' fudges the issue, inasmuch as certainty can be ambiguously construed as (i) a matter of being objectively correct, and (ii) a matter of being subjectively confident. Only if the two are conflated does §2 of this chapter offer any possibility of a solution to the problem posed in §1. For certainty of the order of 100 per cent of type (ii) affords no guarantee at all of certainty of type (i).

Second, if a comparable criterion of certainty were adopted throughout synchronic linguistics, the notion of describing an *état de langue* would be reduced to absurdity. The statement that the French for 'horse' is *chufor* would be accorded a certain degree of descriptive validity (i.e. insofar as *chufor* has the same number of consonants and vowels as the French word for 'horse'). The fact that there is no French word *chufor* could not be held to invalidate it.

Third, it is this attempt to rescue some semblance of synchronic 'reality' for historical hypotheses which forces Saussure to opt for claiming that the task of Proto-Indo-European reconstruction is not to identify the words actually used (in the sense that *cheval* identifies a word actually used in French) but merely to identify the abstract units which enter into their composition. Thus 'one could designate the phonetic elements of a reconstructed language simply by figures or symbols of any kind' ([303]). The figures or symbols in question would be defined simply in terms of contrast and recurrence. Thus a sound could, 'without specifying its phonetic character, be classified and designated by a number in a table of Proto-Indo-European sounds' ([303]).

If this proposal is to be taken at face value, then it might seem that according to Saussure the statement that the Proto-Indo-European word for 'horse' was *akvas* actually goes too far. All that the linguist needs is some such statement as that the Proto-Indo-European word for 'horse' was '15819' (where '1' is defined as 'the same sound, however pronounced, which occurs in both first and fourth positions in the following words ...') Thus we are led to a treatment of sound systems (retrospectively attributed to Saussure by some of his successors) in which the sound system is simply an abstract matrix of contrasts, about the phonetic implementation of which nothing – in theory – need be known at all. But to go this far is to go further than the *Cours* itself takes us.

It is important to see that for Saussure hypotheses about Proto-Indo-European sounds are not 'pure abstractions' because of the realist position he adopts in phonetics. He is committed to the general proposition that the *signifiants* of all languages used a fixed inventory of sounds ([303]) and furthermore to the proposition that 'given any word, one can distinguish clearly its constituent sounds, how many of them there are, and where they begin and end' ([302]). The basic set of sound types, for Saussure, is determined by elementary physiological possibilities of the vocal apparatus, as described in detail in the Appendix to the Introduction of the *Cours*. Therefore, when a Proto-Indo-European sound is identified as being 'the sound which occurs in the following positions in the following words', this is a description which can ultimately, at least in principle, be given a concrete interpretation by reference to the chart of physiologically possible sounds. The statement is to the effect that one of these sounds recurs time and again in the positions stated. The 'sameness' is ultimately a physiological sameness of a known type, even if the precise details are debatable (but within known parameters). In other words, the ultimate justification for such reconstructions is that we know (or assume we know) what sounds the Proto-Indo-European vocal apparatus could produce. If we had any reason for thinking that in fact Proto-Indo-European had been a language of Martian invaders, producing sounds by means of vocal organs with unknown properties, that justification would automatically fall. To claim to identify a Martian word as '15819', in the absence of any chart of Martian phonetics, would, in Saussure's terms, be quite meaningless. There would not even be any guarantee that Martian vocal signs were linear. But if we assume that Proto-Indo-European *signifiants* were linear and that the elements linearly concatenated were drawn from a physiological inventory of known types, we rescue even inaccurate synchronic statements about the word for 'horse' from the limbo of 'pure abstraction'.

CHAPTER IV

Linguistic Evidence in Anthropology and Prehistory

This chapter may be looked upon as taking up the remarks which conclude Chapter II of the Introduction, referring to the 'prejudices, illusions and fantasies' of all kinds which the study of language has fostered, and laying it down as the linguist's task to denounce them. The scepticism Saussure expresses here concerning the extent to which linguistic evidence can throw light on questions of anthropology, ethnography and prehistory clearly relates to his own theoretical position on the relevant linguistic issues. Thus his denial of any inherent connexion between language and race (§1), coupled with his acceptance that language is an important constituent factor in cultural unity (§2), reflects his theoretical commitment to the two propositions that languages are social institutions, not biological legacies, and that they are social institutions based on arbitrary signs. The section on linguistic paleontology (§3), with its warnings against leaping too hastily to conclusions about specific cultural practices, is a disguised sermon about the reliability of historical reconstructions. Most characteristic of all is the refusal in §4 to accept that particular features of linguistic structure may be considered reflections of the 'group mentality' of the language users. Here the reasons offered reflect quite openly Saussure's adherence to the view that sound changes act 'blindly', and that every linguistic system is constructed on the basis of the materials fortuitously bequeathed by random historical processes. Thus he points out, for example, that the Old French construction *le cor Roland* emerged 'purely by chance', and argues that the parallel construction in Semitic may well have done likewise. 'The psychological characteristics of the language community count for little as against facts like the fall of a final vowel or a modification of stress' ([311-12]).

Arguments of this kind throw an interesting if indirect light on the question of the relations between linguistics and other disciplines. Thus when Saussure, speaking *qua* linguist, denies there is any linguistic evidence to support the view that the psychological characteristics of the community determine certain features of linguistic structure, that denial is in fact a disguised assertion of a particular theoretical position within linguistics. It is not a question of what the 'linguistic evidence' shows at all. For the linguistic evidence is equally consonant with the opposite view. Indeed, there is no difficulty at all in principle in reconciling Saussure's claim that sound changes act 'blindly' with the theory that the 'group mentality' will nevertheless favour certain ways of constructing a new linguistic system out of the debris inherited from the past. Saussure, in short, never addresses the question of what counts as linguistic evidence on such matters: for to take that question seriously would be already to concede that there might be systematic factors at work other than those allowed for within the conceptual framework of Saussurean linguistic theory.

CHAPTER V

Language Families and Linguistic Types

The concluding argument of the preceding chapter is here reaffirmed and generalized. It applies, claims Saussure, to the whole question of language typology. 'A language, as we have seen, is not directly subject to the control of the minds of its speakers. Let us conclude by emphasizing one of the consequences of this principle: no family of languages rightly belongs once and for all to a particular linguistic type' ([313]). What 'we have seen', however, is something of a rather different order; namely, that Saussure cannot accept the idea that in different communities there might be different but permanent psychological factors at work which restrict in different ways the available options for combining *signifiants* with *signifiés*. The reason for this reluctance is not difficult to see. To admit the possible existence of such factors would mean acknowledging restrictions on the basic principle of *l'arbitraire du signe*; and Saussurean linguistic theory makes no provision for such restrictions.

Again Saussure's attitude towards 'linguistic evidence' on a point like this speaks for itself. Given a case like the Semitic languages where, as he admits, over a very long period of time the 'persistence of certain characteristics' of linguistic structure is very striking ([315]), Saussure produces two weak counterarguments: (i) that particular characteristics analogous to those which look as if they are 'permanent' in Semitic may appear as relatively transitory features in other languages or language families, and (ii) that even in the Semitic languages one finds occasional exceptions to these supposedly 'permanent' features. By implication, this presumably means that the only features which Saussure would accept as *prima facie* evidence of permanent characteristics inherent in a language family would be: (i) features admitting no exceptions whatever, and (ii) features not found in any other language. In other words, the evidential demands are placed at a level where there is no prospect of meeting them. The question as to why the Semitic languages have preserved these particular characteristics is dismissed with the quasi-tautological remark that this simply means they have undergone less change than many other languages. 'There are no unchangeable features: permanence is due to chance' ([316]). This the reader will recognize as a reiteration of the thesis earlier advanced on pp.[129-34] that languages are not governed by diachronic laws.

*   *   *

The famous concluding sentence of the *Cours*

la linguistique a pour unique et véritable objet la langue envisagée en elle-même et pour elle-même

has been rejected as not authentically Saussurean. Since there appears to be no textual basis for it in the manuscript sources, Saussure's editors have been held responsible, and, by implication, responsible too for the fact that it was subsequently quoted as evidence in support of attributing to Saussure a somewhat narrow and 'exclusive' concept of linguistics (de Mauro 1972: 476-7, n.305). Seen in this light, then, it appears as a final and ineradicable blot on the editorial copybook. Bally and Sechehaye not merely exceeded their brief, but in the end proved incompetent to formulate a clear, unmisleading statement of Saussure's teaching.

'Nothing in the manuscript sources indicates that Saussure uttered this famous pronouncement or, even less, clearly, that it represents the "fundamental idea" of his teaching' (de Mauro 1972: 476). The 'even less' (*encore moins*) epitomizes a philological obsession which has dominated readings of Saussure for the past quarter of a century. Nothing can possibly be authentically Saussurean unless textual evidence other than the *Cours* can be cited in support (however second-hand, implausible or manifestly dubious it may be). The philologists would be fouling their own Saussurean nest, however, to attribute to the editors totally unmotivated fantasies or inventions. It has to be conceded that Bally and Sechehaye did not make the conclusion up '*e nihilo*' (de Mauro 1972: 476). Hence the hypothesis that perhaps 'they thought they were writing something in line with the principle stated on p.[25]: *il faut se placer de prime abord sur le terrain de la langue et la prendre pour norme de toutes les autres manifestations du langage*' (de Mauro 1972: 476).

A simple philological point which this philological reading overlooks is that the phrase *unique et véritable objet* of this last sentence in the *Cours* ([317]) clearly echoes the phrase *véritable et unique objet* ([13]) in the opening sentence of the same text three hundred pages earlier. Whether the two are syntagmatically related may be open to dispute. That they are associatively related can hardly be a subject of contention. Could this be a 'mere coincidence' in a text like the *Cours*? (This particular conjunction of adjectives and nouns occurs nowhere else in the intervening chapters.) The reader will recall that the opening chapter identified various stages through which linguistics had passed *before* identifying its *véritable et unique objet*. That implicitly opens up a question-and-answer format for the *Cours*. Question: 'What is this *objet*?' The question, raised on the first page and then pursued in all its ramifications throughout the following chapters, is eventually answered on the final page. Not only did subsequent Saussurean exegesis object to the eventual answer, but patently failed to recognize the pertinent question.

What might the shades of the editors reply to this ultimate vote of no confidence by posterity? That an attempt to answer the main question raised by someone's teaching is not to be confused with giving a synopsis of that teaching, much less with passing a verdict on it? Or that the full complexity of Saussure's teaching had already been amply reflected in preceding chapters? Perhaps all the reply needed to posterity would be to point out that posterity itself had for decades failed to see anything unSaussurean in that *explicit*. The controversial concluding sentence doubtless has its ambiguities: but they match, with masterly exactness, the ambiguities of the *Cours* itself.

PART TWO

Saussurean Linguistics

… the chauvinism of science is a much greater problem than the problem
of intellectual pollution.

P. Feyerabend

CHAPTER I

Strategy and Programme

Many people must have come to the end of reading the *Cours de linguistique générale* with the uncomfortable feeling that they did not quite know whether they had understood the message or not, in spite of having grasped various general principles and particular arguments along the way. General linguistics, as presented by the *Cours*, seems to emerge as a form of inquiry which is simultaneously possible and impossible. Can the reader even go on to ask: 'But which is it?'

Part of the difficulty is that in spite of its title what Saussure's *Cours de linguistique générale* offers is not a course but a charter. The programme itself is fixed only in broad outline. What is astonishing about the genesis of the text is not that the editors subsequently took material from three sets of university lectures and turned it into a manifesto for an as yet untried approach to language, but, on the contrary, that the manifesto was formulated as lectures for students in the first place. That academic context alone, nevertheless, tells us a great deal.

It is hardly surprising that what emerge as predominant questions in the *Cours* are precisely the questions which would be foremost in the mind of someone who had spent a lifetime teaching the kind of syllabus accepted as constituting Indo-European linguistic studies in the latter half of the nineteenth century, and was not only worried by its inadequacies, but foresaw the possibility that disciplines such as psychology, physiology, sociology and anthropology might well sponsor forms of linguistic inquiry which would be potential rivals for recognition as the modern science of language. This determined in advance that any eventual Saussurean programme would need to reconcile (i) the need to carve out a defensible scientific territory for linguistics, and (ii) the need to partition that territory internally in such a way as to accommodate within it certain traditional vested interests. These joint interdisciplinary and intradisciplinary requirements circumscribed any answer to what we may call Saussure's 'primary theoretical problems'. Nowhere is there any indication that Saussure had the visionary breadth to found general linguistics *de novo*, in the sense of asking himself where and how the human sciences of the twentieth century would need inquiry into language to be directed. In the *Cours* there is not even a breath of academic ecumenicalism. To the extent that Saussurean linguistics is radical, it is radically conservative.

That would at the same time explain one of the most striking omissions in the whole of the *Cours*: that a work devoted to laying the foundations of general linguistic theory never once addresses the question 'What do we need general linguistic theory for?' The omission tells us a great deal about the Saussurean concept of science. The hidden premiss seems to be that sciences simply are endeavours to bring together and interrelate under a few general laws or principles as many disparate facts as possible pertaining to one subject. The idea that perhaps such an endeavour makes better sense in some subjects than in others, and therefore might need a rather different kind of justification in linguistics than, say, in physics is totally lacking in the *Cours*. Saussure appears to assume, simply, that as all-embracing a systematization as possible is automatically desirable and of value for its own sake. Be that as it may, he was certainly right in thinking that no such systematization had been produced in the nineteenth century.

Although the point of departure for Saussurean theorizing is dissatisfaction with the inheritance of nineteenth-century language studies, and the realization that 'the fundamental problems of general linguistics ... still await a solution' ([19]), the *Cours* at no point claims to provide that solution. But at least, as a first step, it seeks to provide an analysis of what the problems are, and to propose some general principles on the basis of which they might be tackled. That, clearly, is as far as Bally and Sechehaye saw their colleague's thinking as having progressed by the time of his death ([10]); and nothing in the subsequently published manuscript material suggests that judgment was wrong. Consequently it would have been a misrepresentation to attempt in the *Cours* a definitive systematization which removed all doubts and precluded certain possibilities of development. Over a period of years, the possibilities of development and the consequent balance of emphasis in the Saussurean conceptual schema for general linguistics doubtless varied in Saussure's own mind. This, again, the editors were fully aware of: as they say in their Preface, Saussure was someone for whom thinking was a constant process of intellectual renewal ([8-9]), and the variations between the three courses of lectures which he gave over the years 1907-11 bear them out. What they were too modest to mention was a possibility that must certainly have occurred to them as they drafted the *Cours*: that such a draft as theirs might well have helped Saussure, had he lived, to see more clearly just how far his own thinking had progressed, and exactly what there was 'still awaiting a solution'. On the other hand, what they are not likely to have foreseen is that the very incompleteness – even vagueness – of that state of Saussure's thought which the *Cours* represents would subsequently prove one of its major interdisciplinary attractions, and enhance its potential as a stimulus for other disciplines than linguistics.

Saussure had certainly progressed as far as seeing how the two basic needs of his programme could be reconciled. The 'territorial' need in any case could not be satisfied by defining the boundaries of linguistics in terms of subject-matter; for, as subject-matter, language and linguistic phenomena were already shared with other disciplines. What was required here was to identify something essentially 'linguistic' which other disciplines could not plausibly claim to study, in spite of the overlap of subject-matter. At the same time, the 'internal' need was to accommodate within this territory topics of the kind which Indo-Europeanists and dialectologists had already established as focal points of scholarly attention. In short, the programme was one which would rescue the subject from the clutches of historians and philologists, but at the same time establish it in a scientific enclave where it was safe from the encroachments of physiologists, psychologists, sociologists and others.

The base-line of the programmatic answer which the *Cours* proposes is the fundamental distinction drawn between *la langue* and *la parole*. Linguistics is proclaimed to be first and foremost a science of *la langue*. This leads straight to the question *Qu'est-ce que la langue?* In one sense, it strikes the reader as a very odd question indeed; and inevitably so. For initially we have no guarantee, as Calvet observes (Calvet 1975: 139), that it is a question which is meaningful at all. The *Cours*, it should be noted, does not propose *langue* as a linguistic technical term (although in fact for Saussure it is) and then offer to define it. On the contrary, there is a strenuous denial that *la langue* is an illusory abstraction, conjured up by terminological sleight of hand ([31]). This is because for Saussure the claims of a subject to be a science depend essentially on whether or not what it studies really exists. (That is precisely the burden of his complaint against nineteenth-century linguistics. It presupposed belief in all kinds of linguistic entities which do not exist: languages which remain 'the same' in spite of splitting up into different dialects; words which remain 'the same' in spite of changing their pronunciation and meaning; grammatical paradigms which remain 'the same' in spite of losing their flexional distinctions; and so on.) For Saussure, it will not do to anchor linguistic reality to samenesses which exist merely retrospectively in the eye of the historian. Hence, 'What is *la langue*?' *has* to be presented as a factual question (on a par with 'What is electricity?' or 'What is the national debt?'). If there is no such thing as *la langue*, then it will not do as the basis for any kind of science at all.

So *la langue* has to be something real, something about which general truths can be discovered (despite the notorious diversity of actual languages), and something which is essentially involved in the social practices and psychological events normally reckoned to be linguistic in nature. Unfortunately, that conjunction of requirements still does not automatically pick out any one thing which can be identified as *la langue*, and Saussure is therefore obliged simply to postulate that *la langue* is somehow both a social institution in the community and at the same time a cognitive system in the mind of the individual. This awkward equation compels Saussure, in spite of his dislike of abstractions, to 'dematerialize' the linguistic sign and treat *la langue* merely as a structure constituted by a set of relations. For only at that level can it plausibly be claimed that the social institution and the individual cognitive system are 'really' one and the same thing.

It is this same equation which leads to what was later called the 'Saussurean paradox' (Labov 1972: 186) in descriptive linguistics. If *la langue* is stored inside every speaker's head, the testimony of a single individual in principle suffices as data for the linguist's description of *la langue* (even if – and perhaps ideally if – the witness and the linguist are one and the same person). By contrast, data for the description of *parole* can be obtained only by observing speech events as and when they occur in social interaction, because such events are not already stored in the heads of any individuals, even the participants themselves. This conclusion is said to be paradoxical because it reverses the basic Saussurean characterization of *langue* as social, as opposed to *parole* as individual ([30]): for it turns out that to study *la langue* it will suffice to study the individual, whereas to study *la parole* will require collecting evidence from the community.

Whether this so-called 'Saussurean paradox' detected by Labov is paradoxical at all has, however, been questioned. According to Pateman, the paradox is 'little more than an index of Labov's naive conceptions of scientific activity' (Pateman 1983: 113). But *ad hominem* rebuttals of this order merely obscure what is at issue, which is neither a verbal dispute about the use of the term *paradox*, nor a question of the validity of anyone's view of 'scientific activity'. The point is that, whether we call it a 'paradox' or not, the *Cours* appears to be committed to an account of how the individual acquires *la langue* which is at odds with a programme for linguistics which claims that '*la langue*, as distinct from *la parole*, is an object that may be studied independently' ([31]).

More precisely, the 'Saussurean paradox' arises from a conjunction of two separate incompatibilities: (i) between 'average' and 'aggregate' concepts of *la langue*, (ii) between either of these and the role assigned to *la langue* in the Saussurean speech circuit. The latter demands uniformity between speaker and hearer: otherwise communication breaks down. But the account given of *la langue* as a social product of *parole* does not yield uniformity. Saussure hesitates between saying that *la langue* is a communal average (*une sorte de moyenne* ([29])) established between individuals, and saying that it is a communal aggregate (*la somme des images verbales emmagasinées chez tous les individus* ([30])), without appearing to realize *either* that these two are quite different concepts of *la langue*, *or* that neither offers any guarantee that speaker and hearer operate with identical cognitive systems for the purposes of *parole*.

Furthermore, neither the 'average' concept of *la langue* nor the 'aggregate' concept supplies any theoretical warrant for a methodology which assumes that in order to study *la langue* it will suffice to study the individual. For it is impossible to identify a communal average without studying the evidence taken from a reasonable cross-section of the community, and it is impossible to identify a communal aggregate without studying all the evidence the community has to offer. These methodological principles hold regardless of whether we are studying language or any other social practice. But in the *Cours* all such difficulties are simply brushed under the broadest of theoretical carpets by a straight equation between social institution and cognitive system.

The 'Saussurean paradox' is one in a series of what we may term Saussure's 'secondary theoretical problems'. These are the problems internal to the Saussurean programme itself. How – and how satisfactorily – some of them are dealt with has already been queried at various points in the preceding commentary on the text of the *Cours*. For the moment it should be noted that in this instance, as in others, the 'internal' problem arises because of an attempt to deal with an 'external' difficulty: here it is the equation between cognitive system and social institution which is forced on Saussure by the need to present (Saussurean) linguistics as a single, unified science with its own autonomy. If *la langue* were not *both* cognitive system *and* social institution, its study would have to be split into at least two separate enterprises, each answerable to a different set of theoretical assumptions.

Having postulated this unified socio-cognitive entity called *la langue* as the primary focus of linguistic investigation, Saussure next has to map out the internal partition of linguistics and show how all aspects of linguistic study are catered for. For this purpose, the initial dichotomy between *langue* and *parole* has to be supplemented by a further dichotomy between synchrony and diachrony. Thus room can be allowed for the study of linguistic change and of dialectal variation, but without the danger of relapsing into the chaos of nineteenth-century failures to distinguish *faits de langue* from *faits de parole*. However, the necessity to integrate the two dichotomies itself generates more 'secondary theoretical problems'.

A certain preoccupation with this new set of secondary problems surfaces intermittently throughout the *Cours*. It gives rise to the impression that this is a text written by someone with a nagging obsession about time, and specifically about the relationship between temporality and systematicity. Ideally, one feels, Saussure would have liked to be able to adopt the extremely elegant solution of treating time as the common dimension which orders all the relevant sets of relations which linguistics has to deal with. But there are various reasons why this will not work. Chief among them is what we may call the 'real time' trap: sometimes temporal relations match linguistic relations, but sometimes they do not. Thus, for example, it is possible to have two languages, of which L1 is still in use centuries after L2 is defunct, even though L2 represents an *état de langue* which is the 'successor' of L1. Saussure is therefore obliged to construe linguistic time relatively to systems, and distinguish an *axe des successivités* from an *axe des simultanéités*. Even this will not quite work, because 'real time' simultaneity does not guarantee systematicity. So the notion of synchrony has to be replaced ultimately by that of idiosynchrony. Avoiding the 'real time' trap by resorting to linguistic time unfortunately means that the orthogonal axes no longer parallel those which plot the history of language communities: but fictionally they are deemed to. We end up with a *Cours* in which the debris of that ideally elegant treatment of time, uniting linguistic events with linguistic systems in perfect theoretical harmony, remains visibly scattered throughout the text (the failure to discard the terms *synchronique* and *diachronique* in spite of their inappropriateness; the attempt to show that geographical variation reduces to temporal variation; the survival of succession in real time as the principle of linearity, etc.).

It is another aspect of the 'real time' trap which obliges Saussure to adopt what Collingwood might have called a compromise view of linguistic history: a compromise, that is, between 'substantialism' and 'anti-substantialism' (Collingwood 1946: 42ff.). Substantialism is the view that the particular time-bound acts and events which constitute the material of history flow from something which itself remains changeless throughout (a city, a nation, an institution, etc.) The opposite view treats this hypothetically changeless entity which allegedly survives through the changes brought by time as a fiction, myth, category mistake, or something similar. Now for Saussure an *état de langue* does not change simply because over a period of time a great variety of acts of *parole* are performed by a great variety of speakers: on the contrary, it may remain unchanged for generations. To that extent, Saussure takes a substantialist view of the linguistic institution itself. However, there are for Saussure certain historical changes which it must be impossible for an *état de langue* to survive. Otherwise twentieth-century French would still represent the same *état de langue* as second-century Latin. So there is a limit to Saussurean substantialism on one level, even while on another level an unbroken continuity of *parole* between generations of speakers is hypothesized. What is it that can survive unchanged to establish that continuity across successive *états de langue*? Merely linguistic material or substance, according to Saussure; but not linguistic form. Thus it makes perfectly good (Saussurean) sense to say that the *t* of the Latin *terra* has survived in French *terre*, even though the French consonant system is quite different from the Latin consonant system. This is rather like saying that the material of a Roman wall can survive in a twentieth-century French building, even though its architectural context and function may have altered entirely. But any variety of substantialism which claims that elements of linguistic form survive from Latin to modern French Saussure will dismiss as based on historical illusion.

Saussure's compromise view of history is also dictated by the internal partitioning requirements of his programme. A theorist who took an uncompromising anti-substantialist position would have to maintain not only that the word *terra* does not survive from Latin into French (which is Saussure's claim) but that – *pace* Saussure – the initial sound *t* does not survive either. According to the anti-substantialist, the 'survival' of the *t* would be just as much a historian's illusion as the 'survival' of the Latin word in French *terre*: for since neither words nor speech sounds are at all like bricks, stones or other physical objects, it is absurd to claim that sounds can survive whereas words cannot. Thorough-going anti-substantialism of this order, theoretically legitimate though it might be, would leave no slot in the linguistic programme for any traditional form of historical linguistics. This is why Saussure cannot accept it. His compromise at least allows historical phonetics to continue as a 'non-illusory' form of inquiry, and this was bound to please all those linguists who regarded the working out of Indo-European 'sound laws' as one of the great intellectual triumphs of the nineteenth century. At the same time, the compromise allows Saussure to deny the validity of the other much-acclaimed achievement of nineteenth-century comparative and historical linguistics, 'historical grammar'. In this way, the Saussurean programme does not reject historical linguistics altogether, but teaches it a lesson and puts it firmly in its place within a new theoretical framework, based on the rigid separation of synchronic facts from diachronic facts.

Calvet's diagnosis (Calvet 1975: 61) hits the nail on the head when it describes structuralism in linguistics as being born of a rejection of *linguistique externe*, and a desire to abstract *la langue* from the social practice in which it is manifested. Well and good, *provided that we interpret this diagnosis in terms of the exigencies of an academic programme*, and not as reflecting some personal ideological stance on the part of Saussure. Otherwise we confuse the original rationale of a linguistic theory with the reasons for its runaway success in the subsequent intellectual history of the twentieth century. It would be unpardonably naive to suppose that the fortunes of Saussurean structuralism had anything to do with the world's sudden interest in the internal affairs of the academic conduct of language studies. That would be like attributing the success of the Beatles to a worldwide fascination with the local culture of Liverpool.

Perhaps as important as any of the factors which Calvet mentions is simply the extent to which Saussurean structuralism appealed to the profound anti-historicism of the twentieth century. Like the twentieth century's most influential theories in all fields (in art, architecture, politics, sociology, etc.) what Saussure urged could be read as legitimizing a rejection of the cultural past. The historical process as portrayed in the *Cours* is one of disruption of old linguistic systems and their replacement by totally new systems. These new systems are not just the old systems patched up, adapted or transformed: they are original whole creations in their own right, and the very condition for their existence is the collapse of previous systems. Moreover, since all linguistic systems are independent, there is no sense in which one system owes anything to another. Analyses valid for earlier systems are totally inapplicable to their successors: indeed, the most profound analytic mistake that can be made for Saussure is to continue to apply classifications and criteria that are derived from an earlier system, as if the later system were the same. The only reality of a system is the reality it has for its present users: to this reality the past contributes nothing. This implied rejection of the nineteenth century's insistence on always looking back to the past in order to explain the present is, as much as any other single feature, what established Saussure's credentials as a thoroughly 'modern' theorist.

The Saussurean identification of synchrony with the viewpoint of current language users ([117]ff.) is a further factor which requires *la langue* to be construed in terms of an equation between social institution and individual cognitive system. For the working of the social institution in its totality is something which the individual speaker is *in no position to observe*, unless the linguistic community is a very small one indeed. In larger communities, however, we cannot as individuals going about our daily linguistic business claim to be in contact with all our fellow speakers. In that sense, an individual can no more command a view of the totality of *parole* in the community than of the totality of the other social transactions being conducted. The guarantee that all speakers are speaking 'the same language' cannot come from anyone's acquaintance with the totality of the community's *parole*, since in many communities no individual can claim anything remotely approaching such an acquaintance. Hence the need to postulate that somehow all speakers have already acquired a standard representation of *la langue* inside their heads 'rather like a dictionary of which each individual has an identical copy' ([38]). How they manage to do this is something of a mystery, but it is simply assumed that somehow or other they do.

Without this assumption, clearly, the descriptive statements of linguistics could never be scientific statements in the sense in which Saussure was trying to establish linguistics as a science. The reasons why take us back again to the 'Saussurean paradox'. If access to *la langue* could not be obtained through the testimony of individuals, there would be strictly nothing scientific to be said about English, or about French; for since no linguist could possibly set about the Herculean task of observing – let alone analysing – the totality of English or French speech, descriptions would be simply provisional codifications of minute fragments of *parole*. No generalizations about *la langue* would be possible. These are the considerations which dictate Saussure's choice of a model of speech communication.

CHAPTER II
Saussure's Theory of Communication

Every linguistic theory presupposes a theory of communication; and Saussurean linguistics is no exception. However minimal or inexplicitly formulated such a theory of communication may be, it has an essential role to play because nothing else can provide the conceptual underpinnings necessary for a more detailed account of how an interactive social activity like language works. If Saussure had called his *circuit de la parole* instead a *circuit de la communication orale*, this might have avoided the unfortunate impression that the reader is expected to accept *la parole* on trust as a process, before the theorist can supply any clear articulation of the distinction between *la parole* and *la langue*. Calling it a *circuit de la parole* sounds suspiciously like taking one term of a theoretical dichotomy for granted, in order thereby to define the other. If, on the other hand, we read the speech circuit as a general theory of oral communication, it does not prejudge the dichotomy in advance. Furthermore, the place of importance which the circuit is given right at the beginning of the *Cours* would then be seen as the logical place to introduce general theoretical assumptions about a communicational whole which involves both *langue* and *parole*.

The theory of oral communication which Saussure's speech circuit summarizes was by no means new, and did not originate within the disciplinary confines of linguistics. The *Cours* makes no reference to these origins, but as a matter of intellectual history they can scarcely be open to doubt. When the speech-circuit model is scrutinized, it becomes clear enough that although Saussure explicitly divided the circuit into its physiological, psychological and physical sections, those divisions were not based upon contemporary findings in psychology, physiology or physics. At the time the *Cours* was published, the neurological, motor and acoustic processes involved in speech were not sufficiently well understood to offer the basis for such a model. Apart from one passing reference to the work of Broca (which, as noted earlier, is used to support a merely negative conclusion), nothing suggests that Saussure's analysis of oral communication was in any way founded on nineteenth-century advances in the sciences dealing with the actual mechanisms of speech. Its ancestry is more venerable.

Saussure's speech circuit is essentially a schematic summary, not of the directly observable facts of speech activity, nor even of unobservable micro-events hypothesized as taking place during speech, but of a psychological explanation of oral communication of the kind propounded in its classic form in the seventeenth century by John Locke, and sometimes called the 'translation theory' of understanding (Parkinson 1977). Saussure simply takes over two basic claims of this old psychological theory and incorporates them as premises in his model. These are: (i) that communication is a process of 'telementation' (that is, of the transference of thoughts from one human mind to another), and (ii) that a necessary and sufficient condition for successful telementation is that the process of communication, by whatever mechanisms it employs, should result in the hearer's thoughts being identical with the speaker's. Although this theory is perhaps most clearly expounded by Locke in its application to language, elements of it can be traced back much further in the philosophical tradition. Plato's theory of forms, for example, as Cornford (1935:9) points out, reveals an 'underlying assumption ... that every common name must have a fixed meaning, which we think of when we hear the name spoken: speaker and hearer thus have the same object before their minds. Only so can they understand one another at all and any discourse be possible.'

The term 'translation theory' refers to the fact that, according to the theory in question, when language is the vehicle of communication understanding requires a double process of 'translation': a speaker's thoughts are first translated into sounds, and then the sounds uttered are translated back again into thoughts by the hearer. This is clearly the basic idea behind Saussure's account of what happens when A and B engage in discourse. A and B are each responsible for the translation required in their respective sections of the circuit. A cannot translate on behalf of B, nor B on behalf of A: this is of the essence of *la parole*. It is conceived by Saussure as an individual enterprise, as distinct from the social or collective enterprise which constitutes *la langue*. If for any reason either A or B fails in this individual responsibility, or the process of double translation is otherwise prevented, the speech circuit is broken and the speech act abortive.

It is interesting to compare Saussure's model with accounts of speech communication which were still being offered fifty years later by authorities in linguistic theory, phonetics and speech pathology. The family resemblance is unmistakable.

In some modern versions, the metaphor of translation is replaced by that of 'encoding' and 'decoding': as for example, in the following generativist formulation:

Linguistic communication consists in the production of some external, publicly observable, acoustic phenomenon whose phonetic and syntactic structure encodes a speaker's inner, private thoughts or ideas and the decoding of the phonetic and syntactic structure exhibited in such a physical phenomenon by other speakers in the form of an inner, private experience of the same thoughts or ideas. (Katz 1966:98)

Similarly, Crystal describes three phases of the speech chain as 'neurological encoding', 'anatomical-physiological encoding', and 'brain decoding' (Crystal 1980:72ff., 93 ff., 119 ff.).

The code metaphor is not merely 'terminological': it is spelled out in quite elaborate detail. For instance:

We may ... think of the speech chain as a communication system in which ideas to be transmitted are represented by a code that undergoes transformations as speech events proceed from one level to another. We can draw an analogy here between speech and Morse code. In Morse code, certain patterns of dots and dashes stand for different letters of the alphabet; the dots and dashes are a code for the letters. This code can also be transformed from one form to another. For example, a series of dots and dashes on a piece of paper can be converted into an acoustic sequence, like 'beep-bip-bip-beep'. In the same way, the words of our language are a code for concepts and material objects ...

During speech transmission, the speaker's linguistic code of words and sentences is transformed into physiological and physical codes – in other words, into corresponding sets of muscle movements and air vibrations – being reconverted into linguistic code at the listener's end. This is analogous to translating the written 'dash-dash-dash' of Morse code into the sounds, 'beep-beep-beep'. (Denes and Pinson 1963: 7-8)

Some versions (e.g. Moulton 1970:23) restrict the terms 'encoding' and 'decoding' to those parts of the circuit which correspond to Saussure's 'psychological' sections. (Thus the transmission from A's brain to A's speech organs, for example, would not count as part of the 'encoding' process.) Others apply the metaphor to physiological processes as well.

It is evident that the substitution of the code metaphor for the translation metaphor alters nothing in the account of communication, except perhaps to make even more perspicuous the point that the objective is the recovery by B of exactly the same conceptual package (the 'message') as A originally formulated.

More emphatically than Saussure, his generativist successors half a century on stressed the inadequacy of restricting the study of language to the 'public' sections of the speech circuit:

Behaviouristically oriented investigations of linguistic communication focus exclusively on the publicly observable aspects of communication situations: speech sounds, nonverbal behavior of the participants in the situation, and physical properties of the available stimuli. Thus, such investigations neglect the essential aspect of successful linguistic communication, the congruence of speaker's and hearer's thought and ideas that results from verbal exchanges. (Katz 1966: 98)

With all this Saussure would doubtless have agreed.

In Katz's view, as in Saussure's, a linguistics restricted to the analysis of publicly observable features of linguistic activity would simply fail to come to terms with the principal function which a language is called upon to serve:

> To understand the ability of natural languages to serve as instruments for the communication of thoughts and ideas we must understand what it is that permits those who speak them consistently to connect the right sounds with the right meanings. (Katz 1966: 100)

Saussure could scarcely have hoped for a more whole-hearted endorsement from posterity of his assumption that the speech-circuit model provides not only a correct but an essential communication theory for linguistics. Most linguists of the nineteenth century had certainly failed entirely to appreciate the need for any such theoretical basis, having concentrated almost exclusively on the publicly observable features of linguistic activity, and even then in a second-hand form (via written records). By adopting and adapting the Lockean model to the purposes of twentieth-century structuralism, the *Cours* makes a decisive break with the crypto-positivism which had reigned in language studies from Bopp to the Neogrammarians.

The main features in which later versions of the speech circuit do not tally with Saussure's are two; and both are significant with respect to the distinction between *langue* and *parole*. First, later accounts tend to give a more elaborate account of the initial and final phase. For example:

> The first thing the speaker has to do is arrange his thoughts, decide what he wants to say and put what he wants to say into *linguistic form*. The message is put into linguistic form by selecting the right words and phrases to express its meaning, and by placing these words in the correct order required by the grammatical rules of the language. (Denes and Pinson 1963: 4)

According to Moulton (1970: 23) the initial phase of encoding is divisible into three consecutive steps, as follows:

Encoding the message {
1. Semantic encoding.
2. Grammatical encoding.
3. Phonological encoding.

These are matched by a parallel sequence in reverse order at the hearer's end of the chain:

Decoding { 9. Phonological decoding.
the message { 10. Grammatical decoding.
          { 11. Semantic decoding.

All that Saussure has to say about the initial phase is the brief reference to concepts 'triggering' sound patterns in the brain ([28]); while the final phase is described as the 'psychological association' of the *image acoustique* with the 'corresponding concept' ([28]).

The second discrepancy concerns a 'loop' in the speech circuit which Saussure omits, but which later accounts supply. The point here is that A and B are both listeners: 'there are two listeners, not one, because the speaker not only speaks, he also listens to his own voice. In listening, he continuously compares the quality of the sounds he produces with the sound qualities he intended to produce and makes the adjustments necessary to match the results with his intentions' (Denes and Pinson 1963: 6). This 'double listening' is regarded as important in providing models of language disability. Furthermore, it is recognized as a complex process. 'Auditory feedback is perhaps the most noticeable way in which we monitor our own communications, but it is not the only way. There is also *kinesthetic* feedback – the feelings of internal movement and position of our muscles, joints, etc. which we have while we are speaking ... Knowing (at an unconscious level) where our tongues are in our mouths is an important factor in maintaining our clarity of speech' (Crystal 1980: 58-9).

It would be uncharitable to suppose that these two discrepancies highlight matters which scholars of Saussure's generation had simply never thought about. Why is there no inclusion of them in Saussure's speech circuit? The first omission sends us back to the question of the Lockean ancestry of Saussure's model, and raises a point on which Saussure was subsequently criticized by the generativists of the 1960s.

Locke and Saussure both seem to assume that the basic item on which the understanding of oral communication operates is a single, indivisible unit of some kind. For Locke this is the 'word', and for Saussure the *signe linguistique*. (In Locke's case, 'word' has to be put in scare quotes. One commentator claims: 'his definition is such that any sound at all will be a word' (Woozley 1964: 36). This rather sweeping charge seems to have been brought on the ground that since Locke is wrong about words anyway, he might as well be hung for a sheep as a lamb. A charge that would stick with more plausibility is that Locke treats words as identified by (what Saussure would have regarded as) their phonetic 'substance'. But then, so do many people for all practical purposes. To object to this is to object to a very usual way in which the term *word* is ordinarily used.)

But Locke has a reason for adopting this kind of unit, which Saussure ostensibly lacks. It is connected with Locke's account of perception and his taxonomy of ideas. According to Locke, when we hear a word such as *man*, or *horse*, or *sun*, or *water*, or *iron* 'everyone who understands the language frames in his mind a combination of those several simple ideas which he has usually observed, or fancied to exist together under that denomination' (Locke 1706: 2.23.6). No such doctrine of simple ideas is supplied by Saussure, who, unlike Locke, was not engaged in the larger theoretical endeavour of constructing a general, internally consistent account of the human mind. Locke's interest in what we understand by words such as *man, horse, sun, water* and *iron* is connected with his intellectual role as epistemologist to the founders of the Royal Society (Aarsleff 1982). Saussure played no comparable role: he was not committed to any particular alliance with contemporary philosophers of science, much less to taking sides in a debate with very considerable religious implications.

The second discrepancy between Saussure's speech circuit and later models also sends us back to Locke. For a theory of understanding, the feedback loop in the communicational mechanism is simply an irrelevance. B's hearing what A says is in no way on a par with A's hearing what A says. If it were, Saussure would have to claim that A does not grasp the meaning of his own utterance until he hears it. *Quod est absurdum*. This is what supplies the internal logic of Saussure's insistence ([27]) that at least two individuals are needed to complete the speech circuit. In strictly Saussurean terms, talking to oneself does not count as a speech act at all.

There are differences between Locke's version of the translation theory of oral communication and Saussure's. Locke evidently supposed that there could be thought without language, and that the mind could engage in it without the aid of any linguistic instrument. 'Language does not exist, then, because man is a rational being; it exists, according to Locke, because man is "a sociable creature", and language is "the great instrument and common tie of society" ' (Parkinson 1977: 2). Saussure emerges as a sceptic on this score. He does not explicitly discuss the question of whether or to what extent human beings could think without language, but he describes prelinguistic thought as amorphous. 'Psychologically, setting aside its expression in words, our thought is simply a vague, shapeless mass' ([155]). More specifically still, '... were it not for signs, we should be incapable of differentiating any two ideas in a clear and consistent way ... No ideas are established in advance, and nothing is distinct, before the introduction of *la langue*' ([155]). This marks a significant shift of emphasis away from Locke, and meshes with an important historical evolution in the philosophical status of linguistic inquiry, which is characteristic of the late nineteenth and twentieth centuries. The evolution in question tends towards seeing language not as a gratuitous social bonus for purposes of communication, but as a *sine qua non* for the articulation of any analytic structure of ideas whatsoever.

This, in one sense, is the essential message of Saussurean structuralism for the whole of the humanities: language is not peripheral to human understanding of reality. On the contrary, human understanding of reality in every sphere revolves about the social use of linguistic signs.

To this extent it could perhaps be argued that it is unfair to saddle Saussure with a crude, old-fashioned Lockean theory of communication. For Saussure would certainly have denied that the systems of concepts on which communication depends are given independently of the system of vocal signals. In Saussure's theory, therefore, there is strictly no question of 'translation' between two systems: on the contrary, both are constitutive of one and the same *langue*. Although a defence of Saussure along these lines is perfectly justified, and shows that in his case the translation metaphor cannot be pressed too far, it nevertheless remains true that Saussure, like Locke, is forced to concede that knowing the meaning of a word is quite different from knowing its pronunciation. Ultimately, the reason for this is that both Saussure and Locke claim that the linguistic sign is arbitrary. It follows that neither Saussure nor Locke can explain speech communication simply by reference to a shared set of vocal forms. For, as Locke points out, being able to utter a word is no guarantee of understanding it: 'he that uses the word *tarantula*, without having any imagination or idea of what it stands for, pronounces a good word; but so long means nothing at all by it' (Locke 1706: 3.10.32.). But it is only possible to pronounce the word *tarantula* without having any idea of 'what it stands for' because *tarantula* is an arbitrary vocal form, having no natural connexion with the creature of which it happens to be the name. If A and B both use the word *tarantula* but neither knows what it means, or only one of them, then on both Saussure's account and Locke's there is no communication. The speech circuit breaks down at the point where no conceptual 'translation' of the word *tarantula* is available.

Thus far Locke would have agreed with Saussure, inasmuch as both theorists postulate complete symmetry between the encoding and the decoding of the vocal signal. Decoding has to recover exactly what was originally encoded. B's understanding of A is simply a mirror image of A's expressing the thought in the first place. The only differences between expression and comprehension that the Saussurean speech circuit allows are (i) a difference in physiological processing (between phonation and audition), and (ii) a difference in the direction of flow, as it were (the flow between *concept* and *image acoustique* being reversed, as shown by the arrows in Saussure's diagram). A point to note is that whereas this symmetry of encoding and decoding is again for Locke grounded in a general account of how the mind works (of which understanding what other people say is only one part), Saussure gives the reader no general account of how the mind works which could provide a comparable anchorage. So what was originally a motivated feature of

Locke's account survives as an article of faith in Saussure's.

A related difference is that Saussure leaves himself room to dissent from Locke's claim that men talk 'only that they may be understood; which is then only done when, by use or consent, the sound I make by the organs of speech excites in another man's mind who hears it the idea I apply to it in mine when I speak it' (Locke 1706: 3.3.3.). For Saussure is apparently concerned only with giving an account of communication in so far as it is mediated by *la langue*: he has nothing to say about the more general problem of understanding between individuals. So, for example, the word *tarantula* might excite a somewhat different idea in B's mind from the idea excited in A's (because, for instance, B is pathologically afraid of spiders whereas A is not, or because one knows more about tarantulas than the other); but that would not matter for Saussure's purposes provided both A and B were in agreement about the linguistic meaning of the term *tarantula*. At first sight, this restriction might seem to give Saussure's theory of communication an advantage over Locke's. But arguably, on the contrary, it presents Saussure with a pivotal problem never satisfactorily resolved in the *Cours*. To phrase it in terms of Locke's example, the problem would be to determine which of the mental associations connected with tarantulas in the minds of A and B count as 'the linguistic concept "tarantula" ' (in other words, the *signifié* of the sign *tarantula*). This is left unclarified in the *Cours*, apart from vague remarks about signs receiving the collective ratification of the linguistic community. But what this ratification consists in, and how the linguist would discover whether it had been collectively given or collectively withheld, are questions passed over in silence. This silence is, to say the least, awkward for Saussurean linguistics; because if there is no answer *la langue* becomes in practice undescribable. Perhaps it is this silence which, in the end, explains why the *Cours* never appeared in print in Saussure's lifetime.

There is an analogous problem too concerning the vocal form of the speech signal. Phonetically sophisticated post-Saussurean versions of the speech circuit make this quite explicit. 'Although we can regard speech transmission as a chain of events in which a code for certain ideas is transformed from one level or medium to another, it would be a great mistake to think that corresponding events at different levels are the same. There is some relationship to be sure, but the events are far from being identical. For example, there is no guarantee that people will produce sound waves with identical characteristics when they pronounce the same word. In fact, they are more likely to produce sound waves of different characteristics when they pronounce the same word. By the same token, they may very well generate similar sound waves when producing different words' (Denes and Pinson 1963: 8). But there is no mention of this in Saussure.

Once the problem is recognized, it poses an embarrassing question for the whole of Saussure's theory of communication. For that theory is based on identities. Once we allow that oral communication between A and B is based not on identities but on disparities, the notion of *la langue* as a fixed code is immediately vulnerable to objections.

Locke here encounters parallel difficulties about identity of ideas and of words, to which his *Essay* similarly offers no solution. The difference is that Locke, unlike Saussure, is not trying to elaborate a theoretical foundation for linguistics. More importantly, the comparison points up a question which Saussurean commentators have been slow to answer. Why did Saussure apparently try to adapt to his own ends a theory of communication which ostensibly served a quite contrary purpose? To put the point more sharply, why did Saussure take over a (Lockean) theory of communication concerned obviously (in Saussurean terms) with *la parole*, and apply it instead to *la langue*? A facile answer might be that Saussure had read Durkheim – an advantage history denied Locke. But there is more to it than that. For Saussure – unless he were very naive – could hardly have failed to see that by so doing he simply inherited Locke's problems writ (collectively) larger.

Saussure's adoption of this Lockean psychological model consequently cannot be explained away on general epistemological grounds. Bloomfield apparently thought the reason was simply Saussure's ignorance of anything more sophisticated: '(he) seems to have had no psychology beyond the crudest popular notions' (Bloomfield 1923). Bloomfield goes on from this to make the point that Saussure 'exemplifies, in his own person and perhaps unintentionally' the irrelevance of psychology to the study of language. The conclusion Bloomfield should have drawn was almost the opposite: namely, that a theoretical framework for the study of language may be shaped in many important respects by the communicational assumptions underlying it.

Hjelmslev was probably nearer the mark when he observed that pre-Saussurean linguistics treated language as being reducible, in the final analysis, to a constitutive totality of individual linguistic acts (Hjelmslev 1942: 30). Such a view is completely antithetical to any form of structuralism, and Saussure could not accept it. In rejecting it, however, he inherited the obligation to offer at least a minimal account of the individual linguistic act, in order to avoid the charge that his theory was an abstraction which simply failed to come to terms with the realities of everyday speech. Looking at the problem from this angle, one can see why Saussure would have found a modified Lockean model of communication attractive. In effect, it offered two welcome guarantees. In the first place, it established the role of linguistics in the human sciences. By interposing *la langue* between the individual speaker and *la parole* within a Lockean framework, Saussure ensures that the study of language cannot be reduced either to the psychology of individual speech acts, or to social analyses of the communication events which such acts constitute. For the individual acts depend on the existence of a linguistic system, of which neither the psychology nor the sociology of the nineteenth century offered any detailed description. In the second place, reducing *la parole* to the individual implementation of resources provided by *la langue* ensured that within linguistics the study of the latter take priority over the former and be independent of it. Thus built into the speech-circuit model there is what amounts to a double guarantee of autonomy: (i) autonomy of linguistics among the disciplines dealing with human speech behaviour, and (ii) autonomy of the study of *la langue* within linguistics.

Where Saussure's speech circuit marks an advance over Locke is that Locke's account is still basically a form of nomenclaturism (Harris 1980: 67 ff.). For Locke, words 'stand for' ideas in the mind: but the mind forms its ideas independently of language. Saussure rejects this psychocentric surrogationalism in favour of giving theoretical priority to the linguistic sign itself (envisaged as an indissoluble combination of *signifiant* and *signifié*). A compromise with Locke is still visible in one feature, however. 'Concepts' remain, in Saussure's account, the prime movers in the activity which occupies the speech circuit: they 'trigger' a process which would have no other plausible starting point.

This still leaves unanswered the question of how a seventeenth-century theory of understanding could plausibly be resuscitated for the purposes of a 'new' twentieth-century science. For however strong Saussure's interest in seeking a basis for establishing linguistics as an autonomous branch of scientific inquiry, it was not an interest so widely shared by fellow academics that any model suitable for that purpose would automatically have commanded general approval (or, at least, general immunity from criticism). Therefore, to explain why Saussure adopted the speech-circuit model of the individual act does not explain why his choice of model met with such widespread acceptance. Part of the answer to this rarely-asked question lies in a nineteenth-century revolution in another field altogether: technology.

Modern technology is deeply committed to circuit models. Without them, it is no exaggeration to say, technology as the modern world knows it could scarcely exist. (The earliest scientific application of the term *circuit* recorded by the *Oxford English Dictionary* dates from 1800 and relates to electricity.) Bearing this in mind, it is not a naive question to ask why Saussure (unlike Locke) insisted that speech involved a *circuit*; and whether as a matter of fact *circuit* was an appropriate term to choose. For Saussure's predecessors, even those most committed to viewing language as a summation of individual acts of speech, had not described the basic process of communication in this way.

The first point to note is that the speech-circuit model is a transmission model. It represents communication as involving passage through a succession of phases arranged in linear progression along a track or pathway. In this succession there are no gaps. The process is envisaged as a continuous journey or transfer of information from one point in space to another point in space: that is, from a location in A's brain to a location in B's brain or, in the reverse direction, from B's brain to A's. Now a model of this kind undoubtedly receives much support from numerous expressions used in everyday speech to describe the processes of communication. For example, ideas are said to be *put into* words; words are *exchanged*; verbal messages are *put across* or *got over, sent* or *passed on*; and eventually *received* and *taken in*. This way of talking about communication as transmission has been described as 'the conduit metaphor' (Reddy 1979), and it is a metaphor with extensive ramifications in various European languages. The influence of this metaphor in predisposing us to accept any transmission model of speech as plain 'common sense' is not to be underestimated.

Saussure's model, however, purports to be one particular type of transmission model. The very term *circuit* implies a contrast with other geometrical configurations. In principle, circuit models of communication must be distinguished from at least two other configurational types: from rectilinear models on the one hand, and from helical models on the other. The difference between a circuit model and a rectilinear model is the difference between a circle and a straight line. The difference between a circuit model and a helical model is the difference between a circle and a helix or spiral. Of these three types, only helical models (Dance 1967) are formally appropriate to capture the dynamic or developmental aspects of speech communication. Circuit models can make no allowance for the progressive modification of the communication situation through time. For circles always lead back to an original point of departure. The only aspect of temporal progression a circuit model allows for is the time it takes for information to pass from one point in the circuit to another point, and the only aspect of modification allowed for is the alteration in the form of the signal as it passes from one section of the circuit to the next.

There is no doubt, then, that Saussure's model is not a helical model. But is it really even a circuit model? On closer inspection, it becomes obvious that the Saussurean 'circuit', in spite of its name, is made up simply of two rectilinear sections joined together. It envisages no feedback of any kind, except a verbal reply following exactly the same progression as the verbal message first transmitted, but with the direction of flow reversed. It incorporates no guarantee that B's utterance is in any way a direct linguistic 'continuation' of or response to A's. Nor is it a 'single-track' rectilinear model, however. For if it were, Saussurean linguistics would be in principle unable to cope with a situation of the type where A and B, meeting in the street, simultaneously utter the words 'Good morning'. In short, the so-called Saussurean 'circuit' would more accurately be described as a two-track rectilinear model of speech communication. Messages can be transmitted independently along either track. All that is precluded is the simultaneous use of one track for the transmission of two messages travelling in opposite directions.

From the foregoing discussion it should be quite clear that the so-called Saussurean speech circuit is in fact an amalgam of two quite independent concepts. One is the concept of what later theorists called the 'speech chain': that is to say, the biological interlinking of processes which are physically and physiologically distinct. (Saussure mentions a *chaîne acoustique* ([64]) and a *chaîne parlée* ([65],[77]): but only in the context of discussing sound sequences. In other words, Saussure's 'chain' is a phenomenon on the syntagmatic level, and not part of the mechanism which itself makes syntagmatic phenomena possible.) The other concept is that of reciprocal exchange: B's response to A is a processual mirror of A's original speech-contact with B. But it is in no way a necessary condition for the existence of speech chains. Neither speech-chaining nor reciprocality of exchange, separately or conjointly, guarantee the identities on which the Locke-Saussure model of communication relies. The missing link is also the missing loop in Saussure's circuit. The assumption, in other words, is that 'what B hears' is nothing other than 'what A hears'. Since A, as an individual, is in sole and undisputed control of the act of *parole* in question ([30]), it must follow that *if* B is to understand A then B and A must both independently hear the same thing.

Once the logical geometry of the Saussurean speech circuit is analysed in these terms, it becomes evident that the only symmetry between its two rectilinear halves is a symmetry of message conversion. Whether the message travels from A to B or from B to A makes no difference. Somehow or other, what starts off as an idea is converted into a physiological process, which is in turn converted into sound, which is in turn converted back into a different physiological process and back again into an idea. The origin of this type of model is not difficult to discover. It has been universally employed in all the natural sciences to account for observed and measurable correspondences in spatio-temporally connected processes involving continuity between different forms of energy. The prototype, in short, is the concept of energy-conversion; but with the caveat that nothing of communicational relevance is 'lost' on the way.

Why, it may be asked, should energy-conversion strike a linguist of Saussure's generation as a plausible exemplar for explaining speech communication? To answer this, we need look no further than the major technological innovations in communication which transformed everyday life in Western industrial society during the course of the nineteenth and early twentieth centuries. They were telegraphy, telephony and broadcasting: all forms of energy-conversion applied to the transmission of verbal messages. It can hardly be a coincidence that the illustration of A and B talking in the *Cours* shows them schematically linked by what look suspiciously like telephone wires. Nor is it a coincidence that the misapplied term *circuit* which Saussure borrowed for his own model of speech communication comes from the technical vocabulary of the electrical engineer. By representing speech as a closed, causally determined process in every way analogous to the energy-conversion processes of physics and chemistry, linguistics was provided in advance with a forged *carte d'entrée* to the prestigious palace of modern science.

It is also worth noting the socio-political implications of the way the speech circuit presents the role of the individual in speech. It is a model which relies on the existence of a fixed code which belongs to the community as a whole. (The *Cours* refers to *la langue* as a *code* on p.[31].) Membership of the linguistic community is implicitly defined by reference to this code. In speech, therefore, the individual merely makes use of a verbal communication system institutionalized collectively, in just the same way as any member of the community has access to public transport, the post office or any of the other organized communication services of modern society. Even as a sender of messages by way of this public code, the individual's initiative is curiously limited. The speech-circuit model simply postulates that a message comes into the mind of the sender already pre-programmed, as it were, for public transmission. How this is possible Saussure never explains. But that is an obscurity which lies outside the point of entry to the speech circuit itself. So even in this humble initiative as a sender of messages, the individual is already mysteriously indebted to the community. We are dealing with a model which assigns to the individual vis-à-vis *la langue* a role which matches exactly the socio-political role assigned to the individual vis-à-vis the institutions of the modern nation-state. As a member, the individual can do no more than what the community, through its institutions, makes it possible for an individual to do.

Predictably, the internal difficulties with such a model arise from the need to reconcile what is basically a mechanical transmission circuit with the notion that the individual retains at least some control over its operation. Clearly, one has to allow for the fact that an individual may formulate a verbal message mentally, but decide not to utter it. The decision to speak, therefore, together with the decision as to what to say, must both fall within the province of voluntary activity on the part of the speaker. This consideration would seem to dictate that both belong to *parole*: for Saussure says of *parole* that it is 'an individual act of the will and the intelligence' ([30]). He proceeds to distinguish in respect of *parole* '(1) the combinations through which the speaker uses the code provided by the language in order to express his own thought, and (2) the psycho-physical mechanism which enables him to externalize these combinations' ([31]). There are at least two problems here. One is that the key process of *parole* according to this account is the individual speaker's selection of a desired combination of signs. This corresponds to the activities going on at the 'linguistic level' in the Denes and Pinson model described above. Yet there is no part of Saussure's circuit which allows for the execution of this process. The description the reader is given of how the circuit operates ([28]) begins straight away with A's concepts 'triggering' the appropriate sound patterns in the brain. Now 'triggering', presumably, is an automatic process, and one over which the individual has no control. Yet it is precisely this section of the circuit which Saussure identifies ([30]) with *parole*. Likewise, it is presumably because the hearer has no control over how to hear the spoken message that Saussure explicitly allows the passive, 'receptive' section of the circuit linking sound-patterns with concepts to be instrumental in the formation of *la langue* in the individual. So we have the odd situation in which the process of associating concepts with sound patterns apparently belongs to *parole*, whereas its mirror-image, the association of sound patterns with concepts apparently does not. Yet the one is no more 'voluntary' than the other.

Similar conundrums arise in respect of the so-called 'psycho-physical mechanism' permitting the speaker to 'externalize' the selected combinations. This again, apparently, belongs to *parole*: but it is difficult to see in what sense the speaker has any voluntary control over this mechanism. What the speaker can do is decide whether or not to try to exercise the mechanism to achieve certain articulatory results: but it is operation of the mechanism itself which constitutes the flow of activity over that particular section of the speech circuit, and this is not a process subject to acts of will. (A speaker does not, for example, decide to send an articulatory 'message' via one neuromechanical pathway rather than another, or decide whether to pay attention to or ignore the feedback systems which guide the whole articulatory process.) But is the reader, it might be asked, intended to understand that physiological events themselves are part of the *acte de parole*? It would seem so. For the *Cours* here speaks of the impossibility of photographing such an act in all its details ([32]). Now this impossibility is not presented as the logical impossibility of photographing a decision: on the contrary, the difficulty is specifically said to reside in the 'infinite number of muscular movements' involved in phonation. This, as part of *parole*, is contrasted with the much simpler corresponding unit in *langue*, which is the *image acoustique*, comprising only a limited number of elements. What is certainly the case is that once the message has been 'externalized', the speaker no longer has any control at all over the further progression round the speech circuit: there is no question of exercising acts of will over the sound waves. Yet, one might argue, it is precisely when the message has at last emerged from 'inside' the speaker and taken on this spatio-temporally unique but fleeting acoustic form that we can most readily grasp its reality as a fact of *parole* and appreciate that facts of *parole* are separate from facts of *langue*. Along this section of the circuit, however, the transmission is under the control neither of A nor of B. It is at the mercy of all kinds of external factors in the communication situation (gusts of wind, extraneous noise, etc.)

These problems of the speech circuit are intrinsic to it, and are never satisfactorily resolved in the *Cours*. It is difficult on this issue to exculpate Saussure (or his successors) from the charge of commitment to a gross category mistake: a mistake perhaps induced, but certainly compounded, by the decision to adapt a mechanical transmission model in order to explicate concepts which, in the final analysis, are not explicable by reference to mechanical processes at all. What is remarkable is that the attempt should have been made in the first place. That it was, however, bears witness to the extent to which the plausibility of this general picture of speech-communication is indebted to the cultural paradigms of a particular phase in Western civilization. Whether it would appear at all convincing if seen against a totally different cultural background must be doubtful. Its persuasiveness derives essentially from the fact that, at a particular time and place in human history, all the relevant analogues and justifications – metalinguistic, philosophical, technological and political – came together to provide what could be seen in that context as a necessary and sufficient conceptual framework for the analysis of speech.

CHAPTER III

Individuals, Collectivities and Values

The extent to which a Saussurean model of communication relies on *la langue* being a fixed code will already be evident from the discussion in the immediately preceding pages. There the requirement is that the code be fixed in the sense of being invariant across individuals and occasions. But that in turn requires that the code be fixed in a further sense. The point commentators have missed is that Saussurean theory needs a fixed code in this other sense too in order to support Saussure's 'first principle of linguistics': that is, in order to explain why, although the connexion between *signifiant* and *signifié* is arbitrary, it nevertheless cannot in any one *état de langue* vary beyond certain limits. This emerges perhaps most clearly in the remarks on writing on p.[165]. Commenting on the variety of different ways in which the letter *t* may be written, Saussure explains this as due to the fact that in writing, as in speech, values are based on contrasts within a fixed system. 'Since the written sign is arbitrary, its form is of little importance: or rather, is of importance only within certain limits imposed by the system' ([165]). In other words, there is a general semiological connexion between the arbitrariness of signs and their membership of fixed systems. Only a fixed system makes it possible to have signs which, although arbitrary, are not free to vary arbitrarily and thus take on *any* form.

It is important not to confuse this latter question with how, given a fixed code, its stability is maintained – or not maintained, as the case may be – throughout a certain community, length of time or geographical area. To stability questions the *Cours* gives mainly straightforward social (i.e. 'external') answers ([104]ff., [281]ff.). This kind of account could in principle apply to types of social institution other than languages. But the question of what fixes the code belongs to a different order of questions altogether. Here we are dealing not with the *état de langue*, but with the idiosynchronic system itself. To give a 'social' answer in that case would be, from a Saussurean point of view, to plunge the whole of linguistic theory into a never-ending circularity; or, perhaps even worse, to bind linguistics hand and foot in dependence on social anthropology.

The way the problem is dealt with in the *Cours* simultaneously demonstrates the brilliance and the vulnerability of Saussure's theoretical acumen. It also brings us to the theoretical core of structuralism. The Saussurean explanation of what fixes the code is archetypally holistic, and it has to be. Nothing 'outside' *la langue* determines the connexion between a *signifiant* and a *signifié*: so whatever does so must be 'inside'. But 'inside' there is nothing apart from other signs. If *la langue* included at least a few fundamental signs which were fixed on the basis of external relations, it might be possible to explain all the other signs as being somehow fixed relatively to these few invariant ones. But for Saussure there are no such fundamental signs of a non-arbitrary character to be found. The only necessary and sufficient condition for establishing the identity of any individual sign is that it be distinct from other signs. However, this can presumably only be so if the system as a whole is structured in such a way as to allocate to each sign its own unique semiological 'space'. Therefore Saussure accepts that adopting the principle that the linguistic sign is arbitrary forces us to conclude that it can only be the total network of interrelations which establishes individual connexions between *signifiants* and *signifiés*. So the Saussurean answer to the question 'What fixes the code?' is that what fixes the individual signs is their reciprocal interdependence in a system, which in turn is fixed simply by the totality of internal relations between its constituent signs. That explains simultaneously why altering just one set of relations disturbs the whole system, and also why, in spite of the arbitrary connexion between any one *signifiant* and any one *signifié*, it is not easy to break that connexion. Altering just one sign encounters the passive resistance of the entire structure. Thus everything in *la langue* is fixed by its structural interdependence with the rest, in the same way that the rungs of a ladder are held in position by being inserted into the vertical struts, which in turn are held in position by the rungs.

In the *Cours*, Saussure offers both a psychological and a social version of how this holistic fixing of the signs is to be construed. The psychological version is represented by the interface metaphor, which likens the contact between thought and sound to the contact between air and water ([156]). According to this version, the two substances are themselves totally amorphous, and structured only as a result of the contact between them. Although this is, in one sense, the purest possible variety of structuralism, it does not explain very satisfactorily how mere contact between intrinsically amorphous substances can automatically produce a structured system. Saussure supplements it, however, by a social version. This is represented by the economic metaphor. The crucial difference between the two versions is that in the latter there is 'contact' between two already independently structured systems, one monetary and the other comprising goods or services. Striking a balance of correlations between units in two separate systems, according to this second metaphor, is what produces a third system of values, which did not exist before.

The advantage of the latter version is that it makes it much easier to understand why contact should result in a structured system and not in chaos: for contact was not between amorphous masses in the first place. That is also the reason, however, why Saussure might not be entirely happy with this second version. For it suggests that there may be other structures 'outside', which in the end determine the resultant pattern of the system of bi-planar correlations. On the other hand, his theory of 'sound types' needs precisely this foundation if it is to underpin the Saussurean account of the *significant*. That account would be incoherent if it were not supposed that the physiology of the vocal apparatus was given in advance by Nature. To that extent, speech sound is not amorphous, but already structured by the possibilities inherent in something external to the idiosynchronic system.

There is ultimately no compromise available between the two versions of how it is possible for a system to be fixed holistically by bi-planar correlations. Nor does the *Cours* attempt a compromise: it simply offers both. In one case systematicity somehow emerges magically *ex nihilo*, whereas in the other systematicity arises from the attempt to adjust units of one kind to units of another kind. On either version, however, it has to be a systematicity which for Saussure will underwrite the concept of a linguistic *state*.

In recent years, linguistic advocates of the so-called 'dynamic paradigm' have urged that no 'static paradigm', whether specifically Saussurean or not, can come to terms with the fact that languages are inherently unstable and continuously evolving. If this is so – and the *Cours* concedes the point that in languages we never find *l'immobilité absolue* ([193]) – the question must arise whether *la langue*, conceived as a fixed code, corresponds to any linguistic reality at all. How Saussure might have replied to 'dynamic paradigm' critics we can only speculate. But we can suppose that a Saussurean answer would maintain, come what may, that *la langue* is not a concept which has to be – or could be – maintained at the expense of sacrificing the dichotomy between synchrony and diachrony; and furthermore that *la langue* is indeed a linguistic reality and not a theoretical abstraction.

Defenders of Saussure have sometimes urged that a careful reading of the *Cours* shows a full awareness of the allegedly neglected dynamic aspect of *la langue*. De Mauro (1972: 454) cites in this connexion the explicit statement in the *Cours* that 'At no one time does a language possess an entirely fixed system of units' ([234]). One might counter this, however, with other explicit statements from the *Cours*. For example, that each language uses 'a fixed number of distinct speech sounds' ([58]), that 'every language has an inventory of sounds fixed in number' ([303]), that 'each language constitutes a closed system' ([139]), that in writing as in languages, values 'are solely based on contrasts within a fixed system' ([165]). Is it possible to read the *Cours* in a way which allows both static and dynamic linguistic paradigms to co-exist within a Saussurean framework? Can the fixed system be sufficiently elastic to accommodate the observed heterogeneity?

The problem revolves around the controversial Saussurean notion of 'value'. For to *fix* a value presupposes the invariance of certain elements and relations. This is as true in the linguistic case as in the economic case which Saussure offers for comparison ([159-60]). The value of a five-franc coin does not remain the same over a period of years simply because it remains equivalent to five one-franc coins. We cannot suppose Saussure thought that: for that would be to reduce a system of values to a mere mathematics. The whole point of his economic analogy is that coins have to be exchanged for something *other than* coins (bread, clothes, services, etc.).

But nor does the value of a five-franc coin remain constant simply because, for instance, the price of bread remains constant. For there are many other factors affecting its value than the price of just one commodity. On the contrary, a fixed price is *eo ipso* no guarantee of anything without considering whether or not it costs more or less to produce the commodity than it used to. Analogously in the linguistic case, it proves nothing to show that the word *unfashionable* has at all times in its history been divisible into the same three morphemic units, nor even that it has always been defined as meaning 'not fashionable', if what is at issue is whether there have been changes in the system of lexical values to which it belongs. Saussure's economic analogy, therefore, seems at first sight only to render the problem more acute: for economic values seem to vary continuously. On the other hand, purchases are made, deals are struck, business is done. How is this possible?

Two attempts to dissolve or at least to minimize the problem on Saussure's behalf will be considered here. One is the explanation given by Ullmann, and evidently approved by de Mauro (1972: 454-5). This presents Saussure as recognizing that *in fact* linguistic phenomena exhibit continuous variation; but deciding to ignore the variation for certain purposes. Thus 'it is not the language which is synchronistic or diachronistic, but the approach to it, the method of investigation, the science of language' (Ullmann 1959: 36). The duality, in Ullmann's view, 'is not entwined in the linguistic material itself.' Thus, apparently, it is a mistake to see Saussure as caught here in any kind of dilemma. There are simply two points of view, and Saussure recognizes the validity of both. One point of view sees *la langue* as a static system, while the other recognizes change. Therefore, presumably, Saussure's reply to 'dynamic paradigm' critics would be that it is *they* who are confused: for they naively reason from the fact that in real time different synchronic systems co-exist to the conclusion that there are no *états de langue* at all. In other words, theirs is yet another failure to distinguish between *faits de langue* and *faits de parole*.

This apologia, however, dodges the real issue. Although it is perfectly true that for Saussure it would be essential not to mix up in the same analysis synchronic and diachronic facts, there is no justification in the *Cours* for supposing the distinction between synchronic and diachronic to be merely in the eye of the analyst. The separation of synchrony from diachrony is neither just a descriptive convenience nor an artifact of linguistic theorizing. To think otherwise would be to make nonsense of Saussure's objection that the viewpoint of the historical linguist does not correspond to any reality in the experience of the speaker. 'The first thing which strikes one on studying linguistic facts is that the language user is unaware of their succession in time: he is dealing with a state. Hence the linguist who wishes to understand this state must rule out of consideration everything which brought that state about, and pay no attention to diachrony. Only by suppressing the past can he enter into the state of mind of the language user' ([117]). Here is as clear a statement as one could wish. It shows that if the linguist adopts the distinction between synchronic and diachronic, that is not simply for descriptive convenience, nor because there is any analytic obligation to do so, but because that distinction is imposed by the nature of linguistic realities for the linguistic community.

Furthermore, the Ullmann-de Mauro defence of Saussure supplies no genuinely Saussurean answer to the question of what 'fixes' the code. It simply papers over the cracks to suggest *if* one adopts the diachronic point of view *then* the code is not fixed at all. This is no more than a bland attempt to please everybody by turning a blind eye to the fact that Saussurean theory subordinates the distinction between synchronic and diachronic to the prior distinction between *langue* and *parole*. After all, everyone presumably agrees that what was the case yesterday or yesteryear may no longer be the case today. That is *not* the same as having grasped the Saussurean distinction between synchrony and diachrony. It is not a question of saying to oneself: 'Today the situation is as it is; but yesterday it was different. Therefore, one must conclude that change has occurred. However, today I cannot foresee anything about tomorrow. Therefore, at the moment, I cannot say that change is occurring. So today, I describe the situation as "static".' On that reasoning, 'today' (however long it may last) is always static. Some Saussurean commentators give the impression of having to defend – or attack – ratiocination of this order. This merely shows that they have failed to grasp the implications of such classic Saussurean dicta as 'it is *la parole* which causes *la langue* to evolve' ([37]) and 'everything which is diachronic in *la langue* is only so through *la parole* ([138]).

Some advocates of the dynamic paradigm argue that the Saussurean position is in any case based upon a *non sequitur*. For from the fact that speakers are ignorant of the past development of the language they speak, it does not follow that from their point of view the language is static, unless the term 'static' is interpreted broadly enough to include the varied patterns of observable change in progress. But if it *is* thus interpreted, then the Saussurean dichotomy between synchronic and diachronic is immediately threatened, and the notion of *la langue* as a homogeneous system cannot be maintained.

Washabaugh identifies three characteristics of the systematic patterning of language variations which advocates of the dynamic paradigm regard as inexplicable within a Saussurean framework. One is the way in which these patterns show up numerically. 'Only by taking a statistical average of a large number of people do systematic relations appear' (Washabaugh 1974: 29). Investigation of the speech behaviour of individuals, on the other hand, shows that the individual is prone to unsystematic fluctuations. The second characteristic is the diachronic nature of the patterning, which is difficult to account for if one assumes with Saussure that linguistic change depends on the acceptance or rejection by the community of innovations initiated by individuals. The third characteristic is the heterogeneity of the patterning. That is to say, whereas Saussurean linguistics assumes a homogeneous language, uniformly employed by all members of the community, observation suggests that speakers are constantly choosing between alternative sets of forms, but dealing with this non-uniformity in a systematic manner.

Washabaugh argues that the first of these three alleged inadequacies of Saussurean linguistics involves a basic conflict between different views about social facts. One is a Durkheimian view, which treats social facts as discoverable only by statistical methods, since there is no guarantee that any individual is perfectly typical of the community. But Saussure's mature theory of language, Washabaugh holds, is non-Durkheimian or even anti-Durkheimian, since 'for Durkheim there is no such thing as psychological reality of a social fact; there is no analogue to Saussure's *la langue individuelle* or *la faculté du langage*' (Washabaugh 1974: 28). Washabaugh rejects the view that Saussure was influenced by Durkheim as based upon 'hearsay', and claims that the resemblances between Saussure and Durkheim are 'only terminological'.

Washabaugh goes on to argue that the other two alleged inadequacies of the Saussurean paradigm in principle have Saussurean solutions, although Saussure himself did not develop them in detail. The key to these solutions lies in Saussure's recognition of *langage* as a human faculty, common to all individuals but independent of particular languages. This faculty, Washabaugh claims, can be construed as a source of universal constraints accounting for the diachronic and heterogeneous patterns detectable in a community's linguistic behaviour. So, paradoxically, far from denying the validity of a dynamic paradigm, Saussurean linguistics actually provides the dynamic paradigm with a sound theoretical basis, and makes it unnecessary to have recourse to any Durkheimian approach to linguistic facts.

An observant reader cannot fail to notice that at various points in the *Cours* there is an uneasy tension between the role attributed to the individual and the role attributed to the collectivity. Saussure speaks, for example, of individual innovations but of collective ratifications, and this is intimately bound up with the basic dichotomy between what belongs to *parole* and what belongs to *langue*. Nowhere, however, does it emerge very clearly what exactly collective ratification amounts to. For theorists who, like Durkheim, deny that social facts are reducible to sets of facts about individuals, a collectivity has to be something more than a mere aggregate of people. Saussure, on the other hand, often seems to assume that the essential process by which linguistic innovations become generalized is simply the imitation by one individual of another individual. But this would reduce collective ratification to a matter of counting heads, and raise in a rather acute form the descriptive problem of deciding at what percentage level a linguistic practice should be judged to have gained general acceptance by the community. Durkheim's frank commitment to a statistical methodology (Durkheim 1895: 9-10) has no obvious echo in the *Cours*.

Washabaugh's defence of Saussure is certainly a more interesting one than any attempt merely to juggle with the application of the terms 'synchronic' and 'diachronic'. The contrast drawn between Saussurean and Durkheimian approaches to social facts invites a number of comments. A long line of commentators, from Doroszewski (1931) down to Dinneen (1967), have claimed or assumed that Saussure was influenced by Durkheim. But this has also been denied, notably by Koerner (1973: 45-71), who points out that 'there is not a single text from either Saussure himself or from lecture notes taken by his students which mentions the names of Durkheim, Tarde or Walras'. More important for a reading of the *Cours* than debating the evidence for 'influences' at this level is how the concept of social facts which we find in the *Cours* compares with Durkheim's. Via what historical route the two are related, if at all, need not concern us.

Catlin (1938: xv) points out that Durkheim's principal criterion of a social fact, that of 'being general throughout the extent of a given society' at a given stage in the evolution of that society, by implication distinguishes a social fact from a psychological fact which is universal to human nature. So at least on this score there is no basic difference between the Durkheim of *Les règles de la méthode sociologique* and the Saussure of the *Cours*, granted the interpretation of Saussurean *langage* as something 'universal to human nature' and of *langue* as a social product in the sense that every language presupposes a particular culture or community whose purposes it serves. Moreover, the implication is that for Durkheim such facts as are 'universal to human nature', even though they will clearly affect people's social behaviour, lie outside the scope of sociology.

Now if for 'the scope of sociology' we substitute 'the scope of linguistics', Saussure's position is in essence no different. It does not fall within the scope of Saussurean linguistics to investigate universal constraints which derive from factors outside the human language faculty, or, more exactly, which are independent of that semiological faculty which is *la faculté linguistique par excellence* ([27]). The reason why is made quite clear in Saussure's remarks about the 'panchronic' point of view ([134-5]). For Saussure 'there is no panchronic point of view' ([135]). This is *not* a denial of the possibility of formulating generalizations of various kinds about linguistic phenomena; but it is both a denial that *faits de langue* can be identifed on any basis 'outside' *la langue*, and an affirmation that the only generalizations which concern linguistics are those concerning *faits de langue*. Clearly, if there are no *faits de langue* which are panchronic facts, then *a fortiori* there are no psychological facts 'universal to human nature' which can be the concern of linguistics, other than those deriving from the *faculté linguistique*.

Durkheim, like Saussure, sees both languages and currencies as obvious examples of social systems which cannot be explained in terms of a fortunate conformity between individual practices. 'The system of signs I use to express my thought, the system of currency I use to pay my debts, the instruments of credit I utilize in my commercial relations, the practices followed in my profession, etc., function independently of my own use of them. And these statements can be repeated for each member of society. Here, then, are ways of acting, thinking and feeling that present the noteworthy property of existing outside the individual consciousness' (Durkheim 1895:4).

What solves for Durkheim the problem of identifying a distinctive subject-matter for the science of sociology is, as Catlin points out, positing the existence of a collective consciousness. Now the phrase *conscience collective* is by no means unfamiliar to a reader of the *Cours*. But in the *Cours* the role played by this notion is not *overtly* that of making it possible to identify a distinctive subject-matter for the science of linguistics. It does, however, serve a no less crucial function: that of distinguishing synchronic from diachronic linguistics ([140]). And since for Saussure synchronic linguistics takes priority, in that diachrony is defined negatively with respect to synchrony, it becomes clear that *indirectly* the notion of a collective consciousness plays for Saussurean linguistics a theoretical role which is exactly parallel to that which it plays in Durkheimian sociology. Positing *la langue* as a supra-individual system solves for Saussure simultaneously the problems of defining and organizing linguistics internally 'as a science'. Unless there is a collective consciousness, the notion of a supra-individual *system* does not make sense in Saussurean terms, systems being defined holistically. Moreover, without a collective consciousness, diachrony would be reduced to relations of chronological succession. For Saussure, clearly, a collective consciousness has to extend across generations to unite individuals whose linguistic lives may be widely separated in 'real time', and however ignorant such individuals may be of the linguistic practices of their forebears.

Catlin says of Durkheim that he demarcated sociology from psychology by limiting psychology 'by definition to the level of individual consciousness' (Catlin 1938: xxvii). What Saussure did was rather different, although the strategy employed was the same. For even if *la langue* was for Saussure in some sense psychological in nature (at least to the extent that *la langue* exists as a cognitive system in the individual), academic psychology in Saussure's days had no established techniques for studying it, other than those which a 'scientific' linguistics was to provide. A psychology which attempted to study speech in the individual *qua* individual would merely be studying aspects of *parole*. Durkheim, says Catlin, believes 'that he is studying a supermind, immanent in society' (Catlin 1938: xxx), and the description is remarkably apposite to Saussure. Although *la langue* is manifest only in the speech behaviour of individuals, *elle n'existe parfaitement que dans la masse* ([30]).

But Saussure runs into both practical and theoretical difficulties in trying to have his collective linguistic bun and eat it, where Durkheim wisely refrains; and this brings us back once again to the 'Saussurean paradox'. There is no corresponding 'Durkheimian paradox' because Durkheim does not attempt to treat the individual as an idealized representative of the community. The practical consequences of the 'Saussurean paradox' were to have a quite marked effect on the subsequent development of linguistics, which can still be seen today. Although the distinction between *langue* and *parole*, as Giglioli points out, 'seemed at first to draw linguistics and sociology together, actually, unwittingly or not, it produced the contrary result. For if *langue* is defined as a set of grammatical rules existing in the mind of everyone, it becomes unnecessary to bother with the study of actual speech in social interactions' (Giglioli 1972: 7). The reason Durkheim gives for rejecting introspection as a way of discovering the collectivity's conception of a social institution is that it 'does not exist in its entirety in any one individual' (Durkheim 1938: xlvi-xlvii). Now although Saussure's *elle n'existe parfaitement que dans la masse* pays lip-service to this too, it can only be lip-service. Otherwise, Saussure's model of communication would not work. There is no way of resolving a conflict between an account of *la langue* as an instrument of communication which assumes that by definition communication resides in the telementation of messages which are identical for any speaker and any hearer, and a general account of social institutions (including *la langue*) which allows that by definition different individuals may have different – and *in any case* will have only imperfect – degrees of mastery of the institution which unites them. The Durkheimian approach cannot – and makes no attempt to – evade the question of *how* it is possible in practice to study social institutions which are complete only *dans la masse*. Saussure, unfortunately, pretends that the problem does not exist. Or, if it does, it is merely a practical and not a theoretical problem. The trouble is that it automatically does become a theoretical problem in the context of any attempt to lay the foundation of linguistics as a science. To set out the theoretical basis for a science which cannot be done is *eo ipso* to reduce the notion of a science to absurdity.

According to Washabaugh, Saussure borrowed the notion of a language as a social institution from Whitney, not from Durkheim, and he quotes Mounin to the effect that the term *institution* does not appear in Durkheim (Washabaugh 1974: 28). This is simply wrong. On the contrary, Durkheim claimed that it is permissible to 'designate as "institutions" all the beliefs and all the modes of conduct instituted by the collectivity' (Durkheim 1895: xxii). Here we seem to have clear evidence that a language for Durkheim does count as a social institution, since it is difficult to see what a language is if not a 'mode of conduct instituted by the collectivity'. For Saussure, *la langue* is precisely that. It is not instituted by the individual. (Saussure goes out of his way to assert that the individual is powerless to affect *la langue* in any way, apart from producing innovations which may – or may not – be subsequently incorporated into *la langue*.) Nor is it instituted by Nature. Those linguistic theorists who subscribed to what was later called 'the innateness hypothesis' do not find themselves in conflict with Durkheim on this score, since Durkheim's 'modes of conduct' manifestly include conduct based in various ways on human natural abilities. There may be a sense in which speaking English and speaking Chinese are based on the same natural abilities. But no one seriously supposes that the differences between the 'mode of conduct' which comprises speaking English and the 'mode of conduct' which comprises speaking Chinese are to be accounted for in terms of genetic differences.

Durkheim continues in the same passage: 'Sociology can then be defined as the science of institutions, of their genesis and of their functioning' (Durkheim 1895: xxii). It is a definition which could easily be adapted to fit Saussurean linguistics. If for 'institutions' we substitute 'linguistic institutions', we can derive a definition which is eminently Saussurean in spirit: 'Linguistics can then be defined as the science of linguistic institutions, of their genesis and of their functioning.' For just previously Durkheim has spelled out an account of the relationship between the freedoms of the individual and collective constraints which is tailor-made for the *Cours*. He says that the idea of a social constraint 'merely implies that collective ways of acting or thinking have a reality outside the individuals who, at every moment of time, conform to it. These ways of thinking and acting exist in their own right. The individual finds them completely formed, and he cannot evade or change them' (Durkheim 1895: lvi). Similarly, the *Cours* tells us that *la langue* 'is not a function of the speaker' ([30]) and that the individual 'is powerless either to create it or to modify it' ([31]). Where Saussure goes further – as he must in order to fulfil the requirements of his model of communication – is to claim that *la langue* also exists in the brain as 'the product passively registered by the individual' ([30]). There is no talk here of a 'collective brain': brains, for Saussure, are things only individuals have. This important difference between Durkheim and Saussure means that Saussure supplies himself in advance with a purely mechanistic psychological explanation of social conformity. The *mécanisme de la langue* is just that. It operates not at the collective but at the individual level, ensuring that the processes of telementational transference required by the *circuit de la parole* can actually take place.

Durkheim comments on the relationship between the social institution and the individual in terms which make an interesting comparison with the remarks on this topic in the *Cours*. He says 'Because beliefs and social practices thus come to us from without, it does not follow that we receive them passively or without modification. In reflecting on collective institutions and assimilating them for ourselves, we individualize them and impart to them more or less personal characteristics. Similarly, in reflecting on the physical world, each of us colours it after his own fashion, and different individuals adapt themselves differently to the same physical environment. It is for this reason that each one of us creates, in a measure, his own morality, religion and mode of life' (Durkheim 1895: lvi-lvii, n.7). This passage could almost stand without modification as an explication of the Saussurean claim that 'all the individuals linguistically linked in this manner will establish among themselves a kind of mean: all of them will reproduce – doubtless not exactly, but approximately – the same signs linked to the same concepts' ([29]). The difference is that whereas Durkheim recognizes the consequences for sociological investigation, Saussure does not. Saussure uses the appeal to a 'collective consciousness' as a way of circumventing the methodological problems consequential on the fact that the larger the linguistic community the less chance there is that any two individuals will have been 'linguistically linked' in the manner required to reproduce 'approximately' the same system of signs.

The only concession Saussure makes to the problem is to admit that in large communities languages tend to fragment dialectally. But his theoretical move here is then to treat each of the resultant dialects as a separate linguistic system in its own right. This is the thrust of his decision to replace the notion of synchrony by that of idiosynchrony. To identify idiosynchronic systems, it may be necessary to pursue 'a division into dialects and sub-dialects' ([128]). The move is clumsy on at least two counts. First, it is quite unclear how the investigator in the field will be able to identify these sub-dialects which constitute separate idiosynchronic systems: for Saussure does not deny that communication may be possible *across* dialects and sub-dialects of the same language, while at the same time conceding that in some cases it may not be ([275]). But if this is so, communication is no criterion for identifying differences between idiosynchronic systems. Second, how can this be reconciled with Saussure's circuit model of communication? That model was based on the assumption that the interlocutors A and B shared the same idiosynchronic system. But if linguistic communication is possible without that common factor, clearly the model proposed is inadequate as a basis for linguistic theory. We would need at the very least a model which showed how it was possible to translate from A's idiosynchronic system into B's idiosynchronic system: whereas in the Saussurean model it is the single idiosynchronic system itself which takes care of the transmission problem of equivalences.

Here the tension between the collective 'social institution' component of *la langue* and the individual 'cognitive system' component of *la langue* stretches the link to its theoretical breaking point. For there is not much sense to be made of the notion that *la langue* is a social institution if the institution cannot provide the most basic of social requirements, which are those of communication between the members of society. Analogously, it would make little sense to treat a monetary system as a social institution if it failed to provide the members of society with a means of buying and selling things. Once language and communication become theoretically divorced, the key Saussurean concept of *valeur* is itself rendered vacuous; and for just the same reason as in the economic analogy, where a five-franc coin simply has no value if *nothing* can be bought with it. (Obviously, that would not prevent it from having a value in some other sense – aesthetic value, historical value, sentimental value: but these other possible dimensions of value are irrelevant to the case.)

The root of the problem with Saussurean linguistics is that it has not worked out the connexion between language and communication in any theoretically satisfactory way. Although it couples language with communication in an intimate partnership, the two partners are condemned to dancing in perpetuity to the tune of what one linguist has called Saussure's 'hesitation waltz' (Gagnepain 1981: 149). This odd composition is the result of starting linguistic theory from the wrong end. Saussurean linguistics begins by focussing upon the properties of the individual linguistic sign in the abstract, and hoping that somehow at the social end, where signs are put to everyday use, everything will work out satisfactorily in terms of communicational corollaries. Unfortunately, it does not work out at all. But it could have worked out if only

Saussure had grasped the full implications of the economic analogy and seen that values are subordinate to transactions, and not the other way round. He might then have seen the wisdom of starting linguistic theory 'from the opposite end'.

The ultimate historical irony is that Saussure's error had been lucidly exposed in advance by Durkheim. (Perhaps that is one reason for supposing that the linguistic theorist who delivered the Geneva lectures had not read *Les règles de la méthode sociologique*; or, if he had read it, had failed to assimilate it.) Durkheim writes sceptically of the academic economics of his day:

> If value had been studied as any fact of reality ought to be studied, the economist would indicate, first of all, by what characteristics one might recognize the thing so designated, then classify its varieties, investigate by methodological inductions what the causes of its variations are, and finally compare these results in order to obtain a general formula. Theory would be introduced only when science had reached a sufficient stage of advancement. On the contrary, it is introduced at the very outset. In order to construct economic theory, the economist is content to meditate and to focus attention upon his own idea of value, that is, an object capable of being exchanged; he finds therein the idea of utility, scarcity, etc., and with these products of his analysis he constructs his definition. (Durkheim 1895: 25)

Transposed into linguistic terms, that advice would provide a charter for general linguistics of a quite different theoretical stamp from the Magna Carta which the *Cours* was subsequently taken to provide.

Saussurean linguistics stands or falls by the Saussurean concept of linguistic values. This is made eminently clear in the *Cours*, where that concept is presented – rightly – as Saussure's most original contribution to modern thinking about language, and indeed to linguistic thought of any era. For no thinker in the entire Western tradition before Saussure ever proposed a view which could be encapsulated in what is perhaps the most famous and contentious of all the Saussurean dicta: *la langue est un système de pures valeurs* ([116]). Whether we accept that view or not, it is one which extends the scope of Western thinking on the subject in unprecedented and challenging ways.

The greatest challenge of all, doubtless, is to pinpoint exactly where Saussure's concept of linguistic value is radically defective. Like the economists' concept of value, Saussure's does not yield constants *unless* we take the further step of assuming that the system of exchange is closed. Only then is there any assurance of that holism which will guarantee determinate identities to the individual items which are or may be exchanged. Without the logical necessity of closure, there just are no constants of the kind Saussurean synchronic theory postulates: no determinate forms, no determinate meanings, no determinate linguistic structure of any kind. It is hardly coincidental that most of Saussure's academic career had been spent in studying dead languages: for nothing imposes the appearance of closure on a system more convincingly than its recession into the irrecoverable past, where it remains perpetually 'frozen' in the form of writing.

By failing to see that values are subordinate to transactions, not transactions to values, Saussure forced his own thinking about language into a theoretical *impasse*. In the linguistic case no less than in the economic case, values are never 'fixed' except by and for the purpose of particular transactions. To recognize this would have necessitated a radical revision of Saussure's evaluation of *parole*. (It is by no means out of the question that a re-evaluation of this order might have ensued from the projected course of lectures on *linguistique de la parole*.) In any case, reversing out of that theoretical *impasse* is inevitable if the Saussurean concept of *valeur* is to be rescued at all. The fact that last week at Sotheby's I bought a vase by Hamada for £500 does not in any way guarantee *either* that the vase has the same value this week *or* that £500 sterling will this week buy me something equivalent to my Hamada vase. Nor can this dilemma be resolved by invoking such explanations as that, perhaps, 'I paid too much for the vase last week,' or alternatively, that 'I got a bargain'. These are simply historical – i.e. diachronic – comments. There is no sense in which they entail that there was a 'correct' value for the vase which I either paid or failed to pay when I bought it. *Mutatis mutandis*, the same applies to linguistic values: and anyone who fails to understand that fails to understand what kind of activity language is.

What happened when I bought the vase was that *by* paying £500 for it I established its value (in that particular commercial context). That I bought it at auction does not affect the example: the same would apply had I bought it in a shop at the price the dealer asked. (Asking prices are not values, even though they may both reflect and be reflected by values.) The price paid for the vase on that occasion automatically becomes an item in its commercial history. It may affect to some extent the price it fetches when next sold. And irrespective of its commercial history, it may affect the prices paid for other Hamada vases in London auction rooms. None of this validates a theory of economics which posits that buying and selling demands a fixed system of values. Furthermore, all the considerations mentioned carry over to the linguistic analogue: for example, the word *vase*. Was this pottery artifact sold for £500 'really' a vase? Might it not have been a bowl, dish, or even a traditional Japanese form for which there is no exact English term? It was, in any case, a unique piece of pottery, fashioned in a certain manner, and sold on this occasion 'as a vase'. The fact that it was catalogued as a 'vase', like the fact that it was sold for £500, becomes part of its history, and may or may not affect how similar pieces of pottery by Hamada are described in English. The meaning of the English word *vase* is no more fixed than the purchasing power of the pound sterling.

It is disappointing that Saussure managed to get so far with the concept of *valeur*, and yet in the end did not quite get far enough. Saussure, as de Mauro (1972: v) points out, saw a major problem of synchronic linguistics as being the problem of sameness: i.e. identity of linguistic signs. The pronunciation of a word may vary as between different instances, and its exact interpretation may also vary according to context. (Exactly the same variations apply to the cases of buying and selling.) From this Saussure draws the unobjectionable conclusion that, in the linguistic case, neither pronunciation nor interpretation *per se* provide adequate criteria for identifying the same item on all occasions. But Saussure, unfortunately, is committed to a model of speech communication which depends essentially on being able to produce and recognize 'the same' linguistic items irrespective of the occasion. How can such a symmetry between production and recognition be established irrespective of any occasional differences? The notion of *la langue* as a value system is intended to provide the answer. But to do this, it has to be a *fixed* value system; that is, it must be invariant across particular occasions. The sameness of a word resides not in having an identical pronunciation or an identical interpretation on all occasions, but in occupying a determinate and unique place in a total system which is supra-individual. This is the Saussurean solution to a problem which a long line of French writers had discussed, going back to Destutt de Tracy and beyond him to Condillac. The topic in question is sometimes referred to as the 'subjectivity of language' (Aarsleff 1982: 343 ff.), and the problem arises for anyone who accepts a Lockean model of speech communication: it is what Taylor calls 'Locke's puzzle' (Taylor 1984).

The Saussurean solution encounters two potential difficulties, one difficulty hidden behind the other. The more obvious difficulty is that unless the system itself is the same for *all* its users, it can hardly yield for them a uniform identification of linguistic signs. That is why change and variation *across users* must be excluded from the system as such. However, since the investigator has access only to the users, and not directly to the system, a plausible programme of linguistic investigation must explain how to circumvent that difficulty.

The less obvious but more serious difficulty is that one cannot get rid of change and variation merely by banishing them by fiat to the diachronic realm. For there is no sense to be made of the notion that an *état de langue* is simply a changing and variable linguistic continuum, but minus the changes and variations. That would be like trying to explain standing still as being the same as running, but without movement. Not only is the proposal incoherent, but in linguistics it automatically defeats its own purpose.

It leaves the synchronic theorist with no principled way of deciding what belongs to the system and what counts as a change or variation to be ignored. ('But since languages are always changing, however minimally, studying a linguistic state amounts in practice to ignoring unimportant changes' ([142]).) In other words, the invariant signs on which speech communication is deemed to depend remain *descriptively* unidentifiable amid the flux of actual discourse with all its individual idiosyncrasies. It follows that in order to have any explanatory utility, the system has to be envisaged as a *whole*, complete in itself, standing apart from the speech acts which it sponsors and the individuals who use it. Hence, as Calvet points out (Calvet 1975: 61) the theorist, although proclaiming *la langue* to be a social institution, ends up by postulating an abstract linguistic system which stands 'outside' society altogether.

Otherwise, in the constant flux of social interaction, there is no stable totality to provide the linguistic framework within which particular linguistic signs can be located and identified. If it were in principle possible that a given speech act by a given individual could (like buying a Hamada vase) itself introduce a modification into the system of values, that would be tantamount to seeing *la langue* as intrinsically open-ended and indeterminate. But then speech communication would be at the mercy of unpredictable innovation, and the basis for a systematic identification of linguistic signs would be lost. Just as in the economic case, it is only if we postulate that *the economy is a closed system* that it makes sense to speak of fixed currency values and equivalences. Once it is conceded that the supply of goods is constantly changing and that particular economic transactions may affect the availability of goods or the demand for them, then a theory of fixed values is no longer viable.

It would be a mistake to think that Saussure was unaware of the problem. The awareness is most obviously apparent in Chapter V of Part II, where there is an attempt to back away from the awkward question of how it is possible for the linguist to delimit the *état de langue* in its entirety. Saussure's holistic theory of linguistic structure requires such a delimitation. On the other hand, he cannot see any plausible *a priori* basis on which to restrict the range of either associative or syntagmatic relations. So he has to concede that 'an associative group has no particular number of items in it: nor do they occur in any particular order' ([174]) and that 'where syntagmas are concerned ... one must recognize the fact that there is no clear boundary separating *la langue*, as confirmed by communal usage, from *la parole*, marked by freedom of the individual' ([173]).

These are damaging admissions. To concede that 'any given term acts as the centre of a constellation, from which connected terms radiate *ad infinitum*' ([174]) is to concede that associative series are in principle open-ended, while to concede that the items occur in no particular order is to concede that the series themselves are internally unstructured. But series which have *no limit* and *no order* can hardly be the basis of any system of fixed communal values, or supply that *tout solidaire* ([157]) from which, by a process of analysis, the constituent elements are eventually reached. If the series are both open-ended and unstructured, there can be no guarantee that different individuals will not subdivide them in different ways, and thus recognize different associative groups; which amounts to saying that different speakers may be operating with different systems of *valeurs*. Thus in Saussurean terms they will be speaking different *langues*, even though the differences may not be obvious from the data of *parole*.

Similarly, in the case of syntagmatic relations, to concede the impossibility of drawing a boundary between individual initiative and collective usage is to concede that in descriptive syntagmatics the linguist will be unable to tell in many cases whether the facts described are *faits de langue* or *faits de parole*. If the status of linguistics as a science depends precisely on not conflating *langue* and *parole*, this concession is in any case a disaster for Saussure; but it is a double disaster inasmuch as the indeterminacy of syntagmatic relations also entails the impossibility of a fixed system of *valeurs*.

This time the paradox is one well worthy of Zeno. For if linguistic units have a value only in virtue of being determinately placed in relation to one another in the context of larger networks of units, each of which in turn functions interdependently with others in still larger networks, then determining the value of even the smallest unit in the system presupposes the completion of an apparently unlimited process of incremental re-contextualization, involving networks of larger and larger size, with structuring of ever-increasing complexity. *C'est du tout solidaire qu'il faut partir pour obtenir par analyse les éléments qu'il renferme* begins to sound less like an invitation to linguistic analysis and more like a warning against the futility of attempting it.

Thus in the end we see Saussurean holism running up against the apparently insuperable difficulty arising from the absence of any clear analytic criteria for identifying the limits of the system, either in the associative or in the syntagmatic dimension. Along neither road does the linguist come to a Checkpoint Charlie, where visas are demanded for crossing the border from Individual Freedom into Collective Coercion, or vice versa. Given that in Saussurean linguistics parts depend on wholes, and analysis proceeds from the latter to the former, this leads straight to the problem that it becomes impossible for the linguist to identify with any assurance the postulated *entités concrètes de la langue*. Saussure is thus ensnared in a theoretical trap of his own making. Proclaiming on the one hand that in linguistics it is the viewpoint chosen which creates the linguistic object, he fails on the other hand to be able to demonstrate that his recommended viewpoint creates any scientifically identifiable object at all.

It is intrinsic to any theoretical endeavour that failure has the potential
to teach as many valuable lessons as success. Saussure's ultimate failure
to resolve the contradiction between a fixed-code model of languages and
the linguistic freedom of the individual teaches a difficult lesson of the
highest value; perhaps still the most valuable lesson in linguistics that
could possibly be learned. If linguists subsequently ignored or forgot or
evaded it, that is nothing for which the blame can retrospectively be laid
at Saussure's door.

The same lesson is a lesson for other social sciences, and for
epistemology in general. One has only to substitute for *la langue* the
designation of any other social institution to see that a conceptual
framework of the kind proposed in the *Cours* will encounter parallel
problems in other disciplines. In one sense, it would have made no
difference if Saussure had been writing about sartorial systems, kinship
systems, or transport systems. His prophetic subordination of linguistics
to semiology already presages this extension. The basic questions the
Cours deals with are questions which will arise wherever a discipline is
concerned with elucidating the mechanisms by which the individual and
the collectivity are mysteriously united in social interaction. Consequently, the *Cours* can be read as a kind of pioneering enterprise in
theorization, relevant for all disciplines which must, sooner or later, face
Durkheim's challenge to recognize social facts as constituting an
independent order of reality. It is Saussure's *Cours* which, if anything
does, validates Lévi-Strauss's claim that linguistics occupies a 'special
place' among the social sciences (Lévi-Strauss 1945).

The explanatory conflict dramatized in the *Cours* is between holism
and individualism: and that is a conflict which demands a larger
academic stage than any that linguistics alone can offer (d'Agostino
1979, Sampson 1979, Pateman 1980). 'Holism versus individualism in
history and sociology' appeared forty years later as the title of a
well-known paper by Gellner (which makes no mention of Saussure at
all, although its themes are essentially Saussurean). What is even more
interesting from a Saussurean point of view is that the original published
title of Gellner's paper was 'Explanations in History'. It is interesting to
speculate which of these two formulations Bally and Sechehaye would
have preferred if choosing a subtitle for the *Cours*. In either case, they
might have been glad of the kind of epigraph which Gellner provides
when he writes of this very conflict that 'when reductions fail, the fact
that they do so and the reasons why they do so, give us some
understanding of the nature of the unreduced concepts' (Gellner 1959:
490 n.1.): or even 'The problem of explanation in history is also the
problem of the nature of sociology' (Gellner 1959: 489).

Therefore, to recommend reading the *Cours* as a record of failure is not a nonsense. The apt comparison is with certain types of experiment in engineering, where a structure is submitted to progressively increasing stress until finally it collapses. The *Cours* is a text of this order. It takes a very simple structure of explanation, based on just two principles, and proceeds to pile more and more upon this framework, in order to demonstrate just how much it will bear. One should not be surprised by the eventual collapse, but amazed by its unsuspected strength, and intrigued to see just where it will fracture. That is why there is no substitute for reading the *Cours* as it stands; and why, as it stands, it remains one of the most impressive intellectual landmarks of modern thought.

Bibliography

H. Aarsleff, *The Study of Language in England, 1780-1860,* Princeton, 1967.

From Locke to Saussure, London, 1982.

F.B. d'Agostino, 'Individualism and collectivism: the case of language,' *Philosophy of the Social Sciences,* vol. 9, 1979.

G.P. Baker and P.M.S. Hacker, *Wittgenstein: Meaning and Understanding,* Oxford, 1980.

Ch. Bally, 'L'arbitraire du signe: valeur et signification,' *Le français moderne,* vol. 8, 1940.

R. Barthes, *Eléments de sémiologie,* Paris 1964. Tr. A. Lavers and C. Smith, London, 1967.

L. Bloomfield, *An Introduction to the Study of Language,* New York, 1914.

Review of Ferdinand de Saussure, *Cours de linguistique générale, Modern Language Journal,* vol. 8. 1923.

Language, London, 1935.

L.G.A. de Bonald, *Législation primitive,* Paris, 1802.

G. Broadbent, R. Bunt and C. Jencks (eds.), *Signs, Symbols and Architecture,* Chichester, 1980.

E. Buyssens, *Les langages et le discours,* Bruxelles, 1943.

L.-J. Calvet, *Pour et contre Saussure,* Paris, 1975.

G.E.G. Catlin, Introduction to E. Durkheim, *The Rules of Sociological Method,* tr. S.A. Solovay and J.H. Mueller, New York, 1938.

CFS: *Cahiers Ferdinand de Saussure,* Genève, 1941-.

A.N. Chomsky, *Syntactic Structures,* The Hague, 1957.

'Current issues in linguistic theory'. In J.A. Fodor & J.J. Katz, *The Structure of Language,* Englewood Cliffs, 1964.

Aspects of the Theory of Syntax, Cambridge, Mass., 1965.

R.G. Collingwood, *The Idea of History,* Oxford, 1946.

F.M. Cornford, *Plato's Theory of Knowledge,* London, 1935.

D. Crystal, *Introduction to Language Pathology,* London, 1980.

J. Culler, *Saussure,* London, 1976.

F.E.X. Dance, 'A helical model of communication'. In F.E.X. Dance (ed.), *Human Communication Theory,* New York, 1967.

P.B. Denes and E.N. Pinson, *The Speech Chain*, Garden City, N.Y., 1963.

F.P. Dinneen, *An Introduction to General Linguistics*, New York, 1967.

W. Doroszewski, 'Sociologie et linguistique (Durkheim et de Saussure),' *Actes du 2e congrès international de linguistes*, Paris, 1933.

E. Durkheim, *Les règles de la méthode sociologique*, Paris, 1895.
[(Page references are to the standard modern reprint of the second edition, Paris, 1937. English versions of the passages quoted are from the translation by S.A. Solovay and J.H. Mueller, *The Rules of Sociological Method*, New York, 1938.)

U. Eco, *A Theory of Semiotics*, Bloomington, 1976.

R. Engler, 'Théorie et critique d'un principe saussurien: l'arbitraire du signe,' *Cahiers Ferdinand de Saussure*, vol. 19, 1962.
'Compléments à l'arbitraire,' *Cahiers Ferdinand de Saussure*, vol.21, 1964.
Edition critique du 'Cours de linguistique générale' de F. de Saussure, Wiesbaden, 1967.
'La linéarité du signifiant'. In R. Amacker, T. de Mauro and L.J. Prieto (eds.), *Studi saussuriani per Robert Godel*, Bologna, 1974.

J.R. Firth, 'The technique of semantics,' *Transactions of the Philological Society*, 1935.
'Personality and language in society,' *The Sociological Review*, vol. 42, 1950.
'Modes of meaning,' *Essays and Studies*, 1951.
(Page references are to the reprints in: J.R. Firth, *Papers in Linguistics 1934-1951*, London, 1957.)

G. Frege, 'Über Sinn und Bedeutung,' *Zeitschrift für Philosophie und philosophische Kritik*, vol.100, 1892.

H. Frei, 'Saussure contre Saussure?', *Cahiers Ferdinand de Saussure*, vol.9, 1950.

E.C. Fudge, 'Phonology'. In J. Lyons (ed.), *New Horizons in Linguistics*, Harmondsworth, 1970.

J. Gagnepain, 'On language and communication,' *Language & Communication*, vol.1, 1981.

A.H. Gardiner, *The Theory of Speech and Language*, Oxford, 1932.

E. Gellner, 'Holism versus individualism in history and sociology'. In P. Gardiner (ed.), *Theories of History*, Glencoe, 1959. (Page reference to this edition.) Originally published as 'Explanations in history,' *Proceedings of the Aristotelian Society*, 1956.

P.P. Giglioli (ed.), *Langue and Social Context*, Harmondsworth, 1972.

R. Godel, *Les sources manuscrites du Cours de linguistique générale de F. de Saussure*, Genève/Paris, 1957.
'De la théorie du signe aux termes du système,' *Cahiers Ferdinand de Saussure*, vol.22, 1966.

R. Harris, *The Language-Makers*, London, 1980.

A. Henry, 'La linéarité du signifiant'. In J. Dierckx and Y. Lebrun (eds.), *Linguistique contemporaine: hommage à Eric Buyssens*, Bruxelles, 1970.

L. Hjelmslev, 'Langue et parole,' *Cahiers Ferdinand de Saussure*, vol.2, 1942.
Omkring sprogteoriens grundlœggelse, Copenhagen, 1943. Tr. F.J. Whitfield, *Prolegomena to a Theory of Language*, Baltimore, 1953.

C.F. Hockett, 'Two models of grammatical description,' *Word*, vol.10, 1954.

A. Hovelacque, *La linguistique*, 2nd ed., Paris, 1877.

C.M. Hutton, *The type-token relation: abstraction and instantiation in linguistic theory*, Oxford, 1986 (unpublished D.Phil. thesis).

R. Jakobson, *Selected Writings. I: Phonological Studies*, The Hague, 1962.

O. Jespersen, *Language; its Nature, Development and Origin*, London, 1922.
Mankind, Nation and Individual from a Linguistic Point of View, Oslo, 1925.

M. Joos (ed.), *Readings in Linguistics I. The Development of Descriptive Linguistics in America 1925-56*, Chicago, 1957.

J.J. Katz, *The Philosophy of Language*, New York, 1966.

J.J. Katz and P.M. Postal, *An Integrated Theory of Linguistic Descriptions*, Cambridge, Mass., 1964.

E.F.K. Koerner, *F. de Saussure: Origin and Development of his Linguistic Thought*, Vieweg, 1973.

A. Lange-Seidl, *Approaches to Theories for Nonverbal Signs*, Lisse, 1977.

G.C. Lepschy, *A Survey of Structural Linguistics*, London, 1970.

C. Lévi-Strauss, 'L'analyse structurale en linguistique et en anthropologie,' *Word*, vol.1, 1945.

J. Locke, *An Essay Concerning Human Understanding*, 5th ed., London, 1706.

N. Love, 'Psychologistic structuralism and the polylect,' *Language & Communication*, vol. 4, 1984.

J. Lyons, 'Human language'. In R.A. Hinde (ed.), *Non-Verbal Communication*, Cambridge, 1972.
Semantics, vol.1, Cambridge, 1977.

B. Malmberg, 'Le circuit de la parole'. In A. Martinet (ed.), *Le langage*, Paris, 1968.

A. Martinet, 'De quelques unités significatives'. In R. Amacker, T. de Mauro and L.J. Prieto (eds.), *Studi saussuriani per Robert Godel*, Bologna, 1974.

T. de Mauro, *Edition critique du 'Cours de linguistique générale' de F. de Saussure*, Paris, 1972.

C. Metz, *Langage et cinema*, Paris, 1971.

C. Morris, *Signification and Significance*, Cambridge, Mass., 1964.

W.G. Moulton, *A Linguistic Guide to Language Learning*, 2nd ed., Menasha, 1970.

F.M. Müller, *Lectures on the Science of Language*, vol. II, London, 1864.

J.A.H. Murray, *Oxford English Dictionary*, vol.1, Oxford, 1888.

C.K. Ogden and I.A. Richards, *The Meaning of Meaning*, London, 1923.

G.H.R. Parkinson, 'The translation theory of understanding'. In G. Vesey (ed.), *Communication and Understanding*, Hassocks, 1977.

T. Pateman, 'Nature and culture in language and speech: another comment on d'Agostino,' *Philosophy of the Social Sciences*, vol. 10, 1980.

'What is a language?', *Language & Communication*, vol.3, 1983.

H. Paul, *Principien der Sprachgeschichte*, Halle, 1880. 2nd ed. (1886) tr. by H.A. Strong, *Principles of the History of Language*, London, 1890. (Page references are to and quotations from the translation.)

C.S. Peirce, *Collected Papers*, 8 vols., ed. C. Hartshorne and P. Weiss, Cambridge, Mass., 1931-58.

L.J. Prieto, *Messages et signaux*, Paris, 1966.

'La sémiologie'. In A. Martinet (ed.), *Le langage*, Paris, 1968.

M.J. Reddy, 'The conduit metaphor – a case of frame conflict in our language about language'. In A. Ortony (ed.), *Metaphor and Thought*, Cambridge, 1979.

N. Ruwet, 'Linguistique et science de l'homme,' *Esprit*, November 1963.

G. Sampson, 'Comment on d'Agostino,' *Philosophy of the Social Sciences*, vol.9, 1979.

A. Schleicher, *Die deutsche Sprache*, Stuttgart, 1860.

A. Sechehaye, 'Les trois linguistiques saussuriennes,' *Vox Romanica*, vol. 5, 1940.

M. Silverstein (ed.), *Whitney on Language*, Cambridge, Mass., 1971.

H. Spang-Hanssen, *Recent Theories on the Nature of the Language Sign*, Copenhagen, 1954.

N.C.W. Spence, 'A hardy perennial: the problem of *langue* and *parole*,' *Archivum Linguisticum*, vol.9, 1957.

'*Langue* and *parole* yet again,' *Neophilologus*, vol.44, 1962. (Page references are to the reprints in: N.C.W. Spence, *Essays in Linguistics*, München, 1976.)

T.J. Taylor, 'Linguistic origins: Bruner and Condillac on learning how to talk,' *Language & Communication*, vol.4, 1984.

B. Toussaint, *Qu'est-ce que la sémiologie ?*, Toulouse, 1978.

M. Toussaint, *Contre l'arbitraire du signe*, Paris, 1983.

S. Ullmann, *The Principles of Semantics*, 2nd ed., Glasgow, 1959. *Semantics*, Oxford, 1962.

J. Vendryes, 'Sur la dénomination,' *Bulletin de la Société de Linguistique de Paris*, vol.48, 1952.

W. Washabaugh, 'Saussure, Durkheim and sociolinguistic theory,' *Archivum Linguisticum*, vol.5, 1974.

W.D. Whitney, *Language and the Study of Language*, London, 1867.

L. Wittgenstein, *Philosophische Untersuchungen*, tr. G.E.M. Anscombe, 2nd ed., Oxford, 1958.

A.D. Woozley (ed.), *John Locke, An Essay Concerning Human Understanding*, Glasgow, 1964.

Index

'An exceptional book. It is completely different from anything else currently available, refreshing, extremely well-written and original in so many ways . . . It is just the sort of book I would want my students to read . . . It is quite the best introductory book that I have ever come across.' **Philip Martin, De Montfort University**

'Fresh, surprising, never boring, and engagingly humorous, while remaining intellectually serious and challenging . . . This is a terrific book, and I'm very glad that it exists.' **Peggy Kamuf, University of Southern California, Los Angeles**

'This excellent book is very well-written and an outstanding introduction to literary studies. An extremely stimulating introduction.' **Robert Eaglestone, Royal Holloway, University of London**

'I am convinced that Bennett and Royle have written a pathbreaking work and I suspect that this book – so full of laughter, suspense, secrets and pleasure – will have an appeal beyond a strictly academic audience.' **Alan Shima, University of Gothenberg**

'All the chapters in the volume are illuminating, informative and original.' **Robert Mills, King's College London**

'Bennett and Royle offer a different kind of introduction, which directly involves the reader in the problems and pleasures of thinking about literature – its distinctiveness, its strangeness, its power, its inexhaustibility . . . They succeed brilliantly in encouraging readers who are new to theory to appreciate its importance, enjoy its revelations, and understand some of its conceptual apparatus without diminishing the centrality of literary writing itself. This is a book which students in every introductory course on criticism and theory would benefit from having.' **Derek Attridge, University of York**

An Introduction to Literature, Criticism and Theory

An Introduction to Literature, Criticism and Theory

Third edition

ANDREW BENNETT AND
NICHOLAS ROYLE

PEARSON
Longman

Harlow, England • London • New York • Boston • San Francisco • Toronto
Sydney • Tokyo • Singapore • Hong Kong • Seoul • Taipei • New Delhi
Cape Town • Madrid • Mexico City • Amsterdam • Munich • Paris • Milan

PEARSON EDUCATION LIMITED

Edinburgh Gate
Harlow CM20 2JE
United Kingdom
Tel: +44 (0)1279 623623
Fax: +44 (0)1279 431059
Website: www.pearsoned.co.uk

_____

Third edition published in Great Britain in 2004

© International Book Distributors Limited 1995
© Pearson Education Limited 1995, 1999, 2004

The rights of Andrew Bennett (1960–) and Nicholas Royle (1957–)
to be identified as authors of this work have been asserted by
them in accordance with the Copyright, Designs and Patents Act 1988.

ISBN 0 582 82295 5

British Library Cataloguing-in-Publication Data
A CIP catalogue record for this book can be obtained from the British Library

Library of Congress Cataloging-in-Publication Data
A CIP catalog record for this book can be obtained from the Library of Congress

10   9   8   7   6   5   4   3   2   1
08   07   06   05   04

Set by 35 in 11/13pt Bulmer MT
Printed in the United Kingdom by Henry Ling Limited, at the Dorset Press, Dorchester, DT1 1HD

The Publisher's policy is to use paper manufactured from sustainable forests.

Contents

Acknowledgements

We are grateful to Michael Ayres for permission to reproduce his poem 'Bittersweet' published in *Poems, 1987–1992* by Odyssey Poets.

In some instances we have been unable to trace the owners of copyright material and we would appreciate any information that would enable us to do so.

Preface to the first edition

This is a new kind of book. It offers new ways of thinking about literature and about what is involved in reading critically. It is designed to be clear and accessible to those who are beginning to study literature, as well as to more advanced students. Although written with university students in mind, we dare to hope that it might also be of interest to other readers.

Literary theory is an unavoidable part of studying literature and criticism. But theory – especially when it takes the form of 'isms' – can often be intimidating or else, frankly, boring. We have tried to avoid simply giving potted summaries of *isms*. Instead we present brief essays on a range of key critical concepts all of which have more or less familiar names. We put these concepts into practice through readings of particular literary texts. Our primary focus, in other words, is on what is powerful, complex and strange about literary works themselves. Our aim is to explain, entertain, stimulate and challenge.

The book is divided into twenty-four chapters and looks as if it has a certain order or progression. It begins with 'The beginning' and ends with 'The end'. But it has been put together in such a way that it can also be read starting from any one chapter. 'The end', for example, is not a bad place to begin. Each chapter concludes with some suggestions for further reading. There is a glossary of critical and theoretical terms at the back of the book, plus a full bibliography of the texts discussed.

Preface to the second edition

This new edition of *An Introduction to Literature, Criticism and Theory* has been thoroughly revised and, we hope, improved. We have revised all existing chapters, updated and expanded the further reading sections, the glossary and the bibliography, and also added four new chapters: 'Monuments', 'Ghosts', 'Queer' and 'The colony'. These additional chapters reflect the importance of certain new or emerging areas of literary studies, such as queer theory, postcolonial theory, debates about 'the canon' and spectrality. We also hope, however, that the new chapters may complement and reinforce what we believe was already distinctive about the first edition of this book, namely its preoccupation with literature and the literary as such. Our foremost desire has been to explore and analyze the strange, protean forms and effects of the literary and of literature as an institution. This second edition, then, attempts to make explicit in new ways our continuing fascination with literary works themselves – with, for example, their monumental, ghostly, queer and colonizing power.

Preface to the third edition

For this third edition we have, once again, revised and updated the book as thoroughly as possible. Some of the revisions are so small that, we suspect, only Bennett and Royle will ever notice; others are more substantial. We have also added four new chapters: 'Creative writing', 'Moving pictures', 'Mutant' and 'War'. In each case, we have sought to acknowledge and engage with recent developments in literature, criticism and theory in what we hope are refreshing, informative and stimulating ways.

1. The beginning

When will we have begun?

Where – or when – does a literary text begin? This question raises a series of fundamental problems in literary criticism and theory. Does a text begin as the author puts his or her first mark on a piece of paper or keys in the first word on a computer? Does it begin with the first idea about a story or poem, or in the childhood of the writer, for instance? Or does the text only begin as the reader picks up the book? Does the text begin with its title, or with the first word of the so-called 'body' of the text?

We will try to begin with a poem. John Milton's great epic *Paradise Lost* (1667) begins by returning to the beginning:

> Of man's first disobedience, and the fruit
> Of that forbidden tree, whose mortal taste
> Brought death into the world, and all our woe,
> With loss of Eden, till one greater Man
> Restore us, and regain the blissful seat,
> Sing Heav'nly Muse, that on the secret top
> Of Oreb, or of Sinai, didst inspire
> That shepherd, who first taught the chosen seed,
> In the beginning how the heav'ns and earth
> Rose out of chaos: or if Sion hill
> Delight thee more, and Siloa's brook that flowed
> Fast by the oracle of God; I thence
> Invoke thy aid to my advent'rous song,
> That with no middle flight intends to soar
> Above th'Aonian mount, while it pursues
> Things unattempted yet in prose or rhyme.

This extraordinary opening sentence is all about beginnings. Thematically, it establishes the poem to be about the *first* disobedience of Adam and Eve which 'Brought death into the world, and all our woe'. But it is also about itself *as* a beginning: it assures us that this is the first time that such a project has been attempted ('Things unattempted yet in prose or rhyme'). It is as if the opening to a poem could be the equivalent of a moon-landing – one small step for John Milton . . . Rather differently, the opening sentence is about itself as a beginning in the sense that it is asking the 'Heav'nly Muse' for inspiration. It is about the way that poems are conventionally thought to begin – in inspiration. This produces a strange paradox of beginnings: the origin of the poem, inspiration, comes *after* the beginning of the poem. In other ways, too, Milton's opening unsettles any simple notion of opening or beginning. Not only does the poem talk about a beginning, the eating of the fruit of knowledge, but it also refers to a return to a time before that beginning ('regain the blissful seat'), a restoration which will be both the beginning of a new age and a repetition of a previous state.

There is another way in which this beginning is not a beginning: it repeatedly refers us back to other texts. Milton refers to Moses ('That shepherd') in the belief that he 'taught' the children of Israel the creation story – in other words, that he wrote the opening books of the Old Testament. In this respect, the muse that Milton's poem addresses and invokes is a second-hand muse. Contrary to its claims to originality, this opening echoes and alludes to various other openings. 'Of man's first disobedience . . . Sing Heav'nly Muse' repeats the conventional apostrophe of such classical openings as Homer's *Iliad* and Virgil's *Aeneid*; 'In the beginning' repeats the opening to the Gospel according to St John ('In the beginning was the Word'), and so on. Finally, the very syntax of Milton's sentence displaces the beginning of the poem, in particular by holding back the main verb of the sentence – 'Sing' – until line six.

Despite the complications of Milton's opening, however, at least it tries (or pretends to try) to begin at the beginning, rather than in the middle. Beginning in the middle – *in medias res* – is the other way to begin. One of the most famous beginnings-in-the-middle is Dante's opening to *The Divine Comedy* (*c*.1307–20):

> Nel mezzo del cammin di nostra vita
> mi ritrovai per una selva oscura,
> che la diritta via era smarrita.
> (Midway in the journey of our life I found myself in a dark
> wood, for the straight way was lost.)

There are at least three different middles here: the middle of 'our life', the middle of a dark wood, the middle of a narrative. Dante conflates life, journey and narrative, and suggests the uncanny terror of *beginning* at such a moment of middling. In particular, the uncanniness of 'mi ritrovai' suggests the hallucinatory terror of (re-)finding, of retrieving oneself. But Dante's opening might also suggest that there are *no* absolute beginnings – only strange originary middles. No journey, no life, no narrative ever really begins: all have in some sense already begun before they begin. But this is not to say that we can do without the concept of the beginning. Where would we be without a beginning? Where would a text be?

The paradox of the beginning having already begun is wittily presented by Laurence Sterne in the opening of his novel *The Life and Opinions of Tristram Shandy, Gentleman* (1759) in terms of both the beginning of a narrative and the beginning of a life:

> I wish either my father or my mother, or indeed both of them, as they were in duty both equally bound to it, had minded what they were about when they begot me; had they duly consider'd how much depended upon what they were then doing;—that not only the production of a rational Being was concern'd in it, but that possibly the happy formation and temperature of his body, perhaps his genius and the very cast of his mind;—and, for aught they knew to the contrary, even the fortunes of his whole house might take their turn from the humours and dispositions which were then uppermost:—Had they duly weighed and considered all this, and proceeded accordingly,—I am verily persuaded I should have made a quite different figure in the world, from that, in which the reader is likely to see me. (5)

This opening is a comic version of Philip Larkin's equivocal opening line to his poem 'This Be The Verse' (1974): 'They fuck you up, your mum and dad'. Tristram Shandy complains because his parents were thinking of something else at the moment of his conception and he is afraid that in consequence his whole life has been fucked up. As his uncle Toby remarks a few pages later, 'My Tristram's misfortunes began nine months before ever he came into the world' (7). *Tristram Shandy* famously confronts the intractable problem of how to end an autobiography: such a text can never catch up with itself because it takes longer to write about life than it takes to live it. In this sense, no autobiography can ever end. But *Tristram Shandy* is also about how to begin – how to begin at the beginning – and how we begin.

If beginnings always have a context and are therefore determined by what comes before, the opening to *Tristram Shandy* also makes it clear that, in turn, beginnings determine what comes after. This is true of literary as of other beginnings: beginnings augur, acting like promises for what is to come. Such is the force of many well-known literary beginnings. The opening to Jane Austen's *Pride and Prejudice* (1813) is apparently unequivocal: 'It is a truth universally acknowledged, that a single man in possession of a good fortune, must be in want of a wife' (1). This sets the stage for the whole novel. The topic is marriage, the tone is ironic. Austen proclaims the values of universalism ('a truth universally acknowledged'), while satirizing them: what is acknowledged as a truth for upper middle-class men in early nineteenth-century England is not necessarily acknowledged universally. Before going on to provide an 'Explanatory' note on its dialect, Mark Twain's *The Adventures of Huckleberry Finn (Tom Sawyer's Comrade)* (1885) begins with a 'notice':

NOTICE

Persons attempting to find a motive in this narrative will be prosecuted; persons attempting to find a moral in it will be banished; persons attempting to find a plot in it will be shot.

BY ORDER OF THE AUTHOR
PER G.G., CHIEF OF ORDNANCE

At once witty and baffling, the sentence is both an entrance and a barrier to the novel. It reads something like the sentence 'Do not read this sentence', in that it both acknowledges that readers *do* try to find motives and morals in narratives, and comically prohibits such a reading. Herman Melville's *Moby Dick; or, The Whale* (1851) is also framed by a number of what Gérard Genette calls 'peritexts' (Genette 1987) – by a contents page, a dedication, an 'Etymology' (of the word 'Whale') and 'Extracts' (several pages of quotations about whales) – before it begins with the famous words 'Call me Ishmael'. Satirical prevarication and pedantry, combined with blustering assertiveness, characterize the whole novel. Virginia Woolf's *Orlando* (1928) opens (after a dedication, preface, contents page and list of illustrations) with a sentence that equivocates by appearing not to do so: 'He – for there could be no doubt of his sex, though the fashion of the time did something to disguise it – was in the act of slicing at the head of a Moor which swung from the rafters' (13). The sentence begins a book about a person of uncertain or variable gender in a tone of strange uncertainty, with a suggestive mixture of decapitation and castration. By appearing not to, this opening sentence, like the novel as a whole, subtly undermines conventional ideas about gender identity. The first sentence of Ford Madox Ford's *The Good Soldier* (1915) is sheer heart-tugging seduction: 'This is the saddest story I have ever heard' (7). It is the sort of sentence from which a novel might never recover. And Proust's famous understated opening to *Remembrance of Things Past* (1913–27) implies that there is no single beginning: 'Longtemps, je me suis couché de bonne heure' ('For a long time I used to go to bed early', 13). A studied reflection on the past, a sense of intimacy, the power of habit and repetition are what characterize Proust's 3,000-page novel. As these examples suggest, one of the peculiarities of literary openings is that they are never single. The openings to *Huckleberry Finn*, *Moby Dick* and *Orlando* produce multiple beginnings through their 'peritexts', but the other examples also present more than one beginning: *The Good Soldier* suggests both a story and its retelling (as well as other stories that are not as sad), while Proust's opening gives a sense that narrative begins in repetition, that no single event can be said to be a beginning.

As we have begun to see, one of the ways in which a literary text multiplies its beginning is through the deployment of peritexts – titles, subtitles, dedications, epigraphs, introductions, 'notices' and so on. A classic example would be the opening of T.S. Eliot's *The Waste Land* (1922). Before we arrive at the first words of Eliot's poem we encounter a series of multilingual hurdles. To start with, there is the title. The title, like all titles, is uncertainly poised between inside and outside. It both names the poem, as if from outside, and forms part of that poem. 'The Waste Land' both refers to a place or predicament – post-1918 Europe, for example – and names the strange 'land' that Eliot's poem creates (like a waste land, the poem is full of debris from the past, fragmentary memories and quotations). Next we encounter the Latin and Greek of Petronius: 'Nam Sibyllam quidem Cumis ego ipse oculis meis vidi in ampulla pendere, et cum illi pueri dicerent: Σίβυλλα τί Θελεις; respondebat illa: ἀποθαυειν Θέλω' ('For once I myself saw with my own eyes the Sibyl at Cumae hanging in a cage, and when the boys said to her "Sibyl, what do you want?" she replied, "I want to die"'). As an epigraph, this quotation too may be said to be both inside and outside the poem, both a commentary on and a part of the text. The next hurdle is a tribute in Italian to Ezra Pound: 'il miglior fabbro' ('the better craftsman'). Pound, as editor, was responsible for much of the final shape of Eliot's poem and therefore is in part the craftsman of what follows. Even this tribute is a quotation: it comes from Dante's *Purgatorio* and is in this sense too both part of Eliot's poem and not part of it. Finally, there is a subtitle: '1. The Burial of the Dead'. This is a quotation from the Anglican burial service. Then we have what appear to be the first words of the poem:

> April is the cruellest month, breeding
> Lilacs out of the dead land, mixing
> Memory and desire, stirring
> Dull roots with spring rain. (ll.1–4)

But in fact these lines are a pastiche or reworking of the opening to another poem, Chaucer's *The Canterbury Tales* (*c*.1387–1400):

> Whan that April with his shoures sote
> The droghte of Marche hath perced to the rote,
> And bathed every veyne in swich licour,
> Of which vertu engendred is the flour. (ll.1–4)

In these and other ways, Eliot's poem displaces its own beginning. The beginning of the poem is no longer the first stroke of the pen or keyboard. Through emphatic effects of intertextuality (including quotation, allusion, reference and echo), Eliot's poem suggests that originality, the notion of beginning as singular, definable, stable is severely problematic. To ask where or when Eliot's poem begins is to meet with a series of questions concerning the identity of the author, the text and reader, and finally of the Western literary tradition generally.

The Waste Land may seem to be unusually concerned with questions of origins and their displacement. But the kinds of effects of intertextuality that this opening explores are in fact fundamental to literary texts more generally. Literary texts, that is to say, are always constructed by and within a context or tradition. In his well-known essay 'Tradition and the Individual Talent' (1919), Eliot himself argues that 'No poet, no artist of any art, has his [*sic*] complete meaning alone': rather, what is important is the poet's 'relation to the dead poets and artists' (Eliot 1975, 38). A poem, novel or play that does not in some sense relate to previous texts is, in fact, literally unimaginable. The author of such a text would have to invent everything. It would be like inventing a new language from scratch, without any reliance on already existing languages. In this sense, intertextuality (the displacement of origins to other texts, which are in turn displacements of other texts and so on – in other words an undoing of the very idea of pure or straightforward *origins*) is fundamental to the institution of literature. No text makes sense without other texts. Every text is what Roland Barthes calls 'a new tissue of past citations' (Barthes 1981, 39).

Two of the most compelling and most persistent myths of literary texts concern their origins. The first is the idea that the most important aspect of any reading is an imagined meeting of the reader's mind with that of the author – an idea that exemplifies what has been known for the past fifty years as the 'intentional fallacy' (the mistaken belief that what the author intended is the 'real', 'final' meaning of the work and that we can or should know what this is). But if we cannot know the beginnings of a text in terms of what is available to us on the page, how much more difficult it would be to discover the origins of the thought which impels the text. Does an author know where these thoughts come from? Are they in fact thoughts (conscious, coherent, consistent)? Whose 'thoughts' do we read when we read the beginning of *The Waste Land*? Eliot's, Chaucer's, Pound's, Petronius', Dante's? Are they still the poet's thoughts if the poet is said to be 'inspired'? The second common myth involves the priority given to an individual reader's first reading of a text. According to this myth, all literary criticism involves a corruption of the original 'experience' of reading. Once upon a time (so this myth goes) we were able to read a novel (by Charlotte Brontë, say, or J.K. Rowling) and have a completely unadulterated reading experience, unsullied by any critical thinking or complexity. But although we often talk about literary texts as though they have been subjected to only one reading, we all know that this is in many respects simply a convenient fiction. Roland Barthes, in his book *S/Z* (1970), makes a point about the act of rereading as 'an operation contrary to the commercial and ideological habits of our society' and suggests that it is 'tolerated only in certain marginal categories of readers (children, old people and professors)' (Barthes 1990b, 15–16). Professors – who are usually old people, very seldom children, though not infrequently an undecidable mixture of the two – include Roland Barthes, of course, and it is part of his aim to question the very idea of a single or first reading. Rereading, he argues,

> contests the claim which would have us believe that the first reading is a primary, naïve, phenomenal reading which we will only, afterwards, have to 'explicate', to intellectualize (as if there were a beginning of reading, as if everything were not already read: there is no *first* reading . . .). (Barthes 1990b, 16)

Once again, Eliot's *The Waste Land* suggests some of the complexities involved in a first reading. If the opening to Eliot's poem refers to Chaucer's, then when can we properly be said to read 'April is the cruellest month'? Surely we must reread it, once we have read it, with Chaucer's words in mind. In which case the first reading is inadequate. Less dramatically, perhaps, the same may be said of any other literary text: every reading (even a so-called 'first reading') is at least in part a learned or programmed response, conditioned by other and others' readings. In this respect, reading critically is, in T.S. Eliot's words, 'as inevitable as breathing' (Eliot 1975, 37).

The present book is, fundamentally, about questions of origins, about beginning. It is concerned with how we might begin to read, to think about and write about literary texts. In particular, the book is about those uncertain origins – the author, the reader and the text – none of which can ever be taken for granted. Neither author nor reader nor text finally or properly constitutes a beginning. As with 'beginning literary studies' (which we have begun now, haven't we?), the idea that everything begins with the author or with the reader or with one particular text is both deeply compelling and deeply false.

Further reading

The now classic exploration of literary beginnings is Edward Said's *Beginnings* (1975), an exuberant and theoretically astute exploration of openings, originality and origins in literature and theory. A more recent and perhaps more accessible book on beginnings is A.D. Nuttall's *Openings* (1992), which eschews theoretical discussion in favour of a concentrated focus on a small number of classic literary openings. On intertextuality, see Graham Allen's *Intertextuality* (2000) and Mary Orr's *Intertextuality* (2003). For a different perspective on these questions, see Françoise Meltzer's study of the idea of literary originality, *Hot Property* (1994), and for a more 'traditional' and sometimes polemically anti-theoretical approach see Christopher Ricks, *Allusion to the Poets* (2002). On inspiration and the origins of creativity, see Timothy Clark's inspirational book, *The Theory of Inspiration* (1997).

2. Readers and reading

What do you do when you come across a poem like this?

> I met a traveller from an antique land,
> Who said—'Two vast and trunkless legs of stone
> Stand in the desert . . . Near them, on the sand,
> Half sunk a shattered visage lies, whose frown,
> And wrinkled lip, and sneer of cold command,
> Tell that its sculptor well those passions read
> Which yet survive, stamped on these lifeless things,
> The hand that mocked them, and the heart that fed;
> And on the pedestal, these words appear:
> My name is Ozymandias, King of Kings,
> Look on my Works, ye Mighty, and despair!
> Nothing beside remains. Round the decay
> Of that colossal Wreck, boundless and bare
> The lone and level sands stretch far away'.

In Percy Bysshe Shelley's famous sonnet 'Ozymandias' (1818) the narrator speaks of meeting a traveller who reports having seen a vast shattered statue strewn across the desert. The statue is of Ozymandias, the thirteenth-century BC King Rameses II of Egypt (Ozymandias is the Greek name for this king). All that remains of the King of Kings and of his 'works' are a few broken fragments, a couple of legs and an inscription which commands the reader to despair. The poem, then, is about monuments, survival and the transience of even the greatest of us. But we might also notice that the poem is about readers and reading – the traveller reads a piece of writing, an inscription on the pedestal of a fragmented statue. The inscription *commands* the reader. And, rather differently, the word 'read' appears in line six, referring to the way that the sculptor understood the 'passions' of Ozymandias and was able to immortalize them in stone. Both the traveller and the sculptor are explicitly figured as readers, and we might also think about the 'I' of the first line as another kind of reader – a listener to the traveller's tale.

The poem, then, concerns a series of framed acts of reading. The sculptor reads the face of the king, the traveller reads the inscription, the narrative 'I' listens to the tale and, finally, we read the poem. One of the things that we might do with this poem is to think about these acts of reading. The poem can be thought about as what Paul de Man calls an 'allegory of reading': it is not only a poem which can be read, it is also a poem which tells an allegory or subtextual story about reading. One of the crucial questions of reading, for example, is how we can justify any particular reading: how can we tell if a particular reading or interpretation is valid? This is a question that goes to the heart of almost every debate in criticism and theory. In this respect the poem presents a paradox in that the traveller says that only a few fragments of the statue remain, that this is all that is left of Ozymandias and his great works. But if this is the case, how can the traveller know that the sculptor read the king's passions 'well'? In this way Shelley's poem can be understood as telling a story or allegory about one of the central paradoxes of reading. To read 'well' is generally taken as meaning to read accurately or faithfully. But the question of which reading of a text is the most accurate is itself a question of reading.

'Ozymandias', then, opens up a series of questions concerning readers and reading. In addition to the crucial question of how we can validate any reading (how we can know whether it is true or faithful), the poem also engages with other questions. Who is this traveller who reads the inscription, for example? And who is the 'I' who listens to, or 'reads', his story? Is the sculptor's 'mocking' of the king's face a kind of reading? What do such questions lead us to think about the power relations of any reading? Is it in the king's power to command his readers to despair? Or to make them obey? Is the traveller's reading of the inscription different from how that inscription might have been read while the king was alive? And does reading therefore change over time – is reading historically specific? What does all of this suggest about reading more generally? In this chapter we shall begin to explore some of these questions, referring to Shelley's poem as a way of summarizing some of the developments in literary criticism and theory over the past few decades.

Some of the most widely publicized developments in literary theory of the second half of the twentieth century went under the umbrella term 'reader-response criticism'. Such developments are usually understood as a reaction against Anglo-American 'new criticism' of the post-war period. Before we discuss reader-response criticism itself, then, it might be useful briefly to outline the position of new criticism with regard to readers and reading. Associated with such US critics as Cleanth Brooks, W.K. Wimsatt and Monroe Beardsley, and indebted also to the principles of 'practical criticism' associated with the British critics I.A. Richards and F.R. Leavis, new criticism involved a way of reading that emphasized form – the importance of considering 'the words on the page' – rather than factors such as the life of the author and his or her intentions, or the historical and ideological context in which the text was produced. New critics considered that such questions, while no doubt interesting, were irrelevant to a consideration of the text itself: they thought of literary texts as 'autonomous', as self-sufficient and self-contained unities, as aesthetic objects made of words. Correspondingly, new critics argued that to try to take account of readers' reactions or responses in the context of, for example, a poem, was to introduce an alien and fundamentally extraneous factor. They even invented a term for what they saw as the 'error' involved in talking about a reader's response in discussions of literary texts: they called it the 'affective fallacy'. For new critics, then, what was important was to pay scrupulous attention to the words of texts themselves, thus bypassing the subjective impressionism of the reader's response.

Like all critical movements, new criticism created its own special canon of literary works and authors. Shelley, notoriously, was not in the new critical canon: in his influential book *Revaluation* (1936), F.R. Leavis had set the trend by caustically opining that Shelley is 'almost unreadable', and that the effect of his eloquence is 'to hand poetry over to a sensibility that has no more dealings with intelligence than it can help' (Leavis 1972, 171, 175). Thus, for example, in his book *The Romantic Poets*, Graham Hough declares that '*Ozymandias* is an extremely clear and direct poem, advancing to a predetermined end by means of one firmly held image' (Hough 1967, 142). Dismissing the poem in this way is odd in view of the fact that irony, ambiguity and paradox are key elements in the new critical weaponry of reading, and that all three are dramatically at stake in lines ten and eleven of the poem, the inscription on the pedestal. 'Look on my Works, ye Mighty, and despair!' is ironic, for example, from at least two perspectives. First, the line can be read as an example of 'hubris' or excessive pride on the part of Ozymandias, who is thus shown to be absurd. Second, it can be read as ironic from Ozymandias's point of view: knowing that even he will die, Ozymandias inscribes these words for future generations, reminding us that even the greatest will be forgotten in time. These conflicting ironies produce both ambiguity and paradox – ambiguity concerning which reading is more valid, and paradox in the fact that the inscription appears to say two conflicting things.

Beginning in the late 1960s and becoming increasingly influential in the 1970s and early 1980s, reader-response criticism directly questioned the principles of new criticism. For critics and theorists such as Wolfgang Iser, Stanley Fish and Michael Riffaterre, questions of the literary text and its meaning(s) cannot be disengaged from the role that the reader takes. Although these and other reader-response critics have widely different approaches to literary texts, they all agree that the meaning of the text is created through the process of reading. What they object to in the new critical approach is the notion that a certain quality or 'meaning' of a literary text simply lies there in the text waiting for the reader or critic to come along and pull it out. Graham Hough's apparently objective assertion that 'Ozymandias' is 'extremely clear and direct', for example, elides the question of 'to whom?' Hough appears to generalize what is, in fact, his particular view of the poem. As we have tried to suggest, the poem may also be read very differently, as syntactically complex and semantically dense. The new critics' sense that the meaning of a poem is simply *there* involves thinking of meaning (in Terry Eagleton's memorable metaphor) as like a wisdom tooth, 'waiting patiently to be extracted' (Eagleton 1996, 77). Reacting against what we might call the dentistry school of criticism, reader-response critics recognize that the meanings of a text rely, in a dynamic way, on the work of the reader. Given that reading is a necessary dimension of any text, these critics attempt to plot the process of reading and the role of the reader.

Rather than closing down the questions of 'who reads?' and 'what is reading?', however, reader-response criticism has opened a postmodern Pandora's box. Critics such as Norman Holland and David Bleich, for example, are interested in investigating ways in which particular individuals respond to texts, and with exploring ways in which such responses can be related to those individuals' 'identity themes', to their personal psychic dispositions – the individual character of their desires, needs, experiences, resistances and so on. This is often referred to as 'subjective criticism' or 'personal criticism'. Such critics would not be interested in deciding which reading of line eleven of 'Ozymandias' is 'correct' because such correctness or accuracy is beside the point. Norman Holland, for example, argues that 'interpretation is a function of identity' and that 'all of us, as we read, use the literary work to symbolize and finally to replicate ourselves' (Holland 1980, 123, 124). To parody the logic of subjective criticism, we might suppose that a reader whose irregular potty-training has resulted in a pathological hatred of authority-figures will delight in the ironic treatment of the King of Kings in Shelley's poem, while another reader who has early come to associate father-figures with absence and unreliability will see the poem as a poignant confirmation of the inevitable disappearance of all fathers. Although Holland assures his reader that he is not 'positing an isolated solipsistic self' (Holland 1980, 131), this is precisely the danger that other critics have seen in this kind of criticism: such a reliance on the autonomy of the reader's thoughts and feelings seems to lead to a state of delusion epitomized by Ozymandias's hollow words.

Theorists such as Stanley Fish on the other hand argue that any individual reader is necessarily part of a 'community' of readers. Every reader, he suggests, reads according to the conventions of his or her 'interpretive community'. In other words, an individual reader's response, according to this model, is determined by the conventions of reading that he or she has been educated into within a certain socio-historical context. Our recognition of the equivoc-ality of 'Ozymandias', for example, is determined by the fact that we have been taught to look and listen for ambiguity and polysemia in literary texts.

A third influential strand of reader-response criticism is exemplified by the work of Wolfgang Iser. Iser elaborates ways in which the work of reading in-volves an interaction between elements of the text and the act of reading itself. He explores ways in which the text is 'concretized' – given shape or meaning in the act of reading. For Iser, neither the text nor the reader should be studied in isolation. Rather, the text produces certain 'blanks' or 'gaps' that the reader must attempt to complete: the reader 'is drawn into the events and made to supply what is meant from what is not said' (Iser 1995, 24). For Iser, the fact that we know nothing about the traveller in Shelley's poem, for example, 'spurs the reader into action' (24). 'Who is this traveller?' we might ask. 'What does he or she think about what is described in the poem?' The text prompts us imaginatively to fill in or fill out such hermeneutic or interpretative 'gaps'.

During the 1980s and 1990s, the political dimensions of reading became increasingly central to critical debate. Literary texts have been read in terms of power relations, in accordance with Michel Foucault's suggestion that 'power is everywhere' (Foucault 1981, 93) – even in reading. 'Ozymandias', in fact, produces multiple representations of the relationship between power and reading. Most explicitly there is the sculptor's 'reading' of the power of the king. The crucial lines here are lines four to eight:

> Half sunk a shattered visage lies, whose frown,
> And wrinkled lip, and sneer of cold command,
> Tell that its sculptor well those passions read
> Which yet survive, stamped on these lifeless things,
> The hand that mocked them, and the heart that fed . . .

The word 'mocked' means both 'imitated' or 'copied' and 'ridiculed' (a *mis*-representation that represents more accurately or more cruelly). The commanding power of the king – his power, not least, to make the sculptor 'read' his face and to copy it on to stone – is resisted in that very reading, in that mockery. The sculptor's 'reading' is both a copy, a faithful representation, and a reading which makes ridiculous. Reading here is figured as *both* faithful, an action of subservience, *and* a subversive act of resistance to power, a transfer and transformation of power. Alternatively, we might consider ways in which the poem suggests that acts of reading are bound up in the historical specificity of power relations. The reading of the statue and the inscription, in this sense, changes over time. Someone contemporary with the King of Kings might read the commanding inscription – 'Look on my Works, ye Mighty, and despair!' – as a statement of omnipotence. By contrast, a reader who, like the traveller, reads the inscription surrounded by the 'lone and level sands', by the *absence* of those works, their *non*-survival, can only read them ironically. What has remained, what has survived, is the work of the sculptor, the *represented* 'passions' of the king (itself a kind of reading), not his works. The power relations of text and reader have shifted decisively over time. Reading, in this sense, is not always and everywhere the same. As Robert Young comments, Shelley's poem 'demonstrates that meaning, like power, is not stable or fixed, and that even power cannot guarantee a tyranny of meaning: although authors may have intentions when they write, once they have written they cannot control and fix the meaning of any reading' (Young 1991a, 238). Finally, we might extrapolate from this to think about the way in which any reading produces a certain relation of power. Shelley's poem might itself be read as a kind of 'cold command' – a command to read. But any reading of the poem must constitute a form of resistance to such a command, a 'mockery' of that command, by the imposition or 'stamping' of its own interpretation on the poem. Reading *survives* the command of the text.

As part of this emphasis on power-relations, recent criticism has also given increased attention to questions of gender and race. Judith Fetterley, for example, has argued that female readers of classic US fiction (and, by implication, of other literary texts) have been 'immasculated', by which she means that they have traditionally been taught to read 'as men' (Fetterley 1978). Writing in the late 1970s, Fetterley argues that women should begin to liberate themselves from the notion of a 'universal' reader (who is implicitly male) and from an identification with male viewpoints in reading, and to develop specifically female models of reading. At stake here is, in Jonathan Culler's terms, the question of what it would mean to read 'as a woman' (Culler 1983, 43–64): how might 'reading as a woman' be different from 'reading as a man'?

And do we know what it means to read 'as a man'? It might be possible to think about Shelley's poem in terms of gendered reading. If we can assume that the traveller is male (after all, few solitary European travellers were female in the early nineteenth century), then one can see that the poem is not only about male pride, but also about male reading. The poem, indeed, is overwhelmingly masculine, a text from which women have been excluded. Yet few critics have been troubled by questions of sexual difference in relation to 'Ozymandias': in this respect, we might suggest, the critical response has been 'immasculated'. From Fetterley's perspective, we might ask how a non-immasculated reading would respond to the masculine power-play of Shelley's poem.

Critics concerned with questions of race and ethnicity have also developed specific strategies of reading and talking about reading. Theorists such as Gayatri Chakravorty Spivak, Henry Louis Gates Jr and Edward Said, for example, have transformed the nature of contemporary literary studies through their emphasis on questions of colonization, ethnic difference, racial oppression and discrimination, the position of the subaltern, the West and its construction of the 'other', imperialism and Orientalism. Edward Said, for instance, argues for what he calls 'contrapuntal reading' whereby, in reading a text, one 'open[s] it out both to what went into it and to what its author excluded' (Said 1993, 79). Our reading of *Jane Eyre* in terms of race and slavery in Chapter 24 suggests one such 'contrapuntal' reading. Similarly, Henry Louis Gates makes questions of reading central to black literary criticism and theory when he argues that black people in the United States have had to develop particular strategies of reading and interpretation for survival:

> Black people have always been masters of the figurative: saying one thing to mean something quite other has been basic to black survival in oppress-ive Western cultures. Misreading signs could be, and indeed often was, fatal. 'Reading', in this sense, was not play; it was an essential aspect of the 'literacy' training of a child. (Gates 1984, 6)

A reading concerned with questions of race might start from the fact that this English poem deals with a racial other – Egyptian or African – and explore the way in which such otherness is inscribed in the poem. The fact that the land is referred to as 'antique', for example, entirely effaces any possibility of a contemporary civilization and culture there. There is nothing beside the barrenness of the 'lone and level sands'. For this poem, Africa apparently only signifies in terms of a mythical past.

Finally, a poststructuralist or deconstructive reading of 'Ozymandias' might, in addition to these concerns, trace the dispersal or dissolution of the reader's identity in the act of reading and affirm the sense of a radical otherness which undermines all claims to interpretive mastery. For poststructuralists, there is a dynamic significance in the question of which comes first – the text or the reader? Is reading simply something that happens to a text as if by chance, something which leaves a text fundamentally unaltered? If so, then the role of the reader would appear to be determined by the text itself: each literary text would be like a set of instructions, a kind of recipe, for how it should be read. By contrast, the text may be understood as fundamentally incomplete, to be effected in the act of reading. In this case the text is remade and made anew in every reading. Rather than choosing between these two hypotheses, deconstructive theories of reading argue that *both* models are operative, in a peculiar double bind of reading: the reader makes the text and the text makes the reader. Deconstruction explores the space between these two possibilities and it seeks to highlight ways in which every reading and every text is unpredictable. Thus deconstruction is interested in the fact that while any text demands a 'faithful' reading, it also demands an *individual* response. Put differently, reading is at once singular (yours and nobody else's) and general (conforming to patterns of meaning dictated by the text – a text that does not require *you* in order to function). Through analysis of these and other paradoxes, critics such as Paul de Man and J. Hillis Miller suggest ways in which reading is strange, unsettling, even 'impossible'.

How should we read the word 'appear' in line nine of Shelley's poem ('And on the pedestal, these words appear'), for example? What makes these words appear? The word 'appear' might be shown to challenge all conventional preconceptions concerning reading. In particular, it challenges us to rethink the relationship between a text on the one hand simply *appearing*, simply being there like a monument, to be read, appearing from nowhere, and on the other hand a text appearing in the sense of 'seeming', an apparition, made in reading. Is the text *there*, or do we make it appear, do we imagine it? Jacques Derrida has referred to the *delireium* of reading, a pun or 'portmanteau' word which combines the French 'lire' ('to read') with 'delirium', to suggest ways in which reading can be delirious or hallucinatory (Derrida 1979, 94, quoting Blanchot). Just as we can never know how 'well', how accurately or faithfully the sculptor has read the king's passions, neither can we escape the dynamics of reading and delirium. In short, we can never stop reading because we can never finally know if what 'appears' in this poem is us reading or us being read. This is not to suggest we should therefore give up, either in despair or in indifference. Our very lives and identities are at stake. If, as we have argued, 'Ozymandias' is as much about readers and reading as about anything else, then we might see that the relation between reading and being read is strangely twisted: not only do we read the poem but the poem reads us. Like Ozymandias himself, we are fragmented, mute and transient: our 'passions' are read, and perhaps mocked, by the sculptor, in the form of the poem itself. After all, in reading this poem, we perhaps cannot avoid a ventriloquistic articulation, silent or not, of the king's words –

> My name is Ozymandias, King of Kings,
> Look on my Works, ye Mighty, and despair!

How do you read *that*? What happens to you, to your name?

Further reading

Andrew Bennett, ed., *Readers and Reading* (1995), collects some of the most significant essays in reading theory of recent years and includes a wide-ranging introduction to the field; for an important collection of earlier essays, see Suleiman and Crosman, eds, *The Reader in the Text* (1980). Sara Mills, ed., *Gendering the Reader* (1994) approaches reading theory from the perspective of gender and feminism. Two collections of essays which consider reading from a historical perspective are Raven, Small and Tadmor, eds, *The Practice and Representation of Reading in England* (1995) and James L. Machor, ed., *Readers in History* (1993). A concise and accessible summary of reader-response criticism and theory is Elizabeth Freund's book *The Return of the Reader* (1987). For a brilliant if difficult discussion of how reading is figured in literary texts, see Paul de Man's *Allegories of Reading* (1979), and see J. Hillis Miller's *The Ethics of Reading* (1987) for a consideration of the act of reading as a response to an ethical call. Two important books from a psychoanalytically oriented feminist perspective are Mary Jacobus's *Reading Woman* (1986) and Shoshana Felman's *What Does a Woman Want? Reading and Sexual Difference* (1993). For an accessible and entertaining history of reading practices and theories from the earliest records to the present, see Alberto Manguel, *A History of Reading* (1997). For an introduction to poststructuralism, see Robert Young's 'Poststructuralism: The Improper Name', in *Torn Halves* (1996). On close reading, see Lentricchia and DuBois, eds, *Close Reading* (2003). For a powerful if highly idiosyncratic take on reading, see Harold Bloom's *How to Read and Why* (2000).

3.   The author

If you really want to hear about it, the first thing you'll probably want to know is where I was born, and what my lousy childhood was like, and how my parents were occupied and all before they had me, and all that David Copperfield kind of crap, but I don't feel like going into it. (5)

The opening sentence of J.D. Salinger's *The Catcher in the Rye* (1951) suggests a number of ways of thinking about the figure of the author. It is at once compellingly straightforward and strangely cryptic. The sentence gives the impression of a spontaneous, candid speaking voice, directly addressing us and showing a specific concern for our wishes and desires ('If you really want . . . you'll probably want'). We are being addressed very much *on the level* – nothing pretentious here, none of 'that David Copperfield kind of crap'. Despite appearances, however, this opening sentence gives little away, rather it is furtive and evasive: 'I don't feel like going into it'. The most important word in this famous opening sentence may indeed be the word 'it': 'it' is the emphatic but equivocal subject ('If you really want to hear about it . . . I don't feel like going into it'). Is the 'it' at the beginning of the sentence the same as the 'it' at the end?

The ambiguity of 'it' corresponds to another kind of uncertainty. For what is also unclear from this opening sentence is *who is speaking* or, more accurately, *who is writing*. After all, despite the seductiveness of the confiding, colloquial voice here, it would be somewhat naive to pretend that this is *not* writing. The sentence is playing a type of literary game with conventions of novel-openings. Of course we quickly learn that the 'I' here is a 16-year-old American boy called Holden Caulfield, but this is not something that is made clear in the first sentence. All we can presume at this point is that we are reading that particular kind of text called a novel and that it has been written by J.D. Salinger. The literary game that is set in motion by this opening sentence has to do with the relationship between fiction (a novel) and truth (biography or autobiography), as well as between an author and a narrator. This is suggested by the apparently deprecating reference to David Copperfield ('all that David Copperfield kind of crap'). There is, then, a metafictional dimension in this seemingly simple opening sentence – metafictional in the sense that it explicitly refers to itself and draws attention to the fact that a story is being told. The narrator invokes the protagonist of one of the 'classic' English nineteenth-century novels and implies, even by denying it, a correlation with *another* literary text.

Both *David Copperfield* and *The Catcher in the Rye* offer a mixing of novel and (auto)biography. In doing so, they provoke a series of fundamental questions about the relationship between literary texts, narrators, characters and authors. Above all, they provoke the question: who is speaking? In presenting us with the voice of a fictional speaker, these texts draw attention to the figure of the author as a sort of concealed or cryptic, haunting but unspecified presence. Who is behind this 'I'? The opening of *The Catcher in the Rye* thus introduces a general question for literary criticism and theory, the question of the presence of another 'I' – the haunting absent-presence of the 'I' who writes, of the author. The author is a kind of ghost. Salinger's novel provides more than one illustration of this. A few pages further on, for example, Holden Caulfield tells us:

> What really knocks me out is a book that, when you're all done reading it, you wish the author that wrote it was a terrific friend of yours and you could call him up on the phone whenever you felt like it. That doesn't happen much, though. I wouldn't mind calling this Isak Dinesen up. And Ring Lardner, except that D.B. [Holden's brother] told me he's dead. You take that book *Of Human Bondage*, by Somerset Maugham, though. I read it last summer. It's a pretty good book and all, but I wouldn't want to call Somerset Maugham up. I don't know. He just isn't the kind of a guy I'd want to call up, that's all. I'd rather call old Thomas Hardy up. I like that Eustacia Vye. (22)

Again, this passage is delightfully straightforward and yet extraordinarily suggestive. It presents us with what is in many respects an undeniable truth, as well as with what constitutes one of the curious effects of literature: literary texts can generate powerful feelings of identification, not only between reader and character but also, perhaps more enigmatically, between reader and author. You really can be drawn into the feeling that the author is 'a terrific friend of yours' or that your appreciation and understanding of an author is so intense it touches on the telepathic. Holden's reference to getting on the phone to the author is uncannily apposite: the rapport that exists between you and your favourite author is indeed a sort of linguistic tele-link. The author is an absent presence, both there and not there. You may feel that you understand like nobody else what it is that the author is saying; and you may be willing to acknowledge that this author can express your opinions, thoughts and feelings as well as or even better than you yourself could. This is, in fact, precisely how the greatness of Shakespeare is often described. It is what William Hazlitt says, for example, in his 1818 lecture 'On Shakespeare and Milton': 'the striking peculiarity of Shakespeare's mind' is 'its power of communication with all other minds' (Hazlitt 1910, 47).

At the same time, however, this passage from *The Catcher in the Rye* prompts us to reflect on at least two other points. First, it is not (not usually, anyway) a two-way friendship that a reader enjoys with an author. Indeed, this one-waywardness is part of the fantasy of reading: the 'author' is generally *not* someone whose telephone number you can readily acquire and with whom you really can become terrific friends in the way that Caulfield is suggesting. The author, in other words, is not so much an 'actual' author at all: rather, it is your personal projection, *your idea* of the author. Second, it is also the case that the author not only *may be* dead, but in some respects *is* dead, even when alive. Part of the irony and humour of this passage from Salinger's novel consists in the blurring of the distinction between living authors and dead ones. For despite his concern with the problem of giving Ring Lardner a ring, given that Ring Lardner cannot be rung (since he is dead), Holden Caulfield concludes his 'call-an-author' fantasy by saying he would like to 'call old Thomas Hardy up' – as if Hardy, though 'old', still lived. As we might all be reasonably expected to know, Thomas Hardy is (and was, well before 1951) unequivocally dead.

A lot has been said and written over the past few decades about 'the death of the author'. This paradoxical idea refers not to the empirical or literal death of a given author, but to the fact that, in a radical sense, the author is absent from the text. 'The death of the author' became a catch-phrase primarily on account of an essay of that title, written by the French poststructuralist Roland Barthes and first published in 1967. Barthes's essay is flamboyant and provocative. In part, he is arguing against the very common ascription of authority to the figure of the author. People often ask, for example: 'Is that what Shakespeare (or Brontë or Dickens) really meant? Is that what the author intended?' Such questions reflect what W.K. Wimsatt and Monroe Beardsley described, in an essay first published in 1946, as 'the intentional fallacy' (Wimsatt and Beardsley 1995). In what became a conceptual cornerstone of Anglo-American New Criticism, they argued that 'the design or intention of the author is neither available nor desirable as a standard for judging the success of a literary work' (Wimsatt and Beardsley 1995, 90). All we have, they argued, is the text itself, and the work of criticism has no business inquiring into the quite separate question of its author's intentions. Indeed, Wimsatt and Beardsley contend that any answer to the question of what, for example, T.S. Eliot meant by 'Prufrock' 'would have nothing to do' with the poem itself (Wimsatt and Beardsley 1995, 99). Even if we were to go to a living author and ask what he or she meant by a particular text, all we would get would be another *text* (his or her answer), which would then, in turn, be open to interpretation. Just because it comes 'from the horse's mouth' does not mean that the horse is telling the truth, or that the horse *knows* the truth, or indeed that what the horse has to say about the 'words on the page' is any more interesting or illuminating than what anyone else might have to say.

We could also ponder the question of 'authorial intention' in the light of psychoanalysis. 'Conscious intention', in this respect, can always be considered as subject to the unconscious workings of the mind. With psychoanalysis, it is no longer possible simply to privilege consciousness as the sombre judge of what is intended. The jurisdiction of 'authorial intention' falters here: what is not meant can still (in another sense) be meant. 'I didn't mean to hurt you' can always mean 'I did'. Correspondingly, it is important to acknowledge some of the implications of twentieth-century linguistics (Saussure, Chomsky, Pinker) as regards this question of the author and his or her authority. Rather than say that the author is in control of the language that he or she uses, we might consider the idea that the language is as much in control of the author. In this respect, language can be thought of as a kind of system within which any writer must take a designated place: the system and rules of language inevitably dictate the possibilities of what someone can say. An author is not God, after all.

Barthes's essay provides a strong sense of the ways in which we need, if not to ridicule, at least to be sceptical about the idea of the author as the origin and end of the meaning of a text. But rather than solving the problem of interpretive authority, 'The Death of the Author' in certain respects simply transfers it. Barthes ends his essay by declaring that 'the death of the author' coincides with 'the birth of the reader' (Barthes 1977a, 118). But as we suggest in the preceding chapter, such a claim is manifestly problematic: after all, the critique of the notion of the Author (to which Barthes wittily gives a capital 'A', thus highlighting the putatively god-like attributes of this figure) is just as valid as a critique of the notion of the reader (who, in effect, simply acquires in Barthes's account a capital 'R' instead). Nevertheless his essay does offer some crucial and succinct remarks on the idea of the author and it remains a valuable account. Barthes writes:

> We know now that a text is not a line of words releasing a single 'theological' meaning (the 'message' of the Author–God) but a multi-dimensional space in which a variety of writings, none of them original, blend and clash. The text is a tissue of quotations drawn from the innumerable centres of culture . . . Once the Author is removed, the claim to decipher a text becomes quite futile. To give a text an Author is to impose a limit on that text, to furnish it with a final signified, to close the writing. (Barthes 1977a, 146)

In a sense the problem here is evident simply from the two words which frame the above quotation: 'Barthes writes'. We are still talking in terms of the author and there could be little more persuasive indication of the idea that the author is *not* dead (though Roland Barthes, sadly, is) than the use of the present tense: Barthes *writes*. But at the same time we need to be careful here. The 'death of the author', in Barthesian terms, is explicitly figurative or metaphorical, and we could say, by way of a sort of corrective to possible misreading in this context, that the author cannot die precisely because, as we've been suggesting, the author is – always has been and always will be – a ghost. Never fully present or fully absent, a figure of fantasy and elusiveness, the author only ever haunts. It is also important to stress that Barthes is not in fact talking about 'the author' but 'the Author'. Insofar as the metaphorical death makes sense, then, it is the death of a particular *concept* of the Author that is at stake. In this respect Barthes's essay has to be seen in its cultural and historical context, as providing a simplified but forceful articulation of a variety of intellectual positions that emerged in the 1960s, in France and elsewhere.

Barthes's essay should be read alongside Michel Foucault's 'What Is an Author?' (1969), an essay that is undoubtedly more systematic and rigorous than Barthes's in many respects. More drily but more carefully than Barthes, Foucault provides an extraordinary sense of the figure of the author as a *historical construction*. The idea of the author is not a timeless given: the figure and significance of the author varies across time, and from one culture to another, from one discourse to another and so on. As regards works of literature, Foucault is concerned to criticize the notion of the author as 'the principle of a certain unity of writing' (Foucault 1979, 151). In other words, like Barthes, he puts into question the idea that the author is a god-like or (in more Foucauldian terms) saint-like figure, that the author is the presiding authority or principle of coherence for the understanding of a text. He does this primarily by focusing on the historical and ideological determinations of the notion of the author. He notes, for example, that

> There was a time when the texts that we today call 'literary' (narratives, stories, epics, tragedies, comedies) were accepted, put into circulation, and valorized without any question about the identity of their author; their anonymity caused no difficulties since their ancientness, whether real or imagined, was regarded as a sufficient guarantee of their status. (Foucault 1979, 149)

And he emphasizes that, more recently, literary authorship has been integrally bound up with changes in law and questions of copyright and ownership of texts. Finally, like Barthes, Foucault is interested in the potentially revolutionary effects of writing. 'What Is an Author?' affirms the jubilatory – because anti-authoritarian (here the correlations between 'author' and 'authority' become explicit) – energies of a writing or discourse freed of the conventional impositions of authorship. Foucault emphasizes the paradox that, while we think of the author as 'a perpetual surging of invention', in fact 'we make him [or her] function in exactly the opposite fashion'. While we think of the author as endlessly creative, in other words, our practice of reading and criticism makes him or her into a locus of authority which confines meaning and significance to a single univocal strand. Foucault thus concludes: 'The author is therefore the ideological figure by which one marks the manner in which we fear the proliferation of meaning' (159). We want there to be an identifiable author for a text because this comforts us with the notion that there is a particular sense to that text.

Barthes and Foucault, among many others, are interested in thinking about literature in ways that do not depend on regarding the author as the origin of the meaning of a text or as the authoritative 'presence' in that text. Contemporary literary theory draws together threads from psychoanalysis (the 'I' is in many ways *by definition* not in control of itself, since it is determined by what it cannot control, in other words, by the unconscious), linguistics (language *speaks us* as much as we speak language), ethnology (creativity, authorship, etc. are differently constructed and conceived in different cultures) and feminism (the Author with a capital A is in many respects clearly – and oppressively – male: God, the Father, the patriarchal Presence). Nevertheless, the figure of the author remains a decisive force in contemporary culture – for all kinds of reasons, some of them entirely admirable. Thus in women's writing, for example, or in the study of supposedly non-mainstream (i.e. non-white, non-US-or-European, non-middle class, non-heterosexual) writing, there has been and continues to be an emphasis on the person of the author, an emphasis that is in some ways remarkably conventional and 'conformist'. This emphasis is particularly characteristic of what has come to be known as identity politics. Such 'conformism' is understandable especially if, as theorists of such writing sometimes claim, it is presented as the initial step in a longer-term strategy of disturbing, dislocating and transforming anthropocentric, patriarchal, white, bourgeois or 'straight' values. It is also true that what we think about a particular text, how we read and understand it, can probably never be simply dissociated from what we know (or think we know) of its author. The fact that we know (assuming that we do) that John Keats died of tuberculosis at the tragically early age of 25 cannot but affect the way we read those prophetically poignant lines from 'Ode to a Nightingale' (1819), written only two years before his death:

> Now more than ever seems it rich to die,
>   To cease upon the midnight with no pain,
>   While thou art pouring forth thy soul abroad
>   In such an ecstasy!
>   Still wouldst thou sing, and I have ears in vain—
>   To thy high requiem become a sod.

Similarly, the fact that Ezra Pound made fascist propaganda broadcasts on Italian radio cannot but affect the way that we read his *Cantos*. But it is still important to bear in mind that there is something deeply problematic about any straightforward reduction of a text to what we think we know of the author's life, thoughts, habits or ideas. In particular, the attempt to settle questions of interpretation through appeals to the intentions of the author cannot but be viewed with suspicion. It is not a question of simply denying or ignoring authorial intention: some hypothesis of what an author intends is an important element in reading and sense-making. But reading and sense-making invariably overflow 'mere' authorial intention. Correspondingly, we could say, it is not a question (as Barthes polemically argued) of simply 'removing' the author, but rather of acknowledging that s/he has a less central and authoritative, in some ways more ghostly role. In this respect, we might say, the author was dead from the start. Specifically, as Jacques Derrida has argued, an author is 'dead insofar as his [or her] text has a structure of survival even if he [or she] is living' (Derrida 1985a, 183). Like any piece of writing (even a text-message), a literary work is capable of outliving its author. This capacity for the text to live on is part of its structure, of what makes it a text. This is not something that the author can control. More generally, no author owns the meanings or the readings of his or her text.

As we have attempted to show, then, the idea of an author-centred reading is in various ways flawed. No doubt it will never be possible to give up the sense of phantasmatic identification with an author ('I love Emily Brontë', 'John Webster is my hero'). Nor, indeed, are we likely to stop reading literary biographies and being interested in the apparently tangential issues of authors' love affairs, their compositional practices or even, if all else fails, their shopping lists. But the relationship between life and work is highly complex and highly mediated, and a key to the authorial life is by no means necessarily a key to the literary text. Our identifications with and ideas about authors are, in the final analysis, themselves forms of fiction. We may speculate, fantasize and tell ourselves stories about an author; but the author is a sort of phantom. In keeping with the notion that the author is necessarily a ghost, we could suggest that the greatest literary texts are indeed those in which the author appears most ghostly. The most powerful works of literature are those which suggest that they are singular, that no one else could have written them, *and yet* that their authorship is, in more than one sense, a phantom issue. One need think only, for example, of Chaucer's *Canterbury Tales*, the plays of Shakespeare, Emily Brontë's *Wuthering Heights*, Toni Morrison's *The Bluest Eye* or of course J.D. Salinger's *The Catcher in the Rye*, to realize that in a sense they tell us nothing about their authors, even if they are texts in which we feel their elusive presence in an especially forceful way. What Keats says of the poet is true of authors generally. The poet as poet has no identity (Keats 1958, 1:387): he or she lives, and lives on, in the strange space of writing.

Further reading

The brief essay entitled 'The Intentional Fallacy' (Wimsatt and Beardsley 1995) remains a valuable critical reference-point for thinking about authorial intention. For a concise and thought-provoking more recent essay on 'Intention', see Annabel Patterson (1995), and see Irwin (1999). On the figure of the author more generally, Roland Barthes's 'The Death of the Author' (1977a) is vigorous and entertaining but should perhaps be read alongside his somewhat later essays, 'From Work to Text' (Barthes 1977b) and 'Theory of the Text' (in Young 1981), as well as Michel Foucault's classic essay 'What Is an Author?' (1979). For wide-ranging collections of critical and other material on the author, see Seán Burke, ed., *Authorship: From Plato to the Postmodern* (1995), Maurice Biriotti and Nicola Miller, eds, *What is an Author?* (1993), and William Irwin, ed., *The Death and Resurrection of the*

Author? (2002). For collections of essays on authorship in film theory see Caughie, ed. (1980), Gerster and Staiger, eds. (2003) and Wexman, ed. (2003). Mark Rose's *Authors and Owners* (1993) is an influential study of the introduction of copyright law and its influence on the 'invention' of the author in the eighteenth century. Similarly, for a study that challenges poststructuralist thinking on authorship, see Seán Burke's *The Death and Return of the Author* (2nd edn., 1998). Finally, for a general introduction to author theory, see Andrew Bennett, *The Author* (2005).

4.   The text and the world

All of the chapters in this book are, in different ways, about the relationship between texts and the world. How do texts represent the world? Where does a text begin and end? Is an author an inhabitant of the world or the creation of a literary text? To what extent is history a kind of text? And what implications does this have for thinking about literature? Can literary texts do things to the world as well as simply describe it? These are some of the questions with which we engage in this book.

The relation between literary texts and the world has been a central problem in criticism and theory at least since Plato banished poets from his imaginary Republic for allegedly misrepresenting the world. The very phrase 'the text and the world', however, immediately presents a questionable distinction: its very formulation presupposes a difference between a text on the one hand and the world on the other. This distinction is, of course, a very common way of thinking about literature: it is implicit in a certain understanding of mimesis or imitation, and in notions of realism and naturalism, and of representation, as well as in metaphors which figure literary texts as offering a window on to the world or (in Hamlet's words) as holding a mirror up to nature. All of these ways of thinking about literary texts start from an assumed separation of the literary work, the text, from the world. They imply that a literary text is not, in essence, part of the world. Actually, over the centuries, writers have been trying to drive a stake into the heart of this assumption: the text–world dichotomy is like a vampire that will not lie down. The latest and most persistent of these vampire-killers are called poststructuralists. Poststructuralism (including new historicism, feminism, deconstruction, postcolonialism and queer theory) consistently undermines the very terms of this text–world dichotomy. Michel Foucault puts the point in a Nietzschean way: 'if language expresses, it does so not in so far as it is an imitation and duplication of things, but in so far as it manifests . . . the fundamental will of those who speak it' (Foucault 1970, 290). Poststructuralists ask what it means to say that a literary text is different from, separate from the world. Shouldn't we say, rather, that such texts actually make up our world? How can an act of inscription or an act of reading *not* be part of the world? Is there a world without such acts? In a later chapter, we look at the ways in which texts may be considered as performative, as acts of language which themselves *do* things, as well as just talk about things. In this chapter, we shall explore the idea that literary texts are acts that destabilize the very notion of the world and that disturb all assumptions about a separation between world and text.

In order to consider this proposition, we shall discuss Andrew Marvell's poem 'To His Coy Mistress' (1681). The poem presents itself as a work of seduction. The speaker addresses his 'coy mistress' and attempts to persuade her to go to bed with him:

> Had we but world enough, and time,
> This coyness, lady, were no crime.
> We would sit down, and think which way
> To walk, and pass our long love's day.
> 5   Thou by the Indian Ganges' side
> Shouldst rubies find: I by the tide
> Of Humber would complain. I would
> Love you ten years before the flood:
> And you should, if you please, refuse
> 10   Till the conversion of the Jews.
> My vegetable love should grow
> Vaster than empires, and more slow.
> An hundred years should go to praise
> Thine eyes, and on thy forehead gaze.
> 15   Two hundred to adore each breast:
> But thirty thousand to the rest.
> An age at least to every part,
> And the last age should show your heart:
> For, lady, you deserve this state,
> 20   Nor would I love at lower rate.
>
> But at my back I always hear
> Time's wingèd chariot hurrying near:
> And yonder all before us lie
> Deserts of vast eternity.
> 25   Thy beauty shall no more be found;
> Nor, in thy marble vault, shall sound

My echoing song: then worms shall try
That long-preserved virginity:
And your quaint honour turn to dust;
30   And into ashes all my lust.
The grave's a fine and private place,
But none, I think, do there embrace.

Now, therefore, while the youthful hue
Sits on thy skin like morning dew,
35   And while thy willing soul transpires
At every pore with instant fires,
Now let us sport us while we may,
And now, like amorous birds of prey,
Rather at once our time devour,
40   Than languish in his slow-chapped power.
Let us roll all our strength, and all
Our sweetness, up into one ball:
And tear our pleasures with rough strife,
Thorough the iron gates of life.
45   Thus, though we cannot make our sun
Stand still, yet we will make him run.

As soon as we ask even the simplest questions about this poem we come up against the problem of representation, the problem of the relationship between the text and the world. Perhaps the most obvious question that we would want to ask is whether the poem should be read as *really* a poem of seduction: is the speaker the same as the poet and, if so, is this text really addressed to a woman Andrew Marvell knew? Or should we understand the speaker to be a fictional construction and the 'real' addressee to be another reader – us, for example – a reader or readers not explicitly addressed but nevertheless implied by the text? Most readings of the poem assume that the latter is the case, that rather than attempting to seduce a woman, this poem presents a fictional dramatization of such an attempt. In this sense, it may seem that the poem is categorically separate from the 'real' world and from 'real' people. But this poetic attempt at seduction does not just take place between a fictive woman and speaker. In various ways, 'To His Coy Mistress' challenges our thinking on fiction and the real. For example, regardless of whether the mistress is conceived as real or fictive, the poem has effects on us. In particular, such a poem can be considered as performative – in the sense that it performs an act not so much of sexual as of textual seduction. It tries to entice us to read and to read on and to draw us into another world – a world of reading that is both fictional and real.

But Marvell's poem does not stop here. It can be shown to engage with the world through the use of a number of specific discourses. The seduction is mediated not only by reference to other kinds of literary texts (poems of seduction, love poems, the *blazon*, the *carpe diem* or *memento mori* motif and so on), but also in terms of other kinds of discourse (biblical, classical, colonial, philosophical, scientific, military). In this respect, the poem could be seen as an example of what the Russian critic M.M. Bakhtin calls 'heteroglossia', in that it embraces a series of overlapping codes and discourses. This complex jumble of discourses positions the text in relation to 'the world' – even if we try to read the poem as simply fictional.

Indeed, rather than thinking of texts on one side and 'the world' on the other, we might reflect on the idea that everything human that happens in the world is mediated by language. Language, as Jean-Jacques Lecercle puts it, 'always reminds us that it, and no one else, is speaking, that whenever we believe we rule over our words, we are in the grip of an unavoidable but nevertheless delusive illusion' (Lecercle 1990, 265). In this context we could attempt to clarify the notoriously controversial statement by Jacques Derrida, in his book *Of Grammatology* (1976, 158, 163), that 'There is nothing outside the text'. This much quoted and much misunderstood slogan is, in fact, a misleading translation of the French sentence 'Il n'y a pas de hors-texte', which is perhaps better rendered as 'There is no outside-text'. The latter version is preferable because it is easier to see that it is saying something credible. When Derrida makes this statement he is talking about reading. His point is not that there is no such thing as a 'real world' but that there is no access to the real world of, for example, Marvell's poem, except through the language of the poem. In other words, there is no reading of 'To His Coy Mistress' that is not dependent, precisely, on language: the 'real world' of the poem is the poem. We cannot go beyond or transcend the text to Marvell's coy mistress since our only access to her is through the poem. But Derrida is also making a larger, more difficult claim, arguing that there is no way to conceive, imagine or even perceive 'the world' without stubbing our toes on the question of language. Put very crudely, Derrida suggests there is no access to 'the world' except, in the broadest sense, through language. 'Language' here need not be simply verbal, but may include everything that works as a system of signs. Even without words, for example, seduction is an affair of language – there is the language of eyes, gestures, touch, a complex olfactory system of signs and so on. Derrida and other theorists of deconstruction, then, regard the text–world opposition as untenable if also perhaps unavoidable. In this respect, those critics of Derrida who argue that his is a 'pure' textualism which cannot account for power or politics are simply failing to recognize – or choosing to

ignore – the extent to which political, social, economic and historical forces
are bound up in language, in discourse, in representation.

Some of these points may become clear if we take a closer look at a few
details of Marvell's poem. The poem explicitly plays upon an opposition
between text and world. It begins by claiming that if there were 'world enough,
and time', the speaker would spend many hundreds of years praising the
woman's beauty. Thus the opening verse-paragraph immediately establishes
an opposition between words and deeds, between talking and making love,
between language and the body – between the text and the world. And, in a
self-consuming rhetorical gesture, the poem argues against any more discourse, any more talk. It argues for the disposal or rejection of speech in favour
of action – the action of the joining of two bodies. In this sense, the whole
poem may be read in terms of a conflict played out between the text and the
world, an attempt to go beyond its own discourse to the body of the woman. At
the same time, however, and paradoxically, the poem appears to suggest that
this separation of text and world is itself impossible. The poem culminates in
a rejection of speech or discourse and in a militaristic metaphor for the violent
exchange between two bodies ('Let us roll all our strength, and all / Our sweetness, up into one ball: / And tear our pleasures with rough strife / Thorough
the iron gates of life'). But this final rejection of speech in favour of action
simply results in silence, the end of the poem: it does not, cannot, go beyond
talk to the body of the woman. For the speaker, there is no escape from talk,
language, discourse, no pure body without, outside of, this poem.

Nevertheless, at various points in the poem, the speaker does attempt to
point beyond language, to refer to the woman's body – here and now. At the
beginning of the third verse-paragraph, for example, he describes a blush
which suffuses the woman's body:

> Now, therefore, while the youthful hue
> Sits on thy skin like morning dew,
> And while thy willing soul transpires
> At every pore with instant fires,
> Now let us sport us while we may . . .

What we might call the poem's 'fiction of immediacy' (the sense that the
speaker is addressing a woman who is present and that the action of this poem
takes place in 'real time') becomes fully apparent at this point, when the
speaker refers directly to the altering state of the woman's body. In addition to
the insistent deixis of 'Now . . . Now', this sense of immediacy is generated
through complex *rhetorical* strategies. For example, the blush or sweat which

'transpires / At every pore' is read as a sign of the inner 'fires' produced by the 'willing soul' of the woman. In its most direct reference to the woman's body, at this 'instant', here and now, the poem is highly figurative. The complicated metaphoricity of these lines, their sheer insistent textuality, dissolves any illusion of corporeal presence. Moreover, as we have suggested, the speaker *interprets* the woman's blush just as we interpret his lines. The fiction of immediacy in Marvell's poem, the reiterated force of the 'now', is derived above all perhaps from the extraordinary turn that occurs at the start of the second verse-paragraph: 'But at my back I always hear / Time's wingèd chariot hurrying near'. This 'always' evokes the constant imminence of something, an unceasing urgency and apprehension that is always there, always 'hurrying near', regardless of whether we are reading or making love, writing or fighting.

'The text and the world' names a false opposition. Texts cannot but be part of the world. To talk about texts as 'representing' reality simply overlooks ways in which texts are already part of that reality, and ways in which literary texts *produce* our reality, make our worlds. In this respect we may be prompted to ask what is at stake not only in the narrator's but in Marvell's and in Western culture's representations of the female body. In particular, we might ask what is involved in the violence embedded within Marvell's figuration of the woman as a body and as dead – as a corpse. What is the relationship between aesthetic and erotic contemplation in this representation on the one hand and its imagining or the woman's death on the other? In her book *Over Her Dead Body: Death, Femininity and the Aesthetic* (1992), Elisabeth Bronfen has explored the multiple ways in which patriarchy figures the conjunction of femininity with death and the aesthetic, and the fact that the female body as an object of aesthetic contemplation is also bound up with a certain violence towards femininity, towards women. According to this thinking, the very status of Marvell's poem as a classic, as a showcase poetic urn in the imaginary museum of English literary history, its reproduction in classrooms, lecture theatres, anthologies and in books such as our own, produces and reinforces the cultural construction of 'woman' as allied with death and with the aesthetic. Indeed, Bronfen would argue that such a poem and its reception have a crucial social and cultural function since, like other representations of the death of a beautiful woman, the poem exemplifies patriarchy's repression of the fact of the (male) subject's own death by the displaced representation of that death in the 'other' (the woman). The linguist Roman Jakobson famously defines the 'poetic function' of language as 'a focus on the message for its own sake' (Jakobson 1960, 365), and the critical tradition has tended to respond to Marvell's poem in just this way, reading it as a self-reflexive, autonomous work of art which transcends the interests of the world. But if instead we read it as a powerful and influential expression of the cultural construction of femininity, we see that the distinction that is embedded in our chapter title – between the text and the world – has dissolved.

Further reading

Edward Said's *The World, the Text, and the Critic* (1983), especially the title essay, persuasively argues the case for saying that 'a text in being a text is a being in the world'. An earlier and now classic argument for a similar position is contained in the work of Raymond Williams, whose 1961 book *The Long Revolution* (1992) has been deeply influential for British cultural materialism in particular. Roland Barthes's classic book *Mythologies* (1972) demonstrates the cultural construction of 'reality' or 'nature' in fascinating analyses of anything from soap powder to wrestling. Roger Fowler's *Linguistic Criticism* (1986) takes a linguistic perspective on questions raised in this chapter. Whiteside and Issacharoff, eds, *On Referring in Literature* (1987) collects a number of essays on the problem of reference in relation to literary texts. For a challenging but brilliant exploration of questions of mimesis and the materiality of writing, see Tom Cohen's *Anti-Mimesis from Plato to Hitchcock* (1994). Alongside and rather more accessible than Bronfen's *Over Her Dead Body* (1992) is Peter Brooks's lucid and thought-provoking *Body Work* (1993), which also considers the representation of bodies – especially female bodies – in nineteenth- and twentieth-century art and literature. For two powerful and very different accounts of writing and/through the body of a woman, see Luce Irigaray, 'This Sex Which is Not One' (1985) and Hélène Cixous, 'The Laugh of the Medusa' (1990).

5. The uncanny

L iterature is uncanny. What does this mean? To try to define the uncanny
is immediately to encounter one of its decisive paradoxes, namely that
'the uncanny' has to do with a *troubling* of definitions, with a fundamental
disturbance of what we think and feel. The uncanny has to do with a sense
of strangeness, mystery or eeriness. More particularly it concerns a sense of
unfamiliarity which appears at the very heart of the familiar, or else a sense of
familiarity which appears at the very heart of the unfamiliar. The uncanny is
not just a matter of the weird or spooky, but has to do more specifically with a
disturbance of the familiar. Such a disturbance might be hinted at by way of the
word 'familiar' itself. 'Familiar' goes back to the Latin *familia*, a family: we all
have some sense of how odd families can seem (whether or not one is 'part of
the family'). The idea of 'keeping things in the family' or of something that
'runs in the family', for instance, is at once familiar and potentially secretive or
strange. As an adjective 'familiar' means 'well acquainted or intimate', 'having
a thorough knowledge', etc.; but as a noun it carries the more unsettling,
supernatural sense of 'a spirit or demon supposed to come to a person *esp* a
witch, etc, at his or her call' (*Chambers Dictionary*). We might think here, for
example, of the demonic 'familiar' that is said to haunt Bertha Mason in
Charlotte Brontë's *Jane Eyre* (1847) or, more comically, of the 12-year-old
Maud's 'supernatural companion' in Elizabeth Bowen's superb novel *A World
of Love* (1955).

Here are a couple of examples of the uncanny. First: you walk into a room in
a house you have never visited before and suddenly you have the sense that
you *have* been there before and that you even seem to know what will happen
next. This kind of experience has even developed its own name, *déjà vu*. Or,
second example: you are in some public place (a shop perhaps or a train) and

you catch sight of someone whom you think looks rather disturbing, and then you realize that you have caught sight of this person reflected in a window or a mirror and that this person is yourself.

These examples could be described as so-called 'real life' occurrences. But are they in fact 'real life'? If, as we shall see, the uncanny is especially relevant to the study of literature, it also has to do with how the 'literary' and the 'real' can seem to merge into one another. On the one hand, uncanniness could be defined as occurring when 'real', everyday life suddenly takes on a disturbingly 'literary' or 'fictional' quality. On the other hand, literature itself could be defined as the discourse of the uncanny: literature is the kind of writing which most persistently and most provocatively engages with the uncanny aspects of experience, thought and feeling. In some ways this is in keeping with the sort of conception of literature theorized by the Russian formalists of the early twentieth century, especially Viktor Shklovsky. Literature, for the Russian formalists, has to do with *defamiliarization* (*ostranenie*): it makes the familiar strange, it challenges our beliefs and assumptions about the world and about the nature of 'reality'. Bertolt Brecht's argument that theatre should produce 'alienation effects' is an obvious analogy here. For Brecht, no actor is supposed to identify completely with the character he or she plays. Likewise the spectator is encouraged to feel dissociated, uneasy, alienated. In accordance with this, Brecht's concern is to demonstrate that the 'real' is not something that is simply a *given*: it is not something definite and immutable, but is constructed through human perception, language, beliefs and assumptions, and consequently it is something that can be changed. In Brechtian terms, the alienating or defamiliarizing power of drama – and art and literature more generally – lies in its capacity to transform us and the world around us. In this chapter we shall argue that these ideas about the power of art to disturb, defamiliarize or shake our beliefs and assumptions are intimately bound up with the uncanny. The uncanny – in particular as first elaborated by Freud, in his essay of that title (Freud 1985b) – is central to any description of the literary.

The uncanny has to do with making things *uncertain*: it has to do with the sense that things are not as they have come to appear through habit and familiarity, that they may challenge all rationality and logic. Nevertheless, it is possible to suggest a few forms that the uncanny takes:

1. Repetition. For example, strange repetition of a feeling, situation, event or character. Two obvious examples of the uncanny, in this respect, would be the experience of *déjà vu* (the sense that something has happened before), and the idea of the double (or *doppelgänger*).

2. Odd coincidences and, more generally, the sense that things are *fated* to happen. Something might happen, for example, that seems 'too good to be true' or that suggests, despite the fact that you do not believe in God, that someone or something is pulling the strings.

3. Animism. This is the rhetorical term referring to a situation in which what is inanimate or lifeless is given attributes of life or spirit. In the last sentence of Emily Brontë's *Wuthering Heights* (1847), for example, we read of 'the soft wind breathing through the grass' – a potentially uncanny instance of animism.

4. Anthropomorphism – that is to say, a more specific (because specifically human) form of animism. It is the rhetorical figure that refers to a situation in which what is not human is given attributes of human form or shape: the legs of a table or the face of a cliff would be examples of anthropomorphism, though they might not immediately or necessarily provoke a feeling of uncanniness. In a similar fashion, children's toys and fairy tales present many possibilities for thinking about anthropomorphism: we may think of such things (dolls or household utensils coming to life and talking) as decidedly *not* uncanny, but there is perhaps also a strange, potential slipperiness here. It is perhaps not by chance that children and children's toys loom large in certain books and films about the supernatural. (A fairy tale is not as far from a horror story as we might initially suppose.) An uncanny story frequently involves a mingling of such elements. It is crucial to the strange and disturbing atmosphere of Charlotte Perkins Gilman's story *The Yellow Wallpaper* (1892) that the room in which the narrator is confined is a former children's nursery. More immediately and more obviously uncanny, however, would be the anthropomorphic character of the wallpaper in this room. There is, for example, the moment when the narrator tells us about the 'kind of sub-pattern' in the wallpaper: 'in the places where [the wallpaper] isn't faded and where the sun is just so – I can see a strange, provoking, formless sort of figure, that seems to skulk about behind' (18).

5. Automatism. This is a term that can be used when what is human is perceived as merely mechanical: examples of this would be sleepwalking, epileptic fits, trance-states and madness. The narrator of *The Yellow Wallpaper* would clearly fit into this category (especially when she is 'creeping' round and round her room at the end), but a sufficiently careful reading of, say, Keats's trance-like 'Ode to a Nightingale' (1819) might also prove interesting in this context. The question at the end of Keats's poem is about trance and, perhaps, madness. In a sense it is a question

that haunts literature in general: 'Do I wake or sleep?' To suggest briefly one other example, the writing of D.H. Lawrence is full of people in states of trance and seizure. Towards the end of 'The Rocking-Horse Winner' (1912), for instance, there is a description of Paul and his mother: 'The Derby was drawing near, and the boy grew more and more tense. He hardly heard what was spoken to him, he was very frail, and his eyes were really uncanny. His mother had sudden seizures of uneasiness about him' (745). Robots and other automata (such as Terminator), on the other hand, are also potentially uncanny, for the opposite reason: what is perceived as human is in fact mechanical.

6. A sense of radical uncertainty about sexual identity – about whether a person is male or female, or apparently one but actually the other. This is made dramatically clear, for instance, in the uncanny revelation in the course of Neil Jordan's film *The Crying Game* (1992), when an apparently female character turns out to have the genitalia of a man; but we could also think of the uncanniness of gender in, for example, Virginia Woolf's *Orlando* (1927), Jeanette Winterson's *Sexing the Cherry* (1989) and *Written on the Body* (1992), and Jeffrey Eugenides's *Middlesex* (2002).

7. A fear of being buried alive. This may seem a somewhat refined example of the uncanny, but it is relevant insofar as it is related more broadly to images or experiences of claustrophobia, of being unexpectedly and unpleasantly stuck (for instance in an elevator, or in a swamp, or simply in a room with the last person in the world you would like to be left alone with). An extreme but fascinating instance of the uncanny in this context would be Edgar Allan Poe's story 'The Premature Burial' (1844) – about a man who has an obsessive fear of being buried alive and goes to great trouble and expense to have his family crypt designed in such a way as to allow him to escape, in the (one might have thought laughably unlikely) event of being buried alive by mistake. In a broader sense, however, we could reflect on the uncanny feelings encountered in all the aspects of being locked in, of enclosure and confinement, in Brontë's intensely claustrophobic *Wuthering Heights* or in Tennyson's short but extraordinarily evocative poem 'Mariana' (1830).

8. Silence. Intriguingly, this is an example proposed by Freud, though he himself is effectively silent on the subject of what makes it uncanny. The potentially uncanny qualities of silence are particularly evident in a work such as Henry James's *The Turn of the Screw* (1898). There is, for example, the strangely silent encounter on the stairs, between the governess and the dead Peter Quint:

> It was the dead silence of our long gaze at such close quarters that gave the whole horror, huge as it was, its only note of the unnatural. If I had met a murderer in such a place and at such an hour we still at least would have spoken. Something would have passed, in life, between us; if nothing had passed one of us would have moved. The moment was so prolonged that it would have taken but little more to make me doubt if even *I* were in life. I can't express what followed it save by saying that the silence itself . . . became the element into which I saw the figure disappear. (135)

9. Telepathy. This is an uncanny idea not least because it involves the thought that your thoughts are perhaps not your own, however private or concealed you might have assumed them to be. Literature is pervaded by examples of the telepathic. Alongside some of the texts already mentioned, such as *Jane Eyre*, *Wuthering Heights*, 'The Rocking-Horse Winner' and *The Turn of the Screw*, we might think, for instance, of George Eliot's *The Lifted Veil* (1878) – the very title of which gestures towards uncanny relevation. Eliot's narrator, Latimer, describes how he suddenly becomes capable of reading others' thoughts. In this way he presents an uncanny example of one of the most fundamental characteristics of narrative fiction: he becomes a telepathic or (nearly) omniscient narrator.

10. Death. In particular, death as something at once familiar – 'all that lives must die', as Gertrude puts it (*Hamlet*, I, ii, 72) – and absolutely unfamiliar, unthinkable, unimaginable. As the Anglican Book of Common Prayer declares: 'In life we are in the midst of death.'

In sum, then, the uncanny can be described as the thoughts and feelings which may arise on those occasions when the homely becomes unhomely, when the familiar becomes unfamiliar or the unfamiliar becomes strangely familiar. Alternatively, the uncanny is – in the words of the German philosopher F.W.J. Schelling – that which 'ought to have remained . . . secret and hidden but has come to light'. Schelling's definition of the uncanny is quoted by Sigmund Freud in his essay, published in 1919, entitled 'The "Uncanny"' ('Das Unheimliche'). In fact, most of the account of the uncanny which we have given so far is indebted to this extraordinary text. When Freud chose to write an essay on the uncanny he was opening up a very strange can of worms.

Freud's essay is largely focused on literature and in particular on a reading of E.T.A. Hoffmann's story 'The Sand-Man' (1816). In this respect it is slightly unusual, since Freud wrote comparatively little that could be described as literary criticism or literary theory. But few of Freud's essays have had a more pervasive and exciting impact on literary studies. What is especially fascinating about Freud's essay is the way in which it prompts us to ask various questions about *boundaries* and *limits*: How much of Freud's essay is psychoanalysis and how much is literature? Where does reason become imagination and imagination reason? Where does science become fiction and fiction science? Where does literature end and literary criticism or literary theory begin?

It has become something of a truism to note that Freud's writings can be thought about in at least two basic and quite different ways. First, there is the Freud of the so-called popular imagination: Freud the patriarchal, bourgeois, nineteenth-century Viennese Jew, who believed that everything has to do with sex. This Freud has very firm views and spouts these in the form of rather mechanically predictable theories, the most celebrated and fundamental of which is perhaps the Oedipus complex. Second, however, there is the other Freud, a Freud who did not fully realize what he was saying, who was for various reasons (historical as much as personal) unable to see or develop the implications of what he was saying, not least because these implications regularly run counter to his own proposed themes and assumptions. This second Freud is a Freud who is, we could say, different from himself, and who constitutes what is sometimes referred to as 'the new Freud' or 'French Freud' (in acknowledgement of the work done by the French psychoanalyst Jacques Lacan and others), a result in other words of what has been called 'the rereading of Freud' or 'the return to Freud'.

Freud's 'The "Uncanny"' provides one of the most dramatic and stimulating manifestations of these two Freuds. On the one hand there is the Freud who believes (and in some sense *needs* to believe) that literature and psychoanalysis can be simply and clearly separated off from each other, and that psychoanalysis can significantly contribute towards a scientific and objective understanding of literary texts. On the other hand there is the Freud who shows (often only inadvertently) that the 'literary' is stranger and more disturbing than psychoanalysis, science or rationalism in general may be able or willing to acknowledge. The essay gives us two Freuds, or a kind of double-Freud, and this double spends the essay investigating the importance among other things of the idea of the double. What makes the double uncanny? According to Freud's essay, the double is paradoxically both a promise of immortality (look, there's my double, I can be reproduced, I can live forever) and a harbinger of death (look, there I am, no longer me here, but there: I am about to die, or else I must be dead already). The notion of the double undermines the very logic of identity.

All of this is suggested, in fact, by the English title of Freud's essay, where the word 'uncanny' is in quotation marks. This putting-into-quotation-marks itself constitutes potential breeding grounds for the uncanny – for the 'un-canny' is always in quotation marks. The uncanny might thus be thought of as a kind of ghost-effect that haunts all words, however self-evident or 'familiar' they may appear to be. We could illustrate this most easily perhaps by trying to imagine what it would be like if proper names (such as 'London', 'George W. Bush', 'God') were suddenly used only in quotation marks – thus giving a new sense to the phrase 'scare quotes'. Language itself, then, becomes uncanny. Indeed, very often the more *familiar* a word, the more uncanny it can become. Every 'word', for example, is capable of being put into quotation marks and the act of putting it into quotation marks makes that word a little strange, as if different from itself, referring to something or somewhere else. This is a general point, also, about repetition: repetition of a word ('Words, words, words', as Hamlet says) can give rise to a sense of hollowness, strangeness, even spookiness.

Repetition is a key aspect of the uncanny, as Freud's essay makes clear. The uncanny is not simply a matter of the mysterious, bizarre or frightening: as we have tried to suggest, it involves a kind of *duplicity* (both doubling and deception) within the familiar. This logic of the uncanny, whereby the familiar turns into, or becomes contaminated by, the unfamiliar, is evident in the word 'uncanny' (or, in German, '*unheimlich*') itself. 'Uncanny' is the opposite of 'canny', meaning 'skilful', 'shrewd', 'knowing' (from Old English *kunnan*, 'to know', especially in the sense 'to know how to be able to do something'). But the word 'canny' shades into its opposite: in Scottish English in part-icular, 'canny' can suggest *unnatural* or *excessive* skilfulness, shrewdness or knowing. This capacity for a word to contain or to turn into its opposite is what Freud elsewhere talks about as the 'antithetical' meanings of 'primal words' (see Freud 1957a). We consider another example of this in Chapter 30, where 'pleasure' can be seen – at least in certain contexts – to entail its opposite ('pain'). Masochism is the term conventionally used to gloss this contradictory logic according to which pain can be pleasure or pleasure pain.

Analysis of the word 'uncanny' seems ineluctably, even fatalistically, bound up with an experience *of* the uncanny, an experience which disturbs any attempt to remain analytically detached and objective. This is strikingly clear from the early pages of Freud's essay, in which he seeks to show how the German word for 'homely' ('*heimlich*'), with its connotations of 'private', 'hidden', 'secret', inevitably conceals its opposite – the 'unhomely' or *un-heimlich*. From this it may be concluded that the uncanny cannot readily be avoided or denied: ultimately, as was hinted by putting it last on our list of ten, the uncanny is aligned with death. As a form of strange disruption, questioning and uncertainty, the idea of the uncanny may be frightening, but it also continues to be a crucially important and productive area for literary study.

The uncanny, then, is an experience – even though this may have to do with the unthinkable or unimaginable. It is not a theme which a writer uses or which a text possesses. The uncanny is not something simply present like an object in a painting. It is, rather, an effect. In this respect it has to do with how we read or interpret (interestingly, it makes no difference here whether we are talking about something in a book or something in the so-called outside world). In other words, the uncanny has to do, most of all, with effects of reading, with the experience of the reader. The uncanny is not so much *in* the text we are reading: rather, it is like a foreign body within ourselves.

Further reading

For a book-length study dealing with many of the concerns of this chapter, see Nicholas Royle's *The Uncanny* (2003). For two accessible and rather different discussions of the uncanny in literature, see Terry Apter's chapter in *Fantasy Literature* (1982) and J. Hillis Miller's essay on the uncanny and *Wuthering Heights*, in his *Fiction and Repetition* (1982). On the historical background to the concept of the uncanny, see Terry Castle's *The Female Thermometer* (1995) and Mladen Dolar's '"I Shall Be with You on Your Wedding-night"' (1991). Hillel Schwartz's *The Culture of the Copy* (1996) offers some fascinating perspectives on doubles and dual-thinking, from 'identical twins' to 'parallel universes'. For a good collection of essays on various aspects of the uncanny, including the first English translation of Ernst Jentsch's 'On the Psychology of the Uncanny' (1906), see *Home and Family* (1995), ed. Sarah Wood. On defamiliarization, the classic essay is Shklovsky's 'Art as Technique' (1965), but for an earlier engagement with similar ideas, see Shelley's crucial and widely reprinted 1821 essay 'A Defence of Poetry'. On theatre and alienation, 'A Short Organum for the Theatre' (Brecht 1978) is terse and stimulating. On fairy tales and the uncanny, see Jack Zipes (1988). On telepathy and the uncanny, see Royle's *Telepathy and Literature* (1991). Freud's 'The "Uncanny"' remains an extremely rich and surprising text (see Freud 1985b, as well as the new Penguin translation in Freud 2003). For some of the more challenging readings of Freud's essay, see Samuel Weber (1973, 2000), Hélène Cixous (1976), Neil Hertz (1979) and Jane Marie Todd (1986). On 'the return to Freud', see Samuel Weber's fine study of that title (1992). For especially good general introductions to psychoanalysis and literature, see Ellmann, ed., *Psychoanalytic Literary Criticism* (1994) and Wright, *Psychoanalytic Criticism: A Reappraisal* (1998).

6.   Monuments

Thou art a monument without a tomb,
And art alive still while thy book doth live,
And we have wits to read, and praise to give.

Ben Jonson's poem 'To the Memory of My Beloved, The Author, Mr. William Shakespeare, And What He Hath Left Us' was originally published as a preface to the First Folio edition of Shakespeare's collected plays in 1623, just seven years after the Bard's death. In these lines Jonson addresses the topic of this chapter: the nature of the literary monument and the way in which the writings of living authors are posthumously transformed into monuments to those authors' lives and work. The poet is, in Jonson's seemingly paradoxical formulation, a 'monument without a tomb', and is 'alive still' despite his death. The paradox that Jonson explores involves the idea that the poet is both alive and dead: after his death the poet still 'lives' through the 'life' of his 'book', which itself lives just as long as we read it and praise it. Exploring this paradox of the literary afterlife, the poem is performative. It *performs* an act of monumentalization, since it is designed not only to remind the reader of the value of Shakespeare's work (the word 'monument', we may remind ourselves, originates in the Latin *monere*, to remind) but also, in so doing, to establish that value. In fact, the publishing venture to which Jonson contributes his poem plays a crucial part in the monumentalization of the poet: the publication of a posthumous 'Collected Works' is itself a sign of the importance of the dead poet's work, an index of his genius. Contrary to Dryden's sense that the poem was 'an insolent, sparing, and invidious panegyric' (quoted in Donaldson 1988, 718), Jonson's intention seems to have been to 'honour' Shakespeare. This is the first stage in the poet's transcendence of his time and in his establishment as a 'classic'. Shakespeare 'was not of an age', Jonson asserts, 'but for all time!' (l.43).

The Second Folio of Shakespeare's plays, published nine years later in 1632, included an anonymous sixteen-line poem (written in fact by John Milton) entitled 'An Epitaph on the Admirable Dramatic Poet, W. Shakespeare'. Like Jonson's poem, Milton's begins by remarking on the fact that the poet had been buried in Stratford rather than, as might be thought more appropriate, Westminster Abbey (where, as Jonson notes, Chaucer, Spenser and Francis Beaumont are buried). Milton also plays on the opposition of life and death in the idea that Shakespeare has built for himself a 'live-long monument'. But he develops Jonson's notion of the relationship between reading and monumentalization by exploring the idea that we, readers, through our 'wonder and astonishment' at Shakespeare's art, are made 'marble with too much conceiving'. For Milton, we ourselves are monuments to the poet's genius, his living tomb:

> What needs my Shakespeare for his honoured bones
> The labour of an age in piled stones,
> Or that his hallowed relics should be hid
> Under a star-ypointing pyramid?
> Dear son of memory, great heir of fame,
> What need'st thou such weak witness of thy name?
> Thou in our wonder and astonishment
> Hast built thyself a live-long monument.
> For whilst to the shame of slow-endeavouring art,
> Thy easy numbers flow, and that each heart
> Hath from the leaves of thy unvalued book,
> Those Delphic lines with deep impression took,
> Then thou our fancy of itself bereaving,
> Dost make us marble with too much conceiving;
> And so sepulchred in such pomp dost lie,
> That kings for such a tomb would wish to die.

Both Jonson and Milton, then, articulate a series of questions around the idea of the monument, around the idea of the monumentalization of literary texts. How does an author enter the 'canon'? What is the relationship between monumentalization and reading? Do literary texts become static, frozen into their own tombs of eternity, or do they change with time and with each new generation? What is at stake in the literary critical process of canonization and monumentalization? What is gained and what lost? Literary texts, as the epitaphs by Jonson and Milton suggest, are themselves places where such questions are inaugurated, first posed and first pondered.

As we have seen, Jonson and Milton both express a certain ambivalence in their sense of the value of the monument and the process of monumentalization. They assert that Shakespeare needs no physical tomb, a structure that is at once a reminder of life and signifier of death. The third and fourth lines of Milton's poem sneer at the idea that Shakespeare's 'hallowed relics should be hid / Under a star-ypointing pyramid'. The lines suggest that the act of remembering, of monumentalizing the poet, is also an act of hiding, disguising, defacing him, and they remind us that this is precisely what we do when we bury the dead: by burying them we honour them but at the same time we hide them from sight, as if they are as much objects of terror and taboo as they are of veneration and awe. As Jonson and Milton recognize, the acts of monumentalization in which they are engaged when they write on Shakespeare are also acts of burial. And it might be argued that we are engaged in a similar dynamic whenever we read, talk and write about literary texts – not least, of course, when we write works of literary criticism. As Paul de Man has argued in an essay on Shelley, the transformation of literary texts into 'historical and aesthetic objects' involves a certain burial of those texts: what we do with dead poets, he remarks, 'is simply to bury them, to bury them in their own texts made into epitaphs and monumental graves' (de Man 1984, 121). The impulse to honour the dead, that is to say, is at the same time an impulse to bury them, to do away with them, to forget them, to be done with them. This, it might be said, is the fundamental tension of the institution of literary studies, an irreducible conflict between at once remembering and forgetting the dead.

The paradox is broached rather differently in Frank Kermode's *The Classic* (1975), a book that has itself become a minor classic in discussions of literary value, the canon and the nature of the institutionalization of literature. Kermode comments on the tension between endurance and changeability that constitutes the canon: 'the books we call classic possess intrinsic qualities that endure, but possess also an openness to accommodation which keeps them alive under endlessly varying dispositions' (Kermode 1975, 44). Just as Jonson defines Shakespeare as 'not of an age but for all time', so Kermode is attempting to think about the way that such a text or such an oeuvre 'speaks' to all generations and is as such 'timeless'. But he also suggests that it can only be 'timeless' by signifying differently at different times, so that it is, as such, time-bound. For Kermode, it is the possibility of a certain 'openness' to interpretation, what he terms the text's 'accommodation', which allows what we call a 'classic' to survive. Kermode evokes a sense of the classic as the living dead, surviving endlessly on new readers. His account has certain implications for notions of authorial intention and for ideas about the limits of interpretation: if a literary text can be read and reread at different times, in accordance with their varying (conscious *and* unconscious) interests, prejudices, ideas and conventions, then it would seem that the text cannot be limited to a single or univocal interpretation. If this position is correct, Kermode comments, we must somehow 'cope with the paradox that the classic changes, yet retains its identity'. And this has the further consequence that the text must be 'capable of saying more than its author meant', even if it were the case that saying 'more than he meant was what he meant to do'. Strange as it might seem, a 'classic' author may have meant what he or she cannot have known that he or she meant. Ultimately, Kermode suggests, 'the text is under the absolute control of no thinking subject' and is 'not a message from one mind to another' (Kermode 1975, 80, 139).

These ideas about the canon, about literary survival and about the nature of the 'classic', bring us back to questions of meaning, interpretation and authorial intention which we address elsewhere in this book. But here we are also concerned with another question, one that is equally fundamental to this book and to the practice and discipline of literary criticism more generally: the question of literary value. Readers will no doubt have noticed the way in which Bennett and Royle repeatedly employs terms of valuation: we refer, for example, to Milton's 'great epic poem' in Chapter 1, to Elizabeth Bowen's 'superb' novel in Chapter 5, to the opening paragraph of *Middlemarch* as 'extraordinary' in Chapter 8, to Sheridan's *The School for Scandal* as 'one of the greatest eighteenth-century English comedies' in Chapter 12. We also repeatedly use such terms as 'haunting', 'powerful', 'disturbing', 'singular' to suggest our positive valuation of texts, and seem to ascribe value, more or less explicitly, to aspects of texts that we see as funny, complex, undecidable, unsettling, and so on. In other words, Bennett and Royle, like any other work of literary criticism or theory, is benetted and embroiled in value judgements. This situation is unavoidable: even if we were to exclude value-laden terms from our critical vocabulary, we (have to) choose certain texts to read and talk about and such choices can in themselves be taken to imply judgements of value. Indeed, it may be said that the primary aim of critical discourse, the impulse for talking about books, is to persuade someone else to appreciate what the critic finds valuable about a literary text.

The bases on which judgements about literary value are made, however, are not easy to define. One of the most intriguing things about T.S. Eliot's classic essay 'What is a Classic?' (1945) is the way that he repeatedly uses the word 'mature' as a kind of talisman to express what he sees as valuable in literary texts. Indeed for Eliot, in this essay at least, it amounts to the very definition of a classic: 'If there is one word on which we can fix, which will suggest the maximum of what I mean by the term "a classic", it is the word *maturity*' (Eliot 1975, 116). He then goes on to use the words 'mature' (as adjective and verb) and 'maturity' a total of 23 times in the same paragraph: ripeness is certainly all, it would seem, as far as Eliot is concerned. Eliot's essay was written in 1944: it would be strange now to find a critic so confident about the values to be ascribed to the notion of 'maturity'. In general, it might be said, 'mature' is no longer part of the critical vocabulary of value. And what strikes us now about Eliot's use of the word is the fact that he nowhere says what he means by it, what he means when he says that a literary text is 'mature'. We can all tell when a peach is ripe but can we tell a mature poem from an immature one? What do we do with it – squeeze it? Is Shelley's *Adonais* mature? Is it more or less mature than Pope's *Essay on Man*, or Spenser's *Epithalamion*, or Eliot's *The Waste Land*? Is maturity even seen as valuable any more? As a critical term, 'mature' has become risible. And yet, for Eliot, it is crucial to his project of exploring the notion of the 'classic' and to his concept of literary value. This is not to say that Eliot was foolish or irresponsible in his terminology: rather, it exemplifies the fact that critical vocabularies change over time while always being in any case somewhat porous, unstable, contentious. In the eighteenth century, the vocabulary of value included ideas of proportion, probability and propriety; the Romantics developed a vocabulary of the sublime, imagination and originality; while nearer to our time, the New Critics valued complexity, paradox, irony and tension in poems, and postmodern critics valorize disjunction, fragmentation, heteroglossia, aporia, decentring.

Alongside changes in critical vocabulary, there are changes in how literary monuments are perceived and valued. The most obvious example would be the reception of Shakespeare himself. While Jonson and Milton declared, very soon after his death in 1616, that Shakespeare had earned a place in the literary canon, in fact his reputation developed much more slowly and patchily than this would suggest. Indeed, during much of the eighteenth century his work was criticized as brilliant but faulty: he was seen as a poet of 'nature' rather than learning, and was faulted for his versification and diction, his endless punning, his handling of plot and characterization, the improbability of his narratives, for not obeying the unities of time and place, and so on (see Vickers 1981, 1–86). It was only towards the end of the eighteenth century that an unalloyed and arguably uncritical sense of Shakespeare's monumental and timeless genius became commonplace. Indeed, throughout the eighteenth and even into the nineteenth century his plays were regularly rewritten to iron out his faults and make him more amenable to contemporary tastes. Thus *King Lear* was never performed on the English stage in its original form during the eighteenth century because its ending was held to be too gloomy – a happier, more appropriate ending was written for it by Nahum Tate in 1681 and became the standard acting text. In the present day, the perception and valuation of Shakespeare remains deeply indebted to the Romantic conception of his work as sublime, even sacred. At the same time, this conception of Shakespeare has undergone radical demystification and deconstruction in the work of such critics as Terence Hawkes, Jonathan Dollimore, Joel Fineman, Catherine Belsey, John Drakakis, Margreta de Grazia and others.

In recent years, much attention has been given to the construction of the literary canon. In particular, critics have explored the ways in which the canon is bound up with questions of education, class, economics, race, ethnicity, colonization, sexual and gender difference, and so on. This has led to a large-scale reassessment of both the canon itself and how evaluations take place. The notion of literary value as an inviolable essence has disintegrated. Our sense of the apparently impersonal and autonomous realm of the aesthetic has been irrevocably complicated. More than ever we are made aware of how far our own individual judgements are subject to social, political and institutional constraints. More than ever we are made aware of how far the canon is a fabrication. Thus, for example, critics have devoted much energy in recent years to discovering or rediscovering women writers and writers from different racial and ethnic backgrounds whose work has been neglected. In the case of women writers, it is often argued that such authors have been overlooked precisely because they are women, since, with a few notable exceptions (Austen, the Brontës, Woolf, Plath, for example), the patriarchal ethos of the literary critical establishment has tended to efface or marginalize women's writing in general. The publication of such anthologies as Gilbert and Gubar's *Norton Anthology of Literature by Women* (1985), Roger Lonsdale's *Eighteenth-Century Women Poets* (1989), Andrew Ashfield's *Romantic Women Poets* (1995, 1998), and Angela Leighton and Margaret Reynolds's *Victorian Women Poets: An Anthology* (1995), have altered the shape of the canon in and beyond the academy. More generally, what Elaine Showalter calls 'gynocriticism' and publishing ventures such as Virago and the Woman's Press have altered our literary historical maps by rediscovering numerous forgotten (or never recognized) authors, and critics have devoted a great deal of energy to the work of re-editing their writings, as well as to the critical, biblio- and biographical tasks of new evaluations.

Such reassessments and rediscoveries force us to face a series of difficult and complex questions concerning literary value and critical evaluation. Is literary value eternal and unchanging or is it contingent and dependent on readers and the institutions of criticism? Are we simply constructing new, exclusive canons when we discover 'neglected' writers, or are we rethinking the whole idea of 'the canon' and canonization? Is there such a thing as literary value? If so, how can it be described and defined? What are we doing when we make such judgements? Is there, as Steven Connor argues, an 'imperative' or 'necessity' of value (Connor 1992, 8)?

The recent rethinking of the canon, then, involves both a reassessment of which texts should be in the canon and a rethinking of the idea of the canon itself. Such reassessments have hardly gone unchallenged. One of the most stubbornly provocative challenges to what, in his view, has become the modern critical orthodoxy, is Harold Bloom's *The Western Canon* (1994). Bloom's 'single aim' is to 'preserve poetry as fully and purely as possible' against the politicizing of what he calls the 'school of resentment'. For Bloom, the school of resentment is typified by those critics who argue that the literary critical institution has valorized the work of 'dead white males' at the expense of the work of marginalized writers – women, say, or Afro-Caribbeans or Hispanics or gays or the working classes (Bloom 1994, 18). For these 'resentful' critics, the work of criticism cannot be disengaged from the work of social and political critique since the traditional canon operates as an ideological justification of the values (often racist, heterosexist, patriarchal, colonial and elitist) of the male, Western, establishment figures which it enshrines. For Bloom, by contrast, literature is and should be an antisocial body of work. Literary texts, he argues, even work *against* political and social improvement: indeed, for Bloom, great writers 'are subversive of all values'. Reading their work with a view to forming our 'social, political, or personal moral values' would merely make us 'monsters of selfishness and exploitation' (29). The canon, for Bloom, is élitist and discriminatory or it is nothing. Accordingly, his book is itself élitist. Bloom lists the 3,000 books and authors that he claims make up the Western canon. He then narrows this down to 26 books/authors to which his volume is devoted. In the final analysis, though, Bloom's canon comes down to a single author by whose work all else must be judged. We will not be surprised by now to learn that that author is William Shakespeare. Bloom's argument for the Western canon relies, finally, on Shakespeare's unique genius:

> Shakespeare's eminence is, I am certain, the rock upon which the School of Resentment must at last founder. How can they have it both ways? If it is arbitrary that Shakespeare centres the Canon, then they need to show why the dominant social class selected him rather than, say, Ben Jonson, for that

arbitrary role. Or if history and not the ruling circles exalted Shakespeare, what was it in Shakespeare that so captivated the mighty Demiurge, economic and social history? Clearly this line of inquiry begins to border on the fantastic; how much simpler to admit that there is a *qualitative* difference, a difference in kind, between Shakespeare and every other writer, even Chaucer, even Tolstoy, or whoever. Originality is the great scandal that resentment cannot accommodate, and Shakespeare remains the most original writer we will ever know. (Bloom 1994, 25)

Bloom is compelling. The apparent continuity in the valuation of Shakespeare from the eighteenth century to the present does indeed seem to validate such a judgement of his work as a unique and uniquely original phenomenon, and this is confirmed by what seems to be our instinctive sense on reading him that we are encountering something original, unique, 'for all time'. It is hard to get round our sense, our intuitive sense, on reading Shakespeare, that his work is simply, unquestionably richer, more complex, more endlessly fertile, than that of other writers, even of other 'canonical' writers.

And yet, and yet . . . Still we might have nagging doubts. How do we know that our 'intuition' is not itself a learned response, that our 'instinctive' sense of Shakespeare's genius is not, itself, a result of our schooling? If we see our appreciation of Shakespeare as an effect of social conditioning, we might feel that his work does not have the eternal qualities we thought it did. Moreover, we might notice that Bloom's 'explanation', his offering of the case of Shakespeare as a final arbiter for his judgement about aesthetic judgement, tells us nothing about the grounds for such claims: indeed, the questions that Bloom poses for the 'school of resentment' might also be asked of his own work, since his account of Shakespeare as *different*, as *original* and so on, is no more an explanation than the 'history' or 'class' which his opponents offer. Bloom's is, finally (and proudly), a monumentalizing gesture: his very language allies Shakespeare with the material of the tomb itself in its metaphor of the 'rock', and eternalizes him and abstracts him from history in its comment that he is 'the most original writer we will ever know'. We are led back, then, to the question with which we began this chapter: is that what we want of our writers? Monuments?

It might seem ironic that what would appear to be the deeply conservative, reactionary, élitist position of Harold Bloom should find confirmation in the writings of that monument of socialism, Karl Marx. And yet Marx himself affirms the sense that, as far as art goes, the crucial question is not how artists reflect on or are influenced by their time but rather just the strange fact of their survival:

the difficulty lies not in understanding that the Greek arts and epic are bound up with certain forms of social development. The difficulty is that they still afford us artistic pleasure and that in a certain respect they count as a norm and as an unattainable model. (Quoted in Guillory 1993, 322)

This, then, is what remains to be explained: the way that literary works remain with us, haunt us, still, beyond the conditions of their production, whatever may be our legitimate concerns for human and social justice. Just this remaining, this endurance of the haunting singularity of the literary text, is what keeps us coming back to it as our preoccupations, desires, prejudices and commitments change. What baffles and enthrals – what Bloom is responding to in his flawed but deeply productive defence of the canon – is the singularity and uncanny *force* of the literary. It is this characterization of Shakespeare as a 'monument without a tomb' – a monumentalizing *and* anti-monumentalizing phrase – that Bloom shares with Jonson. And it is the undecidable nature of such gestures, the sense that we bury poets as we raise monuments of reading to them and our sense that, still, they hold over us an uncanny, haunting power, which brings us to them, brings us back to them.

Further reading

Much, often highly polemical work, has been published on the so-called 'canon wars' in the last few years, evincing the high institutional and pedagogical stakes involved in how canons are formed and regarded. Barbara Herrnstein Smith's *Contingencies of Value* (1988) offers a persuasive proposal for a pragmatic sense of literary value and the canon. John Guillory's *Cultural Capital* (1993) is a densely argued polemic for the 'inevitability of the social practice of judgement' and of the inextricability of aesthetic and economic 'value'; Guillory is influenced by the work of the French sociologist Pierre Bourdieu, whose *Distinction: A Social Critique of the Judgement of Taste* (1984) offers an important account of the social, cultural, economic and political issues embedded in decisions about the value of literary and other works. Henry Louis Gates's *Loose Canons* (1992) engages with issues raised in this chapter, especially regarding racial and ethnic difference. On postcolonialism and the canon see John Thieme, *Postcolonial Con-texts* (2001). For studies of the creation of the English canon, see Kramnick, *Making the English Canon* (1998) and Ross, *The Making of the English Literary Canon* (1998). Within the specifically English critical tradition of the twentieth century, perhaps the most influential and opinionated work is that of F.R. Leavis, who is happy in, for example, *The Great Tradition* (1948) sweepingly to dismiss great swathes of literature (an author such as Laurence Sterne is relegated to a dismissive footnote) and to try to reduce the novel tradition to just four writers: an amusing and enlightening book to read, still, for insights into the rhetoric of *doxa* and unreflective prejudice in canon formation.

7.   Narrative

Stories are everywhere: in movies, sitcoms, cartoons, commercials, poems, newspaper articles, novels. We all make use of stories every day and our lives are shaped by stories – stories about what happened in our dreams or at the dentist, stories about how we fell in love or the origins of the universe, stories about war and about peace, stories to commemorate the dead and to confirm a sense of who we are. In this chapter, we propose to circle around the following propositions:

1. Stories are everywhere.
2. Not only do we tell stories, but stories tell us: if stories are everywhere, we are also in stories.
3. The telling of a story is always bound up with power, with questions of authority, property and domination.
4. Stories are multiple: there is always more than one story.
5. Stories always have something to tell us about stories themselves: they always involve self-reflexive and metafictional dimensions.

Roland Barthes suggests that falling in love involves telling ourselves stories about falling in love: in this sense, he argues, 'mass culture is a machine for showing desire' (Barthes 1990c, 136). Disagreements, arguments, even wars, are often the result of conflicting stories concerning, for example, the rights to a piece of land: the real reason for both the first Gulf War (1991) and the second Gulf War (2003) may have been oil, but the technical justification for going to war turned on the story of who owned or should own a particular piece of Kuwait in the first instance and the existence or otherwise of Weapons of Mass Destruction in the second. Academic, 'objective' or 'scientific' discourses are constructed as stories. The historian Hayden White has given special emphasis to the fact that history is written in the form of certain kinds of narrative, that the task of the historian is to 'charge . . . events' with 'a comprehensible plot structure' (White 1978, 92). Science is composed of stories: astronomy attempts to narrate the beginnings of the universe; geology seeks to tell the story of the formation of mountains and plains, rivers, valleys and lakes; and like Rudyard Kipling's 'Just So' stories, evolutionary psychology purports to tell us the story of how we came to be as we are. For many centuries, millions of people have come to understandings about their place in the world, the meaning of their lives and the nature of politics, ethics and justice through stories about the lives of Christ, Buddha or the prophet Mohammed. The narrative of class struggle and emancipation from peasant society to the dictatorship of the proletariat has had a profound influence in the past 150 years. And in the twentieth century, Sigmund Freud produced a new and scandalous story about the nature of childhood. To say that Christianity, Buddhism, Islam, Marxism and psychoanalysis involve stories is not to suggest that they are merely fictive. Rather, it is to register the fact that there are few aspects of life which are not bound up with strategies and effects of narrative.

The simplest way to define narrative is as a series of events in a specific order – with a beginning, a middle and an end. We might think about James Joyce's short story 'The Dead', from *Dubliners* (1914), to illustrate the point. Put very simply, the story begins with the arrival of Gabriel and his wife Gretta at a party, tells of the events of the party and the couple's walk home, and ends as they fall asleep in their hotel. What is important in this description is the temporal ordering of what happens. By contrast, lyric poems, for example, are not typically thought to express or depict a series of temporally ordered series of events. One of the ways in which lyric poetry is defined, in fact, is by the absence of any such representation of events – lyric poems characteristically use the present tense and exploit a sense of the presence of the speaker in the act of meditating or speaking. Percy Bysshe Shelley's 'To a Sky-Lark' (1820) recounts no events, but is an effusion of the poet's sense of the bird's 'unpremeditated art' which he attempts both to define and in some ways to reproduce. Similarly, while Seamus Heaney's 'bog poems' from *North* (1975) might dig up buried narratives of victimization, sacrifice and atonement, their lyric tone gives a sense of an individual poet responding, now, to what he sees. Narrative, however, is characterized by its foregrounding of a series of events or actions which are connected in time. What happens at the end of 'The Dead' is determined by what happened earlier. The events are recounted more or less chronologically in Joyce's story, in that the order of the telling follows the order of the told: first we learn of Gabriel and Gretta's arrival, then of the party, and finally of the hotel. But narratives also invariably involve what the narratologist Gérard Genette has called anachronisms – flashbacks, jumps forwards (or prolepses), the slowing down and speeding up of events and other distortions of the linear time-sequence (Genette 1986). Texts such as Virginia Woolf's 'The Mark on the Wall' (1921) dislodge our sense of temporal sequence. The story begins: 'Perhaps it was the middle of January in the present year' (Woolf 1982, 41). This suggests that the events recounted span a number of months, but by the end we have the sense that the story follows the wanderings of the narrator's consciousness over only a number of minutes or, at most, hours. Despite this and many other distortions of chronological order, however, Woolf's text is only readable insofar as it exploits our *expectations* of narrative sequence. Indeed, these distortions themselves can only be conceived against a background of linear chronological sequence.

Time, then, is crucial to narrative. But as the novelist E.M. Forster recognizes in *Aspects of the Novel* (1927), the temporal ordering of events is not the whole story. Forster makes a memorable distinction between 'The king died and then the queen died' on the one hand, and 'The king died, and then the queen died of grief' on the other (Forster 1976, 87). While the first 'narrative' includes two events related in time, he proposes, the second includes another 'connection', the crucial element of causality. The first simply lists two events, while the second provides the thread of a narrative by showing how they are related. The logical or causal connections between one event and another constitute fundamental aspects of every narrative. An obvious example would be detective stories. Detective stories rely, above all, on our expectation and desire for connection. They produce quite complex routes to a revelation of whodunnit, routes both determined and detected by the logic of cause and effect.

The beginning–middle–end sequence of a narrative also tends to emphasize what is known as a teleological progression – the *end* (in Greek, *telos*) itself as the place to get to. A lyric poem does not seem to rely on its ending to provide coherence: the end is not typically the place where all will be resolved. By contrast, we often think of a good story as one that we just cannot put down, a novel we compulsively read to find out what happens at the end. The narrative theorist Peter Brooks has studied ways in which readers' desires are directed towards the end, ways in which narratives are structured towards, or as a series of digressions from, an ending:

> we are able to read present moments – in literature and, by extension, in life – as endowed with narrative meaning only because we read them in anticipation of the structuring power of those endings that will retrospectively give them the order and significance of plot. (Brooks 1984, 94)

Likewise, Brooks has elaborated the paradoxical ways in which the dénouement or tying up of a story is worked towards through the paradox of digression. Thus, for example, while we may find a novel, film or play frustrating if it contains too many digressions from the main plot, we enjoy the suspense involved in delaying a dénouement. 'Suspense' movies, thrillers and so on, in particular, exploit this strangely masochistic pleasure that we take in delay. One of the paradoxical attractions of a good story, in fact, is often understood to be its balancing of digression, on the one hand, with progression towards an end, on the other.

But what is this end which we so much desire? (We may find out in more detail below, in Chapter 32.) Brooks and others have suggested that narratives move from a state of equilibrium or stasis through a disturbance of this stability, and back to a state of equilibrium at the end. The end of a narrative, the state of equilibrium, occurs when the criminal is discovered, when the lovers get married, or when the tragic hero dies. In addition, this end is characteristically the place of revelation and understanding. A part of the equilibrium that endings apparently offer is the satisfaction of epistemophilia, the reader's desire to know. And because of the conventional emphasis on hermeneutic discovery at the end, endings tend to be particularly over-determined places: we look to the end to provide answers to questions that the text has raised. In modernist narratives such as Woolf's 'The Mark on the Wall', however, these answers tend to be withheld or else treated ironically. The ending of Woolf's story is paradoxical, in fact, in that it resolves the question with which the story starts out – what is the mark on the wall? – by telling us that it is a snail. But this 'answer' to the question simply parodies those conventional realist endings that seem to clear up our confusions and satisfy our curiosity. So what if it is a snail? To say that the mark is a snail is an example of what is called an aporia – an impassable moment or point in narrative, a hermeneutic abyss. If we ask what Woolf's story is 'about', we realize that it is about itself as a story. The ending tells everything, it gives us 'the answer', and it tells us nothing: it is not for this 'answer' that we have read the story. Our epistemophilia proves to be perverted.

One of the most fundamental distinctions in narrative theory is that between 'story' and 'discourse'. As Jonathan Culler has suggested, a fundamental premiss of narratology is that narrative has a double structure: the level of the told (story) and the level of telling (discourse) (Culler 1981). These levels have been given different names by different theorists – the Russian formalists call them *fabula* and *sjuzhet*; the French structuralists call them either *récit* (or *histoire*) and *discours*, and so on. 'Story', in this sense, involves the events or actions which the narrator would like us to believe occurred, the events (explicitly or implicitly) *represented*. 'Discourse', on the other hand, involves the way in which these events are recounted, how they get told, the organization of the *telling*. In fact, of course, these two levels can never be entirely separated, and much narrative theory has been concerned to describe ways in which they interact. Thus Charlotte Brontë's *Jane Eyre* and Joyce's 'The Dead', for example, present the events of the narrative more or less in the order that they are alleged to have occurred. By contrast, texts such as Emily Brontë's *Wuthering Heights* and Woolf's 'The Mark on the Wall' move forward and backward in time and shift from the level of telling to that of the told in complex and unnerving ways. Many modernist and postmodernist texts experiment with the relation between these two levels, to denaturalize or defamiliarize our sense of how narratives function. A text such as Robert Coover's short story 'The Babysitter' from *Pricksongs and Descants* (1969), for instance, presents several slightly different accounts of what appears to be the same evening from a number of different perspectives: the contradictions and dislocations produced within and between these accounts, however, make it impossible, finally, to determine the precise nature or order of the evening's events. Alain Robbe-Grillet's novels, such as *The Voyeur* (1955) and *Jealousy* (1957), also recount the 'same' series of events over and over again, but from the 'same' narratorial perspective: each telling, however, is subtly different, thus dissolving our sense of any one, true, narrative of events. Rather than reading such texts simply as exceptions or aberrations, we might consider ways in which they metafictionally reflect on the multiplicity of any narrative – its susceptibility to different readings, its differing narrative perspectives, its shifting senses of place and time.

Everything that we have said about narrative up to this point has concerned the sense of its linearity: narrative involves a linear series of actions connected in time and through causality. In addition to this linearity, we might consider another important aspect of narrative, namely the relation between teller and listener or reader. Indeed, rather than appealing to the idea of a sequence of events, Barbara Herrnstein Smith has argued that we need to ground our understanding of narrative in terms of 'someone telling someone else that something happened' (Smith 1981, 228). The significance of this proposition is that it redirects our focus from the events or actions themselves to the relationship between the author or teller and the reader or listener. As Jonathan Culler has put it, 'To tell a story is to claim a certain authority, which listeners grant' (Culler 1997, 89). Much of the work in narrative theory has involved attempts to discriminate among different kinds of narrators (first person or third person, objective or subjective, reliable or unreliable, so-called 'omniscient' or not, together with questions concerning his or her 'point of view', his or her 'voice' and so on). Our understanding of a text is pervaded by our sense of the character, trustworthiness and objectivity of the figure who is narrating. Moreover, it is often very important to discriminate between the narratorial point of view and that of the so-called implied author – a particularly important distinction in certain ironic texts, for example. Although Jonathan Swift's essay 'A Modest Proposal' (1729) would not usually be considered as a narrative, it does provide one of the classic examples of narratorial irony. In this essay, the narrator proposes that in order to deal with poverty and hunger in Ireland and to prevent children of the poor from being a burden to their parents, such children should be sold to the rich as food – a solution that would be 'innocent, cheap, easy, and effectual' (509). The narrator appears to make his proposal seriously but we necessarily conceive of an 'implied author' who has very different views and motives, and who is making a political point about the immorality of the English government in its attitude towards poverty in Ireland. Our understanding of the ironic force of the text necessitates a discrimination between the two voices or personae of the narrator and the implied author.

A consideration of the relationship between teller and listener or reader leads in turn to questions of power and property. One of the most famous storytellers is Scheherazade from *A Thousand and One Nights*. In these classical Arabic narratives, Scheherazade has been sentenced to death by the king but is able to stave off her execution by telling him stories. By ending her story each night at a particularly exciting point, she is able to delay her death for another day because the king wants to find out what happens next. What makes *A Thousand and One Nights* so intriguing for narrative theorists has to do with its enactment of forms of power. As Ross Chambers proposes, 'To tell a story is to exercise power' (Chambers 1984, 50). Chambers argues that storytelling is often used, as in the case of Scheherazade, as an 'oppositional' practice, a practice of resistance used by the weak against the strong: 'oppositional narrative', he claims, 'in exploiting the narrative situation, discovers a power, not to change the essential structure of narrative situations, but to *change its other* (the "narratee" if one will), through the achievement and maintenance of authority, in ways that are potentially radical' (Chambers 1991, 11). In this respect, we might consider the motives and effects of Gretta's story of her dead lover in 'The Dead': perhaps the ending of Joyce's narrative should be understood in terms of the diffusion of Gabriel's egoistic, domineering and even rapacious desire for his wife by Gretta's narration of her love story. Gretta, subject to patriarchal society's insistence on the husband's rights to the wife's body, displaces her husband's unwanted attention by telling him a story. The violence of Gabriel's desire is expressed in references to his longing 'to be master of her strange mood . . . to cry to her from his soul, to crush her body against him, to overmaster her' (248). By the middle of Gretta's narration, Gabriel sees himself, by contrast with the lover of her story, as a 'ludicrous figure . . . idealizing his own clownish lusts' and a 'pitiable fatuous fellow' (251). And by the end, all lusts and all passions and anger, all mastery and desire, have dissolved: 'Gabriel held her hand for a moment longer, irresolutely, and then shy of intruding on her grief, let it fall gently and walked quietly to the window' (253). This conflict of stories – Gabriel's about himself and Gretta's about her dead lover – results in a disturbance of power relations. In this sense, just as much as 'The Mark on the Wall', or the stories of Coover and Robbe-Grillet, 'The Dead' is self-reflexively about the power of stories. More often, of course, it is the dominant ideology which is able to tell stories about, for example, how it got to be the dominant ideology. In the Soviet Union, it was the Bolsheviks and later the Stalinists who got to write the history books. But there is an important difference between these two forms of power: the power exerted by Scheherazade and by Gretta is a specifically *narrative* power. The only way that these storytellers can avoid death on the one hand and violent passion on the other is by making their stories good, by making them compelling to the point of distraction. By contrast, as far as the Soviet Union was concerned, the Stalinist version of history did not even have to be plausible, because its lessons would be enforced in other ways. *Narrative* power, then, may be the only strategy left for the weak and dispossessed: without narrative power, they may not be heard.

The social and political importance of stories is eloquently expressed by the old man in Chinua Achebe's novel *Anthills of the Savannah* (1987): 'The sounding of the battle-drum is important; the fierce waging of the war itself is important; and the telling of the story afterwards – each is important in its own way' (123–4). But, the man continues, the story is 'chief among his fellows':

> 'The story is our escort; without it we are blind. Does the blind man own his escort? No, neither do we the story; rather it is the story that owns us and directs us. It is the thing that makes us different from cattle; it is the mark on the face that sets one people apart from their neighbours.' (124)

Stories own us, and tell us, Achebe suggests, as much as we own or tell stories.

There are many questions of narrative, then, which may be considered in relation to literature: temporality, linearity and causality, so-called omniscience, point of view, desire and power. But most of all, perhaps, it is the relation between narrative and 'non-' or 'anti-narrative' elements that fascinate and disturb. Aspects such as description, digression, suspense, aporia and self-reflection, temporal and causal disorders are often what are most compelling in narrative. A text such as Woolf's 'The Mark on the Wall', indeed, *has* no narrative outside of description and aporetic reflections on the nature of narrative. Correspondingly, Joyce's 'The Dead' depends to a large extent on moments of what Joyce refers to elsewhere as 'epiphany', moments of revelation or understanding, moments that appear to stand outside time, outside of narrative. As Gabriel watches his wife listening to a piece of music as they prepare to leave the party, there is just such a moment – a moment of revelation which is also a moment of mystery. Gretta, standing listening to a song is, for Gabriel, full of 'grace and mystery . . . as if she were a symbol of something' (240). Like Scheherazade's, Joyce's storytelling holds off, and hangs on, death. And as the snow falls on the world outside the hotel window at the end of the story, as Gabriel falls into unconsciousness and the narrative slips away, there is another moment of epiphany, a dissolution of time, of space, of life, of identity, desire and narrative.

Further reading

Gérard Genette's *Narrative Discourse* (1986) is a systematic and influential account of the structure of narrative. Another modern classic which takes as its focus questions of narrative perspective is Dorrit Cohn's *Transparent Minds* (1978). Wallace Martin's *Recent Theories of Narrative* (1986) and Shlomith Rimmon-Kenan's *Narrative Fiction* (2002) both provide excellent and very clear introductions to narrative theory, while J. Hillis Miller's essay 'Narrative' (1990) presents a concise and accessible summary of a number of paradoxes in narrative. Peter Brooks's *Reading for the Plot* (1984) explores ways in which narrative may be thought about in relation to readers' desires; on the 'epistemophilic urge' in narrative, see his *Body Work* (1993). A good short summary of feminist perspectives on narrative theory is Margaret Homans's 'Feminist Fictions and Feminist Theories of Narrative' (1994); see also Lidia Curti, *Female Stories, Female Bodies* (1998). James Phelan has collected some useful and provocative essays on narrative and its relationship to issues of reading in *Reading Narrative* (1989). Seymour Chatman's *Coming to Terms* (1990) is an incisive summary of narrative theory in relation to literary texts and film, and is especially useful in its discussion of ideas of narrative perspective and point of view. For a critique of traditional narratology from a poststructuralist perspective, see Andrew Gibson, *Towards a Postmodern Theory of Narrative* (1996). For a valuable and wide-ranging collection of essays on narrative theory, from Plato to Trin Minh-Ha, focusing in particular on 'classic' structuralist approaches and poststructuralist provocations, see Martin McQuillan, ed., *The Narrative Reader* (2000).

8.   Character

Characters are the life of literature: they are the objects of our curiosity and fascination, affection and dislike, admiration and condemnation. Indeed, so intense is our relationship with literary characters that they often cease to be simply 'objects'. Through the power of identification, through sympathy and antipathy, they can become part of how we conceive ourselves, a part of who we are. More than two thousand years ago, writing about drama in the *Poetics*, Aristotle argued that character is 'secondary' to what he calls the 'first essential' or 'lifeblood' of tragedy – the plot – and that characters are included 'for the sake of the action' (Aristotle 1965, 40). Considerably more recently in an essay on the modern novel, 'The Art of Fiction' (1884), the novelist Henry James asked, 'What is character but the determination of incident? What is incident but the illustration of character?' (James 1986, 174). While Aristotle makes character 'secondary' to plot, James suggests that the two are equal and mutually defining. Indeed, the novels and plays we respond to most strongly almost invariably have forceful characters as well as an intriguing plot. Our memory of a particular novel or play often depends as much on our sense of a particular character as on the ingenuities of the plot. Characters in books have even become part of our everyday language. Oedipus, for example, has given his name to a condition fundamental to psychoanalytic theory, whereby little boys want to kill their fathers and sleep with their mothers. Mrs Malaprop in Sheridan's play *The Rivals* (1775) has given us the word 'malapropism' when someone uses, for example, the word 'illiterate' to mean 'obliterate' (see I.2.178). A 'romeo' denotes a certain kind of amorous young man resembling the hero of Shakespeare's *Romeo and Juliet* (*c*.1595). When we refer to someone as a 'scrooge', we mean a miser, but when we do so we are alluding, knowingly or not, to the protagonist of Charles

Dickens's *A Christmas Carol* (1843), for whom Christmas is a fatuous waste of time and money. Vladimir Nabokov's novel *Lolita* (1958) has given us a term for what the *OED* defines as 'a sexually precocious schoolgirl', as well as a word which especially through the Internet has acquired an association with the sexual abuse of children. There is even a day named after a fictional character, 'Bloomsday' (16th June), after Leopold Bloom in James Joyce's *Ulysses* (1922).

But what is a person or a character in a literary work? What does it mean to talk about a character as 'vivid' or 'life-like'? How do writers construct characters and produce the illusion of living beings? What is the relationship between a person in a literary text and a person outside it? As we shall try to demonstrate, these are questions that books themselves – in particular plays, novels and short stories – consistently explore. In this chapter, we shall focus, in particular, on the nineteenth-century realist tradition. It is, we suggest, this tradition which has culminated in the kinds of assumptions that we often hold about people and characters today. And it is against such preconceptions that modernist and postmodernist texts tend to work.

Charles Dickens's novels are indisputably from the nineteenth century. Whether or not they can be described as 'realist', though, is very definitely a matter of dispute. But this very uncertainty makes the novels particularly intriguing for a discussion of character since they tend both to exploit and to explode 'realist' conventions of characterization. *Great Expectations* (1860–1) opens with the orphan-hero, Pip, examining the writing on his parents' gravestones in order to attempt to determine the 'character' of his mother and father:

> As I never saw my father or my mother, and never saw any likeness of either of them (for their days were long before the days of photographs), my first fancies regarding what they were like, were unreasonably derived from their tombstones. The shape of the letters on my father's, gave me an odd idea that he was a square, stout, dark man, with curly black hair. From the character and turn of the inscription, '*Also Georgiana Wife of the Above*', I drew a childish conclusion that my mother was freckled and sickly. (35)

The comedy of this passage is partly produced by the double sense of 'character' – as the shape of an inscribed letter on a tombstone and as the personality of a human being. The text implies that our knowledge of people is determined by writing, by the character of written words. Although he is 'unreasonable', in taking the shape of letters to denote character, Pip is not simply mistaken in recognizing that our sense of our self and of other people is developed through language. For as this passage clearly indicates, we construct ourselves through and in words, in the image-making, story-generating power of language. In this respect, it is significant that the opening to *Great Expectations* explores one of the major themes of literary texts: the question 'who am I?' One fascination of characters in fiction and drama, as well as one of their most 'characteristic' activities, is to suggest answers to this question, not only for themselves, but also for us.

To talk about a novel such as *Great Expectations* as 'realist' is in part to suggest that its characters are 'life-like', that they are like 'real' people. But what does this mean? The first requirement for such a character is to have a plausible name and to say and do things that seem convincingly like the kinds of things people say and do in so-called 'real life'. The second requirement is a certain complexity. Without this complexity, a character appears merely 'one-dimensional', cardboard or (in E.M. Forster's terms) 'flat' (Forster 1976, 73). To be life-like, a fictional character should have a number of different traits – traits or qualities which may be conflicting or contradictory: he or she should be, to some extent, unpredictable, his or her words and actions should appear to originate in multiple impulses. Thirdly, however, these tensions, contradictions, multiplicities should cohere in a single identity. Thus 'life-likeness' appears to involve both multiplicity and unity at the same time. In the classic nineteenth-century realist novel *Middlemarch* (1871–2), for example, there is a character called Lydgate of whom George Eliot observes: 'He had two selves within him', but these selves must 'learn to accommodate each other' in a 'persistent self' (182). It is this tension, between complexity and unity, that makes a character like Lydgate both interesting and credible. The importance of such unity in realist texts is made clear by works like Robert Louis Stevenson's *The Strange Case of Dr Jekyll and Mr Hyde* (1886) or, less melodramatically, Joseph Conrad's 'The Secret Sharer' (1910): these narratives can be called 'limit texts' in that they use the framework of life-like or realistic characters to explore what happens when the self is demonically split or doubled. In doing so, such texts challenge the basis of realism itself.

Realist characterization presupposes a 'mimetic' model of literary texts whereby what is primary or original is a real person, and a character in a book is simply a copy of such a person. Such a model does not allow for a reversal of this relationship: it does not allow for the possibility that, for example, a person in 'real life' might be convincing to the extent that he or she resembles a person in a book. On the face of it, such a reversal may sound rather strange or counterintuitive: we would normally want to give priority to a 'person' and say that characters in books are more or less like 'real' people. In fact, however, as the example of *Great Expectations* suggests, it is easy to demonstrate that things also work the other way round. Indeed, literary history contains various dramatic instances where 'life' copies fiction. After the publication of Goethe's *The Sorrows of Young Werther* in Germany in 1774, for example, there was a fashion among young men in Europe for suicide, an act modelled on the suicide of the eponymous hero of that novel. Similarly, J.D. Salinger's novel *The Catcher in the Rye* (1951) was held responsible for the antisocial behaviour of numerous young men in the United States in the 1950s and early 1960s who identified with the disaffected hero Holden Caulfield. The young, in fact, are often considered (by the old) to be in danger of mimetic dissipation, to endanger themselves, their families and society because they identify with and then copy the actions and attitudes of disreputable people in books or, more recently, in film and video.

This paradox of character whereby people in books are like 'real' people who are, in turn, like people in books, is suggested by the words 'person' and 'character' themselves. We have been using these words more or less interchangeably, though with an implicit and conventional emphasis on the 'reality' of a person and the 'fictionality' of a character. But the words are worth examining in more detail. According to *Chambers Dictionary*, 'person' signifies both 'a living soul or self-conscious being' and 'a character represented, as on the stage'. Indeed, 'person' goes back to the Latin word *persona*, the mask worn by an actor in a play on the classical stage. The English language uses the word 'persona' to signify a kind of mask or disguise, a pretended or assumed character. The word 'person', then, is bound up with questions of fictionality, disguise, representation and mask. To know a person, or to know who a person is, involves understanding a mask. In this respect, the notion of person is inseparable from the literary. This is not to say that 'real' people are actually fictional. Rather it is to suggest that there is a complex, destabilizing and perhaps finally undecidable interweaving of the 'real' and the 'fictional': our lives, our *real* lives, are governed and directed by the stories we read, write and tell ourselves.

There is a similar enigma about the word 'character': just as the word 'person' has a double and paradoxical signification, so 'character' means both a letter or sign, a mark of writing, and the 'essential' qualities of a 'person'. Again, the etymology of the word is suggestive: from the Greek word *kharattein*, to engrave, the word becomes a mark or sign, a person's title and hence a distinguishing mark – that which distinguishes one person from another – and from this a 'fictional' person or a person on stage. Pip's characterological reading of his parents' tombstones, then, is perhaps not so far off the mark. And in *Hamlet*, when Polonius tells his son Laertes that he should remember his 'precepts' or advice, he plays on this double sense, using 'character' as a verb:

'And these few precepts in thy memory / Look thou character' (I.iii.58–9). In this way, Shakespeare's play suggests how intimately 'character' is bound up with inscription, with signs, with writing.

We have argued that the realist novel tends to rely on a particular conception of what a person is – that a person is a complex but unified whole. We might develop this further by suggesting that the realist model of character involves a fundamental dualism of inside (mind, soul or self) and outside (body, face and other external features). The 'inside' that we associate with being human has many different forms. In the nineteenth century this was often described in terms of 'spiritual life' or 'soul'. More recently, it has just as often (and perhaps more helpfully) been understood in terms of the unconscious. The following extracts from the first paragraph of George Eliot's novel *Middlemarch* will allow us to explore this in more detail:

Miss Brooke had that kind of beauty which seems to be thrown into relief by poor dress. Her hand and wrist were so finely formed that she could wear sleeves not less bare of style than those in which the Blessed Virgin appeared to Italian painters; and her profile as well as her stature and bearing seemed to gain the more dignity from her plain garments, which by the side of provincial fashion gave her the impressiveness of a fine quotation from the Bible,—or from one of our elder poets,—in a paragraph from today's newspaper. She was usually spoken of as being remarkably clever, but with the addition that her sister Celia had more common-sense. Nevertheless, Celia wore scarcely more trimmings; and it was only to close observers that her dress differed from her sister's, and had a shade of coquetry in its arrangements; for Miss Brooke's plain dressing was due to mixed conditions, in most of which her sister shared. The pride of being ladies had something to do with it: the Brooke connections, though not exactly aristocratic, were unquestionably 'good' [. . .] Young women of such birth, living in a quiet country-house, and attending a village church hardly larger than a parlour, naturally regarded frippery as the ambition of a huckster's daughter. Then there was well-bred economy, which in those days made show in dress the first item to be deducted from, when any margin was required for expenses more distinctive of rank. Such reasons would have been enough to account for plain dress, quite apart from religious feeling; but in Miss Brooke's case, religion alone would have determined it [. . .] and to her the destinies of mankind, seen by the light of Christianity, made the solicitudes of feminine fashion appear an occupation for Bedlam. She could not reconcile the anxieties of a spiritual life involving eternal consequences, with a keen interest in guimp and artificial protrusions of drapery. [. . .] (29–30)

This extraordinary opening paragraph, with its ironic insistence on the importance of clothes despite Dorothea Brooke's spiritual aspirations, clearly acknowledges that physical appearance (outside) works as a sign of character (inside). What is indicated here is an opposition that is fundamental in realist texts: that there is an inside and an outside to a person, that these are separate, but that one may be understood to have a crucial influence on the other. The opening to *Middlemarch* concentrates almost obsessively on Dorothea's clothes because it is her clothes that allow us insight into her character. As this suggests, another convention of characterological realism is that character is hidden or obscure, that in order to know another person – let alone ourselves – we must decipher the outer appearance. Eliot constantly manipulates and plays with the mechanisms of such realism, above all with that form of telepathy or mind-reading whereby a narrator can describe a character from the outside but can also know (and keep secrets about) that character's inner thoughts and feelings, conscious or unconscious. At the same time, by evoking Dorothea's appearance in terms of how 'the Blessed Virgin appeared to Italian painters' and by comparing her 'plain garments' to 'the impressiveness of a fine quotation', Eliot subtly foregrounds a sense of the painterly and the textual. We are drawn and caught up in intriguing uncertainties about where representation (a picture or text) begins or ends.

From Dorothea's clothes, then, Eliot weaves a fine and intricate web of character – in terms of the familial, social and political, and in terms of the moral and religious. Indeed, one of the most striking sentences of the excerpt focuses ironically on this concern with clothes: 'She could not reconcile the anxieties of a spiritual life involving eternal consequences, with a keen interest in guimp and artificial protrusions of drapery.' The passage as a whole makes it clear, however, that Dorothea's puritan plainness is simply the reverse side of a 'keen interest in guimp'. Her preference for 'plain dressing' is itself a complex and considered statement of fashion. It is at this point, in particular, that Eliot's ironic presentation of Dorothea involves a subtle questioning of the conventional opposition between a 'spiritual life' on the one hand and the 'artificial protrusions of drapery' on the other. The passage suggests that this opposition is itself artificial, that whatever people 'really' are cannot be separated from how they appear. It suggests that people are constituted by an interplay of inner and outer, but that it is not a question of one being the truth and the other mere surface. So while realist conventions of character may rely on the opposition between inner and outer, mind or spirit and body, and so on, Eliot's description of Dorothea also shows how this opposition can be questioned from within the realist tradition itself.

This brings us to one of the central questions raised by many novels: How can we know a person? As we have seen, realist novels such as George Eliot's attempt to answer this question by presenting people as knowable by a number of 'outward' signs of 'inner' worth. Appearances, however, can be deceptive. Indeed, many novels and plays are concerned with the problem of deception or disguise, with discriminating between an appearance that is a true sign of inner value and one that is not. The realist tradition often relies on the possibility of such deception, while also presupposing the possibility of finally discovering the worth or value of a person by reading the outward signs. The exposure, despite appearances, of Bulstrode's hypocrisy, for example, and the final validation of Lydgate's good character are central to the plot of *Middlemarch*. But the fact that a 'person' is itself, in some sense, a 'mask', means that even if we think we 'know' the soul or self of a person, his or her true identity, there is always a possibility, even if that person is ourself, that such an identity is itself a form of mask. This irreducible uncertainty may partly account for realism's obsessive concern with the question: 'Who am I?'

The stories of Raymond Carver (1938–88), like many so-called postmodern texts, relentlessly play with such conventions of characterological construction and perception. In 'Cathedral' (1983), for example, the somewhat obtuse, belligerent, intolerant, discriminatory narrator finds it both comic and unnerving to think about how a blind man, a friend of his wife who has been invited to pass the evening in their home, looks – even while (or because) he cannot look. The narrator is struck by the fact that the blind man does not wear dark glasses. This disturbs him, since although at first sight the blind man's eyes 'looked like anyone else's eyes', on closer inspection (and the narrator takes the opportunity for a lengthy session of unreciprocable inspection) they seem 'Creepy': 'As I stared at his face, I saw the left pupil turn in toward his nose while the other made an effort to keep in one place. But it was only an effort, for that eye was on the roam without his knowing it or wanting it to be' (297). The story culminates in a dope-smoking session in which the blind man teaches the narrator the advantages of drawing with closed eyes, of the necessary visual imagination of the blind. On one level, the story performs a conventional reversal of the blind and the seeing, figuring the blind man as the seer. But on another level, Carver explores conventions of characterological construction by querying the equation of the look of someone with their identity (the eyes, conventionally the most telling indicator of character are, for our view of the blind man, just 'creepy' signifiers of mechanical dysfunction, disconnected from intention, emotion, will), and by prompting an awareness that in this story it is the one who is *not* seen – either by us as readers or by the blind man – who most fully exposes himself, exposes his 'character', in all its belligerence, intolerance and obtuseness.

As we have seen, it is difficult in an absolute sense to separate real from fictional characters. To read about a character is to imagine and create a character in reading: it is to create a person. And as we have tried to show, reading characters involves learning to acknowledge that a person can never finally be singular – that there is always multiplicity, ambiguity, otherness and unconsciousness. Our final point concerns what it means to 'identify' with characters in fiction. It seems difficult, if not impossible, to enjoy a novel or play without, at some level, identifying with the characters in it. In fact, the most obvious definition of the 'hero' or 'heroine' of a novel or play would be the person with whom we 'identify', with whom we sympathize or empathize, or whose position or role we imaginatively inhabit. The anti-hero, by contrast, is the character with whom we might identify, but only in wilful resistance to prevailing codes of morality and behaviour. 'Identification' in any case is never as simple as we might think. To identify with a person in a novel or play is to identify *oneself*, to produce an identity for oneself. It is to give oneself a world of fictional people, to start to let one's identity merge with that of a fiction. It is, finally, also to create a character for oneself, to create oneself as a character.

Further reading

Two very good and reasonably accessible accounts of character are Harold Bloom's 'The Analysis of Character' (1990) and Hélène Cixous's 'The Character of "Character" ' (1974). A classic if somewhat reductive account of character may be found in Chapters 3 and 4 of Forster's *Aspects of the Novel* (1976), first published in 1927. For a lucid discussion of character in the nineteenth- and early twentieth-century novel, see Martin Price, *Forms of Life* (1983). A very different kind of approach is exemplified in Thomas Docherty's *Reading (Absent) Character* (1983), which focuses in particular on the *nouveau roman* and postmodern writing generally, in order to move beyond a 'mimetic' theory of character to one in which characterization is seen as 'a process of reading and writing'. For an excellent, if difficult, argument for the deconstruction of character which challenges the humanist perspective of a unified self and argues for 'an esthetic and ethic of the fragmented self ', see Leo Bersani's important book *A Future for Astyanax: Character and Desire in Literature* (1978). J. Hillis Miller's chapter on 'Character' in *Ariadne's Thread* (1992) brilliantly weaves literary with critical, theoretical and philosophical reflections on character. On the question of identification in psychoanalysis and literature, see Diana Fuss, *Identification Papers* (1995).

9. Voice

Nothing is stranger, or more familiar, than the idea of a voice. In George Eliot's *Daniel Deronda* (1876), a character called Mrs Meyrick observes that 'A mother hears something like a lisp in her children's talk to the very last' (423). In Shakespeare's *King Lear* (1605), the blinded Gloucester recognizes Lear from his voice: 'The trick of that voice I do well remember; / Is't not the King?' (IV, vi, 106–7). In both of these examples we have what appear to be confirmations of the persistence of identity, expressed in the singular or peculiar nature (the 'trick') of a person's voice. But in each of these exchanges we are also presented with a kind of strangeness as well: in the context of Eliot's novel, for example, we may reflect on the irony of the fact that what the mother recognizes in her children, what it is in their voice that confirms the persistence of their identity, is something that cannot be heard, a lisp perceived only by the mother. Moreover there is something strange in the idea that an adult's speech should be, in a dream-like or hallucinatory fashion, haunted by the past in this way. In the example from Shakespeare, on the other hand, it is difficult for us not to be aware of the terrible precariousness of recognition and, by implication, of identity: Gloucester may believe that he recognizes, and may indeed recognize, the trick of the king's voice, but we are all too aware of the fact that he can never again *see* the king, never confirm the king's identity by sight. And ironically, Gloucester is only reunited with Lear thanks to help from his son Edgar, whose voice (disguised as Tom o' Bedlam) Gloucester *fails* to recognize.

The examples from Eliot and Shakespeare appear, at least initially, to be about the familiarity and individuality of voice. But like literary texts more generally, they are also concerned with the ways in which a voice may be strange and disturbing. We may enjoy a novel like Raymond Chandler's *The*

Little Sister (1949) partly on account of the distinctive, gritty, cinematographic voice-over of Marlowe the narrator, but one of the things that makes this novel haunting and powerful, as well as comical, is its sensitivity to the strangeness of voices. Thus for example we have Miss Mavis Weld, apparently concerned about her brother: 'She clutched her bag to her bosom with tight little fingers. "You mean something has happened to him?" Her voice faded off into a sort of sad whisper, like a mortician asking for a down payment' (39). Or we have Marlowe recounting a phone call: 'The phone rang before I had quite started to worry about Mr Lester B. Clausen. I reached for it absently. The voice I heard was an abrupt voice, but thick and clogged, as if it was being strained through a curtain or somebody's long white beard' (41).

The power of a voice is made dramatically clear by the British Government's censorship of the Sinn Fein leader, Gerry Adams: for a number of years (until September 1994) his voice was, in effect, illegal. His words, when broadcast, had to be spoken by an actor. Few voices could be said to have haunted the British media at that time as forcefully as Gerry Adams's. But a concern with what is powerful, haunting and strange about voices is hardly a recent phenomenon. One need only think of the importance of oracles, and the intimate links between voice and prophecy in the Bible and other classical texts. Consider, for instance, the voice that announces in I Corinthians 13: 'Though I speak with the tongues of men and of angels, and have not charity, I am become as sounding brass, or a tinkling cymbal. / And though I have the gift of prophecy, and understand all mysteries, and all knowledge; and though I have all faith, so that I could remove mountains, and have not charity, I am nothing' (1–2). Or think of the apocalyptic voices at the end of the Bible, in the Book of Revelation – for example of the angel who comes down from heaven, whose 'face was as it were the sun, and his feet as pillars of fire' and who

> cried with a loud voice, as when a lion roareth: and when he had cried, seven thunders uttered their voices.
>
> And when the seven thunders had uttered their voices, I was about to write: and I heard a voice from heaven saying unto me, Seal up those things which the seven thunders uttered, and write them not.

In both of these biblical quotations voice is described in terms that identify it with the non-human – with musical instruments (sounding brass or tinkling cymbal), with the sound of a lion or with the sound of thunder. It is also presented in terms of multiplicity (speaking in tongues, the voices of the seven thunders) and what we might call the uncanny (the voice that has the gift of prophecy and is apparently omniscient; the voice that is forbidden, that must be sealed up). All of these characteristics are important for thinking about literary texts more generally. Literature, in fact, might be defined as being the space in which, more than anywhere else, the power, beauty and strangeness of the voice is both evoked or bodied forth *and* described, talked about, analyzed. In this respect, reading literary texts involves attending to extraordinary voices.

One of the most obvious extremes of voice in literature is in relation to music – in other words, the idea that voice becomes pure sound, turns into music. Here we may recall Walter Pater's suggestion that all art constantly aspires towards the condition of music: this is as much true of the 'smoky kind of voice' (202) whose singing transfixes and transforms the life of the narrator in Jean Rhys's story 'Let Them Call It Jazz' (1962) as it is of the glozing, serpentine voice that seduces Eve in Milton's *Paradise Lost* (Book IX, 532ff.), or of the song of the skylark or of the nightingale to which Shelley and Keats respectively aspire in their great song-like odes. At the same time, however, we are all perfectly aware that literary texts are *not* (simply) music or song. Part of what makes texts literary is indeed their peculiar, paradoxical relation to music (not least in lyric poems and ballads, originally performed with or as music). That is to say, poems or short stories or other texts may aspire towards the condition of music, but they are necessarily stuck in their so-called linguistic predicament. Thus Coleridge's 'Kubla Khan' (1798) is concerned with the demonic power of music played by 'A damsel with a dulcimer' and with the paradoxical desire to 'build' the very things that the poem has described (a pleasure-dome and caves of ice) 'with music':

> A damsel with a dulcimer
> In a vision once I saw:
> It was an Abyssinian maid,
> And on her dulcimer she played,
> Singing of Mount Abora.
> Could I revive within me
> Her symphony and song,
> 　To such a deep delight 'twould win me,
> That with music loud and long,
> I would build that dome in air,
> That sunny dome! those caves of ice!

In Shelley's ode 'To a Sky-Lark' (1820), on the other hand, the speaker ends by implying that he is unteachable:

> Teach me half the gladness
> That thy brain must know,
> Such harmonious madness
> From my lips would flow
> The world should listen then—as I am listening now.

Shelley's ode thus aspires to the 'harmonious madness' it can never voice. Similarly, Keats's Ode of 1819 can acknowledge the 'ecstasy' of the night-ingale's 'voice', but the speaker also recognizes that he can never triumph in the desire to 'dissolve' his identity with that voice. Being stuck in this respect is no doubt a fundamental *condition* of literature. Not surprisingly then, literary texts call to be thought about not only in terms of how they *body forth* voices but also in terms of how they reflect, comment on and analyze what 'voice' *means*. As Eve's temptation by the snaky sibilants of Satan suggests, in Milton's *Paradise Lost*, a voice can be astonishingly seductive. Interestingly, a voice can become *more* seductive by referring to the fact that it is being seductive. (The contemporary commercial success of phone-sex may also testify to this.) Voice seduces: as the etymology of seduction may suggest (*se-*, aside, *ducere*, to lead), it leads us aside or draws us away.

What does it mean to talk about voice in relation to literary texts? Take the opening of a short story by Raymond Carver, entitled 'Fat' (1963). It begins:

> I am sitting over coffee and cigarettes at my friend Rita's and I am telling her about it.
> Here is what I tell her.
> It is late of a slow Wednesday when Herb seats the fat man at my station.
> This fat man is the fattest person I have ever seen, though he is neat-appearing and well dressed enough. Everything about him is big. But it is the fingers I remember best. When I stop at the table near his to see to the old couple, I first notice the fingers. They look three times the size of a normal person's fingers – long, thick, creamy fingers. (64)

This is, in some ways at least, a descriptively straightforward opening. But once we reflect on it, we find that it is doing many different and quite sophist-icated things. The first point to observe is that this is a first person narration with a strong sense of a speaking voice: we are drawn away by what we might call the 'reality effect' of a speaking voice that is produced in part through the conversational language – the lexical items and syntax, the topic, use of the present tense, repetition – and in part through the explicit reference to the fact that the narrator is speaking and 'telling' us something. The opening sentences, in a quite subtle way, put the reader in the position of the narrator's friend Rita

('I am telling her . . . Here is what I tell . . .'). Despite the seductively 'realistic' or 'everyday' quality of voice here, something fairly complex is going on: we are presented with a narrator who, even in the apparently straightforward language of the opening two sentences, makes it clear that this is a self-referential or metafictional story, a story that is at least at some level a story *about* story-telling. The seductiveness of an apparently casual speaking voice tends to distract attention from this dimension of the text. Moreover, without really drawing attention to the fact, we have up till now been referring to the 'I' of the story as the narrator. In other words, we have been making an implicit distinction between narrator and author. This is a first-person narration and the narrator, we quickly learn, is a waitress. What we are being presented with, in other words, is the 'voice' of a girl or young woman. At the same time, however, there is a sort of double-voicing here to the extent that we may recognize this text as being characteristic of Raymond Carver's work. In this respect, we could say, there is also the phantasmatic voice of Carver lurking in these lines. We hear the 'voice' of Carver in a figurative, ghostly sense (like a signature tune).

Rather differently, there is Thomas Hardy's poem, 'The Voice':

> Woman much missed, how you call to me, call to me,
> Saying that now you are not as you were
> When you had changed from the one who was all to me,
> But as at first, when our day was fair.
>
> Can it be you that I hear? Let me view you, then,
> Standing as when I drew near to the town
> Where you would wait for me: yes, as I knew you then,
> Even to the original air-blue gown!
>
> Or is it only the breeze, in its listlessness
> Travelling across the wet mead to me here,
> You being ever dissolved to wan wistlessness,
> Heard no more again far or near?
>
> > Thus I; faltering forward,
> > Leaves around me failing,
> > Wind oozing thin through the thorn from norward,
> > And the woman calling.

Written in December 1912, 'The Voice' belongs to the series of so-called '1912–13 poems' that Hardy wrote following his first wife's death earlier that year. It is difficult, in other words, not to read this poem as autobiographical

– to understand it as a poem about the poet's experience of mourning follow-ing his wife's death. But the poem is more than simply autobiographical: it is about the radical uncertainty of human identity and experience, their falter-ing. 'The Voice' not only describes the uncanny experience of hearing a dead person's voice but in some sense transfers the call to us in turn. The poem functions as a kind of strange textual switchboard. Again, we can respond to the poem in quite straightforward terms – it is a poem about someone who is out walking in an autumn or early winter landscape and who thinks he hears the voice of a woman whom he once loved (who was 'all' to him) but who is no longer above ground ('heard no more again far or near'). As its title suggests then, it is about 'the voice' he hears. But it is also a poem about voice more gen-erally, and about the relationship between poetry and hearing a woman's call. (This may in turn recall the notion of inspiration in classical Greek and Roman times, in other words hearing the voice, music or song of a female Muse or Muses.) This is evident, for example, in the opening line: 'Woman much missed, how you call to me, call to me'. What we are presented with here is an affirmation of the spooky actuality of hearing a dead woman's voice – an affirmation which the poem proceeds to question ('Can it be you that I hear?'), but which it concludes by reaffirming ('Thus I; faltering forward . . . And the woman calling'). This opening line, however, is at the same time grammatic-ally ambiguous: 'how' suggests a questioning as well as an exclamation. 'Call to me, call to me', on the other hand, can be read as an echo (as *two* voices, even if the second is a double of the first) or as changing from an exclamation – 'how you call to me' – to a demand: 'call to me'.

The ending of the poem suggests either that the speaker is off his head, hearing voices, or that the dead really do come back and it is indeed possible to hear voices from beyond the grave. But it also suggests something about literary texts in general. Every one of the writers who has been discussed in this chapter is dead. But as we indicate in our discussion of 'the death of the author' (in Chapter 3), every literary text can be thought of as involving a voice from beyond the grave, since every text is at least potentially capable of outliv-ing the person who originally gives voice to it. The woman in Hardy's poem is in this respect a figure of the poet *par excellence*. Do we hear Hardy's voice in 'The Voice' or not? Or – to reflect on the poem in a quite different way altogether, that is to say in the light of what Harold Bloom calls 'the anxiety of influence' – do we perhaps hear Keats's voice in this poem? Bloom's celebrated theory (Bloom 1973) is that what impels poets to write is not so much the desire to reflect on the world as the desire to respond to and to chal-lenge the voices of the dead. For Bloom, any 'strong' poem will always involve an encounter between the 'living' poet – in this case Hardy – and the dead – in this case perhaps most obviously Keats, whose 'Ode to a Nightingale' is also explicitly concerned with the 'dissolving' qualities of voice and identity. From a Bloomian perspective, Hardy's reference to 'You being ever dissolved to wan wistlessness' might be read not so much as an address to the poet's dead wife (strange enough as that gesture may itself seem) but rather as an eerie and ambivalent 'replay' of Keats's lines:

> That I might drink, and leave the world unseen,
>   And with thee fade away into the forest dim:
> Fade far away, dissolve, and quite forget
>   What thou amongst the leaves hast never known . . .

Keats's voice might, in this sense, be said to haunt 'The Voice' as much as it does other Hardy poems, such as 'The Darkling Thrush' (1900) – the very title of which explicitly refers us to Keats's ode ('Darkling I listen . . .'). In poems such as 'The Voice' and 'The Darkling Thrush', in other words, we can recognize the 'trick' of Hardy's voice in terms of an idiomatic tone (lugubrious, plaintive, ironic etc.) and idiomatic rhymes and neologisms ('listlessness', 'wistlessness'). But this is 'voice' in a figurative, ghostly sense. Moreover, it is 'voice' as plural – haunted by, for example, the voice or voices of other poets such as Keats.

The examples of Carver and Hardy are helpful because they highlight a number of important ideas for thinking about voice in relation to literature. First they suggest that the question of voice is never simple, even (or perhaps especially) when it appears to be. Second, and more specifically, they suggest that literary texts not only *present* voices but also have things to say *about* what voices are and how we might or might not hear them. Third, there is invariably more than one voice in a literary text, even if it is a matter of a voice ostensibly just talking or responding to itself.

This final point can be thought about further in at least two ways. On the one hand – and this has been an important feature of recent literary theoretical concerns – there is the importance of seeing literature as a space in which one encounters multiple voices. Literary texts call upon us to think about them in terms of many voices – for instance, in terms of what M.M. Bakhtin calls *heteroglossia* or of what he, Julia Kristeva, Roland Barthes and others refer to as *polyphony*. Literature is, as Salman Rushdie has observed, 'the one place in any society where, within the secrecy of our own heads, we can hear *voices talking about everything in every possible way*' (Rushdie 1990, 16). Saleem, the narrator of Rushdie's novel *Midnight's Children* (1981), is an excellent example: he is telepathic, like every so-called omniscient narrator in a work of fiction, and he is continually hearing multiple voices. As he remarks: 'I was a radio receiver, and could turn the volume down or up; I could select individual voices; I could even, by an effort of will, switch off my newly-discovered inner ear' (164).

On the other hand – and this has been a related and similarly important feature of recent critical and theoretical concerns – literature encourages us to think about the idea that there may in fact be no such thing as *a* voice, a single, unified voice (whether that of an author, a narrator, a reader or anyone else). Rather, there is difference and multiplicity *within* every voice. There is, then, not only the kind of socio-literary polyphony that Bakhtin describes, and which he illustrates for example by looking at the way Dickens orchestrates, inhabits and detaches himself from the role of various speakers in his novel *Little Dorrit* (Bakhtin 1992, 203–5). But in addition to this, and more fundamentally, any one voice is in fact made up of multiple voices. There is difference and polyphony *within* every voice. We have tried to suggest this by looking at some of the ways in which the voice of an author or poet is always phantasmagoric or ghostly and itself in turn always haunted. We might conclude, however, with a thought proffered in one of the 'Adagia' (or 'aphorisms') of the poet Wallace Stevens: 'When the mind is like a hall in which thought is like a voice speaking, the voice is always that of someone else' (168).

Further reading

For two traditional but in some respects still stimulating accounts of voice and literature, see Yvor Winters, 'The Audible Reading of Poetry' (1957), and Francis Berry, *Poetry and the Physical Voice* (1962). A more recent and theoretically informed account is provided by Furniss and Bath (1996), in their chapter on 'Hearing Voices in Poetic Texts'. Roland Barthes has very engaging, thought-provoking things to say about voice, for example in *S/Z* (Barthes 1990b). On heteroglossia, see M.M. Bakhtin, *The Dialogic Imagination* (1981). For Kristeva and polyphony, see for example the essay 'Word, Dialogue and Novel' (Kristeva 1986). For a challenging but brilliant account of the strangeness of the narrator's 'I' in a literary text, see Maurice Blanchot's 'The Narrative Voice' (Blanchot 1981). On voice in relation to print and reading, see Griffiths, *The Printed Voice of Victorian Poetry* (1989). On poetry, voice and hearing, see Geoffrey Hartman's eclectic and stimulating essay, 'Words and Wounds' (Hartman 1981), and, for a more technical, difficult but fascinating study, see Garrett Stewart's *Reading Voices* (1990). Steven Connor's remarkable study *Dumbstruck – A Cultural History of Ventriloquism* (2000) offers a wide-ranging account of voice especially in relation to spiritualism and teletechnology. The philosopher David Appelbaum's *Voice* (1990) is a brilliant and idiosyncratic study of such dimensions of 'voice' as the cough, laugh, breath and babble. Oliver Sacks's *Seeing Voices* (1991) is a thought-provoking exploration specifically in the context of deafness, while Wesling and Slawek's *Literary Voice* (1995) draws on philosophy, linguistics and other disciplines to defend literary voice against 'modern philosophy's critique of the spoken'. Finally, from a specifically psychoanalytic perspective, see Mladen Dolar's essay 'The Object Voice' (1996).

10. Figures and tropes

It's not for nothing that they call Elvis Presley 'The King' and Eric Clapton 'God'. But the force of these acts of renaming depends on the assumption that no one takes them literally. No one supposes that the United States has become a monarchy and put Elvis Presley on the throne. No one, not even the most loyal of fans, believes that Eric Clapton created the world in six days and rested on the seventh. They may believe that his guitar-playing is transplendent, but even those whose judgement is blurred by an unholy mixture of illegal substances and Clapton's heavenly guitar solos are unlikely to take him for the Almighty Himself. These renamings of Presley and Clapton, then, involve the kind of exaggeration or verbal extravagance known as hyperbole. By the same token, few are likely to take as gospel Pink's theologically unorthodox statement in her recent hit single that 'If God is a DJ / Life is a dance floor / Love is the rhythm / You are the music'. To refer to Elvis as 'The King' or Clapton as 'God', or to think in turn of God as a DJ, is to use figurative language.

Literary language is sometimes defined in terms of its deviations from or distortions of ordinary language. Like many generalizations, this idea is both useful and misleading. It suggests that literary texts are characterized by the use of figures of speech or tropes. And it defines figures and tropes in opposition to or as deviations from 'ordinary' or 'literal' language. Thus *Chambers Dictionary* defines a rhetorical figure as 'a deviation from the ordinary mode of expression', and trope as 'a figure of speech, properly one in which a word or expression is used in other than its literal sense'. Such figures include, for example, hyperbole, metaphor, metonymy and anthropomorphism. Metaphor is the general term for the figure of resemblance, whereby one thing is likened to another. Metonymy is a general term for the figure of association or contiguity, whereby one thing is talked about by referring to something associated with it. Anthropomorphism is the general term used to refer to the non-human as if it were human. So-called 'ordinary' language, by contrast, is thought to use far more literal language, language that calls a spade a spade.

As the examples of Presley, Clapton and Pink suggest, however, the figurative is by no means restricted to literary texts: rather, it saturates all language. Friedrich Nietzsche famously argued that even truth itself is figurative. In his essay 'On Truth and Lie in an Extra-Moral Sense', Nietzsche asks 'What, then, is truth?' and offers the following answer:

> A mobile army of metaphors, metonyms, and anthropomorphisms – in short, a sum of human relations, which have been enhanced, transposed, and embellished poetically and rhetorically, and which after long use seem firm, canonical, and obligatory to a people: truths are illusions about which one has forgotten that this is what they are; metaphors which are worn out and without sensuous power; coins which have lost their pictures and now matter only as metal, no longer as coins. (Nietzsche 1980, 46–7)

When we think that we speak 'truthfully', without the distortions of figuration, Nietzsche suggests, we only deceive ourselves. The language of truth, language supposedly purified of figures and tropes, is simply language to which we have become so habituated that we no longer recognize it as figurative. This suggests that our world is constituted figuratively, that we relate to ourselves, to other people, to the world, through figures of speech. The manipulation and exploitation of figurative language may therefore be understood to have fundamental implications for the political, social, even economic constitution of our world. The very way that we understand the world may be said to be mediated by the kinds of figures that we use to speak about it. We could think about this in terms of any everyday aspect (aspect is a visual metaphor) of life – for example, the names of newspapers, those 'organs' (a metaphor) that help to *organize* (the same organic metaphor) our world: the *Herald, Guardian, Sun, Mirror, Telegraph, Tribune* and so on. While such discourses as history, philosophy, psychology, economics and so on may, at least in principle, attempt to rid themselves of figurative language, it is precisely figuration, which is anyway unavoidable, which is at the centre of the discipline of literary studies. This unavoidability is suggested in the passage from Nietzsche, with its concluding figuration of metaphors as coins. Nietzsche explicitly relies on the figurative to demystify language and thus to formulate a definition of the truth. As Paul de Man remarks, tropes are not 'a derived, marginal, or aberrant form of language but the linguistic paradigm par excellence': figurative language 'characterizes language as such' (de Man 1979, 105).

Central to literary criticism and theory, then, are such questions as: What are the effects of rhetorical figures in literary texts? What purpose do they serve? And how do they function? One of the most common misconceptions about literary texts is that their figurative language is simply decorative, something added to the text to make it more readable, more dramatic, or more 'colourful'. It is certainly true that the perceived presence of figurative language often seems to increase at points of emotional and dramatic intensity, like the soaring violins at moments of sexual passion or dramatic tension in a Hollywood film. Thus D.H. Lawrence, for example, is known for his so-called 'purple passages'. But simply to suggest that figures are 'added' to literary language, like the musical soundtrack to a movie, does not get us very far. The soaring violin theory of rhetorical figures is misguided because, as Nietzsche suggests, language is inescapably figurative: the meaning of a text cannot be separated from its expression, its figures.

Figuration is fundamental to our world, to our lives. An alteration in the way we figure the world also involves an alteration in the way that the world works. Take Ralph Ellison's *Invisible Man* (1952), for example. This novel uses invisibility as a figure (both metaphorical and literal) for the marginality, the oppression, effacement and dehumanization of black people in the United States. Here is the opening to the prologue to Ellison's great novel:

> I am an invisible man. No, I am not a spook like those who haunted Edgar Allan Poe; nor am I one of your Hollywood-movie ectoplasms. I am a man of substance, of flesh and bone, fiber and liquids – and I might even be said to possess a mind. I am invisible, understand, simply because people refuse to see me. Like the bodiless heads you see sometimes in circus sideshows, it is as though I have been surrounded by mirrors and hard, distorting glass. When they approach me they see only my surroundings, themselves, or figments of their imagination – indeed, everything and anything except me. (3)

Visibility and invisibility figure the social, political and economic effacement and consequent oppression of blacks in the United States. The man is invisible because he cannot escape the preconceptions that others have concerning him. These preconceptions are produced by a 'perception' of his skin colour. This so-called perception is itself an effect of the kind of rhetorical figure we call synecdoche, whereby a part – here, the skin – stands for the whole – a man.

But simply to categorize someone as 'black' (or 'white') is in a sense laughably reductive and inaccurate. Likewise, to say that someone is 'coloured' is in a sense to say nothing at all, because the skin, hair, nails, eyes, teeth of each one of us is a multichromatic assemblage of different hues. The categories of black, white and coloured operate as instances of synecdoche. What people 'see' is a form of metaphor, a figment or figure of imagination – a 'phantom in other people's minds . . . a figure in a nightmare which the sleeper tries with all his strength to destroy' (3). It is in this way that Ellison's narrator is invisible, for while people think that they see – they think they see a black man – in fact they see nothing, they are blinded by metaphor. Ellison's novel suggests that such habitual blindness may be challenged and in turn transformed by acts of language. It presents a metaphor or allegory of the invisible man to counter the worn coin of representation. After all, the effacement of the black man is, in a crucial sense, constituted through acts of language. Without the vocabulary of prejudice and racism, any such effacement would be inconceivable. Racism is an effect of language. In particular, the passage from Ellison cited above suggests that racism is an effect of synecdochic substitution – skin pigment for personal identity, individual for collective or racial identity. The invisible man can be seen again, his invisibility perceived, through alternative metaphors, through rhetorical figures.

The opening of Ellison's novel, then, gives us one answer to the question of how figures and tropes function in literary and other texts: they can make us see what is otherwise invisible, concealed by prejudice, effaced by habit. They seek to change the world. To recall the term used by Viktor Shklovsky and other Russian formalist critics writing in the 1920s, figurative language has the capacity to 'defamiliarize' our world – to refigure, reform, revolutionize.

What kinds of effects can be produced through figuration and how far can a reading of such figures go? Let us consider another example, a poem by the nineteenth-century New England poet Emily Dickinson. In Dickinson's work, figures, like language considered more generally, tremble on the edge of meaning. One reason why her poetry is particularly appropriate in a discussion of figurative language is that it characteristically 'deconstructs' or defamiliarizes its own rhetorical figures: her poetry constitutes a subtle yet decisive assault on figuration itself. This poem (no. 328) was written around 1862:

> A Bird came down the Walk—
> He did not know I saw—
> He bit an Angleworm in halves
> And ate the fellow, raw,

5   And then he drank a Dew
From a convenient Grass—
And then hopped sidewise to the Wall
To let a Beetle pass—

He glanced with rapid eyes
10   That hurried all around—
They looked like frightened Beads, I thought—
He stirred his Velvet Head

Like one in danger, Cautious,
I offered him a Crumb
15   And he unrolled his feathers
And rowed him softer home—

Than Oars divide the Ocean,
Too silver for a seam—
Or Butterflies, off Banks of Noon
20   Leap, plashless as they swim.

In language at once direct and elusive, the poem describes a bird eating a worm, taking a drink and flying away. The rhetorical figure which stands out in the opening lines is personification or anthropomorphism. Both the bird ('he') and the worm (the 'fellow') of the first stanza are described as if they were human. But the anthropomorphic insistence of the first half of the poem becomes strangely convoluted as it goes on to explore the specificity of simile (a is like b) as a species of metaphor (a is b, in other words the 'like' is unstated). In line eleven we learn that the bird's eyes 'looked like frightened Beads'. But this simile is not as simple as it looks. It remains unclear whether 'looked like' means that the eyes actively *looked* (they looked, in the way that beads look, assuming that they do), or whether the bird's eyes, to the narrator, looked *like* beads. The simile is itself ambiguous. Moreover, *what* the eyes looked like – the beads – also undergoes an uncanny metamorphosis. To refer to beads as 'frightened' is to employ the rhetorical figure called animism, whereby an inanimate object is given the attributes of life. Far from clarifying the look of the bird's eyes, the simile makes it *less* concrete, less visible or imaginable, by making a comparison with something that cannot possibly be seen. It is entirely incorrect to say that the bird's eyes 'looked like' frightened beads, since *frightened* beads are not available to the gaze at all, and beads cannot look. The simile, a peculiar example of a 'transferred epithet', disturbs the sense of who or what is frightened and confounds the distinction between the figurative and the literal, image and word, the imagined and the visible.

The last two stanzas of the poem increase these uncertainties. In the penultimate stanza, rowing on an ocean is the 'vehicle' for the metaphor, the 'tenor' or 'meaning' of which is flying. But once again the figure is ambiguous: the ocean metaphor is inadequate, the line suggests, to express the softness, the silvery delicacy of the movement of the bird's flight. Where a boat would leave a wake in the water, a kind of seam, the bird leaves none in the air. But while 'Too silver for a seam' may be 'translated' as meaning something like 'too delicate for a wake or track in water', the line may also be understood to be referring to the delicacy of figurative language and its relation to the world. Critics usually distinguish simile within metaphor more generally by pointing out that phrases such as 'like' or 'as' mark simile as explicitly figurative. Through another kind of figure known as paronomasia – produced by the homophone 'seam'/'seem' – the poem reflects silently on figuration itself. Metaphors seem to be unmarked, too silver, too subtle, for a seam, or for the word 'seem' (or 'as' or 'like'), too delicate for the mark of figuration. Just as there is no seam left behind after the bird's flight – it flies as if by magic – metaphor also leaves no mark, no 'seem' and no seam. Or, to put it more paradoxically but more accurately, like the word 'plashless', a word which negates 'plash' but does so only by referring to it, metaphor both does and does not leave a mark.

The extraordinary ending to the poem involves another metaphor for the bird's flight – the flight of a butterfly – but presents this in terms of swimming. The bird is like a butterfly leaping off a bank into the water so delicately that there is no (s)plash. With the phrase 'Banks of Noon', however, Dickinson's poem disturbs the basis of metaphorical transformation itself. 'Banks of Noon' is no more comprehensible than the 'frightened Beads' encountered earlier. The metaphorical transitions are short-circuited, for while it is possible to see that a bird's flight is 'like' rowing a boat, it is unclear how a bank of noon can be 'like' anything physical – are we to believe that 'noon' can be a kind of river bank, for example? The phrase highlights the deceptiveness of figuration, its potential for linguistic effects of *trompe l'œil* and hallucination. It dramatizes the ease, the inevitability with which language slides away from referential assumptions. On the other hand, 'Banks of Noon' can be considered in terms of another kind of phenomenon – intertextuality – whereby a text is woven out of words and phrases from elsewhere. In this respect, the phrase recalls the Shakespearean 'bank and shoal of time' from Macbeth's murderous speech (*Macbeth* I.vii.6) – giving the sense of the present as a kind of isthmus within the ocean of eternity – and suggests the end or the edge of time, time strangely suspended or delayed. The ending of Dickinson's poem suggests that figurative language entails a series of displacements and substitutions which both produce and withhold the illusion of reference. In these and other ways, Dickinson's poem suggests that figures make and unmake our world, give us meaning and take it away.

In our discussion of Dickinson's poem, we have drawn attention to the self-reflexive possibilities of figuration, to the way that figures can turn reflexively back on themselves, trope themselves, so that the text remarks on its own language. To end our discussion of figures, we shall turn briefly to another text which may also be shown to register the uncanny potential of figurative language. In our chapter on narrative we referred briefly to James Joyce's great long short story 'The Dead'. The story begins with the following sentence: 'Lily, the caretaker's daughter, was literally run off her feet' (199). In fact, Lily is not *literally* run off her feet at all. Strangely, we say 'literally run off her feet' to mean *not* literally but figuratively run off her feet. The use of the word 'literal' here, like the phrase about feet, is metaphorical. In this respect, we can see that the opening sentence to the story produces a play of figuration which refers indirectly both to the subject of the story, death, and to its telling. 'Literally run off her feet' is a dead metaphor, a metaphor which has become so common that its identity as figurative has largely been lost: dead metaphors are Nietzsche's worn coins of language. We can say 'I was literally run off my feet' without recognizing that we are using a metaphor at all, that far from using the phrase literally, we are exploiting a figure of speech. The metaphorical use of the word 'literally' in this phrase is a good example of the evocative possibilities of 'catachresis', the rhetorical term for a misuse or abuse of language. 'The Dead', which is above all about death, is also about dead language, dead metaphors.

Joyce's story ends with the return of a 'figure from the dead' (251), the haunting memory of Gretta's dead boyfriend, Michael Furey. In the final pages, Gretta's husband Gabriel looks out of the window of a hotel as his wife sleeps. The last paragraph of the story is couched in intense, swooning, highly figurative prose:

> A few light taps upon the pane made him turn to the window. It had begun to snow again. He watched sleepily the flakes, silver and dark, falling obliquely against the lamplight. The time had come for him to set out on his journey westward. Yes, the newspapers were right: snow was general all over Ireland. It was falling on every part of the dark central plain, on the treeless hills, falling softly upon the Bog of Allen and, farther westward, softly falling into the dark mutinous Shannon waves. It was falling, too, upon every part of the lonely churchyard on the hill where Michael Furey lay buried. It lay thickly drifted on the crooked crosses and headstones, on the spears of the little grate, on the barren thorns. His soul swooned slowly as he heard the snow falling faintly through the universe and faintly falling, like the descent of their last end, upon all the living and the dead. (255–6)

The most remarkable, the most pressing feature of this paragraph is, perhaps, repetition. In particular, the word 'falling' occurs seven times: falling obliquely, falling, falling softly, softly falling, falling, falling faintly, faintly falling. This verbal repetition produces a mesmeric sense of descent, sleep, fading and death. What Joyce appears to be evoking here, through figurative effects of language – repetition, alliteration, assonance and sibilance, syntactic inversion or chiasmus ('falling faintly, faintly falling') – is a fading out, a falling off, of language itself. 'The Dead' is about the death of (figurative *and* literal) language.

To borrow Joyce's metaphor and reverse it, it is indeed the metaphorical death of language (rather than the death of metaphorical language) that gives the story life. And it is, more generally, the productive tensions of figurative language that give life to literary texts. In this chapter, we have tried to suggest that, like literature itself, literary criticism begins and ends with figuration. In reading we should try to figure out ways in which figures at once generate and disturb literary texts. Like Marvell's lover in his desire to stop the sun, if we cannot escape figures, still we can make them run.

Further reading

For a very engaging and informative further guide to figures and tropes, see Arthur Quinn's little book *Figures of Speech* (1993). See Paul Ricoeur's *The Rule of Metaphor* (1978) for a difficult but comprehensive work on metaphor from the perspective of a philosopher. For literary critical approaches, see Hawkes's useful book *Metaphor* (1972) and Brooke-Rose's *A Grammar of Metaphor* (1958). A classic structuralist account of figuration or 'poetic' language is Roman Jakobson's 'Closing Statement: Linguistics and Poetics' (1960). De Man's *Allegories of Reading* (1979) is a challenging and influential account of the conflicts of rhetoric and grammar produced by close readings of a number of literary and philosophical texts. For an excellent but very demanding series of rhetorical readings in a de Manian vein, see Cynthia Chase, *Decomposing Figures* (1986). Derrida's 'White Mythology' (1982) is a dense and difficult but by now classic argument against the notion that there could be any simple escape from figurative language. Richard Rand's 'Geraldine' (in Young 1981) offers a complex and very stimulating exposition of figures and tropes through a reading of Coleridge. Other useful books are Todorov, *Introduction to Poetics* (1981) and Lakoff and Johnson, *Metaphors We Live By* (1980). 'Silva Rhetoricae' is a very helpful website for figures of speech, at http://www.humanities.byu.edu/rhetoric/silva.htm.

11. Creative writing

Is this it then? Is this 'creative writing'? What is 'creative writing' anyway, and what is a chapter on creative writing doing in a book on literature, criticism and theory? What is it that writing creates? And what is the difference between 'creative writing' and 'literature'?

In what follows we would like to explore two general propositions: (1) 'creative writing' doesn't appear from nowhere. It has a history and is closely bound up with both the contemporary university and the current state of English (both as a language and as a subject of study). In particular, the recent surge in the popularity of 'creative writing' courses is intricately entwined with the history of the term 'literature' and with recent developments in literary criticism and theory. (2) Despite appearances perhaps, 'creative writing' often serves to delimit the liberating and exhilarating, but also fearful possibilities of language. In this, it shares something with the dictionary, which offers the following definition of 'creative':

> Specifically of literature and art, thus also of a writer or artist: inventive, imaginative; exhibiting imagination as well as intellect, and thus differentiated from the merely critical, 'academic', journalistic, professional, mechanical, etc., in literary or artistic production. So **creative writing**, such writing. (*OED*, sense 1b)

Let us note first of all that the *OED* has no hesitation in identifying 'creative writing' with 'literature' and 'art'. The *OED* definition is predicated on the basis of a firm distinction between 'imagination' and 'intellect'. Thus 'creative' is differentiated from other sorts of writing ('the merely critical, "academic", journalistic, professional, mechanical, etc.'). But how seriously can we take this distinction? Is there nothing 'creative' about other sorts of writing?

Definitions, as we know, are never 'merely academic': they are forms and conduits of power. We might note one further intriguing detail in this dictionary definition, namely the scare quotes around 'academic'. 'Creative writing', this might suggest, is both 'academic' and non-academic. As the deceptive simplicity of the *OED* definition is perhaps beginning to make clear, 'creative writing' has a strange relation to the academy and to the academic. In fact, creative writing appears to have been institutionalized, in more than one sense of that word, since the incorporation of 'creative writing courses' within educational institutions is inevitably a form of appropriation and control. As early as 1958 we find the *Oxford Magazine* (4 December, no.164/2, cited in *OED*) declaring that 'In America established, or at any rate committed, writers have been absorbed, permanently or temporarily, into the apparatus of creative writing workshops.' This 'apparatus', establishing itself across British universities and elsewhere, has become increasingly powerful. Few practising writers (novelists and poets in particular) today can become commercially successful without becoming a part of this apparatus, however temporarily or unwillingly. But there is also a more radical way of construing this apparatus or 'creative writing machine', namely as the means by which the dangerous and disruptive possibilities of language, and of 'writing' in particular, are (apparently) contained, reduced, locked up. What does it mean that the unpredictable powers of creativity, of creative writing, are being incorporated into and assessed by the university? What is going on in the desire or apparent need to turn creative writing into an 'apparatus', a useful tool or machine?

To begin to respond to such questions, we have first of all to reckon with the ways that the emergence of 'creative writing' is linked to the history of the concept of literature. As the *OED* definition makes clear, 'creative writing' is inseparable from the question of literature. It has been fashionable in recent years, especially in the field of cultural studies, to regard literature as one sort of discourse or cultural product among others, such as philosophical discourse, or a film, or a restaurant menu. But in this context, Bennett and Royle, we like to think, is nothing if not unfashionable. Our concern is with the idea that there is in fact something distinctive about literature and that, in short, literature is not commensurable with other sorts of discourse. One reason for this is quite simple: literature in a sense does not exist. It has no essence. It is not a case of X being a literary text, and Y being non-literary. Literariness is more spectral and elusive. Any text conventionally considered as literary (Geoffrey Chaucer's 'The Wife of Bath's Prologue and Tale', say) can be read as non-literary (for example, as an account of female sexuality in the Middle Ages); and conversely, any text conventionally considered as non-literary (a political speech, say) can be read as literary (for example, in terms of an enactment of the strange ways of language, the workings of metaphor and other rhetorical figures). As Jacques Derrida has put it: 'There is no literature without a *suspended* relation to meaning and reference' (Derrida 1992a, 48). It is not that literature does not refer – for instance, we have to construe 'wife' and 'Bath' in relation to a world of 'meaning and reference', we have to make some sort of sense of these two words. But literature has to do with a certain *suspendedness* of such referring, as well as a *dependence* on what is referred to.

To take another example: how should we read the phrase 'midnight's children', in the title of Salman Rushdie's 1981 novel? We are impelled by a desire to go beyond suspense, for example in order to be able to state categorically and definitively that the words 'midnight's children' refer to the moment on the 14th/15th of August 1947 when India became independent and to the children who happened to be born just at that time. But the peculiar literariness of the title-phrase consists, *at the same time*, in the fact that it is enigmatic, resistant to any final stable determination. One could not, after all, even hope to exhaust the readings of the title without an exhaustive reading of the text to which that title refers. Strangely suggesting that children are *of* or *belonging to* a time ('midnight' with its connotations of the witching hour, darkness and mystery, the peculiarly decisive yet uncertain, spooky border between day and night), that there could be children of time but perhaps not space and that a book could itself somehow *be* these children, Rushdie's title conjures the bizarre telepathic mass of fictional narrative opened up in its name. *Midnight's Children*, after all, is not – or not only – social or political history: it is a novel, a work of literature or (notice how odd this might sound) creative writing.

As we argue elsewhere in this book (see the chapter entitled 'Mutant'), 'literature' is a comparatively modern invention. The emergence of creative writing in the mid-twentieth century in the US, and more recent institutional expansions in the UK and elsewhere, are part and parcel of the process whereby the question 'what is literature?' or 'what is literariness?' becomes a central topic in literary texts themselves, as well as in literary criticism and theory. It is in this context that we might situate the proliferation, in the twentieth century, of poems about poetry and novels about novels. We might recall here Wallace Stevens's declaration in his great long poem *The Man with the Blue Guitar* (1938): 'Poetry is the subject of the poem, / From this the poem issues and / To this returns' (Stevens 176); or Samuel Beckett's characterization of the work of James Joyce: 'writing is not *about* something; *it is that something itself*' (Beckett 1983, 27). Significantly also, in this context, the last decades of the twentieth century witnessed the appearance of the term 'metafiction', to designate 'fiction about fiction', 'self-conscious' or 'self-reflexive fiction' (from 1960, according to the *OED*). And the term 'postmodern' is of course bound

up with this increasingly explicit attention to the nature of the literary, to
the literariness of the literary. But we should not oversimplify this. No doubt
literary works have, to greater or lesser extents, always drawn attention to
themselves, foregrounding their own strange nature: think of Shakespeare's
plays within plays, in *Hamlet* or *A Midsummer Night's Dream*, or Cervantes's
Don Quixote, or Sterne's *Tristram Shandy*, or Diderot's *Jacques le fataliste*,
or Wordsworth's *The Prelude*. Nevertheless it also seems clear that creative
writing is itself a new and different kind of foregrounding. It is as if 'Creative
Writing' were calling out: 'Look at me, come and write literature here, come
and experience the literary, it'll be fun! This way to the creative writing class!'
This particular institutionalized flagging of literature could also be regarded
as a flagging in the sense of 'becoming exhausted' – and here we might think of
Gilles Deleuze's marvellous essay on 'the exhausted' (in Deleuze 1998) as a
way of understanding contemporary literature (especially in the wake of
Samuel Beckett). In all sorts of ways, in fact, we might see literature (and therefore creative writing) as coming to an end, its very existence increasingly
threatened for example by the ubiquities of visual, digital and text cultures
(film, TV, video, DVD, texting, email, the Internet, gaming). It is not without
reason that J. Hillis Miller opens his recent book *On Literature* (2002) with
the words: 'The end of literature is at hand. Literature's time is almost up'
(Miller 2002, 1).

But we do not necessarily want to link the rise of creative writing with the
'end of literature'. (As Hillis Miller's book goes on to make clear, things are in
fact more complex than his initial apocalyptic pronouncement might suggest.)
Instead, we would like to conclude by proposing six ways in which creative
writing offers new challenges and insights in relation to thinking about literature and literary studies.

1. 'Creative writing' is not simply opposed to 'critical writing'. We might
   most readily understand this in terms of the notion of metalanguage.
   Metalanguage is language about language, a discourse that takes another
   discourse as its object. Literature might thus be viewed as the 'object-
   discourse' for which literary criticism or theory functions as a metalanguage. But the logic of metalanguage is everywhere. It was already operating
   in the title phrase of this paper: 'Creative writing', this chapter, is not in any
   simple or conventional sense an *example of* creative writing. 'Creative writing' signifies rather that this is a chapter *about* creative writing. Wherever
   we encounter talking about talking, stories about stories, poems about
   poetry, statements (like this one) that refer to themselves, we are engaged in
   effects of metalanguage. But there is something odd about metalanguage,

something that makes it a double-bind, that is to say at once necessary and impossible. A metalinguistic or metadiscursive text (for example, a work of literary criticism or theory) cannot proceed to take another text (a work of literature or creative writing) as its object without that 'object' being at the same time, in this very gesture, part of the 'meta-text'. Metalanguage is never pure, it always entails a logic of being apart from *and* immersed in its object-language. The acknowledgement that you cannot write about another text without either doing something to it or its doing something to your 'own' writing (if only by virtue of your quoting it, and therefore quoting it out of context, in a new and different context) led Roland Barthes to his celebrated declaration: '*Let the commentary be itself a text*' (Barthes 1981, 44). Is Barthes a creative writer? The difficulty of responding to this question has to do, at least in part, with the ways in which his work unsettles, plays with and over the putative borders and distinctions between creative and critical writing. His texts (like those of Maurice Blanchot, Jacques Derrida and Hélène Cixous) call for new forms, styles and inventions both in literary criticism or theory *and* in literature or creative writing. This is not to suggest, however, that creative and critical writing are really just the same thing. Such is the other side of the double-bind: metalanguage is *necessary*, as well as impossible. Critical writing does not involve 'a suspended relation to meaning and reference' in the way that literary or creative writing does.

2. One does not know, as one writes or as the writing comes, one cannot know if it is creative or not, if it will have been creative or not. Who will have been the judge of whether such and such a piece of writing is or is not 'creative'? Isn't 'creative writing' necessarily predicated on an experience of reading that is to come, like a promise? 'I promise to be creative', you might say. But unlike other kinds of promises, it may not be in your own power to determine whether or not you will be 'creative'. Following Cixous, we could say that the only 'creative writing' worthy of the name entails the experience of what is beyond us, beyond our capabilities, impossible. She declares: 'The only book that is worth writing is the one we don't have the courage or strength to write. The book that hurts us (we who are writing), that makes us tremble, redden, bleed' (Cixous 1993, 32).

3. Creative writing, if there is any, entails what Timothy Clark (in his study of the idea of inspiration) calls 'a crisis of subjectivity' (Clark 1997). He suggests we might think about this in terms of the blank page facing the would-be writer. This 'blank page' has been conceived in various ways. The seventeenth-century poet Thomas Traherne, for example, described it metaphorically, in terms of infancy: 'An empty book is like an infant's

soul, in which anything may be written. It is capable of all things, but containeth nothing' (Traherne 1991, 187). Clark, on the other hand, describes the blank page as a 'virtual space' that is 'neither in the psyche of the writer nor . . . outside it': this 'space of composition', as he calls it, 'skews distinctions of inner and outer', of 'self and other' (Clark 1997, 22, 27). Writing, creative writing, is transformative, performative in ways that cannot be calculated or foreseen. The writer does not simply precede the writing. The figure of 'the writer' is in crucial respects always 'phantasmatic', never simply 'empirical' or given (see Clark 1997, 24–6). As Blanchot puts it: 'Writing is nothing if it does not involve the writer in a movement full of risks that will change him [or her] in one way or another' (Blanchot 1995, 244). One of the things that makes creative writing, in the context of the university, so distinctive and potentially troublesome is that it entails an explicit engagement with these forms of the transformative and performative, the risky and incalculable.

4. If creative writing involves an openness to otherness, to what has traditionally been called 'inspiration' or 'the muse' or 'God', it nevertheless also involves something singular, something like a signature, something that seems unique. It is something 'akin to style', as Raymond Carver remarks in his brief but powerful essay 'On Writing', 'but it isn't style alone. It is the writer's particular and unmistakable signature on everything he [or she] writes. It is his [or her] world and no other . . . [The writer] has some special way of looking at things and . . . gives expression to that way of looking' (Carver 1986, 22). It is thus possible to read a phrase or sentence or two by, say, William Blake (the Argument to 'The Marriage of Heaven and Hell') or Emily Dickinson (Poem 214) or Franz Kafka (Aphorism 43 in *The Collected Aphorisms*), and recognize in this the sort of style or signature to which Carver is referring:

> Rintrah roars and shakes his fires in the burdened air;
> Hungry clouds swag on the deep.

> I taste a liquor never brewed—
> From Tankards scooped in Pearl—

> As yet the hounds are still playing in the courtyard, but their prey will not escape, however fast it may already be charging through the forest.

In each case it is a question of these lines, these phrases marking the distinctive 'style' of a writer. No one but Blake could talk about Rintrah roaring or hungry clouds *swagging* on the deep; no one but Dickinson could achieve quite this combination of the wondrous, the visceral and the abstract; no one but Kafka offers quite this sense of inescapable claustrophobia and doom. We might here recall what Coleridge said of first encountering two lines from Wordsworth's 'Winander Boy': 'had I met these lines running wild in the deserts of Arabia, I should have instantly screamed out "Wordsworth!"' (Coleridge 1956–71, 1:453).

In an extraordinary essay entitled 'He Stuttered', Gilles Deleuze describes this sort of signature or singularity in terms of the invention of a new kind of language, a kind of foreign language within a language. He writes:

> a great writer is always like a foreigner in the language in which he expresses himself, even if this is his native tongue. At the limit, he draws his strength from a mute and unknown minority that belongs only to him. He is a foreigner in his own language: he does not mix another language with his own language, he carves out a nonpreexistent foreign language *within* his own language. He makes the language itself scream, stutter, stammer, or murmur. (Deleuze 1998, 109–10)

This foreign language is never purely the writer's own, of course: it is always made up of words from elsewhere and might always turn out to have been the wrong language. Such is the anguish and uncertainty evoked by Roland Barthes when he writes, of himself, as if he were a character in a novel: 'Writing a certain text, he experiences a guilty emotion of jargon, as if he could not escape from a mad discourse no matter how individual he made his utterance: and what if all his life *he had chosen the wrong language!*' (Barthes 1977, 114–15).

5. Creative writing happens, if it happens, in a strange nursery. This is another way in which, as a course or subject, 'creative writing' inhabits a quite disturbing and peculiar place within the university: the university is perhaps no longer to be understood as an adult venue, or even as a place in which you mature or 'grow up'. As Sigmund Freud remarks in 'Creative Writers and Day-Dreaming' (1907): 'every child at play behaves like a creative writer' (Freud 1985f, 131). The greater the creative artist, in Freud's view, the more he (or she) remains childlike. As he declares in another essay, on Leonardo da Vinci: 'all great [artists] are bound to retain some infantile part. Even as an adult [Leonardo] continued to play, and this was another reason why he often appeared uncanny and incomprehensible to his contemporaries' (Freud 1985g, 220).

6. Creative writing, if there is any, is urgent despatch, with radically uncertain address. Paul Celan's description of a poem as 'a message in a bottle' (Celan 1986, 34; quoted in Clark 1997, 272) is apt here. A work of creative writing is a sort of letter, perhaps a letter-bomb. Elizabeth Bowen says of her first experience of reading Rider Haggard's strange novel *She*: 'After *She* . . . I was prepared to handle any book like a bomb' (Bowen 1986, 250). If you are thinking of writing a novel, it is 'Not a bad plan to think [it's] going to be a letter' (Forster 1976, 162), suggests E.M. Forster – but a letter being read, we might add, after you're dead. Creative writing: keep it compact, think of that iceberg Ernest Hemingway talked about (seven-eighths of the text should be invisible: see Hemingway 2000, 1694), hurry up, it's a matter of life and death, write now. As the Jewish proverb has it: 'Sleep faster! We need the pillows' (quoted in Bloom 1994, 448).

Further reading

The Station Hill Blanchot Reader (1999) brings together an excellent selection of Maurice Blanchot's fiction as well as of his remarkable meditations on the nature of writing, critical and creative. For two of Barthes's most influential and provocative essays on the unstable or dissolving boundaries between literature, criticism and theory, see Barthes 1977c, 1981. For two fine collections of Hélène Cixous's extraordinary essays on writing, see Cixous 1993, 1998. Gilles Deleuze's *Essays Critical and Clinical* (Deleuze 1998) contains numerous fascinating pieces, including 'Literature and Life', 'He Stuttered' and 'The Exhausted'. Timothy Clark's *The Theory of Inspiration* (Clark 1997) offers a rich and stimulating historical and theoretical account of the nature of inspiration and literary composition, especially from the eighteenth century to the present. For an important broader account of creativity, especially engaging with more scientific perspectives, see Margaret A. Boden's *The Creative Mind* (Boden 2004). On the concept and practice of metafiction, there is a good collection of essays entitled *Metafiction*, edited by Mark Currie (1995). On issues relating to literature, politics and the university, see Derrida's brilliant essay on 'The University without Condition' (Derrida 2002a). Finally, on the relationship between creative writing and psychoanalysis, see Freud's 'Creative Writers and Day-Dreaming' (Freud 1985f); on Freud himself as a writer, see Mahony 1987, Edmundson 1990 and Young 1999; and for a particularly 'wild' but fascinating exploration of the implications and effects of psychoanalysis for creativity, see Chasseguet-Smirget 1984.

12. Laughter

'We are very sorry, indeed, to learn what happened,' said a BBC spokesman on hearing about the *death of a Goodies fan while watching the show*. 'He just laughed heartily and too long,' said his wife. 'After 25 minutes of laughing he gave a tremendous belly laugh, slumped on the settee, and died. (He) loved the Goodies, and it was one of the best for a long time' . . . (*The Guardian*, 26 March 1975)

The man's death was, no doubt, a great misfortune. But, as the response of his wife might suggest, there was also something quite funny, and even appropriate about it. The word 'funny' here is oddly ambiguous: how funny it is, after all, that a word ('funny') should mean both 'amusing' and 'strange'. The peculiar appropriateness of the death of this Goodies fan consists not only in the fact that it was a particularly *good* episode of the comedy programme ('one of the best for a long time'), but also in the way in which it is suggestive of a more general and perhaps more intimate link between laughter and death. When we say that someone 'died laughing' or 'laughed themselves to death' we are, in most circumstances, speaking metaphorically. What is funny (in both senses) about the case of the Goodies fan is that it involves a literalization of this metaphor. To take a metaphor literally (which can also be called 'catachresis' or 'misapplication of a word') is an example of a rhetorical device that is often very effective as a means of generating laughter. In this respect it would seem that the man's death conforms to the conventions of comedy. But of course there is also a darker side to this, the side that involves 'funny' in the sense of 'funny peculiar'. In other words, what this newspaper report also prompts us to ask is: why do we talk about 'dying with laughter' or 'laughing oneself to death'? Why do we talk about actors 'corpsing', in other words of being unable to speak their lines because of a sudden fit of hysterical laughter? Are all these instances *simply* metaphorical? Is there something about laughter that, in a profound if ticklish way, puts it in touch with death? Let us leave these questions in suspense for a little while.

What about laughter and literature? We often think of literature as very (or, dare one say, 'deadly') serious, especially if we are studying it. In part this is because (as we suggest in greater detail in Chapter 19) literature is linked to notions of the sacred, to a sense of hushed respect. But literature is also about pleasure, play and laughter. In this chapter we shall attempt to provide an account of some of the ways in which laughter has been theorized, down the centuries, and attempt to illustrate these theories in relation to particular literary texts. Finally, we shall focus on the idea of literature as a space in which the notion of seriousness itself, and the distinctions between the 'serious' and 'non-serious', are fundamentally unsettled, thrown into question, discombobulated.

There are few things worse than the prospect of trying to talk about laughter, or trying to define what is humorous. It is something of a lost cause from the start. It automatically seems to put us – if we dare risk a slightly risible analogy at this point – in the position of the frog, in the story about the frog, the chicken and the librarian. A chicken walks into the local town library, goes up to the librarian's desk and says: 'Bok!' So the librarian gives the chicken a book. The chicken goes away, but comes back the next day, goes up to the librarian's desk and says: 'Bok, bok!' So the librarian gives the chicken two books, the chicken goes away, comes back the next day: 'Bok, bok, bok!' So the librarian provides the chicken with three more books. And the next day 'Bok, bok, bok, bok!' and so on until the fifth day, when the chicken comes in and says to the librarian, 'Bok, bok, bok, bok, bok!' The librarian hands over five books but then decides to follow the chicken, at a surreptitious distance, out of the library. The librarian follows as the chicken goes down the street, across the road and down a smaller street, then through an unbolted wooden door, down a passageway, into a garden, across the garden to a small lake, across a narrow bridge to an island in the middle, where the chicken puts the books down in front of a frog who says: 'Reddit, reddit, reddit, reddit, reddit.'

If there is laughter here it would be the result of a number of things. First, there is the ridiculous anthropomorphism: chickens do not go to libraries, librarians do not respond to chickens as if they were simply 'members of the public', frogs do not read books. Second, there is the pleasure of recognition as we realize that the 'bok, bok' of a chicken could after all be heard as a request for a book, or for two books, and that the croaking of a frog might indeed be construed as 'read it, read it'. Third, there is the sense of a so-called shaggy dog story, the feeling that the story could go on indefinitely, that the chicken could, at least in principle, order up the entire holdings of the British Library. Bok, bok, bok . . . Here laughter would be linked to suspense, and more specifically perhaps to the hysterical effect of a potentially permanent postponement of a resolution. It is this which in part at least constitutes the comic force of a play such as Beckett's *Waiting for Godot* (1953). But by the same token it would also be what haunts or menaces every tragedy: comedy in this sense could be defined as the overturning of the tragic. But there is also, by contrast, something comical about the very corniness (so to speak) of the joke, its 'cheepness' and groan-making quality. In this respect the joke relies on a certain surprise – the surprise of the punchline – *and* a certain recognition: you know that a punchline is going to come and what sort of punchline it will be, but you cannot tell exactly what it will be. There is a childlike pleasure involved in laughing at something at once surprising and familiar. Indeed, Freud argues in his brilliant (but oddly unamusing) book *Jokes and Their Relation to the Unconscious* (1905), 'everything comic is based fundamentally on degradation [or "stepping down"] to being a child' (Freud 1976, 292). Finally, this ridiculous story about the frog, the chicken and the librarian suggests something about the relations between laughter, reading and mystery. For perhaps what is also funny about the story is the implicit hyperbole whereby anyone (let alone a frog) could be expected to have read *everything*. In this respect we can never be in the position of the frog or – to put it more specifically in terms of our argument in this chapter – there is never a truly froglike position from which to provide a serious account of laughter. Any theory of laughter, we would like to suggest, is necessarily infected, undermined, displaced by the experience of laughter itself.

Let us consider a couple of the basic theories of laughter. The first is the 'superiority theory' of laughter. It is succinctly and famously formulated by the seventeenth-century English philosopher Thomas Hobbes: 'The passion of laughter is nothing else but *sudden glory* arising from some sudden *conception* of some *eminency* in ourselves, by *comparison* with the *infirmity* of others, or with our own formerly' (Hobbes 1840, 46). We laugh, according to this argument, out of a sense of superiority – the 'sudden glory' or 'conception of eminency' in relation to the stupidity or weakness of others, or of ourselves at some point in the past. Thus, for example, we may laugh at the man who slips over on the banana skin, or we may laugh at Bottom, in *A Midsummer Night's Dream*, because he is such an ass, or we may laugh with Swift at the small-mindedness of other human beings, for example in Book I of *Gulliver's Travels* (1726).

The second theory is what we could call the 'nothing theory' or the 'no theory' theory. This may be illustrated by way of the Monty Python sketch in which a woman called Miss Anne Elk (John Cleese in drag) is interviewed because she is supposed to have a new theory about the brontosaurus. Miss Elk will not disclose her theory but seems instead concerned simply to say over and over again that she *has* a theory and that the theory is hers: 'my theory that I have, that is to say, which is mine, is mine'. Chris, the interviewer (Graham Chapman), becoming exasperated, says: 'Yes, I know it's yours, what is it?' Looking rather nervously around the studio, Anne Elk replies: 'Where?' (Monty Python's Flying Circus 1989, 119) When Miss Elk does finally enunciate her theory it is truly bathetic – in fact, no theory at all:

> *Miss Elk*   Ready?
> *Presenter*   Yes.
> *Miss Elk*   My theory by A. Elk. Brackets Miss, brackets. This theory goes as follows and begins now. All brontosauruses are thin at one end, much much thicker in the middle and then thin again at the far end. That is my theory, it is mine, and belongs to me and I own it, and what it is too.
> *Presenter*   That's *it*, is it?
> *Miss Elk*   Spot on, Chris. (119)

In more sombre and philosophical terms, the 'nothing theory' or 'no theory' theory is suggested, for instance, by Immanuel Kant's proposition that '*Laughter is an affection arising from a strained expectation being suddenly reduced to nothing*' (Kant 1988, 199). Laughter is nothing more than the bursting of a bubble. When we laugh, according to this argument, we are laughing in a sort of 'absurd' vacuum: 'merely' laughing, with nothing to support us. In a fascinating essay entitled 'The Laughter of Being', Mikkel Borch-Jacobsen suggests a radicalization of this Kantian formulation. Following the work of the French writer Georges Bataille in particular, he argues that 'There is no theory of laughter, only an experience' (Borch-Jacobsen 1987, 742). Moreover, this experience is of a decidedly 'funny' sort – for it is an experience of, precisely, *nothing*. As Bataille puts it: '[when I laugh,] I am in fact nothing more than the laughter which takes hold of me' (Bataille 1973, 364, cited by Borch-Jacobsen, 744).

Let us turn from 'theory' to consider some literary examples. Laughter can be dependent on the visual – and literature is full of instances of visual comedy. But laughter, at least in literature, is perhaps more fundamentally a matter of language. One of the greatest eighteenth-century English comedies is Richard Brinsley Sheridan's play, *The School for Scandal* (first performed in 1777).

It contains numerous classic moments of visual comedy (characters in disguise, characters hiding themselves behind screens, characters being thrust hastily into closets and so on), but the comic power of Sheridan's play consists above all in its language. This starts from the very title of the play – with its satirical implication that scandalmongering is something to be taught – and from the names of its characters – a woman called Lady Sneerwell, her servant, Snake, a gentleman called Sir Benjamin Backbite and so forth. We could consider a brief exchange between Lady Sneerwell and Mr Snake on the subject of her 'superiority' over other slanderers and scandalmongers such as Mrs Clackitt:

> *Lady Sneerwell*   Why truly Mrs Clackitt has a very pretty talent – and a great deal of industry.
> *Snake*   True, madam, and has been tolerably successful in her day. To my knowledge she has been the cause of six matches being broken off and three sons disinherited, of four forced elopements, and as many close confinements, nine separate maintenances, and two divorces. Nay, I have more than once traced her causing a *tête-à-tête* in the *Town and Country Magazine*, when the parties perhaps had never seen each other's face before in the course of their lives.
> *Lady Sneerwell*   She certainly has talents, but her *manner* is gross.
> *Snake*   'Tis very true. She generally designs well, has a free tongue, and a bold invention; but her colouring is too dark and her outlines often extravagant. She wants that delicacy of hint and mellowness of sneer which distinguishes your ladyship's scandal.
> *Lady Sneerwell*   You are partial, Snake. (I, i, 10–26)

We can imagine the comic possibilities of the characters' gestures and appearance, but what is most comic is in the language itself – in the satirical observation on what it means to be 'tolerably successful', in the incongruity or absurdity of evaluating who has the more beautiful 'sneer', in the snaking sibilance of Snake's last sentence, in the playful truth of Lady Sneerwell's final remark.

The play called *The School for Scandal* is, then, fundamentally wordplay. Indeed, we could say, literature in general has to do with wordplay or – to use a more technical-sounding term – with paronomasia. This is in part what makes it potentially so subversive and disturbing. Could there really be a character called Snake? Or a woman called Lady Sneerwell? What kind of world do they belong to? Literature is a matter of linguistic as well as social scandal. It poses a constant challenge to the realms of so-called 'good sense' and represents an affront to what could be called the ideology of seriousness.

Paronomasia is indeed so originary a dimension of literary works that one is tempted to agree with the narrator of Samuel Beckett's *Murphy* (1938) and say: 'In the beginning was the pun' (41). Even Shakespeare becomes open to criticism on this front. Literary critics may not have much of a reputation for being amusing – but critical indignation at Shakespeare's soft spot for the 'quibble' (or 'pun') gives rise to what we think is one of the funniest paragraphs in the history of literary criticism. Here is Samuel Johnson's fascinating and irresistible paragraph from his Preface to Shakespeare (1765):

> A quibble is to Shakespeare what luminous vapours are to the traveller; he follows it at all adventures; it is sure to lead him out of his way and sure to engulf him in the mire. It has some malignant power over his mind, and its fascinations are irresistible. Whatever be the dignity or profundity of his disquisition, whether he be enlarging knowledge or exalting affection, whether he be amusing attention with incidents or enchaining it in suspense, let but a quibble spring up before him, and he leaves his work unfinished. A quibble is the golden apple for which he will always turn aside from his career or stoop from his elevation. A quibble, poor and barren as it is, gave him such delight that he was content to purchase it by the sacrifice of reason, propriety, and truth. A quibble was to him the fatal Cleopatra for which he lost the world and was content to lose it. (Johnson 1969, 68)

It is perhaps difficult not to find the 'dignity' and 'profundity' of Johnson's 'disquisition' amusing: he quibbles about quibbling in terms as extravagant as any in Shakespeare. In the process he also delightfully intimates what is often so compelling about such wordplay, namely its playful mixing of sex and death: the quibble is the apple of Shakespeare's I, the obscure object of desire, at once 'barren' and 'the fatal Cleopatra'.

We will now consider another, rather different kind of literary work, Geoffrey Chaucer's 'The Miller's Tale'. This is the story set in Oxford, about the superstitious old carpenter John, his beautiful young wife Alisoun, and their handsome lodger, Nicholas. Along with a rather absurd rival called Absolon, Nicholas is after the young wife. Chaucer's tale recounts, with superb comic concision, how Nicholas persuades John that the end of the world is coming, in order to distract him so that he can get into bed with the old man's wife. John ends up with a broken arm, but Nicholas finally fares worse. That same night, Alisoun has already humiliated Absolon: he craves a kiss from her and she agrees, but in the dark Absolon finds himself kissing her arse, not her mouth. When Nicholas tries to repeat this jape, and indeed embellish it with a thundering fart, he receives a burning hot poker up his bum. In order to try to describe what makes Chaucer's 'The Miller's Tale' one of the greatest comic poems ever written we could point to the visual comedy of John the Carpenter up in the rooftop cutting the cable and crashing down, convinced that the flood is coming and that he'll be safe in the 'kneeding-tubbe' that will be his mini Noah's ark. This fall might be seen as a literalization and structural equivalent of the fall of the tragic hero. In this respect comedy is not the *opposite* of tragedy but the same, viewed from a different perspective. While we identify with the tragic hero or heroine, we stand apart from or above the comic victim. Chaucer's poem, then, offers a clear example of the Hobbesian motif: we laugh because we are not stupid like John the Carpenter. The Carpenter falls. We remain where we are, superior, riding high.

But we must at the same time acknowledge that all of this is in a sense only happening *in language*, as something being narrated. And indeed the comic force of 'The Miller's Tale' is very specifically linguistic. It is not only a matter of the brutally eloquent account of John's cuckolding, or the satirical portrayal of Absolon's fashion-conscious, prancing character, or the bawdy language of pissing and 'letting flee' monumental farts. It is also, and most crucially, that the whole story seems to be structured like a joke condensed from or into the single word, 'water'. The whole text turns on the double signification of the word 'water': for Nicholas it's a screamed request for an anodyne to salve his sizzling arse, for John it signifies that the flood is upon them. The two parts of the story are explosively assembled in the wordplay or paronomasia around this single word:

> The hote culter brende so his toute,
> And for the smert he wende for to dye.
> As he were wood, for wo he gan to crye—
> 'Help! water! water! help, for Goddes herte!'
> This carpenter out of his slomber sterte,
> And herde oon cryen 'water!' as he were wood,
> And thoghte, 'Allas, now comth Nowelis flood!'
> He sit him up withouten wordes mo,
> And with his ax he smoot the corde atwo,
> And doun goth al . . .

>   (lines 709–18)

[The hot poker burnt his bum so badly he thought he was going to die of the pain. Like a lunatic he cried out in woe: 'Help! Water! Water! Help, for God's sake!' Hearing someone madly cry 'Water!' the carpenter started out of his sleep and thought 'Oh no! It's Noah's flood!' He sits up like a shot and cuts the rope with his axe, and everything gives way . . .]

The visual comedy of the fall (whether from the roof in Chaucer, or on a banana skin in *Tom and Jerry*), and the accompanying emphasis on high and low, seems to have a 'funny' counterpart in the terms of rhetorical figures and tropes. Thus what creates laughter in a text is often either hyperbole (exaggeration) or litotes (understatement). Some examples of hyperbole would be the sorts of comparative metaphor for which Raymond Chandler's work is celebrated. In *The Little Sister* (1949), for instance, we encounter the gorgeous Miss Gonzales who, Marlowe tells us, 'smelled the way the Taj Mahal looked by moonlight' (70), had a 'mouth as red as a new fire engine' (158) and who proceeds to make 'a couple of drinks in a couple of glasses you could almost have stood umbrellas in' (70). Correspondingly we are told of a man wearing 'sky-blue gaberdine slacks . . . and a two-tone leisure jacket which would have been revolting on a zebra' (84) and a police lieutenant called Maglachan who 'had a jaw like a park bench' (167). Litotes, on the other hand, is a pervasive trope in Jonathan Swift's *A Modest Proposal* (1729), a text which also illustrates the fundamental, if in many ways disturbing, power of irony as a comic dimension of literary texts. *A Modest Proposal* works by understatement and irony. It modestly (or litotically) proposes that a solution to poverty and population management in Ireland might be the killing of small children, then selling and eating them.

Outside of literature, we might say, it is possible to entertain perfectly serious ideas about laughter, about jokes, comedy and humour. Thus Freud's *Jokes and their Relation to the Unconscious* (Freud 1976) is a fascinating work, not only for the similarities it reveals between the structure of jokes and dreams (and by implication, therefore, the structure of works of literature as well), but also for the basic and in some ways disturbing truth it offers as regards the nature of most jokes. Freud argues that jokes tend to be sexist, 'dirty', violent, racist: they transgress social taboos and 'lift' repression. But literature, conversely, might be defined as the space in which the seriousness of Freud's or anyone else's claims are ironized, satirized, parodied or otherwise put into question. For literature is the discourse that is, perhaps more than any other, concerned with questioning and unsettling assumptions about what is serious and what is not serious. Such a questioning and unsettling is especially characteristic of what is widely referred to as 'the postmodern'. Postmodern works such as the stories of Kafka, the plays of Samuel Beckett or the novels of Ian McEwan present a disquieting, irresolvable mixture of the serious and non-serious, tragic and comic, macabre and laughable. This uncomfortable mixture, however, might also be seen to be at play in Shakespeare's tragedies, for example, or indeed in Chaucer's 'The Miller's Tale', which ends with a scene in which everyone is laughing but where it is no longer clear what kind of laughter it is or who is laughing at what or who. As we have suggested, the study of literature is in various ways policed by a kind of ideology of seriousness. There is a strong tendency to accept the rules, to adhere to boundaries and categories, to say: the study of literature is a serious affair. Or to say: X is a serious text or a serious moment in a text, whereas Y is not serious. No doubt in the context of the novel, 'realism' has been and in many ways continues to be the very embodiment of a certain 'seriousness'. But the postmodern prompts us to ask various questions in this respect: how seriously, for example, should we take 'realism' or 'reality effects' in literature? What does seriousness imply or assume? Who are the police and what is the nature of their authority?

Laughter can both liberate and mystify. It can be diabolical. It can be at once offensive (laughing at sexist or racist jokes, for instance) and inoffensive (it was 'only a joke'). It can be cruel, a means of exclusion or of exerting power over people ('then she just laughed in my face'). But it can also be joyous, a means of sharing and of confirming one's sense of 'social community'. As Freud observes of jokes: 'Every joke calls for a public of its own and laughing at the same jokes is evidence of far-reaching psychical conformity' (Freud 1976, 203–4). Laughter can be undecidably 'real' and 'unreal', 'genuine' and 'false'. It can be tiring, it can have you on your hands and knees. It can be uncontrollable, as if with a life of its own. In the engulfment of uncontrollable laughter we lose a sense of who or what we are. We are reduced to nothing. Every pretension to mastery or superiority collapses and dissolves. Laughter becomes the obliteration of identity. It is this obliteration – when one is truly engulfed in laughter, when one is nothing *but* this laughter – that perhaps gives laughter its strange intimacy with death.

Further reading

For two classic accounts of laughter and the comic, see Henri Bergson, *Laughter: An Essay on the Meaning of the Comic* (1921) and Sigmund Freud, *Jokes and their Relation to the Unconscious* (1976). Freud also has a short but extremely interesting essay on the nature of humour (in Freud 1985d). Bergson's essay is reprinted in Sypher, ed., *Comedy* (1956) which also reprints George Meredith's eloquent 'An Essay on Comedy' (1877). Simon Critchley's *On Humour* (2002) is an astute, lucid and entertaining little book, dealing in further detail with many of the topics discussed in the present chapter. Arthur Koestler's *The Act of Creation* (1964) contains some engaging and thoughtful material on 'the jester' and the nature of laughter. On quibbling in Shakespeare, see M.M. Mahood's *Shakespeare's Wordplay* (1957) and, especially in a sexual context, Eric Partridge's classic *Shakespeare's Bawdy* (2001, first published in 1947). For an account of Chaucer in a similar vein, see Thomas W. Ross (1972). For a wide-ranging and challenging collection of essays on puns and wordplay, see Jonathan Culler, ed., *On Puns* (1988a). For a varied collection of essays on comedy from a historical perspective, see Cordner, Holland and Kerrigan, eds, *English Comedy* (1994). Borch-Jacobsen's complex but excellent account of theories of laughter, 'The Laughter of Being', appears in a 'Laughter' special issue of *Modern Language Notes* (1987). Of particular interest in the same issue are Samuel Weber's 'Laughing in the Meanwhile' (1987) and Jean-Luc Nancy's 'Wild Laughter in the Throat of Death' (1987); see also Nancy's interrogation of his own question 'Is it possible to be in the presence of laughter?' in 'Laughter, Presence' (1993). From a feminist perspective, see Gray, *Women and Laughter* (1994).

13. The tragic

Tragedy tears us apart, it shatters our sense of ourselves and the world. The terrifying power of tragedy is suggested by Sir Philip Sidney when he speaks, in *An Apology for Poetry* (1595), of

> high and excellent Tragedy, that openeth the greatest wounds, and showeth forth the ulcers that are covered with tissue; that maketh kings fear to be tyrants, and tyrants manifest their tyrannical humours; that, with stirring the affects of admiration and commiseration, teacheth the uncertainty of this world, and upon how weak foundations gilden roofs are builded . . . (98)

Tragedy has to do with strangeness. It involves an overwhelming sense of what Sidney calls 'the uncertainty of this world'. It involves – as Aristotle suggested, more than 2,300 years ago – a paradoxical combination of emotions, at once pity and fear or (as Sidney says) 'admiration and commiseration'. Tragedy involves an encounter not only with the death of a character on stage (or in the pages of a book) but also with the idea of our own deaths. Tragedy resists simple explanations. As A.C. Bradley observed, in 1904: 'tragedy would not be tragedy if it were not a painful mystery' (38). In this chapter we propose to elucidate this sense of 'painful mystery' and to consider some examples of tragic literature, ranging from Shakespeare to the present.

When we think of tragedy in the context of literature in English, no doubt we think first of Shakespeare and especially of the 'great tragedies', *Hamlet* (1600–1), *Othello* (1604), *King Lear* (1605) and *Macbeth* (1606). With such plays in mind, and adapting Aristotle's definition in the *Poetics*, we could suggest that tragedy comprises four basic elements. The first is that there is a central character (the protagonist), someone who is 'noble' and with whom we are able to sympathize or identify. The second is that this character should suffer and (preferably) die, and that his or her downfall or death should roughly coincide with the end of the play. The third is that the downfall or death of the central character should be felt by the spectator or reader to be both inevitable and 'right' but at the same time in some sense unjustifiable and unacceptable. The fourth element can be referred to as apocalypticism. As we have already indicated, it is not just the death of the protagonist that we are presented with in a tragedy: in identifying with the protagonist who dies, we are also drawn into thinking about our own death. And because the protagonist's death is invariably shattering to other characters, tragedy always engages with a broader sense of death and destruction, a shattering of society or the world as a whole.

Without these four elements there cannot be a tragedy. From an Aristotelian perspective we might want to propose additional elements, in particular the notions of *peripeteia* ('reversal'), *anagnorisis* ('revelation' or 'coming to self-knowledge') and *hamartia* ('tragic flaw' or 'error'). *Peripeteia* is a useful term for referring to the reversals or sudden changes in fortune that a character or characters may experience – Lear's being made homeless, for instance, or Othello's being transformed by 'the green-ey'd monster' (III, iii, 166) of jealousy. Aristotle introduced the term in the context of tragedy, though it is also apposite in other contexts, including comedy (where a character may experience a reversal or sudden change for the good). *Anagnorisis* refers to the idea of a moment of revelation or recognition, especially the moment when a protagonist experiences a sudden awakening to the truth or to self-knowledge. A tragic work may contain more than one such moment: Hamlet's life, for instance, might be described as a sort of *anagnorisis* 'block', a ghostly series of apparent but ineffective *anagnorises* starting with his exclamation 'O my prophetic soul!' (I, v, 40) on discovering the murderous truth about his father's death and realizing that this is what he had imagined, deep in his 'prophetic soul'. Classically, though, a tragedy tends to be construed as having one crucial or climactic moment of *anagnorisis*. In Sophocles's *Oedipus the King*, for example, this can be very specifically located in lines 1306–08, as Oedipus finally realizes that he is himself the criminal he has been seeking:

> O god—
> all come true, all burst to light!
> O light—now let me look my last on you!
> I stand revealed at last.

Finally, *hamartia* refers to the idea of tragic characters having a particular flaw or weakness, or making an error of judgement which leads to their downfall or death. Thus, for example, each of the male protagonists of Shakespeare's 'great tragedies' could be considered in terms of a fundamental moral or psychological weakness. Hamlet's irresolution, Othello's jealousy, Lear's pride and Macbeth's ambition might then be seen as a key element in each of these works. A primary aim in this chapter, however, is to stress the ways in which the tragic entails a fundamental sense of what remains painful, mysterious or uncertain. That is to say, to focus on a character's 'tragic flaw' or 'error' tends to suggest something straightforwardly *causal*: Hamlet's irresoluteness is the cause of his tragedy and so on. This is not to say that Hamlet's irresolution or Othello's jealousy are unimportant. These 'flaws' or 'weaknesses' are crucial – they are integral to what we think and feel about Hamlet and Othello as characters and therefore to what we think and feel about their tragic fates. But what constitutes the tragic is always stranger and more painful than is suggested by the inevitably moralistic and reductive claim that, for instance, Othello should not have allowed himself to get so jealous and worked up. His jealousy has a crucial but partial and perhaps finally uncertain significance in terms of the tragic power of the play. About to murder his beloved wife, Othello begins what is one of the most anguished and intolerable soliloquies in Shakespeare's work: 'It is the cause, it is the cause, my soul;/Let me not name it to you, you chaste stars,/It is the cause' (V, ii, 1–3). 'Cause' here may mean 'crime', 'legal or other case' or 'reason'. What is conveyed in these lines is a sense of what *cannot be named*, a profound strangeness and uncertainty regarding the very sense of this repeated and equivocal word, 'cause'. Tragedy, we want to suggest, and as *Othello* pointedly demonstrates, is not only about the sense of particular causes or explanations but also, and more importantly, about a painful absence or uncertainty of cause.

Tragedy (and here we use the word to embrace both Shakespearean and more recent forms) is not only inimical to the pleasure-button-pushing mentality of Hollywood or Broadway, but also at odds with the very idea of identity and meaning. As Howard Barker puts it, in a series of aphoristic statements entitled 'Asides for a Tragic Theatre' (1986):

> In tragedy, the audience is disunited . . . Tragedy is not about reconciliation . . . Tragedy offends the sensibilities. It drags the unconscious into the public place . . . After the carnival, after the removal of the masks, you are precisely who you were before. After the tragedy, you are not certain who you are. (Barker 1989, 13)

Tragedy is offensive, it generates disunity and exposes disharmony. Like psychoanalytic theory (itself of course crucially indebted to Sophocles's *Oedipus the King*), tragedy makes the unconscious public. It leaves us uncertain about our very identities, uncertain about how we feel, about what has happened to us.

Finally, there is something apocalyptic about the tragic, not only in the sense that it consistently entails an experience of unmanageable disorder but also in that this experience of disorder is linked to a more general kind of *revelation* (the meaning of the original Greek word 'apocalypsis'). The apocalyptic revelation at the heart of the tragic has to do with a sense that no God or gods are looking down on the world to see that justice is done, or that, if there are gods, they are profoundly careless, indifferent, even sadistic. The heavens may be occupied or vacant, but the world is terrible and *makes no sense*. To illustrate this idea in relation to *King Lear*, for example, we could look to a few lines spoken by Albany – addressed to his wife Goneril and concerned with the 'vile' behaviour of herself and her sister Regan towards their father, the King:

> If that the heavens do not their visible spirits
> Send quickly down to tame these vile offenses,
> It will come,
> Humanity must perforce prey on itself
> Like monsters of the deep. (IV, ii, 46–50)

The tragic revelation of *King Lear* concerns the sense that humanity is indeed monstrous and that there are no 'visible spirits' or any other sort of spirits that might properly or profitably be called down from the heavens. One of the shortest, yet perhaps most powerful lines in Shakespeare – 'It will come' – is apocalyptic both in terms of the dark revelation of the idea that there are no gods or divine justice and in terms of the sense of an impending or accumulating cataclysm of general destruction and death. The word 'come' is crucial here – as indeed it is in the final passages of several of Shakespeare's tragedies – in part because it resonates with the apocalypticism of the end of the Bible: 'He which testifieth these things saith, Surely I come quickly. Amen. Even so, come, Lord Jesus' (Revelation 22:20). Tragedy says 'come' in a double sense: it summons us, it engages our feelings of sympathy and identification, it demands that our emotions be involved in what is happening. But at the same time tragedy says: we have to suffer, we are going to die, there is no justice and there is no afterlife. It, death and cataclysm, will come. In this way, tragedy engages with the limits of sense, verges on the senseless. Because what tragedy is about *is* senseless, meaningless – the unjust and yet unavoidable shattering of life. This would be another way of trying to highlight the mysterious and paradoxical nature of the tragic. When Ludovico says, of the bed displaying the corpses of Othello and Desdemona, 'Let it be hid' (*Othello*, V, ii, 365), Shakespeare's play paradoxically conceals or encrypts this intolerable sight that tragedy calls us to witness. Correspondingly, in *King Lear*, the death of Cordelia and Lear's madness of grief are figured in apocalyptic terms – Kent asks, 'Is this the promis'd end?' Edgar retorts, 'Or image of that horror?' (V, iii, 264–5) – but what the tragedy finally and paradoxically reveals is perhaps rather the ethical and spiritual horror of a world in which violence, torture and terror recur unendingly. What is revealed in *King Lear*, in other words, is the sense that there is no image of the end except as this unendingness.

With these rather dark thoughts in mind, let us try to say a little more about the first three elements of a tragedy. First of all, there is the idea of the central character with whom one strongly sympathizes or identifies. 'Sympathy' here entails primarily the idea of 'entering into another's feelings or mind' (*Chambers*). It carries clear connotations of the original Greek terms 'syn', *with*, and 'pathos', *suffering* – that is to say, 'sympathy' as 'suffering with'. It is important to distinguish this from 'feeling sorry for'. In tragedy, sympathy with a character is indistinguishable from a logic of identification, of identifying with that character and experiencing and suffering with her or him. The tragic has to do with a sense of *loss* of identity – the sense that (in Barker's words) 'you are not certain who you are'. We might try to clarify this a little more by remarking on the paradoxical nature of sympathy specifically in relation to drama. Sympathy involves going out of ourselves, and sharing or identifying with the position of another. Putting it slightly differently, it involves a sense of going out of ourselves but, at the same time, *putting ourselves on stage*. In this respect we have an intriguing example of *chiasmus*, which can be formulated as follows: there is no drama without sympathy, but there is no sympathy without drama. This proposition may also help us to appreciate why, in historical terms, tragedy has so consistently been associated with the dramatic. More than any other genre, tragedy explores the limits of the experience of sympathy, as it broaches self-obliteration and death. In a manner especially suited to the stage, tragedy is exposure to death – to that extreme of sympathy or identification where, putting oneself on stage, one loses a sense of oneself and *becomes* the one who dies.

It is only on the basis of this first element (sympathy) that the second (the suffering and death of a character) can be described as tragic. This seems logical enough, but the third element of a tragedy is distinctly paradoxical: the death that occurs at the end of a tragedy is experienced as being at once unavoidable and unjust. This is sometimes talked about as tragic inevitability. Every tragic work will generate a sense of the inevitable or (to use a term that is perhaps too easily loaded with religious connotations) the *fated*. The tragic invariably concerns a sense of what is *foreseeable* but *unavoidable*. But what is unavoidable (Desdemona in *Othello* must die, Tess in Hardy's novel must die, Ikem and Chris in Achebe's *Anthills of the Savannah* must die) is also unacceptable: the tragic seems to involve a peculiar contradiction whereby death is inevitable and therefore (however painfully) appropriate *but at the same time* unjust, unacceptable and therefore inappropriate. Consider, for example, the moment in the final scene of *Hamlet* when Hamlet confides to Horatio: 'If it be now, 'tis not to come; if it be not to come, it will be now; if it be not now, yet it will come – the readiness is all' (V, ii, 220–2). At this moment we, like Horatio, may not *want* Hamlet to die, but at the same time it is hard to imagine that there could be any other outcome to this dark 'coming' to 'readiness' about which Hamlet is speaking here. The paradoxical nature of this third element of the tragic is analogous to the Aristotelian notion of cartharsis. 'Catharsis' is generally understood to refer to the 'cleansing' effect of watching (or reading) a tragedy and to involve the combination of two kinds of emotion (pity and fear). The cathartic effects of watching (or reading) are linked to the peculiar fact that tragedy can give pleasure. Likewise, as we noted earlier, the combination of pity and fear seems contradictory. After all, how can one feel pity and fear at the same time? If there were a simple answer to this question we would no longer be thinking within the terms of the tragic, since the tragic comprises precisely this kind of contradictoriness of feeling. Pity (*pathos* in ancient Greek) is understood by Aristotle in terms of a movement towards the spectacle of destruction and death on stage (or page), while fear or terror (*phobos* in ancient Greek) is a movement away from it. In this way, the spectator or reader is torn apart. And it is in this sense that we can say that the tragic is not rationalizable, rather it is an *affront* to our desires for meaning and coherence.

In thinking about a particular drama or other work in terms of the tragic, then, perhaps the most obvious thing to do in the first instance is to consider the question of sympathy and/or identification. One could for example think about such questions as the following: how does a tragic text generate sympathy? Which character or characters elicit our sympathy? What is it that *happens* in the text that produces a feeling of sympathy or identification on our part? It is not only a question of character (what is he or she *like* as an individual?) and plot (what happens to him or her, the poor sod?) but also, and more fundamentally, a matter of how character and plot are created *in language*. In short, it is worth trying to think about which particular passages, which particular speeches, and even which particular phrases or words help to generate sympathy in the spectator or reader. To get a clearer sense of this it may be useful to give an example in which one might reasonably suppose that sympathy is at work, and to offer a paraphrase. Take Lady Macbeth's words of murderous guilt as overheard by the Doctor and Gentlewoman. (It is, of course, an illustration of the disturbing power of this tragedy that Shakespeare is able to make us sympathize or identify with a psychopathic murderer.) Lady Macbeth says: 'Here's the smell of the blood still. All the perfumes of Arabia will not sweeten this little hand. O, O, O!' (V, i, 50–2). Lady Macbeth does *not* say: 'Oh what a bore, this smelly blood. Not even industrial cleansing fluid will get this off my hands. Hell, what am I supposed to do?' There are numerous observations one might make regarding the extraordinary *pathos* of Lady Macbeth's language – in its Shakespearean form, that is. The first word she says, 'Here', is significant precisely because it draws us into absolute proximity with her. 'There' would have a quite different effect. The deictic 'Here' suggests how a play such as *Macbeth* establishes and maintains sympathy or identification through the presentation or indication of psychological interiority, in other words the *inside* perspective of a given character's thoughts and feelings. The 'smell of the blood' and the felt persistency of the word 'still' may be mere somnambulistic hallucination, but the spectator or reader is here being presented with intimate, indeed appalling, knowledge of Lady Macbeth's thoughts and sense-impressions. Through the strangeness of soliloquy (the theatrical device that most explicitly facilitates our access to the interior world of a character's thoughts and feelings), we feel in turn the pouring out of guilt in 'All the perfumes of Arabia . . .' and the stammering nullity of 'O, O, O!' We cannot claim to truly understand or identify with Lady Macbeth (that would be sleepwalking madness), but her language, pitifully overheard by other characters and by spectators or readers alike, generates sympathy. Sympathy, in short, is something that calls to be described and analyzed not only at the macro-level of character and plot but also, and more importantly, at the micro-level of individual words, phrases, sentences.

Finally, we could consider the question of the tragic in some of its more contemporary forms. One can think of many sorts of literary works that are tragedies of one kind or another – and often showing obvious conformities with the model we have outlined. But it is also evident that tragedy has undergone certain changes in the past century or so. There are various reasons for this. One reason has to do with the notion of 'the death of God'. Tragedy, that is to say, is bound to be different if it is considered, at the outset, from a secular perspective. Shakespearean tragedy might be said to be modern to the extent that it seems to dramatize the terrible revelation of a secular and arbitrary world, a purposeless universe of suffering and death. Thomas Hardy's novels

– *The Mayor of Casterbridge* (1886), *The Woodlanders* (1887), *Tess of the d'Urbervilles* (1891) and *Jude the Obscure* (1895), for example – might be regarded as limit-texts in this respect: they are remarkably close to the sort of model of tragedy that we have outlined in this chapter but their tragic force consists less in a dramatic revelation that there is no God or ultimate justice and more in an ironic toying with the very grounds of such a revelation. If, as Paul Fussell has argued, irony is the 'dominating form of modern understanding' (Fussell 1975, 35), this is especially clear in the sort of ironization of tragedy evident in Thomas Hardy's work. The fact that these novels incorporate allusions to what Hardy calls the Immanent Will, the 'intangible Cause' or 'Unfulfilled Intention', as well as to more familiar classical deities, is simply part of this ironization. In terms of drama itself, there have been quite traditional examples of the tragic – one might think of Arthur Miller's great allegorical work, *The Crucible* (1953), for example – but more characteristic of the past century have been the kind of secular tragicomedies of Chekhov or Beckett.

A second reason why tragedy is not what it used to be concerns the transformations that have taken place over the past two hundred years or so regarding the notions of the individual and society. If modern tragedies tend to be about ordinary people rather than kings or queens, they also show how far the lives of such 'ordinary people' are bound up, determined and constrained by broader social, economic and political realities. One of the first modern tragedies in European drama, Henrik Ibsen's *A Doll's House* (1879), for example, is not simply about the break-up of the 'doll' Nora's marriage: it is about the ways in which the patriarchal institution and conventions of marriage effectively *programme* this tragic break-up. Particularly in the wake of Ibsen's work, in other words, there is a fundamental shift from a classical idea of tragedy as inevitable and beyond human control to the modern idea of a tragedy as something humanly engineered and happening in a world in which something could and should be done, for instance about sexual inequality, racism and so on. In his autobiography, Bertrand Russell remarks that 'One of the things that makes literature so consoling, is that its tragedies are all in the past, and have the completeness and repose that comes of being beyond the reach of our endeavours' (Russell 1968, 169). Russell's observation may be appropriate for thinking about tragedy in its classical modes; but it is quite inadequate and misleading for thinking about modern tragedy. New historicist and poststructuralist critics, in particular, have been concerned to underline what many of the more recent examples of tragic works of literature make clear, namely that what Russell comfortably refers to as 'the past' is precisely what is in question. And if the past is in question, so is the present. Whose past are we talking about? From whose perspective? With whose interests at stake?

We could illustrate this by referring briefly to a couple of contemporary works of tragic literature. The first example is a novel about the United States. Toni Morrison's *The Bluest Eye* (1970) contains the basic elements of tragedy – even if this includes a modification of Shakespearean 'suffering and death' into Morrisonian 'suffering and terrible abuse'. It is set in Ohio, and the narrative begins in 1941. It recounts the story of a young black girl called Pecola and how she comes to be sexually abused by her grimly named father, Cholly Breedlove. Morrison's novel may be set in the past but its power as a tragic text consists partly in the fact that it is making an explicit political statement not only about racism in contemporary US society but also about the perception of history itself. The novel involves a lucid but terrible elaboration of *why* this man called Breedlove should have abused his daughter. By stressing the ways in which Breedlove himself had in the past been racially and physically abused in turn, Morrison's novel provides a complex historical account of racism and violence. *The Bluest Eye* is tragic but the villain is paradoxically part of the tragedy. Morrison's novel broaches a despairing realism quite foreign to Shakespearean tragedy. *King Lear* concludes with Edgar's words:

> The weight of this sad time we must obey,
> Speak what we feel, not what we ought to say:
> The oldest hath borne most; we that are young
> Shall never see so much, nor live so long. (V, ii, 324–7)

His words may sound like a hollow formality or formalism – even as they ironically refer to the importance of saying 'what we feel, not what we ought to say' – but there is at least an implicit affirmation here of some kind of future. Toni Morrison's novel concludes more blankly: 'It's too late. At least on the edge of my town, among the garbage and the sunflowers of my town, it's much, much, much too late' (190).

The second example is Chinua Achebe's *Anthills of the Savannah* (1987). Achebe's novel is at once more and less than a tragedy in a classical or Shakespearean sense. It is set in a semi-fictional present-day African state and recounts the process by which one of the protagonists, a newspaper editor called Ikem Osodi, is 'fatally wounded' (169) by the military authorities, and the other male protagonist, the Commissioner for Information, Chris Oriko, gets shot by a policeman who is apparently about to rape a schoolgirl. The narrator adopts the perspective of Chris's lover, the mourning Beatrice:

The explanation of the tragedy of Chris and Ikem in terms of petty human calculation or personal accident had begun to give way in her throbbing mind to an altogether more terrifying but more plausible theory of premeditation. The image of Chris as just another stranger who chanced upon death on the Great North Road or Ikem as an early victim of a waxing police state was no longer satisfactory. Were they not in fact trailed travellers whose journeys from start to finish had been carefully programmed in advance by an alienated history? If so, how many more doomed voyagers were already in transit or just setting out, faces fresh with illusions of duty-free travel and happy landings ahead of them? (220)

Though in many respects tragic, *Anthills of the Savannah* suggests a powerful circumscription and questioning of classical notions of tragedy – not least in the light of what Achebe calls 'an alienated history'. Like Morrison's *The Bluest Eye*, it is an explicitly political novel, directly focusing on the contemporary while exploring ways of rethinking the past. Both novels suggest, in their different ways, the extent to which tragedy is – humanly and unacceptably – 'carefully programmed'. In its broadest implications, the 'alienated history' to which Achebe's novel refers is perhaps alien to the very forms of Western thought, prompting us to reflect on the idea that 'history' and 'tragedy' are themselves Western concepts.

Further reading

Aristotle's *Poetics* is the single most important account of tragedy in Western history. Drakakis and Liebler's *Tragedy* (1998) has a very useful introduction and provides an excellent range of critical material, from Hegel to Derrida. For a psychoanalytic understanding of tragedy, see André Green's now classic *The Tragic Effect* (1979). For an influential account of how the sense of the tragic in the modern world has all but disappeared, see George Steiner's *The Death of Tragedy* (1961). And by way of equally influential riposte, see Raymond William's *Modern Tragedy* (1969), which vigorously demonstrates how tragedy has changed and will continue to do so. Of the most recent studies of the tragic, Jonathan Dollimore's *Radical Tragedy* (2nd edn, 1989) is particularly challenging, stimulating and wide-ranging. Specifically on Shakespeare, *Shakespearean Tragedy* (1992), ed. John Drakakis, contains a good deal of valuable critical material. On the peculiar relations between the tragic and pleasurable, see Nuttall (1996) and Eagleton (2003).

14. History

What is the relationship between a literary text and history? Broadly speaking critics have produced four answers to this question:

1. Literary texts belong to no particular time, they are universal and transcend history: the historical context of their production and reception has no bearing on the literary work which is aesthetically autonomous, having its own laws, being a world unto itself.
2. The historical context of a literary work – the circumstances surrounding its production – is integral to a proper understanding of it: the text is produced within a specific historical context but in its literariness it remains separate from that context.
3. Literary works can help us to understand the time in which they are set: realist texts in particular provide imaginative representations of specific historical moments, events or periods.
4. Literary texts are bound up with other discourses and rhetorical structures: they are part of a history that is still in the process of being written.

These four models of literature and history characterize various schools of criticism. The first model is often associated with new criticism or more generally with formalism, especially influential in literary studies in the middle decades of the twentieth century. New critics are concerned with literary texts as artifacts which transcend the contingencies of any particular time or place and which resist what they see as a reduction of the aesthetic whole to a specific historical context. Thus, for example, R.S. Crane argues in an essay first published in 1935 that literary history is essentially part of 'the general history of culture' (Crane 1967, 20), while a 'program of literary studies based on criticism' would focus on 'imaginative works considered with respect to those qualities which can truly be said to be timeless . . . in the sense that they can be adequately discerned and evaluated in the light of general principles quite apart from any knowledge of their origin or historical filiation' (18). The second model is the kind of approach favoured by philological or what we might call 'background' critics. Such critics are concerned to describe and analyze literary texts through a consideration of their historical 'background', whether biographical, linguistic, cultural or political. The titles of Basil Willey's two classic studies from 1934 and 1940 respectively indicate this approach: *The Seventeenth Century Background: Studies in the Thought of the Age in Relation to Poetry and Religion* and *The Eighteenth Century Background: Studies on the Idea of Nature in the Thought of the Period.* For such critics, knowledge of a literary text's historical circumstances forms the basis for an understanding of that text. The third model tends to be associated more with traditional historical scholarship than with literary criticism, as it assumes that literary texts are in some respect subordinate to their historical context. It also tends to assume that literary texts provide undistorted 'reflections' of their time. Thus, for example, in his book *Religion and the Decline of Magic* (1971), Keith Thomas appeals to Shakespeare's works on a number of occasions to justify his arguments. Discussing the practice of cursing, Thomas points out that 'In Shakespeare's plays, the curses pronounced by the characters invariably work', and argues that this is 'not just for dramatic effect' but that 'it was a moral necessity that the poor and the injured should be believed to have this power of retaliation when all else failed' (Thomas 1971, 507). We might call this model the 'reflective' approach. The last model is associated with a new kind of concern with the historical dimensions of literary studies particularly since the early 1980s. This model is specifically associated with new historicist critics in the United States and with cultural materialist critics in Britain (for convenience, we shall use the term 'new historicist' in this chapter to cover both varieties). In both cases, this new interest in history has been refracted through the concerns of both Marxism and post-structuralism to produce a complex model of the literary. In this chapter we shall focus on strategies of reading developed by new historicism in order to consider ways in which literary texts may be thought about in historical terms.

New historicists argue that to ask about the relationship between literature and history is the wrong question. The form of the question presupposes that there is literature on the one side and history on the other. Despite their differences, 'new critics', 'background critics' and 'reflectionists' tend to rely on precisely such a polarity: they assume that the categories of 'literature' and 'history' are intrinsically separate. They distinguish, more or less explicitly, between the need for the interpretation of literary texts on the one hand, and the transparency of history on the other. In an essay entitled 'Literary Theory, Criticism, and History' (1961), for example, René Wellek argues that 'Literary study differs from historical study in having to deal not with documents but with monuments' and that the literary critic 'has direct access to his [*sic*] object', while the historian 'has to reconstruct a long-past event on the basis of eye-witness accounts' (Wellek 1963, 14–15). For old-historicist critics, history is not so much textual as more simply a series of empirically verifiable events. And they also assume that it is possible for our knowledge of both historical events and literary texts to be detached and objective, outside the forces of history.

New historicism may be understood as a reaction against such presuppositions: put briefly, it may be defined as a recognition of the extent to which history is textual, as a rejection of the autonomy of the literary text and as an attempted displacement of the objectivity of interpretation in general. As the quasi-founder of new historicism, Stephen Greenblatt, remarks in an essay entitled 'Toward a Poetics of Culture', 'methodological self-consciousness is one of the distinguishing marks of the new historicism in cultural studies as opposed to a historicism based upon faith in the transparency of signs and interpretive procedures' (Greenblatt 1990a, 158). Thus, new historicists argue that the production of literary texts is a cultural practice different only in its specific mode or formulation from other practices – from furniture-making to teaching to warfare to printing. No absolute distinction can be made between literary and other cultural practices. As Stephen Greenblatt puts it, art is 'made up along with other products, practices, discourses of a given culture' (Greenblatt 1988, 13). Literary texts are embedded within the social and economic circumstances in which they are produced and consumed. But what is important for new historicists is that these circumstances are not stable in themselves and are susceptible to being rewritten and transformed. From this perspective, literary texts are part of a larger circulation of social energies, both products of and influences on a particular culture or ideology. What is new about new historicism in particular is its recognition that history is the 'history of the present', that history is in the making, that, rather than being monumental and closed, history is radically open to transformation and rewriting.

New historicists argue that any 'knowledge' of the past is necessarily mediated by *texts* or, to put it differently, that history is in many respects textual. In this, at least, they are in agreement with Jacques Derrida who declared in *Of Grammatology* in 1967: 'The age already in the *past* is in fact constituted in every respect as a *text*' (Derrida 1976, lxxxix). A number of major consequences follow from such an assertion. In the first place, there can be no knowledge of the past without interpretation. (This is also one of the ways in which new historicism is specifically Nietzschean: as Nietzsche said, 'facts is precisely what there is not, only interpretations' (Nietzsche 1968, section 481).) Just as literary texts need to be read, so do the 'facts' of history. Thus, theorists such as Hayden White suggest that our knowledge of the past is determined by particular narrative configurations – that in talking about the past we tell stories. 'Properly understood', White remarks,

> histories ought never to be read as unambiguous signs of the events they report, but rather as symbolic structures, extended metaphors, that 'liken' the events reported in them to some form with which we have already become familiar in our literary culture . . . By the very constitution of a set of events in such a way as to make a comprehensible story out of them, the historian charges those events with the symbolic significance of a comprehensible plot structure. (White 1978, 91–2)

In this respect, the strategies and tools of critical analysis – the consideration of figures and tropes, a critical awareness of the rhetorical elements of language and so on – are as appropriate to a critical study of history as they are to literary studies.

From a new historicist perspective, any reading of a literary text is a question of negotiation, a negotiation between text and reader within the context of a history or histories that cannot be closed or finalized. Indeed, Stephen Greenblatt argues that literary works themselves should be understood in terms of negotiation, rather than in the conventional (romantic) sense of a 'pure act of untrammeled creation' – negotiations which are 'a subtle, elusive set of exchanges, a network of trades and trade-offs, a jostling of competing representations' (Greenblatt 1988, 7). 'The work of art', declares Greenblatt, 'is the product of a negotiation between a creator or class of creators, equipped with a complex, communally shared repertoire of conventions, and the institutions and practices of society' (Greenblatt 1990a, 158). Greenblatt and other new historicist critics reject any attempt to produce a 'whole' or final reading and argue for readings which are apparently disjunctive or fragmented. Similarly, questioning the boundaries of text and world, of art and society, such critics work 'at the margins of the text' in order to gain 'insight into the half-hidden cultural transactions through which great works of art are empowered' (Greenblatt 1988, 4). A critic might study legal documents, for example, or arguments concerning the politics of kingship, or handbooks on the education of children, or accounts of exotic travels and exploration and so on, in order to get a purchase on a particular work of literature. But such texts are not to be construed as either the background or the essential key to understanding the literary text. Rather, like plays, poems and novels, they are to be understood as texts through which questions of politics and power can be negotiated.

Such negotiation concerns, not least, our reading. If 'history' necessarily entails interpretation, then such acts of reading will themselves be embedded within a particular social and cultural situation. There is no escape from history even if this history is regarded as multiple and in a process of unceasing transformation. New historicism argues that we are inescapably implicated – even in the fantasy of academic objectivity and detachment – in structures and strategies of power. Power is produced and reproduced in research, teaching and learning as it is in any other practice or discourse. As Michel Foucault remarks, power is 'omnipresent' as 'the moving substrate of force relations which, by virtue of their inequality, constantly engender states of power', states of power which are, however, 'always local and unstable'. 'Power', Foucault goes on, 'is everywhere' (Foucault 1981, 93).

In order to consider how such an approach might work in practice, we propose to discuss a poem by the English romantic poet William Wordsworth entitled 'Alice Fell, or Poverty'. The poem was written on the 12th and 13th March 1802, and first published in 1807. It is a seemingly uncomplicated account of an incident that was recounted to Wordsworth by his friend Robert Grahame. As the subtitle indicates, the poem presents itself as an allegory concerning poverty:

> The Post-boy drove with fierce career,
> For threat'ning clouds the moon had drowned;
> When suddenly I seemed to hear
> A moan, a lamentable sound.
>
> 5 As if the wind blew many ways
> I heard the sound, and more and more:
> It seemed to follow with the Chaise,
> And still I heard it as before.
>
> At length I to the Boy called out,
> 10 He stopped his horses at the word;
> But neither cry, nor voice, nor shout,
> Nor aught else like it could be heard.
>
> The Boy then smacked his whip, and fast
> The horses scampered through the rain;
> 15 And soon I heard upon the blast
> The voice, and bade him halt again.

Said I, alighting on the ground,
'What can it be, this piteous moan?'
And there a little Girl I found,
20   Sitting behind the Chaise, alone.

'My Cloak!' the word was last and first,
And loud and bitterly she wept,
As if her very heart would burst;
And down from off the Chaise she leapt.

25   'What ails you, Child?' She sobbed, 'Look here!'
I saw it in the wheel entangled,
A weather beaten Rag as e'er
From any garden scare-crow dangled.

'Twas twisted betwixt nave and spoke;
30   Her help she lent, and with good heed
Together we released the Cloak;
A wretched, wretched rag indeed!

'And wither are you going, Child,
Tonight along these lonesome ways?'
35   'To Durham' answered she half wild—
'Then come with me into the chaise.'

She sate like one past all relief;
Sob after sob she forth did send
In wretchedness, as if her grief
40   Could never, never, have an end.

'My child, in Durham do you dwell?'
She checked herself in her distress,
And said, 'My name is Alice Fell;
I'm fatherless and motherless.

45   And I to Durham, Sir, belong.'
And then, as if the thought would choke
Her very heart, her grief grew strong;
And all was for her tattered Cloak.

The chaise drove on; our journey's end
50   Was nigh; and, sitting by my side,
As if she'd lost her only friend
She wept, nor would be pacified.

Up to the Tavern-door we post;
Of Alice and her grief I told;
55   And I gave money to the Host,
To buy a new Cloak for the old.

'And let it be a duffil grey,
As warm a cloak as man can sell!'
Proud Creature was she the next day,
60   The little Orphan, Alice Fell!

From a new historicist perspective we might try to situate this poem in relation to other contemporary discourses which deal with poverty, charity and property. We could, for example, investigate the rhetorical strategies and discursive conventions of debates surrounding the Poor Law, economics, poverty and charity at the turn of the nineteenth century. One such text is Adam Smith's *The Wealth of Nations*, first published in 1776, one of the most influential works of political economy in the early nineteenth century. In this work, Smith twice refers to beggars, once when he argues that 'Before the invention of the art of printing, a scholar and a beggar seem to have been terms very nearly synonymous' (Smith 1986, 237), and once when he considers beggars as the only people who do not take part in the circulation of exchange and barter. In this latter passage, from the second chapter of his multi-volume work, Smith argues that there is 'a certain propensity in human nature' which is 'to truck, barter, and exchange one thing for another' (117). It is this 'propensity' which distinguishes humans from animals: 'When an animal wants to obtain something either of a man or of another animal, it has no other means of persuasion but to gain the favour of those whose service it requires' (118). But humans – unlike animals, consistently dependent on others – cannot constantly expect others' benevolence. Instead, a man must 'interest [another person's] self-love in his favour': 'Nobody but a beggar chooses to depend chiefly upon the benevolence of his fellow-citizens' (118–19). Although Smith goes on to say that even beggars take part in the circulation of monetary exchange by buying goods with the money that they are given, in this extraordinary passage he has managed to dehumanize beggars, to put them outside of humanity, on the level of the animal. By arguing that human relations are relations of exchange, based on the principle of 'self-love', however, Smith suggests an apparent paradox in the discourse of charity: he claims that 'the charity of well-disposed people' supplies the beggar with 'the whole fund of his subsistence' (119), but does not explain *why* such people should give to beggars. According to his own arguments, people would only give to beggars if they were to gain something in return. There is, in this sense, no pure gift, no possibility of a gift. A number of significant rhetorical manoeuvres, then, may be seen to be at work in Smith's discourse of charity and begging. In the first place, beggars are dehumanized. Secondly, charity becomes a paradoxical or perverse, even an impossible act. Thirdly, by saying 'a beggar *chooses* to depend', Smith implies freedom of choice where economic necessity may be at stake. Finally, and most generally, Smith makes it clear that questions of charity and begging are part of a larger discourse of property and the exchange of property, indeed, part of a specific ideology of free-market liberalism.

We might think about these points in relation to Wordsworth's poem for, although Alice Fell does not actually beg and is not referred to as a beggar, the poem puts her in the position of a beggar, and is specifically concerned with that particular kind of exchange of property named 'charity'. What we might then seek to do is not to produce a thematic reading of the poem: rather, we might consider how the rhetorical strategies at work in Smith's account of beggars, property and charity are reproduced and transformed in those of the poem.

We might start by thinking about ways in which the poem articulates questions of property. Property in 'Alice Fell' is not simply a question of the cloak, but of poetry itself as property. The very origins of the narrative are bound up with questions of ownership in that the story originated with Wordsworth's friend Robert Grahame. Moreover, Dorothy Wordsworth, the poet's sister, wrote an account of the same incident in her journal before Wordsworth wrote his poem. Dorothy's account goes as follows:

> Mr. Graham said he wished Wm had been with him the other day – he was riding in a post chaise and he heard a strange cry that he could not understand, the sound continued and he called to the chaise driver to stop. It was a little girl that was crying as if her heart would burst. She had got up behind the chaise and her cloak had been caught by the wheel and was jammed in and it hung there. She was crying after it. Poor thing. Mr. Graham took her into the chaise and the cloak was released from the wheel but the child's misery did not cease for her cloak was torn to rags; it had been a miserable cloak before, but she had no other and it was the greatest sorrow that could befal her. Her name was Alice Fell. She had no parents, and belonged to the next Town. At the next Town Mr. G. left money with some respectable people in the town to buy her a new cloak. (Wordsworth 1984, 702)

As with a number of William's most famous lyrics, 'Alice Fell' resembles Dorothy's journalistic account in many ways: both poem and journal entry are concerned with the strangeness of the girl's cry, with the girl's continuing misery, with the ragged state of her cloak. More specifically, there are numerous verbal echoes of the journal entry in William's poem, most strikingly, the poem's 'she wept, / As if her heart would burst' and the journal's 'crying as if her heart would burst'. In this respect, William may be said to have appropriated the story from his friend and from his sister. This leads us to the question of what property it is that constitutes this text as a poem. Is it *properly* a poem? How is it different from Grahame's oral account or from Dorothy's journal entry? And where does the poem originate, who owns it and authorizes it? We might want to follow these questions through to an investigation of the institution of literature itself. How is the canon produced, for example, what factors are at work in canon-formation in England such that women's diaries have tended to be excluded, canonically marginalized? Can it be said that in choosing the form of the journal-entry to record the story Dorothy is excluding herself from the public discourse of literature? How is Dorothy's account both reproduced and effaced in William's poem and in the critical tradition, and why? Rather differently, we could argue that Dorothy's diary entry is not simply supplementary to the poem but is an essential part of it. Indeed, it becomes difficult to distinguish property as regards the cloak and property as regards the Wordsworths. In these respects, questions of property cannot be considered to be simply the context or the thematic focus of the poem: the poem originates in certain problematic exchanges, transfers or gifts of narrative property.

The poem is also 'about' an exchange of property. The girl loses her cloak in the wheel of the carriage, and the speaker gives her enough money to buy a new one. But along with this exchange go a series of property disturbances. The girl's proper name, Alice Fell, for example, is curious. It is not a name Wordsworth invented, it seems. But is it 'historical' or 'literary'? The poem, indeed, exacerbates the sense of uncertainty regarding the strange properties of this proper name. Not only is it transferred from the title to the main body of the poem, or from the girl to the poem, but it also has a curious grammatical status in itself: it is suspended between a name and a minimal sentence, a kind of mini-narrative in itself – Alice fell. The poem is not only called 'Alice Fell', but is also about the fall of Alice. And once we recognize that there is something strange about the girl's name, we might also notice that 'Alice Fell' is haunted by the figure of a 'fallen woman', a woman outside 'respectable' society. Dorothy's text seems to pick up on this in its use of the verb 'befal', just prior to naming the girl herself. Conversely, we may recall that 'fell' also means the skin or hide of an animal, so that Alice might be like her cloak, a kind of rag, caught up and torn apart by the moving carriage.

Finally, 'fell' as 'wild', as 'fierce, savage, cruel, ruthless, dreadful, terrible' or 'intensely painful' and even (of poison) 'deadly', or 'shrewd, clever, cunning' (*OED*) gives us a sense of the outcast, inhuman, dangerous, improper nature of this figure, and perhaps partly explains her – and the poem's – haunting power: she is, as the narrator himself declares, 'half wild' (l.35). The dehumanization at work in Smith's account of beggars is also wildly at work in Wordsworth's poem.

If the poem is about the exchange of property, it is also about the question of charity. Every act of charity may be understood as an implicit assertion that the end of suffering is possible. Dorothy's account of the incident recognizes that, after the girl's cloak was released, her 'misery did not cease'. One of the key stanzas of Wordsworth's poem in this respect is stanza seven:

> She sate like one past all relief;
> Sob after sob she forth did send
> In wretchedness, as if her grief
> Could never, never, have an end.

The phrases 'like' and 'as if' point to the unspeakable possibility that the girl really is 'past all relief', and that her 'grief / Could never, never, have an end'. Much of the force of the poem may be said to reside precisely in this terrifying possibility – that nothing can be done, that charity cannot finally help. In this respect, it is significant that unlike Dorothy's account, the poem ends in a blustering statement of self-satisfaction: in the final stanza, the girl is said to be 'proud' on account of her new cloak. But the girl's poverty and orphanhood remain and the pride appears to be as much a projection of the speaker's emotions as the girl's. The *speaker* apparently does have reason to be proud – he can feel proud of his charitable action. Attributing pride to the girl simply increases the speaker's own reasons to be proud. It might be argued that the poem works against itself, implicitly exposing the self-deceptive nature of the charitable act. Given this logic of projection, the poem clearly suggests that self-deception is necessary to charity or that, in Adam Smith's terms, there is no pure gift, that in giving the cloak, the speaker receives the satisfaction of pride. Moreover, the poem's triumphant ending implies that charity can end suffering. But this sense of triumph and of an ending are simultaneously undone: we must give and to do so we must believe that our gift will help to end suffering, but suffering is never-ending. The hardly audible, ghostly historical counter-voice of the poem cries that, as an orphan, Alice Fell cannot but suffer (etymologically, 'orphan' means 'one who has lost'). Her suffering is never-ending because it cannot be ended. Unlike the speaker, who is on a journey that will end (see line 49, 'our journey's end'), the suffering of Alice Fell has no end. Just as the speaker is haunted by a strange voice at the beginning of the poem, so he is haunted by the uncanny disembodied voice of suffering, haunted by what he knows but cannot know – that suffering and the improper or 'fell' (wild, inhuman, fallen) disturbances of property are never ending.

Stephen Greenblatt argues that culture 'is a particular network of negotiations for the exchange of material goods, ideas, and – through institutions like enslavement, adoption, or marriage – people'. Greenblatt also contends that 'Great writers are precisely masters of these codes, specialists in cultural exchange' (Greenblatt 1990b, 229–30). Our account has sought to locate Wordsworth's poem in relation to the discourses of property and charity as articulated in one particular text. Wordsworth, we might say, is a master of – and is mastered by – the codes of property and charity. New historicism seeks to explore such mastery, while remaining alert to ways in which such codes continue to play themselves out in the discourses of the present – including, not least, the discourses of history and criticism.

Further reading

For eloquent and readable accounts of a historicized theory of culture, see Stephen Greenblatt's essays 'Towards a Poetics of Culture' (1990a) and 'Culture' (1990b). See his *Shakespearean Negotiations* (1988) and *Marvelous Possessions* (1991) for witty and penetrating readings of various Renaissance texts, and see also Catherine Gallagher and Greenblatt's *Practising New Historicism* (2000). For an important if somewhat intricate discussion of such issues in the context of the Romantic period, see James Chandler's *England in 1819* (1998). Useful collections of new historicist and cultural materialist essays include Dollimore and Sinfield, eds, *Political Shakespeare* (1994), Wilson and Dutton, eds, *New Historicism and Renaissance Drama* (1992), Veeser, ed., *The New Historicism* (1989) and *The New Historicism Reader* (1994), Ryan, ed., *New Historicism and Culture Materialism* (1996), and most recently Tamsin Spargo, ed., *Reading the Past* (2000). For a complex but important study of history and contemporary historiography, see Robert Young, *White Mythologies* (1990). For a good but demanding overview of historicisms old and new, see Paul Hamilton's *Historicism* (1996). For a sharp and engaging account of new historicism and cultural materialism, see Brannigan (1998). Todd (1988) provides a valuable feminist account of literary history.

15. Me

W ho are we? What am I? What is an 'I'? What does it mean to say 'me'? What is the relationship between an 'I' in a literary text and an 'I' out- side it? One of the central ideas of this book is literature's capacity to question, defamiliarize and even transform the sense of who or what we are. In the next few pages we would like to elaborate further on this, by trying to look at the nature of personal identity or 'me' both in broadly historical and theoretical terms and more specifically in terms of what literary texts themselves suggest.

In Flannery O'Connor's story 'Revelation' (1961) a woman called Mrs Turpin has a traumatic and bizarre reaction when a strange girl sitting in a doctor's waiting room tells her: 'Go back to hell where you came from, you old wart hog' (217). Mrs Turpin is scandalized by this statement and that same evening, back at the farm, by herself, hosing down the pigs, she demands an explanation. Being Christian and superstitious (as well as grotesquely racist and class-prejudiced), Mrs Turpin regards the girl's words as a message from God:

> 'What do you send me a message like that for?' she said in a low fierce voice,
> barely above a whisper but with the force of a shout in its concentrated fury.
> 'How am I a hog and me both?' (222)

What is striking here is not only the woman's confusion and indignation at the apparently contradictory idea that she might be a human being and an old wart hog at the same time, but also the fact that her 'fury' is expressed in a direct, personal address to God. Mrs Turpin's sense of outrage becomes outrageous in turn, as her questions addressed to God culminate in a questioning *of* God: 'A final surge of fury shook her and she roared, "Who do you think you are?"'

(223) The strangeness of putting this question to God comes from the fact that it is a question that should only be asked of another human. Only humans are supposed to be able to reflect on who they are and at the same time be obliged to take seriously a questioning of their own identity. If the question 'Who do you think you are?' is one that cannot or should not be asked of God, nor is it a question one would normally ask of a wart hog. In this respect it would seem that there is something characteristically human about the question. 'Who do you think you are?' is the question that humans ask of others and try to answer about themselves. As Socrates said, 'The unexamined life is not worth living' (Plato, *Apology*, 38a). And the definition of being human must remain in the form of a questioning: Mrs Turpin's 'concentrated fury' is, in this respect, pitifully, comically human.

At the same time, it could be said that this question ('Who do you think you are?') is most clearly raised and most fully explored in works of literature. This might in fact be another general definition: literature is the space in which questions about the nature of personal identity are most provocatively articulated. In the nineteenth century and earlier in the twentieth century, literary critics used to talk about 'the person' and 'the individual'. In more recent years, however, there has been a tendency to refer to 'the human subject' or just 'the subject'. This may sound jargonistic but there are good reasons, in fact, for talking about 'the subject' rather than, say, 'the person' or 'the individual'. The French poststructuralist Michel Foucault has written: 'There are two meanings of the word "subject": subject to someone else by control and dependence, and tied to one's own identity by a conscience or self-knowledge' (Foucault 1983, 212, cited by During 1992, 153). The word 'person', by contrast, perhaps too easily retains connotations of the 'I' or 'me' as detached from everything, a *free agent*. Likewise, the term 'individual' (etymologically from the Latin *individuus*, 'undivided' or 'not divisible') suggests a sense of the 'I' as simply free, as being at one with itself and autonomous or self-ruling. It is this idea of the sovereignty of the 'I' that Freud gestures towards and ironizes when he speaks of 'His Majesty the Ego' (Freud 1985f, 138).

The term 'subject' is useful, then, in that it encourages a more critical attentiveness to the ways in which the 'I' is *not* autonomous, to the fact that it does not exist in a sort of vacuum. Rather an 'I' or 'me' is always *subject* to forces and effects both outside itself (environmental, social, cultural, economic, educational, etc.) and 'within' itself (in particular in terms of what is called the unconscious or, in more recent philosophical terms, otherness). We are subjects in the sense of being 'subject to' others 'by control or dependence' (in Foucault's phrase) right from birth and even before: not only are we radically dependent on the father who sires us and the mother who bears us, but also on the environment (ecological, economic, familial, social, etc.) into which we are born, as well as on the multiple forms of authority and government which condition our upbringing. A 'me' born to a single mother in Soweto is not the same kind of 'me' as a 'me' born to a duchess in Kensington, but they are both in their different ways *subjects*. Of course if the Kensington 'me' had been in line for the throne, things would have looked slightly different: in Britain, at least, one is subject not only to the authority of one's parent or parents, one's local authorities, the police and central government, but also – at least on paper – to the Queen (thus one is 'a British subject') and, beyond her, to the Christian God. That, then, is one way in which every 'I' is necessarily and fundamentally a *subject*. Rather differently, being a subject has specifically to do with language. You cannot be an 'I' without having a proper name, and in English-speaking countries you usually acquire a proper name around the time of birth or even before. We are born into language, we are born – more precisely – into patriarchal language, into being identified by a patronym, by a paternal proper name. (Even the mother's maiden name is, of course, a patronym.) We are also endowed with a forename and again this is not something *we* choose, it is something to which we are *subject* – even if, in Britain for example, people do legally have the right to change their names at the age of eighteen. Juliet's complaint is haunting and even tragic precisely because it highlights the way in which we are *subject to* names, even if we wish to ignore or disown them:

> Oh Romeo, Romeo, wherefore art thou Romeo?
> Deny thy father and refuse thy name;
> Or, if thou wilt not, be but sworn my love,
> And I'll no longer be a Capulet.
> (*Romeo and Juliet*, II, ii, 33–6)

More broadly, questions of personal or individual identity are indissociably bound up with language. We may like to suppose that there is some 'me' outside language or that there is some way of thinking about ourselves which involves a non-linguistic 'me'. But the *idea* of this non-linguistic 'me' must found itself in language – beginning with the name itself, or with the words 'I', 'me', 'mine', 'myself' and so on. We cannot, in any *meaningful* way, escape the fact that we are *subject to* language. As Jacques Derrida has put it: 'From the moment that there is meaning there are nothing but signs. We think only in signs' (Derrida 1976, 50).

We can also consider this topic from a more explicitly historical perspective. The idea of the 'I' or 'me', in other words, is not unchanging and

unchangeable. It is in many respects historically and ideologically determined. The way we think about 'I' today is inevitably different from the way in
which 'I' was thought about and defined in, say, seventeenth-century France
by René Descartes. The principle of the Cartesian cogito ('I think therefore I
am') – that is to say, the model of the *rational subject* which Descartes theorizes
in his *Discourse on Method* (1637; 1977) – in many respects continues to
govern Western thinking. But there are other ways of thinking, and other
ways of thinking about thinking. In the mid-twentieth century, for example,
the German philosopher Martin Heidegger declared: 'Thinking begins
only when we have come to know that reason, glorified for centuries, is the
most stiffnecked adversary of thought' (Heidegger 1977, 112, cited by
Judovitz 1988, 186). Likewise, and more recently, Jacques Derrida has been
consistently concerned to demonstrate that, as he puts it: 'reason is only one
species of thought – which does not mean that thought is "irrational"'
(Derrida 1983, 16).

But perhaps the most obvious way of illustrating the changes over the past
century in thinking about thinking, and in thinking about the model of the
rational subject, is in terms of psychoanalysis. Psychoanalysis has changed
the way in which we are obliged to think about 'the subject'. In the light of the
psychoanalytic theory of the unconscious, the proposition 'cogito ergo sum'
('I think therefore I am') becomes manifestly problematic. I do not, and perhaps strictly speaking never can, know precisely *why* or *how* I think what
I think, if only because of the extent to which what I think is necessarily determined by forces and effects of which I am (in many ways thankfully) unaware.
In a short essay written as an encyclopaedia entry on 'Psychoanalysis' first
published in 1923, Freud suggests that the unconscious is evident not only in
dreams but in

> such events as the temporary forgetting of familiar words and names, for-
> getting to carry out prescribed tasks, everyday slips of the tongue and of the
> pen, misreadings, losses and mislayings of objects, certain errors, instances
> of apparently accidental self-injury, and finally habitual movements carried
> out seemingly without intention or in play, tunes hummed 'thoughtlessly',
> and so on. (Freud 1986, 136–7)

The significance of Freud's theory of the unconscious thus consists in the
demonstration that the subject who thinks (the subject of 'I think') is composed of forces and effects which are at least in part unconscious. 'I',
let us remind ourselves, is not 'God' – even if it may be *subject to* fantasies
of being so.

Psychoanalysis, then, has been a particularly disturbing but valuable discourse because it has promoted an awareness of the extent to which any 'I' or human subject is *decentred*: I, in other words, can never be simply or precisely who or what I think. What makes this idea disturbing and at the same time valuable is that it involves a dislocation of notions of human mastery and autonomy of self. It introduces instead the humility of recognizing that the human subject is not centred in itself, let alone centred in relation to the surrounding world or solar system. In an essay on 'The Resistances to Psychoanalysis' (1925), Freud talks about the 'emotional' difficulties people have in accepting the ideas of psychoanalysis and draws analogies between this and the theories of Darwin and Copernicus. In the case of psychoanalysis, he says, 'powerful human feelings are hurt by the subject-matter of the theory. Darwin's theory of descent met with the same fate, since it tore down the barrier that had been arrogantly set up between men and beasts.' Freud goes on to suggest that 'the psychoanalytic view of the relation of the conscious ego to an overpowering unconscious was a severe blow to human self-love', and that, 'as the *psychological* blow to men's narcissism', it compares 'with the *biological* blow delivered by the theory of descent and the earlier *cosmological* blow aimed at it by the discovery of Copernicus' (Freud 1986, 272–3). In this sense, psychoanalysis complements the Copernican revolution and nineteenth-century evolutionary theory in providing a powerful critique of anthropocentric or humanist values and ideas. Psychoanalysis demonstrates in uncomfortably clear terms how the 'arrogance' or narcissism of anthropocentrism – that is to say, every kind of thinking, including every kind of philosophy and politics, which puts the human at the centre of the earth and solar system, if not of the universe – is both unwarranted and unsustainable.

The Cartesian 'I think therefore I am' can be further considered specifically in relation to language. Language determines the 'I' and the 'I think'. This can be illustrated simply by reflecting on the idea that Descartes's formulation was first published in Latin ('cogito ergo sum'). We anglophone subjects are already adrift in effects of language and translation, but so too was Descartes himself: after all, his works appeared not in some form of seventeenth-century French but in a foreign, 'dead' language. He was subject to the scholarly protocols of his own time and the requirement to write (and in some sense presumably think) in Latin. What is at stake in this logic of being *subject to language* is a conception of language as not simply *instrumental*: language is not simply something that we *use*. Language governs what we (can) say as much as we govern or *use* language. Language is not simply an instrument: we are, unavoidably, *agents* of language. Moreover we are, more precisely perhaps, secret or double agents of language: we do not necessarily know, from one moment to the next, *how* we are being used by language or where it might be leading us. As in the most compelling kind of espionage story, however, this is not a situation we can get out of. As the narrator neatly puts it, in Margaret Atwood's short story 'Giving Birth' (1977): 'These are the only words I have, I'm stuck with them, stuck in them' (225–6). The 'in' is, no doubt, more difficult to reflect on than the 'with', but it is no less important.

How do these various questions and ideas relate to literary works more generally? First of all let us emphasize that, if literature is concerned with exploring and reflecting on the nature of personal identity, it is also a space of exhilarating, even anarchic openness and imaginative or transformational possibility. Literature can be thought of as being, in Derrida's words, 'the institution which allows one to *say everything*, in *every way*' (Derrida 1992a, 36). In particular there is this astonishing, anarchic freedom in literature: at least in principle, the author of a literary work can be any 'I' he or she wishes to. To put it like this is to imply that the author is an 'I' before or outside the literary work. But who is to say that there is an 'I' anywhere that is not in part *literary*? This rather strange question is a focus of one of the greatest comical literary or philosophical works in the twentieth century, Samuel Beckett's *The Unnamable* (first published in English in 1959). This text is preoccupied with the idea that it is the 'I' itself that is in a sense the unnamable: the 'I' that speaks, or that seems to speak, is never true, never precisely itself, never the same, for example, as the 'I' who has spoken or the 'I' that writes 'I'. *The Unnamable*, then, starts off from the apparently simple but perhaps unfathomable remark, 'I, say I', and from the paradox that 'I seem to speak, it is not I, about me, it is not about me' (293). Nearly fifty pages later the narrator is still impelled to observe that 'on the subject of me properly so called . . . so far as I know I have received no information up to date' (338). In Beckett's wonderfully funny, but also dark and unnerving text, the Cartesian-rationalistic 'I think' becomes: 'I only think, if that is the name for this vertiginous panic as of hornets smoked out of their nest, once a certain degree of terror has been exceeded' (353). As with so much of Beckett's writing, this sentence is at once quite straight-forward and semantically dense, unsettling, surprisingly resistant to a single interpretation. We might note, for example, the explicit attention to the uncer-tainties of language ('if that is the name') and of the relationship between terror and thinking. To think about this sentence can induce vertiginous panic and become terrifying. It succinctly illustrates literature's complex and unsettling effects when it comes to thinking about thinking – when it comes to thinking about identity and about the 'I' that claims to think.

We could conclude by trying to say a little more about the ways in which, as we suggested earlier, the 'I' or 'me' is in fact historically determined. One very broad but decisive example of this would be the question of the 'I' or 'me' in relation to romantic and post-romantic literature. In *Of Grammatology* (1967), Derrida argues that the importance of Jean-Jacques Rousseau's work consists in the fact that he 'starts from a new model of presence: the subject's self-presence within *consciousness* or *feeling*' (Derrida 1976, 98). European romanticism in general might be characterized in terms of this kind of 'new model of presence', and in particular in terms of a new emphasis on the centrality and importance of the 'I' as a subject who both thinks and feels. This could be exemplified by a celebrated stanza written by George Gordon Byron on the back of a manuscript-page of canto 1 of *Don Juan* (1819–24):

> I would to heaven that I were so much clay,
>   As I am blood, bone, marrow, passion, feeling—
> Because at least the past were pass'd away—
>   And for the future—(but I write this reeling,
> Having got drunk exceedingly to-day,
>   So that I seem to stand upon the ceiling)
> I say—the future is a serious matter—
> And so—for God's sake—hock and soda-water!

The new emphasis on the 'I' in romantic culture is consistently articulated in terms of the polarity or gulf between a subject ('I feel') and an object (the clouds, a skylark, a nightingale). The (impossible) desire for a fusion between subject and object (the idea for example of being, in Matthew Arnold's words, 'in harmony with nature') is one of the most striking characteristics of the work of the English romantic poets. It is clear, for instance, in Keats's 'Ode to a Nightingale', in which the speaker is eventually compelled to admit defeat in his attempt to fuse or dissolve into the nightingale's song: the word 'forlorn' is 'like a bell / To toll me back from thee to my sole self'. This emphasis on the 'sole self' broaches the notion of solipsism – that is to say the refusal or inability to believe in the reality of anything outside or beyond the self. The idea of such an isolation of the self has its representatives in classical philosophy and literature, but it is particularly pervasive in nineteenth- and twentieth-century European culture. It is evoked by the pathos, or bathos, of the opening lines of Matthew Arnold's poem, 'To Marguerite – Continued' (1849):

> Yes! in the sea of life enisled,
> With echoing straits between us thrown,
> Dotting the shoreless watery wild,
> We mortal millions live *alone*.

It is also implicit in the work of Freud, to the extent that psychoanalysis suggests that everything comes down to the power and significance of *projection*, of the qualities, moods or emotions which we *project on to* people and things. Wallace Stevens sums this up when he says:

> few people realize on that occasion, which comes to all of us, when we look at the blue sky for the first time, that is to say: not merely see it, but look at it and experience it . . . – few people realize that they are looking at the world of their own thoughts and the world of their own feelings. (Stevens 1951, 65-6)

But as we hope will by now be clear, solipsism is a myth, a delusion or mirage. Solipsism presupposes the idea of something like what Wittgenstein calls a private language (Wittgenstein 1984). There is no such thing as a private language: the phrase 'private language' is an oxymoron. Language is social or, at least, language comes from elsewhere, from others and from otherness in general. Even to say, as a self-avowed solipsist might, 'I do not believe in the reality of anything apart from myself', is to demonstrate a dependence on what is not 'me', not oneself. It is to demonstrate that one is *subject to* language. As the voice, or one of the voices, in *The Unnamable* puts it: 'I'm in words, made of words, others' words . . .' (390).

Literature, like art more generally, has always been concerned with aspects of what can be called the unconscious or 'not me' or other: it is and has always been centrally concerned with dreams and fantasy, hallucinations and visions, madness, trance, and other kinds of impersonality or absences of self. But we could say that romantic and post-romantic literature has been increasingly sensitive to the role of otherness and increasingly aware of what might be described as our obligations in relation to otherness. Beckett's writing is perhaps only the most philosophically refined recent example of post-romantic literature which is concerned to explore, deflate and transform our understanding of the question, 'Who do you think you are?' In this respect his work might be seen to anticipate and encapsulate much of what is called poststructuralism. Poststructuralism demonstrates that the 'I' or human subject is necessarily decentred. It argues against the reductiveness (and even the possibility) of rationalism, in particular through its attention to what is other (though not simply 'irrational') as regards Western 'rational' thinking. And it persistently shows up the presumptuousness of the model of an autonomous, supposedly masterful human being, and thus points beyond 'merely' literary questions, exposing the barbarities of anthropocentrism in general. Some of this may be felt in a faltering, haunting few words from *The Unnamable*:

if only I knew if I've lived, if I live, if I'll live, that would simplify everything, impossible to find out, that's where you're buggered, I haven't stirred, that's all I know, no, I know something else, it's not I, I always forget that, I resume, you must resume . . . (417)

Further reading

For some very clear and stimulating introductory accounts of psychoanalysis and its implications for 'me', see Freud 1986; for a complex and challenging analysis of Freudian thinking on the idea of the subject, see Borch-Jacobsen, *The Freudian Subject* (1988). For a careful and thought-provoking discussion of the human subject from the perspective of the social sciences, see Paul Hirst and Penny Woolley, *Social Relations and Human Attributes* (1982). A highly influential account of romanticism stressing the importance of conflicts and disjunctions between subject and object, me and the world, etc., is M.H. Abram's classic study, *The Mirror and the Lamp* (1953). Another influential discussion of these issues, this time from the perspective of the history of philosophy (particularly from Descartes to the Romantic period) is Charles Taylor's wide-ranging and informative *Sources of the Self* (1989). For two very good general accounts of poststructuralism, see Robert Young's Introduction to *Untying the Text* (1981) and Josué Harari's Introduction to *Textual Strategies* (1979); and see Joel Fineman's *The Subjectivity Effect in Western Literary Tradition* (1991) for a theoretically and critically astute exploration of such issues in a number of literary (especially Shakespearean) texts.

16. Ghosts

What has literature to do with ghosts? Before we consider this question we need to think about a prior question: what is a ghost? The word 'ghost' is related to and originates in the German *Geist*, a word that *Chambers Dictionary* defines as 'spirit, any inspiring or dominating principle'. The *OED* gives, as its first and fourth definitions of 'ghost', the 'soul or spirit, as the principle of life' and 'A person'. In these respects, the ghost is fundamental to our thinking about the human: to be human is to have a spirit, a soul, a *Geist* or ghost. But the more common modern sense of 'ghost' (albeit only listed seventh in the *OED*) involves the idea of a spectre, an apparition of the dead, a revenant, the dead returned to a kind of spectral existence – an entity not alive but also not quite, not finally, dead. Ghosts disturb our sense of the separation of the living from the dead – which is why they can be so frightening, so uncanny. These conflicting senses of the word 'ghost' suggest that ghosts are both exterior and central to our sense of the human. Ghosts are paradoxical since they are both fundamental to the human, fundamentally human, and a denial or disturbance of the human, the very being of the inhuman. We propose to devote this chapter, to dedicate it, to the living-dead, to the ghost(s) of literature. And we propose that this scandal of the ghost, its paradoxy, is embedded in the very thing that we call literature, inscribed in multiple and haunting ways, in novels, poems and plays.

Ghosts have a history. They are not what they used to be. Ghosts, in a sense, *are* history. They do not, after all, come from nowhere, even if they may appear to do just that. They are always inscribed *in a context*: they at once belong to and haunt the idea of a place (hence 'spirit of place' or *genius loci*), and belong to and haunt the idea of a time (what we could call a 'spirit of time' or rather differently what is called the 'spirit of the age' or *Zeitgeist*). In other words, it is possible to trace a history of ghosts, as well as to think about history itself as ghostly, as what can in some form or other always come back. We might, for example, pursue a history of ghosts in terms of what J. Hillis Miller calls 'the disappearance of God' (Miller 1963) in the nineteenth century. If the Christian God is, as Karl Marx claimed, 'Spectre No. 1' (Marx 1976, 157), it is fair to suppose that this 'disappearance' has altered the conception of ghosts, holy or otherwise. Correspondingly, we might pursue a history of ghosts in terms of the nineteenth-century emergence of psychology and, in particular, psychoanalysis. Ghosts, that is to say, move into one's head. In the course of the nineteenth century the ghost is internalized: it becomes a psychological symptom, and no longer an entity issuing commandments on a mountain-top or a thing that goes bump in the night.

In particular, psychoanalytic accounts of ghosts have revolutionized literary studies. We might illustrate this in terms of what is arguably the greatest 'ghost work' in English literature, Shakespeare's *Hamlet* (1600–1601). The play itself is cryptic and elusive about the apparition and truthfulness of the figure of the ghost of Hamlet's father: why is it, for instance, that when the ghost appears in Act III, scene iv, it is only seen by Hamlet and not by his mother? But it is also clear that the play's representation of the ghost is grounded in the Christian mythology of Shakespeare's time – hence Hamlet's fear that 'The spirit that I have seen / May be a devil' who 'Abuses me to damn me' (II, ii, 598–9, 603). In twentieth-century psychoanalytic readings such as those advanced by Jacques Lacan or Nicolas Abraham, however, the ghost has become something very different. Lacan develops the ghostly or phantasmatic dimensions of the basic Freudian reading of the play as Oedipal drama: Hamlet cannot take revenge on his murderous uncle Claudius because he is haunted by the sense that what Claudius has done is what he would have wanted to do – kill his father and go to bed with his mother. In Lacan's scandalous and brilliant development of this reading of *Hamlet* (in a seminar in 1959), the ghost has to do with the phallus. As 'an imaginary object which the child comes to accept as being in the father's possession' (Wright 1992, 318), the phallus is in a sense the very symbol of paternity. For Lacan, the reason for Hamlet's inability to kill Claudius (until, at least, the moment of 'complete sacrifice', i.e. of his own death) is that 'one cannot strike the phallus, because the phallus, even the real phallus, is a *ghost*' (Lacan 1977b, 50–1). In this way, Lacan makes *Hamlet* an allegory of phallocentric culture: phallocentrism (everything in a culture that serves to equate the symbolic power of the father, the phallus, with authority, the proper, presence, truth itself) becomes a sort of farcical but terrible ghost story. In Lacan's reading, Hamlet's being haunted by his father is an allegory of the nature of the ego. In an appalling pun, he calls Hamlet an 'hommelette', a little man, a son, who is both dependent on his namesake King Hamlet and has his 'ego' scrambled – like an egg – by this haunting. As Maud Ellmann neatly summarizes it: 'the ego is a ghost' (Ellmann 1994, 17). There are problems with what Lacan does with a literary work like *Hamlet*, in particular in seeming to appropriate it simply as an allegorical means of presenting the 'truth' of psychoanalysis. But his thinking has proved extremely productive and stimulating for critics and theorists concerned to analyze the ghostliness of identity in literary texts and to question the nature and terms of the phallocentric ghost story in which we continue to have our being.

In the work of Nicolas Abraham, on the other hand, *Hamlet* is a central text for his theory that ghosts have to do with unspeakable secrets. The only reason why people think they see ghosts is because the dead take secrets with them when they die. In his essay 'Notes on the Phantom: A Complement to Freud's Metapsychology' (1975), Abraham observes that 'the theme of the dead – who, having suffered repression by their family or society, cannot enjoy, even in death, a state of authenticity – appears to be omnipresent (whether overtly expressed or disguised) on the fringes of religions and, failing that, in rational systems' (Abraham 1994, 171). Ghosts are everywhere, a painful fact of life. Abraham contends that 'the "phantom" [or "ghost"], whatever its form, is nothing but an invention of the living'. People see ghosts because 'the dead were shamed during their lifetime or . . . took unspeakable secrets to the grave'. These secrets remain, like a crypt, a gap, in the unconscious of the living. The ghost or phantom thus embodies 'the gap produced in us by the concealment of some part of a loved object's life . . . what haunts are not the dead, but the gaps left within us by the secrets of others' (171).

Abraham's account is helpful in illuminating the strangeness of Shakespeare's *Hamlet*, its obscure but persisting sense of secrets taken to the grave, of what the ghost calls the untellable 'secrets of my prison-house' (I, v, 14). But his 'Notes on the Phantom' also opens up new ways of thinking about ghosts in literature more generally: in effect, it inaugurates a theory of literature as a theory of ghosts. We can think of this ghostliness, first, in the relatively straightforward sense described by a character called Stella Rodney in Elizabeth Bowen's *The Heat of the Day* (1948): '"What's unfinished haunts one; what's unhealed haunts one"' (322). From the great fourteenth-century Middle English dream-elegy *Pearl* to Don DeLillo's very different dream-elegy *The Body Artist* (2001), literature is a place of ghosts, of what's unfinished, unhealed and even untellable. But more precisely, and perhaps more eerily, Abraham's work alerts us to a ghostliness about which characters, and even authors themselves, are unaware. Here we encounter the strangeness of the ghostly secret as, in Esther Rashkin's words, 'a situation or drama that is transmitted without being stated and without the sender's or receiver's awareness of its transmission' (Rashkin 1992, 4).

If psychoanalysis has been important in providing new ways of thinking about ghosts, however, this has not happened in a vacuum. As we suggested earlier, it is in fact part of a more general shift in how ghosts have been figured, theorized and experienced since the end of the nineteenth century. The emergence of psychology and psychoanalysis has its ghostly counterpart in literature, especially in the emergence of psychological realism and the psychological novel. Nowhere is this clearer than in the fiction of Henry James (1843–1916). In an essay on his ghost stories, published in 1921, Virginia Woolf writes:

> Henry James's ghosts have nothing in common with the violent old ghosts – the blood-stained sea captains, the white horses, the headless ladies of dark lanes and windy commons. They have their origin within us. They are present whenever the significant overflows our powers of expressing it; whenever the ordinary appears ringed by the strange. (Woolf 1988, 324)

Stories such as *The Turn of the Screw* (1898), 'The Beast in the Jungle' (1903) and 'The Jolly Corner' (1908) conjure and explore the ghostliness of experience in profoundly unsettling ways. All of these stories bear witness to the ungovernable, overflowing strangeness which Woolf evokes. More particularly, they also illustrate the sense of ghostly secrets, of what Abraham called the 'gaps left within us by the secrets of others', together with a sense of the ghostliness of the ego (or 'I') itself.

The last of these stories, 'The Jolly Corner', is especially forceful in its evocation of the idea of the 'I' as ghost. As in a number of other ghost stories – for example, Emily Brontë's *Wuthering Heights* (1848), Nathaniel Hawthorne's *The House of the Seven Gables* (1851) and George Douglas Brown's *The House with the Green Shutters* (1901) – 'The Jolly Corner' is both the name of a house and the name of the text itself. The literary work is a haunted house. 'The Jolly Corner' recounts how a 56-year-old, wealthy New Yorker called Spencer Brydon, long settled in Europe, makes a 'strangely belated return to America' (190), having been absent 33 years. He goes back to his childhood home, 'his house on the jolly corner, as he usually, and quite fondly, described it' (191). Rented out and a source of income for decades, the house is now, ostensibly, empty. Brydon becomes obsessed with the place, with visiting and wandering around it, increasingly caught up by the sense that it contains some ghostly secret of the past. Following a dense but queerly captivating third-person so-called omniscient narration, we are drawn into a hunt, in which the protagonist turns out to be both hunter and hunted, haunter and haunted. As the narrator asks, with the bizarre tone of detachment characteristic of the text as a whole: 'People enough, first and last, had been in terror of apparitions, but who had ever before become himself, in the apparitional world, an incalculable terror?' (202). Of course – and this is where fiction is itself most manifestly a *haunt* – this 'apparitional world' to which James refers only appears through writing. The very strangeness of fiction may be said to consist in this idea of a 'medium', a text, in which the apparitional and non-apparitional are made of the same stuff, indistinguishable. As E.M. Forster put it, in *Aspects of the Novel* (1927): 'Once in the realm of the fictitious, what difference is there between an apparition and a mortgage?' (Forster 1976, 103).

Despite appearances, then, we don't want to limit our talk about ghost stories just to ghost stories. Indeed we would like to suggest that the greater the literary work, the more ghostly it is. This might be one way of understanding what Derrida is getting at when he proclaims, in his book *Spectres of Marx*, that 'A masterpiece always moves, by definition, in the manner of a ghost' (Derrida 1994, 18). Playing on the earlier Latin sense of 'genius' as 'spirit', he says that a masterpiece is 'a work of *genius*, a *thing* of the *spirit* which precisely seems to *engineer itself* [*s'ingénier*]' (18). Masterpieces, such as *Beowulf* or *Hamlet* (which is the example Derrida is discussing) or James's 'The Jolly Corner' or Beckett's *Molloy*, are *works* that give a sense of having been spirited up, of working by themselves. Great works call to be read and reread while never ceasing to be strange, to resist reading, interpretation and translation. This is one basis for thinking about canonicity in Harold Bloom's terms: the canon is always a spectral affair. As he declares, in *The Western Canon*: 'One ancient test for the canonical remains fiercely valid: unless it demands rereading, the work does not qualify' (Bloom 1994, 30). A great work will always seem uncanny, at once strange and familiar; a surprising, unique addition to the canon and yet somehow foreseen, programmed by the canon; at once readable and defiant, elusive, baffling. For Bloom, writing itself is essentially about a relationship (always one of anxiety, according to him) with the dead, with earlier great writers. The point is most succinctly made by Bloom's precursor, T.S. Eliot, when he says in his essay 'Tradition and the Individual Talent' (1919) that the 'best', 'most individual' parts of a literary work are 'those in which the dead poets . . . assert their immortality most vigorously' (Eliot 1975b, 38). It is a relationship eerily evoked in Eliot's 'Little Gidding' (1943), where the speaker describes an encounter in which he 'caught the sudden look of some dead master/ . . . The eyes of a familiar compound ghost / Both intimate and unidentifiable' (Eliot 1975a, 193). For Bloom, as for Eliot, poetry is also a ghostly discourse in a more general sense. This is hauntingly exemplified by Wallace Stevens's 'Large Red Man Reading' (1948), in which the subject of the poem, the reader himself, evokes ghosts: 'There were ghosts that returned to earth to hear his phrases, / As he sat there reading, aloud, the great blue tabulae. / They were those from the wilderness of stars that had expected more' (423). We are all haunted: experience itself is never enough; and it is the ghostly discourse of literature which most sharply testifies to this.

One problem with talking about the canon in the way Bloom does is that it appears to be ahistorical: in other words, literature seems to belong to a time-less realm, the canon seems to be impervious to the material effects of social, political, economic and cultural history. Our argument in the present chapter, however, is that while literature is indeed 'ghost work', its haunt is historical. The ghosts of the twentieth century are not the same as those of the nine-teenth, and so on. We might, for example, reflect on the links between ghosts and technology. In the context of Western culture in the third millennium, and from the point of view of so-called common sense, we may like to believe that we do not believe in ghosts any more; but in important respects the world has become and is continuing to become increasingly ghostly. As Jacques Derrida has observed:

> Contrary to what we might believe, the experience of ghosts is not tied to a bygone historical period, like the landscape of Scottish manors, etc., but . . . is accentuated, accelerated by modern technologies like film, tele-vision, the telephone. These technologies inhabit, as it were, a phantom structure . . . When the very *first* perception of an image is linked to a structure of reproduction, then we are dealing with the realm of phantoms. (Derrida 1989, 61)

This recalls, or calls up, the image of Derrida in Ken McMullen's film *Ghost Dance* (1989) being asked if he believes in ghosts and replying: 'That's a hard question because, you see, I am a ghost.' In a film, everyone is a ghost. If the ghost is the revenant, that which uncannily returns without ever being prop-erly present in the first place, it becomes clear that, more than ever, we live in the midst of ghosts: the voice on the telephone is only ever the reproduction of a voice, the image on television or movie-screen only ever a reproduction. Freud conveys his amazement at the surreal nature of telephones when he remarks in *Civilization and Its Discontents* (1930) that 'With the help of the telephone [one] can hear at distances which would be [regarded] as unattain-able even in a fairytale' (1985e, 279). But since Freud's day, we have witnessed the new ghostly arrivals of the space age, the answer-phone, video-recorder, camcorder, personal computer, email, the Internet and World Wide Web, virtual reality, genetic engineering, nanotechnology, hyperspace and so forth.

Whether in literature, psychoanalysis or philosophy, contemporary thought is irrevocably hooked up to developments in technology and tele-communications. Contemporary literature faces new kinds of challenge in terms of how to represent, assimilate or think the increasing ghostliness of culture. The question of literature today is inseparable from an increasingly prevalent, indeed unavoidable encounter with a technics of the ghost. DeLillo's *The Body Artist*, for example, with its haunting evocations of ghost-voices and ghost-images in telephones, answering machines, voice-recorders, webcams and video projections, suggests that calling up ghosts in the twenty-first century is inseparable from such new technologies.

We would like to conclude by trying to explore some of these ideas in rela-tion to Toni Morrison's novel *Beloved*. This novel, first published in 1987, is set in America, in the years leading up to and following the abolition of slavery. It is about the unspeakable reality of slavery, about ghosts and the way in which US culture continues to be haunted by the atrocities of its past. The narrat-ive of the novel rests on the dynamic of ghostly secrets and the untellable. 'Beloved' is a baby murdered by her mother, Sethe, because the mother sees death for her daughter as preferable to slavery; 'Beloved' is also a beautiful 'shining' ghost of a woman who, years later, haunts the lives of Sethe and her other daughter, Denver, and Sethe's drifting partner Paul D. The novel, in its very title, is a ghost, or gathering of ghosts. *Beloved* is about

> what it took to drag the teeth of that saw under the little chin; to feel the baby blood pump like oil in [Sethe's] hands; to hold her face so her head would stay on; to squeeze her so she could absorb, still, the death spasms that shot through that adored body, plump and sweet with life. (251)

This, 250 pages into the text, is the most 'graphic' description we are given of what nevertheless haunts the book from the title onwards. The haunting is inscribed in the passage just quoted, for example, in the eerie double sense of 'still' (as adverb 'yet' and verb 'stop'): this gross moment is a still, stilled moment, caught in time, which still haunts, is still to be absorbed. On the final page of the novel we encounter the statement that 'This is not a story to pass on' (275). This statement suggests that the story should not or cannot be told, but also that it is not one we can pass by. The history of the United States is an untellable ghost story that must not, however, be forgotten. Every house in the US is a haunted house. As Baby Suggs says in grimly comic response to her daughter-in-law Sethe's suggestion that they vacate the baby-haunted house known only by its number (124): ' "Not a house in the country ain't packed to its rafters with some dead Negro's grief. We lucky this ghost is a baby. My husband's spirit was to come back in here? or yours? Don't talk to me" ' (5).

Beloved is set in the nineteenth century and is faithful to the modes of ghost-liness, spirits, tele-culture and telecommunications available at that time: the text opens with an attempted exorcism and an instance of apparent telekinesis ('The sideboard took a step forward but nothing else did': 4); there are allu-sions to telegraphy and the recently invented Morse code (110), to 'long-distance love' (95) and even to photography (275). But in other ways *Beloved* is a profoundly contemporary novel, a work of the late twentieth century not only in style and form but also in terms of its conception and implacable analysis of ghosts. In particular, it is written out of or through a psychoana-lytically inflected understanding of deferred meaning, a sense of trauma as ghostly, as that which comes back again and again, which continues, haunt-ingly. Morrison's novel is about the unspeakable not only now but in the future, slavery as a legacy *still*, not as something belonging to what we call the history books.

Marx in 1848 saw communism as 'a spectre . . . haunting Europe' (the famous opening words of *The Communist Manifesto*). One hundred and fifty years later, Derrida too sees communism as spectral. Hence its rapport with deconstruction. Deconstruction, as Derrida describes it, is concerned to think about the sense that 'everyone reads, acts, writes with *his or her* ghosts' (Derrida 1994, 139), to think about presence (and absence) as necessarily haunted, about meaning as spectralized. In these respects, deconstruction offers perhaps the most important contemporary theory of ghosts. Commun-ism is like democracy itself: 'it has always been and will remain spectral: it is always still to come' (Derrida 1994, 99).

Further reading

For two helpful and wide-ranging accounts of the ghostly in literature from a 'gothic' perspective, see David Punter, *The Literature of Terror*, 2nd edition (1996), and Fred Botting, *Gothic* (1997). Terry Castle (1995) has a good chapter on eighteenth- and nineteenth-century conceptions of ghosts, entitled 'Spectral Politics: Apparition Belief and the Romantic Imagination'. For a lucid and helpful exposition of Lacan's notoriously difficult essay on *Hamlet*, see Bruce Fink (1996). More generally, for some very good, clear and accessible readings of literature-with-Lacan, see Linda Ruth Williams (1995). More complex Lacanian accounts of the literary may be found in the brilliant work of Shoshana Felman (1987) and Jacqueline Rose (1996). Nicolas Abraham's 'Notes on the Phantom: A Complement to Freud's Metapsychology' and 'The Phantom of Hamlet *or* The Sixth Act, *preceded by* The Intermission of "Truth"' are collected in *The Shell and the Kernel* (1994). For a difficult but thought-provoking elaboration of Abraham's work on ghosts, see Esther Rashkin, *Family Secrets and the Psychoanalysis of Narrative* (1992). For a very rich but demanding account of spectrality and politics, focusing on *Hamlet* and the writings of Karl Marx, see Jacques Derrida, *Spectres of Marx* (1994). For the links between psychoanalysis, technology and telecommunications, see Derrida's challenging but fascinating *Archive Fever* (1995); for an account of the cultural and philosophical importance of the telephone, see Avital Ronell's *The Telephone Book* (1989). Peter Nicholls's essay, 'The Belated Postmodern: History, Phantoms and Toni Morrison' (1996), offers a subtle and stimulating reading of *Beloved* by way of many of the notions of the ghostly discussed in this chapter. For ghosts and Victorian literature, see Julian Wolfreys (2002); for ghosts and modernism, see Jean-Michel Rabaté (1996) and Helen Sword (2002); and for a good collection of essays on ghosts in relation to deconstruction, psychoanalysis and history, see Buse and Stott (1999).

17. Moving pictures

What do movies tell us about literature? Over recent decades cinema has increasingly come to be incorporated into university literature courses and literature professors have been pronouncing on films, as well as on novels, poems and plays. But what do we learn about literature when we watch and talk about film? And what do we learn about moving pictures when we study literature? We are all familiar (if not bored to tears) with talk of 'the film of the book' and even 'the book of the film', with discussion of how the film-version is or is not faithful to the 'original' book-version, of whether the film is as good as the book or vice versa. We want to get away from such talk: to put it simply, the film of the book is a film, it's not a book. We need a different vocabulary and different critical perspectives. Film is, nevertheless, inextricably tied in with the study of literature. Thinking about film provides innovative ways of thinking about literature, and vice versa. While the study of one informs, stimulates and provokes the study of the other, however, we do not want to suggest that the specificity of literature can or should be done away with. Our purpose in this chapter is, above all, to elucidate and explore the nature of the literary through thinking about film.

Sadly, there is no video or DVD of Wordsworth's great nineteenth-century autobiographical epic, *The Prelude*, available at your local video store. Nevertheless, in talking about moving pictures, we would like to focus on this poem. First published after the poet's death in 1850, *The Prelude* was written and revised between 1798 and 1839. Wordsworth began writing it, in other words, almost a hundred years before the first film (shown by the Lumière brothers in 1895). Not only has *The Prelude* not been turned into a movie, then, but it would be unreasonable to expect Wordsworth to be interested in the technologies of film production. Except for the fact that the word 'cinema' derives from the Greek *kinema*, 'motion', and that such precursors of the cinema as the panorama, the 'eidophusikon' and the 'diorama' were invented and became popular during Wordsworth's lifetime, the idea might seem quite deranged. But, as we hope to make clear, things are not as simple as this. *The Prelude*, we want to suggest, is composed or organized around a series of 'stills', moments taken from the moving picture of the poet's own mind, the cinema of his life. Wordsworth's poem is often regarded as the first great auto-biographical narrative in English, an account of 'the growth of a poet's mind' that – in the 1805 version we will concentrate on here – stretches over thirteen books and roughly nine thousand lines of blank verse. Vital to an understanding and appreciation of *The Prelude* are Wordsworth's 'spots of time', which are concerned with the effects of childhood memories on later life.

At a key moment in Book 11 of *The Prelude*, Wordsworth arrests the movement of his narrative, to speculate on its workings:

> There are in our existence spots of time,
> Which with distinct preeminence retain
> A renovating virtue, whence, depressed
> By false opinion and contentious thought,
> Or aught of heavier or more deadly weight
> In trivial occupations and the round
> Of ordinary intercourse, our minds
> Are nourished and invisibly repaired . . .
> > Life with me,
> As far as memory can look back, is full
> Of this beneficent influence.
> > > (*The Prelude* 1805, Book 11: 257–78)

There are certain memories, especially from early childhood, which stay with us, and have a capacity to renew, to 'nourish' and 'invisibly repair' our minds. 'As far as memory can look back': Wordsworth presents his autobiography and indeed his life in visual terms, and evokes these 'spots of time' as a kind of montage of moving pictures. 'Spots of time' are intensely visual and emphatically moving. They are arresting and affecting, moving in their stillness.

Wordsworth's 'spots of time' can be related to moving pictures in at least three ways. A spot of time is mobile, a matter of motion, a shifting scene. Second, it entails a moving or agitation of the mind and feelings. (The word 'emotion', we may recall, is from the Latin *ēmovēre*, to stir up, to create motion.) Finally, in a way that is not only or not simply anachronistic, we might suggest that a spot of time resembles a movie or movie-clip in terms of its apparently closed-off or framed quality (it's a 'spot'), and in terms more generally of what it allows us to think about the nature and experience of time itself. Above all perhaps, Wordsworth's 'spots of time' prefigure modern cinema in terms of what Gilles Deleuze calls 'the time-image' (Deleuze 1989). We will try to elucidate this idea in greater detail shortly.

Wordsworth famously declares in the Preface to *Lyrical Ballads* (1800) that poetry 'takes its origin from emotion recollected in tranquillity' (Wordsworth 1984, 611), suggesting that it involves at once a stilling and a revision or re-gathering of what has been moving. The phrase 'spots of time' likewise sug-gests something paradoxical, a strange fixing of time in place, *as* place. What, we may ask, is the 'time' of a 'spot of time'? In order to start thinking about this we need to reckon with the ways in which Wordsworth's poetry exploits the sheer slipperiness of poetic language. Even the brief 'spots of time' passage quoted a moment ago was written and revised over a period of years. In the earliest version, in 1799, the spots of time are said to have 'a fructifying virtue', a little later 'a vivifying virtue', and in a third version 'a renovating virtue' (see *The Prelude*, 428, n.2). For all their apparent stillness or tranquillity, these 'spots of time' are in motion, pictured in unstable, altering, moving language.

Let us zoom in on one of these 'spots of time', namely the passage in which Wordsworth recalls the experience, as a young boy, of stealing ravens' eggs:

> Nor less in springtime, when on southern banks
> The shining sun had from her knot of leaves
> 335   Decoyed the primrose flower, and when the vales
> And woods were warm, was I a plunderer then
> In the high places, on the lonesome peaks,
> Where'er among the mountains and the winds
> The mother-bird had built her lodge. Though mean
> 340   My object and inglorious, yet the end
> Was not ignoble. Oh, when I have hung
> Above the raven's nest, by knots of grass
> Or half-inch fissures in the slippery rock
> But ill sustained, and almost, as it seemed,
> 345   Suspended by the blast which blew amain,
> Shouldering the naked crag, oh, at that time
> While on the perilous ridge I hung alone,
> With what strange utterance did the loud dry wind
> Blow through my ears; the sky seemed not a sky
> 350   Of earth, and with what motion moved the clouds!
>
> The mind of man is framed even like a breath
> And harmony of music . . .
>
> (*The Prelude* 1805, Book 1: 333–52)

This 'spot of time' apparently ends with the words 'with what motion moved the clouds!' We have quoted the words that follow on from it in order to draw attention to the remarkable, often unfathomable breaks that characteristically splice together Wordsworth's poetry. Having concluded his moving picture of this spot of time, he starts a new verse-paragraph, now in a quite different tone and place: 'The mind of man is framed even like a breath / And harmony of music'. But the boy Wordsworth is literally left hanging, clinging to the tiny fissures in the rock and seeming to be held in place largely by the wind itself. With the extraordinary editing of this moment, with this singular cliff-hanger, we are offered a fitting example of what Paul de Man calls Wordsworth's 'sheer language' (de Man 1984, 92). 'Sheer language' means language alone, working by itself, in the sense that our only access – and indeed *Wordsworth's* only access – to these memories of stealing ravens' eggs is in and through language. But we might also hear in 'sheer language' the sense of something precipitous, vertiginously headlong. The blank on the page immediately following 'with what motion moved the clouds!' figures a sort of abyss.

Wordsworth chooses to stop the spot, leaves himself (a portrait of the poet as a young thief) on a perilous ridge, just about hanging on by 'knots of grass / Or half-inch fissures in the slippery rock'. 'Oh, when I have hung / Above': which way up is he? What is the point of view? This last question actually enfolds three questions, each of them as relevant to film as to literary studies: (1) What is the point of view in a literal sense? From what position or angle is this being seen? (2) What is the narrative point of view? Who is seeing it and who is describing it, and from what perspective or perspectives? (3) What is the temporal perspective? How are issues of past, present and future involved here? From what position in time is this 'spot of time' to be viewed? One of the most important differences between literary narrative and film narrative is that, with the former, the reader is almost always presented with a knowledge of what is going on in the thoughts and feelings of a specific narrator or character. With literary narrative you get 'inside information' as to what is going on in the mind and body of a character. This is particularly the case when the story is told by a so-called omniscient or (perhaps more accurately) telepathic narrator. More generally, however, a fictional exposure of 'secret' interiority is at the very heart of literature and there is something eerie about this – about the idea of being able to read the mind of the author, a narrator or character. This interiority is fundamentally alien to film: the 'eye of the camera' is doomed to the visible. The only way that film can provide 'inside information' is through strategies or techniques from literature (the 'telling' voice-over, in particular).

Being John Malkovich (dir. Spike Jonze, 1999) is a witty, at moments hilarious movie that ironically acknowledges and foregrounds these limits of film and film discourse. The film involves the discovery and exploitation of a 'portal' through which people are able to enter the head of the 'real-life' actor and have the chance of 'being John Malkovich'. One of the most memorable scenes is when Malkovich himself insists on going through the portal and finds himself (as it were) in a dreamlike restaurant-cum-nightclub surrounded by other John Malkovichs. At a table where a couple of John Malkovichs are dining, he looks over the restaurant menu and sees that it consists entirely of dishes called 'Malkovich'. Everywhere he is confronted by a proliferation of John Malkovichs, all of them saying (or singing) over and over again the single word 'Malkovich', 'Malkovich', 'Malkovich'. In this cinematic hall of mirrors everyone is the same, the name says it all, and interiority is rendered comically non-existent.

Wordsworth's account of stealing ravens' eggs allows us a particularly intimate sense of the poet's interior world. While Spike Jonze's film seems at once to celebrate and ridicule the mad narcissism of a stammering 'Malkovich, Malkovich, Malkovich', Wordsworth's poetry offers us a rather different experience of what Keats called the 'egotistical sublime' (Keats 1958, 1:387). As William Hazlitt once remarked: Wordsworth 'sees nothing but himself and the universe . . . His egotism is in some respects a madness' (Hazlitt 1930–34, 5:163). This conception of Wordsworth corresponds, perhaps rather unnervingly, to how Hugo Münsterberg described the impact of cinema in his 1916 book, *The Photoplay: A Psychological Study*: 'the massive outer world has lost its weight, it has been freed from space, time, and causality, and has been clothed in the forms of our own consciousness' (Münsterberg 1916, 220, quoted in Armstrong 240). We might be tempted to think of Wordsworth's account of stealing ravens' eggs as profoundly ego-centred: what else would you expect from that self-regarding genre known as autobiography? But we would argue that the poem also goes far beyond this obsession with self. Besides the strange and disorienting ambiguity of the literal 'point of view' of the 'plunderer' (above or below the sky, upside down or right way up?), for example, there are the temporal disjunctions of the scene. This 'spot of time' is both 'at that time' (1.346), in the past, and at the same time it is in this strange 'here and now' of sheer language, being written or being read, still. It is also, crucially, a moving picture that entails an intimate sense of the unknowable and incalculable. It involves a logic of unforeseeable *becoming*: 'spots of time' work 'invisibly', we are told, and go on working, work on, in the future. The scene shifts inwardly, from the present perfect tense ('when I have hung' [1.341]) to simple past ('I hung'). The place of the present 'I', the 'I' that recollects, speaks or writes, gives way to an image of alien suspension, an 'I' blown through with 'strange utterance', lost to an alien sky: 'With what strange utterance did the loud dry wind / Blow through my ears; the sky seemed not a sky / Of earth, and with what motion moved the clouds!'

Alfred Hitchcock's *Vertigo* (1958) is also a masterpiece of suspense. In the opening sequence the protagonist Scottie (James Stewart) is seen hanging on for dear life to the ripped guttering of a San Francisco rooftop as a police officer, having tried to help him, plummets to his death. As Susan White puts it: 'we never see (or hear about) Scottie's rescue – in a sense [he] remains hanging over the edge of the precipice throughout the film' (White 1991, 911). Something similar happens in *The Prelude*: in a sense the boy trying to steal ravens' eggs remains hanging there throughout the rest of that epic poem. The moment in *Vertigo* is, we might say, weirdly Wordsworthian. On the one hand it is difficult not to project (the word is as much cinematic as psychoanalytic) back on to the past, on to literary works of the pre-film era, critical ideas and perspectives generated by film. On the other, it is striking how many of our current ways of thinking were in fact already quite firmly established in the nineteenth century.

Had he still been living when cinema began, Wordsworth would have been at once fascinated and appalled. With its intimations of cinematicity, however, *The Prelude* also suggests that he would not have been entirely surprised either. Wordsworth's poem communicates the power of ocularcentrism, of what he calls 'The state . . . / In which the eye was master of the heart . . . The most despotic of our senses' (Book 11: 170–3). The quasi-hypnotic draw of twenty-first-century 'visual culture' (TV, video, cinema, DVD, computer games, and so on) was, we might say, already in play in Wordsworth's day. Thus the poet reminisces, for example, about 'Still craving combinations of new forms, / New pleasure, wider empire for the sight' (Book 11: 191–2). And while, in his amazing account of life in London (in Book 7), he conveys a moral disapproval of such newfangled visual pleasures as panoramas and 'mimic sights that ape / The absolute presence of reality' (Book 7: 248–9), his own depiction of the city and its inhabitants is achieved through a series of moving pictures. In this way he evokes London as 'the quick dance / Of colours, lights and forms, the Babel din, / The endless stream of men and moving things' (Book 7: 156–8). And in one of the most memorable encounters anywhere in his poetry, Wordsworth picks out – or feels uncannily picked out by – a blind beggar 'amid the moving pageant' (Book 7: 610). The 'spectacle' at the centre of this 'moving pageant' is reproduced and interiorized in turn as a moving picture, a kind of monstrous mill in Wordsworth's mind: 'My mind did at this spectacle turn round / As with the might of waters . . . I looked, / As if admonished from another world' (ll. 616–23).

In another 'spot of time' in *The Prelude*, Wordsworth recalls when, aged five, he is out riding with a servant (or 'guide') called James, becomes separated from him and stumbles on alone, down to a valley where 'in former times / A murderer had been hung in iron chains' (Book 11: 288–9). Nearby he comes across the eerie graffiti of 'fresh and visible' letters scored in the turf where 'Some unknown hand had carved the murderer's name' (l.293). He quickly quits this 'spot', 'reascending the bare common' (ll.301–2), approaching 'A naked pool that lay beneath the hills' (l.303) overlooked by a summit with a stone beacon on top. Closer at hand, he sees a windblown girl bearing a pitcher on her head. And, all of a sudden, he is halted at this sight:

> It was, in truth,
> An ordinary sight, but I should need
> Colours and words that are unknown to man
> To paint the visionary dreariness
> Which, while I looked all round for my lost guide,
> Did at that time invest the naked pool,
> The beacon on the lonely eminence,
> The woman, and her garments vexed and tossed
> By the strong wind. (Book 11: 307–15)

Wordsworth writes of painting with colours and words that are unknown (not yet, perhaps never to be, invented), as if it were a matter of something fixed, the landscape painting of a visionary dreariness (in effect, a seeing of seeing, a vision of visionariness); and yet, as with the earlier passage we encountered ('with what motion moved the clouds!'), it is at the same time explicitly a question of a moving picture (the girl's 'garments vexed and tossed / By the strong wind'). Wordsworth's 'spots of time' are concerned with senses of movement that have yet to be captured in colours or words.

In this respect his writing offers a singular twist to the classic tradition of *ut pictura poesis*, in which painting and poetry are regarded as 'sister arts', painting being seen as a kind of mute poetry and poetry a speaking picture. In his *Lectures on Rhetoric and Belles Lettres* (1759–83), Hugh Blair echoes this tradition when he argues that 'a true poet makes us imagine that we see [the object or natural landscape] before our eyes; he catches the distinguishing features; he gives it the colours of life and reality; he places it in such a light that a painter could copy it after him' (Blair 1842, 549). Wordsworth's concern is rather with the sense of an impossible word-painting, with a sense of the impossibility of *ekphrasis* (a verbal representation of the visual). He is moved by a vision he can neither paint nor describe, that is not yet realized or realizable.

In this way we might suggest that Wordsworth's spots of time are concerned with that sense of 'moving' evoked in the 'Intimations' ode, where the child is described as 'Moving about in worlds not realized'. They are (about) moving pictures, visions in process, still to be realized, as well as sights that move, disturb, exhilarate, stir the emotions.

Our attempt to explore the moving pictures of Wordsworth's 'spots of time' is in part inspired by the work of the philosopher Gilles Deleuze (1925–95). Deleuze has provided perhaps the most provocative account of cinema in recent decades. His books *Cinema 1: The Movement-Image* (Deleuze 1986) and *Cinema 2: The Time-Image* (Deleuze 1989) are complex and challenging, in particular because he argues that cinema alters the very nature of thinking, writing and philosophy. Elaborating on the work of Henri Bergson, Deleuze contends that the universe becomes 'a cinema in itself, a metacinema' (Deleuze 1986, 59). With cinema, Deleuze argues, we see 'seeing'. It is no longer a question of 'point of view', of *someone's* (a character's or a director's) point of view. The eye of the camera is not an 'I'. As Claire Colebrook glosses it: 'What makes the machine-like movement of the cinema so important is that the camera can "see" or "perceive" without imposing concepts. The camera does not organise images from a fixed point but itself moves across movements' (Colebrook 2002, 32). Related to this is what Deleuze calls the 'time-image', that is to say the way in which cinema presents us with a thinking or experience of time cut off from any question of a succession of past-present-future.

The time-image is not an image *of* something, it is what comes about with the effects of 'false continuity and irrational cuts' (Deleuze 1989, xi), for example with a certain disjunctiveness of seeing and hearing. Such disjunctiveness is evident from the very start of Hitchcock's *Vertigo*, as we are presented with the spiralling graphics and seeing of seeing in Kim Novak's eye, Bernard Herrmann's madly melodramatic, 'irrational' soundtrack accompanying us into the opening realization of vertigo in the image of Scottie hanging from the rooftop. The opening of *Vertigo* illustrates the distinctiveness of the cinematic image which, according to Deleuze, involves 'a dissociation of the visual and the sound' (Deleuze 1989, 256). And although it is a poem, something like this vertginous 'dissociation' might be read back into Wordsworth's juxtaposition of the unearthly sky and moving motion of the clouds and the 'strange utterance' of 'the loud dry wind' as his younger self clings to the 'slippery rock' in *The Prelude*.

Deleuze's work engages with new kinds of thinking, writing and becoming. His books on cinema, along with his writings on literary texts, challenge us with the question: how should we think, read and write about literature *after* cinema, or with what we have learnt from cinema in mind? And, indeed, what new kinds of literary writing might be envisaged? Leo Tolstoy appears to have foreseen such questions when he commented in 1908, a year before he died and almost twenty years before the first talkies:

> [cinema] will make a revolution in our life – in the life of writers . . . We shall have to adapt ourselves to the shadowy screen and to the cold machine. A new form of writing will be necessary . . . This swift change of scene, this blending of emotion and experience – it is much better than the heavy, long-drawn-out kind of writing to which we are accustomed. It is closer to life. In life, too, changes and transitions flash before our eyes, and emotions of the soul are like a hurricane. The cinema has divined the mystery of motion. And that is its greatness. (Tolstoy, quoted in Murphet and Rainford 2003, 1)

As Colin MacCabe remarks, in a recent essay entitled 'On Impurity: the Dialectics of Cinema and Literature', 'it is impossible to give a serious account of any twentieth-century writer without reference to cinema' (MacCabe 2003, 16). This is the case not only with such cinematically self-conscious writers as John Dos Passos, Gabriel García Márquez or Salman Rushdie, but also with writers such as Virginia Woolf, James Joyce and T.S. Eliot. In an interview entitled 'The Brain Is the Screen' (1986), Deleuze uses cinema to make some illuminating remarks about works of art in general. He offers a compelling vision of the nature of literary works, the future of moving pictures and 'new emotions':

> A work of art always entails the creation of new spaces and times (it's not a question of recounting a story in a well-determined space and time; rather, it is the rhythms, the lighting, and the space-times themselves that must become the true characters). A work should bring forth the problems and questions that concern us rather than provide answers. A work of art is a new syntax, one that is much more important than vocabulary and that excavates a foreign language in language. Syntax in cinema amounts to the linkages and relinkages of images, but also to the relation between sound and the visual image. If one had to define culture, one could say that it [consists in] perceiving that works of art are much more concrete, moving, and funny than commercial products. In creative works there is a multiplication of emotion, a liberation of emotion, and even the invention of new emotions. This distinguishes creative works from the prefabricated emotions of commerce. (Deleuze 2000, 370)

If it is impossible to read modernist and postmodern literature without engaging with questions of cinema, it is also the case that we can no longer read

Wordsworth without doing so through the kinds of thinking that cinema makes possible. At the same time, it is part of the cryptic and enduring power of Wordsworth's poetry, and of his 'spots of time' in particular, that they can continue to give us new ways of thinking about emotions, liberating and inventing in moving pictures.

Further reading

Literature and Visual Technologies: Writing After Cinema, eds Murphet and Rainford (2003), is a valuable collection of essays on the comparatively new field of reading film through literature and literature through film. For two critical works that, like the present chapter, are concerned with thinking about literature in relation to the history and prehistory of cinema, see Bill Readings's 'Milton at the Movies' (in Readings and Schaber 1993) and Grahame Smith's *Dickens and the Dream of Cinema* (2003). Gilles Deleuze's *Cinema 2: The Time-Image* (1989) is a fascinating and profound study, though certainly not easy on first encounter. Claire Colebrook's introductory book, *Gilles Deleuze* (2002), is a lucid and invaluable guide to this difficult but important thinker. For a recent collection of essays more specifically focusing on Deleuze and the literary, see Buchanan and Marks (2000). On the power of the eye and vision, see (so to speak) Martin Jay's monumental *The Denigration of Vision in Twentieth-Century French Thought* (1993), and, more generally in relation to textuality, the fine range of essays collected in *Vision and Textuality* (eds Melville and Readings, 1995). For a recent study of feeling, affect and being moved, see Eve Kosofsky Sedgwick's *Touching Feeling* (2003). For excellent accounts of the long-standing literary-critical tradition of interest in the interaction of word and image, see Mitchell 'Iconology' (1986) and 'Picture Theory' (1994), Krieger, 'Ekphrasis' (1992), and Heffernan, 'Museum of Words' (1993).

18. Sexual difference

John laughs at me, of course, but one expects that in marriage.

John is practical in the extreme. He has no patience with faith, an intense horror of superstition, and he scoffs openly at any talk of things not to be felt and seen and put down in figures.

John is a physician, and *perhaps*—(I would not say it to a living soul, of course, but this is dead paper and a great relief to my mind)—*perhaps* that is one reason I do not get well faster.

You see he does not believe I am sick! (9–10)

This passage from Charlotte Perkins Gilman's short story *The Yellow Wallpaper* (1892) presents a number of important issues concerning sexual difference. In particular it dramatizes conventional presuppositions about the differences between men and women. The phrase 'of course' may signal that the first sentence is satirical and ironic, but the implication remains: a woman is subordinate to her husband and cannot expect to be taken seriously. The differences between men and women, in this passage, are primarily a matter of recognizing certain kinds of gender stereotypes. Such stereotypes depend to a considerable extent on a conceptual opposition: man versus woman. And, like other binary oppositions, this involves a hierarchy. John, the man, is active, 'practical', dominant, unemotional. The narrator, the woman, appears to be passive, non-practical, subordinate, emotional. The opposition between the man and the woman is underscored by the insistent stress on the man's actions, qualities and characteristics (John does this, John is such-and-such) and the corresponding *absence* of information regarding the woman. Gilman is exposing a hierarchy, in other words, involving the dominance of the man and the subordination of the woman. *The Yellow Wallpaper* has become something of a modern classic as regards the literary representation of women and the idea of what Elaine Showalter has called, in a book of that name, 'A Literature of Their Own'.

The Yellow Wallpaper is a first-person narrative which tells the story of a woman whose husband insists that, because she is ill, she must remain confined in a room with revolting yellow wallpaper in a large old house where the couple and their baby are staying for the summer. The woman narrates the frightening process whereby she comes to believe that there is some *other* woman in the room, a woman behind or inside the wallpaper. The text culminates with the demonic turn by which she has *become* the woman behind the wallpaper but has got out. The husband comes into the room to discover his wife creeping around the walls: 'Now why should that man have fainted? But he did, and right across my path by the wall, so that I had to creep over him every time!' (36)

The Yellow Wallpaper offers a particularly striking example of what Sandra Gilbert and Susan Gubar talk about as 'the madwoman in the attic' (Gilbert and Gubar 1979). The story is a dramatic and powerfully ironic account of how a woman is repressed, confined and ultimately driven crazy, specifically by her husband, but more generally by the violence of patriarchy. It is no coincidence, therefore, that *The Yellow Wallpaper* should have been written by a woman known in her own lifetime for her contribution to the women's movement in the United States and, in particular, for her work of non-fiction, *Women and Economics* (1898). *The Yellow Wallpaper* can be read as a powerful satire on patriarchal society and values. In particular it emphasizes the ways in which violence against women need not be physical in a literal sense, but can nevertheless be all-pervading. It is what we could call the soft face of oppression that is satirically presented, for example, when the narrator notes: '[John] is very careful and loving, and hardly lets me stir without special direction' (12). Or when she says: 'It is so hard to talk with John about my case, because he is so wise, and because he loves me so' (23). As these remarks indicate, the text is also about the woman's collusion in her confinement and in her oppressed state. The text explores the ways in which the problem of patriarchy has not only to do with the behaviour of men but also, just as urgently, with that of women.

All literary texts can be thought about in terms of how they represent gender difference and how far they may be said to reinforce or question gender-role stereotypes. Take, for example, an early sixteenth-century sonnet, such as Thomas Wyatt's 'Whoso List to Hunt':

Whoso list to hunt, I know where is an hind,
But as for me, alas, I may no more.
The vain travail hath wearied me so sore
I am of them that farthest cometh behind.
Yet may I, by no means, my wearied mind
Draw from the deer, but as she fleeth afore,
Fainting I follow. I leave off therefore,
Since in a net I seek to hold the wind.
Who list her hunt, I put him out of doubt,
As well as I, may spend his time in vain.
And graven with diamonds in letters plain
There is written, her fair neck round about,
'*Noli me tangere*, for Caesar's I am,
And wild for to hold, though I seem tame.'

Wyatt's sonnet figures men and women in a number of gender-stereotypical ways. Man is the hunter, woman is the hunted. Man is the subject, active, full of 'travail', whereas woman is the object, indeed she is not even figured as human but instead as simply 'an hind', a female deer. Moreover Wyatt's poem integrates this gender-stereotyping within its very structure of address. The poem, that is to say, is addressed to men (to those who wish, or 'list', to hunt), not to women: in this way it appears to offer a classic example of the construction or assumption of the reader as male. Gilman's short story and Wyatt's sonnet are radically different kinds of text, written at completely different periods and from within almost unimaginably heterogeneous cultures (England in the early sixteenth century, the United States in the late nineteenth century). Yet they do offer significant parallels. Both in their quite different ways invite us to reflect critically on the question of gender and more particularly on the power of gender-stereotypes. In both texts, we encounter such stereotypes (I am a woman and therefore subordinate, passive, hysterical, an object, etc.), but we are also provoked to a questioning of the very idea of gender opposition as such.

On one level, then, there is a valuable and perhaps unavoidable reading of literary texts in terms of essentialism: there is essentially one form of sexual difference and that is the difference between male and female, boys and girls, men and women. The notion of essentialism here consists primarily in anatomical or biological difference: the man has a penis, whereas the woman does not, or the woman has a pudendum, breasts and a child-bearing capacity whereas the man has none of these. Various kinds of gender-stereotypes are then articulated, as it were, on to this essentialism: the male is strong, active, rational, the female is weak, passive, irrational and so forth. Within the logic of this description – which has dominated the history of Western culture – having a penis seems to have been so important that it becomes appropriate to speak of its *symbolic* significance, in other words to speak of the *phallus*. Texts or particular aspects of texts can then be described not only in terms of the patriarchal but also in terms of the phallocentric or phallogocentric. Patriarchy involves upholding the supposed priority of the male. In Gilman's text, for example, John is the head (or patriarch) of the family, he makes the decisions and rules the household. The notion of phallocentrism, on the other hand, involves some of the more subtle, more symbolic and perhaps more fundamental ways in which the phallus can be equated with power, authority, presence, and the right to possession. The 'logo' of 'phallogocentrism' points us towards the argument (promoted by theorists such as Jacques Derrida, Hélène Cixous and Luce Irigaray) that the very notions of truth, reason, rationality, the proper, meaning, etc. are phallocentric. Jonathan Culler has summarized this as follows:

> Numerous aspects of criticism, including the preference for metaphor over metonymy, the conception of the author, and the concern to distinguish legitimate from illegitimate meanings, can be seen as part of the promotion of the paternal. Phallogocentrism unites an interest in patriarchal authority, unity of meaning, and certainty of origin. (Culler 1983, 61)

It is in this context, then, that the French theorist Irigaray speculates on the possibilities of kinds of language that would somehow break with the masculine. As she remarks:

> a feminine language would undo the unique meaning, the proper meaning of words, of nouns: which still regulates all discourse. In order for there to be a proper meaning, there must indeed be a unity somewhere. But if feminine language cannot be brought back to any unity, it cannot be simply described or defined. (Irigaray 1977, 65)

As may already be clear from these very brief accounts of phallocentrism and phallogocentrism, reading literary texts in terms of sexual difference can be more complex and demanding than simply recognizing the gender oppositions and hierarchies to be found at work in a text. As feminist criticism has established, such kinds of recognition are crucial. Inevitably perhaps, we tend to start from an essentialist position and our reading of literary texts is guided by this. But what is most important about literary representations of gender is not merely that a particular text can be shown to be sexist or phallocentric, or even feminist. Rather it is that literary texts call into question many of our essentialist ideas about gender.

In other words it could be argued that there is no such thing as a feminist, or a masculinist or a sexist, literary work *in itself*: it all depends on how it is read. An obvious example here would be the work of D.H. Lawrence. Kate Millett's *Sexual Politics* (1969) was a groundbreaking book because of the acuity and passion with which it attacked Lawrence's (and other male writers') work for its 'phallic consciousness' (238) and degradation of women. Millett's account still makes powerful reading, but it is also in important respects reductive – especially in its author-centred representations of the novels it discusses. For Millett, that is to say, the aim of literary criticism is to criticize the male author – a figure whose male voice, male presence and male ideas are unequivocally clear, for Millett, in everything Lawrence wrote. More recently, however, critics have tended to focus more on the tensions and paradoxes within Lawrence's writings in themselves, rather than on the author-figure thought to be looming behind them. Critics such as Leo Bersani (1978) and Jonathan Dollimore (1991) have thus emphasized the idea of Lawrence's texts as in many ways working *against themselves* and as unsettling various assumptions that we may have (or Lawrence may have had) about gender as such. Thus Dollimore, for example, focuses on the fact that 'so much [in Lawrence's work] is fantasized from the position of the woman . . . and in a voice that is at once *blindingly heterosexist and desperately homoerotic*' (Dollimore 1991, 275).

We can consider these points by looking again at the Gilman and Wyatt texts. As we have suggested, *The Yellow Wallpaper* reads, on one level at least, as a literary case-study in the oppression and repression of a middle-class white woman in the United States in the late nineteenth century. It may be read as a dynamic feminist demand for liberation from the maddening claustrophobia of patriarchy. But the text is at the same time powerfully equivocal. For instance, simply in terms of the narrative and its conclusion, we must ask ourselves: how much of an affirmation is it, if the only possible liberation for a woman is madness? Is it possible to speak on behalf of women from the position of madness? If, as the narrative of Gilman's text implies, the only way out of patriarchy is to fall, or creep, into madness, is there in fact any way out at all? Isn't *The Yellow Wallpaper* as much caught up in the net of the patriarchal as, say, Henry Miller's *Sexus* (1949)? Such questions are not meant as a way of *closing down* the Gilman text by reducing it to the transmission of a merely negative message about the position of women in relation to patriarchy. Rather they are questions which the text itself can be said to pose:

to read *The Yellow Wallpaper* critically is to engage with its equivocality, with its ironic and complex refigurations of essentialist notions of gender.

In this context it is not surprising that some of the most provocative feminist criticism since the mid-1970s has been closely bound up with what is referred to as deconstruction. Deconstruction could be defined as a strategy of disruption and transformation with regard to every and any kind of essentialism. 'Essentialism' here would include, for example, the assumption that everyone is irreversibly either male or female, that the literal is inescapably different from the figurative, that speech is fundamentally different from writing and so on. In particular, deconstruction involves the desedimentation of those conceptual oppositions through which essentialism operates. In the first place this has meant inverting the hierarchy of male and female, masculine and feminine, father and mother, phallic and (for example) clitoral, along with related couplings such as strong and weak, active and passive, rational and irrational, practical and impractical, presence and absence. Deconstruction, however, entails not only the inversion or overturning of hierarchies but also the transformation of the basis on which they have operated. This might be thought about in relation to the passage from *The Yellow Wallpaper* with which we began this chapter. The narrator tells us: 'John is practical in the extreme. He has no patience with faith, an intense horror of superstition, and he scoffs openly at any talk of things not to be felt and seen and put down in figures' (9). What we have here is an apparently straightforward assertion of the physician husband's practicality and rationalism, implicitly contrasted with the narrator's own lack of these qualities. But on another level the passage might be said to disturb and even transform the very basis on which we presume to talk about the practical and impractical, the rational and irrational. After all, as George Eliot's great novel *Daniel Deronda* (1876) rhetorically asks: 'Who supposes that it is an impossible contradiction to be superstitious and rationalising at the same time?' (48). Indeed, as Gilman's text here intimates, rationalism can be construed as in turn a kind of superstition. To 'scoff openly', as John does, suggests exaggeration and defensiveness. To have 'an intense horror of superstition' is itself perhaps a mark of superstitiousness. There is, in short, a disturbance of the grounds of reason (here and elsewhere) in Gilman's text: this is deconstructive in the sense that it is specifically concerned with a suspension of the logic of non-contradiction. It is interested in disturbing what is perhaps the founding claim of Western philosophy, namely Aristotle's proposal that 'it is impossible for anything at the same time to be and not to be' (Aristotle 1941, 737). This 'law of contradiction' is, as Paul de Man puts it, 'the most certain of all principles' (de Man 1979, 120).

Deconstructive feminism puts this founding claim into question. It is rather like the Freudian argument that the unconscious knows no contradictions: one can dream of a compound figure, for example, someone who is (say) both your mother and not your mother but someone else at the same time. Feminism in its deconstructive mode, then, undermines the very basis on which identity and non-identity are constructed. A deconstructive reading of *The Yellow Wallpaper*, for example, might elaborate on the logic whereby the narrator is both mad and not mad at the same time. The narrator both is and is not the woman behind the wallpaper. The narrator both is and is not herself.

Since the late 1960s, feminism has revolutionized literary and cultural studies. But, as recent critical work such as Judith Butler's suggests, the political force of feminism remains limited so long as it promotes itself as an 'identity politics' (politics based on identifying oneself with a particular, usually marginalized and oppressed, group). The problem with the essentialism or (in Butler's terms) the *foundationalism* of 'identity politics' is that 'it presumes, fixes, and constrains the very "subjects" that it hopes to represent and liberate' (Butler 1990, 148). The subjects who empower themselves through 'identity politics' are in some sense disempowered by their very subjection to it. This, in part, is why we have titled this chapter 'Sexual difference' rather than, say, 'Gender and identity'. What the term 'sexual difference' may usefully gesture towards, then, is the idea that identity itself is perhaps most productively and critically seen as fissured, haunted, at odds with itself. As Derrida has remarked, 'an identity is never given, received, or attained': the assertion of identity always betrays a '*disorder of identity*' (Derrida 1998b, 28, 14). 'Sexual difference' involves not only difference *between* but difference *within*. We are, in Julia Kristeva's phrase, 'strangers to ourselves' (Kristeva 1991). *The Yellow Wallpaper* could be seen to enact or allegorize this notion of difference *within*. That is to say, it subverts the idea of identity itself, in its presentation of a woman who is, in a sense, uncannily double, always already inhabited by another, in this case the woman behind the wallpaper. The text thus prompts us to ask: what is a woman (and conversely, what is a man) if she is double within herself?

This sort of disruption or subversion of identity is further suggested at the level of *writing* itself. The narrator of *The Yellow Wallpaper* presents herself as a writer. This is indicated in the passage we cited at the beginning of this chapter: 'I would not say it to a living soul, of course, but this is dead paper and a great relief to my mind.' The narrator attests to her own 'imaginative power and habit of story-making' (15). With this in mind we could suggest the following hypothesis: wherever there is writing, sexual or gender identity becomes equivocal, questionable, open to transformation. The hypothesis might be considered in relation to Thomas Wyatt's 'Whoso list to hunt'. We have suggested earlier how clearly this poem seems to categorize and distinguish between men and women, even to the extent of postulating its very addressee as a male. A conventional response to this poem is, in the first instance at least, firmly guided by essentialist and oppositional thinking: man vs. woman, hunter vs. hunted, etc. Originally, of course, Wyatt's poem would have circulated privately among a small group of aristocratic men. And indeed, as Marguerite Waller has remarked in her reading of this poem, even in the twentieth century the critical tendency has been to deny 'the position of any reader who is not male, heterosexual, and politically privileged' (Waller 1987, 6). But there are other ways in which to think about this poem and to appreciate that, like other literary works, it can be seen to call into question many of our essentialist ideas and assumptions. For example, through its implicit elision of a female reader it provokes the questions: How should a woman read this poem? Is it possible that the apparent *absence* of women as addressees might be construed as a testament to the idea that a woman reader is precisely what the poem calls for but cannot have, and that this strange absence is figured in the rhetoric of the poem itself, for instance in the image of trying to hold the wind in a net? Is the wind that is woman more or less powerful than the net? Is the net of patriarchy that we mentioned earlier only so much wind in turn?

Or to put these questions in a somewhat different form: To whom does writing belong? The idea that writing (and therefore literature in general) is a site of questioning and possible transformation of sexual or gender identity applies to both the Wyatt sonnet as a whole and to its final couplet in particular:

> '*Noli me tangere*, for Caesar's I am,
> And wild for to hold, though I seem tame.'

Whose words are these? To whom are they addressed? Such writing, 'graven with diamonds in letters plain', renders paradoxical the distinctions between man and woman, man and man (the speaker and Caesar), the touchable and untouchable, wild and tame, addressor and addressee.

Literary texts at once encourage *and* exceed the parameters of essentialist or identity-oriented readings. By rendering the nature of sexual identity fundamentally questionable they provide a particularly disturbing as well as exhilarating space in which to reflect on the question that Foucault asks in the context of the memoirs of Herculine Barbin, a nineteenth-century French hermaphrodite: 'Do we truly need a true sex?' (Foucault 1980b, 3).

Further reading

Joseph Bristow's *Sexuality* (1997) provides a very clear and helpful account of contemporary theories of sexual desire and how these frame issues of identity and difference; see also Glover and Kaplan, *Genders* (2000). Specifically on literature, sexuality and modernism, see Joseph Allen Boone's *Libidinal Currents: Sexuality and the Shaping of Modernism* (1998). For accessible and clear accounts of contemporary feminist criticism and theory, see Toril Moi, *Sexual/Textual Politics* (1985) and Rita Felshi, *Literature After Feminism* (2003). For a more challenging and radical view, see Judith Butler's *Gender Trouble* (1990) and *Bodies that Matter* (1993). *Speaking of Gender* (Showalter, ed., 1989) is a good collection of essays on gender, and Warhol and Herndl, eds, *Feminisms* (1997) is a comprehensive collection of over seventy classic and more recent essays on different aspects of feminist literary criticism and theory. Another good collection, oriented towards rethinking gender from within, is *Sexual Sameness* (Bristow 1992b). See, too, in this context, Jonathan Dollimore's wide-ranging and provocative study, *Sexual Dissidence* (1991). Finally, for an important historical account of 'woman', see Denise Riley, *Am I That Name?* (1988).

19. God

John Lennon, playing his celestially white piano, begins the song entitled 'God' (1970) by singing: 'God is a concept / by which we measure / our pain'. What kind of concept is God? In this chapter we propose to explore this question and its relation to literature. In doing this we shall try to emphasize not only that literature is pervasively concerned with religious themes but also that the ways in which we think, read and write about literature are likewise pervaded by religious – and particularly Judaeo-Christian – ideas. The concept of God, in other words, has as much to do with the practice of literary criticism as with the nature of literature. Let us give three very brief instances. The most famous atheist in the history of English poetry, Percy Bysshe Shelley, asserts that 'A poem is the very image of life expressed in its eternal truth' (Shelley 1977, 485): in the phrase 'eternal truth', Shelley is being religious. In his Preface to *Poems* (1853), Matthew Arnold writes of the name 'Shakespeare' that it is 'a name the greatest perhaps of all poetical names; a name never to be mentioned without reverence' (Arnold 1965, 599): with the word 'reverence', Arnold is being religious. Finally, in his essay 'Tradition and the Individual Talent' (1919), T.S. Eliot declares that 'The progress of an artist is a continual self-sacrifice, a continual extinction of personality' (Eliot 1975, 40): by appealing to 'self-sacrifice', Eliot is being religious.

We would like to try to approach the question of 'God' and literary studies by presenting, in a gesture familiar from religious discourse, a series of six edicts. As we hope will become clear, these edicts are not cut in stone. Nor do they add up to a list of systematic principles or rules. Although we write in the rhetorical form of the edict, we wish to make clear that, with respect to God at least, we have absolutely no authority whatsoever to proclaim anything at all. Our aim, as elsewhere in this book, is to provoke questions and further discussion, not to close them off or close them down.

First edict: God is an anthropomorphism

As we have noted elsewhere (for instance in Chapter 5), anthropomorphism is the rhetorical term by which something that is *not* human is attributed with the form or shape (Greek, *morphe*) of the human (*anthropos*). More specifically, as Nietzsche, Freud and others have argued, God is a projection of the human ego on to the surrounding universe. And it comes as no surprise to find that this ego or 'me' writ extremely large is, almost invariably, male. It is in this context that Freud suggests that God (here primarily the Judaeo-Christian God) is a kind of hyperbolic father-figure. He proposes that God is 'a father-substitute; or, more correctly . . . he is an exalted father . . . he is a copy of the father as he is seen and experienced in childhood' (Freud 1985c, 399). God is the figure of authority, the great progenitor, the Big Daddy who is sometimes angry (Old Testament), sometimes loving (New Testament). If one thinks for a moment about the idea of God as 'she', one might quickly sense the whole edifice of traditional Christianity tremble. This is no doubt the reason for the frisson of amusement that may accompany the reading of this car-sticker: 'When God made men-drivers she was only joking!' God, then, is not it: God is 'he' or, if you want to get people's backs up, 'she'. Either way, God would seem to be inconceivable without anthropomorphism.

Second edict: God is dead

This proposition is linked most often with the philosophy of Nietzsche, but it can be understood more generally in relation to the impact on European culture of Biblical (especially German) scholarship and of (mainly British and German) fossil discoveries and subsequent developments in the theory of evolution in the nineteenth century. By the mid-nineteenth century it had become clear, at least to a significant number of educated European people, that the Bible was a tendentious collection of writings, many of which simply could no longer be trusted in terms of their historical fact and accuracy. The study of fossils made it impossible to suppose that the earth could be, as the Bible propounds, only a few thousand years old. Most famously, Charles Darwin's *The Origin of Species* (1859) offered a far more empirically and historically convincing account of how human beings came about and, at the same time, served to cut God out of the equation. Poets and novelists of all sorts were obliged to reckon with what J. Hillis Miller (in a book of that title) refers to as 'the disappearance of God'. It is this sense of disappearance that Matthew Arnold evokes in 'Dover Beach' (written around 1851), when he describes the retreating 'sea of faith':

The Sea of Faith
Was once, too, at the full, and round earth's shore
Lay like the folds of a bright girdle furled.
But now I only hear
Its melancholy, long, withdrawing roar,
Retreating, to the breath
Of the night wind, down the vast edges drear
And naked shingles of the world.

European culture, at least according to this story, has become increasingly secularized.

Of course things are inevitably more complex than this. Even to acknowledge, for example, that 'God is dead' is to think in anthropomorphic terms, and to imply that 'He' was once alive rather than that 'He' never existed. The notion of the death of God runs into difficulties in many ways similar to those regarding the notion of the death of the author (see Chapter 3, above). As Virginia Woolf notes, in a somewhat different context: 'It is far harder to kill a phantom than a reality' (Woolf 1942, 151).

Third edict: to acknowledge the idea that God is an anthropomorphism or that he is dead is not the same as getting rid of him

As Roland Barthes makes clear, the idea of God is inescapably linked to ideas of truth, presence, revelation and meaning in general. In this respect, the issue of God is liable to creep into the discussion of literary texts, wherever questions of meaning, truth and so on are at stake. Barthes sees the notion of the author as interdependent with that of God. And he presses for a theory and practice of literature that would no longer be theological, declaring:

> The space of writing is to be ranged over, not pierced; writing ceaselessly posits meaning ceaselessly to evaporate it, carrying out a systematic exemption of meaning. In precisely this way literature (it would be better from now on to say *writing*), by refusing to assign a 'secret', an ultimate meaning, to the text (and to the world as text), liberates what may be called an anti-theological activity, an activity that is truly revolutionary since to refuse to fix meaning is, in the end, to refuse God and his hypostases – reason, science, law. (Barthes 1977a, 147)

The intimate linkage between 'God' and 'meaning' is implicit in the Bible, in the opening sentence of the Gospel according to St John: 'In the beginning was the Word, and the Word was with God, and the Word was God' (St John

1:1). The original Greek for 'Word' here is 'logos', which means not only 'word' but also 'sense' or 'meaning'. It is in this context that we might consider the notion of what Jacques Derrida has called logocentrism, in other words the entire system (of Western thought, culture and philosophy) that is implicitly or explicitly governed by notions of essential and stable meaning and ultimately by what Derrida refers to as a transcendental signified (God, for example). To put this more specifically in terms of literary texts, we could say that perhaps our greatest desire in reading a poem or a novel is to know what it 'means'. Knowing what the text 'means' has often been seen as synonymous, for example, with knowing what the author (who here becomes a sort of substitute for God) meant by writing it. No doubt a crucial part of reading and doing criticism concerns precisely such a 'theological' activity. What Barthes helps us to see, however, is that this activity is *theological* in the sense that it presupposes a single, stable and authoritative centre.

Barthes's account is extremely appealing – for instance in its associating literature, or *writing*, with the 'truly revolutionary' – but it is also in certain respects problematic. While he is doubtless right to link literature with notions of revolution, anarchy, transgression and liberation, things are trickier than his account may suggest. Barthes's own phraseology remains, at least to some extent, complicit with what it claims to be rejecting or refusing. Just as an atheist could be said to be complying with a kind of theistic thinking through the very gesture of denial (you cannot say, for example, that God does not exist without presupposing a kind of ultimate knowledge of the universe), so the idea of 'an *anti*-theological activity' inevitably remains bound up with an understanding of the 'theological' to which it is being opposed. Similarly Barthes's use of the word 'truly' ('truly revolutionary') could be said to reinstate the notions of 'reason, science, law' precisely at the moment that he is claiming to denounce or refuse them. This is not to say that the general value and significance of Barthes's observations can be discounted. Rather it is to suggest that non-theological thinking is considerably more difficult than one might imagine. It is in this respect that we could recall Nietzsche's supposition that we shall not get rid of God so long as 'we still believe in grammar' (Nietzsche 2003, 48). Like many of Nietzsche's more disturbing aphoristic remarks, this assertion borders on the unthinkable: What could one say about anything if there were no rules governing how to speak or what to say?

Fourth edict: religion is everywhere

It perhaps becomes clearer how deeply Western culture is theologically embedded if we reflect on the way we structure time. In the most fundamental way, the year is based on the Christian religion. Every year (1789 or 2010, for example) is *anno Domini*, 'in the year of our Lord'. Things in, say, Europe and the United States would look very different without a Christian framework: imagine, to begin with, a concept of the year that does not involve Christmas or Easter, or a concept of the week that does not have a Sunday. Christianity, in short, is more pervasive and insidious than many people, including non-practising Christians, agnostics or indeed atheists, might suppose.

How should we think about this in relation to reading and writing about literary texts? In many ways, searching for religious and particularly Christian ideas and motifs in the field of literary studies is like being the Edgar Allan Poe character in 'The Purloined Letter' who is faced with a map and cannot see the name of the country he is looking at because the letters of the name are so big. Being critical of religion is also more unusual than one might think. As Jonathan Culler points out, in an essay entitled 'Political Criticism: Confronting Religion': 'literature departments these days contain people with all manner of views – Marxists, Lacanians, deconstructionists, feminists – but seldom anyone who seriously attacks religion' (Culler 1988b, 78). Culler goes on to provide a forceful summary of the responsibilities of the teacher and critic in this context:

> The essential step is to take up the relation of our teaching and writing to religious discourse and to maintain a critical attitude when discussing religious themes – that is, not to assume that theistic beliefs deserve respect, any more than we would assume that sexist or racist beliefs deserve respect. This might involve us in comparing Christianity with other mythologies when we teach works imbued with religion, or making the sadism and sexism of religious discourse an explicit object of discussion, as we now tend to do when teaching works containing overtly racist language. (Culler 1988b, 80)

Fifth edict: literature has an evil streak

Rather than innocently pretend that literature in its creativity and *joie de vivre* is somehow innately *good*, or ludicrously claim, as did critics such as Matthew Arnold (in the nineteenth century) and F.R. Leavis (in the twentieth), that reading and studying literature in some 'natural' way make you a 'better' person, we should recognize instead that literary creativity has at least as much to do with evil as with good. In his influential and characteristically religious essay 'The Function of Criticism at the Present Time' (1864), Matthew Arnold described literature as 'the promised land' that contains 'the best that is known and thought in the world' (Arnold 1964, 34, 33). Very much within this Christian-spiritualistic critical tradition, F.R. Leavis propounded a theory of literature as the embodiment of 'our spiritual tradition . . . the "picked experience of ages"' (Leavis and Thompson 1964, 82). Such conceptions epitomize the sorts of spurious claims traditionally made of what Leo Bersani has described (and devastatingly criticized) as 'the authoritative, even redemptive virtues of literature' (Bersani 1990, 1). Indeed, it may be said that there is something diabolical about the literary. As Georges Bataille makes clear in his pathbreaking study, *Literature and Evil* (1953), a collusion between creation, imagination and evil is characteristic of literary works in general. 'Literature is not innocent', writes Bataille: 'Literature, like the infringement of moral laws, is dangerous' (Bataille 1985, x, 25).

We can illustrate this by considering the example of John Milton's *Paradise Lost* (1667). In the following lines from Book I, Milton describes the unsettling ability that devils have of being able to change instantaneously from the size of giants to the size of pygmies or to the size of 'fairy elves':

> . . . they but now who seemed
> In bigness to surpass Earth's giant sons
> Now less than smallest dwarfs, in narrow room
> Throng numberless, like that Pygmean race
> Beyond the Indian mount, or fairy elves,
> Whose midnight revels, by a forest side
> Or fountain some belated peasant sees,
> Or dreams he sees, while overhead the moon
> Sits arbitress, and nearer to the earth
> Wheels her pale course: they on their mirth and dance
> Intent, with jocund music charm his ear;
> At once with joy and fear his heart rebounds. (ll.777–88)

Unfolding the comparison of devils with 'fairy elves', these lines have to do with seduction and uncertainty, the charming power of music (or, by extension, poetry) – to which even the moon seems drawn – and the rebounding undecidability of 'joy and fear', the moment in which one does not know what one sees (or dreams one sees). Is one charmed by this vision or not? Milton leaves the comparison there, on the point of the rebound. And in a sense the whole of *Paradise Lost* is inscribed in the moment of this rebounding heart.

The passage from *Paradise Lost* demonstrates the workings of a powerful ambivalence and what we might call an aesthetic tribute (or subordination) to the devilish. This may help to explain William Blake's famous remark about *Paradise Lost*, in 'The Marriage of Heaven and Hell' (1790–3), that 'The reason Milton wrote in fetters when he wrote of Angels & God, and at liberty when of Devils & Hell, is because he was a true Poet and of the Devil's party without knowing it.' One of the most controversial literary critics of the late twentieth century, Harold Bloom, has elaborated an entire theory of poetry (Bloom 1973) in accordance with this Blakean insight: for Bloom, Milton's Satan is the very epitome of the strong modern (i.e. Miltonic and post-Miltonic) poet. In any case it seems clear that Milton's great epic poem, and Blake's poetry in turn, is profoundly indebted to a kind of aesthetic of evil. As Bataille shows, evil and the literary imagination are in cahoots. We could illustrate this quite succinctly in terms of Shakespeare's *Othello*, by supposing that this play were retitled *Iago*: Iago may indeed be abominable, but he is just as clearly the imaginative focus of Shakespeare's play, the embodiment of its creativity and dramatic energy.

A corresponding sense of the literary aesthetic of evil is suggested by Henry James when he offers an explanation of the power of *The Turn of the Screw* (1898), in his comments on that short but enthralling horror novel in a preface to *The Aspern Papers*: 'Only make the reader's general vision of evil intense enough', James says, '. . . Make him [*sic*] *think* the evil, make him think it for himself . . .' (James 1986, 343). Putting our fifth edict in slightly different terms, then, we could say that literature tends towards the demonic: it is about entrancement, possession, being invaded or taken over. The word 'demonic' in this context is significantly ambiguous and is best left that way: a demon is 'an evil spirit' or 'devil', but can also be 'a friendly spirit or good genius' (*Chambers*). To argue that literature has an evil streak is not to imply a moral denunciation of literary works any more than it is to provide support for the liberalist notion that reading literature makes you a better person. Literary texts are dangerous. No one, we might suggest, can be more palpably aware of this fact than the author of *The Satanic Verses* (1988) who, following the novel's publication, notoriously became subject to a *fatwa* (a death sentence pronounced by a Muslim judicial authority). Reading literary texts engages us, in a disturbing but creative and singular way, in the obligation to 'think the evil for oneself'. The paradoxically creative force of evil in literary texts is what makes them in turn the exemplary space for experiencing the undecidable and for thinking about ethics. Far from being immoral or even amoral, literature involves us in what Bataille calls a 'hypermorality' (Bataille 1985, ix). It confronts us with questions which call for different kinds of decision-making and critical responsibilities. Is *The Satanic Verses* an evil work? Is it any more evil than *Paradise Lost*, say, or Mary Shelley's *Frankenstein* (1818) or Elizabeth Bowen's *The House in Paris* (1935)? To rush to decisions in response to such questions is to turn a blind eye to the enigmatic powers of the literary and to ignore what could be called its peculiar ethical imperative.

Sixth edict: literature is sacred

This would be another side to what is paradoxical about the literary. Salman Rushdie's Herbert Read Memorial Lecture, 'Is Nothing Sacred?' was given in his absence by Harold Pinter, at the Institute for Contemporary Arts in London, on 6 February 1990: Rushdie himself was at that time in enforced hiding as a result of the *fatwa* and unable to appear in public for the occasion. Rushdie's lecture starts off by stating that nothing is sacred:

> nothing is sacred in and of itself. . . . Ideas, texts, even people can be made sacred – the word is from the Latin *sacrare*, 'to set apart as holy' – but . . . the act of making sacred is in truth an event in history. It is the product of the many and complex pressures of the time in which the act occurs. And events in history must always be subject to questioning, deconstruction, even to declaration of their obsolescence. (Rushdie 1990, 3)

But the lecture then moves on to cast doubt on this idea that nothing is sacred. Rushdie suggests that he may be obliged 'to set aside as holy the idea of the absolute freedom of the imagination and alongside it [his] own notions of the World, the Text and the Good' (5). He goes on to speculate on the idea that art can and must offer us something like 'a secular definition of transcendence' where transcendence is defined as 'that flight of the human spirit outside the confines of its material, physical existence which all of us, secular or religious, experience on at least a few occasions' (7). Finally Rushdie withdraws and appears to want to retract these earlier claims about art and, in particular, literature. He declares: 'now I find myself backing away from the idea of sacralizing literature with which I flirted at the beginning of this text; I cannot bear the idea of the writer as secular prophet' (14).

The shifts in Rushdie's position, the different kinds of flirtation going on in this brief text, 'Is Nothing Sacred?' are neatly illustrative of the seemingly paradoxical, contradictory nature of the concept of literature. We may, as readers or students or teachers, be powerfully motivated by a sense of the secular (and even, to phrase it more provocatively, by a sense that religion has been the greatest evil in human history, that it is nothing more than what Don Cuppit calls a 'hatred machine' (Cuppit 1997, 98)). But so long as we are concerned with the question of literature we are concerned with what is sacred. The murder in 1991 of Hitoshi Igarashi, the Japanese translator of Rushdie's novel *The Satanic Verses*, may allow us to reflect sombrely on the terrible blindness by which certain people have arrived at the belief that *The Satanic Verses* is an evil work, a blasphemous book which cannot or should not be read as fictional (or in that sense '*literary*') at all. But it also tragically gestures towards what may after all be the *something* that is sacred about literature, namely its untranslatability. Jacques Derrida has spoken of this, in the context of the German writer and philosopher Walter Benjamin, as follows:

> if there is something untranslatable in literature (and, in a certain way, literature is the untranslatable), then it is sacred. If there is any literature, it is sacred; it entails sacralization. This is surely the relation we have to literature, in spite of all our denegations in this regard. The process of sacralization is underway whenever one says to oneself in dealing with a text: Basically, I can't transpose this text such as it is into another language; there is an idiom here; it is a work; all the efforts at translation that I might make, that it itself calls forth and demands, will remain, in a certain way and at a given moment, vain or limited. This text, then, is a sacred text. (Derrida 1985b, 148)

Quite apart from the fact that, as critics such as Terry Eagleton (1996) have stressed, literary studies in Britain, for example, in many ways arose out of the desire or need to find a substitute for religion, literature is sacred in its singularity. As soon as we set it apart (*sacrare*) and recognize the singularity or uniqueness of a work, its demand that it be translated and its insistence on being untranslatable, we are engaging with the sacred.

> To be, or not to be, that is the question . . .

> Season of mists and mellow fruitfulness,
>   Close bosom-friend of the maturing sun . . .

> Sexual intercourse began
> In nineteen sixty-three . . .

Further reading

Salman Rushdie's 'Is Nothing Sacred?' (1990) is an accessible and very stimulating essay on literature and the sacred. Jonathan Culler's 'Political Criticism: Confronting Religion' (1988b) is clear and provocative, as is the book on which his discussion is centrally focused, William Empson's *Milton's God* (1965). On religion and the historical emergence of English Studies in Britain, see Eagleton 1996. For a very challenging reading of Nietzsche's 'God is dead', see Heidegger 1977. For a collection of complex but fascinating essays on God and language, religion, law, philosophy and politics, see Jacques Derrida's *Acts of Religion* (Derrida 2002b). For two excellent studies which consider the Bible itself from a literary critical perspective, see Robert Alter, *The Art of Biblical Narrative* (1981) and *The Art of Biblical Poetry* (1985). For a useful collection of texts concerned with historical perspectives on the question of evil, see Rorty (2001). A useful general survey of theology in relation to the work of various contemporary theorists and philosophers can be found in Graham Ward (1996). For three recent and powerful books on some of the paradoxes of religion today, see Don Cupitt, *After God* (1997), Hent de Vries, *Philosophy and the Turn to Religion* (1999) and Derrida and Vattimo, eds, *Religion* (1998).

20. Ideology

'I know the human being and fish can coexist peacefully.'
What does President George W. Bush's hallucinatory assertion tell us about literature and ideology? The literary critic and theorist Paul de Man suggests one answer in a well-known, if perhaps somewhat obscure statement from his 1982 essay 'The Resistance to Theory': 'What we call ideology is precisely the confusion of linguistic with natural reality'. De Man's remark places literature, the art of language, at the centre of political or 'ideological' debate: as de Man himself asserts, it means that, 'more than any other mode of inquiry', literary criticism and theory (what de Man calls 'the linguistics of literariness') is itself 'a powerful and indispensable tool in the unmasking of ideological aberrations' (de Man 1986, 11). One way to think about de Man's assertion is to consider the extent to which the 'ideological aberrations', as some might call them, of the President of the United States of America are linked up with the linguistic aberrations of his speech. We are all perhaps familiar with such 'Bushisms' as 'They misunderestimated me', 'They said this issue wouldn't resignate with the People', or 'I don't need to be subliminabable'. But what kind of new environmentalism is involved in Bush's dream-like comment about humans and fish? Equally, we might ask what kinds of redefinition are involved in the tortuous phrase (in Bush's 2004 State of the Nation speech) about Iraq's 'weapons of mass destruction program related activities', or what kind of economic policy is being promulgated in the financially bizarre assertion that 'if most of the [tax] breaks go to wealthy people it's because most of the people who pay taxes are wealthy'? (For these and other Bushisms, see www.bushisms.com.) In each case, the language itself is bound up with the ideological aberrations of a US President whose 'environmentalism' is nothing less than catastrophic

for the planet, whose justification for the 2003 war against Iraq was blown apart by the fact that no WMDs were found in that country, and whose economic policy involves the political tautology of tax cuts for the rich and increasing poverty for the poor. The linguistic aberrations of Bush's speech, in other words, may themselves be said to articulate the illogicality, vanity, evasions or sheer ignorance of disastrous environmental, foreign and welfare policies – that is to say, of a certain view of the world, of a certain ideology.

But what is this thing called 'ideology'? The word has something of a bad name: the 'crude' Marxist notion of ideology is of 'false consciousness', 'the system of ideas and representations which dominate the mind of a man [*sic*] or a social group' (Althusser 1977, 149), as contrasted with the underlying reality of economic and class relations. The influential theorist Louis Althusser summarizes Marx's notion of ideology by contrasting it with 'the concrete history of concrete material individuals': ideology, instead, is a 'pure dream', it is 'empty and vain' and 'an imaginary assemblage'. 'Ideology', Althusser continues, 'represents the imaginary relationship of individuals to their real conditions of existence' (Althusser 1977, 151, 153). In classical Marxism – which, as we shall see, Althusser radically develops – ideology is an imagined representation of reality: it is false, distorted by definition. Ideology is not, Terry Eagleton remarks, 'a set of doctrines': rather, it 'signifies the way men [*sic*] live out their roles in class-society, the values, ideas and images which tie them by their social functions and so prevent them from a true knowledge of society as a whole' (Eagleton 1976, 16–17).

For many traditional non-Marxist critics, thinking about ideology is something that gets in the way of reading literature: focusing on the political or ideological dimensions of a literary text results in a reductive simplification of its true value, a value that transcends local or contingent questions of class, race or gender. For such critics, the opening to the present chapter would be 'ideological' in a bad sense – it is, they might say, politically biased, not the way to write objective, academic literary criticism. Once again, but differently, ideology is a distortion.

Finally, from a poststructuralist perspective, the notion of ideology is fundamentally suspect, since it relies on a questionable opposition of true and false, of reality and false consciousness. By this view, ideology appears too easily as a master term for totalizing readings of literary texts. In this chapter, however, we shall attempt to suggest ways in which the work of the neo-Marxist critic Louis Althusser has effectively produced a poststructuralist Marxism by substantially modifying the 'crude' opposition of disguised or distorted representations on the one hand and an underlying political and material reality on the other.

In a famous essay entitled 'Ideology and Ideological State Apparatuses' (1969), Louis Althusser seeks to describe ways in which the state exerts its power outside such institutions as the army, the courts, the police, etc. – that is to say, in culture and society generally. The central insight of this essay is that ideology is bound up with the constitution of the subject, that 'man is an ideological animal by nature' – meaning that people constitute or define themselves *as humans* through ideology. Althusser argues that

> the category of the subject is constitutive of all ideology, but at the same time . . . the category of the subject is only constitutive of all ideology insofar as all ideology has the function (which defines it) of 'constituting' concrete individuals as subjects. (Althusser 1977, 160)

To put it simply: subjects – people – make their own ideology at the same time as ideology makes them subjects. The implications of this idea are enormous because it means that 'ideology' goes to the heart of personal identity, of how we conceive ourselves as subjects in the world and all that this involves. Althusser avoids a reductive opposition of ideology and reality by suggesting that ideology *makes* our reality in constituting us as subjects. Ideology, Althusser argues, 'hails or interpellates concrete individuals as concrete subjects' (162): it calls us or calls to us as subjects and we recognize ourselves as subjects in our response to this call. To become human, to identify oneself as a subject, then, is an effect of ideology. For Althusser, the function of Art generally is, as he remarks in 'A Letter on Art', 'to make us see', and what it allows us to see, what it forces us to see, is 'the ideology from which it is born' (Althusser 1977, 204). What is most terrifying and compelling about this is the fact that being a subject feels so real, so natural – and yet, as Althusser remarks, this very 'reality' or 'naturalness' of being a subject is itself an 'ideological effect'.

This is heady stuff, and rather abstract – if also, as Althusser suggests, terribly real. How can we begin to think about the workings of ideology in literary texts? Etienne Balibar and Pierre Macherey take us some way towards an understanding of the question in their important essay 'On Literature as an Ideological Form' (1981). They argue that literary texts produce the illusion of 'unity'. Such writing is, for them, itself ideological. For Balibar and Macherey a 'material analysis' needs to look for 'signs of contradictions' which appear 'as unevenly resolved conflicts in the text' (87). For these critics, indeed, literature *begins* with 'the imaginary solution of implacable ideological contradictions': literature is there because 'such a solution is impossible' (88). In capitalist society, literature itself is an 'ideological form', both produced by and producing ideology. The task of the critic would be to look beyond the unity that the literary text strives to present, and forcefully to explore the contradictions embedded within it. The strange case of detective fiction illustrates this point very well. The genre produces its own consoling fictions, its own ideology. While we may think of crime as eternally recurring, for example, as an unavoidable function of any sociopolitical context, detective fiction allows us to perceive it as both solvable and the result of the actions of specific, isolated and morally culpable individuals.

Tony Bennett has argued that a thoroughgoing Althusserian criticism would not simply restore or reveal the contradictions that are already in texts: rather, it would 'read contradictions into the text' in such a way that it would 'effect a work of transformation on those forms of signification which are said to be ideological' (Bennett 1979, 146–7). In this respect, an 'ideological criticism' is not one that understands the reality of a text better. Rather it is criticism that changes the text. Such a reading of, say, an Agatha Christie detective novel would not simply seek to expose ways in which such writing conforms to and reinforces the status quo of bourgeois capitalism. Instead, it would recognize reading as an intervention in and transformation of that text itself. Bennett argues that there can be no notion of '*the* text' underlying any reading: texts have 'historically specific functions and effects' (Bennett 1979, 148), they change in time, and what changes them is reading.

In order to think about some of these points and questions, we shall briefly consider Edgar Allan Poe's story 'The Purloined Letter' (1845). This story, and Poe's earlier 'The Murders in the Rue Morgue' (1841) and 'The Mystery of Marie Roget' (1842–3), are often considered to be the first examples of modern detective fiction. Set in Paris, the narrative concerns a detective named August C. Dupin, who is asked to solve a mystery concerning the theft of a letter from the 'royal apartments' belonging to 'a personage of the most exalted station' (495), that is to say, presumably, the Queen of France. The contents of the letter have the potential to compromise the Queen and leave her open to blackmail. As she is reading the letter she is interrupted by her husband, from whom the letter must be concealed. She does not have time to hide the letter so she lays it on the table as she talks to her husband, relying on the fact that it is *not* concealed to hide the fact that it *must* be concealed. While they are talking, another person, 'Minister D.', enters the room, notices the letter and manages to exchange it for a worthless letter that he happens to be holding. The Queen sees this exchange but can do nothing to stop it without drawing attention to the secret letter. She is now open to blackmail and her letter must be discreetly retrieved by the head of the police service. The police have surreptitiously searched Minister D.'s house but have been unable to find the letter. Dupin is asked to help. He goes to the minister's house and manages to spot the letter, turned inside out, but revealed for all to see, hanging from the Minister's mantelpiece. Later, by returning to the house with a copy of the letter and arranging for the minister to be distracted while he is there, Dupin manages to substitute his copy for the genuine article and retrieve the now doubly purloined letter.

Detective fiction may be understood to have a conservative ideological form because of its generic investment in the restoration of the status quo. A detective story typically involves a disturbance of order in the wake of an originary event of physical violence or theft of property, followed by the re-establishment of order by the discovery of the criminal – after which the jewels are returned or the murderer is punished (or both). Moreover, the genre conventionally relies on the idea of the criminal as an autonomous individual: he or she must be morally responsible for his or her actions and must not be insane. This is because the genre depends, on the one hand, on an outcome in which society's and the reader's desire for moral restitution is fulfilled and, on the other hand, on the detective's ability rationally to deduce the criminal's motives. If the criminal is mad, he or she cannot be punished (he or she must be cured), and his or her motives and actions cannot be rationally deduced because they will be, by definition, irrational. Similarly, any critique of society or social institutions is likely to be counterproductive in a work of detective fiction because of the danger that 'society', rather than a particular individual, will itself come to be seen as the culprit. This is a dilemma which is particularly acute in, for example, contemporary feminist detective fiction: the novels of such writers as Sara Paretsky, Amanda Cross and Gillian Slovo are concerned as much with exposing the gross injustices of patriarchal society as with finding a specific criminal. In such cases there is a sense in which the criminal cannot finally be punished and the status quo restored because it is that very status quo which is responsible for the crime. Encoded within classic detective fiction, then, is a reactionary political agenda. This ideological form of the genre might be said to be an unspoken but necessary part of any conventional detective story. From this point of view, one could say that 'The Purloined Letter' involves the re-establishment of power relations, the assertion of the culprit as autonomous and independent, and the implementation of reason to restore the status quo.

But what is particularly interesting about Poe's story from this perspective is not so much the way in which it institutes and reinforces the ideological formation of a certain literary genre, as it is the fact that this formation also entails a number of paradoxes, sites of disturbance and displacement. One of the key elements of the story is the identification of the detective with the criminal. Dupin explains that he was able to discover the letter by identifying himself with Minister D. and, in particular, by identifying the minister's mode of thinking as both rational and poetic (like Dupin, he is both mathematician and poet). The story establishes what we might call 'inspired reasoning' – as contrasted with the rational approach of the regular police – as the characteristic technique for both detective and criminal in detective fiction. But the story also initiates a central paradox of the genre whereby the detective not only identifies with but is in some ways identical to the criminal. In this sense, it is no accident that the letter is, in fact, 'purloined' twice – once by the minister and once by Dupin. The detective in this story, and in detective fiction more generally, must obey the double bind of identity with, but difference from, the criminal. This intrinsic generic paradox suggests ways in which the ideological conservativism of the genre, its investment in a restoration of the status quo and reinforcement of an absolute distinction between criminal and non-criminal, may be undermined. Similarly, in establishing 'inspired reasoning' as the *modus operandi* for both detective and criminal, Poe's story opens the way for its own deconstruction. While detective and criminal, author and reader all need to employ reason to attain their ends, such reason is continually disturbed by its 'other', inspiration or unreason. It comes as no surprise, therefore, that Poe was also obsessed with occultism, spiritualism and the uncanny. Nor is it any surprise to discover that the inventor of Sherlock Holmes, Arthur Conan Doyle, was on the one hand a trained physician and, on the other, a keen amateur in the study of telepathy and the after-life. The detective in this context combines a doctor's empirical and scientific acumen with a telepath's ability to read the criminal's mind. More generally, detective fiction seems to be continually threatened with its generic other – the gothic, tales of psychic phenomena, spiritualism – as is suggested by such gothic tales as Doyle's *The Hound of the Baskervilles* (1902), for example, or such apparently supernatural tales as his 'The Parasite' (1893). Finally, the genre of detective fiction is organized through a precarious relation with social critique. As we have pointed out, classic detective fiction must distance itself from an ideological critique of society which, however, can never be finally erased. Detective fiction can only exist if there are crimes to detect, and if there are crimes to detect society cannot be perfect. Some of the most interesting exponents of detective fiction – Dashiel Hammett, Raymond Chandler, or more recently Paul Auster, William McIlvanney, Sara Paretsky, Philip Kerr, Ian Rankin – gain much of their narrative energy from precisely such a tension – the possibility that the constitution of their narratives as detective fiction will be dissolved by their unavoidable engagement in social and political critique.

Our final point concerning Poe's story and its relation to ideology concerns the way in which it is based on the idea that what is most open or revealed, most 'obvious', may itself be the most deceptive or most concealing. The fact that Minister D. conceals the purloined letter precisely by *not* hiding it, by leaving it where all can see it (the place where no one – except Dupin – will look, because it is too exposed), makes 'The Purloined Letter' an allegory of ideological formation. Ideology may be defined in terms of the obvious, in terms of common sense. It is, in the West, 'common sense' that a 'normal' subject or person is autonomous, for example, that crime is the result of individual actions, or that such an individual operates through rational motivation. But at the same time each of these obvious, self-evident or commonsensical points disguises a very specific concept of the self, an ideology.

Rather than offering an escape from ideology, then, literary texts may be considered as places where the structures and fractures of ideology are both produced and reproduced. Literary texts do not simply or passively 'express' or reflect the ideology of their particular time and place. Rather, they are sites of conflict and difference, places where values and preconceptions, beliefs and prejudices, knowledge and social structures are represented and, in the process, opened to transformation.

Further reading

Althusser's 'Ideology and the Ideological State Apparatuses' (1977) is a basic text for a consideration of the fundamental importance of ideology in the constitution of the human subject. The classic Althusserian account of literature is Macherey's astute and highly readable *A Theory of Literary Production* (1978); see also Balibar and Macherey (1981). For a more up-to-date account, drawing on numerous Althusser texts posthumously published in French, see Warren Montag (2003). A good brief account of ideology is the entry in Williams, *Keywords* (1976). More recent, more detailed and exhaustive is Terry Eagleton's *The Ideology of the Aesthetic* (1990). Three good short introductions to the subject are Terry Eagleton's *Ideology: An Introduction* (1991), David Hawkes's *Ideology* (1996) and James Decker's *Ideology* (2004); and for useful collections of essays, see Eagleton, ed., *Ideology* (1994) and Mulhern, ed., *Contemporary Marxist Literary Criticism* (1992). A valuable work on the ideology of detective fiction in particular is Stephen Knight's *Form and Ideology in Detective Fiction* (1980). Poe's *The Purloined Letter* has itself become a site of intense ideological conflict and theoretical speculation following important essays by Lacan and Derrida: see Muller and Richardson, eds, *The Purloined Poe* (1988).

21. Desire

In 1954 Alan Turing, the inventor of one of the first modern electronic computers (the 'Turing Machine'), killed himself. Two years earlier, he had been prosecuted for 'gross indecency' – that is, for having sex with another man. His crime had been to desire the wrong person, to have the wrong desire. The man who, with others, has transformed our world by the manipulation of a binary system (on/off), was prosecuted and persecuted thanks to another binary system – right/wrong, good/evil, moral/immoral, legal/illegal, heterosexual/homosexual, normal/perverse. There is a terrible irony here. Turing's machine and its descendants exploit a simple polarity to develop the most complex patterns imaginable (and those beyond imagination). Society's programme of ethics and legality, by contrast, can often seem to be based on rigid and unforgiving binary oppositions. Desire: right or wrong.

Is it possible that desire is more complex? The most influential philosopher of desire in the twentieth century has been Sigmund Freud. For Freud, all desire goes back to the child's original desire for the mother, for the mother's breast. This desire is so strong that it produces an absolute identification: '"I am the breast",' wrote Freud, ventriloquizing the unspoken words of the infant (Freud 1975b, 299). Beyond this originary desire, however, Freud tends to see the precise structure of desire as determined by socialization, by the way in which the child is brought up. In such texts as *On Sexuality: Three Essays on the Theory of Sexuality* (1905/1977), Freud argues that desire is 'essentially' mobile – it has no essence, no proper object, beyond the child's hallucinatory desire for the breast. Most justifications for the proscription of desire – against homosexual acts, for example – rely on assertions about what is 'natural'. But if we accept Freud's arguments, we find that the appeal to the natural is highly questionable.

The mobility of desire is demonstrated by a text such as Shakespeare's comedy *Twelfth Night* (*c.*1601). While his *Romeo and Juliet* (*c.*1595) may seem to reproduce the myth of an absolute and eternal love between one man and one woman, *Twelfth Night* is concerned rather with the contingency and mobility of desire. Duke Orsino sees himself as a true lover, a man overwhelmed by love and constant only in his desire:

> For such as I am, all true lovers are,
> Unstaid and skittish in all motions else,
> Save in the constant image of the creature
> That is belov'd. (II, iv, 17–20)

In love with an image of the woman he claims to love, Orsino is at the same time in love with the image of himself in love. A philosopher of love – most of his speeches meditate, often absurdly, on the nature of love and the lover – Orsino is unaware that 'true love', including his own, is ultimately love of love, that desire is desire for its own image. In spite of himself, Orsino illustrates the accuracy of Nietzsche's aphorism: 'In the end one loves one's desire and not what is desired' (Nietzsche 1989, 93). In fact, by the end of the play it has become clear that Orsino's desire is radically mobile and contingent. Orsino uses his servant Cesario as a messenger between himself and Lady Olivia, the woman he desires. Cesario is really a woman called Viola, dressed as a man, and is herself in love with the Duke. At the end of the play, Olivia marries Viola's twin brother and Viola reveals that she is really a woman. At this point, unabashed by the ease with which his desire can move from one object to another, Orsino proposes marriage to Viola. The 'true lover' in Shakespeare's play turns out to have mobile and vicarious desires, and even gender seems to be more a comedy of convention than a matter of nature. Does Orsino finally desire Viola or Cesario?

In the context of literature more generally, we can begin to think about the importance of desire in two fundamental ways. In the first place, we would suggest that every literary text is in some way *about* desire. To say this, however, is not to suggest that it is everywhere and always the same desire. As Michel Foucault's influential three-volume *A History of Sexuality* (1981–8) makes particularly clear, desire is bound up with all sorts of social and institutional practices and discourses – with questions of law, gender and sexuality, with the discourses of medicine, theology, economics and so on. Thinking about desire in literary texts – about representations of desire – inevitably opens on to questions of historical context. For example, nowadays we may take for granted the term 'homosexual' and the notion of homosexual desire.

But as we show in more detail in Chapter 22, below, the term and indeed the concept is relatively recent. The first entry for 'homosexual' in the *OED* is from 1892. Critics such as Joseph Bristow have demonstrated that a critical appreciation of a play such as Oscar Wilde's *The Importance of Being Earnest* (1895) is crucially dependent on an understanding of the historical emergence of a homosexual lifestyle at the end of the nineteenth century (Bristow 1992a). While the term 'homosexual' can refer to both men and women, its entry into the English language in the late nineteenth century did not result in a sudden visibility for lesbians, however. Indeed, the most striking aspect of lesbianism in 'straight' culture generally has been the denial of its existence. In 1885, for example, Queen Victoria is said to have reacted to the suggestion that there should be a law for women corresponding to the new law against 'gross indecency' between men by remarking, simply, 'no woman could ever do that' (quoted in Castle 1992, 128). Similarly, Leonard Woolf's mother responded to Radclyffe Hall's lesbian novel *The Well of Loneliness* (1928) by saying 'I am seventy-six – but until I read this book I did not know that such things went on at all. I do not think they do' (quoted in Knopp 1992, 118). And, in literary criticism, it is only since the 1980s, despite pioneering studies such as Jeannette Foster's *Sex Variant Women in Literature* from 1958, that a critical vocabulary for talking about lesbian writing has begun to emerge. As far as 'straight' culture goes, critics such as Joseph Allan Boone, for example, have shown how the very *form* of conventional nineteenth-century narrative is bound up with the Victorian social dynamics of courtship and marriage (Boone 1987). According to Boone, the traditional marriage plot 'owes much of its idealizing appeal to its manipulation of form to evoke an illusion of order and resolution': this 'illusory' sense of order, he suggests, itself 'glosses over the contradictions, the inequalities, concealed in the institution of marriage' (Boone 1987, 9).

But literary texts are not only about how and why characters desire each other and what happens to those desires. Literary texts also produce or solicit desire. They make us desire, in reading. Literary texts, we might say, are (in Deleuze and Guattari's phrase) 'machines of desire'. Not only do they generate desire (such as the desire to read on), but they are generated by it (by the desire, for example, to tell). In this respect it might be useful to turn Freud's famous question of female desire, 'what does a woman want?' (quoted in Jones 1958, 2:468) – and Gayatri Spivak's reformulation of it as 'what does a man want?' – into a question about literary texts: What does a text want? Does it want to tell us something or conceal something? Does it want to make us want it? How? And so on. But if texts can be thought to desire, readers desire, too: we desire solutions, we desire to get to the end of the story, we desire insight or wisdom, pleasure or sadness, laughter or anger. The fundamental paradox of reading, however, is that we always desire an end (a resolution, an explanation, the triumph of good), but that this end is not the end of desire. As Boone has shown, classic nineteenth-century narrative ends with the apparent satisfaction of desire (the reader's, the character's or preferably both). But as Freud has taught us, this end of desire is not the end of the story: as he speculates in 'Civilization and Its Discontents', there is something in the very nature of sexual life which 'denies us full satisfaction' (Freud 1985e, 295).

Perhaps the most important post-Freudian theorist of desire, especially in the context of literary studies, is the French psychoanalyst Jacques Lacan. His particular concern is with what he terms the 'paradoxical, deviant, erratic, eccentric, even scandalous character' of desire (Lacan 1977a, 286, quoted in Bowie 1991, 134). Lacan's texts are notoriously difficult to read, in part because they claim to (or are condemned to) speak on behalf of this strange figure of desire. Any attempt to summarize or explain what he has to say about desire is bound to be misguided – precisely to the extent that it will appear to be putting this scandalous figure in a conceptual strait-jacket. With that proviso in mind, however, we could be a bit scandalous in our own fashion and summarize Lacan's characterization of desire as follows: Lacan elaborates on Freud's contention that there is something about the nature of desire that is incompatible with satisfaction. His account of desire is more radical than Freud's, however. Freud emphasizes the ways in which we can never get what we want: we may think we have got it (pouring ourselves a gin and tonic, paying for a new car), but actually desire will always have moved on again (to the next gin and tonic, the chance to get on the road and drive and so on). Waiting for a final fulfilment of desire is, indeed, like waiting for Godot in Samuel Beckett's play. For Freud, this endlessly deferred complete satisfaction is seen simply as an unavoidable, if rather poignant aspect of what it is to be human. For Lacan, on the other hand, the nature of desire is at once more alien and more subversive. This can be illustrated in two ways. First, for Lacan, the alien or alienating character of desire is not something that happens to come along and make life difficult for people. Instead, people have become alienated before they even become people (or 'subjects' in psychoanalytic terms). The human subject is always already 'split' – divided within itself by the scandalous nature of desire. Second, Lacan gives much greater emphasis than Freud to the role of language in relation to desire. One of Lacan's most famous dicta is that 'the unconscious is structured like a language' (see, for example, Lacan 1977a). For Lacan, language is not something that we can use in order to try to make ourselves more comfortable with the alien nature of desire: desire speaks

through language and it speaks us. We are, in a way, the senseless puppets of
desire as much when we speak or write as when we fall in love.

The interdependence of desire and language in turn is an overt concern of
many literary texts. In such texts, there is a recognition that language or meaning
can never finally be closed or completed and that desire can never be fulfilled.
Robert Browning's poem 'Two in the Campagna', from 1855, is one such text:

1

I wonder do you feel today
  As I have felt since, hand in hand,
We sat down on the grass, to stray
  In spirit better through the land,
5   This morn of Rome and May?

2

For me, I touched a thought, I know,
  Has tantalized me many times,
(Like turns of thread the spiders throw
  Mocking across our path) for rhymes
10   To catch at and let go.

3

Help me to hold it! First it left
  The yellowing fennel, run to seed
There, branching from the brickwork's cleft,
  Some old tomb's ruin: yonder weed
15   Took up the floating weft,

4

Where one small orange cup amassed
  Five beetles,—blind and green they grope
Among the honey-meal: and last,
  Everywhere on the grassy slope
20   I traced it. Hold it fast!

5

The champaign with its endless fleece
  Of feathery grasses everywhere!
Silence and passion, joy and peace,
  An everlasting wash of air—
25   Rome's ghost since her decease.

6

Such life here, through such lengths of hours,
  Such miracles performed in play,
Such primal naked forms of flowers,
  Such letting nature have her way
30   While heaven looks from its towers!

7

How say you? Let us, O my dove,
 Let us be unashamed of soul,
As earth lies bare to heaven above!
 How is it under our control
35 To love or not to love?

8

I would that you were all to me,
 You that are just so much, no more.
Nor yours nor mine, nor slave nor free!
 Where does the fault lie? What the core
40 O' the wound, since wound must be?

9

I would I could adopt your will,
 See with your eyes, and set my heart
Beating by yours, and drink my fill
 At your soul's springs,—your part my part
45 In life, for good and ill.

10

No. I yearn upward, touch you close,
 Then stand away. I kiss your cheek,
Catch your soul's warmth,—I pluck the rose
 And love it more than tongue can speak—
50 Then the good minute goes.

11

Already how am I so far
 Out of that minute? Must I go
Still like the thistle-ball, no bar,
 Onward, whenever light winds blow,
55 Fixed by no friendly star?

12

Just when I seemed about to learn!
 Where is the thread now? Off again!
The old trick! Only I discern—
 Infinite passion, and the pain
60 Of finite hearts that yearn.

The poem is about the impossibility of capturing the moment of desire, of capturing or 'holding' desire, of fulfilling and so ending it. The speaker desires the 'good minute' – analogous to what James Joyce later calls 'epiphany' and Virginia Woolf 'moments of being' – but recognizes its inevitable escape. The second stanza makes it clear that this is also a poem about language, about the tantalizing nature of a moment which poetry attempts to but cannot capture.

In stanza ten, the speaker 'pluck[s] the rose / And love[s] it more than tongue can speak'; but the moment passes immediately and he asks 'Already how am I so far / Out of that minute?' Exploring the central trope of romantic love – the loss of identity in a merging with the other, the desire evoked in stanza nine in particular – Browning's poem suggests the impossibility and inevitable failure of this desire. The poem traces the paradoxes of romantic love while discerning the impossibility of expressing in language the flux of life, the fluidity and fragility of experience.

If literature and theory alike demonstrate that desire is mobile, endlessly displaced, they also suggest that it is 'mediated', produced through imitation and simulation. Particularly influential in this context has been the recent work of Eve Kosofsky Sedgwick. Developing the ideas of the French post-structuralist critic René Girard, Sedgwick has argued that desire is everywhere mediated, that desire is structured by a triangular relation of rivalry. Take three people: A, B and C. A, let us say, desires B. Why? Normally, we would assume that A desires B because B is desirable (at least to A). For Girard and Sedgwick, however, things are rather different. For them, A desires B because B is desired by C. We learn to desire, Girard and Sedgwick argue, by copying others' desires, and our desire is produced, fundamentally, in response to the desire of another. 'The great novelists', Girard claims, 'reveal the imitative nature of desire' and expose what he terms 'the lie of spontaneous desire' (Girard 1965, 14, 16). Now, Sedgwick further points out that most of the examples in Girard's book, *Deceit, Desire, and the Novel* (1965), involve a specific relation of gender, wherein B is a woman and A and C men: the woman is the object of desire, while the two men are rivals. Love stories often concern the rivalry of two men for a woman, in which the rivalry itself indeed becomes more important than the desire for the woman. For Sedgwick, in fact, Western culture in general is structured by a 'crisis of homo/heterosexual definition': 'an understanding of virtually any aspect of modern Western culture must be, not merely incomplete, but damaged in its central substance to the degree that it does not incorporate a critical analysis of modern homo/heterosexual definition' (Sedgwick 1991, 1). Sedgwick develops these insights to suggest that, in Western discourse, in stories, novels, films and so on, relationships are most commonly structured in terms of what she calls 'homosocial desire'. Homosocial desire is not the same as homosexual desire. It does not need to be explicitly expressed as desire, and it is not necessarily physical. In fact, homosocial desire is often concerned rigorously to exclude the possibility of homosexual relations. The traditional male preserves of locker-room, board-room and clubroom are sites of homosocial bonding which, at the same time, may be virulently homophobic. But in male-dominated society, such relations are fundamental: in all such societies, Sedgwick claims, 'there is a special relationship between male homosocial (*including* homosexual) desire and the structures for maintaining and transmitting patriarchal power' (Sedgwick 1985, 25). Sedgwick argues that a large proportion of the stories, films, songs and other narratives by which Western society imaginatively structures desire can be read as narratives of homosocial desire: while such narratives take as their overt subject the desire of a man for a woman, again and again the really important relationship is that between two men, either as rivals or as colleagues, friends, or associates. Developing the idea first proposed by the French structuralist anthropologist Claude Lévi-Strauss, that in many societies women tend to be tokens of exchange, Sedgwick argues that women are effaced in this triangular structure, as mere objects for barter. At some level, then, patriarchal society excludes women even from relations of desire. Homosocial desire in our society, Sedgwick suggests, is both the most required and the most carefully regimented desire.

Sedgwick offers a highly provocative model for thinking about desire in narrative. According to this model, the workings of desire are inextricably linked to the homophobic, homosocial and patriarchal structures of society. Many canonical works of literature might be reread in these terms. This is not to suggest that the Great Tradition is full of closet homosexuality, for example, just waiting to be 'outed' (although we make some attempt in this regard in our 'Queer' chapter, below). Rather, it is to suggest that homosocial desire in all its forms is central to the workings of what we might like to think of simply as 'heterosexual' writing. The notions of heterosexual and homosexual need to be rethought. Shakespeare's *Hamlet* (c.1601), for example, concerns not only the murder of Hamlet's father and its revenge, but also a relation of rivalry between Prince Hamlet (as a surrogate for his father, King Hamlet) and Hamlet's uncle, Claudius (the dead King's brother), over the Queen. Emily Brontë's *Wuthering Heights* (1847) may gain much of its power from the barely hidden conflicts of homosocial desire between Heathcliff and other men, resulting in rivalry and extraordinary violence. In its focus on the triangle of two men (Eugene Wrayburn and Bradley Headstone) and one woman (Lizzie Hexam), Charles Dickens's *Our Mutual Friend* (1865) is a superb, if disturbing, example of the potentially murderous erotic dynamic that exists between men. Thomas Hardy's *Tess of the D'Urbevilles* (1891), a novel that appears to focus on the eponymous and tragic heroine, is also structured by rivalry between two men who desire her, Angel Clare and Alec D'Urbeville. D.H. Lawrence's *Women in Love* (1921), while overtly about two men and their love for two women, is also, and perhaps more importantly, about the relationship between the two men, Gerald and Birkin.

Desire, then, is both a fundamental topic of literary texts and fundamental to reading. But one of the things that literary texts consistently suggest is that desire is paradoxical, mobile, mediated. And perhaps the homophobia that may have ultimately resulted in the death of Alan Turing can itself be understood in terms of a distortion or displacement of desire – a fear of homosexuality, a fear of the other, which is bound up in society's anxieties about such mobilities and mediations. One of the responsibilities of contemporary literary criticism and theory lies in the exposure, questioning and transformation of the rigid oppositions that result in such fear and oppression.

Further reading

Foucault's *The History of Sexuality: An Introduction* (1981) is a crucial starting point for thinking about desire. Similarly influential is Deleuze and Guattari's difficult but compelling *Anti-Oedipus* (1983). Peter Brooks offers fascinating accounts of the reader's desire in *Reading for the Plot* (1984) and *Body Work* (1993), while Catherine Belsey presents a readable poststructuralist account of a number of literary texts of desire in her *Desire: Love Stories in Western Culture* (1994). Leo Bersani's *A Future for Astyanax: Character and Desire in Literature* (1976) remains a brilliant and thought-provoking point of reference for exploring the representation and effects of desire in literary texts. For three excellent brief accounts of the work of Lacan, see the introductory books by Bowie (1991), Weber (1992) and Rabaté (2001). On the discourse of homosexual desire and homophobia, see Jonathan Dollimore's influential book *Sexual Dissidence* (1991), and for a collection of essays on lesbian criticism and theory, see Munt, ed., *New Lesbian Criticism* (1992). On the importance of heterosexual desire for the development of the novel in the nineteenth century, see Joseph Allen Boone, *Tradition and Counter Tradition* (1987). For historically wide-ranging discussions of issues of desire, see Dollimore's *Death, Desire and Loss in Western Culture* (1998) and *Sex, Literature and Censorship* (2001).

22. Queer

Queer's a queer word.

The entry of the word 'queer' into the English language is itself a study in the queer ways of words. *Chambers Dictionary* defines the adjective as follows: 'odd, singular, quaint: open to suspicion: counterfeit: slightly mad: having a sensation of coming sickness: sick, ill (*dialect*): homosexual (*slang*)'. What's queer about this synonymatic definition is the way in which it includes three apparently unrelated senses for the 'same' word – clustering around ideas of strangeness, sickness and homosexuality. One question immediately arises: how do you get from 'queer' as 'singular' or 'quaint' or 'slightly mad' or 'ill' to 'queer' as 'homosexual'? While the answer may to some seem to be self-evident, the process is worth examining in greater detail. The *Oxford English Dictionary* shows the slippage from one sense to the other in action: its extensive historical account of the word reveals that in fact there was a delay of more than four hundred years between the introduction of the 'odd' or 'singular' sense of the word into English and the introduction of its 'homosexual' sense. The first entry for 'queer' in the *OED* comes from the early sixteenth century (Dunbar's 'Heir cumis awin quir Clerk', from 1508), while the first entry for the word in its homosexual sense is from 1922 in a publication by the Children's Bureau of the US Department of Labor. The latter comes from the straight (but also rather queer) language of a report entitled *The Practical Value of the Scientific Study of Juvenile Delinquents*, which refers to the idea that 'A young man, easily ascertainable to be unusually fine in other characteristics, is probably "queer" in sex tendency'. The sentence, immortalized as an entry in the *OED* simply by virtue of its priority as the first recorded usage of the word, is intriguing for a number of reasons. It makes stereotypical assumptions about certain 'characteristics', it expresses the idea that queerness is written on the body and implicitly identifies it with delinquency or illness. But it also holds the word at arm's length – with so-called 'scare-quotes' – as if the term is not fully accepted or acceptable, or as if the word is still in process, moving from a sense of oddness to a (related) sense of homosexuality. Homosexuality is 'queer', then, because of the perceived queerness of queers, their difference from 'us' (scientists, US Department of Labor officials, sociologists, and so on): queers are a category apart, a self-defining and identifiable group determined precisely by the queer difference of its members from the regime of the normal – from what Adrienne Rich, the contemporary lesbian poet and critic, calls 'compulsory hetero-sexuality' (Rich 1986).

But the story of 'queer' is not over yet. For the next seventy years or so, 'queer' gained currency in the English language in the United States and elsewhere as (usually) a derogatory term for (usually male) homosexual; it was combined with 'coot' to form the dismissive phrase 'queer as a coot'; and, in the 1960s and 1970s, was combined with 'bashing' to denote (and doubtless to help legitimize) verbal and physical violence against those who were, or who were perceived to be, homosexual. In the late 1980s and early 1990s, however, partly in response to the spread of AIDS among gay men, the word took a queer turn: homosexuals themselves began to 'reclaim' the word, to use it in place of the genderspecific and arguably effete term 'gay' or the clinical and cheerless 'homosexual' or the polite and even mythological-sounding 'lesbian'. 'Queer' becomes a term of pride and celebratory self-assertion, of difference affirmed and affirmative difference. The very reason for the use of 'queer' to denote homosexuality in the first place – the sense that homo-sexuality is associated with singularity and difference – is also inherited in this act of linguistic reappropriation, but the values afforded such strangeness are reversed. The fact that queers are different from 'straight' people is seen as a source of power and pride – and 'straight' now becomes a term with poten-tially negative connotations (conventional, dull, unadventurous). 'Queer' also has the advantage of being an inclusive term which gains in prestige and power just in so much as it shakes up our codes and codings of male and female, or masculinity and femininity, or bi-, hetero- and homo-. As Eve Kosofsky Sedgwick comments, 'queer' can refer to 'the open mesh of possibilities, gaps, overlaps, dissonances and resonances, lapses and excesses of meaning when the constituent elements of anyone's gender, of anyone's sexuality aren't made (or *can't be* made) to signify monolithically' (Sedgwick 1994, 8). Essentially, then, 'queer' challenges all gender and sexual essentialisms.

In homage to this brilliant queering of 'queer', its (re)appropriation as a device for the social and political empowerment of certain more or less defined, more or less discrete, more or less oppressed sexual identities, and linking up with our comments elsewhere on the association of literary texts with the uncanny or the strange, we would like to suggest that literature is itself a little (and sometimes more than a little) queer. By this we mean two things. Firstly, we want to suggest that there is an eminent tradition of queer writing in English, writing by men and women who are more or less permanently, more or less openly, more or less explicitly, queer and writing about queerness. For reasons that will become clear, this tradition is all but invisible before the late nineteenth century, although it arguably includes Marlowe, Shakespeare, the debauchee Lord Rochester, the eighteenth-century poet Katherine Philips, Henry Mackenzie (author of the novel of exquisite sensitivity *The Man of Feeling* [1771]), Matthew Lewis (author of the Gothic high-camp novel *The Monk* [1796]), Lord Byron, Walt Whitman and Herman Melville. But the literary canon from the late nineteenth century onwards is full of authors who are queer, who write homoerotic poetry or write about the experience of homosexual desire – including Gerard Manley Hopkins, Algernon Swinburne, Oscar Wilde, A.E. Housman, Virginia Woolf, Vita Sackville-West, Djuna Barnes, D.H. Lawrence, Dorothy Richardson, Charlotte Mew, H.D., Katherine Mansfield, Rosamund Lehmann, Radclyffe Hall, T.E. Lawrence, E.M. Forster, Elizabeth Bowen, W.H. Auden, Christopher Isherwood, Compton Mackenzie, Tennessee Williams, Alan Ginsberg, Gore Vidal, Truman Capote, James Baldwin, Patrick White, William Burroughs, Edmund White, Thom Gunn, Adrienne Rich, Joe Orton, Alice Walker, Jeanette Winterson, John Ashbery, Hanif Kureishi and innumerable others. We might say that there is a canon of queer writers in modern literature, except that the 'straight' canon is itself everywhere inhabited by queers (many of the writers listed above, that is to say, are central to the canon of literature in English, whether they are read as queer or straight).

Our second reason for talking about literature as 'a little (and sometimes more than a little) queer' is to suggest that literary texts in general might be open to what has been called 'queer reading'. Some of the strangeness or uncanniness, some of the power and fascination of literary texts, that is to say, has to do with the singular space which they offer for thinking (differently) about gender and sexuality. This point is illustrated by the work of Eve Sedgwick, one of the most influential queer theorists of recent years, whose notion of 'homosocial desire' we discuss, above, in our chapter on 'Desire'. In an essay entitled 'The Beast in the Closet' (first published in 1986), Sedgwick discusses Henry James's short story 'The Beast in the Jungle' (1903). James's story is an apparently 'straight' story about John Marcher, a confirmed bachelor, who has a terrible and overwhelming secret (the 'beast' of the title), a secret

which never is, never could be, articulated, but which is nevertheless understood by his friend May Bartram, a woman who supports him and who, it is
clear, could – or should – have been his lover or wife. In a stunning reading of
the story, Sedgwick examines a number of aspects of the story and its discursive contexts. She discusses the figure of the bachelor in the late nineteenth
century, for example, as a role that allowed certain men to avoid the rigorous
demands of the compulsorily heterosexual society in which they lived. (James
himself, Sedgwick argues, was a bachelor whose complex sexuality seems to
have been notable as much for the obstinacy of its heterosexuality as for anything else.) Sedgwick considers the dynamics of 'male homosexual panic'
as the unmanageable fear of homosexuality among heterosexuals, a fear that
would also appear to be based on the heterosexual male's fear of his own
desire for other men. Sedgwick then examines certain linguistic and rhetorical
aspects of the apparently heterosexual story and shows how, viewed in this
light, the story turns queer. Thus Sedgwick notes that the story uses the word
'queer' on a number of occasions to denote John Marcher's condition: while it
is clear that the primary sense of the word denotes a certain 'strangeness' (after
all, the homosexual sense of 'queer' was not an explicit part of its official
meaning in 1903), nevertheless, as we have seen, the move within 'queer' from
'strange' to 'homosexual' is never far away – and is not as queer as it might
seem. In this respect, James's use of the word may be seen to be haunted by
its semantic developments a few years later and to raise the spectre of an
unacknowledged difficulty concerning Marcher's sexual identity. Sedgwick
also notes a number of less specific 'lexical pointers', all of which are 'highly
equivocal' but which add up to a queering of the whole story. Phrases such
as Marcher's 'singularity', 'the thing [May Bartram] knew, which grew to be
at last . . . never mentioned between them save as "the real truth" about
him', 'his queer consciousness', 'dreadful things . . . I couldn't name', 'his
unhappy perversion', and so on (quoted in Sedgwick 1994, 203), convey a
strong sense of specifically *sexual* disturbance in Marcher's character. In a
complex and enthralling piece of literary critical detective-work, Sedgwick
develops a reading of the text which compellingly suggests the 'cataclysm'
of Marcher's condition to be that of (in Oscar Wilde's poignant formulation)
the 'love that dare not speak its name', the unacknowledged and unacknow-
ledgeable homosexuality of his queerness. As far as the normative values of
straight society are concerned, queerness is devastatingly and catastro-
phically *queer*: the 'straight' Marcher's problem is his inability to deal with
the problem of (his) queerness.

In her reading of the story, however, Sedgwick is not attempting to argue,
definitively, that Marcher (or James, for that matter) is in any simple sense

homosexual. Instead, she is queering the narrative by thinking through its linguistic and conceptual slippages and their engagements with the discourse that emerges out of and indeed energizes the otherwise bland, monolithic certainties of heterosexuality. Sedgwick attempts to bring out (from the closet, so to speak) the extent to which the discourse of homosexuality – the heterosexual discourse of homosexuality, that is to say, the way that homosexuality is conceived and expressed by so-called 'heterosexuals' – may be read in a text that is apparently concerned with very different matters. And Sedgwick's reading powerfully demonstrates that the discourse of heterosexuality is itself dependent upon that of homosexuality, governed, even defined, by that which it excludes. There is something rather queer, in other words, about being straight.

As well as opening up new ways of reading 'straight' literary texts, then, queer theory – such as recent work by Michel Foucault, Eve Sedgwick, Judith Butler, Leo Bersani, Alan Sinfield, Jonathan Dollimore, Joseph Bristow and others – has begun to challenge our ideas about gender and sexuality by querying (or queerying) the very basis of the categories we use to talk about ourselves, us queers and us straights. Queer theory, that is to say, queers the pitch as far as sexuality is concerned. As a number of theorists have commented, there is something rather curious, rather queer, about the way in which we divide our human and social worlds into two supposedly discrete (if not always discreet) categories. Of all the possible categories that are available to us to define ourselves and others – our wealth (or lack of it), class, height, hair colour, dietary preferences, shoe size, baldness or otherwise, political or religious beliefs, aesthetic preferences, choice of holiday destination or hi-fi manufacturer – the one that our culture has fixed upon to define us most profoundly, in some respects perhaps even beyond that of ethnic origin, race or skin colour, is that of sexual preference, the sex of the person whom we desire. This is the case not least because, as Leo Bersani remarks, 'Unlike racism, homophobia is entirely a response to an internal possibility' (Bersani 1995, 27).

David Halperin observes that 'it is not immediately evident that differences in sexual preference are by their very nature more revealing about the temperament of individual human beings, more significant determinants of personal identity, than, for example, differences in dietary preference' (Halperin 1990, 26). The comment invites us to imagine a world, or a society, in which one's identity would be defined by one's choice of food, a world in which, say, vegetarians would regularly be discriminated against in terms of their careers (they would not be allowed to join the army, for example, for fear that they might seduce others into vegetarianism); would be subject to physical and verbal abuse while walking quietly in the streets of our cities (veggie-bashing, it would be called, and would be caused by veggiephobia, the fear of being forced to eat a plate of vegetables or even of finding out that one is, deep down, oneself a vegetarian); would be disqualified from adopting children because of the fear that such children would lack a balanced diet in the crucial early years of their physical and mental development; would often socialize in special veggie bars and clubs avoided by carnivores; and would be, or would be thought to be, immediately recognizable by the way they walked, their clothes, their hairstyles, and their general demeanour. This imagined world might remind us of the pervasiveness and power of sexual preference as a determiner of our everyday lives. Indeed, the absurdity of this fictional scenario brings home how deeply embedded in our thinking is our definition of gender and sexual preference. Michel Foucault makes the point forcefully in an interview when he remarks that 'ever since Christianity, the West has not stopped saying: "To know who you are, find out about your sex." Sex has always been the focal point where, besides the future of our species, our "truth" as human subjects is tied up' (Foucault 1980a, 3). In this context we might think about how odd it is, how queer, that our social worlds and our social prejudices are organized around a choice – the sex of our sexual partners – which in some ways is similar to choices about eating, or not eating, meat.

One of the major projects of queer theory has been to examine the ways in which, in fact, the categories of desire by which we regulate our social and sexual worlds are not as fixed and immutable, not as 'natural' and self-evident, as we might like to think. Indeed, according to the influential argument of Michel Foucault, our ideas about hetero- and homo-sexuality are a function of the 'invention' of homosexuality in the late nineteenth century. While the precise historical configurations of any such 'invention' have been challenged by historians of sexuality, many of whom see the late seventeenth and eighteenth centuries as the crucial period of redefinition and 'crystallization' (see Sedgwick 1985, 83; Glover and Kaplan 2000, 91–3), Foucault's argument has been highly important in the development of queer theory. But it is crucial to understand that when Foucault claims that homosexuality was invented at a particular time in the recent past he is not arguing that men did not love, desire and have sex with other men, or women with women, before that time. Rather, he is suggesting that the apparently unequivocal distinction between *being* homosexual or *being* straight – the sense that you *are* one or the other, and the sense that *who you are* is defined by that distinction – is an aspect of sexual relationships and personal identity which has developed only very recently within certain institutional and discursive practices. According to Foucault, during the nineteenth century a series of shifts in the discourses of medicine, law, religion, politics and social analysis combined to produce the homosexual as a discrete identity. In particular, while medicine began to define a certain type of behaviour and certain desires as characteristic of a certain 'type' of person (the so-called 'invert'), the law redefined sexual acts between men as 'gross indecency' (an offence instituted in the so-called 'Labouchère Amendment' added to a law passed in the United Kingdom in 1885 which was primarily concerned with the regulation of prostitution). The new law criminalized sex between men (it simply ignored sex between women), by contrast with an older law, against 'sodomy', which covered certain forms of sex between men and women as well as various other kinds of 'unspeakable' acts, sexual and otherwise. Thus, for example, Jeffrey Weeks points out that nineteenth-century society imprisoned together atheists, the mute and sodomites, suggesting a strange homology of criminality (Weeks 1998, 693). As a result, the homosexual comes to be seen, within certain legal and medical discourses, as a particular type of person, as having a particular identity. In an eloquent and forceful passage from *The History of Sexuality: An Introduction*, Foucault argues as follows:

> As defined by the ancient civil or canonical codes, sodomy was a category of forbidden acts; their perpetrator was nothing more than the juridical subject of them. The nineteenth-century homosexual became a personage, a past, a case history, and a childhood, in addition to being a type of life, a life form, and a morphology, with an indiscreet anatomy and possibly a mysterious physiology. Nothing that went into his total composition was unaffected by his sexuality. It was everywhere present in him: at the root of all his actions because it was their insidious and indefinitely active principle; written immodestly on his face and body because it was a secret that always gave itself away. It was coinsubstantial with him, less as a habitual sin than as a singular nature . . . Homosexuality appeared as one of the forms of sexuality when it was transposed from the practice of sodomy onto a kind of interior androgyny, a hermaphrodism of the soul. The sodomite had been a temporary aberration; the homosexual was now a species. (Foucault 1981, 43)

Foucault is arguing that within 'the ancient civil or canonical codes' homosexuality as an *identity* is more or less invisible before the mid to late nineteenth century. In other words, in the context of thinking about, say, Shakespeare, asking the question of whether or not he was homosexual is, in effect, an anachronism, inappropriate to the specific ways in which sexuality and sexual identity were constructed, experienced and defined in the late sixteenth and early seventeenth centuries.

The notion of the historically and culturally constructed nature of sexuality, the idea that sexualities are differently defined and differently experienced at different times, is taken one step further by the influential theorist of gender and sexuality Judith Butler. For Butler, gender and sexuality are performative, rather than fixed or determined by biology or 'nature': gender identity 'is performatively constituted by the very "expressions" that are said to be its results' (Butler 1990, 25). 'I'm queer' is not simply a descriptive statement but makes something happen: it not only states but affirms and even creates the identity it refers to. According to this argument, in fact, the more of a man or the more of a woman you are, the more obviously your masculinity or femininity is a performative construct, the more overtly it is acted out. Both gender and sexuality, for Butler, are always kinds of drag acts so that theatrical drag acts play out the implicit logic of sex and gender identity according to which our lives are, more generally, determined. As an example of such a performance of gender and sexuality Butler reminds us of Aretha Franklin's line 'you make me feel like a natural woman'. As Butler remarks, on first sight the line seems to be affirming the notion of the naturalness of gender and sexuality: the singer's love for the man makes her a *natural* woman. Butler comments that the line seems to indicate that 'there is no breakage, no discontinuity between "sex" as biological facticity and essence, or between gender and sexuality' (Butler 1991, 27). But when we think a little more carefully we see that this naturalness is both something that is *learnt* or *produced* ('you *make* me feel . . .'), and something that is *imitated* ('you make me feel *like* . . .'). Playing out and articulating the performative logic of gender and sexuality, Aretha Franklin is singing about it, wittingly or not, as a kind of 'heterosexual drag' (28). This, for Butler, is indicative of the way that all sexualities – homo-, hetero-, bi- and other – are forms of drag, performances of sex and of gender.

'Shakespeare', declares Harold Bloom, 'largely invented us' (Bloom 1994, 40). One way of understanding this claim would be in relation to the cultural construction of gender and sexuality. Reading Shakespeare can help us to think about ways in which sexuality is an unstable site of conflict and transgression, historically contingent, mobile, a performance. Writing at a time before categories of homo- and heterosexual desire had been institutionalized, medicalized, rigidified and policed, Shakespeare's writing questions what it means to be a man or a woman, and what it means, as a man and as a woman, to desire men and to desire women. We might end by thinking about Shakespeare's sonnet 20, a key text in debates surrounding his representations of sexuality and sexual identity: in this sonnet, as Bruce Smith comments, 'for the poet, for his readers, and presumably for the young man', issues of love and sexuality 'reach a crisis' (Smith 1994, 249). Here is a poem that has fascinated (and indeed horrified) readers and critics through the centuries, a poem by a man addressed to a man, his 'master mistress', which thinks about masculinity and femininity and thinks about the different ways in which they inhabit male and female bodies, thinks about how homo- and hetero-eroticism are performed, played out in language. It is a poem that both plays on stereotypes of gender and sexuality (including misogyny) and, at the same time, disorients them, queers them, plays with the idea of a 'natural' gender and sexuality but also with the idea of the constructedness of such identities. This is a natural wo/man: a man who is all man, by nature 'pricked out', but who is at the same time, curiously, queerly, female, his 'woman's face' by 'nature' 'painted':

> A woman's face, with nature's own hand painted,
> Hast thou, the master mistress of my passion—
> A woman's gentle heart, but not acquainted
> With shifting change, as is false women's fashion;
> An eye more bright than theirs, less false in rolling,
> Gilding the object whereupon it gazeth;
> A man in hue all hues in his controlling,
> Which steals men's eyes and women's souls amazeth.
> And for a woman wert thou first created,
> Till nature as she wrought thee fell a-doting,
> And by addition me of thee defeated,
> By adding one thing to my purpose nothing.
> But since she pricked thee out for women's pleasure,
> Mine be thy love, and thy love's use their treasure.

Further reading

Eve Kosofsky Sedgwick's books *Between Men* (1985), *The Epistemology of the Closet* (1991) and *Tendencies* (1994) present highly influential accounts of homosocial and homosexual desire focusing on a series of (mainly) nineteenth- and twentieth-century texts. The opening two chapters of the groundbreaking *Between Men* offer a good starting point. Alan Sinfield's brisk, polemical and entertaining books *Cultural Politics – Queer Reading* (1994) and *The Wilde Century: Effeminacy, Oscar Wilde and the Queer Moment* (1994) provide good accounts of many of the ideas encountered in this chapter. Donald E. Hall's *Queer Theories* (2003) offers a good short introduction to the field. A more detailed and scholarly discussion of queer sexuality in Renaissance England is Bruce Smith's *Homosexual Desire in*

Shakespeare's England (1994). For a thought-provoking study of nineteenth-century US literature in this context, see Scott S. Derrick (1997). Correspondingly, for a study of 'effeminate England' since 1885, see Joseph Bristow (1995). For a brilliant and often excoriating examination of some of the presuppositions and prejudices surrounding cultural representations of homosexuality (including those of 'queer theorists' themselves), see Leo Bersani's *Homos* (1995). For an important recent account of the historicism of queer theory and the history of homosexuality, see Halperin *How to Do the History of Homosexuality* (2002).

23. Suspense

I n a moment, we shall say something that may be rather shocking. In the meantime, we propose to describe two kinds of suspense, resolved and unresolved. 'Resolved' suspense is usually associated with thrillers, detective stories, gothic novels, tales of mystery and the supernatural, and romances. The Italian novelist and literary theorist Umberto Eco uses the term 'closed texts' for such narratives, as contrasted with 'open texts' which leave the reader in doubt or uncertainty (Eco 1979). In closed texts, the murderer is found, the mystery resolved, the ghost exposed as a mechanical illusion, or the lovers are able to consummate their love. In these cases, suspense relies for its resolution on the revelation of a secret or secrets. Resolved suspense can also be created by delaying an event that we know will happen. This is especially clear in examples from cinema. We feel certain that the woman behind the shower curtain cannot escape the raised dagger of the psycho-killer, but for a few seemingly endless moments the fulfilment of this expectation is delayed. Similarly, in *Fatal Attraction* (1987) the pet rabbit is never going to avoid the boiling pot, and in *Silence of the Lambs* (1991) it is only a matter of time before Hannibal the cannibal lives up to his name and gets his unjust dessert. Here suspense is not so much created by a hermeneutic gap, by the reader's ignorance, as by our expectation of an event which is delayed: we are pretty sure *what* is going to happen, we just don't know *when*. These are kinds of narrative suspense, then, that can be defined in terms of expectation, delay and resolution.

One of the most notorious instances of literary suspense is Henry James's novella *The Turn of the Screw* (1898). In this story, the reader's expectation of an ending is screwed to an excruciating pitch of tension (the story is, excruciatingly, about suspense itself, as its title might indicate). The suspense of this haunting story rests largely on whether it is about actual ghosts and real evil, or is simply a psychological case-study of a disturbed mind. Critics have tended to argue for one reading or the other. Recently, however, critics have recognized that the choice of interpretation – the choice, finally, of which story we think we are reading – is irresolvable. As Roslyn Jolly comments, 'critics have become increasingly aware that the irresolvability of the tale's ambiguity puts on trial their own readerly skills and assumptions about meaning in narrative' (Jolly 1993, 102). Indeed, critics have realized that this uncanny and unsettling suspense of interpretation is itself part of what makes the story so terrifying: *The Turn of the Screw* is *suspended* between two mutually exclusive readings. While the tale builds up to an extraordinary pitch of narrative suspense, our sense of what happens at the end of the story may never finally be resolved. James manages to exploit a fundamentally ambivalent narrative structure (the story is told by the governess herself, so there is no one to tell us whether or not she is mad), and to 'end' his story in a kind of *open* suspense, a suspense without end. In particular, James continually provides us with pointers or markers to a final resolution, with suggestions of ghosts, telepathy and evil on the one hand, and of madness on the other, making us wait for a final resolution of ambiguities which never arrives. In Chapter 9, for example, the governess says of the two children, Miles and Flora, that 'There were moments when, by an irresistible impulse, I found myself catching them up and pressing them to my heart' (131). The sentence foreshadows in a suspenseful and undecidable way the extraordinary ending of the story, where the governess does, literally, 'catch' Miles: 'I caught him, yes, I held him – it may be imagined with what a passion' (198). In both cases, however, the *force* of this catching – how forceful it is, and how conscious or rational, what its intention is – is suspended. Is the governess protecting Miles or smothering him? We are left, then, in a state of hermeneutic suspense, of interpretative uncertainty – unable to know, finally, how to read James's story. Suspense, in this case, is open.

Another way to think about this is in terms of a suspense which, according to Jacques Derrida, is peculiarly literary: 'There is no literature', claims Derrida, 'without a *suspended* relation to meaning and reference' (Derrida 1992a, 48). There may be a temptation to think of the irresolution of James's suspense simply as carelessness or as a mistake – the author has not made his meaning clear. As Derrida suggests, however, literary texts can be characterized precisely in terms of unresolved suspense. And this suspense concerns, in the first place, the very status of the worlds to which literary texts refer. Critics use various terms to describe suspenseful effects in reading: ambiguity, ambivalence, equivocality, indeterminacy, undecidability, uncertainty, aporia, gap, hiatus. All of these words may be applied to the effects of suspense achieved by James's story.

In addition to such narrative suspense, effects of suspense can be produced on a more local and less melodramatic scale by aspects of syntax and versification, by the very language of the text. James, in fact, is famous for a peculiarly suspenseful sentence structure which complements the intensity of narrative suspense in stories such as *The Turn of the Screw*. The story opens in the form of a 'frame narrative': a group of people get together to tell stories, one of which is that of the governess. Here is the opening sentence of the story:

> The story had held us, round the fire, sufficiently breathless, but except the obvious remark that it was gruesome, as, on Christmas eve in an old house, a strange tale should essentially be, I remember no comment uttered till somebody happened to say that it was the only case he had met in which such a visitation had fallen on a child. (81)

Not only is this sentence *about* suspense – the suspense of being 'held' by a story, the holding of breath and the withholding of comments – but it is also syntactically structured by suspense. The final word, 'child', is the kernel of the sentence, its centre, but the word is withheld until the end. Before that, the sentence develops through multiple subclauses and syntactical digressions. Henry James's prose, then, the syntax of his sentences, is highly suspenseful.

The Turn of the Screw turns on suspense – indeed turns, self-reflexively, on the very idea of 'turns'. Chapter 9, again, is exemplary. The governess is reading Henry Fielding's *Amelia* alone at night: 'I found myself, at the turn of a page and with his spell all scattered, looking straight up . . .' (133). She leaves her room and walks into the hall, where at 'the great turn of the staircase' (134) she sees, for the third time, the ghost of Peter Quint. The chapter ends with a description of this ghost disappearing into 'the silence itself': 'I definitely saw it turn, as I might have seen the low wretch to which it had once belonged turn on receipt of an order' as it disappears 'into the darkness in which the next bend was lost' (135). The 'next bend' may be in the darkness of the staircase, but it is also the next chapter of the story, the dark bend or turn of narrative. It is not only the governess, then, who sees or hallucinates a ghostly presence in the turns: our own reading is suspended on the turns of the narrative.

Verse also relies on turns. The fact that the word 'verse' comes from the Latin *vertere*, 'to turn', might alert us to the way in which verse is wedded to the turns of line endings, suspenseful places of ghostly pausation. In addition to the suspense as we turn from one line to the next, verse produces its own forms of suspense through the exploitation of the possibilities of rhythm. Comparatively rudimentary verse-forms, such as those of nursery rhymes and ballads, for example, are notable for the way in which they generate suspense through rhythmical repetition, by building into the poetry the expectation of a repetition. The opening to the traditional Scottish ballad 'Sir Patrick Spens' is one such example:

> The King sits in Dumferling toune,
>   Drinking the blude-reid wine:
> O whar will I get a guid sailor,
>   To sail this schip of mine?

Much of the force of this powerfully haunting poem (one that, in many ways, anticipates such pseudo-medieval ballads as Coleridge's 'The Ancient Mariner' and Keats's 'La Belle Dame sans Merci') is achieved through the regularity of its metrical arrangement (the regular four-beat first line and three-beat second line, which continues throughout the poem). Together with the regular rhyming of lines two and four of each stanza, the prosody of the poem adds up – in the expectation and fulfilment of rhythmical suspense – to one of the most compelling of its pleasures.

Effects of rhythmical suspense are also explored in more intricate ways by poets such as Thomas Hardy. Hardy's poetry is notable not least for the wide range of its verse-forms. 'Neutral Tones' (written in 1867, first published in 1898) enacts various effects of suspense through rhythm:

> We stood by a pond that winter day,
> And the sun was white, as though chidden of God,
> And a few leaves lay on the starving sod;
>   —They had fallen from an ash, and were gray.

> 5   Your eyes on me were as eyes that rove
> Over tedious riddles of years ago;
> And some words played between us to and fro
>   On which lost the more by our love.

> The smile on your mouth was the deadest thing
> 10   Alive enough to have strength to die;
> And a grin of bitterness swept thereby
>   Like an ominous bird a-wing . . .

> Since then, keen lessons that love deceives,
> And wrings with wrong, have shaped to me
> 15   Your face, and the God-curst sun, and a tree,
> And a pond edged with grayish leaves.

While not strictly regular, the rhythm of the first three lines of each stanza is more or less regular, consisting of four sets of one or two weak (or 'short') [.] stresses followed by one strong (or long) one [—]: Wĕ stōod | bў ă pōnd | thăt wĭn | tĕr dāy. The final line of each stanza, however, lacks one 'foot', having only three combinations of weak and strong stress: Thĕy hăd fāllen | frŏm ăn asĥ, | ănd wĕre grāy. The regularity of the first three lines of each stanza is disappointed. This gives an effect of blankness, of something missing, of incomplete suspense. This effect is related to the theme of the poem, its sense of blank hopelessness: the poem is concerned with something missing, a lack, a loss, which is inexpressible. This, then, is just one example of the many ways in which poetry is able to create effects of suspense in rhythm such that the *form* of the poem is inseparable from its *content*.

As we have already suggested, poetry can also exploit line endings for effects of suspense. The neo-classical poetry of Alexander Pope, for example, plays on the suspenseful formalities of rhyming couplets. The following lines from Pope's poem 'An Essay on Criticism' (1711) generate suspense through rhyme, rhythm and antithesis:

> *True wit* is *Nature* to Advantage drest,
> What oft was *Thought*, but ne'er so well Exprest . . .
> (lines 297–8)

The fact that the whole of Pope's long poem is in the form of rhyming couplets means that the first line creates the expectation of a second line which will end in the rhyme 'est'. And we are not disappointed. The second line both develops and explains the first, creating an analogy between thought and nature on the one hand, and clothing and expression on the other, to define 'true wit'. Owing to the regularity of the verse-form, the first line creates an expectation of such an answering line and, although the lines are end-stopped (they do not continue syntactically from one line to the next), they produce the expectation of such an answer: the sense of the first line is suspended until its completion in the next.

Writing almost a century later, William Wordsworth also exploits the suspenseful effects of verse, in particular of line endings, but does so very differently. Consider, for example, 'A Slumber did my Spirit Seal' (1800):

> A slumber did my spirit seal;
>   I had no human fears:
> She seemed a thing that could not feel
>   The touch of earthly years.
>
> 5 No motion has she now, no force;
>   She neither hears nor sees,
> Rolled round in earth's diurnal course
>   With rocks and stones and trees.

This poem is usually understood to be about a young girl who has died, and critics usually relate it to other poems which were written by Wordsworth at about the same time and which concern a girl named Lucy. The speaker appears to be lamenting not only the girl's death, but also his own ignorance, the fact that he remained unaware that she might die when she was alive. Unlike Pope's poem in almost every other respect, Wordsworth's is similar in that most of its lines are end-stopped. Crucially, however, line three is run on or enjambed: there is no punctuation after the word 'feel', and the next line is required for syntactical completion. In fact, the end of this line exploits not only syntactical but also hermeneutic suspense. After all, it would be possible to read line three as syntactically complete: 'She seemed a thing that could not feel'. But this produces a very different meaning from what we find if we continue to the next line – 'She seemed a thing that could not feel / The touch of earthly years'. There is a significant difference between not being able to feel, and not being able to feel 'the touch of earthly years'. The first possibility gives us the sense that she – like, apparently, the speaker, in line one – is anaesthetized, closed off, to all sensation and all emotion. The second possibility gives us the sense that this was a young girl who seemed as if she would never grow old or die. What the poem achieves with this line-break, this turn, is to generate and hold both meanings in suspense. While the latter is no doubt the 'correct' reading – we cannot simply ignore line four, once we have read it – the apparent completion offered by line three in isolation remains to haunt this latter sense.

As with our discussion of Henry James, we find that examples of resolved or closed suspense can in fact be read as open – as examples of the unresolved. Wordsworth's poem prompts a number of suspenseful questions. In the very opening line of the poem, for example, it is not clear whether 'my spirit' sealed a slumber or a slumber sealed 'my spirit': in any case it is very difficult to know what the three words ('slumber', 'spirit', 'seal'), either separately or together, are referring to. Likewise, while we have assumed that the referent of 'she' in line three is a girl, Lucy, the word can also be understood to refer back to 'my spirit' in line one. There is, in fact, no final way of determining which reading is 'correct'. While we may want to choose one reading over the other, we have no way to justify such a choice: the point is undecidable or equivocal. And the difference has significant implications for any reading of the poem. In the first place, while the poem appears to be about the relationship between the speaker and a girl, the equivocal reference of 'she' means that we can no longer be sure that the object of the speaker's interest is a person outside of himself, rather than his own 'spirit'. As Paul de Man comments in his reading of this poem in his essay 'The Rhetoric of Temporality', 'Wordsworth is one of the few poets who can write proleptically about their own death and speak, as it were, from beyond their own graves. The "she" in the poem is in fact large enough to encompass Wordsworth as well' (de Man 1983, 225). Rather differently, it may be that this equivocal reference suggests something very important about mourning itself – that in mourning, the object of our grief is neither simply inside nor simply outside the one who mourns. The suspense of reference in this context might be connected to another of the themes of the poem – closure. The speaker talks of his spirit being 'sealed', of 'she' being untouchable in the first stanza, and in the second of 'she' being without motion, force or sensory perception, 'rolled round' with the earth as if sealed in a grave. This sense of closure may even be reinforced by the end-stopped rhymes of each stanza. In all of these ways, the poem is 'about' a sense of closure – being sealed, enclosed, finished, dead. And yet the closure that the poem so intensively suggests is in dynamic tension with the undecidable suspense of reference – with, indeed, the poem's *meaning*. Far from being closed, in fact, the poem is undecidably suspended. Once we recognize the central importance of the tension between what we have called closed and open suspense in the poem, it becomes available as a means with which to map many of the poem's features. In particular, we might recognize that the poem is suspended by the uncanny gap of time between stanza one and stanza two, that moment outside the poem when 'she' dies, the unspoken, perhaps unspeakable event of a death which at once haunts and generates the poem. Wordsworth's poem thus enacts a drama of suspense, an allegory of closure *and* undecidability.

Ambiguity and undecidability have been central to Anglo-American literary criticism and theory in the twentieth century. One of the most influential works has been William Empson's *Seven Types of Ambiguity* (1930; 3rd edn 1953). In the middle decades of the century, partly as a response to Empson's book, the so-called new critics focused on ambiguity as a major concern of literary texts. More recently, poststructuralist critics have emphasized the notion of undecidability. The difference between new critical ambiguity and poststructuralist undecidability, though apparently minimal, is perhaps fundamental. For the new critics, ambiguity produces a complex but organic whole, a unity wherein ambiguity brings together disparate elements. For poststructuralist critics, by contrast, undecidability opens up a gap, a rift in the text which can never be fully sealed. Undecidability opens the text to multiple readings, it destabilizes the reader's sense of the certainty of any particular reading, and ultimately threatens to undermine the very stability of any reading position, the very identity of any reader (as Søren Kierkegaard remarks, 'the moment of decision is madness'). Suspensions of meaning bypass the reductive and constricting determination of what is now recognized to be the illusion of a single, final, determined 'meaning'. To think in terms of undecidability, however, is not to advocate the equal legitimacy of any and every interpretation: to acknowledge and explore aporias or suspensions of meaning involves the responsibilities of the most thoughtful and scrupulous kinds of reading.

Readers tend to want to resolve suspense: like foreplay, suspense carried on beyond a certain point seems to be undesirable, indeed intolerable. We want answers, and we want them soon. And there are all sorts of ways of terminating suspense, of closing it or resolving it. We can appeal to the notion of authorial intention and try to argue that Wordsworth 'meant' this or that, or we can appeal to 'historical evidence' and try to establish whether Lucy 'really is' the referent of this poem, or in line with the dentistry school of literary criticism to which we referred in Chapter 2, we can simply argue for a single extractable molar of meaning for the text. In every such case, however, we would be suppressing the suspendedness of that 'suspended relation to meaning and reference' that Derrida talks about. Rather than immediately attempting to resolve suspense, then, we might think about literary texts as themselves sites of suspense, places where suspense can occur without being closed off, without being finished. We might consider that it is the function of literary texts to go beyond the trite, the comforting, the easy resolution of suspense, to take us to imagined places where suspense cannot be resolved, where questions are more complex and more challenging than can be reduced to a single determined meaning. In this respect, there are reasons to welcome undecidability, this challenge to our desire to master the text.

Further reading

For a brilliant exploration of Wordsworth's line endings, see Christopher Ricks's 'William Wordsworth 1' (1984). For two fine introductory works on rhythm and metre, see Derek Attridge's *Poetic Rhythm* (1992) and Thomas

Carper and Derek Attridge's *Meter and Meaning* (2003). An excellent and imaginative exploration of prosody in terms of the sounds of English poetry is John Hollander's *Vision and Resonance* (1985). On suspense in the sense of ambiguity or undecidability, there is, perhaps, no better place to start than William Empson's classic *Seven Types of Ambiguity* (1953), first published in 1930. On the idea of literature as suspended in relation to meaning and reference, see the interview with Jacques Derrida in his *Acts of Literature* (1992a). A classic argument concerning the 'undecidability' of contending meanings in literary texts is J. Hillis Miller's 'The Figure in the Carpet' (1980). For a rather different approach, see D.A. Miller, ' "Cage aux folles": Sensation and Gender in Wilkie Collins's *The Woman in White*' (1989), which offers a fascinating consideration of the physiological effects of suspense fiction on readers.

24. Racial difference

You might reasonably expect a chapter on racial difference to focus on, for example, William Faulkner's great novel of social aspiration and race prejudice *Absalom, Absalom!* (1936) or Toni Morrison's closely related slave narrative, *Beloved* (1987). Our intention here, however, is to argue that questions of race, slavery and racial violence are everywhere, and that they pervade even the most apparently 'innocent' literary works. In this way we will be guided by the provocative and incisive words of the American poet John Ashbery: 'Remnants of the old atrocity subsist, but they are converted into ingenious shifts in scenery, a sort of "English Garden" effect, to give the required air of naturalness, pathos and hope' (Ashbery, *Three Poems* (1956), cited in Wood 2002, 1).

Charlotte Brontë's *Jane Eyre* (1847) is one of the classic nineteenth-century novels in English. It describes a love affair between the eponymous heroine, a governess, and her aristocratic master, Rochester. The novel ends with the marriage of Jane and Rochester after Jane has become both professionally and economically independent. Jane's struggle for independence marks the novel as centrally engaged with the oppression of women in nineteenth-century England and with the possibility of their liberation from constricting roles of subservience to their male 'masters'. Alongside the question of gender, however, *Jane Eyre* raises other questions. These are questions of racial difference and they will form the focal point of this chapter. Jane and Rochester are unable to marry because Rochester is already married to Bertha Mason, a creole woman from the West Indies. This woman, who is mad, is kept locked up in Rochester's attic. Occasionally she escapes, and at one point attempts to set light to Rochester's bed while he is in it. Finally, in a pyromaniacal frenzy, she sets light to the house and dies in the blaze. Her death leaves the way clear for Jane and Rochester to marry, although not before Rochester is blinded and crippled in trying to save Bertha from the fire.

While the novel has long been recognized as an exploration and critique of the position of women in nineteenth-century society, more recently critics have begun to see questions of racial and ethnic difference as central to the novel. The delayed recognition of the importance of these questions is telling. As in the English literary tradition more generally, such questions have been marginalized or effaced. They have simply not been seen or have been ignored. Such an effacement is, in fact, inscribed in the novel itself. Indeed, representations of race in *Jane Eyre* may be said to constitute a sort of textual unconscious: like the repressed contents of the Freudian unconscious, they repeatedly return in disguised form. In the following passage, for example, racial and ethnic difference becomes part of the flirtatious courtship ritual of Jane and Rochester. At one point, Jane, the narrator, sees Rochester smile: 'I thought his smile was such as a sultan might, in a blissful and fond moment, bestow on a slave his gold and gems had enriched.' This image of sultan and slave then develops into a whole discourse on slavery and racial otherness:

'I would not exchange this one little English girl for the Grand Turk's whole seraglio—gazelle-eyes, houri forms, and all!'

The Eastern allusion bit me again. 'I'll not stand you an inch in the stead of a seraglio', I said; 'so don't consider me an equivalent for one. If you have a fancy for anything in that line, away with you, sir, to the bazaars of Stamboul, without delay, and lay out in extensive slave-purchases some of that spare cash you seem at a loss to spend satisfactorily here.'

'And what will you do, Janet, while I am bargaining for so many tons of flesh and such an assortment of black eyes?'

'I'll be preparing myself to go out as a missionary to preach liberty to them that are enslaved—your harem inmates amongst the rest. I'll get admitted there, and I'll stir up mutiny; and you, three-tailed bashaw as you are, sir, shall in a trice find yourself fettered amongst our hands: nor will I, for one, consent to cut your bonds till you have signed a charter, the most liberal that despot ever yet conferred.' (197–8)

Ironically, Jane is to gain her financial independence and her freedom from what Rochester calls her 'governessing slavery' (298) when she inherits a fortune derived, we can only assume, from the slave-trade of the West Indies. Moreover, although she seriously contemplates it, she does not finally leave England with another man, St John Rivers, who wishes to marry her and take her with him as a missionary to India. Most importantly, however, this passage presents us with the intersection of the discourses of sexual desire and racial otherness. These discourses organize the novel but do so in a way that the novel itself seems to repress. Both Jane and Rochester figure the racially other as sexually active and even passionate, while at the same time being available for purchase, like goods to be bought in a market. By contrast, Jane herself is repeatedly figured in terms of resisting both her own sexual desires and the financial temptations of Rochester's wealth: her sexuality is governed by self-control and she cannot be bought. The passage also brings together questions of sexuality and gender, race and economics, through its references to slavery. Slavery, the buying and selling of the dehumanized and racially other, is central to the novel's plot in that Jane gains her financial and therefore social independence after inheriting a fortune made in the Caribbean, where slavery had been the main source of wealth. Rather differently, the novel repeatedly figures slavery through metaphors of chains and imprisonment. A few paragraphs after the above quotation, for example, Rochester expresses a desire to imprison Jane when he says that ' "when once I have fairly seized you, to have and to hold, I'll just – figuratively speaking – attach you to a chain like this" (touching his watch-guard)' (299). The expression 'figuratively speaking' denies but at the same time exposes the structure of gender and race relations organizing the novel: it exposes the fact that Rochester is *not* only speaking 'figuratively'. Indeed, the phrase marks a textual anxiety concerning the precise status of slavery in the novel – literal or figurative. And this anxiety is compounded by the fact that while Rochester is flirtatiously threatening Jane with enchainment, incarcerated in his attic, imprisoned in chains, is his wife, the racially other Bertha.

A brief reading of a second passage might clarify some of these issues concerning the novel's representations of race. The first time that Jane and the reader see Bertha is a crucial moment. Jane and Rochester are prevented from marrying by the revelation that he is already married. Rochester tells Jane the truth and, in order to excuse his attempted bigamy, takes her into the attic to look at Bertha:

> In the deep shade, at the farther end of the room, a figure ran backwards and forwards. What it was, whether beast or human being, one could not, at first sight tell: it grovelled, seemingly, on all fours; it snatched and growled like some strange wild animal: but it was covered with clothing, and a quantity of dark, grizzled hair, wild as a mane, hid its head and face. (321)

No longer a woman, Bertha is the other of humanity, unrecognizable as human, a beast with a purely animal physiognomy. Almost invisible, Bertha cannot be seen. Invisibility, as this suggests, and as we observe in our reading of the opening to Ralph Ellison's *Invisible Man* in Chapter 10, above, is the condition of racial otherness. As Henry Louis Gates has commented, 'The trope of blackness in Western discourse has signified absence at least since Plato' (Gates 1984, 315). In this novel, Bertha cannot and must not be seen. Despite (or because of) her invisibility as an individual, Bertha embodies the very idea of difference for Rochester and for the novel itself. Rochester explicitly contrasts Bertha with Jane: 'look at the difference! Compare these clear eyes with the red balls yonder – this face with that mask – this form with that bulk' (322). By contrasting the two women, Rochester makes it clear that Bertha should be understood as the other of Jane. But, as we have seen elsewhere, otherness is a tricky business. If you say that one thing is the opposite of another, you are at the same time asserting their mutual dependence, in that it is pointless to contrast two things from different categories. You would not say that a cricket match is the *opposite* of a submarine, for example, if only because there are no obvious points of comparison. What is being asserted in Rochester's comparison, then, is not only difference but also likeness: in particular, they are both women who are, in different ways, imprisoned, and both are partners for Rochester. Bertha is what Jane is not but *could be*. While it is only opposition that is announced, *Jane Eyre* is haunted by the possibility that Bertha is not simply other to but also, in some ways, identical with Jane.

In these respects, then, *Jane Eyre* articulates how racial otherness is constituted – both absolutely other, non-human, bestial, and at the same time an integral element in what defines racial sameness, in this case Englishness and, or as, whiteness. And it is this ambiguous status of the other (racial or otherwise) that makes it so threatening, so disturbing, so dangerous. This dangerous (racial) other, far from being unusual is, in fact, quite common in canonical works of English literature. Figures of the racially other – more or less threatening, more or less destructive – appear as, for example, the Moor in Shakespeare's *Othello* (*c.*1602), the Jew in *The Merchant of Venice* (*c.*1596), Caliban in *The Tempest* (1611), Man Friday in Daniel Defoe's *Robinson Crusoe* (1719), some of Lord Byron's dashing, exotic heroes and anti-heroes, the Malay in Thomas De Quincey's *Confessions of an English Opium Eater* (1822), Heathcliff in Emily Brontë's *Wuthering Heights* (1847), Daniel Deronda in George Eliot's novel of that name (1876), and various figures in the colonial stories and novels of Rudyard Kipling (1865–1936), Joseph Conrad (1857–1924), E.M. Forster (1879–1970) and Graham Greene (1904–1991), to name only some of the most famous examples. Far from being a marginal concern of English Literature, in fact, racial difference is central.

But the internationalizing of contemporary 'English' literature in and as the literatures of the English-speaking 'world' – in the literatures of (for example)

Australia, Canada, the Caribbean, Hong Kong, India, New Zealand, Nigeria, Pakistan, South Africa, Sri Lanka, the USA, the West Indies – has also permanently altered our conception of such 'otherness'. The emphatic multiculturalism of the postcolonial canon suggests, indeed, that the racial, linguistic and cultural 'other' may indeed be conceived as the white Anglo-Saxon writer him- or herself. At the same time, the geo-political, cultural and racial heterogeneity of postcolonial discourses itself provokes a questioning of the apparently stable, established values of canonicity, with its assumptions of paternity and inheritance, its homogenizing linearity of influence, and its cultural exclusivity.

We have tried to suggest elsewhere in the present book that many of the major developments in literary criticism and theory of the past few years have been associated with what is known as a critique of the subject – with a deconstruction of the stable, coherent and autonomous 'self'. This critique investigates the idea that there is nothing *essential* about the nature of any individual or about the human more generally. It is not for nothing that this critique of the subject and of essentialism has been mounted. Our brief reading of the dehumanization of Bertha in *Jane Eyre* has begun to suggest that Western humanism necessarily defines itself through terms of race, by constructing a racial other which then stands in opposition to the humanity of the racially homogeneous. Such essentializing of race is at once philosophically untenable and very dangerous. Racism is, before anything else, the delusion of essentialism. As Robert Young points out, the invention of modern concepts of 'human nature', together with ideas about the universal nature of humanity and the human mind, occurred during the centuries characterized in the West by colonization, 'those particularly violent centuries in the history of the world now known as the era of Western colonization' (Young 1990, 121). Critics such as Frantz Fanon, Edward Said, Gayatri Spivak and Homi Bhabha have argued that the Western discourse of colonialism is constituted by the other subject – by alterities of race, colour or ethnic origin. Western notions of human identity itself as universal or unchanging may be recognized as a historical construct constituted by the exclusion, marginalization and oppression of racial others.

Literary studies is far from free of the discursive marginalization of racial and ethnic others. For example, it was long thought possible for writers and critics to appeal to 'universal' values. A notorious instance of this is a series of comments made by the nineteenth-century politician, literary critic and historian Thomas Babington Macaulay in his *Minute on Law and Education* (1835). This Minute, presented to the Committee of Public Instruction for Bengal, was destined to have a decisive influence on the education of the indigenous population in colonial India. Macaulay argues for the teaching of

English and against the teaching of Arabic and Sanscrit to the Indian population. His argument relies on assertions concerning the aesthetic value of
Western culture:

> I have no knowledge of either Sanscrit or Arabic. But I have done what I
> could to form a correct estimate of their value. I have read translations of the
> most celebrated Arabic and Sanscrit works. I have conversed, both here
> and at home, with men distinguished by their proficiency in the Eastern
> tongues. I am quite ready to take the oriental learning at the valuation of the
> orientalists themselves. I have never found one among them who could
> deny that a single shelf of a good European library was worth the whole
> native literature of India or Arabia. The intrinsic superiority of the Western
> literature is indeed fully admitted by those members of the committee who
> support the oriental plan of education. . . . It is, I believe, no exaggeration
> to say that all the historical information which has been collected in the
> Sanscrit language is less valuable than what may be found in the paltry
> abridgements used at preparatory schools in England. In every branch of
> physical or moral philosophy, the relative position of the two nations is
> nearly the same. (Quoted in Said 1983, 12)

While expressing appalling prejudice, this passage appeals to standards of
objectivity, academic authority and apparently rational statements about
'intrinsic superiority'. The passage is evidence that, as Frantz Fanon remarks,
for the native, 'objectivity is always directed against him' (quoted in Said
1993, 196) – that 'objectivity' is ideological. In Macaulay's statement, such
objectivity is, in fact, blatantly ideological in its dependence on judgements
of aesthetic value. By their very nature, such statements can *only* be culturally, ethnically and historically specific. To judge the aesthetic standards of
one culture by those of another is self-evidently problematic. Judged by the
standards of Japanese Noh drama, for example, Shakespeare's plays are
absurdly verbose and thoroughly incompetent. And yet the history of Western aesthetics is dominated by precisely such notions of the universality of art.

To end this chapter, we would like to suggest two ways of going beyond
such ways of reading and writing. Implicit in our discussion has been the idea
that there is a connection between the differences of race and of gender. In this
respect, Patrick Williams and Laura Chrisman argue that any 'discussion of
ethnicity is always also by implication a discussion of gender and sexuality'.
The reason for this is, not least, that 'Women, as the biological "carriers"
of the "race", occupy a primary and complex role in representations of
ethnicity . . . and it is women's exercise of their sexuality which is an often
unacknowledged major concern underlying such representations' (Williams

and Chrisman 1993, 17). In Western literature black women have been doubly effaced. As novels such as Alice Walker's *The Color Purple* (1982) and Toni Morrison's *The Bluest Eye* (1970) make clear, black women are silenced both as black and as female. But it is precisely this doubled otherness which might help us begin to move beyond racial essentialism, beyond the repressive politics of identity. In an attempt to get beyond a constricting notion of identity and of a simple and reductive notion of otherness, Mae Gwendolyn Henderson has argued that black women's writing is 'interlocutionary, or dialogic' owing to their position as 'not only the "Other" of the Same, but also as the "other" of the other(s), [which] implies . . . a relationship of difference and identification with the "other(s)"' (Henderson 1993, 258–9). The value of this analysis is that it allows us to recognize the plurality of identity, to recognize that any identity is constituted by a multiplicity of positions and differences. Black women's writing, in particular, being marginalized twice over, figuring the other of the other, reinforces a sense of the polymorphic nature of identity. In addition, Henry Louis Gates has argued that all black texts are necessarily 'two toned', or 'double-voiced', that they both engage with white canonical discourse and, at the same time, express a black consciousness. This, for Gates, leads to a discourse which is duplicitous, potentially subversive, one that undermines the universalizing and essentializing tendencies of hegemonic white discourse: 'Black people have always been masters of the figurative: saying one thing to mean something quite other has been basic to black survival in oppressive Western cultures' (Gates 1984, 6).

Our second suggestion for displacing the monolithic and oppressive assumptions about racial difference is the possibility of *reading* otherwise – the possibility of what Edward Said calls 'contrapuntal reading' (Said 1993, 78). A number of critics and theorists have suggested different ways of reading, guided by an acceptance of multiplicity, a questioning of binary oppositions and an affirmation of radical otherness. Said suggests that we might read such texts as Brontë's *Jane Eyre* or Jane Austen's *Mansfield Park* 'with an understanding of what is involved when an author shows . . . that a colonial sugar plantation is . . . important to the process of maintaining a particular style of life in England' (78). Such a reading, a contrapuntal reading, two-toned or double-voiced, cannot ignore the discourse of slavery by which Jane's liberation as a woman is mediated.

Further reading

Frantz Fanon's impassioned and politically charged *The Wretched of the Earth* (1967) is the classic work on race, nationalism and decolonization. For good recent discussions of race and culture, see David Marriott, *On Black Men* (2000), and Brian Nero, *Race* (2003). For a valuable and thought-provoking account of racism in relation to the emergence and functioning of the modern nation-state, see David Theo Goldberg (2002). For a wide-ranging and polemical study of the links between race and sexuality, especially in the context of slavery, see Marcus Wood (2002). Much of the most interesting work on race and ethnicity in literature has been that associated with studies of postcolonialism: two important collections of essays are Homi Bhabha, ed., *Nation and Narration* (1990) and Williams and Chrisman, eds, *Colonial Discourse and Post-Colonial Theory* (1993). The work of Spivak, who comes at the subject of race and ethnicity from a specifically feminist position, has been particularly influential: see her *In Other Worlds* (1987). For another collection of poststructuralist essays, see Henry Louis Gates, ed., *'Race', Writing and Difference* (1986). Gates's *The Signifying Monkey* (1988) is the most sustained elaboration of his theory of writing and racial difference from the perspective of black writing in the United States. From a more specifically feminist perspective, see Toni Morrison's brief and highly readable *Playing in the Dark: Whiteness and the Literary Imagination* (1993). In a British context in particular, see James Procter's *Dwelling Places: Postwar Black British Writing* (2003) and the useful anthology *Writing Black Britain*, ed. Procter (2000).

25. The colony

Colonialism, postcolonialism, neocolonialism: three *isms* that depend upon the figure of the colony. In the Preface to this book we remark that theory – particularly when it takes the form of *isms* – can seem intimidating or simply boring. Deeply desiring to be neither, we also have good theoretical reasons for feeling wary of *isms*. As Martin Heidegger put it: 'Every mere *ism* is a misunderstanding and the death of history' (Heidegger 1967, 60–1). This assertion draws attention to the ways in which *isms* inevitably encourage generalization, abstractness, a lack of critical clarity and of historical awareness. But saying this of course does not make *isms* go away. *Isms* are convenient, as well as deadly. Here are three convenient, if deadly, definitions: 'colonialism' is 'the policy or practice of obtaining, or maintaining hold over, colonies, *esp* with the purpose of exploiting them' (*Chambers Dictionary*); 'postcolonialism' is concerned with what 'occur[s] or exist[s] after the end of colonial rule' (*Shorter OED*); 'neocolonialism' is concerned with the *continuing effects* of colonialism after the end of colonial rule, and thus with a questioning of the break implied by the *post-* of 'postcolonial'. Much *ism*-izing energy has been spent on the distinctions or lack of distinctions between these various terms. For example, the authors of *The Empire Writes Back* (1989) argue that the term 'postcolonial' should be seen as covering 'all the culture affected by the imperial process from the moment of colonization to the present day' (Ashcroft, Griffiths and Tiffin 1989, 2). This definition mingles colonialism and 'postcoloniality', and also mixes itself up with the arguably more rigorous and precise conception of 'neocolonialism' as involving 'the half-hidden narratives of colonialism's success in its continuing operations' (Young 1991b, 3). Rather than engage directly with these various *isms*, we propose in this chapter to try to reflect on them indirectly, by focusing on what is common to them all (the colony) and by considering a series of related topics: language, time, point of view, writing, law, justice and drama.

The word 'colony' itself is suggestive: in etymological terms a patriarchal and agricultural metaphor (Latin *colonia* a colony, from *colonus* a husbandsman, from *colere* to till), 'colony' is, according to *Chambers*, 'a name vaguely applied to a state's dependencies overseas or abroad . . . ; a body of persons settled in a foreign country, or forming a separate ethnic, cultural or occupational group; the settlement so formed; the place they inhabit'. One thing is already clear from this definition: the colony, and all the *isms* it colonizes, has to do with the colonizing power and effects of language itself, with language *as* colonization. There is no concept of the colony in the English language that does not depend on the colonization of English by Latin – which is also to say, the colonization of Latin by English. Correspondingly, we might ask, is US English colonized by British English or is it the other way round? Colonization here, as always, works in two directions: to colonize is, however imperceptibly or insidiously, to be colonized. If, as William Burroughs claimed, language is a virus, this is because it is a colonizer. In particular as 'dependency overseas or abroad' or 'settlement in a foreign country', a colony always involves the imposition of a foreign language; and all the colonialist wars in history (there are perhaps no other) are also wars in and over language. Indeed, as some linguists like to say, a language is a dialect with an army and a navy. Finally, however, we may suppose that there is no way of thinking about any of these matters *in one's own language* without being already *colonized by* language. Colonization is at the origin: we are always already dependants of language, colonized by one or more languages.

To be 'always already' is to be unsure, among other things, about one's sense of time. In this and other respects, the notion of colony has a strange relation to time. As its etymology indicates, 'colony' is fundamentally a spatial term: originally it has to do with tilling the land. When we think about colonies we think, first perhaps, of space, of the appropriation and exploitation of land. But questions of time are just as important in a (post- or neo-) colonialist context. Indeed, as we indicated a few moments ago, the very terms 'post-' and 'neo-' are temporal, concerned with what comes after or continues to haunt the colony. Literary texts offer especially good illustrations of how the colony deranges and disorders the sense not only of place but also of time. We could consider this, for example, in relation to Conrad's *Heart of Darkness* (1902). On the one hand, there is a clear and irrefutable historical context for the narrative: it is a novel about the European (especially Belgian and British) colonial exploitation of Africa (especially the Congo) in the late nineteenth century. On the other hand, however, and *at the same time*, the novel conveys a particularly strong sense of this journey to the colonial heart of darkness as a journey into another time. As Marlow recounts:

> Going up that river was like travelling back to the earliest beginnings of the world . . . The broadening waters flowed through a mob of wooded islands; you lost your way on that river as you would in a desert, and butted all day long against shoals, trying to find the channel, till you thought yourself bewitched and cut off for ever from everything you had once known—somewhere—far away—in another existence perhaps. (48)

Conrad's novel is both historically specific (it illuminates the barbarity of European colonialism in Africa) and pervasively dreamlike (at once timeless and primordial). Jean Rhys's *Wide Sargasso Sea* (1966) also characterizes the colony as unsettling any 'homely' sense of time, in particular by evoking the strange timelessness of dreaming and trance. For the unnamed Mr Rochester (the colonizer who is also colonized by his time in the West Indies) the unnamed Windward island, where he and Antoinette spend their honeymoon, is 'quite unreal and like a dream' (49). Indeed his colonial experience as a whole may be described as 'all . . . a nightmare' (76). But the strangeness works in two directions. Thus England in turn is repeatedly evoked in terms of the timelessness of a dream for Antoinette (49, 70). Just as *Heart of Darkness* traces a disturbing, circular structure which returns the narrative, finally, to London as the 'heart of darkness', so Rhys's novel complicates our sense of time in more general narrative terms. Its disordering of temporality has to do, above all, with its status as a prequel to Charlotte Brontë's *Jane Eyre*. Post- but also pre-*Jane Eyre*, it exposes the colonialist dimensions of the earlier novel *before the event*.

Finally, we could consider the example of Chinua Achebe's *Things Fall Apart* (1958). Achebe's novel recounts the rise and fall of a man called Okonkwo, and tells how Christian white men come to colonize and largely destroy the culture and identity of the Igbo tribe to which he belongs. Like *Heart of Darkness* and *Wide Sargasso Sea*, *Things Fall Apart* is temporally deranged and deranging: it is impelled by Achebe's own 'decolonizing' mission of seeking to write an alternative version of Conrad's novel, specifically from the perspective of the *colonized*. Yet Achebe's narrator is obliged to occupy a sort of double-time – at once from the late nineteenth-century time of the novel's action (narrating as if from *within* the Igbo tribe) and from the mid-twentieth-century time of its telling (narrating from a position *outside* the tribe and from a considerable distance in time). Achebe's novel is an extraordinary meditation on the difficulty of saying *when* 'things fall apart', of determining when, for example, colonization happens, or when the colonial becomes post-colonial. This difficulty is marked, above all, in the title of the novel, with its haunting suspension in the present tense, and in the fact that it is a quotation. The phrase 'things fall apart' is taken from W.B. Yeats's 'The Second Coming' (1919), a poem that is inseparable from Christian mythology and inseparable in turn from the colonialist context of the First World War and the Irish Troubles. Achebe's novel, from its title onwards, is written (however critically or ironically) in the language of the Christian colonizer.

If from a literary perspective the twentieth century is 'the age of Kafka', as Harold Bloom asserts (Bloom 1994, 448), Kafka's work is perhaps not the most obvious to turn to for thinking about issues of the colony. Let us, how-ever, consider a short story that may help to dislodge this assumption. 'In the Penal Colony' (*In der Strafkolonie*) was written in October 1914 and first pub-lished shortly after the First World War, in 1919. It is one of Kafka's grimmest and least funny stories. Set in an unnamed penal colony, on an unnamed island, it focuses on a number of unnamed characters and is told – primarily from the perspective of an unnamed 'explorer' – by an uncannily knowledge-able or telepathic third-person narrator. The explorer has been invited by the Commandant of the colony to witness the execution of a soldier who has been 'condemned to death for disobedience and insulting behaviour to a superior' (140). The story focuses on the gruesome and terrifying machine that is to bring this execution about, and on the 'officer' whose proud, even sacred, responsibility it is to explain the machine to the explorer and ensure it does its work. By a characteristically eerie Kafkaesque twist, the officer ends up freeing the prisoner and putting himself to death in his place; the story concludes with the explorer leaving the island on a boat with an unnamed ferryman.

The interest of Kafka's narrative in terms of issues of (post- or neo-) colon-ialism has to do with four related ideas: point of view, writing, law and justice. First, it dramatizes the problem and importance of 'point of view', both in a narratological and also in a more broadly cultural and political sense. It offers a basis for thinking about questions such as: From what perspective or point of view can or should one think about, say, Shakespeare's *Othello* (1604), Austen's *Mansfield Park* (1814), Forster's *A Passage to India* (1924), Rushdie's *Midnight's Children* (1981) or indeed any other literary work that engages with colonial differences? And more broadly, from what point of view does one make ethical and other judgements about other people, other societies and cultures? Kafka's story does this by *exploring* (a word in our critical vocabulary that suddenly takes on a new 'colonizing' dimension) the explorer's dilemma from his own point of view: 'The explorer thought to himself: It's always a ticklish matter to intervene decisively in other people's affairs. He was neither a member of the penal colony nor a citizen of the state to which it belonged' (151). The explorer is a foreigner, a stranger, but he is also described as being 'conditioned by European ways of thought' (155). How should the man respond to the seemingly undeniable 'injustice of the procedure and the inhumanity of the execution' (151)? Kafka's text does not offer any simple answer to this question, focusing instead on the increasingly intolerable suspense of withholding judgement. At the same time the story generates an overwhelming sense of the explorer's unique position and responsibility: he is seen as 'an illustrious foreigner' (155) in a privileged position to pass comment and influence events. Indeed Kafka's story gives a further, more incisive inflection to the dilemma. For while there *is* judgement and decision within the story (the explorer makes clear his strong disapproval of the machine and the punishment; the officer in turn makes a firm decision to free the condemned man and take his place), the reader is left finally with what is in some respects the most 'ticklish matter' of all, namely: who is the narrator of this story, what point of view does he or she have on everything that goes on in the text, and what, in the light of this, is our own point of view? As Gilles Deleuze and Félix Guattari have observed, 'It is by the power of his non-critique that Kafka is so dangerous' (Deleuze and Guattari 1986, 60). 'In the Penal Colony' dramatizes an extraordinary experience of solitude, by posing the question of point of view as a necessary but radically uncertain experience of *responsibility* for each and any reader. To read the story is to be colonized by this dangerous power.

Second, Kafka's text foregrounds the importance of writing itself, of textuality. One of the continuing controversies within the general area of postcolonialist thinking concerns the theoretical complexity of some of its best-known practitioners. Thus postcolonialist theory is perceived as being 'depressingly difficult' (Williams and Chrisman 1993, ix), above all on account of its seemingly abstract, unworldly focus on 'discourse' and 'textuality'. Edward Said, Gayatri Spivak and Homi Bhabha in particular have come to be seen as what Dennis Walder calls 'the three police officers of the postcolonial' (Walder 1998, 4). In his engaging book *Post-Colonial Literatures in English*, Walder seeks to evade the long arm of the law while trying to keep his sights trained on postcolonial literary works themselves. This is a bold but also risky strategy. As Ania Loomba puts it: 'Many writings on colonial or postcolonial discourse may not expressly privilege the textual, but they implicitly do so by interpreting colonial relations through literary texts alone' (Loomba 1998, 95). As Kafka's story suggests, when it comes to thinking about the colony, there is no getting away from the founding complexity of questions of textuality, from the uncanny character of writing, from the limits of the readable. For law itself is inseparable from textuality, writing, inscription. Moreover, Kafka's story is also a disturbing account of law in terms of different, even mutually unintelligible, incommensurable languages or discourses: different characters speak, read and fail to understand different languages. The punishment for the condemned man in Kafka's story involves a Harrow which inserts innumerable needles into the prisoner's body and gradually inscribes in his flesh 'whatever commandment [he] has disobeyed' (144). The officer patiently explains:

> 'there are two kinds of needles arranged in multiple patterns. Each long needle has a short one beside it. The long needle does the writing, and the short needle sprays a jet of water to wash away the blood and keep the inscription clear.' (147)

The words being inscribed in this case are 'HONOUR THY SUPERIORS!' (144). For the condemned man the sentence is unreadable, unknown, until it is literally written on his body, by which time he will be at the point of death, beyond all sense of honour, beyond any sense at all.

Finally, Kafka's story provokes the thought that every colony is a penal colony. Every colony entails the imposition of codes of law, justice and punishment from elsewhere, from back 'home' or from a foreign country. This is indeed a central issue in many colonial or postcolonial novels. Forster's *A Passage to India*, for example, turns on the question of justice and the law, culminating in the drama of the trial scene and the attempt to have Dr Aziz found guilty of attempted rape. Likewise in Rhys's *Wide Sargasso Sea*, everything depends on the colonizing power of 'English law' (see 5, 11, 69) and what Christophine calls the 'damn cold lie' of that English word, ' "justice" ' (94). Similarly we may recall that *Heart of Darkness* concludes with Marlow's meditation on the idea that Kurtz had 'wanted only justice' (111), while *Things Fall Apart* ends with the self-justificatory cogitations of the District Commissioner who is to write a mere paragraph about what we as readers have spent a book experiencing and who has decided, 'after much thought', to entitle his work *The Pacification of the Primitive Tribes of the Lower Niger* (148). 'Be just': these are the key words of Kafka's brief and terrifying text, 'In the Penal Colony'. The dictum appears, according to the officer, among the papers of the former Commandant of the colony. But the explorer cannot read it:

> Now the officer began to spell it, letter by letter, and then read out the words. ' "BE JUST!" is what is written there,' he said, 'surely you can read it now.' . . . [T]he explorer made no remark, yet it was clear that he still could not decipher it. (161)

Issues of law and justice are at the heart of all (post- or neo-) colonial literature. On the one hand, as 'In the Penal Colony' suggests, these issues are
always context-specific; they can, and perhaps must, call for a dangerous
experience of solitude in any and every reader. The reader is judge: Be just!
The reader is put in the impossible position of trying to see from the perspective of both the explorer and the narrator at the same time and, alone, to judge
accordingly. On the other hand, such texts also remind us of the extent to
which ethical and juridical decisions are determined within a context of
specific national and state identities. Thus Kafka's text might lead us to think
about the need for a revolution in the very concept of international law, beyond
the boundaries of any state or colony. As Jacques Derrida has proposed in
Spectres of Marx: 'international law should extend and diversify its field to
include, if at least it is to be consistent with the idea of democracy and of
human rights it proclaims, the *worldwide* economic and social field, beyond
the sovereignty of States' (Derrida 1994, 84).

In Plato's philosophical colony, his imagined Republic, mimetic art,
including poetry and drama, is to be excluded. Such art is dangerous because
it 'waters and fosters' false feelings (Plato 1961, 832): it embodies the
uncomfortable truth that imitation is formative. This recalls the idea, proposed at the outset of this chapter, that language and colonization are inextricable. To imitate is to be uncertainly colonized *and* colonizing. We could
consider this further in relation to the important essay called 'Of Mimicry
and Man: The Ambivalence of Colonial Discourse', by Homi Bhabha, one
of the 'police officers' mentioned earlier. Bhabha demonstrates how post-
Enlightenment English colonialism is dependent on a logic of imitation or
mimicry: the colonized other is obliged to mimic the language, and to varying degrees to imitate the customs, gestures and even dress of the colonizers.
This mimicry, however, is never pure: mimicry, Bhabha argues, 'is at once
resemblance and menace' (Bhabha 1996, 362). There is a fundamental
ambivalence in the act of colonial appropriation: the colonizer at once desires
and fears that the colonized be like him (or, less frequently, her). Colonial
mimicry, in other words, is governed by a logic of what Bhabha describes
as 'almost the same, *but not quite*' (361). In order to succeed, colonial appropriation must fail. As Angela Smith describes it, in the context of V.S.
Naipaul's *The Mimic Men* and Rhys's *Wide Sargasso Sea*: 'The presence of
the colonial other imitating the white male colonizer disrupts the authority of the colonizer's language, and [reveals] an inherent absurdity in the
colonial enterprise' (Smith 1997, xviii). The appeal and effectiveness of
Homi Bhabha's argument is that it undermines the 'authoritative discourse'
(362) of colonialism from within: by imitating this discourse, the colonized

subject shows it to be different from itself, never at home with its own inner-most desires.

One of the understated effects of Bhabha's essay is to suggest how import-ant the notions of theatre, acting and drama are for thinking about (post- or neo-) colonialism. Indeed it encourages us to reflect more broadly on the extent to which personal identity is based on imitation, is inherently theatrical. These are hardly new concerns in the context of literature. Work by critics such as Francis Barker and Peter Hulme (1985) and Paul Brown (1994), for example, has emphasized how deeply Shakespeare's *The Tempest* (1611) is a play about these issues. A play about strange derangements in the experience of time as well as place, and pervasively concerned with questions of leg-itimacy, authority and justice, *The Tempest* is also profoundly engaged with the 'colonial' paradoxes of language, acting and identity. It is a play not least about teaching and mimicry. Just as Prospero is Miranda's 'schoolmaster' (I, ii, 172), so she in turn becomes the teacher of Caliban, the 'slave' whom they find when first coming to the island. In a celebrated exchange near the beginning of the play, she reminds Caliban: 'I pitied thee, / Took pains to make thee speak, taught thee each hour / One thing or other' (I, ii, 355–7). Caliban retorts: 'You taught me language; and my profit on 't / Is, I know how to curse. The red plague rid you / For learning me your language!' (I, ii, 365–7). There are a number of paradoxes in play here. This exchange suggests how thor-oughly language determines who or what we are or might become: there is no escape from the colonizing and mimicking power of language as it annexes one subject (Caliban) after another (Miranda). As the quibble on 'red' and 'rid' intimates, one cannot be rid of what is read, what is read cannot readily be unread: language in *The Tempest* is itself a sort of plague. Caliban's capacity to curse, indeed his very capacity to embody any meaning at all, is an effect of linguistic colonization. Yet his cursing at the same time can only ever be based on a reflection or mimicking of the colonizers and, no doubt, of their own 'innermost desires'. Caliban presents Miranda and Prospero with a disturbing and uncertain mirroring of themselves which nothing in the play can finally efface. This is evident in the very syntax and versification of Prospero's final declaration of recognition regarding Caliban: 'this thing of darkness I / Acknowledge mine' (V, i, 275–6). The inverted syntax and the hesitancy of the enjambment underscore this ambivalent sense of Prospero as not merely owning but also, and paradoxically, *being* 'this thing of darkness'.

As Barker and Hulme have emphasized, *The Tempest* is, in various para-doxical and intractable respects, 'a play imbricated within the discourse of colonialism' (204). It is also, as we have tried to make clear, a play about acting, imitation and mimicry. Finally, we would like to suggest that *The Tempest* is also a kind of colony in itself. Indeed in a sense this is just what every dramatic work is. It establishes itself in a strange time and place of its own, linked to but distinct from the rest of the world: the dramatic work is a site of derangement, mimicry, power and transformation. As Captain Phillip, the Governor of New South Wales, observes, in Timberlake Wertenbaker's *Our Country's Good* (1988): 'A play is a world in itself, a tiny colony we could almost say' (Act 2, Scene 2). Engaged in casting a different and complex theatrical light on that penal colony the British called Australia, *Our Country's Good* is also, like any other dramatic work, strangely resistant to being seen merely as a representation or part of the world in which it is set. In its very title, like Shakespeare's *The Tempest* or *A Midsummer Night's Dream*, it establishes a peculiar colony, it 'gives to airy nothing / A local habitation and a name' (*A Midsummer Night's Dream*, V, i, 16–17).

Further reading

Much valuable material is available in anthologies such as Ashcroft, Griffiths and Tiffin, eds, *The Post-Colonial Studies Reader* (1995) and Williams and Chrisman, eds, *Colonial Discourse and Post-Colonial Theory* (1993). For two excellent introductory works, see Ania Loomba's *Colonialism/Post-colonialism* (1998) and Robert Young's *Postcolonialism: A History* (2001). Loomba is particularly stimulating for the emphasis she gives to how far issues of gender and sexuality are implicated in (post- or neo-) colonialism. Young provides more detailed coverage of some of these issues in his earlier book *Colonial Desire: Hybridity in Theory, Culture and Race* (1995). For another recent work that is original, thought-provoking and extremely good in its expositions, see Nicholas Harrison's *Postcolonial Criticism* (2003). Related to issues of gender and sexuality (and indeed apposite in the context of the tacitly homoerotic dimensions of Kafka's 'In the Penal Colony'), increasing critical attention has recently been given to the links between the colony and queerness. On this, see, for example, Christopher Lane's challenging but fascinating *The Ruling Passion: British Colonial Allegory and the Paradox of Homosexual Desire* (1995) or Yonatan Touval's playful and thought-provoking essay on *A Passage to India*, 'Colonial Queer Something' (1997). Finally, Edward Said's work on (post- and neo-) colonial issues is both very accessible and highly influential: his most important books are *Orientalism* (1978) and *Culture and Imperialism* (1993).

26. Mutant

We became hominid about five million years ago and 'human' in the sense of *homo erectus* about three million years later. *Homo sapiens*, though, only developed about 30–40,000 years ago. Why it was that our genetic cousins, the Neanderthals, died out just a few thousand years after the arrival of *homo sapiens*, is one of evolution's enigmas. 'Wherever humans advanced,' Henry Gee explains, 'Neanderthals retreated.' In what he calls 'a sudden spasm',

> humanity (the winners) acquired all the external trappings we think of as defining our own tribe. The Neanderthals, in contrast, just pottered around, doing the same kind of timeless nothing-in-particular they'd done for 300,000 years, for all the world like an extended episode of Winnie-the-Pooh (only with real Heffalumps). (Gee 1996, 38)

Just think of it, that could be us: a world of endless honey-pots and pooh-sticks, with only Heffalumps and Eeyore's chronic depression to worry about, and with just Tigger, Piglet, the god-like Christopher Robin and a few others for company.

Since humans won out, though, things have tended to be a little more complicated, humans being what they are. But what are human beings? What is it like to be human? We don't ask this just because we belong to that species known as academics. Instead it is an inevitable question for anyone who calls herself a human being. In this chapter, we want to look at what it means to be human, but also at what it means to be a mutant or a monster, and to discuss ways in which literature is bound up with these questions. Literature has had a crucial role in configuring the nature and limits of the human. Beginning with Beowulf (*c*.1000), English literature is a history of monsters. We could think, for example, about the extent to which the literary canon is strewn with dehumanized or otherwise mutated people. Samuel Beckett writes plays that feature disembodied voices, people that spend their time crawling in mud, that live in dustbins or that are just mouths. Wallace Stevens is interested in what he calls the 'inhuman person' (in 'Gigantomachia'), and W.B. Yeats yearns to be a mechanical bird of hammered gold in 'Sailing to Byzantium' (1927). In *Women in Love* (1921) D.H. Lawrence talks repeatedly about his characters 'lapsing out' (for example Lawrence 1960, 48, 199) and all four of the main characters voice a 'grudge against the human being': for Ursula in particular, 'that which the word "human" stood for was despicable and repugnant' (275). Thomas Hardy is impelled to set the human dramas of *The Return of the Native* (1878) against the inhuman geological time-scale of Egdon Heath, and the passions and betrayals of *The Woodlanders* (1887) against grotesquely anthropomorphized woodlands. Wordsworth risks scorn by recording the apparently dehumanized, crazed babblings of an idiot boy (in 'The Idiot Boy' (1798)), and becomes strangely fixated by the figure of the leech gatherer, a figure like a 'huge Stone' or a 'Sea-beast', in 'Resolution and Independence' (written 1802). The seventeenth-century poet George Herbert wants to be a tree ('I read, and sigh, and wish I were a tree': 'Affliction I' (1633)). Shakespeare mixes up humans with fairies in *A Midsummer Night's Dream* (1596), spirits and the misshapen monster Caliban in *The Tempest* (1611), and presents us with 'inhuman' characters in plays such as *Richard III* (1592–3), *The Merchant of Venice* (1598) and *Othello* (1604). Western literature as a whole can seem to bulk up like a vast mutation out of the animal, vegetable, astral, bestial, petrific, spirit and parahuman transformations that are recounted in Ovid's *Metamorphoses* (1 BC) and Apuleius's *The Golden Ass* (2nd century AD).

To study literature is necessarily to engage with the mutant. 'Mutant', from the Latin for 'change', is essentially bound up with inessentiality, with mutability, and with otherness. Contemporary literature in particular is especially concerned with variations on the mutant. But what is it about biotechnology and nanotechnology, about eugenics and genetic engineering, the cyborg and the robot, about monsters and mutants and their interactions with people that is at once so compelling and so terrifying? 'We are all chimeras', Donna Harraway portentously declares in her influential feminist 'Cyborg Manifesto' (1985). Twentieth-century humans, she asserts, are 'theorised and fabricated hybrids of machine and organism; in short we are cyborgs' (Harraway 2000, 70). What is this fascination with the human as (also) other, this yearning to *be* other, to be unthinking or animal, hybrid or cyborg, mechanical or mutant, virtual, immutable, stony, inhuman, or dead?

In this chapter we would like to explore the workings of such compulsions and terrors in the context of literature and other so-called 'humanities' subjects, and the fascination that the limits of the human seem to hold for humans. Literature is, above all, about the human, about what it means to be human, and therefore about the non-human, about what it might mean not to be human. Literature allows us to think the limits of the human, even to unthink our often-unthinking attachment to notions of the human and humanity. Finally, literature itself may be conceived as a monstrous or mutant discourse, a humanism that is also inhuman, alien. In each of the texts mentioned above, there seems to be an engagement with the human that is expressed in terms of a fascination with the inhuman, or with a human becoming non-human, ahuman, abhuman or parahuman. As our reference to biotechnology, nanotechnology, genetics and so on suggests, there is a peculiarly millennial, peculiarly topical dimension to these questions. This is perhaps most clearly evident in cinema, with its devotion to mutant, computerized, cyborg or alien beings such as the Terminator (a creature recently mutated into the 'real life' Governor of California, the 'Governator'), ET, Blade Runner or Robocop, those appearing in *Star Trek*, *Star Wars*, *Close Encounters*, *Alien*, *Men in Black* and *The Matrix* (in all their various mutations), as well as those that have morphed into familiar figures from countless Frankenstein remakes, vampire and horror flicks, and gothic comic books or 'graphic novels'. In all of these movies, Hollywood plays out a cultural desire for and fear of the parahuman and non-human, of the 'invasion of the body snatchers', the invasion of the boundaries of the human: each of the films mentioned presents a battle between the human and the non- or para- or quasi- or post-human. And in each case, human will and imagination, feeling and compassion, is what survives. All of these films attempt, in the end, to confirm the idea that we are each of us unique, sentient and compassionate – that we are 'human'. Despite the state-of-the-art special effects, the hyper-modern and futuristic scenarios, the avant-garde narratives and the balletic digitized violence, films like the *Matrix* series are deeply traditional, deeply concerned with traditional 'human values', with humanity.

But the concern with how humans are made, and with what makes them human rather than mutant or monstrous, is also a preoccupation of contemporary literature. Jeffrey Eugenides's Pulitzer Prize-winning novel *Middlesex* (2002) is a potent and witty example. As if impelled by an attempt to wipe from memory the more sinister reverberations of his eugenic name, Eugenides has produced perhaps the first novel based around Richard Dawkins's theory of the 'selfish gene' (the idea that it's genes that survive, not individuals, or as Eugenides puts it, 'what humans forget, cells remember' (Eugenides 2002,

99)). *Middlesex* tells the story of a genetic mutation – in this case a shared recessive gene, a mutated gene of the fifth chromosome, in the narrator's incestuously married grandparents – which finally results in Calliope's (or Cal's) birth as a hermaphrodite. And the novel is about the genetic, familial, social and political events that lead up to that monstrous birth and the personal and familial consequences that grow out of it. While Eugenides's novel is impressively informed about the biology of genetic mutation, it is also concerned with the social monstering of the mutant, with the different ways in which people respond to those that are different (with rage, desire, disgust, sympathy, rejection, violence, fascination, surgery).

The fascination with the human and the limits of the human in literature is a strange outgrowth of what is called humanism. Humanism involves the belief that human beings have 'unique capacities and abilities, to be cultivated and celebrated for their own sake' (Audi 1999, 397). It entails a resistance to superstitious or religious conceptions of the human on the one hand, and to the reduction of the human to animality or the organic, on the other. 'Man is an invention of recent date', Michel Foucault famously opines in *The Order of Discourse*; but concomitantly it is a 'mutation', he says, that may be 'nearing its end' (Foucault 1970, 386–7). The development of modern humanism, of the idea of 'man' as the ultimate value and as autonomous, individual, self-willing and self-moving, is argued (by Foucault and others) to have occurred between about the sixteenth and the eighteenth centuries. As we have seen (in Chapter 24, above), critics such as Robert Young suggest that the formation of notions of the human and human nature, of 'humanity and the universal qualities of the human mind as the common good of an ethical civilization', coincided with the development of Western colonialism (Young 1990, 121). And it is not by chance that the invention of the human takes place at a time when European imperial expansion makes it necessary to distinguish fundamentally between European colonizers and colonized natives (who can then be appropriated, enslaved, exploited, slaughtered). Indeed, inventions of the human, definitions of 'man' or 'mankind', always seem to be bound up with the exploitation of their others (whether these others are defined in animal, gender, ethnic or racial, class or religious terms). Humanism, the logic of humanity, in other words, is also a dehumanizing discourse. The humanist dimensions of literature are fully manifested only at the end of the eighteenth century when the literary work comes to be associated with an autonomous individual, the 'author', who produces (or 'creates') an 'original' body of 'imaginative' or (as it is now often termed) 'creative' writing. 'Literature was specialized towards *imaginative writing*', Raymond Williams remarks, 'within the basic assumptions of Romanticism', just as the modern sense of 'individual', so central to the new humanism and to the new conception of literature, is linked to the Enlightenment phase of scientific, political and economic thought that finds its full expression in the eighteenth century (Williams 1983, 186, 164). Literary criticism, especially as it has been formulated since the nineteenth century, is often fundamentally humanist in orientation: F.R. Leavis, for example, proclaims that 'there *is* a "human culture" to be aimed at that must be achieved by cultivating a certain autonomy of the human spirit' (quoted in Day 1996, 111). And recent literary theory (including Marxism, psychoanalysis, structuralism, poststructuralism and deconstruction) has often challenged the anthropocentrism of such criticism precisely with respect to its allegiance to the tenets of humanism.

Literature, like philosophy and religion, is obsessed with what it means to be human – whether it's in the form of Philip Roth's sense of the human as morally stained in *The Human Stain* (2000), or in the form of George Eliot's marvellously intricate meditations on human character and spirit in such novels as *The Mill on the Floss* (1860) and *Daniel Deronda* (1876), or in the form of Jonathan Swift's misanthropic vision of people as bestial, ignorant, irrational Yahoos in *Gulliver's Travels* (1726). But the question of the human is provoked in literary texts above all by means of what is not human, and in post-romantic literature in particular by the presentation of monsters and mutants. By presenting beings that are specifically and spectacularly *not* human, that are precisely configured as deviations from the human, literary texts allow us to find ourselves, in Wallace Stevens's words, 'more truly and more strange' ('Tea at the Palaz of Hoon' (1921)).

Perhaps the most compelling and most influential of literary monsters is Mary Shelley's creature in her first novel, *Frankenstein* (1818). But *Frankenstein* is also the subject of one of the commonest misapprehensions in English literature, namely that Frankenstein is the name of a monster. This is almost as common as the error of thinking that Wordsworth's poetry is about daffodils, that James Joyce's *Ulysses* is unreadable, or that John Fowles's *The Magus* is a great novel. In fact, though, there are very few daffodils in Wordsworth, *Ulysses* is a wonderful if challenging novel (and a piece of cake compared to *Finnegans Wake*), *The Magus* is verbose, dull, self-regarding and (too often) overrated – and Mary Shelley's Frankenstein is as human as the rest of us. Victor Frankenstein is a young Genovese man of 'distinguished' birth who leaves his family to study at the University of Ingolstadt in Upper Bavaria and there becomes fascinated by the possibility of creating a living being. The monster that Victor Frankenstein creates in fact has no name: this itself is doubtless one reason for the confusion and for the popular idea that Frankenstein is the name of a monster. Naming the monster of Mary Shelley's novel 'Frankenstein', then, is an egregious if understandable mistake.

But it is worth contemplating the error, it is worth thinking about how and why it has been such an important dimension of the novel's reception over the years since its first publication in 1818, why the inventor's name has mutated, morphed, into that of his creature. The error might be seen as valuable and instructive for at least two reasons. In the first place, the idea that 'Frankenstein' is the name of a monster marks an important division between the popular idea of Mary Shelley's novel and the novel itself – the popular idea as disseminated by theatre and film versions, by the appearance of the monster in comic books and cartoons, in advertising and TV comedy sketches, in rock music and on the Internet, rather than any actual reading of Shelley's book. In this popular conception of Shelley's novel, in this common misreading or non-reading of her text, the name 'Frankenstein' often works as shorthand for 'Frankenstein's Monster' or 'Frankenstein's Creature'. In a sense there are two *Frankensteins* – two 'texts' called *Frankenstein* – one being the novel written by Mary Shelley, the other being something like an infection, a virus or outgrowth, a mutant transformation of the novel and its dispersal into popular culture, into popular mythology. The fact that there is a veritable glut of entries (2,666 items are listed) in D.F. Glut's *The Frankenstein Catalogue (Being a Comprehensive History of Novels, Translations, Adaptations, Stories, Critical Works, Popular Articles, Series, Fumetti, Verse, Stage Plays, Films, Cartoons, Puppetry, Radio and Television Programs, Comics, Satire and Humor, Spoken and Musical Recordings, Tapes and Sheet Music featuring Frankenstein's Monster and/or Descended from Mary Shelley's Novel)* (1984) gives an indication of the monstrosity of the novel, its uncontrolled, uncontrollable outgrowth. This leads us to our second point, which is that the misnaming of Shelley's monster nevertheless expresses a truth. It would be true to say that '*Frankenstein* is a monster'. *Frankenstein* – the novel – *is* a kind of mutant or monster, *is*, in a sense, monstrous. Victor refers to his own tale as 'my hideous narration', and it is a tale that Walton, who hears it, describes as one to 'congeal' or 'curdle' the blood (Shelley 1994, 222, 233). One contemporary reviewer even referred to the novel itself as a 'monstrous literary abortion' (quoted in Botting 1995, 5).

The way that the novel is constructed seems in fact to bear an uncanny resemblance to the way that a monster is formed. Both Mary Shelley and Victor Frankenstein are wisely rather unforthcoming about the mechanics of creating a monster (you can find out how to construct a nuclear bomb by surfing the Internet, but you can't find out how to build Frankenstein's monster). All we can gather is that the technique involves the collection of assorted body parts from dead people and their reconstruction and revivification through a (vaguely defined) process of surgery, galvanism and electrification. Victor Frankenstein, we are told, 'pursue[s] nature to her hiding places . . . among the unhallowed damps of the grave'; he 'collect[s] bones from charnel houses' and 'disturb[s], with profane fingers, the tremendous secrets of the human frame'. His laboratory, his 'workshop of filthy creation' is 'a solitary chamber, or rather cell' where he collects materials furnished from the 'dissecting room and the slaughter house' (Shelley 1994, 83). In principle, though less gruesomely, *Frankenstein* is constructed in the same way. In her 1831 Introduction to the novel, Mary Shelley declares that 'everything has a beginning' but that that beginning must necessarily be 'linked to something that went before'. Referring to the Hindu belief that the world is supported by an elephant but that the elephant in turn is supported by a tortoise, Shelley argues that literary 'invention' 'does not consist in creating out of a void, but out of chaos'. Literary creation, in other words, like the creation of a monster or indeed like the theological act of creation, 'can give form to dark, shapeless substances but cannot bring into being the substance itself'. Shelley's comments alert us to the fact that making a literary text is akin to other forms of making, including most pertinently, the making of monsters. In this respect, too, her novel is a kind of monster, mutated or created out of her reading. Shelley draws on contemporary scientific and medical works by Erasmus Darwin, Humphry Davy and others. She alludes to and quotes contemporary poets such as Wordsworth, Coleridge, Goethe, and her lover Percy Bysshe Shelley, as well as Milton and other canonical writers. She engages with works of social, political and moral philosophy by her father William Godwin and her mother Mary Wollstonecraft, and with classical works of historiography by Plutarch and Volney. And before all of these there is the grounding intertext of that great mutant book of creation, the Bible. In other words, just as Frankenstein's creature is constructed out of pieces hewn from dead bodies, the novel is largely constructed – thematically, verbally, conceptually, intellectually – from the huge corpus of Shelley's reading, from the writings of the living and the dead. And the novel comes across, sometimes rather awkwardly, monstrously, like something created out of different genres (the gothic novel or novels of sensibility, moral or theological disquisitions, novels of ideas), just as it brings together the rational investigation of Enlightenment science with the other of that rationality, the discourse of the superstitious, the monstrous, the gothic, the uncanny. The Soviet critic M.M. Bakhtin's word for this is 'heteroglossia', the distribution within a text of different discourses or genres or 'voices', while Julia Kristeva, Roland Barthes and others call it 'intertextuality': our words for it are 'monstrism' and 'mutant'.

This genesis and reception of Shelley's novel, then, offers a dramatic instance of a more general law of literature. Literature, we might say, is a monstrous or mutant form, a mutant discourse. Literary texts don't appear out of nowhere. As we suggest elsewhere in this book, recent literary criticism and theory has been much concerned with intertextuality, with ways in which a poem or novel is constructed out of other cultural and literary discourses, the ways in which texts, ideas and words mutate, ceaselessly evolving and transforming the possibilities of literary forms. This is why literary studies, this unruly, improper discipline, is in fact truly, properly 'interdisciplinary'. The study of literature involves, from the start, a mixing and contamination of disciplines and genres. Literary criticism and theory are themselves mutant, and any significantly 'new' or 'original' critical or theoretical work produces a mutation in the discipline. *Frankenstein* can perhaps also help us to grasp how literary texts are mutated in their reception. Perhaps more virulently than any other nineteenth-century text, the germ of *Frankenstein* has been passed on in endless mutations. Mutation, in this respect, is central to the process that we call canonization: for canonization to occur, a text must be inherited, transformed, responded to, deformed, developed, and imitated – in future texts, in the literary and other traditions to which it gives birth, in being read. Neither Mary Shelley nor Victor Frankenstein is in control of the monsters s/he creates. And this is what is monstrous about the monster. It is precisely this fear that we won't be able to control what we create – a fear that Christians project on to God's relationship with his unruly angel, Satan – that defines the contemporary concern with GM products (so-called 'Frankenstein Foods'). And it is a fear expressed in debates surrounding our current crisis of humanity, the development of 'gene therapy' and the suspicion that these technologies will result in the production of genetically modified people (as if we weren't all genetically modified anyway).

Criticism and theory have recently been much taken with mutants and monsters: 'English' sometimes seem to read like an emerging tetralogy, a study or discourse of monsters. But what is a monster? The *OED* – that monster of a book – is of course essential reading for students of the monster. The English 'monster' mutated from the Latin 'monere', to warn, a word related to 'monare', 'to show': the monster is something shown, in other words, as a warning. But the complex of senses in which 'monster' has been used in English, the way in which the word has mutated out of this original sense of warning, is also instructive: the monster is something 'extraordinary, or unnatural; a prodigy, a marvel'; it is 'an animal or plant deviating in one or more of its parts from the normal type . . . a misshapen birth, an abortion'; it is 'an imaginary animal . . . having a form either partly brute and partly human, or compounded of elements from two or more animals'; it is 'a person of inhuman and horrible cruelty or wickedness'; and it is 'an animal of huge size' and by association 'anything of vast and unwieldy proportions'. For Charles Darwin, a 'monstrosity' is 'some considerable deviation of structure, generally injurious to or not useful to the species' (Darwin 1866, 46). All of these senses are useful for a theory of the monster, but what they make clear, finally, is the fact that the monster isn't so much *un*natural as something that comes *out* of nature, something that goes through and beyond nature. The monster is both natural and unnatural, a grotesque development of, an outgrowth from or in nature. And it is for this reason that the monster must be abhorred, rejected, abjected, excluded. But let's be clear about this: the monster is excluded, abjected, not because it is entirely other but because it is at least in part *identical* with that by which it is excluded – with, in this case, the human. As Diana Fuss comments in this context, 'sameness, not difference, provokes our greatest anxiety' (Fuss 1996: 3). The monster is both of nature and beyond it: as the *OED* informs us in one citation, 'the vegetable kingdom abounds with monsters'. The monster is, indeed, the most natural thing in the world, and fundamentally allied with birth. Babies are monsters: David Lynch's wonderfully dark *Eraserhead* (1976) knows this, knows what we fear inside (literally) ourselves and in others; the pregnant Desdemona in *Middlesex* knows it too as she 'prepares to meet the creature hidden in her womb' (Eugenides 2002, 123); and 'monstrous birth' is also of course the subject of the play from which the name Desdemona has itself sprouted (see *Othello* 1.3.386).

In the same way, the mutant, the potentially monstrous genetic deformation, is primordially a function of birth. In biology, in the theory of evolution, and in genetics, mutation is a necessary part of the evolution of the species. The word 'mutant' suggests a deformation, transformation, alteration: 'I am fully convinced that species are not immutable', declares Darwin at the beginning of *The Origin of the Species* (Darwin 1866, 6). Without mutation, change, metamorphosis, morphing, no species could develop. Evolution *is*, therefore, mutation, and we are all mutations from our parents, as they were mutations from theirs (children typically have about 100 genetic differences from their parents, 100 mutations (Ridley 1994, 44)). The mutant *is* 'nature', *is* what we all are: you're a mutant, we tell you; and your mother was a mutant before you.

Dictionaries are dangerous books. For the fourteen-year-old Calliope in *Middlesex* it is the dictionary that finally allows her to begin to understand what she is, to begin to confront everything that she fears about herself and everything that she desires to know. She has heard the gender alignment consultant at the clinic use the word 'hypospadias' in relation to her condition as he probes and photographs her, so she checks out the word in Webster's

Dictionary. Presenting its definition, the dictionary directs Calliope to look up 'eunuch'. The entry for that word in turn directs her to 'hermaphrodite'. A hermaphrodite has the 'sex organs and many of the secondary characteristics of both male and female', Calliope reads, and the word includes 'anything comprised of a combination of diverse or contradictory elements'. Then the dictionary directs her to 'see synonyms at MONSTER'. 'The synonym was official, authoritative', Calliope thinks:

> it was the verdict that the culture gave on a person like her. *Monster*. That was what she was. That was what Dr. Luce and his colleagues had been saying. It explained so much, really. It explained her mother crying in the next room. It explained the false cheer in Milton's voice. It explained why her parents had brought her to New York, so that the doctors could work in secret. It explained the photographs, too. What did people do when they came upon Bigfoot or the Loch Ness Monster? They tried to get a picture. For a second Callie saw herself that way. As a lumbering, shaggy creature pausing at the edge of the woods. As a humped convolvulus rearing its dragon's head from an icy lake. (Eugenides 2002, 431–2)

Further reading

For three recent collections of essays on the question of the human see Fuss, ed., *Human, All Too Human* (1996), Brewster et al., eds, *Inhuman Reflections* (2000), and Neil Badmington, ed., *Posthumanism* (2000). Tony Davies's *Humanism* (1997) is a good short introduction to the historical development of ideas of humanism, while John Gray's *Straw Dogs: Thoughts on Humans and Other Animals* (2002) is a provocative critique of the fondly held idea of the human and of humanism in Western culture. On monsters, see Clark and Royle, eds, *Monstrism* (2002), and there is a good short chapter on the monster and the gothic in Punter and Byron, *The Gothic* (2003). On monsters and aliens in popular culture, see Elaine Graham's *Representations of the Post/Human* (2002). On the abhuman, see Kelly Hurley's *The Gothic Body* (1996). Tzvetan Todorov's *On Human Diversity* (1993) examines the question of definitions of the human from the Enlightenment onwards, calling for a new and newly enlightened humanism.

27. The performative

'I confess my ignorance': *Chambers Dictionary* gives this as an example of a performative. The word 'performative', declared J.L. Austin in 1956, 'is a new word and an ugly word, and perhaps it does not mean anything very much. But at any rate there is one thing in its favour, it is not a profound word' (Austin 1970, 233). The present chapter is concerned to sort out what this rather odd, perhaps unprofound word does mean. A performative is a statement that not only describes an action but actually performs that action. A performative is, in principle at least, the opposite of a constative statement. A constative statement involves a description of how things seem to be, a statement or assertion of something that can be true or false. 'The teachers are ignorant', for example.

All language can be thought about in terms of the constative and the performative. On the one hand, there is language as *descriptive*, as saying something about something. On the other, there is language as performative, as not only saying something but *doing* or *performing* something at the same time. 'I do' (as words spoken by the prospective wife or husband in answer to a particular question in the marriage service), 'I declare this meeting inquorate', 'I promise to pay the bearer the sum of twenty pounds': these are all examples in which language is clearly supposed to be doing something. If it were not, marriage would be impossible, committee meetings would never end (or, more happily, might never take place at all) and a twenty-pound note would be quite worthless, a mere curiosity. The distinction between constative and performative statements is derived from a particular strand of Anglo-American philosophy known as speech-act theory. Speech-act theory is most famously associated with the work of the Oxford philosopher J.L. Austin and in particular with his book entitled *How to do Things with Words* (1962). It has become an important area of contemporary philosophy and linguistics but has also proved extra-ordinarily provocative in the field of literary criticism and theory.

At first this idea may seem baffling. Surely, we may tell ourselves, literary texts are simply 'words on a page' and moreover words that relate to fictional or poetic worlds, not to the so-called real world in which marriage ceremonies are genuinely performed, committee meetings truly take place and money is real. But the truth of the matter is a little more complicated than this. Literary texts can indeed be considered from the perspective of the performative. Thus we may recall that the very word 'poetry' comes from the Greek verb *poieein*, 'to make', 'to create': this suggests that poetry might in fact be a making or *doing*, as much as a saying or *stating*.

In order to start exploring this idea in more detail, we will look at one or two poems which are particularly interesting in the context of the performative. First of all, John Keats's 'This Living Hand' (written in *c*.1819):

> This living hand, now warm and capable
> Of earnest grasping, would, if it were cold
> And in the icy silence of the tomb,
> So haunt thy days and chill thy dreaming nights
> That thou would wish thine own heart dry of blood
> So in my veins red life might stream again,
> And thou be conscience-calm'd—see here it is—
> I hold it towards you—

These chilling lines, which as it happens were not published until 1892, more than seventy years after Keats's death, are apparently *about* this death. The text functions as a bizarre and complex kind of curse or threat: it suggests that if the writer were dead (if this hand were no longer living but cold and in the grave), 'you' – the reader – would be so haunted that you would be willing to die in order that the writer could live again. The last words then weirdly suggest that this hand really is still living, despite the fact that we know the poet is dead: 'see here it is—I hold it towards you—'.

Keats's poem may or may not be 'unfinished': we only have the text as recorded in the margin of a manuscript of another poem. Our doubt as to whether it is a fragment or a finished poem is part of a more general sense of uncertainty. 'This Living Hand' promotes a strong sense of the strangeness of writing as such. It testifies on the one hand (as it were) to the fact that a hand, the writer's or anyone else's, is always capable of being outlived by the writing which it produces. Paradoxically, what lives on is the writing and not the hand. On the other hand (so to speak), the poem insists – in a quite threatening and disturbing way – on the power that language has to be *deictic*, to point (like, precisely, a hand) and to say 'this' ('This living hand') and 'here' ('here it is'), now, in a strangely 'icy' present. We may not know how we feel about this poem, we may not know how to understand or earnestly 'grasp' it. But however we may want to think about it, one thing seems clear: the poem is *doing* something to us as readers. It is performative in at least two ways: first, in that it is a threat and, second, in that it *enacts* the curious logic of holding out a hand ('This living hand') to us as readers, here and now. Austin notes, in *How to do Things with Words*, that the classic examples of performatives are 'all with verbs in the first person singular present indicative active . . . Examples are "I name", "I do", "I bet", "I give"' (Austin 1962, 56). And he adds that another 'useful criterion' for a performative statement is the presence, whether explicit or implicit, of the word 'hereby' (57). Keats's poem, whether considered as finished or unfinished, is clearly saying in some sense: I hereby threaten and haunt you.

Here is another example ('we hereby offer it to you'), a three-line poem by the contemporary English poet Michael Ayres, entitled 'Bittersweet' (1993):

> Survivors again. I never thought we'd make it.
> I never thought I could be forgotten,
> Or that it would be so bittersweet.

There are intriguing similarities between the Keats and Ayres poems. Both are concerned with the idea of survival and both can be read as poems about themselves, in other words as poems that are self-reflexive or self-referential. And like 'This Living Hand', 'Bittersweet' is self-reflexive in a decidedly paradoxical sense. The deployment of the title-word 'bittersweet' at the very end of the poem establishes the self-reflexive or self-referential dimension: it invites us to suppose that what 'would be so bittersweet' would be the poem of that title, the poem we are or have just been reading. The word 'bittersweet' at the end of the poem leads us back to the beginning of the poem, or rather to the very title of the poem, in a way that calls to mind Coleridge's favourite image for a story – that of the ouroboros, or snake with its tail in its mouth. If the sense of time in this poem is paradoxical, so too of course is the very word 'bittersweet'. This word is an oxymoron – an apparent contradiction in terms, comparable to Milton's phrase 'darkness visible' (*Paradise Lost*, I, 63). Finally, Ayres's poem is paradoxical as regards the idea of being forgotten. The 'I' of this poem declares, 'I never thought I could be forgotten'. This can be read as saying 'I never thought I could be forgotten and look, sure enough,

I haven't been', but it can also be read as saying the opposite: 'I never thought I could be forgotten but the truth is that I have been.' The more plausible of these interpretations would perhaps be the latter, but if we read the poem in this way we encounter what appears to be its central paradox: being a survivor involves being forgotten. How should we make sense of this? One way would be to say that this is a love poem about the bittersweet experience of surviving some crisis or great difficulty in a relationship: the 'I' of the poem survives but only at the cost of no longer being the 'I' he (or she) used to be. We are left, in this case, with the enigma of an 'I' who has been forgotten, but who nevertheless survives in writing, that is to say, in the very words of the poem. If 'I' simply depends on writing, then perhaps so does the 'we' referred to in the first line. This 'we', in turn, could be read not only as referring to the speaker and the speaker's lover, for example, but also as referring to *ourselves*, the poem's readers. In this sense the poem would be doing something to us, turning us into survivors: reading becomes bittersweet.

As if haunted by an aftertaste, we could carry on trying to describe here what 'This Living Hand' and 'Bittersweet' seem to be doing as poems. The basic point, however, is precisely that: they are not poems that are simply descriptive, they are also performative. Keats's text pulls us into its strange and icy grasp, Ayres's poem makes reading bittersweet. Both poems are indeed kinds of riddle. Each is saying, in effect: without your being able fully to understand it, this is a poem about the fact that you have read it. Each of these poems draws particular attention to the fact that it is writing and that it can survive its author, like a monument. In this respect both poems exploit the monumentalizing character of writing in a way similar to that of Shakespeare's sonnet 55:

> Not marble, nor the gilded monuments
> Of princes, shall outlive this pow'rful rime,
> But you shall shine more bright in these contents
> Than unswept stone, besmear'd with sluttish time.
> When wasteful war shall statues overturn,
> And broils root out the work of masonry,
> Nor Mars his sword nor war's quick fire shall burn
> The living record of your memory.
> 'Gainst death and all-oblivious enmity
> Shall you pace forth; your praise shall still find room,
> Even in the eyes of all posterity
> That wear this world out to the ending doom.
>   So till the judgment that yourself arise,
>   You live in this, and dwell in lovers' eyes.

This is a love poem which asserts that it will 'outlive' marble, gilded monuments, masonry and so on. It is thus concerned with the idea that writing – and this text in particular – has a capacity for monumentalization greater than that of anything else that humans might create. Because the poem itself will last until the end of the world ('the ending doom'), so will the memory of the lover who is being addressed. The haunting irony of Shakespeare's poem is that it constitutes not only the 'living record' of the lover's 'memory' but also the very existence of this lover: 'You live in this, and dwell in lovers' eyes.' The poem is not simply a 'record'. Rather, the lover ('you') only exists thanks to these fourteen lines. Poetry, then, in keeping with its etymology, can be performative in the most radical way: it can create 'you'.

The notion of the performative is extremely helpful for thinking about literature, then, because it allows us to appreciate that literary texts not only describe but perform. Literary texts not only say but do things: they do things with words and do things to us. More precisely they do things *by* saying. After declaring, in his poem 'In Memory of W.B. Yeats (d. Jan. 1939)', that 'poetry makes nothing happen', the poet W.H. Auden qualifies and even contradicts this by observing that 'it survives', as 'A way of happening, a mouth'. Alongside this we could juxtapose a remark made by Jacques Derrida, who says: 'promising is inevitable as soon as we open our mouths – or rather as soon as there is a text' (Derrida 1986a, 98). A promise is, of course, a classic example of a performative. This is not to say that we should scan poems or other literary texts for examples of the poet, author, narrator or characters literally making promises to the reader or to other characters. Rather it is a matter of recognizing that literary texts are, in their very structure, promises. To recall an example that Derrida gives: 'A title is always a promise' (Derrida 1986a, 115). Even (or especially) with its title, a literary text has begun to promise. As soon as there is a text, perhaps before anyone (the poet, author, narrator or character) even opens their mouth, the performativity of a promise is underway. In order to get a sharper sense of the way a title works as a promise, we could consider how a text might be read if it had a different title from the one it has been given. Imagine Shakespeare's *King Lear* if it were retitled *Cordelia*, or Sylvia Plath's 'Daddy' if it were retitled 'Why I Love a Fascist'. Tom Stoppard captures this bizarrerie in his script for *Shakespeare in Love* (1998, dir. Peter Madden) where the Bard's working title for *Romeo and Juliet* is *Romeo and Ethel the Pirate's Daughter*. And we might wonder how differently we would conceive T.S. Eliot's *The Waste Land* had Ezra Pound not persuaded his friend to alter the title from *He Do the Police in Different Voices*. With a different title, a quite different kind of promise is being made: the work starts doing something quite different to us.

Let us conclude with a few words about one of these examples, Sylvia Plath's poem 'Daddy'. This poem is about the speaker's love and hatred of her father and describes the process by which she comes to exorcise him – by 'killing' him twice and finally driving a stake through his heart. 'Daddy' neatly encapsulates many of the points we have been discussing in this chapter. If 'Daddy' is a particularly crucial word for this poem, starting from its very title, so too is the word 'do'. Plath's text is fundamentally about *doing* and most of all, we can suggest, about doing by saying, about doing things with words. 'You do not do', the poem emphatically opens. 'I do, I do', the speaker exclaims. A powerfully disturbing rhetorical mixture of a marriage and an execution, Plath's poem appears at once to describe *and perform* the process by which the speaker can finally disconnect herself from the addressee ('The black telephone's off at the root') and conclude finally: 'Daddy, daddy, you bastard, I'm through'. The force of the poem involves the sense that the speaker is exorcising her father as she speaks, that these words are what finally get rid of him. The text is like a poetic equivalent of psychoanalysis as 'the talking cure'.

We have been dealing mainly with poems in this chapter, since they provide an especially clear sense of how the 'I' of the text, or how the text itself, can be seen to create and transform – to perform. But as the example of titles indicates, the idea of the performative is of fundamental importance for all literary texts. A simple way of illustrating this would be to say that every literary text is a kind of letter. It is a text addressed privately to each of us, me or you in isolation, at the same time as being a letter that has been made public, published. To read a literary text is to agree to the idea of a possible relationship. The literary text – whether poem, play, short story or novel – is a letter, and by reading it you become its recipient. Pursuing this analogy between a literary text and a letter, J. Hillis Miller argues that what is particularly striking about the performative dimension of literature is that it is in some ways fundamentally unpredictable. Literary texts give an exemplary 'twist' to the conventional, Austinian notion of the performative. Miller writes: 'The "twist" lies in the fact that the performative power of the letter is not foreseen or intended. This is contrary to the strict concept of a performative utterance as defined by Austin' (Miller 1991, 172). We have tried to suggest the workings of such a 'twist' in the paradoxical and 'riddling' effects of the poems we have looked at: poems are performative but not in ways that we can necessarily expect or completely, earnestly grasp. Indeed the 'twist' may consist in the very failure intimated here. Every performative (a promise or threat or whatever) is haunted by the necessary possibility that it will fail or go astray. The 'twist' of performatives in literature might be illustrated in relation to the final words of Sylvia Plath's poem 'Daddy': 'Daddy, daddy, you bastard, I'm through'. Something appears to be happening here, but what? Is calling daddy 'bastard' a way of renouncing his legitimacy and thus, as it were, excommunicating him? What does 'I'm through' mean? Can the 'I' say this, while still addressing 'daddy'? Does 'I'm through' mean 'I *am* finished' or 'I *have* finished'? Or does it mean, paradoxically, that the 'I' is finally *through to* 'daddy', only now, beyond the last word of the poem, finally able to address him?

Further reading

J. Hillis Miller's work on performatives is particularly accessible. See his excellent studies *Tropes, Parables, Performatives* (1991) and *Speech Acts in Literature* (2001). For an essay specifically focusing on the poetic and the riddle, see his 'Deconstruction and a Poem' (Miller 2000). More difficult but also extremely good are the essays of Paul de Man, for instance in his *Allegories of Reading* (1979). De Man gives some startling accounts of literary texts as works of persuasion. From a more psychoanalytically oriented perspective, see also Shoshana Felman's challenging but thought-provoking study, *The Literary Speech Act* (1983). On the performative in the context of British and German Romanticism, see Esterhammer's fine book *The Romantic Performative* (2000). Judith Butler's work, especially *Gender Trouble* (1990), *Bodies That Matter* (1993) and *Excitable Speech* (1997), offers a complex but compelling account of identity, gender and politics in general as 'performative' in ways explicitly indebted to J.L. Austin, even if he would not readily have recognized them. Jonathan Culler has a helpful and stimulating account of Butler and performative language in his *Literary Theory: A Very Short Introduction* (1997).

28. Secrets

Why do we read works of literature? What do we hope to get out of reading a novel, for example? In an essay entitled 'Secrets and Narrative Sequence', Frank Kermode writes: 'To read a novel expecting the satisfactions of closure and the receipt of a message is what most people find enough to do; they are easier with this method because it resembles the one that works for ordinary acts of communication' (Kermode 1983, 138). Most people, according to Kermode, read novels in the hope of reading something that adds up to a complete whole – a story with a clear structure and 'message'. They are looking for a good story line – something to get their teeth into on a long train-journey, for example, something which has a strong sense of what Kermode calls 'narrative sequence'. This is what is implied by the term 'consumer-fiction': to read a novel is to consume it. If a good novel is like a good meal, some novels are no doubt easier to chew and swallow than others. Stephen King's *The Shining* would be fast food in comparison with the feast of Henry James's *The Golden Bowl*. Kermode is working with a very basic model: novels can be compared with 'ordinary acts of communication' (by which he presumably means things like successfully negotiating your order with the person behind the service counter at Burger King) and most novel-reading is as simple and as sequential as abc. There are, however, things which get in the way of narrative sequence, and these are what Kermode calls *secrets*: 'secrets', he argues, 'are at odds with sequence' (138). What he is referring to here is the idea of textual details, specific aspects of the language of a text, particular patterns of images or rhetorical figures that a reader may not even notice on a 'consumerist' reading, but that are nevertheless present and which can provoke a sense of mystery. Thus Kermode focuses on the enigmatic, repeated but apparently superfluous references to black and white in Joseph Conrad's *Under Western Eyes* (1911).

It may be that what draws many people towards the study of literature (the desire not only to consume the novels of, say, James, Conrad or Stephen King, but also to reflect on their cultural, historical and ideological context, on how these novels work and what effects they produce) is a fascination with the possibilities of secrets. As we shall try to show in this chapter, the relationship between literature, secrecy and secrets is fundamental. Indeed, we would like to suggest that in many respects the question, 'What is literature?' can be considered as synonymous with the question, 'What is a secret?'

A secret is what is concealed, deliberately or inadvertently hidden, kept separate and apart. (The word 'secret' comes from the Latin *secernere*, where *se-* signifies 'apart' and *cernere* is 'to separate'.) Even the most rapidly consumed of novels involve secrets, if only because narratives are linear and the contents of a work cannot be presented all at once. Every narrative can be defined as a process of unfolding and revelation. It is precisely because there are things that remain hidden from us, and because we want to know what these things are, that we continue to read. This is the general context in which Roland Barthes elaborates his notion of the 'hermeneutic code'. The hermeneutic code concerns everything in a text that has to do with the creation of an enigma and its possible clarification and explanation. In this respect it is perhaps helpful to recall that etymologically the word 'enigma' is linked to fable and storytelling. It derives from the Greek verb *ainissesthai*, 'to speak allusively or obscurely', from *ainos*, 'a fable'. The most obvious example of enigma in the context of literary narratives is the whodunnit detective story: the question 'whodunnit?' forms the central enigma of the text and the hermeneutic code involves 'the various (formal) terms by which an enigma can be distinguished, suggested, formulated, held in suspense, and finally disclosed' (Barthes 1990b, 19). Why is this character doing this, for instance phoning the police or watching a letter burn on the fire? What is the significance of such and such an object, for instance the concrete-mixer in the cellar? How does this moment in the narrative throw light on the enigma of the crime? What is about to be revealed? All these questions are hermeneutic – they have to do with a work of interpretation and the hope or expectation or desire that the text will provide the answers. The mystery story or whodunnit is a particularly striking example, since (as its name indicates) it is explicitly concerned with drawing the reader into a mystery, and with manipulating her or him into asking questions, being watchful for 'clues' and looking for an explanation. In this sense, the pleasure of detective stories involves reading as itself a form of detecting.

But the mystery story or whodunnit is only one example of something that is much more general about the relationship between narratives and secrets. For, in an important sense, Chandler's *The Little Sister* (1949) or William McIlvanney's *Laidlaw* (1977) are no different from, say, D.H. Lawrence's *The Virgin and the Gipsy* (1930) or Toni Morrison's *The Bluest Eye* (1970). These novels likewise involve various kinds of mystery and concealment: they inevitably hold back a full revelation of what happens, releasing this information only gradually. More importantly perhaps, they generate a sense of mystery and secrecy through the very institution of the so-called omniscient narrator. The idea of such a narrator is basically magical or occult (the word 'occult', it may be noted, literally means 'hidden', 'secret'): such narratives are structured by powers of foresight. For it is invariably part of what is called omniscient narration (including what is known as 'realist fiction') that the narrator 'knows' the future and that this power of foresight is implicitly or explicitly articulated at numerous moments in a given narrative.

The Virgin and the Gipsy, for example, opens as follows:

> When the vicar's wife went off with a young and penniless man the scandal knew no bounds. Her two little girls were only seven and nine years old respectively. And the vicar was such a good husband. True, his hair was grey. But his moustache was dark, he was handsome, and still full of furtive passion for his unrestrained and beautiful wife.
>
> Why did she go? Why did she burst away with such an *éclat* of revulsion, like a touch of madness?
>
> Nobody gave any answer. Only the pious said she was a bad woman. While some of the good women kept silent. They knew.
>
> The two little girls never knew. (167)

This passage not only plays on the idea of secrecy as something related to a particular character (the vicar's 'furtive passion') but, through its apparent omniscient narration, sets up various kinds of secret knowledge. The 'good women kept silent' because they 'knew': 'knew what?' we ask ourselves. 'The two little girls never knew': this, too, the narrator knows though does not, at least for the moment, reveal to us. What is it that the narrator knows? What is it that the two little girls 'never knew'? The 'never' in particular is a subtle and eerie word, suggesting that the perspective from which the narrator speaks is in fact posthumous as regards the girls themselves. On rereading – that is to say, with the benefits of readerly hindsight – we may find this word 'never' even more peculiar, since the two girls who 'never knew' do not die, in fact, in the course of the narrative. In this context one might want to ask: What planet, or fictional world, does this narrator come from?

Of course, narrators are just linguistic fabrications, textual creatures. Nevertheless, we are drawn into their worlds and a crucial part of the magic, sorcery or 'occultism' of literary narratives has to do with the mysterious but seductive 'reality' of the narrator. An omniscient narrator is a strange figure, by its very nature. The strangeness consists not only in the basic idea of omniscience itself, but also in what is concealed within that omniscience. Omniscience is itself a fiction, a strange invention of literary critics drawing on the obviously problematic identification between an author or narrator and the Christian God. (As the *OED* makes clear, the word 'omniscient' originally referred specifically to 'the omniscient Being, the Deity'.) Narrators may appear to be all-knowing but they are certainly not all-telling. A narrator is always secretive, in other words, and this secretiveness concerns both the notion of storytelling-as-gradual-revelation and the question of what we do not and perhaps can never know about this narrator. Thus we may recognize that one of the most secretive or enigmatic aspects of a literary narrative may concern the character of its narrator (so-called omniscient or not): what, for example, are we to make of the narrator of Henry James's *Washington Square*, or Joseph Conrad's *Heart of Darkness*, or Virginia Woolf's *Mrs Dalloway*?

Toni Morrison's *The Bluest Eye*, on the other hand, involves the final revelation that the two primary narrators (a so-called omniscient narrator and one of the characters, Claudia) are apparently the same: such a revelation does not serve to clarify or rationalize the nature of the storytelling but, on the contrary, exacerbates the reader's sense of the narrator-as-enigma. *The Bluest Eye* indeed begins with mystery – with the enigmatic presentation (and equally enigmatic repetition or re-presentation) of the text of what appears to be a US school primer: 'Here is the house. It is green and white. It has a red door. It is very pretty. Here is the family' (7). In a forcefully disjunctive way this opening switches, without any explanation, to a passage of italicized text which starts: 'Quiet as it's kept, there were no marigolds in the fall of 1941. We thought, at the time, that it was because Pecola was having her father's baby that the marigolds did not grow' (9). There is a sense here of a narrator speaking knowledgeably from a position of hindsight ('We thought, at the time'), of someone who knows things which may or may not be revealed as the narrative unfolds. More provocatively, however, we are left with the mysteriousness of the first four words, 'Quiet as it's kept'. What is 'it', Who or what is keeping quiet? Why are we being alerted to what appears to be secret and why should it be kept quiet? Is the narrator imparting information to the reader or keeping quiet about it?

If a logic of secrecy, concealment and revelation is crucial to the workings of any novel, it is also evident in less obviously narrative texts such as lyric poetry.

Consider the following poem (No. 180), written around 1859, by Emily Dickinson:

> Our lives are Swiss—
> So still—so Cool—
> Till some odd afternoon
> The Alps neglect their Curtains
> And we look farther on!
>
> *Italy* stands the other side!
> While like a guard between—
> The solemn Alps—
> The siren Alps—
> Forever intervene!

This poem is about what is concealed or hidden from us: it gestures towards something secret. It suggests that there are moments of revelation or epiphany ('some odd afternoon') when we are able to 'look farther on' – beyond the Alps. These moments, or this moment (since technically only one 'odd afternoon' is mentioned), might be compared to what Wordsworth calls 'spots of time' or Hardy 'moments of vision'. Dickinson's poem appears, at least on one level, to describe or relate such a moment and to attribute great significance to it. But if there is a revelation, if the secret and perhaps the meaning of our lives is being referred to here, what is it? The poem says only that 'we look farther on' and that '*Italy* stands the other side': it remains unclear what it is that is being revealed at this moment when 'The Alps neglect their Curtains'. Is it '*Italy*' simply? But what does '*Italy*' mean? The word 'Forever' in the final line of the poem underlines the strangeness of what is going on here and the continuing or unresolved *enigma* of what the poem has to tell us. The definiteness and absoluteness of 'forever' confirms, in effect, the sense that this poem at once reveals and can never reveal its secret.

Dickinson's poem could in fact be described as exemplary of literary texts in general. In particular it dramatizes the fact that the notion of a secret is paradoxical. Jacques Derrida has formulated the paradox as follows: '*There is something secret*. But it does not conceal itself' (Derrida 1992b, 21). In an essay called 'Derrida's Topographies', J. Hillis Miller offers a helpful account of this paradox. On the one hand, Miller points out, 'We normally think of a secret as in principle discoverable' (Miller 1994, 16): Kermode's 'satisfactions of closure' and 'the receipt of a message' and Barthes's 'hermeneutic code' make sense only if we accept this principle. There is closure and there is a message to the extent that 'All is revealed'. There is a valid hermeneutic effort or labour of interpretation because there is something to be interpreted, seized, comprehended. On the other hand, however, there is the question of what

Miller calls a 'true secret'. He notes: 'a true secret, if there is such a thing, cannot ever, by any means, be revealed' (17). And Miller then elaborates on the Derridean paradox: 'A true secret . . . is not hidden somewhere . . . A true secret is all on the surface. This superficiality cannot by any hermeneutic procedures, material or linguistic, be gone behind. A literary text (and any text may be taken as literary) says what it says' (17). Thus, in Dickinson's poem, there would be the enigmatic, perhaps ultimately cryptic status of '*Italy*': there is nothing 'within' or 'behind' this appositely italicized '*Italy*'. The text says (only) what it says: '*Italy* stands the other side!' It does not say that 'Italy' symbolizes 'romance' or that it represents 'revolution' or even that it can be taken as a synonym for 'the secret'. However superficial or profound or elliptical, it simply says what it says. In these terms, then, it is not only a question of literature as involving secrets that are concealed and that are gradually or finally brought to light. It is also – and perhaps more enigmatically – a matter of a secrecy that does not involve any kind of concealment at all.

A literary text 'says what it says': it says, for example, that 'we look farther on!' Or it says, at the very outset, what its title is. Perhaps the secrecy of literary works begins with titles themselves. Perhaps what makes a work 'literary' is in part that its title remains enigmatic. A literary text says that it is called 'The Virgin and the Gipsy' or 'The Bluest Eye' or, say, 'The Shining'. What do these titles refer to? Does Lawrence's text, for example, finally and clearly establish what is to be understood by 'the dark, tremulous potent secret of . . . virginity' (207), or what is meant by the idea of a gipsy, of a figure that is apparently outside 'the vast and gruesome clutch of our law' (236)? And what is the status and significance of the conjunctive ('and') in the title of this Lawrence text? What does 'and' mean? Conversely, what is signified by 'the bluest eye' and in the eyes of which reader or beholder? Or again, what do those two words, 'the shining', have to tell us? Each of these examples, in fact, resists what Kermode refers to as 'the satisfactions of closure' and 'the receipt of a message'. It is their readability *and* their resistance to being read that makes them 'literary', in Hillis Miller's terms. This is in part at least why the question 'What is literature?' is inseparable from the question 'What is a secret?'

It has been traditional to think of meaning as something behind or within the words of a text. Reading has conventionally been thought of on the basis of a surface-depth model, with the words of the text as the surface and the meaning lurking somewhere inside or underneath. The text has secrets and often explicitly conveys and exploits the idea that it has the power to disclose or preserve these secrets. With poststructuralist accounts of literature, however, there has been an important shift away from this surface-depth model. This is not to say that the surface-depth model is no longer relevant. Indeed it is very difficult to think about meaning or about reading without relying to a considerable extent on the values and assumptions of this model. Moreover, as we have been trying to suggest, virtually every literary text can be seen to work with this model. This is, in short, the theory and practice of secrets as (in principle) discoverable. Poststructuralism, however, is generally suspicious about any reading of a literary text that would equate a secret with the 'true' or 'ultimate' meaning. Poststructuralism pays particular attention to the paradoxical nature of secrets – to the fact that secrets can be undiscoverable and yet at the same time unconcealed. In this sense the secrets of a literary text may be right in front of our eyes and yet they remain secret, like 'the purloined letter' on the mantelpiece in Edgar Allan Poe's story of that title, or like the solemn, siren Alps, some odd afternoon.

To conclude, we could briefly consider secrets in two further ways. At the beginning of this chapter we put forward the hypothesis that what attracts many people to the study of literature is a fascination with the idea of secrets. We have sought to elaborate on this by considering some of the many respects in which literary texts are bound up with the enigmatic, mysterious, secret and (in a double sense) occult. And we have attempted to emphasize the important paradox whereby secrets can be discoverable but that a 'true secret', if there is such a thing, can never be discovered. Our focus has been on texts and on how they compel, manipulate and fascinate their readers. But there is also another perspective from which to think about literature and secrets. This would be from that of the reader rather than the text, and in particular as regards the notion of a reader who is interested not so much in the idea of secrets *in the text* (whodunnit? what is going to happen next? and so on) but rather in the possibilities of secrets *within herself* or *within himself*, secrets that may have to do with dreams, memories, fantasies, speculations and desires set off by the text, thoughts and feelings that may never have been experienced before – that is to say, in a surprising way, secret thoughts and feelings. It is in this context that literary texts can be acknowledged as having uncanny powers, including an ability to alter people's very sense of themselves, of their identity and 'place'.

Secondly, we might try to think about the possibility of a 'true secret' within ourselves, about the paradox of what a 'true secret' might be. This touches on what we refer to in the following chapter as 'the unpresentable'. The name which is sometimes given to this notion of a true secret is 'death'. The Ghost of Hamlet's father comes to Hamlet and says:

> But that I am forbid
> To tell the secrets of my prison-house,
> I could a tale unfold whose lightest word

Would harrow up thy soul, freeze thy young blood,
Make thy two eyes like stars start from their spheres,
Thy knotted and combined locks to part,
And each particular hair to stand an end
Like quills upon the fretful porpentine.
But this eternal blazon must not be
To ears of flesh and blood. (I, v, 14–21)

The Ghost at once tells and does not tell. The Ghost keeps the secrets of its prison-house even as it evokes the effects of their disclosure. This is another way of talking about the enigma of literature: whether in the form of Shakespearean tragedy or a contemporary whodunnit, literature is about what cannot be told, and in particular about that impossible package holiday which Hamlet refers to as that 'undiscover'd country, from whose bourn / No traveller returns' (III, i, 78–9). This undiscovered country is neither inside us nor outside us. It is a secret that does not conceal itself: the fact that we are going to die but that, as Freud puts it, 'It is indeed impossible to imagine our own death; and whenever we attempt to do so we can perceive that we are in fact still present as spectators' (Freud 1985a, 77).

Further reading

Besides the readable and stimulating essay on 'Secrets and Narrative Sequence' (1983), Frank Kermode has written an important study entitled *The Genesis of Secrecy* (1979) which deals with various questions about, for example, 'why narratives are obscure', why we prefer an enigma to 'a muddle', and so on. Barthes's *S/Z* (1990b) contains brilliant insights into senses of secrecy and enigma in reading. Especially in its focus on silence and the unspoken, Pierre Macherey's *A Theory of Literary Production* (1978) is a powerful account of literary secrets in relation to politics and ideology. From a quite different, intensively psychoanalytic perspective, Esther Rashkin's *Family Secrets* (1992) is a thought-provoking though somewhat cryptic study of mainly nineteenth-century literary works. Jacques Derrida has written numerous essays about secrets: see, in particular, the fascinating but difficult 'Fors' (Derrida 1986b) and 'Passions' (Derrida 1992b), as well as the highly illuminating discussions in *A Taste for the Secret* (Derrida and Ferraris, 2001). In his essay on 'Derrida's Topographies' (1994), on the other hand, J. Hillis Miller provides an excellent account of Derrida's work on secrets (especially 'Fors') and more generally a valuable and accessible introduction to 'Derrida and literature'.

29. The postmodern

Since this book does not attempt to introduce different critical schools or historical periods of literature, it may seem inappropriate to include a chapter on the postmodern. In the following pages, however, we wish to suggest that this topic provides us with an invaluable set of terms for thinking about literary and other cultural texts, that to a significant degree it involves ways of thinking which are unavoidable in the twenty-first century.

The word 'postmodern' itself seems odd, paradoxically evoking what is after ('post') the contemporary ('modern'). How can something be *after* the contemporary? In this respect, in as much as they are confronting the importance of paradox in relation to the contemporary study of literature, other chapters in this book are also dealing with the postmodern. But this paradox of the time of the postmodern also points to the fact that, strictly speaking, the postmodern should not be thought of as a term of periodization: the postmodern challenges our thinking about time, challenges us to see the present in the past, the future in the present, the present in a kind of no-time.

No doubt all periodizing terms (the Renaissance, the early modern period, the Romantic period, and so on) resist definition, but there is perhaps something additionally resistant, peculiar and (for many) maddening about the 'postmodern'. Indeed, the postmodern appears to welcome and embrace a thinking of itself in terms of multiplicity. It resists the totalizing gesture of a metalanguage, the attempt to describe it as a set of coherent explanatory theories. Rather than trying to explain it in terms of a fixed philosophical position or as a kind of knowledge, we shall instead present a 'postmodern vocabulary' in order to suggest its mobile, fragmented and paradoxical nature.

A postmodern vocabulary

Undecidability

Undecidability involves the impossibility of deciding between two or more competing interpretations. As we point out in Chapter 18, classical logic is founded on the law of non-contradiction: something cannot be both A and not A at the same time. The postmodern gives particular emphasis to ways in which this law may be productively questioned or suspended. A classical example of this is the Cretan liar paradox. If someone says 'I am a liar', how can we tell if that person is lying or not? Our ability to make a decision about the validity of such a statement is, at least temporarily, suspended. According to classical logic, the Cretan liar paradox is an isolated and particular instance of a paradoxical statement. For the postmodern, by contrast, the suspension of the law of non-contradiction is endemic. In the postmodern, all absolute values – such as the traditional values of God, Truth, Reason, the Law and so on – become sites of questioning, of rethinking, of new kinds of affirmation. The postmodern, that is to say, does not simply reject the possibility of making decisions. Rather, it gives new attention to the value of the undecidable. What the new critics of the middle of the twentieth century called ambiguity or paradox is now considered in terms of undecidability. The difference is that for the new critics literary texts tended to exploit the polysemic potential of language to create a unified whole in which ambiguity produced an enriching of the text's final unity. For postmodern critics, by contrast, undecidability radically undermines the very principle of unity: these critics celebrate multiplicity, heterogeneity, difference. Undecidability splits the text, disorders it. Undecidability dislodges the principle of a single final meaning in a literary text. It haunts. As Derrida puts it, there is no decision, nor any kind of moral or political responsibility, that is not haunted by the *'experience and experiment of the undecidable'* (Derrida 1988, 116).

A new enlightenment

Theorists of the postmodern are drawn into that exhilarating as well as terrifying 'play' of a text thrown up by its forms of undecidability. For those nervous of the postmodern, this is deemed to amount simply to nihilism and chaos. But for postmodernists it is precisely those monolithic, unthinking assumptions about a fixed grounding for political, ethical and textual decisions that lead to abhorrent results. It is the belief in a transcendent explanatory system – such as God, national identity or historical materialism, to name just three

– which leads to terror, persecution and oppression. In each case, there is a transcendental value (God, the Nation-State, a certain reading of the writings of Marx) which can justify any excess. Postmodernists suggest that reason itself has been used to justify all sorts of oppression. Reason may be said to lie behind the Stalinist terror, for example, in the form of a rational or 'scientific' development of Marx's thinking. Alternatively, in the science of eugenics, 'rational' argument or so-called empirical science helped to justify the Jewish holocaust on grounds of racial difference. This is why, writing in 1944, Theodor Adorno and Max Horkheimer argue that 'Enlightenment is totalitarian' (quoted in Docherty 1993, 5). 'Enlightenment' here can be understood very generally as a way of characterizing Western thought since the seventeenth century. Very simply, the notion of the Enlightenment entails the assertion of the power of reason over both superstition and nature, the belief that a combination of abstract reason and empirical science will lead to knowledge and eventually to political and social progress. By contrast, the postmodern is sceptical about claims of progress in history, not least because of the necessary marginalization (of the apparently non-progressive) which it entails.

A common misunderstanding of the postmodern is that it involves simply an assertion and celebration of the irrational. The postmodern can more helpfully be understood, however, as a *suspension and deconstruction* of the opposition between the rational and the irrational. Irrationalism in itself is only another form of rationalism because it is dependent for its definition on its opposite (only someone who is *rational* could conceive of someone or something as *irrational* and the irrational can only be defined in opposition to the rational). The postmodern could be seen as concerned rather with what Jacques Derrida calls 'a new enlightenment' (Derrida 1988, 141) concerned to explore the value and importance of ways of thinking that cannot be reduced to an opposition between the rational and the irrational.

Dissemination

Postmodern resistance to totalizing forces such as rationalism or irrationalism means that its characteristic form is fragmentary. Fragmentation, in fact, is commonly associated with the romantic and modern periods: poems such as Percy Bysshe Shelley's 'Ozymandias' (1818) from the romantic period and T.S. Eliot's *The Waste Land* (1922) from the modern period are crucially concerned with the notion of the fragment. In this sense, fragmentation is not unique to the postmodern. But the postmodern entails a new kind of critique of the very ideas of fragment and totality. This has taken the form of, among

other things, a fundamental questioning of the notion of originality and correspondingly a new kind of emphasis on citation and intertextuality, parody and
pastiche. In this respect, originality, which has been of particular importance
as an aesthetic value since the eighteenth century, is seen as a kind of ideological fetish, rather than the overriding criterion in aesthetic judgements.
Moreover, we might remark a significant difference between notions of
fragmentation in the postmodern and those in romanticism and modernism:
fragmentation in the postmodern does not depend on the possibility of an
original 'unity' which has been lost. The romantics and modernists, by contrast, tend to figure fragmentation in terms of the loss of an original wholeness.
Another way of thinking about postmodern fragmentation is in terms of
dissemination. Dissemination involves a sense of scattering (as in a scattering
of seeds or 'semes'), a scattering of origins and ends, of identity, centre and
presence. Postmodern fragmentation is without origins, it is dissemination
without any assurance of a centre or destination.

Little and grand narratives

One of the best-known distinctions in the postmodern is that made by Jean-
François Lyotard concerning what he calls 'grand' narratives and 'little' narratives. 'Grand narratives' such as Christianity, Marxism, the Enlightenment
attempt to provide a framework for everything. Such narratives follow a
'teleological' movement towards a time of equality and justice: after the last
judgement, the revolution, or the scientific conquest of nature, injustice,
unreason and evil will end. Lyotard argues that the contemporary 'world-
view', by contrast, is characterized by 'little narratives'. Contemporary
Western discourse is characteristically unstable, fragmented, dispersed – not
a *world-view* at all. 'Little narratives' present local explanations of individual
events or phenomena but do not claim to explain everything. Little narratives
are fragmentary, non-totalizing and non-teleological. Lyotard claims that, in
the West, grand narratives have all but lost their efficacy, that their legitimacy
and their powers of legitimation have been dispersed. Legitimation is now
plural, local and contingent. No supreme authority – Marx, Hegel or God
– can sit in judgement. In his provocatively titled book *The Gulf War Did Not
Take Place* (1995), for example, Jean Baudrillard offers an analysis of the way
that the first Gulf War was as much a function of televisual and other media
representations as of anything else. Despite the controversial nature of his
title, Baudrillard is not so much suggesting that there was no war as that in
an unprecedented way its very actuality was and remains indissoluble from
media representations.

The phenomenon described here has also been described by the phrase 'legitimation crisis', borrowed from the German thinker Jürgen Habermas. Habermas uses this phrase to denote a situation in which all 'master codes' or grand narratives, all conventions, institutions, final authorities have been put into a state of crisis. And in the last century or so, the announcements of the death of God, 'man' and the author have successively dramatized this dissolution of authority.

Simulation

The Western philosophical tradition of aesthetics has relied heavily on a distinction between the real and its copy. This goes back at least as far as Plato, who argued that painters, actors, dramatists and so on, all produce representations or 'imitations' of the real world. (In fact, Plato argues that even a bed is an imitation of the concept or idea of a bed, so that a picture of a bed is a second-degree copy of an essential but unobtainable bed, the essence of bedness.) This way of thinking has given rise to a hierarchical opposition between the real and the copy. And the hierarchy corresponds to that of nature and fabrication, or nature and artifice. The postmodern, however, challenges such hierarchies and shows how the set of values associated with these oppositions can be questioned. As the film *Falling Down* (1993) starring Michael Douglas makes clear, the photograph of the hamburger in the fast-food restaurant is infinitely superior to the rather sad and surprisingly expensive artifact that you have just bought. Even nature, in this postmodern reversal, is subject to improvement. To adopt Umberto Eco's words, 'technology can give us more reality than nature can' (Eco 1993, 203). Films such as *The Truman Show* (1998) and *The Matrix* (1998) demonstrate a postmodern fascination with the technologies of virtual reality. In the first a man unwittingly lives his life in the fabricated studio world of a 24-hour-a-day soap opera, while in the second human kind has been enslaved by robots who feed off their energy, keeping them subservient by plugging them into a virtual world, the matrix.

Another way of thinking about this phenomenon is to use Jean Baudrillard's term 'simulation' (or 'the simulacrum'). Simulation is contrasted with representation. The latter works on the basis that there is a distinction between what the linguist Ferdinand de Saussure calls the signifier and the signified, between a word or 'sound-image', and the idea or the 'mental concept' that it represents. In classical terms, there is an absolute distinction between the word 'hamburger' and what that word represents. Similarly, common sense tells us that there is a clear and necessary distinction between a photograph of a hamburger and a hamburger. Simulation, by contrast, short-circuits such distinctions. Saturated by images – on computers, TV, advertising hoardings, magazines, newspapers and so on – the 'real' becomes unthinkable without the copy. In other words, simulation involves the disturbing idea that the copy is not a copy of something real; the real is inextricable from the significance and effects of the copy. That hamburger that looks so tempting is far more delicious than any you could ever taste. But, paradoxically, when you taste *your* hamburger, you are at the same time tasting what is created by advertising images of hamburgers. If Coke really is it, then, it is because our experience of drinking Coca Cola cannot be disengaged from the seductive lifestyle images of its advertising, from those insidious effects of the brand name, whereby the desirability of a given product is in a sense *branded* into our consciousness and unconscious. This leads to the world of what Jean Baudrillard calls the hyperreal, in which reality is fabricated by technology. As Baudrillard puts it 'simulation is no longer that of a territory, a referential being or substance. It is the generation by models of a real without origin or reality; a hyperreal . . . Henceforth it is the map that precedes the territory' (Baudrillard 1988, 166).

Depthlessness

Another way of talking about simulation or the simulacrum is in terms of depthlessness. If one governing opposition for Western thought has been between the real and the copy, between nature and artifice, another has been between surface and depth. An obvious example of this would be the notion of 'expression', which involves the idea that the words which we write or speak *express* something 'inside' our heads (thoughts and feelings). The words are the surface, whereas our thoughts or consciousness represent depth. Similarly, the idea of the self, the very possibility of being human, has conventionally relied on such an opposition: the subject or self is constituted as a relation between surface and depth, inside and outside.

Fredric Jameson provides a useful account of four depth models that, he argues, have dominated the West in the twentieth century (Jameson 1993, 70):

1. Marxism: Marxism crucially depends on the notion of ideology. Put simply, this involves the idea that we do not see the reality of the world around us but only what we have been indoctrinated into seeing.
2. Psychoanalysis: Freud's theories are based on the distinction between the conscious and the unconscious, whereby the unconscious is held to be

the truth behind or beneath the distorted representation which we call consciousness.

3. Existentialism: in its various forms, existentialism relies on a distinction between, on the one hand, authentic existence and, on the other hand, inauthenticity: authenticity is the truth of selfhood underlying the distortions effected by a state of inauthenticity.

4. Semiotics: as we have seen, Saussurean notions of language presuppose a distinction between the signifier on the one hand and the signified on the other. The word or sound-image indicates an underlying idea or mental concept.

In each case, the authentic or real is understood to be hidden or disguised, while the surface phenomenon, the facade, is an inauthentic distortion or arbitrary offshoot of the underlying truth. With the postmodern, all of these surface-depth models are shaken up. The postmodern suspends, dislocates and transforms the oppositional structures presupposed by major Western modes of thought – by classical Marxism, psychoanalysis, existentialism, semiotics.

Pastiche

Jameson also distinguishes between parody and pastiche. Both rely on imitation of earlier texts or objects. In parody, there is an impulse to ridicule by exaggerating the distance of the original text from 'normal' discourse. The postmodern, however, no longer accepts the notion of 'normal' language: pastiche is 'blank' parody in which there is no single model followed, no single impulse such as ridicule and no sense of a distance from any norm (see Jameson 1992, 166–7). Postmodern architecture, for example, borrows elements from various earlier periods of architecture and puts them in eclectic juxtaposition. In what the architectural critic Charles Jencks has termed 'radical eclecticism' (Jencks 1993, 283), there is no single stable reference. Similarly, a Madonna video parodies, for example, *film noir*, Marilyn Monroe, contemporary pornography, avant-garde erotic art and Catholic icons, in an apparently random dissonance of combination. Rather differently, the music of contemporary 'Bollywood' films supplies a potent mix of classical and folk music from the Indian subcontinent with the so-called 'Western' rhythms and sounds of soul, jazz, rock'n'roll, pop, disco, 1970s blaxpoitation funk, trip hop, techno, ambient and house music. It is just such a sense of eclecticism that distinguishes contemporary culture for Lyotard:

> Eclecticism is the degree zero of contemporary general culture: one listens to reggae, watches a western, eats McDonald's food for lunch and local cuisine for dinner, wears Paris perfume in Tokyo and retro clothes in Hong Kong; knowledge is a matter for TV games. (Lyotard 1992, 145)

This hybridization, a radical intertexuality mixing forms, genres, conventions, media, dissolves boundaries between high and low art, between the serious and the ludic. Genre becomes explicitly unstable, especially in such texts as Vladimir Nabakov's *Pale Fire* (1963), which mixes up a poem with a literary-critical analysis and political thriller, John Fowles's *The French Lieutenant's Woman* (1969), which uses history textbooks to tell a love story, D.M. Thomas's *The White Hotel* (1981), which exploits the genres of poetry and psychoanalytic case-study, or David Eggers's *A Heartbreaking Work of Staggering Genius* (2000), which infuriatingly resists our desire to categorize it as either autobiography or novel ('Based on a true story', the book proclaims on its cover). Two of the most creative and powerful television drama series yet produced are exemplary in this respect: David Lynch's *Twin Peaks* (1990) mixes up the detective story with forms such as horror, avant-garde or art-house movies, soap opera and so on, while Dennis Potter's *The Singing Detective* (1986) dissolves the borders between the detective story, Hollywood musicals, psychological dramas, and the *Bildungsroman*.

The unpresentable

Since the postmodern challenges the distinction between mimesis or copy and the real, it contests the modes of its own representation, of representation itself. Thus it paradoxically *defines* itself in terms of liminal phenomena which defy both categorization and, finally, expression – the unpresentable, or in some of its other formulations, the sublime (Lyotard), the abject (Kristeva), the unnamable (Beckett). Thus Samuel Beckett's writing, for example, may be said to be constituted by the paradoxical impossibility and necessity of discourse – 'I can't go on, I'll go on' (*The Unnamable*, 418).

If in 'going on' there are no clear rules of representation, mimesis, temporality, then the artist is working within the terms of the radically undecidable, or the yet to be decided, as Lyotard remarks:

> The postmodern would be that which, in the modern, puts forward the unpresentable in presentation itself: that which denies itself the solace of good forms, the consensus of a taste which would make it possible to share collectively the nostalgia for the unattainable; that which searches for new

presentations, not in order to enjoy them but in order to impart a stronger sense of the unpresentable . . . the artist and the writer, then, are working without rules in order to formulate the rules of what *will have been done*. Hence the fact that work and text have the characters of an *event* . . . *Post modern* would have to be understood according to the paradox of the future (*post*) anterior (*modo*). (Lyotard 1992, 149–50)

The unpresentable is an effect, not least, of a disturbance of temporality, of the linear progression of time. The postmodern is grammatically specified as inhabiting the future perfect, what will have been. There is no pure present on the basis of which re-presentation may take place.

Decentring

Everything that we have said in this chapter may be summarized in terms of the notion of decentring. The postmodern challenges the 'logo-centric' (the authority of the word, the possibility of final meanings or of being in the presence of pure 'sense'). It challenges the ethnocentric (the authority of one ethnic 'identity' or culture – such as Europe or 'the West' or Islam or Hinduism). It challenges the phallocentric (everything that privileges the symbolic power and significance of the phallus). As Ihab Hassan remarks, the postmodern may be summarized by a list of words prefixed by 'de-' and 'di-': 'deconstruction, decentring, dissemination, dispersal, displacement, difference, discontinuity, demystification, delegitimation, disappearance' (Hassan 1989, 309).

In place of the centre, but not in its place, there is alterity, otherness, a multiplicity and dispersal of centres, origins, presences.

Further reading

An excellent introduction to postmodernism is Christopher Butler's *Post-modernisn: A Very Short Introduction* (2002). Good collections of essays include Brooker's *Modernism/Postmodernism* (1992), Docherty's *Postmodernism* (1993), and Drolet's *The Postmodernism Reader* (2003). Bertens and Natoloi, eds, *Postmodernism: The Key Figures* (2001) provides useful entries on the key thinkers. Lyotard's *The Postmodern Condition* (1984) is, by now (paradoxically), a classic text to start with – 'Answering the Question: What is Postmodernism?' (1992) is particularly useful. His more recent *Postmodern Fables* (1997) offers a series of brief, elliptical and often enigmatic essays on postmodern topics. Jameson's 'The Politics of Theory' (1988) and Linda

Hutcheon's books *A Poetics of Postmodernism* (1988) and *The Politics of Postmodernism* (1989) provide strong, politicized accounts of the postmodern. Steven Connor offers an excellent overview of the postmodern in his *Postmodernist Culture* (1997). For an engaging study of the postmodern in relation to romance, romanticism and politics, see Elam (1992). For two accounts of the postmodern specifically in the context of literary narrative and narrative theory, see Andrew Gibson (1996) and Mark Currie (1998). Readings and Schaber, eds, *Postmodernism Across the Ages* (1993) is a useful collection of essays which seek to challenge the common assumption that postmodernism is a period term referring to the current time.

30. Pleasure

Whether in a seminar or at the pub, often the first thing that gets asked about a book is: Did you enjoy it? This is not just a way of making conversation, but also suggests the fundamental importance of pleasure when it comes to reading. In fact, the question 'Did you enjoy it?' far from breaking the ice and starting a passionate discussion, is generally followed by a terse 'Yes' or 'No' and then forgotten. We may talk about things we enjoy in a work of literature – the gripping narrative, the appealing characters, the power of the language, the comedy and pathos – but we do not very often talk about the enjoyment itself, about what enjoyment or pleasure *is*. There are at least two reasons for this. In the first place, pleasure, enjoyment, emotional and indeed erotic excitement are extremely difficult, or even impossible, to talk about. Secondly, and no doubt related to this, such pleasures tend to border on the transgressive or taboo. But as we hope to show in the course of this chapter, pleasure is crucial to, and even synonymous with, literature itself. This is perhaps why Sir Philip Sidney declares that the purpose of poetry is 'to teach and delight' (Sidney 2002, 86) and why, in his 1802 Preface to *Lyrical Ballads*, William Wordsworth uses the word 'pleasure' (and its cognates) more than fifty times, proposing that the 'end of poetry is to produce excitement in coexistence with an overabundance of pleasure' (Wordsworth 1984, 609). This is not to construe the literary as 'mere' play, as simply hedonistic or self-indulgent. Instead we will seek to describe a sense of pleasure and of literature that may be both disconcerting and subversive.

Take a text that might seem relatively innocuous, a story called 'Bliss' (1920) by the New Zealand writer Katherine Mansfield. 'Bliss' concerns a 30-year-old woman called Bertha Young and her feelings of extreme pleasure before and during a dinner-party at her home. She and her husband Harry entertain an erotically powerful blonde called Pearl Fulton, a ludicrous poet called Eddie Warren and a more or less equally risible couple, Mr and Mrs Norman Knight. Bertha is consistently described as feeling a 'fire of bliss' (311) inside her: 'Everything was good – was right. All that happened seemed to fill again her brimming cup of bliss' (311). She is 'as much in love as ever' (308) with her husband, but she has also fallen in love with the beautiful Pearl Fulton: 'she always did fall in love with beautiful women who had something strange about them' (307). Whether it is the lovely appearance of the dinner table or the blossoming pear tree which Bertha takes Pearl to look at from the drawing-room balcony, everything helps to give Bertha the feeling of being (like Keats in 'Ode to a Nightingale') 'too happy' (308). The story ends with an excruciating moment of revelation, however, as Bertha inadvertently discovers that her husband and Pearl Fulton are lovers: unaware that Bertha can see them, the couple exchange intimacies in the hall. Bertha's feelings of bliss are finally, brutally effaced.

This is how 'Bliss' begins:

> Although Bertha Young was thirty she still had moments like this when she wanted to run instead of walk, to take dancing steps on and off the pavement, to bowl a hoop, to throw something up in the air and catch it again, or to stand still and laugh at—nothing—at nothing, simply.
> What can you do if you are thirty and, turning the corner of your own street, you are overcome, suddenly, by a feeling of bliss—absolute bliss!—as though you'd suddenly swallowed a bright piece of that late afternoon sun and it burned in your bosom, sending out a little shower of sparks into every particle, into every finger and toe? (305)

Bertha can scarcely contain herself, she is overcome by such a feeling of bliss that she does not know what to do. The passage suggests a number of significant things about the nature of pleasure. First, there is an evocation of laughter which may complement some of the remarks we make about laughter in Chapter 12: Bertha wants 'to stand still and laugh at—nothing—at nothing, simply'. Laughter, the desire to laugh, is one manifestation of Bertha's feelings of extreme pleasure or 'bliss'. But more precisely laughter is identified with a sense of 'nothing, simply'. We may recall here Georges Bataille's remark: '[when I laugh,] I am in fact nothing other than the laughter which takes hold of me' (Bataille 1973, 364). There is, for Bertha, the desire to laugh but a desire for laughter that would be 'at nothing', a sense of laughter as pointless, as itself nothing.

Second, and related to this, there is the sense of bliss (like the force of uncontrollable laughter) as something by which a subject – Bertha Young – is 'overcome'. The subject is no longer in control, but rather is in danger of shattering, as if into a 'shower of sparks'. Third, the passage suggests a striking correlation between 'bliss' and the inexpressible. The language of the extract resorts to the metaphorical, figurative and paradoxical (it was '*as though* you'd suddenly swallowed a bright piece of that late afternoon sun') precisely because it would appear that there is no other way of describing this 'feeling of bliss'. This feeling of bliss is like having a foreign body inside you (as if you'd suddenly swallowed a piece of the sun): it's alien to yourself but burning inside you. Fourth, and leading on from this, there is the suggestion that pleasure can be painful at the same time: the burning bosom here might be compared with the 'aching Pleasure' evoked in Keats's 'Ode to Melancholy'.

Finally, and perhaps most crucially, the passage draws the reader into the experience that is being described. It intimates a subtle kind of performative (see Chapter 27), that is to say we can think about the passage as not only describing something but also *doing something*. Pleasure, up to and perhaps even beyond the extreme form of pleasure to which the narrator gives the name 'bliss', is not just a topic or theme *in* the text: it also *is* the text, it is the title of the text and it is a potential effect of reading. The text draws us into a sense of what Wordsworth refers to when he declares, of his experience of the first days of the French Revolution, in *The Prelude*: 'Bliss was it in that dawn to be alive' (Book XI, 108). Through its evocations of the loveliness of the world (a blue dish, a pear tree in blossom), Mansfield's story affirms and calls on us to affirm the inexpressible pleasures of being alive: it evokes a revolution in sensibility. It also gives us the pleasure of reading as romance, reading about romance, about the subtleties of erotic feelings between people. It gives us the pleasures of identification, irony, suspense and social satire. And 'Bliss' gives us all of these things in language: the experience of pleasure is an experience of words, a pleasure in words, even as it points towards a sense of pleasure that is inexpressible, beyond words.

The pleasure of reading 'Bliss' starts with the deceptive simplicity of its narrative perspective. We are confronted here with an apparently omniscient or telepathic narrator who is capable of inhabiting the mind, body and feelings of the protagonist. This is what narrative theorists call 'free indirect discourse', in which we are presented with a voice practising impersonation or ventriloquism, a voice that is undecidably both the narrator's and the character's. Bertha Young's thoughts and feelings are conveyed not only through a third-person narration ('she still had moments', 'she wanted to run') but also, in the second paragraph of the extract, in the second-person ('you are overcome'). This is unusual – though an important characteristic of Mansfield's work generally – and strangely insidious: the 'you', after all, may not finally stop short of *you*, the reader. The subtle, almost imperceptible way in which the text draws us into the experience of what is being described can be illustrated in the very opening words of the story: 'Although Bertha Young was thirty she still had moments like this.' The word 'this' seems to call on the reader to acknowledge or accept something already evident, already presented to her or him. Discreetly, deftly, it draws the reader into the immediate here and now of the experience of bliss.

Another aspect of the pleasure of Mansfield's story has to do with its creation of irony and suspense. The text works through suspense, through the pleasure of suspension and an ominous suspension of pleasure. For while the narrative perspective invites us to identify with Bertha and her feelings of bliss, the text also generates other, more specifically readerly kinds of pleasure. Bertha's feelings of 'bliss', for example, are at various moments represented in ironic terms. The reader is given a strong sense that – despite the repeated evocations of the 'fire of bliss', the incredible beauty of the table, the pear tree and so on – Bertha Young may have a rather limited experience of bliss, especially in sexual terms. Near the end of the story we are told that, as people are about to start leaving the party, 'For the first time in her life Bertha Young desired her husband' (314). Bliss in this case seems to have been postponed. The reader takes pleasure, then, in being able to identify with the protagonist but to experience at the same time a sense of ironic detachment. Above all, the reader's pleasure is generated by the pervasive sense that something is going to happen, that the narrator knows something (and soon perhaps the reader will know something too) which fundamentally complicates Bertha's feelings of 'bliss'. Bliss, then, seems to involve a state of suspension – for Bertha, for the reader and, differently, for the very structure of narration.

On this basis we can perhaps formulate one or two more general propositions about pleasure and literature. Literature is about the possibilities of pleasure. It is about the idea that readerly pleasure is erotic. Literature is erotic (even if it is not literally concerned with erotic or sexual topics or themes) because it is always concerned with seducing the reader. Literary texts can seduce us, or, put more strongly, they need to seduce us. In a sense there is no reason to read a literary text, it serves no purpose, has no function. And this is why, as Ross Chambers has argued, in his book *Story and Situation: Narrative Seduction and the Power of Fiction* (1984), the essential 'power' of a literary text is its power of seduction. In particular, a literary text can seduce us through a logic of what Freud calls 'disavowal'. Disavowal involves the situation in which someone knows that such and such is not true but nevertheless thinks, speaks or acts as if it is true. Disavowal involves thinking: 'I know, but still . . .' The process of disavowal whereby we can be seduced into the world of literature, into fictional worlds, has been neatly phrased by Roland Barthes in his book, *The Pleasure of the Text* (1973): the reader *disavows*, in other words he or she keeps thinking, '*I know these are only words, but all the same* . . .' (Barthes 1990a, 47). The logic of disavowal perhaps offers a more precise way of thinking about how we read works of literature than Coleridge's famous idea of a 'willing suspension of disbelief' (Coleridge 1975, 169): the notion of disavowal more dramatically highlights the contradictoriness of what is going on in the act of reading. The work of the text, its task of seduction, is to ensure this disavowal, to put the reader into this state of what is at once 'truth' and 'fiction'.

This principle of disavowal – of reading a work of fiction as though it were not only words – permits us to suggest a way of distinguishing between literature and pornography. Both have a capacity for erotic and sexual stimulation but the difference between them could be said to consist in the fact that a literary work does not allow the reader to forget the process by which he or she is being seduced, whereas pornography calls for the abolition of the 'as though' altogether. In other words, pornography entails what John Forrester (following Jean Baudrillard) describes as 'a fantasy of a real in which representation does not exist, i.e. a real without seduction' (Forrester 1990, 332). Katherine Mansfield's 'Bliss' is not likely to be classified as pornography; but it is certainly about erotic and sexual feelings – both in what it tells and in its telling. More particularly, the story explores some of the limits of pleasure: it dramatizes the ways in which pleasure is concerned with strangeness (the nothingness of laughter), paradox (the inarticulable) and contradiction (disavowal). Fundamental to this is what Mansfield's text suggests about the curious temporality of pleasure. To recall the opening words once more: 'Although Bertha Young was thirty she still had moments like this when she wanted to run instead of walk, to take dancing steps on and off the pavement, to bowl a hoop, to throw something up in the air and catch it again, or to stand still and laugh at—nothing—at nothing, simply.' This sentence is set in the past tense, but the 'this' ('moments like this') suggests something immediate, here and now. In fact, the time of 'this' is uncertain and strange: it is as if the present of 'moments like this' is already gone. 'Moments like this' are presented in the past tense in such a way as to suggest that they are already 'moments like that' or 'moments like those'. The ambiguity of the this-ness of 'this' is compounded by multiplicity: Bertha wanted to run, to dance, to bowl a hoop, to throw and catch something, to stand still and laugh. Are these all different moments or are they different ways of figuring one single moment ('moments like this [one]')? The sense of time, in the context of extreme pleasure or 'bliss', seems to involve an undecidable, uncontainable multiplicity. Time cannot contain itself when it comes to bliss.

Katherine Mansfield's special focus on moments of intense feeling belongs to a specific historical context and in particular to the literary and cultural aftermath of late nineteenth-century aestheticism. This is to suggest that pleasure and bliss can be thought about in historical terms: they are experienced and represented differently at different times. A full-scale account of the aestheticism of such figures as Walter Pater, Oscar Wilde, Algernon Swinburne, Aubrey Beardsley and others need not detain us here. Its principal concerns were with the idea of art for art's sake, beauty as truth, and the appeal of the moment for the moment's sake (there is no past, no future, only the present moment). In the late nineteenth century the aesthetes made of pleasure a philosophy, a moral creed, a way of being. At the heart of aestheticism is a focus on the beauty and power of the moment. It is concerned with the experience and expression of the intense pleasure of the present. The most succinct and eloquent text for an understanding of aestheticism is Walter Pater's Conclusion to his book *The Renaissance* (1873). This Conclusion, only a few pages in length, offers us a way of understanding the work of many modernist writers, including Joseph Conrad, James Joyce, D.H. Lawrence, Virginia Woolf, Elizabeth Bowen, Ezra Pound, Wallace Stevens, T.S. Eliot and Mansfield herself. All of these writers are singularly concerned with the power of particular moments. On the one hand they are concerned with exploring a sense that the only time of *any* feeling or experience (painful or pleasurable) is right now, this very moment now. On the other hand, however, these writers are concerned with showing that even the present moment is already a ghost of itself. In the Conclusion to *The Renaissance*, Pater puts this concisely when he describes the present moment as 'gone while we try to apprehend it'. The present moment is that 'of which it may ever be more truly said that it has ceased to be than that it is' (196). Pater's Conclusion urges us to make the most of the ecstatic and passionate possibilities of experience, given the 'awful brevity' of our lives: life is defined as 'this short day of frost and sun' (197) and (one of the things that made Pater's text quite scandalous at the time of its first publication) there is no sense of any afterlife or consolations beyond the grave. Here is the conclusion to Pater's Conclusion:

> our one chance lies in expanding that interval [i.e. life], in getting as many pulsations as possible into the given time. Great passions may give us this quickened sense of life, ecstasy and sorrow of love, the various forms of enthusiastic activity, disinterested or otherwise, which come naturally to

many of us. Only be sure it is passion – that it does yield you this fruit of a quickened, multiplied consciousness. Of such wisdom, the poetic passion, the desire of beauty, the love of art for its own sake, has most. For art comes to you proposing frankly to give nothing but the highest quality to your moments as they pass, and simply for those moments' sake. (198–9)

Pater's unprecedented emphasis on the present moment played a crucial role in the development of aestheticism in Britain, the United States and elsewhere. It haunts modernist writing in turn – whether in the form of epiphanies (in James Joyce's *A Portrait of the Artist as a Young Man* for example), or of what Virginia Woolf famously refers to as 'moments of being', or of what Mansfield, at the start of 'Bliss', refers to as 'moments like this'. All of these writers in their different ways are concerned with the uncontainable, delirious, ecstatic, inexpressible quality of individual moments, of time as (only) now. It is not simply a question of a *'carpe diem'* ('seize the day') motif in modern literature. Rather, it is a matter of how the present moment resists any attempt to appropriate or 'seize' it. It is a matter of how moments of extreme pleasure (including orgasm) are at the same time moments of loss: such moments involve, indeed, a kind of dissolution and more generally suggest a sense of experience in terms of what Pater calls 'that continual vanishing away, that strange, perpetual weaving and unweaving of ourselves' (196).

In other words, as Mansfield's story suggests, pleasure can be thought about in terms of a subversion of identity. It is for this reason, among others, that it is not possible to say that the kinds of pleasures with which this chapter is concerned are simply hedonistic. Nor can one say that the kind of thinking and experience valued by Pater constitutes mere self-indulgence or a contemptible neglect of political and social realities. As a way of illustrating this we will focus on what is perhaps the most important and most pleasurable work on the topic of pleasure and literature in recent years, Roland Barthes's *The Pleasure of the Text*. Barthes stresses that 'hedonism has been repressed by nearly every philosophy' (Barthes 1990a, 57) and he is at pleasurable pains to argue against such repression. The value and originality of his study consists not in the politically suspect project of advocating hedonism in a traditional sense but rather in the critical delineation of the paradoxes of pleasure, specifically in the experience of reading. Barthes offers a sort of critical anatomy of pleasure in reading. In particular, he distinguishes between two sorts of pleasure: pleasure of the 'comfortable' sort and pleasure of a more disturbing and subversive kind. Barthes writes:

Text of pleasure: the text that contents, fills, grants euphoria; the text that comes from culture and does not break with it, is linked to a *comfortable* practice of reading. Text of bliss: the text that imposes a state of loss, the text that discomforts (perhaps to the point of a certain boredom), unsettles the reader's historical, cultural, psychological assumptions, the consistency of his tastes, values, memories, brings to a crisis his relation with language. (14)

Barthes's book suggests, then, that there are two ways in which we could think about pleasure. One is basically recuperative: it does not break with culture but rather reinforces traditional or comfortable notions of meaning, society, ideology, etc. The other sense of pleasure ('bliss') is more unsettling and strange. No doubt all literary and other cultural texts are susceptible to being read in both of these ways. Barthes's own emphasis, however, falls on 'bliss' ('jouissance' in French). 'Bliss' has to do with the inexpressible: 'pleasure can be expressed in words, bliss cannot' (21). Bliss has to do with a deconstruction of the political: it is thus engaged in 'de-politicizing what is apparently political, and in politicizing what apparently is not' (44). Or as Barthes puts it: 'The text is (should be) that uninhibited person who shows his behind to the *Political Father*' (53). Above all, bliss has to do with the subversion of identity itself. As with the uncontrollable force of laughter or the moment of orgasm, the extreme pleasure of bliss involves a collapse of self, a (momentary) dissolution of identity. The subject is thus 'never anything but a "living contradiction"': a split subject, who simultaneously enjoys, through the text, the consistency of his selfhood and its collapse, its fall' (21).

By way of conclusion, we would like to suggest that – while Barthes refers to the reader as 'he' – the 'living contradiction' he describes may be thought about as, in the final analysis, undecidably gendered. Partly what makes Barthes's work unusual and challenging is that it explicitly centres on the importance of 'emotion', defining this as 'a disturbance, a bordering on collapse' (25). For Barthes, we could say, the pleasure of reading inevitably involves 'getting hysterical'. But the collapse of selfhood, the shattering force of bliss which he talks about, is a collapse in which it is no longer clear whether there is a subject, or what gender it might belong to. Mansfield's story can also be considered in these terms. Insofar as it is a text about 'women and hysteria', it suggests that 'getting hysterical' (306) is just as much a male as a female tendency. 'Bliss', that is to say, is as much about male hysteria as it is about female hysteria. This is evident, in particular, in Mansfield's characterization of Eddie Warren, the poet who is '(as usual) in a state of acute distress', and whose first words, frenetically peppered with italics, provide a hysterical account of his journey to the Youngs':

> 'I have had such a *dreadful* experience with a taxi-man; he was *most* sinister. I couldn't get him to *stop*. The *more* I knocked and called the *faster* he went. And *in* the moonlight this *bizarre* figure with the *flattened* head *crouching* over the *lit-tle* wheel . . .' (309)

But it is also evident in Mansfield's characterization of Bertha's husband Harry, who is one moment 'rush[ing] into battle where no battle was' (310) and at others 'extravagantly [i.e. hysterically] cool and collected' (310, 315). More radically, however, 'Bliss' is a story about the condition of 'living contradiction' which Barthes evokes. It suggests that that extreme of pleasure called 'bliss' is our undoing, including the undoing of gender-identity.

The story concludes with Harry locking up and Bertha recalling Pearl Fulton's final words to her ('Your lovely pear tree!'):

> And then she was gone, with Eddie following, like the black cat following the grey cat.
> 'I'll shut up shop,' said Harry, extravagantly cool and collected.
> 'Your lovely pear tree—pear tree—pear tree!'
> Bertha simply ran over to the long windows.
> 'Oh, what is going to happen now?' she cried.
> But the pear tree was as lovely as ever and as full of flower and as still. (315)

'Bliss' ends with this 'still'. It leaves the question of bliss itself in suspense, inexpressible, unbearable. As Barthes remarks: 'Pleasure's force of *suspension* can never be overstated' (Barthes 1990a, 65). Pleasure remains resistant and enigmatic, like 'literature'. The pleasure of literature is perhaps less to do with the fact that it 'holds a mirror up to nature', offering a reflection of 'life', and more to do with an experience of 'living contradiction' – with what suspends or momentarily shatters our sense of ourselves. It is subversive, finally, in suggesting that nothing is obvious, that, as Stephen Melville puts it : 'nothing is obvious either in advance or after the fact' (Melville 1986, xxvi).

Further reading

For a contemporary classic account, see Michel Foucault's *The Use of Pleasure* (*The History of Sexuality*, vol. 2, 1985). On pleasure and reading in general, see Roland Barthes's *The Pleasure of the Text* (1990a). For reading and seduction, Ross Chambers's *Story and Situation: Narrative Seduction and the Power of Fiction* (1984) is a fascinating and quite accessible work. Jean Baudrillard's *Seduction* (1990) is an important study but difficult. On the power of the moment in modern literature a good place to start is Morris Beja's clear and very readable *Epiphany in the Modern Novel* (1971). For an advanced study of pleasure and self, see Carolyn J. Dean's *The Self and Its Pleasures* (1992). On literature and the gendering of hysteria, see Elaine Showalter's fine essay 'On Hysterical Narrative' (1993). For a useful collection of essays on pleasure in relation to cultural studies, see Stephen Regan, ed., *The Politics of Pleasure* (1992). On the politics of enjoyment, in particular regarding enjoyment as something ordered, imposed or 'superegotistical', see Slavoj Žižek, *For They Know Not What They Do: Enjoyment as a Political Factor* (1991).

31. War

Here's a poem that you probably won't like very much:

I

Half a league, half a league,
　Half a league onward,
All in the valley of Death
　Rode the six hundred.
5 'Forward, the Light Brigade!
Charge for the guns!' he said:
Into the valley of Death
　Rode the six hundred.

II

'Forward, the Light Brigade!'
10 Was there a man dismayed?
Not though the soldier knew
　Some one had blundered:
Their's not to make reply,
Their's not to reason why,
15 Their's but to do and die:
Into the valley of Death
　Rode the six hundred.

III

Cannon to the right of them,
Cannon to the left of them,

20   Cannon in front of them
       Volleyed and thundered;
    Stormed at with shot and shell,
    Boldly they rode and well,
    Into the jaws of Death,
25   Into the mouths of hell
       Rode the six hundred.

IV

    Flashed all their sabres bare,
    Flashed as they turned in air
    Sabring the gunner there,
30   Charging an army, while
       All the world wondered:
    Plunged in the battery-smoke
    Right through the line they broke;
    Cossack and Russian
35   Reeled from the sabre-stroke
       Shattered and sundered.
    Then they rode back, but not
       Not the six hundred.

V

    Cannon to the right of them,
40   Cannon to the left of them,
    Cannon behind them
       Volleyed and thundered;
    Stormed at with shot and shell,
    While horse and hero fell,
45   They that had fought so well
    Came through the jaws of Death
    Back from the mouth of hell,
    All that was left of them,
       Left of the six hundred.

VI

50   When can their glory fade?
    O the wild charge they made!
       All the world wondered.
    Honour the charge they made!
    Honour the Light Brigade,
55   Noble six hundred!

The poem recounts an incident from the Crimean War (1854–6) in which, after a 'blunder' by an officer, 600 lightly armed British infantrymen charged the Russian artillery, resulting in more than 400 British deaths. 'The Charge of the Light Brigade' was written on 2 December 1854 by Alfred, Lord Tennyson, the poet laureate – 'in a few minutes', he says, after reading a report of the incident in the *Times* newspaper. It is a famous poem that is invariably included in anthologies, so you'll probably know it or know of it. If you had gone to an English school in the early twentieth century you might well have been made to memorize and recite it. But what is it about the poem that you (probably) don't like and indeed that you may disapprove of? There are two things in particular. First, there are its militaristic repetitions and rhythms. This means that, despite its intricately varied form, the poem can seem somewhat crude or unsophisticated. And the formal, public nature of the poem might seem a little dated as well – just the kind of thing you might expect of a nineteenth-century poet laureate. Second, there is the sentiment that underlies the poem: it seems unreservedly to celebrate warfare, heroism, and perhaps above all an unthinking and unquestioning adherence to one's duty. Tennyson's poem seems to glorify the actions of those compatriots who fight and die in war, even – or especially – in the context of a futile, misguided, suicidal military manoeuvre. Someone has blundered, but the poem is not particularly interested in who that might be, or in holding anyone responsible for the error. Instead, Tennyson simply seeks to praise the soldierly virtues of those who carried out orders. For these reasons, the poem has come to seem (as one critic puts it) 'mildly ludicrous, slightly contemptible' (McGann 1985, 190–1).

You'll probably like Wilfred Owen's 'Futility' rather better:

> Move him into the sun—
> Gently its touch awoke him once,
> At home, whispering of fields half-sown.
> Always it woke him, even in France,
> 5   Until this morning and this snow.
> If anything might rouse him now
> The kind old sun will know.
>
> Think how it wakes the seeds—
> Woke once the clays of a cold star.
> 10   Are limbs, so dear achieved, are sides
> Full-nerved, still warm, too hard to stir?
> Was it for this the clay grew tall?
> —O what made fatuous sunbeams toil
> To break earth's sleep at all?

This First World War poem was written in May 1918 and published posthumously in 1920. It gradually becomes clear that the 'him' of the first line is in fact a dead soldier. Like Tennyson's poem, Owen's is very well known and like Tennyson's it focuses on a futile death. Like Tennyson's, Owen's is a poem of commemoration or mourning. In other respects, though, 'Futility' seems very different. It takes the form of an intimately personal, even private lyric, expressing the sadness of an individual (a soldier, rather than a newspaper reader, we might surmise from the intimacy and directness of the poem). This contrasts with Tennyson's more detached, formal and public expression of pride, a kind of triumphant mourning. For Owen, as he famously said in a planned Preface to his poems, the poetry 'is in the pity'. In its own way, Owen's poem is just as much a piece of propaganda as Tennyson's jingoistic ballad. It is a matter of anti-war propaganda in this case – though it has been read by some critics as being, in its nostalgic evocation of 'home', a kind of pro-British propaganda (see for example Pittock 2001). 'Futility' works as public propaganda through its very privateness. It works as propaganda by appearing not to. Only at the very end of the poem does it become evident why it is called 'Futility'. The poem involves an almost abstract meditation on the futility of war, moving from the expression of mourning for an individual soldier to the question of the futility of human life. It shifts from curiously muted imperatives ('move him', 'Think how') to a series of plangently rhetorical questions. There is no narrative beyond this movement of the speaker's thoughts and we know next to nothing about the individual who died, an individual who in fact seems to stand (in a kind of synecdoche) for the many others, many British at least, who died in the First World War. The poem's form itself disavows any suggestion of militarism or of the celebration of battle: the subtly varied rhymes and half-rhymes ('sun', 'once', 'half-sown', 'France', 'snow', 'now', 'know') and the gently tripping rhythm ('Think how it wakes the seeds— / Woke once the clays of a cold star') themselves abrogate the strident uniformity of militarism. Even nationalism is subdued to a longing for English fields. The poem won't march in step, so to speak.

We think you'll like Owen's poem more than Tennyson's (though we might be wrong, of course, especially if you have the military in mind as a career option). In other words, we imagine you will be more inclined to assent to Owen's understated critique of war and militarism. It is easier to identify with the quiet, meditative, lyric poise of its individualized elegiac voice, its anti-militaristic rhythms. Such a preference would be in keeping with a more general change in literary and cultural taste over the last 150 years, especially in the wake of two world wars and, for the US, the national trauma of Vietnam. The public, nationalistic celebration of military heroism of the nineteenth century has given way to a more contemporary appreciation of the significance of private sorrow and a resistance to the futility of war, any war, all war.

But things were not always so. Literature begins with war, with the rage of war. *Menis*: wrath, fury, rage. The first word of the first great poem in the Western literary tradition, Homer's *Iliad* (*c*.700 BC), declares its topic: the rage of Achilles. The Western tradition, in other words, starts up in rage and blood, the rage for war, the rage for rage – godlike, swift-footed, murderous Achilles' rage:

> Rage—Goddess, sing the rage of Peleus' son Achilles,
> murderous, doomed, that cost the Achaeans countless losses,
> hurling down to the House of Death so many sturdy souls,
> great fighters' souls, but made the bodies carrion,
> feasts for the dogs and birds,
> and the will of Zeus was moving towards its end.
> Begin, Muse, when the two first broke and clashed,
> Agamemnon lord of men and brilliant Achilles.
>   (Homer 1990: Book 1, lines 1–8)

What is striking about such a beginning, and about Homer's poem as a whole, is its keen enthusiasm for war, a celebration of war that is joined with loud regret for its murderous, bloody losses. The poet calls on the goddess, his muse, to 'sing the rage' of Achilles, attempting to summon up poetry that will itself be warrior-like, belligerent. Homer's narrative is driven by its tale of war, just as its readers are, and at the same time it is sickened by its own violence, just as its readers are. The language itself, in Robert Fagles's evocative translation, has a belligerence that is at once appalling, and appalled. Here, even at the very start of the Western literary tradition, there is a sense that war is all, that war is total and never ending. The *Iliad* is thoroughly immersed in warfare, with up to half of its 17,000 lines concerned with battles. Its set-piece battle-scenes and intricate, bloody evocations of hand-to-hand fighting make the *Iliad* seem like a multiplex conflation of *Bridge Over the River Kwai*, *Star Wars*, *Apocalypse Now*, *Saving Private Ryan*, and *Fight Club* – but in the hexameters of Homeric Greek verse rather than as a Dolby®-enhanced cinematic experience. The opening to the *Iliad* takes place in the tenth year of the Achaean siege of Troy, and the sense that the war might never end is voiced early on by Agamemnon: 'We are still fighting it, / no end in sight' (Book 2, lines 142–3). Indeed, the end of Homer's poem is not the end of the war: victory and defeat are still looming. We leave, we are left, at the end of the *Iliad*, with the death of Hector, the Trojan leader. 'The *Iliad* is a poem that lives and moves and has its being in war', comments the classical scholar Bernard Knox, 'in that world of organized violence in which a man justifies his existence most clearly by killing others' (Homer 1990, 35). This war, Homer's war, is a war without end.

Amazingly, for much of the twentieth century the *Iliad* was read as anything but a war poem (see Tatum 2003, 49–50). In his classic study of the poem *Tradition and Design in the 'Iliad'* (1930), for example, Maurice Bowra analyzes it as a 'profoundly moral story' that is 'tragic in character' (26). Why is it that a poem about a war has systematically been read differently, as if it was 'really' about something else, not about war at all? It may be that the answer has to do with the poem's obsessive focus on the very stuff of war, on rage, violence, blood and bodies in pieces, and with our desire to think of poetry in other terms, as celebrating other virtues, less polemical kinds of thinking. It may at least partly be explained, in other words, by the delight that the poem takes in gore, savagery, rage, violence. Here are some samples from Book 16, if you can stomach them:

> Brave Petroclus first—
> just as Areilycus swerved in sudden flight
> he gored him in the hip with a slashing spear
> and the bronze lancehead hammered through his flesh,
> the shaft splintering bone as he pitched face-first,
> pounding the ground—
> And the veteran Menelaus wounded Thoas,
> raking his chest where the shield-rim left it bare,
> and loosed his limbs—
> And Amphiclus went for Meges
> but Meges saw him coming and got in first by far,
> spearing him up the thigh where it joins the body,
> the point where a man's muscle bunches thickest:
> the tough sinews shredded around the weapon's point
> as the dark swirled down his eyes—
> . . .
> Idomeneus skewered Erymas straight through the mouth,
> the merciless brazen spearpoint raking through,
> up under the brain to split his glistening skull—
> teeth shattered out, both eyes brimmed to the lids
> with a gush of blood and both nostrils spurting,
> mouth gaping, blowing convulsive sprays of blood
> and death's dark cloud closed down around his corpse.
> (Homer 1990, Book 16, lines 362–74, 407–13)

In this respect, Homer's poem is the equivalent not of the sanitized violence of a Hollywood war movie, nor even of the discretely edited images from 'war torn' countries that are beamed into your sitting room by CNN or the BBC, but of Goya's shocking images of the Spanish War of Independence in *Disasters of War* (1810–14): bodies in pieces, bodies hacked, sliced, torn apart, decapitated, dismembered, disembowelled. Homer's words, like Goya's pictures, are grotesque in their realism, appalling in their unflinching, even zealous, recording of human suffering, in their representation of *people* violently objectified as violated, hacked and pierced *bodies*.

So what is a war poem presenting us with? What are Homer, Tennyson and Owen commemorating? To what are they testifying or bearing witness? The question of commemoration and testimony, of poetry as bearing witness and the associated questions of trauma and trauma theory, have become important dimensions of literary studies in the past decade or so, both in relation to cultural representations of war and, more especially, in relation to holocaust studies. 'How is the act of *writing* tied up with the act of *bearing witness*?' asks Shoshana Felman in *Testimony: Crises of Witnessing in Literature, Psychoanalysis, and History* (1992). 'Is the act of *reading* literary texts itself inherently related to the act of *facing horror*?' she ponders (2). Writing of Claude Lanzmann's film *Shoah* (1985), a film of first-hand testimonies by witnesses of – mostly victims of – the Holocaust, Felman defines our era as an '*age of testimony*', one in which witnessing itself 'has undergone a major trauma'. Lanzmann's film, Felman argues, presents 'a historical crisis of witnessing' out of which witnessing becomes 'in all senses of the word, a *critical* activity' (Felman 1992, 206). For Felman, this 'crisis' involves the sense that bearing witness to something of such unimaginable horror as the Holocaust puts the act of witnessing itself under extreme pressure. Susan Gubar expresses at least part of the difficulty in the subtitle to her recent book *Poetry After Auschwitz: Remembering What One Never Knew* (2003): the problem of testimony in the context of the Holocaust has to do with the difficulty of fully or properly 'knowing' what has been witnessed, even by those most directly involved as victims – or indeed as persecutors.

But the crisis of witnessing also involves the idea that, as Jacques Derrida puts it, testimony 'always goes hand in hand with at least the *possibility* of fiction, perjury, lie' (Derrida 2000, 27). As Derrida makes clear, this is *not* to say that all testimony is fiction, perjury, lie, not to dissolve the crucial distinction between truth and lie, truth and fiction, but to suggest nevertheless that they are inextricably linked. This is evident, not least, from the writings of the Holocaust, writings by victims and witnesses such as Primo Levi, who themselves struggle to make sense, to form narratives, out of their experiences, to piece their experiences together into coherent shapes. Levi's *If This Is A Man* (published in the US as *Survival in Auschwitz*) (1958) is an extraordinary account of his time in Auschwitz – 'Auschwitz, *anus mundi*, ultimate drainage site of the German universe', as he calls it (Levi 1989, 65). Explaining the 'fragmentary character' of the book, Levi recounts that, at the time, the need to tell his story involved 'an immediate and violent impulse, to the point of competing with . . . other elementary needs'. The shaping of these fragments into a book only occurred later. The book could only retrospectively lend coherence to what took place in the arsehole of the world (Levi 1987, 15–16). Levi even proposes, in his later meditation on witnessing the Holocaust *The Drowned and the Saved* (1986), that the witnesses to the full horror of Auschwitz are precisely those who can never bear witness, since they are those who went under, who 'drowned', who were killed. As Paul Celan writes, in what is perhaps the most succinct but inexhaustibly provoking remark on this topic: 'No one / bears witness for / the witness' (Celan 1971, 241). The witness is always, in some sense, deprived. There is something eerie and ghostly about the solitude of bearing witness.

Derrida adds another perception to our thinking of testimony, however, a perception which is fundamental to the question of the *Shoah*, the destruction or burning, the Holocaust of World War Two in particular, but which will also take us back to the question of war literature, and to the poems of Tennyson, Owen and Homer. As Derrida argues, testimony involves a 'universalizable singularity' (Derrida 2000, 94). A testimony must in the first place be singular, unique:

> I am the only one to have seen this unique thing [the witness says], the only one to have heard or to have been put in the presence of this or that, at a determinate, indivisible instant; and you must believe me because you must believe me – this is the difference, essential to testimony, between belief and proof – you must believe me because I am irreplaceable. (40)

But at the same time, this singularity, this irreplaceability of testimony, of the witness, must also be 'exemplary', must also stand as an example. The witness implicitly announces that:

> I swear to tell the truth, where I have been the only one to see or hear and where I am the only one who can attest to it, this is true to the extent that anyone *in my place*, at that instant, would have seen or heard or touched the same thing and could repeat exemplarily, universally, the truth of my testimony. The exemplarity of the 'instant', that which makes it an

'instance', if you like, is that it is singular, singular *and* universal, singular *and* universalizable. The singular must be universalizable; this is the testimonial condition. (41; translation modified)

Let us return to our three war poems and briefly consider how each is caught up in its own way with problems of testimony and exemplarity. The force of Homer's narration of violent hackings and gory deaths involves the specificity of those violations, the uniqueness of each slash, each stab. But the force also inheres in the exemplarity of these actions and these scenes, which means that one stab or slash has to take the place of thousands (just as in Hollywood movies, for different, for financial reasons, a handful of soldiers must take the place of thousands). The emotional, visceral effect on us as readers is surely to make us imagine what it would be like to receive or to deliver such violations of the body. And it is the terrible specificity, the graphic violence of the images that gives them their sense of authenticity, even as we understand that these acts take place in the realm of myth, that 'Homer' (whoever he was or they were) is not a witness, that 'Homer' is part of the myth. Part of what is remarkable about these scenes, perhaps, is our uncertainty about their undecidably mythic status (remembering that, as such critics as Paul Veyne have argued, in Ancient Greek culture myths were at the same time believed in and not believed in, seen as both true and not true (see Veyne 1988)). By contrast, through the intimacy of his language, his touching lyricism, Owen evokes a sense that this one soldier's death stands for the deaths of thousands of others and that the speaker's authentically personal witnessing of this death can stand as a wider argument about the futility of war. The 'Futility' of the title is not just of this death but of all war deaths. But in this case, it is on account of the 'authenticity effect' (as we might call it), the sense that the speaker has been a witness to this particular individual death, that he can speak with authority about war. Finally, Tennyson makes the opposite argument, an argument for war or at least for its heroism, when he witnesses, as a newspaper reader, the heroism of soldiers even in the face of blundering officers. And it is precisely because his witnessing is not unique and indeed not direct that his poem may seem to those living in the contemporary 'age of testimony' to be false, phoney, unconvincing, crass.

The different testamentary structures of the poems of Tennyson, Owen and Homer open up another question, the question of the 'aesthetic' pleasure that we might take from scenes of death, sacrifice, savagery. Why do we like to read and imagine such scenes? What is it about such scenes that is so compelling, even as they repel? It is in dealing with paradoxical questions such as these that psychoanalysis can be especially helpful. Freud's

'Psychopathic Characters on the Stage' (1904), for example, offers a rich exploration of drama and *agon* (or conflict), and of the reader's or speaker's suffering as a form of 'compensation' (Freud 1985h, 123). In fact, war haunts the work of Sigmund Freud. There are writings that specifically focus on its meanings and psychological effects, such as 'Thoughts for the Times on War and Death' (1915), 'Mourning and Melancholia' (1917), 'On Transience' (1916) and 'Why War?' (1933). But war is in fact everywhere in Freud's thinking. Freud is a great theorist of war and of *agon* more generally. Amongst his most remarkable, devastating essays in this context is 'Civilization and Its Discontents' (1930). Here he offers a compelling explanation for our delight in – and, to use Seamus Heaney's phrase from 'Punishment' (1975), our 'civilized outrage' at – images of war. Freud argues that aggression goes deep but that it conflicts with our sense of 'civilization', our sense of ourselves as civilized, cultured, rational and reasonable beings. In 'Civilization and Its Discontents', he argues that human beings are driven by what he calls the 'pleasure principle' but that the 'programme of becoming happy . . . cannot be fulfilled', and indeed that 'what we call our civilization is largely responsible for our misery' (Freud 1985e, 271, 274). Freud suggests that there is a fundamental conflict or contradiction between our primitive instincts – in particular our aggressiveness – and our desire or need for civilization (by which he means both what he calls 'Eros', the 'instinct' of love, fellowship, community, and the need for security). Rather than simply being 'gentle creatures who want to be loved', Freud tells us, human beings are, 'on the contrary, creatures among whose instinctual endowments is to be reckoned a powerful share of aggressiveness' (302). It is 'not easy for men to give up the satisfaction of this inclination to aggression', Freud argues, and they 'do not feel comfortable without it' (304–5). The reason for our unhappiness, Freud suggests, is that 'civilization' demands that we forego our 'natural aggressive instinct, the hostility of each against all and of all against each' (313). 'The price we pay for our advance in civilization', he declares, 'is a loss of happiness through the heightening of the sense of guilt' (327). In so-called 'civilized' society, our instinctual aggression is turned inward, it becomes that kind of psychic violence of the 'conscience' experienced as feelings of 'guilt'. Freud's analysis of human aggression and its conflict with the social or 'civilized' might help us to understand something of the problem of the literature of war, and our ambivalence in reading it.

Freud helps us to think differently about literature and war – more polemically, perhaps ('polemic' comes from the Greek *polemos*, war). In particular his work serves to challenge two perhaps rather naïve, sentimental or unhistorical conceptions about war literature. In the first place it allows us to question the assumption that war is the opposite of peace and that peace is the natural or normal condition of society. 'War and Peace': Leo Tolstoy's title can easily be read as articulating a contrast, an opposition. But it can also, and perhaps more productively, be construed as a conjunction, a joining up. We might thus start to explore the idea that there is no literature that is not war literature. War in the *Iliad*, remember, never ends. And war in 'post-war' Europe and beyond has never stopped – in colonial, neo-colonial and post-colonial arenas; as the 'cold war' (in which 'real' war was displaced to other, mostly developing, countries); in tribal conflicts, civil wars and inter-ethnic killings in Europe and across the globe; and as the so-called 'war against terrorism', our new war of religion. Second, Freud's work encourages us to question the assumption that the literature of war is, or should be, somehow 'naturally' or normally against war, anti-war, pacifist or non-combatant. In fact something of the opposite is true: the history of Western literature is a history of warfare and belligerence, of *agon* and *polemos*. From Homer's *Iliad* to Virgil's *Aeneid* to Chaucer's *Troilus and Criseyde* to Milton's *Paradise Lost*, the epic tradition in particular, that most elevated of genres, has celebrated the heroes of warfare and celebrated the victory of the mighty. And traces of war are found in more recent epics even when they appear to be about other things than war. We could consider, for example, William Wordsworth's *The Prelude* (with its turning point of the French Revolution), Keats's *Hyperion* (a poem on the war of the gods), Byron's *Don Juan* (with its fascination with the Napoleonic wars), Walt Whitman's *Leaves of Grass* (which according to Whitman himself 'revolves around' the American Civil War), Ezra Pound's *The Cantos* (which spans two world wars), or David Jones's *In Parenthesis* (recounting the poet's experience as a soldier in the First World War).

We might remember Doris Lessing's remark that it is 'sentimental to discuss the subject of war, or peace, without acknowledging that a great many people enjoy war – not only the idea of it, but the fighting itself' and that this is true 'even of people whose experiences in war were terrible, and which ruined their lives' (quoted in Tatum 2003, 116). That certainly seems to have been the case in the early twentieth century, at the beginning of its first 'great' war: Bertrand Russell expresses pacifist horror at finding in 1914 that 'the anticipation of carnage was delightful to something like ninety per cent of the population' (Russell 1968, 2:17). It is for this reason, perhaps, that literature is not simply *against* war, the poetry is not only in the 'pity'. And an understanding of this fact will perhaps better help us to understand the strange double-talk and double-dealings of literature, and to appreciate the deep, troubled and incessant conjunction of literature and war.

Further reading

For fascinating recent work on literature and the Holocaust see Geoffrey Hartman's *Scars of the Spirit* (2002), Daniel Schwartz's *Imagining the Holocaust* (1999), and Susan Gubar's *Poetry After Auschwitz* (2003). More generally on trauma in relation to psychoanalysis, literature and history, see Cathy Caruth's *Unclaimed Experience* (1996). For a psychoanalytic approach to the question of aggression and war, see the title essay in Jacqueline Rose's *Why War?* (1993). James Tatum's excellent study of the culture of war in *The Mourner's Song* (2003) focuses in particular on Homer and the Vietnam war and touches on a number of points raised in this chapter. There are very many interesting and valuable studies of literature and the First World War in particular: see, for example, Paul Fussell's *The Great War and Modern Memory* (1975), Samuel Hynes's *A War Imagined: The First World War and English Culture* (1990) and Allyson Booth's *Postcards from the Trenches* (1996).

32.   The end

Fin. The British comedians French and Saunders do a parody of Ingmar
Bergman films, in which they occupy an isolated clifftop house and
moan at one another about alienation, death and damnation. The skit – shot,
naturally, in black and white – concludes as the two women look out at the
dismal grey seascape and see the letters 'FIN' appear amid the waves. One
turns to the other and asks, 'What does it mean?' As with all witticisms
perhaps, amusement here depends on a force of recognition: 'fin' is not a
dorsal fin or an abbreviation for 'Finland' but is immediately recognizable
as a word (rather pretentiously taken from the French language) meaning
'The End'. And we all know what 'The End' means. It's obvious. Or is it?
What is an end?

In 'Little Gidding' (1942), T.S. Eliot observes that 'to make an end is to
make a beginning. / The end is where we start from.' Certainly when it comes
to reflecting critically on our reading of a literary text, thinking about the end
is a good way of starting. We can ask ourselves various questions: How does
the text end? What effects does this ending have? Where does the text leave *us*
as readers? More specifically, what *kind* of ending does the text have? Is it
abrupt, surprising, inevitable, apocalyptic, bathetic? And why? All of these
are questions which assume that the end or ending is indeed final, conclusive,
closed. But what happens when we think about texts as having open endings?
In what ways might the text be seen as having an ending that is haunting,
ambiguous, suspenseful, unfinished, equivocal, undecidable? Inevitably perhaps, the end of a literary text is both obvious and not so obvious – in some
senses closed, but in others open. In any case, a particularly helpful way of
reflecting on the overall force of a literary text is to analyze the nature and
impact of its ending.

To provide a typology or systematic account of different kinds of endings, in poems, plays, short stories and novels, would be an endless task, since every ending is different from every other and each calls on the reader to respond to this singularity. It may be a characteristic of many short stories that they end with a twist, and it may be a characteristic of many sonnets that they end with a rhyming couplet, but every short story and every sonnet still has to be thought about on its own terms. In this way we might take the final line of Adrienne Rich's poem, 'A Valediction Forbidding Mourning' (1970), to be emblematic: 'To do something very common, in my own way.' Every poem, every literary work, must have an ending – however open, suspended or apparently non-conclusive – but each one has its own way of doing this 'very common' thing.

More than this, every literary work is open to rereading, and the way in which its ending is appreciated or understood will vary, however imperceptibly, not only from one reader to another but from one reading to another. The idea of rereading can help us to clarify two important points about endings. First, to consider the end, to reflect critically on how a text ends and what effects it produces, is already to reread and, consequently, to recognize that there is no single end to a literary work: the end is always multiple. It is always possible to consider the end as happening in a number of different ways and in the light of more than one reading. Second, to reflect critically on how a text ends, and what impact it produces, is inevitably to think back, to think again and in effect to reread everything that has led up to this end. Thus it may be argued that, rather than being unusual or perverse, rereading is perhaps unavoidable. In this sense we never get to the end of a text.

Literary texts call for rereading in various ways. Elizabeth Taylor's short story 'Mr Wharton' (1965) is about a girl called Pat Provis who has left her home near Nottingham to work in London, and about her mother Hilda who insists on coming down to help her move into a new flat in the suburbs. Pat rather reluctantly puts up with her mother's presence and begrudgingly accepts her maternal attentions and assistance. A significant topic of conversation, when Pat gets back from her day working as a secretary in an office, is how disgusting her boss, Mr Wharton, is. He is one of those sorts of men who (in Pat's words) go out for lunch, 'eat and drink themselves stupid, and then go home and tell their wives what a hard day they've had' (229). The story ends with Hilda Provis on the train back to Nottingham and her daughter returning home to the flat. Here is the twist:

> In a positive deluge, Pat and Mr Wharton drove up to Number Twenty. He, too, had an umbrella, and held it carefully over her as they went down the garden path and round the side of the house.

> 'Excusez-moi,' she said, stooping to get the key from under the dustbin.
> 'Could be a nice view on a nice day,' he said.
> 'Could be,' she agreed, putting the key in the door. (234)

The revelation that Pat and her boss are apparently having (or are about to begin having) an affair overturns the sense that we had been given that Pat finds Mr Wharton repulsive. The twist, then, calls for a rethinking or rereading of the text, even as it provides a final justification or clarification as to why the text should be entitled 'Mr Wharton'. It is also worth stressing, however, that while this is an apparently straightforward, even banal example of what Jeffrey Archer would call a story with 'a twist in the tale', and while it ends in a clear and specific way, still the ending is open and multiple. It is not, for example, entirely clear how these two characters feel about one another or what kind of relationship is involved. More generally, this ending forces us to rethink everything in the story up to that point: we cannot help but revise our reading of the text. Finally, it is important to recognize that the end of Taylor's text, like that of many literary works, is explicitly future-oriented. The words 'Could be' mark an openness to the future in relation to the recounted time of the narrative but they also mark an openness of ending and of interpretation.

Other texts call for other kinds of thinking about ends and rereading. Samuel Taylor Coleridge's 'The Rime of the Ancient Mariner' (1798; revised 1817) ends with a description of the effect of the tale of the Ancient Mariner on the Wedding-Guest who has been forced to listen to it:

> He went like one that hath been stunned,
> And is of sense forlorn:
> A sadder and a wiser man,
> He rose the morrow morn. (ll.622–5)

The final stanzas of Coleridge's poem constitute a sort of epilogue. We might reasonably ask ourselves what status such an epilogue has in relation to the idea of the end of a work: does the end come before the epilogue or is the epilogue itself the end? As in many of Shakespeare's plays (*As You Like It, All's Well That Ends Well* and *The Tempest*, for instance), the epilogue functions as a kind of supplement, and thus conforms to the paradoxical logic of both coming *after* the end and at the same time *being the end*. Such a supplement is paradoxical in that it both completes and adds to the story. More generally, such endings are self-referential: just as the epilogues to Shakespeare's plays are explicitly about the fact that (as the King puts it, at the end of *All's Well That Ends Well*) 'the play is done', so the end of 'The Rime of the Ancient

Mariner' specifically talks about the telling of the tale and the effect of this telling on its listener ('He went like one that hath been stunned / And is of sense forlorn'). The Mariner's tale, in other words, has already ended. Or has it? These are the words that come after his tale is told:

> 'Since then, at an uncertain hour,
> That agony returns:
> And till my ghastly tale is told,
> This heart within me burns.
>
> I pass, like night, from land to land;
> I have strange power of speech;
> That moment that his face I see,
> I know the man that must hear me:
> To him my tale I teach.' (ll.582–90)

In a transfixing and haunting way, the tale of the Ancient Mariner both ends and does not end. The 'ghastly tale is told' but what the tale tells is that it can never finally be told: it is at once the product and the articulation of an interminably recurring 'agony'. It is a tale about demonization, about being possessed by an 'agony' and by 'strange power of speech': it is a tale about its own telling and, in situating the reader in the position of the Wedding-Guest, it suggests that the end is only a beginning. Reading, or rereading, is interminable. From start to finish, reading is *it*: to recall the bizarre first word of Coleridge's poem, 'It is an Ancient Mariner . . .' (l.1).

In a very different fashion, Jean Rhys's novel *Wide Sargasso Sea* (1966) ends with the Creole female narrator (Bertha or, more correctly perhaps, Antoinette) preparing to set fire to the house in England belonging to the male narrator (the never specifically named Mr Rochester). Antoinette/Bertha waits for her guard, Grace Poole, to fall asleep:

> I waited a long time after I heard her snore, then I got up, took the keys and unlocked the door. I was outside holding my candle. Now at last I know why I was brought here and what I have to do. There must have been a draught for the flame flickered and I thought it was out. But I shielded it with my hand and it burned up again to light me along the dark passage. (124)

Rhys's novel depends on the reader's acknowledgement of an intertextual relationship with Charlotte Brontë's *Jane Eyre*, but it is only at the end that the two dramatically collide. One of the things that makes this final passage so extraordinary is the fact that it is *not* final. Rather, it leads us directly into another text, into the fire that engulfs Thornfield Hall and kills Bertha Mason, in *Jane Eyre*. More fundamentally still, it puts a light to all our assumptions about Brontë's novel, it calls on us to reread and rethink the whole of *Jane Eyre* and its place and significance in the (white, middle-class or aristocratic) English literary canon. With the end of *Wide Sargasso Sea*, *Jane Eyre* can never be the same again.

The end of *Wide Sargasso Sea* is both an end and not an end. It is both closed and open. It is closed or conclusive in the sense that it leads us to the dramatic and terrible moment of setting fire to the house, and of the narrator in effect setting fire to herself. And it is open in the sense that it leads us into a radically different encounter with another text. *Wide Sargasso Sea* dislocates everything in *Jane Eyre* that marginalizes or silences the otherness of a non-white (in this case West Indian Creole) subject and everything that marginal-izes or silences the otherness of madness. The ending of Rhys's novel is also open in the sense that it calls for a rereading or for rereadings that are, in prin-ciple, limitless. What is involved here is a notion of intertextuality not only in its weak sense (*Wide Sargasso Sea* 'quotes' or alludes to *Jane Eyre*) but also in the strong sense of a text's strictly unbounded capacity for referring to or link-ing up with other texts. Thus the text of *Wide Sargasso Sea* is linked up not only with the text of *Jane Eyre*, for example, but with any and every other text that might be classified as representative of 'the traditional English novel', with any and every other text that portrays what Gilbert and Gubar call 'the madwoman in the attic', with any and every text that ends with fire or entails a holocaust, and so on. The end of Rhys's text is open, above all perhaps, in the sense that it is future-oriented. The novel ends with a suspension of time: 'Now at last I know why I was brought here and what I have to do.' It leads us towards a terrible event, it leads us (in short) towards death, but it leaves us on the threshold – or rather, to recall the very last words of the text, it leaves us with suspended movement, in a 'dark passage'. It leaves us waiting to make connections, of potentially limitless kinds – for example with the Talking Heads (or Tom Jones and the Cardigans), burning down the house, or with Prodigy's 'Firestarter'.

Jane Eyre itself 'ends' with intertextuality. Specifically it cites the end of what is probably the most intertextually pervasive book in Western culture, the Bible: ' "Amen; even so come, Lord Jesus!" ' (Revelation 22:20). The end of *Jane Eyre*, like the end of *Wide Sargasso Sea*, would then seem to confirm a sense that texts are inevitably linked up with other texts and that there is no simple end (or beginning) to any text. It may be, in fact, that to emphasize texts as unfinished and unfinishable is characteristically modern or, perhaps, postmodern. The writings of Franz Kafka and Samuel Beckett are often thought of as being especially representative of twentieth-century European literature. In this respect it should not seem surprising that Kafka's novels are unfinished and that they are about experiencing the interminable, or that Beckett's great trilogy (*Molloy, Malone Dies, The Unnamable*) ends with the paradoxical words, 'I can't go on, I'll go on' (418). Poststructuralism in particular challenges us to think critically about the ways in which the idea of the end is in various ways paradoxical. It calls on us to acknowledge – rather than to deny or ignore, or explain so as to defuse, as more traditional literary criticism has done – the intractable complexities of aporia, suspense and the undecidable.

We can briefly illustrate this in terms of the endings of two very different twentieth-century novels, Elizabeth Bowen's *The Death of the Heart* (1938) and J.D. Salinger's *The Catcher in the Rye* (1951). Bowen's magnificent novel ends with a housemaid called Matchett taking a taxi to an obscure hotel somewhere in Kensington, intending to collect and take home the heartbroken heroine of the novel, the 16-year-old orphan called Portia:

> Matchett straightened her hat with both hands, gripped her bag more firmly, mounted the steps. Below the steps the grey road was all stucco and echoes—an occasional taxi, an occasional bus. Reflections of evening made unlit windows ghostly; lit lights showed drawing-rooms pallid and bare . . .
> Through the glass door, Matchett saw lights, chairs, pillars—but there was no buttons, no one. She thought: 'Well, what a place!' Ignoring the bell, because this place was public, she pushed on the brass knob with an air of authority. (318)

Bowen's novel ends with this endless moment of suspense – before Matchett enters the hotel. In this way Bowen's novel dramatizes the idea that the end of a text always figures a threshold, a place that is liminal and uncertain. Moreover it is a threshold which we can never go beyond: Matchett never goes into the hotel. Her intention (of collecting Portia) is never fulfilled.

Uncertainty or undecidability also marks the end of *The Catcher in the Rye*. Its final chapter is a kind of epilogue, which begins with Holden Caulfield declaring 'That's all I'm going to tell about' and goes on to conclude:

> . . . D.B. [Holden's brother] asked me what I thought about all this stuff I just finished telling you about. I didn't know what the hell to say. If you want to know the truth, I don't *know* what I think about it. I'm sorry I told so many people about it. About all I know is, I sort of *miss* everybody I told about. Even old Stradlater and Ackley, for instance. I think I even miss that

> goddam Maurice. It's funny. Don't ever tell anybody anything. If you do,
> you start missing everybody. (220)

The ending of Salinger's novel emphasizes that the narrator is in some kind of psychiatric institution but leaves in suspense the question of whether or not he will stay there or what will happen if he leaves. The final passage is equivocal and paradoxical: it suggests that the story or 'stuff' is 'finished' but that there is more 'to tell about'. We are presented not only with the narrator's own powerful ambivalence ('I don't *know* what I think') but also with a sense of uncertainty as to whether or not we as readers have really been told anything or where we are being left. What kind of end is this? Is it an end?

Poststructuralism entails a kind of thinking that tries to proceed by putting the very idea of the end into question. 'End' here involves not only the sense of 'conclusion' (the end of a text, for instance) but also the sense of 'goal' and 'purpose' (the goal or purpose of reading a text, for instance). As regards the sense of 'the end' as 'the conclusion of the text', poststructuralism shows how this is problematic and even impossible: as we have been trying to make clear, intertextuality and rereading (or rereadability) mean that, in important respects, there is no end to any text. As regards the sense of 'the end' as 'the goal' or 'purpose', poststructuralism again highlights what is paradoxical. At issue here is the very nature of human desire and the paradox of the idea that, as we argue in greater detail in Chapter 21, desire is endless. Jacques Derrida, for example, emphasizes that we cannot do without the notion of end as goal or purpose (or, in its Greek form, *telos*). Nor can we do without the idea of a fulfilment or plenitude of desire. As he puts it: 'Plenitude is the end (the goal), but were it attained, it would be the end (death)' (Derrida 1988, 129).

The poetry of John Ashbery is suggestive in this context. In a poem entitled 'Soonest Mended' (1970), he writes:

> To step free at last, minuscule on the gigantic plateau—
> This was our ambition: to be small and clear and free.

Part of what makes Ashbery's poetry 'postmodern' is that it repeatedly articulates the desire to 'step free at last' but at the same time repeatedly ironizes, dislocates, writes off this gesture or 'ambition'. Ashbery has described his poems as being like dreams, and as texts for a reader to pick up, to start reading and put down again at whatever point she or he chooses: like dreams, Ashbery's poems tend to give no coherent or comforting sense of how or why they end, and yet they also convey a strong sense of the desire and need to think in terms of ends.

In the end, of course, the end is death and, more generally perhaps, the end of the world. It is not surprising, in this respect, that *Jane Eyre* should end with a quotation from the end of the book which tells of the end of the world ('The Book of Revelation' or, in Greek, 'The Apocalypse'). As Frank Kermode demonstrates, in his brief classic *The Sense of an Ending* (1967), 'the paradigms of apocalypse continue to lie under our ways of making sense of the world' (Kermode 1967, 28). Thus, for example, the great systems of Western philosophy – such as Christianity and Marxism – make sense of the world by imagining a future in which the world is fundamentally different, in which *our* world has ended forever. Christianity and Marxism, then, engage with desires that can be called apocalyptic. Such desires are crucial, also, for an appreciation of literature. Literature offers at once an imaginative experiencing and a critical questioning of the end, and it does so in ways that can be both at once exhilarating and unnerving. Literary texts, and particularly the ends of literary texts, open on to the future. And as Derrida has observed: 'The future can only be anticipated in the form of an absolute danger' (Derrida 1976, 5). The end is coming, this is it, it's now, right now, any moment now.

Further reading

Frank Kermode's *The Sense of an Ending* (1967) is a remarkable and thought-provoking account of literature and what he sees as the human need for ends. Norman Cohn's *The Pursuit of the Millennium* (1970) remains a standard and accessible work of reference for the apocalyptic nature of religious and political systems (especially Christianity and Nazism). Jacques Derrida's entire œuvre can be described as a sustained meditation on 'the end': see, in particular, 'The Ends of Man', in *Margins of Philosophy* (Derrida 1982), 'No Apocalypse, Not Now (full speed ahead, seven missiles, seven missives)' (1984), and 'Of an Apocalyptic Tone' (Derrida 1992c). On the way that poems end, see Barbara Herrnstein Smith, *Poetic Closure* (1968). For a highly engaging account of gender and culture at the *fin de siècle*, see Elaine Showalter's *Sexual Anarchy* (1991). Finally, see D.A. Miller, *Narrative and its Discontents* (1981), a fascinating book on the endings of traditional nineteenth-century novels. And then, to end yet again, death: see Peter Brooks's remarkable cogitations on death, narrative and the end-of-the-story, in the essay 'Freud's Masterplot' (in Brooks 1984), and Garrett Stewart's brilliant study of ending it all in fiction, *Death Sentences* (1984).

Glossary

Affective fallacy: term used by W.K. Wimsatt and Monroe Beardsley to designate what they see as the error of making subjective responses (cognitive or emotional) the criteria for interpretive, critical or aesthetic judgements.

Allegory: (Gk. 'other speaking') a narrative which – through allusion, metaphor, symbolism, etc. – can be read not simply on its own terms but as telling another, quite different story at the same time.

Alliteration: repeated consonant sounds, particularly at the beginning of words, e.g. 'kiddies' clobber', 'mountains of moonstone'. (See also *assonance*.)

Allusion: a reference, often only implicit or indirect, to another work of literature or art, person, event, etc.

Ambiguity: where a word, phrase or text may be interpreted in more than one way, but often taken to suggest an uncertainty between two (rather than three or more) meanings or readings. (See also *equivocality, polysemia, undecidability*.)

Animism: the rhetorical figure whereby something inanimate or lifeless is given attributes of life or spirit, e.g. Emily Brontë, *Wuthering Heights*: 'I believe at Wuthering Heights the kitchen is forced to retreat altogether into another quarter . . . the chairs, high-backed, primitive structures, painted green, one or two heavy black ones lurking in the shade . . .'; or the opening of Shelley's 'Ode to the West Wind': 'O wild West Wind, thou breath of Autumn's being . . .'

Anthropocentrism: refers to everything in a culture that asserts or assumes that the human (Gk. *anthropos*, 'man') is at the centre – whether of the universe, the world, or the meaning of a text.

Anthropomorphism: the rhetorical figure whereby the non-human is described in human terms (e.g. the legs of a table, the face of truth).

Aporia: a rhetorical figure for doubt. Especially associated with deconstructive thinking, an aporia may arise when the reader encounters two or more contradictory codes, 'messages' or 'meanings' in a text. It involves an impasse or site of undecidability. (See also *undecidability*.)

Assonance: correspondence or 'rhyming' of vowel sounds, e.g. eat, sleep; ooze, droop.

Bathos: artistic falling-away; a sense of disappointment or anti-climax, expressed by the writer or felt by the reader, e.g. the bathos in Matthew Arnold's 'The Buried Life', in the use of the word 'melancholy' at the culmination of a sentence which might have been expected to conclude on a note of triumph or joy: 'Yet still . . . / As from an infinitely distant land, / Come airs, and floating echoes, and convey / A melancholy into all our day'.

Catachresis: (Gk. 'misuse') rhetorical term for misuse or misapplication of language.

Catharsis: (Gk. 'purgation', 'purification') according to Aristotle, something that can happen to a spectator or reader at the end of a tragedy, due to a release of emotional tension arising from the experience of a paradoxical mixture of pity and terror.

Chiasmus: (from the Gk. letter χ) a rhetorical figure involving repetition and reversal, e.g. 'If you fail to plan, you plan to fail'. More broadly the term is used to refer to forms of intercrossing or reversal whereby each of the two sides of a conceptual opposition (e.g. man/woman, text/world, etc.) is shown to be reversible and paradoxically to be present and functionally active in its opposite.

Close reading: 'method' of reading emphasized by new critics which pays careful attention to 'the words on the page' rather than the historical and ideological context, the biography or intentions of the author and so on. Close reading, despite its name, brackets questions of readers and reading as arbitrary and irrelevant to the text as an artifact (see *affective fallacy*). It assumes that the function of reading and criticism is simply to read carefully what is already 'there' in the text.

Closure: an ending, the process of ending.

Connotation: an association, idea or image evoked by a word or phrase. Roughly equivalent to 'suggestion', connotation is distinct from denotation (what words denote or signify).

Couplet: two successive rhyming lines in a poem, e.g. Alexander Pope's 'Epigram Engraved on the Collar of a Dog I Gave to His Royal Highness': 'I am his Highness' Dog at Kew: / Pray tell me, sir, whose dog are you?'

Crypt: (Gk. *kryptein*, to hide) a term developed by the psychoanalysts Nicolas Abraham and Maria Torok to describe effects of transgenerational haunting. A crypt is a sort of 'false unconscious', the means by which a child is unknowingly preoccupied by a secret or secrets transmitted by a parent.

Cultural materialism: cultural materialism may be considered as the British version of new historicism. Both schools of criticism are characterized by newly theorized and politicized readings of history and of literary texts. While new historicism is particularly concerned with the textuality of history, however, cultural materialism, influenced by Raymond Williams's version of Marxist criticism, focuses on the material conditions of the production and reception of literary texts. Cultural materialists are thus concerned to expose the ideological and political dimensions of such texts.

Deconstruction: a term particularly associated with the work of Jacques Derrida. Roughly speaking, deconstruction is desedimentation: to deconstruct is to shake up and transform.

Defamiliarization: the Russian formalist critic Viktor Shklovsky uses the term *ostranenie*, usually translated as 'making strange' or 'defamiliarization', to denote what he sees as the primary function of literary texts – to make the familiar unfamiliar, to renew the old, or make the habitual appear fresh or strange.

Deixis: a term from linguistics, referring to the use of words concerning the place and time of utterance, e.g. 'this', 'here'.

Dénouement: (Fr: 'unknotting') either the events following the climax of a plot, or the resolution of this plot's complications at the end of a short story, novel or play.

Discourse: can mean simply 'speech or language generally', or 'language as we use it'. But the term is often used in more theoretical contexts to signify the use of language associated with a particular institution, cultural identity, profession, practice or discipline. In this way each discourse is one of a number of discourses (the discourse of the colonizer, for instance, as distinct from that of the colonized). Whether general or particular, discourse is always inscribed within relations of power, within the structures and strictures of institutions.

Double bind: a double bind involves the kind of double or contradictory statement or order which deconstructive criticism tends to focus on, e.g. the sentence 'This sentence is not true' is both true and not true at the same time (if it's true then it's not true and if it's not true then it's true). Rather differently, the sentence 'Do not read this sentence' involves an order which can only be obeyed if it is disobeyed (we have to read the sentence in order to know that we should not read it).

Ekphrasis: (Gk. 'description') narrowly defined, ekphrasis involves the attempt to describe a visual work of art in words; more generally, however, ekphrasis denotes any attempt to encapsulate a visual image or perception or effect in language.

Elegy: (Gk. 'lament') a poem of mourning for an individual or a lament for a tragic event; the adjective 'elegiac' may be used to describe a sense of mourning or loss encountered in any text – poem or prose.

End-stopping: where lines of poetry end with punctuation, usually with strong punctuation such as full-stops, semi-colons or colons, e.g. in the penultimate section of Wallace Stevens's 'An Ordinary Evening in New Haven': 'The wind has blown the silence of summer away. / It buzzes beyond the horizon or in the ground: / In mud under ponds, where the sky used to be reflected'. End-stopping is the opposite of *enjambment*.

Enjambment: the phenomenon whereby one line of poetry carries over into the next line without any punctuation whatever. Especially characteristic of poetry such as Milton's, Wordsworth's and Shelley's.

Epic: long narrative dealing with heroic deeds usually employing elevated language and traditionally involving a heroic or 'superhuman' protagonist, e.g. *The Odyssey, Paradise Lost.*

Epistemophilia: (Gk. 'a love of knowledge') epistemophilia is the desire for knowledge which literary texts produce in readers – the desire for the 'truth' or 'meaning' of the text, for example. Peter Brooks argues that epistemophilia is a dimension of the sex drive, and that it involves a 'dynamic of curiosity' which may be thought to be 'the foundation of all intellectual activity' (Brooks 1993, xiii).

Equivocality: like 'ambiguity', this suggests that a word, phrase, etc. has more than one meaning but, while 'ambiguous' suggests that it may be possible to decide on one primary meaning, 'equivocal' suggests that the meaning cannot be resolved. (See also *undecidability, polysemia*.)

Essentialism: refers to ways of conceiving people, cultures, etc. as having certain innate, natural or universal characteristics. Essentialism is strongly contested in most contemporary literary theory. The following three statements are all examples of essentialist thinking: (1) 'I have a personality and individuality which is completely unaffected by anything out there in the "real" world, such as language, economics, education, nationality, etc.'; (2) 'Women are more intelligent, caring and sensitive than men'; and (3) 'At bottom, you are either white or black, and that's all there is to it'.

Fabula: (also referred to as 'story' or *'histoire'*) the events of a narrative.

Feminist criticism: feminist criticism seeks on the one hand to investigate and analyze the differing representations of women and men in literary texts and, on the other hand, to rethink literary history by exploring an often marginalized tradition of women's writing. Feminist criticism is concerned to question and challenge conventional notions of masculinity and femininity; to explore ways in which such conventions are inscribed in a largely patriarchal canon; and to consider the extent to which writing, language and even literary form itself are themselves bound up with issues of gender difference.

Figure (of speech), figurative language: this is usually defined in negative terms – that is to say, as non-literal language. Figurative language involves the entire field of what is known as rhetoric and includes, for example, metaphor, simile, hyperbole, anthropomorphism, etc.

Formalism: refers generally to kinds of criticism that emphasize the importance of the formal dimensions of literary texts, such as prose style, rhyme, narrative structure, verse-form and so on. In this respect formalism is seen to stress the importance of form as (supposedly) distinct from content, meaning, social and historical context, etc. The term can be encountered in two quite different contexts, namely Russian formalism and the formalist concerns of American New Criticism (or 'close reading'). In fact the Russian formalists were not simply formalist: their close attention to the specificity of literary form was consistently subordinate to more general political, even revolutionary concerns.

Genre: a kind; a literary type or style. Poetry, drama, novel may be subdivided into lyric (including elegy, ode, song, sonnet, etc.), epic, tragedy, comedy, short story, biography, etc.

Hermeneutic: a term formerly used to designate attempts to establish a set of rules governing the interpretation of the Bible in the nineteenth century; in the context of contemporary criticism, the term refers to theories of interpretation more generally.

Heteroglossia: (Gk. 'other/different tongues') term used by Mikhail Bakhtin to describe the variety of voices or languages within a novel, but can be used of any text to give the sense that language-use does not come from one origin but is multiple and diverse, a mixing of heterogeneous discourses, sociolects, etc. (See also *polyphony*.)

Humanism: any system of thought that accords human beings central importance can be called humanism. Humanism involves the belief that humans are unique among animals (that they are not, in a sense, animals at all), as well as a resistance to superstitious or religious thinking.

Hyperbole: a figure of speech which involves exaggeration, excess or extravagance, e.g. 'I'm starving' instead of simply 'I am hungry', 'incredible' instead of 'very good'.

Ideology: while the term 'ideology' has a long history, its most common usage in contemporary literary criticism and theory originates in Marx's distinction between base and superstructure and refers to the way in which literary texts may be said to engage with – to reinforce or resist – the governing social, cultural and especially political ideas, images and representations of a society. Ideology, in the work of writers such as Louis Althusser and Pierre Macherey, is seen as fundamental to the very production of subjectivity itself, and for these writers, all cultural signification (including that of literary texts) is 'ideological'. According to this thinking, ideology reflects the fact that no writer is merely 'free' to express him- or herself, but is necessarily constrained by the conditions of the production of his or her text, by his or her social, cultural, economic and political circumstances. Ideology is thus held to be ineradicably inscribed in the literary text and the task of the critic is to analyze the work's often disguised or hidden ideological subtext.

Implied reader: Wolfgang Iser uses this term to denote a hypothetical reader towards whom the text is directed. The implied reader is to be distinguished from the so-called 'real reader'.

Indeterminacy: see *undecidability*.

In medias res: (L. 'in the middle of things') starting a story in the middle of the action.

Intentional fallacy: W.K. Wimsatt and Monroe Beardsley's term for what they see as the mistake of attempting to interpret a literary text by appealing to the supposed intentions of its author.

Interpretation: usually understood to involve an attempt to define the meaning or meanings of a specific text, with the assumption that a text has a limited meaning or meanings.

Intertextuality: a term coined by Julia Kristeva to refer to the fact that texts are constituted by a 'tissue of citations', that every word of every text refers to other texts and so on, limitlessly. Often used in an imprecise or weak sense to talk about echoes or allusions.

Irony: a rhetorical figure referring to the sense that there is a discrepancy between words and their meanings, between actions and their results, or between appearance and reality: most simply, saying one thing and meaning another.

Jouissance: (Fr. 'bliss', 'pleasure', including sexual bliss or orgasm) a term introduced into psychoanalytic theory by Jacques Lacan, to refer to extreme pleasure, but also to that excess whereby pleasure slides into its opposite. Roland Barthes uses the term to suggest an experience of reading as textual bliss. Similarly, Jacques Derrida suggests that the effect of deconstruction is to liberate forbidden jouissance.

Logocentrism: term introduced by Jacques Derrida in order to refer to everything in Western culture that puts *logos* (the Gk. term for 'word', more broadly translatable as 'meaning' or 'sense') at the centre. As Derrida argues, there is no simple escape from logocentric thinking.

Lyric: usually a fairly short poem supposedly expressing the thoughts and emotions of a speaker. Lyrics tend to be non-narrative in form.

Metafiction: a short story or novel which exploits the idea that it is (only) fiction, a fiction about fiction. Arguably, however, there are metafictional dimensions in any work of fiction. (See also *self-reflexivity*.)

Metaphor: a basic trope or figure of speech in which one thing is described in terms of its resemblance to another thing, e.g. the verb 'to fly' in 'she flew into his arms'. (See also *simile*.)

Metonymy: a basic trope or figure of speech in which the name of an attribute of an object is given for the object itself (e.g. in 'the pen is mightier than the sword', pen is a metonym for writing; sword is a metonym, for fighting or war).

Metre: the pattern of stressed and unstressed syllables in verse – one of the primary characteristics which may be said to distinguish verse from prose.

Mimesis: (Gk. 'imitation') the idea that literature attempts to represent 'life' or 'the world' more or less accurately, as it 'actually' is, etc. (See also *realism*.)

Monologue: a text (or part of a text) consisting of the speech of a single person (usually a fictional narrator, character or persona) speaking in actual or virtual solitude. In drama, referred to as a 'soliloquy'.

Narrative: may be defined in terms of the recounting of a series of events and the establishing of some (causal/temporal) relation between them.

Narratology: the field of critical and theoretical inquiry concerned with analysis of the underlying narrative structure or form of literary and other texts. Originating in the structuralist desire to produce a quasi-mathematical modelling of the deep structure of all narrative texts, recent developments in the field have encompassed poststructuralism, psychoanalytic criticism, feminism and other tendencies and have tended to move away from such scientism to examine the cultural and political significance of the workings of specific narrative texts in their historical context.

Narrator: the person or persona (as distinguished from the author) who is telling a story. Narrators can be variously categorized: a so-called omniscient narrator appears to know everything, an intrusive narrator gives his or her own comments and opinions on the story, an unreliable narrator cannot be trusted for some reason (e.g. he or she is prejudiced, exaggerating, lying), a first-person narrator presents himself or herself in the story as 'I', a third-person narrator speaks of his or her characters as 'she', 'he', etc.

New historicism: like its British version, cultural materialism, new historicism in the USA is concerned with a newly politicized and theorized historical criticism. While cultural materialism traces its roots back to Raymond Williams, new historicism is particularly influenced by Foucault's investigations of the workings of the institutions and discursive practices of medicine, psychology, the law, the university and so on, by which subjects are constructed, by which ideas are formed, and within which contexts literary texts are produced. New historicists are concerned with what Louis Montrose, in a now famous chiasmus, calls the 'historicity of texts and the textuality of history' (in Veeser 1989): history is itself 'textual' and open to interpretation, while literary texts are subject to the circulation of political and other currents of power.

Oxymoron: (Gk. 'wise foolishness') a trope which combines contradictory words or ideas, e.g. 'bittersweet', 'darkness visible'.

Paradox: an apparently contradictory or strange statement of how things are: that which is apparently illogical or absurd but may be understood to be meaningful or 'true'.

Parody: an imitation of another work of literature (usually with exaggeration) in order to make it seem ridiculous and/or amusing.

Paronomasia: word play. (See also *pun*.)

Pastiche: a work made up of imitation of other work(s); unlike parody, pastiche is not necessarily designed to ridicule.

Performative: pertaining generally to performance and, in the context of drama, to the active, dynamic effects of theatre. More specifically in the context of speech-act theory and the analysis of literary texts, however, 'performative' is an adjective referring to the capacity that statements have for *doing* as well as *saying* things. A promise or an act of naming, for example, is a performative.

Phallocentrism: refers to everything in a culture that asserts or assumes that the phallus (the symbolic significance of a penis and more generally the patriarchy linked to this) is at the centre.

Phallogocentrism: a term conflating logocentrism and phallocentrism, used to refer to everything in language or meaning (*logos*) which is phallocentric. See also 'logocentrism' and 'phallocentrism'.

Point of view: refers to the way in which the narrator 'sees' or interprets her or his material: also referred to as 'narrative perspective'.

Polyphony: literally, 'having many voices': the idea that, rather than originating in a 'single voice' (cf. 'univocal'), a literary text has multiple origins or voices. Cf. 'heteroglossia, 'intertextuality'.

Polysemia or polysemy: (Gk. 'many meanings') the quality of having several or many meanings.

Poststructuralism: Term used to describe those kinds of thinking and writing that disturb or exceed the 'merely' rational or scientific, self-assuredly 'systematic' work of structuralists. It is primarily associated with the work of Derrida, Lacan, Foucault, Deleuze and Guattari, Cixous and (post-1967) Barthes. Poststructuralism entails a rigorous and, in principle, interminable questioning of every centrism (logocentrism, ethnocentrism, anthropocentrism, etc.), of all origins and ends, meaning and intention, paradigm or system.

Protagonist: the leading character in a story (hero or heroine).

Pun: a play on words alike or nearly alike in sound but different in meaning (e.g. the word 'grave' in 'Ask for me tomorrow and you shall find me a grave man', *Romeo and Juliet*, III, i).

Queer theory: taking as its starting point an assumption about the constructedness of human sexualities, queer theory argues that sexuality is neither 'innate' nor 'natural' but subject to social, cultural, religious, educational, intellectual and other influences. Following Michel Foucault, theorists such as Eve Kosofsky Sedgwick, Judith Butler, Jonathan Dollimore and Joseph Bristow examine ways in which masculinity and femininity, and homo- and heterosexuality, are represented in literary and other texts and question traditional notions of the stability of such categories. In the work of such critics, 'queer theory' is in fact central to any thinking about literary representation, homosexual, heterosexual or other.

Realism: a descriptive term particularly associated with the nineteenth-century novel to refer to the idea that texts appear to represent 'the world' 'as it really is'.

Rhyme: like assonance and alliteration, rhymes are everywhere, in prose as well as in strictly 'poetic' texts. There are several varieties of rhyme, of which the most common are (i) full rhyme, e.g. 'cat'/'sat'; (ii) half-rhyme or off-rhyme, e.g. 'beat'/'keep', 'crime'/'scream'; (iii) internal rhyme, where a rhyme occurs within a line of verse, e.g. the '-ell' rhymes in Keats's ode 'To Autumn': 'To swell the gourd, and plump the hazel shells / With a sweet kernel; to set budding . . . /'; (iv) eye-rhyme, which should be seen but not heard, e.g. 'love'/'prove'; (v) masculine or strong rhymes, that is, words of one syllable, e.g. 'cat'/'sat', etc.; (vi) feminine or weak rhymes, which extend over more than one syllable, e.g. 'follow'/'hollow', 'qualify'/'mollify', etc.

Satire: the humorous presentation of human folly or vice in such a way as to make it look ridiculous, e.g. Jonathan Swift's *A Modest Proposal*.

Self-reflexivity: the phenomenon whereby a piece of writing refers to or reflects on itself. Often used interchangeably with 'self-referentiality'. (See also *metafiction*.)

Sibilance: an emphatic presence of 's' or 'z' sounds.

Simile: a trope in which one thing is likened to another, specifically through the use of 'like' or 'as' (a species of metaphor): in 'The barge she sat in, like a burnish'd throne / Burn'd on the water' (*Antony and Cleopatra*, II, ii) there is a metaphor in 'The barge . . . burn'd' (it is not literally on fire), and a simile in 'the barge . . . like a burnish'd throne'.

Simulacrum: (L. 'to make like') in the postmodernism of Jean Baudrillard the simulacrum is defined in terms of the substitution of the sign of the real for the real itself, in terms of a copy without origin.

Sjuzhet: (Russian 'plot') term used by the Russian formalist critics and borrowed by certain narratologists to denote the way in which a story is told, its 'discourse' or telling, as opposed to the events of the narrative, the *fabula* or story.

Sonnet: a lyric poem of (usually) fourteen lines, most commonly divided into units of eight lines (octave) plus six (sestet), or of three quatrains (four lines each) and a couplet.

Stanza: a grouping of lines of verse, usually forming a self-contained pattern of rhymed lines – thus stanzas of a poem are normally of equal length.

Symbol: a figure in which one object represents another object (often an abstract quality): conventional symbols include, for example, scales for justice, a dove for peace, a goat for lust, a lion for strength, a rose for beauty or love, etc. A symbol is a kind of metaphor in which the subject of the metaphor is not made explicit, and may be mysterious or undecidable.

Teleology: literally, 'to do with the study of the end, goal or purpose'. In contemporary literary studies, 'teleology' has to do with the idea that we think about texts (or about our activities as readers) as having a particular kind or particular kinds of *telos* (goal, purpose or end). One way of defining deconstruction or poststructuralism would be as a sustained questioning of the meaning, value and effects of teleological assumptions and ideas.

Trauma theory: ('trauma' from Gk. 'a wound') trauma theory is concerned with ways in which traumatic events are represented in language. It is particularly concerned with the difficulty or impossibility of such representations, particularly in the context of a sense of the unspeakable or untellable and of Freud's notion of *Nachträglichkeit* or deferred action, whereby the trauma may properly be said to be experienced only after it is retrospectively (re)interpreted.

Trope: (Gk. 'turn'): any rhetorical figure or device.

Undecidability: the phenomenon or experience of being unable to come to a decision when faced with two or more possible readings or interpretations. In a weak and imprecise sense, used interchangeably with 'indeterminacy'. 'Indeterminacy' is a negative term, however, implying that a decision (about being unable to determine a reading or interpretation) has already been reached. 'Undecidability', on the other hand, stresses the active, continuing challenge of being unable to decide.

Univocal: the quality of supposedly having only one meaning. 'The cat sat on the mat' might (and at some level must) be considered as a statement with univocal meaning: everyone knows what it is referring to. But at another level univocality is always open to question, in particular insofar as the context of a statement is never stable but is always susceptible to alteration or recontextualization. For example: Does 'cat' mean 'lion' here? One person's sense of 'mat' may not be someone else's (it may be their prize Persian rug). And so on.

Select bibliography of other introductory texts and reference works

Introductions

Barry, Peter. 2002. *Beginning Theory: An Introduction to Literary and Cultural Studies*. 2nd edn. Manchester: Manchester University Press.

Belsey, Catherine. 1980. *Critical Practice*. London: Methuen.

Culler, Jonathan. 1983. *On Deconstruction: Theory and Criticism after Structuralism*. London: Methuen.

Culler, Jonathan. 1997. *Literary Theory: A Very Short Introduction*. Oxford: Oxford University Press.

Eagleton, Terry. 1996. *Literary Theory: An Introduction*. 2nd edn. Oxford: Basil Blackwell.

Furniss, Tom and Michael Bath. 1996. *Reading Poetry: An Introduction*. London: Harvester Wheatsheaf.

Jefferson, Ann and David Robey. 1986. *Modern Literary Theory: A Comparative Introduction*. 2nd edn. London: Batsford.

Lentricchia, Frank and Thomas McLaughlin, eds. 1995. *Critical Terms for Literary Study*. 2nd edn. London and Chicago: Chicago University Press.

Selden, Raman, Peter Widdowson and Peter Brooker. 1997. *A Reader's Guide to Contemporary Literary Theory*. 4th edn. Hemel Hempstead: Prentice Hall.

Reference works

Brogan, T.V.F. 1994. *The New Princeton Handbook of Poetic Terms*. Princeton: Princeton University Press.

Coyle, Martin, Peter Garside, Malcolm Kelsall and John Peck, eds. 1990. *Encyclopaedia of Literature and Criticism*. London and New York: Routledge.

Cuddon, J.A., ed. 1992. *The Penguin Dictionary of Literary Terms and Literary Theory*. Harmondsworth: Penguin.

Evans, Dylan. 1996. *An Introductory Dictionary of Lacanian Psychoanalysis.* London: Routledge.

Gray, Martin. 1992. *A Dictionary of Literary Terms.* 2nd edn. Harlow, Essex and Beirut: Longman York Press.

Groden, Michael and Martin Kreiswirth, eds. 1994. *The Johns Hopkins Guide to Literary Theory and Criticism.* Baltimore: Johns Hopkins University Press.

Laplanche, J. and J.-B. Pontalis. 1973. *The Language of Psycho-Analysis,* trans. Donald Nicholson-Smith. London: Hogarth Press and the Institute of Psycho-Analysis.

Macey, David. 2000. *The Penguin Dictionary of Critical Theory.* London: Penguin.

Makaryk, Irena R., ed. 1993. *Encyclopaedia of Contemporary Literary Theory: Approaches, Scholars, Terms.* Toronto: University of Toronto Press.

Sim, Stuart. 1995. *The A–Z Guide to Modern Literary and Cultural Theorists.* Hemel Hempstead: Prentice Hall/Harvester Wheatsheaf.

Wolfreys, Julian, ed. 2002. *The Edinburgh Encyclopaedia of Modern Criticism and Theory.* Edinburgh: Edinburgh University Press.

Wright, Elizabeth, ed. 1992. *Feminism and Psychoanalysis: A Critical Dictionary.* Oxford and Cambridge, Mass.: Basil Blackwell.

Literary works discussed

Achebe, Chinua. *Things Fall Apart*. London: Heinemann, 1986.

Achebe, Chinua. *Anthills of the Savannah*. London: Heinemann, 1987.

Anon. 'Sir Patrick Spens', in *The Penguin Book of Ballads*, ed. Geoffrey Grigson. Harmondsworth: Penguin, 1975.

Arnold, Matthew. Preface to *Poems* (1835), 'To Marguerite – Continued', 'Dover Beach', in *The Poems of Matthew Arnold*, ed. Kenneth Allott. London: Longman, 1965.

Ashbery, John. 'Soonest Mended', in *The Double Dream of Spring*. New York: Ecco Press, 1975.

Atwood, Margaret. 'Giving Birth', in *Dancing Girls and Other Stories*. London: Virago, 1985.

Auden, W.H. 'In Memory of W.B. Yeats (d. Jan. 1939)', in *Collected Poems*, ed. Edward Mendelson. London: Faber and Faber, 1991.

Austen, Jane. *Pride and Prejudice*, ed. Frank W. Bradbrook. London: Oxford University Press, 1970.

Ayres, Michael. 'Bittersweet', in *Poems 1987–1992*. Nether Stowey, Somerset: Odyssey Poets, 1994.

Beckett, Samuel. *Molloy, Malone Dies, The Unnamable*. London: Calder and Boyars, 1959.

Beckett, Samuel. *Murphy*. London: Picador, 1973.

Beckett, Samuel. *Waiting for Godot*. London: Faber and Faber, 1986.

Blake, William. 'The Marriage of Heaven and Hell', in *Blake: The Complete Poems*, 2nd edn, ed. W.H. Stevenson. London: Longman, 1989.

Bowen, Elizabeth. *The Heal of the Day*. Harmondsworth: Penguin, 1976.

Bowen, Elizabeth. *The Death of the Heart*. Harmondsworth: Penguin, 1987.

Bowen, Elizabeth. *A World of Love*. Harmondsworth: Penguin, 1988.

Brontë, Charlotte. *Jane Eyre*. Harmondsworth: Penguin, 1966.

Brontë, Emily. *Wuthering Heights*. Harmondsworth: Penguin, 1965.

Browning, Robert. 'Two in the Campagna', in *Robert Browning: Selected Poetry*, ed. Daniel Karlin. Harmondsworth: Penguin, 1989.

Byron. *Poetical Works*. Oxford: Oxford University Press, 1970.

Carver, Raymond. 'Fat' and 'Cathedral' in *Where I'm Calling From: The Selected Stories*. London: Harvill, 1993.

Chandler, Raymond. *The Little Sister*. New York: Vintage Books, 1988.

Chaucer, Geoffrey. *The Canterbury Tales: Nine Tales and the General Prologue*, eds V.A. Kolve and Glending Olson. New York: Norton, 1989.

Coleridge, S.T. *Collected Letters of Samuel Taylor Coleridge*, 6 vols, ed. Earl Leslie Griggs. Oxford: Oxford University Press, 1956–71.

Coleridge, S.T. 'The Rime of the Ancient Mariner', 'Kubla Khan', in *The Oxford Authors Samuel Taylor Coleridge*, ed. H.J. Jackson. Oxford: Oxford University Press, 1985.

Conrad, Joseph. *Heart of Darkness*. Harmondsworth: Penguin Popular Classics, 1994.

Dante Alighieri. *The Divine Comedy. Inferno I: Italian Text and Translation*, trans. Charles S. Singleton. New Jersey: Princeton University Press, 1970.

DeLillo, Don. *The Body Artist*. London: Picador, 2001.

Dickens, Charles. *Great Expectations*. Harmondsworth: Penguin, 1965.

Dickinson, Emily. 'Our Lives are Swiss', 'I taste a liquor never brewed', 'A Bird came Down the Walk', in *The Complete Poems of Emily Dickinson*, ed. Thomas H. Johnson. London: Faber and Faber, 1970.

Eliot, George. *Middlemarch*. Harmondsworth: Penguin, 1965.

Eliot, George. *The Lifted Veil*. London: Virago, 1985.

Eliot, George. *Daniel Deronda*. Harmondsworth: Penguin, 1987.

Eliot, T.S. *The Waste Land*, 'Little Gidding', in *Complete Poems and Plays*. London: Faber and Faber, 1975a.

Ellison, Ralph. *Invisible Man*. New York: Random House, 1952.

Eugenides, Jeffrey. *Middlesex*. London: Bloomsbury, 2003.

Ford, Ford Madox. *The Good Soldier* in *The Bodley Head Ford Madox Ford*, vol. 1. London: Bodley Head, 1962.

Gilman, Charlotte Perkins. *The Yellow Wallpaper*. London: Virago, 1981.

Hardy, Thomas. 'Neutral Tones', 'The Voice', 'The Darkling Thrush', in *The Oxford Authors Thomas Hardy*, ed. Samuel Hynes. Oxford: Oxford University Press, 1984.

Hazlitt, William. *The Complete Works of William Hazlitt*, 21 vols, ed. P.P. Howe. London: Dent, 1930–34.

Heaney, Seamus. *North*. London: Faber and Faber, 1975.

Homer. *The Iliad*, trans. Robert Fagles, introduction and notes by Bernard Knox. New York: Penguin, 1990.

Ibsen, Henrik. *Four Major Plays*. Oxford: Oxford University Press, 1981.

James, Henry. *The Turn of the Screw*, in *The Bodley Head Henry James*, vol. XI, ed. Leon Edel. London: Bodley Head, 1974.

James, Henry. 'The Jolly Corner', in *Major American Short Stories*, ed. A. Walton Litz. Oxford: Oxford University Press, 1994.

Jonson, Ben. *A Critical Edition of the Major Works*, ed. Ian Donaldson. Oxford: Oxford University Press, 1988.

Joyce, James. 'The Dead', in *Dubliners*. London: Everyman, 1991.

Kafka, Franz. *The Collected Aphorisms*, trans. Malcolm Pasley. Syrens: London, 1994.

Kafka, Franz. 'In the Penal Colony', in *The Complete Short Stories of Franz Kafka*, ed. Nabu N. Glatzer. London: Minerva, 1992.

Keats, John. *The Letters of John Keats, 1814-1821*, 2 vols, ed. Hyder Edward Rollins. Cambridge, Mass.: Harvard University Press, 1958.

Keats, John. 'Ode to a Nightingale', 'Ode on Melancholy', 'This Living Hand', in *The Poems of John Keats*, ed. Jack Stillinger. London: Heinemann, 1978.

Larkin, Philip. 'This Be The Verse', in *Collected Poems*, ed. Anthony Thwaite. London: Faber and Faber, 1988.

Lawrence, D.H. 'The Rocking-Horse Winner', in *The Collected Short Stories of D.H. Lawrence*. London: Heinemann, 1974.

Lawrence, D.H. *St. Mawr. The Virgin and the Gipsy*. Harmondsworth: Penguin, 1950.

Mansfield, Katherine. 'Bliss', in *The Stories of Katherine Mansfield*, ed. Antony Alpers. Oxford: Oxford University Press, 1984.

Marvell, Andrew. 'To His Coy Mistress', in *The Oxford Authors Andrew Marvell*, ed. Frank Kermode and Keith Walker. Oxford: Oxford University Press, 1990.

Melville, Herman. *Moby Dick; or, The Whale*, ed. Harold Beaver. Harmondsworth: Penguin, 1972.

Miller, Arthur. *The Crucible*. Harmondsworth: Penguin, 1988.

Milton, John. *Complete Shorter Poems*, ed. John Carey. London: Longman, 1971.

Milton, John. *Paradise Lost*, ed. Scott Elledge, 2nd edn. New York: Norton, 1993.

Monty Python's Flying Circus. *Just the Words*, 2 vols. London: Methuen, 1989.

Morrison, Toni. *The Bluest Eye*. London: Triad/Panther, 1981.

Morrison, Toni. *Beloved*. London: Picador, 1988.

O'Connor, Flannery. 'Revelation', in *The Secret Self: Short Stories by Women*, ed. Hermione Lee. London: Everyman, 1991.

Owen, Wilfred. 'Futility', in *The Poems of Wilfred Owen*, ed. John Stallworthy. London: Hogarth, 1985.

Pater, Walter. *The Renaissance*. New York: Modern Library, 1919.

Plath, Sylvia. 'Daddy', in *Collected Poems*, ed. Ted Hughes. London: Faber and Faber, 1981.

Poe, Edgar Allan. 'The Premature Burial', 'The Purloined Letter', in *Tales of Mystery and Imagination*. London: Dent, 1984.

Pope, Alexander. 'An Essay on Criticism', in *The Poems of Alexander Pope*, ed. John Butt. London: Methuen, 1963.

Proust, Marcel. *A la recherche du temps perdu*. Paris: Gallimard, 1954.

Rhys, Jean. 'Let Them Call It Jazz', in *The Secret Self: Short Stories by Women*, ed. Hermione Lee. London: Everyman, 1991.

Rhys, Jean. *Wide Sargasso Sea*, ed. Angela Smith. Harmondsworth: Penguin, 1997.

Rich, Adrienne. 'A Valediction Forbidding Mourning', in *The Fact of a Doorframe: Poems Selected and New, 1950–84*. New York: Norton, 1984.

Rushdie, Salman. *Midnight's Children*. London: Picador, 1982.

Rushdie, Salman. *The Satanic Verses*. New York: Viking, 1988.

Salinger, J.D. *The Catcher in the Rye*. Harmondsworth: Penguin, 1987.

Shakespeare, William. All's Well That Ends Well, Romeo and Juliet, Twelfth Night, Hamlet, Othello, King Lear, Macbeth, The Tempest, Sonnet 20, Sonnet 55, in *The Riverside Shakespeare*. Boston: Houghton Mifflin, 1974.

Shelley, Mary Wollstonecraft. *Frankenstein; Or, The Modern Prometheus*, eds D.L. Macdonald and Kathleen Scherf. Peterborough, Ontario: Broadview, 1994.

Shelley, Percy Bysshe. 'Ozymandias', 'To a Sky-Lark', 'A Defence of Poetry', in *Shelley's Poetry and Prose*, eds Donald H. Reiman and Sharon B. Powers. New York: Norton, 1977.

Sheridan, Richard Brinsley. *The Rivals*, ed. Elizabeth Duthie. London: Ernest Benn, 1979.

Sheridan, Richard Brinsley. *The School for Scandal*, ed. F.W. Bateson. New York: Norton, 1979.

Sidney, Sir Philip. *An Apology for Poetry*, ed. Geoffrey Shepherd. London: Nelson, 1965.

Sophocles. *The Three Theban Plays: Antigone, Oedipus the King, Oedipus at Colonus*, trans. Robert Fagles. Harmondsworth: Penguin, 1984.

Sterne, Laurence. *The Life and Opinions of Tristram Shandy, Gentleman*, ed. Ian Campbell Ross. Oxford: Clarendon Press, 1983.

Stevens, Wallace. 'Large Red Man Reading', 'The Man with the Blue Guitar' and 'Tea at the Palaz of Hoon', in *The Collected Poems of Wallace Stevens*. New York: Alfred Knopf, 1954.

Stevens, Wallace. 'Adagia', in *Opus Posthumous*. New York: Alfred A. Knopf, 1957.

Swift, Jonathan. 'A Modest Proposal', in *The Writings of Jonathan Swift*, eds Robert A. Greenberg and William Bowman Piper. New York: Norton, 1973.

Taylor, Elizabeth. 'Mr Wharton', in *The Secret Self: Short Stories by Women*, ed. Hermione Lee. London: Everyman, 1991.

Tennyson, Alfred Lord. 'The Charge of the Light Brigade', in *The Poems of Tennyson*, ed. Christopher Ricks. London: Longman, 1987.

Traherne, Thomas. 'Centuries of Meditations', in *Selected Poems and Prose*, ed. Alan Bradford. Harmondsworth: Penguin, 1991.

Twain, Mark. *The Adventures of Huckleberry Finn*, eds Walter Blair and Victor Fischer. Berkeley: University of California Press, 1988.

Wertenbaker, Timberlake. *Our Country's Good*. London: Methuen, 1988.

Winterson, Jeanette. *Sexing the Cherry*. London: Bloomsbury, 1989.

Winterson, Jeanette. *Written on the Body*. London: Jonathan Cape, 1992.

Woolf, Virginia. 'The Mark on the Wall', in *A Haunted House and Other Short Stories*. London: Grafton, 1982.

Woolf, Virginia. *Orlando: A Biography*. Oxford: Oxford University Press, 1992.

Wordsworth, William. *The Prelude 1799, 1805, 1850*, eds Jonathan Wordsworth, M.H. Abrams and Stephen Gill. London: Norton, 1979.

Wordsworth, William. 'Alice Fell', 'A Slumber did my Spirit Seal', *Intimations* 'Ode', in *The Oxford Authors William Wordsworth*, ed. Stephen Gill. Oxford: Oxford University Press, 1984.

Wyatt, Sir Thomas. 'Whoso List to Hunt', in *Collected Poems*, ed. Joost Daalder. London: Oxford University Press, 1975.

Bibliography of critical and theoretical works

Abraham, Nicolas. 1994. 'Notes on the Phantom: A Complement to Freud's Metapsychology' (1975) and 'The Phantom of Hamlet or The Sixth Act, *preceded by* The Intermission of "Truth"' (1975), in *The Shell and the Kernel: Renewals of Psychoanalysis*, Nicolas Abraham and Maria Torok, trans. Nicholas Rand. Chicago: Chicago University Press.

Abrams, M.H. 1953. *The Mirror and the Lamp: Romantic Theory and the Critical Tradition*. Oxford: Oxford University Press.

Allen, Graham. 2000. *Intertextuality*. London: Routledge.

Alter, Robert. 1981. *The Art of Biblical Narrative*. London: George Allen and Unwin.

Alter, Robert. 1985. *The Art of Biblical Poetry*. New York: Basic Books.

Althusser, Louis. 1969. 'Ideology and Ideological State Apparatuses' and 'A Letter on Art', in *Lenin and Philosophy and Other Essays*, trans. Ben Brewster, 2nd edn. London: New Left Books, 1977.

Appelbaum, David. 1990. *Voice*. New York: State University of New York.

Apter, Terry E. 1982. 'The Uncanny', in *Fantasy Literature: An Approach to Reality*. London: Macmillan.

Aristotle. 1941. *The Basic Works of Aristotle*, ed. Richard McKeon. New York: Random House.

Aristotle. 1965. *On the Art of Poetry*, in *Classical Literary Criticism*, Trans. T.S. Dorsch. Harmondsworth: Penguin.

Armstrong, Tim. 1998. *Modernism, Technology and the Body: A Cultural Study*. Cambridge: Cambridge University Press.

Arnold, Matthew. 1964. 'The Function of Criticism at the Present Time', in *Essays in Criticism*. New York: Everyman's Library.

Ashcroft, Bill, Gareth Griffiths and Helen Tiffin, eds. 1989. *The Empire Writes Back*. London: Routledge.

Ashcroft, Bill, Gareth Griffiths and Helen Tiffin, eds. 1995. *The Post-Colonial Studies Reader*. London: Routledge.

Attridge, Derek. 1992. *Poetic Rhythm*. Cambridge: Cambridge University Press.

Audi, Robert, ed. 1999. *The Cambridge Dictionary of Philosophy*, 2nd edn. Cambridge: Cambridge University Press.

Austin, J.L. 1962. *How to do Things with Words*. Oxford: Clarendon Press.

Austin, J.L. 1970. 'Performative Utterances', in *Philosophical Papers*, 2nd edn, eds J.O. Urmson and G.J. Warnock. Oxford: Oxford University Press.

Badmington, Neil, ed. 2000. *Posthumanism*. London: Palgrave.

Bakhtin, M.M. 1981. *The Dialogic Imagination: Four Essays*, trans. M. Holquist and C. Emerson. Austin: University of Texas Press.

Bakhtin, M.M. 1992. From 'Discourse in the Novel', in *Modern Literary Theory: A Reader*, eds Philip Rice and Patricia Waugh. London: Edward Arnold.

Baldick, Chris. 1987. *In Frankenstein's Shadow: Myth, Monstrosity, and Nineteenth-Century Writing*. Oxford: Oxford University Press.

Balibar, Etienne and Pierre Macherey. 1981. 'On Literature as an Ideological Form', in *Untying the Text: A Post-Structuralist Reader*, ed. Robert Young. London: Routledge and Kegan Paul.

Barker, Francis and Peter Hulme. 1985. 'Nymphs and Reapers Heavily Vanish: The Discursive Con-Texts of *The Tempest*', in *Alternative Shakespeares*, ed. John Drakakis. London: Routledge.

Barker, Howard. 1989. *Arguments for a Theatre*. London: John Calder.

Barthes, Roland. 1972. *Mythologies*, trans. Annette Lavers. London: Jonathan Cape.

Barthes, Roland. 1977a. 'The Death of the Author', in *Image Music Text*, trans. Stephen Heath. London: Fontana.

Barthes, Roland. 1977b. 'From Work to Text', in *Image Music Text*, trans. Stephen Heath. London: Fontana.

Barthes, Roland. 1977c. *Roland Barthes by Roland Barthes*, trans. Richard Howard. New York: Hill and Wang.

Barthes, Roland. 1981. 'Theory of the Text', in *Untying the Text: A Post-Structuralist Reader*, ed. Robert Young. London: Routledge and Kegan Paul.

Barthes, Roland. 1990a. *The Pleasure of the Text*, trans. Richard Miller. Oxford: Basil Blackwell.

Barthes, Roland. 1990b. *S/Z*, trans. Richard Miller. Oxford: Basil Blackwell.

Barthes, Roland. 1990c. *A Lover's Discourse: Fragments*, trans. Richard Howard. Harmondsworth: Penguin.

Bataille, Georges. 1973. *Oeuvres Complètes*, vol. V. Paris: Gallimard.

Bataille, Georges. 1985. *Literature and Evil*, trans. Alistair Hamilton. London: Marion Boyars.

Baudrillard, Jean. 1988. 'Simulacra and Simulations', in *Selected Writings*, ed. Mark Poster. Cambridge: Polity.

Baudrillard, Jean. 1990. *Seduction*, trans. Brian Singer. London: Macmillan.

Baudrillard, Jean. 1995. *The Gulf War Did Not Take Place*, trans. Paul Patton. Sydney: Power Publications.

Beckett, Samuel. 1983. *Disjecta: Miscellaneous Writings and a Dramatic Fragment.* London: John Calder.

Beja, Morris. 1971. *Epiphany in the Modern Novel.* London: Peter Owen.

Belsey, Catherine. 1994. *Desire: Love Stories in Western Culture.* Oxford: Blackwell.

Bertens, Hans, and Joseph Natoli, eds. 2001. *Postmodernism: The Key Figures.* Oxford: Blackwell.

Bennett, Andrew, ed. 1995. *Readers and Reading.* London: Longman.

Bennett, Andrew. *The Author.* London: Routledge. 2005.

Bennett, Tony. 1979. *Formalism and Marxism.* London: Methuen.

Bergson, Henri. 1921. *Laughter: An Essay on the Meaning of the Comic,* trans. Cloudesley Brereton and Fred Rothwell. London: Macmillan.

Berry, Francis. 1962. *Poetry and the Physical Voice.* London: Routledge and Kegan Paul.

Bersani, Leo. 1978. *A Future for Astyanax: Character and Desire in Literature.* Boston: Little Brown.

Bersani, Leo. 1990. *The Culture of Redemption.* Cambridge, Mass.: Harvard University Press.

Bersani, Leo. 1995. *Homos.* Cambridge, Mass.: Harvard University Press.

Bhabha, Homi, ed. 1990. *Nation and Narration.* London: Routledge.

Bhabha, Homi K. 1996. 'Of Mimicry and Man: The Ambivalence of Colonial Discourse', in eds Philip Rice and Patricia Waugh, *Modern Literary Theory: A Reader,* 3rd edn. London: Edward Arnold.

Biriotti, Maurice and Nicola Miller, eds. 1993. *What is an Author?* Manchester: Manchester University Press.

Blanchot, Maurice. 1981. 'The Narrative Voice (the "he", the neuter)', in *The Gaze of Orpheus and Other Literary Essays,* trans. Lydia Davis. New York: Station Hill.

Blanchot, Maurice. 1995. *The Work of Fire,* trans. Charlotte Mandell. Stanford: Stanford University Press.

Blanchot, Maurice. 1999. *The Station Hill Blanchot Reader: Fiction and Literary Essays,* trans. Lydia Davis, Paul Auster and Robert Lamberton, ed. George Quasha. Barrytown, New York: Station Hill Press.

Blair, Hugh. 1842. *Lectures on Rhetoric and Belles Lettres,* ed. William Milner.

Bloom, Harold. 1973. *The Anxiety of Influence: A Theory of Poetry.* Oxford: Oxford University Press.

Bloom, Harold. 1990. 'The Analysis of Character', in *Holden Caulfield,* ed. Harold Bloom. New York: Chelsea House.

Bloom, Harold. 1994. *The Western Canon: The Book and School of the Ages.* London: Macmillan.

Bloom, Harold. 2000. *How to Read and Why.* London: Fourth Estate.

Boden, Margaret A. 2004. *The Creative Mind: Myths and Mechanisms,* 2nd edn. London and New York: Routledge.

Boone, Joseph Allen. 1987. *Tradition and Counter Tradition: Love and the Form of Fiction.* Chicago: University of Chicago Press.

Boone, Joseph Allen. 1988. *Libidinal Currents. Sexuality and the Shaping of Modernism*. Chicago: Chicago University Press.

Booth, Allyson. 1996. *Postcards from the Trenches: Negotiating the Space Between Modernism and the First World War*. New York: Oxford University Press.

Borch-Jacobsen, Mikkel. 1987. 'The Laughter of Being', in *Modern Language Notes*, 102, no. 4: 737–60.

Borch-Jacobsen, Mikkel. 1988. *The Freudian Subject*, trans. Catherine Porter. Stanford: Stanford University Press.

Botting, Fred, ed. 1995. *Frankenstein: New Casebook*. Basingstoke: Macmillan.

Botting, Fred. 1997. *Gothic*. London: Routledge.

Bourdieu, Pierre. 1984. *Distinction: A Social Critique of the Judgment of Taste*, trans. Richard Nice. Cambridge, Mass.: Harvard University Press.

Bowen, Elizabeth. 1986. *The Mulberry Tree*. London: Virago.

Bowie, Malcolm. 1991. *Lacan*. London: Fontana.

Bowra, Maurice. 1930. *Tradition and Design in 'The Iliad'*. London: Oxford University Press.

Bradley, A.C. 1904. *Shakespearean Tragedy: Lectures on Hamlet, Othello, King Lear, Macbeth*. London: Macmillan.

Brannigan, John. 1998. *New Historicism and Cultural Materialism*. London: Macmillan.

Brecht, Bertolt. 1978. 'A Short Organum for the Theatre', in *Brecht on Theatre: The Development of an Aesthetic*, ed. and trans. John Willett. London: Eyre Methuen.

Brewster, Scott, John L. Joughin, David Owen and Richard Walker, eds. 2000. *Inhuman Reflections: Thinking the Limits of the Human*. Manchester: Manchester University Press.

Bristow, Joseph. 1992a. 'Introduction' to Oscar Wilde, *The Importance of Being Earnest and Related Writings*. London: Routledge.

Bristow, Joseph, ed. 1992b. *Sexual Sameness: Textual Differences in Lesbian and Gay Writing*. London: Routledge.

Bristow, Joseph. 1995. *Effeminate England: Homoerotic Writing after 1885*. Buckingham: Open University Press.

Bristow, Joseph. 1997. *Sexuality*. London: Routledge.

Bronfen, Elisabeth. 1992. *Over Her Dead Body: Death, Femininity and the Aesthetic*. Manchester: Manchester University Press.

Brooke-Rose, Christine. 1958. *A Grammar of Metaphor*. London: Secker and Warburg.

Brooker, Peter, ed. 1992. *Modernism/Postmodernism*. London: Longman.

Brooks, Peter. 1984. *Reading for the Plot: Design and Intention in Narrative*. Oxford: Oxford University Press.

Brooks, Peter. 1993. *Body Work: Objects of Desire in Modern Narrative*. Cambridge, Mass.: Harvard University Press.

Brown, Paul. 1994. ' "This thing of darkness I acknowledge mine": *The Tempest* and the Discourse of Colonialism', in *Political Shakespeare: Essays in Cultural*

Materialism, eds Jonathan Dollimore and Alan Sinfield, 2nd edn. Manchester: Manchester University Press.

Buchanan, Ian and John Marks. 2000. *Deleuze and Literature*. Edinburgh: Edinburgh University Press.

Burke, Seán. 1998. *The Death and Return of the Author: Criticism and Subjectivity in Barthes, Foucault and Derrida*, 2nd edn. Edinburgh: Edinburgh University Press.

Burke, Seán, ed. 1995. *Authorship: From Plato to the Postmodern: A Reader*. Edinburgh: Edinburgh University Press.

Buse, Peter and Andrew Stott, eds. 1999. *Ghosts: Deconstruction, Psychoanalysis, History*. Basingstoke: Macmillan.

Butler, Judith. 1990. *Gender Trouble: Feminism and the Subversion of Identity*. London: Routledge.

Butler, Judith. 1991. 'Imitation and Gender Insubordination', in *Inside/Out: Lesbian Theories, Gay Theories*, ed. Diana Fuss. New York: Routledge.

Butler, Judith. 1993. *Bodies that Matter: On the Discursive Limits of 'Sex'*. New York: Routledge.

Butler, Judith. 1997. *Excitable Speech: A Politics of the Performative*. New York: Routledge.

Carper, Thomas and Derek Attridge. 2003. *Meter and Meaning: An Introduction to Rhythm in Poetry*. New York: Routledge.

Caruth, Cathy. 1996. *Unclaimed Experience: Trauma, Narrative, and History*. Baltimore: Johns Hopkins University Press.

Carver, Raymond. 1986. 'On Writing', in *Fires: Essays, Poems, Stories*. London: Picador.

Castle, Terry. 1992. 'Sylvia Townsend Warner and the Counterplot of Lesbian Fiction', in *Sexual Sameness: Textual Differences in Lesbian and Gay Writing*, ed. Joseph Bristow. London: Routledge.

Castle, Terry. 1995. *The Female Thermometer: Eighteenth-Century Culture and the Invention of the Uncanny*. Oxford: Oxford University Press.

Caughie, John, ed. 1981. *Theories of Authorship: A Reader*. London: Routledge and Kegan Paul.

Celan, Paul. 1986. *Collected Prose*, trans. Rosemarie Waldrop. Manchester: Carcanet Press.

Chambers, Ross. 1984. *Story and Situation: Narrative Seduction and the Power of Fiction*. Manchester: Manchester University Press.

Chambers, Ross. 1991. *Room for Maneuver: Reading (the) Oppositional (in) Narrative*. Chicago: University of Chicago Press.

Chandler, James. 1998. *England in 1819: The Politics of Literary Culture and the Case of Romantic Historicism*. Chicago: University of Chicago Press.

Chase, Cynthia. 1986. *Decomposing Figures: Rhetorical Readings in the Romantic Tradition*. Baltimore: The Johns Hopkins University Press.

Chasseguet-Smirget, Janine. 1985. *Creativity and Perversion*. Foreword by Otto Kernberg. London: Free Association Books.

Chatman, Seymour. 1990. *Coming to Terms: The Rhetoric of Narrative in Fiction and Film*. Ithaca: Cornell University Press.

Chomsky, Noam. 1957. *Syntactic Structures*. S-Gravenhage: Mouton.

Cixous, Hélène. 1974. 'The Character of "Character"', *New Literary History*, 5: 383–402.

Cixous, Hélène. 1976. 'Fiction and Its Phantoms: A Reading of Freud's *Das Unheimliche*', *New Literary History*, 7: 525–48.

Cixous, Hélène. 1990. 'The Laugh of the Medusa', trans. Keith Cohen and Paula Cohen, in *New French Feminisms: An Anthology*, eds Elaine Marks and Isabelle de Courtirvon. Amherst: University of Massachusetts Press.

Cixous, Hélène. 1993. *Three Steps on the Ladder of Writing*, trans. Sarah Cornell and Susan Sellers. New York: Columbia University Press.

Cixous, Hélène. 1998. *Stigmata: Escaping Texts*, trans. Eric Prenowitz. London and New York: Routledge.

Clark, Timothy. 1997. *The Theory of Inspiration: Composition as a Crisis of Subjectivity in Romantic and Post-Romantic Writing*. Manchester: Manchester University Press.

Clark, Timothy and Nicholas Royle, eds. 2002. 'Monstrism', *The Oxford Literary Review* 23.

Cohen, Tom. 1994. *Anti-Mimesis from Plato to Hitchcoch*. Cambridge: Cambridge University Press.

Cohn, Dorrit. 1978. *Transparent Minds: Narrative Modes for Presenting Consciousness in Fiction*. Princeton, NJ: Princeton University Press, 1978.

Cohn, Norman. 1970. *The Pursuit of the Millennium: Revolutionary Millenarians and Mystical Anarchists of the Middle Ages*. Oxford: Oxford University Press.

Colebrook, Claire. 2002. *Gilles Deleuze*. London and New York: Routledge.

Coleridge, Samuel Taylor. 1975. *Biographia Literaria, or Biographical Sketches of my Literary Life and Opinions*, ed. George Watson. London: Dent.

Connor, Steven. 1992. *Theory and Cultural Value*. Oxford: Blackwell.

Connor, Steven. 1997. *Postmodernist Culture: An Introduction to Theories of the Contemporary*, 2nd edn. Oxford: Blackwell.

Connor, Steven. 2000. *Dumbstruck – A Cultural History of Ventriloquism*. Oxford: Oxford University Press.

Cordner, Michael, Peter Holland and John Kerrigan, eds. 1994. *English Comedy*. Cambridge: Cambridge University Press.

Crane, R.S. 1967. 'History Versus Criticism in the Study of Literature', in *The Idea of the Humanities and Other Essays Critical and Historical*, vol. 2. Chicago: University of Chicago Press.

Critchley, Simon. 2002. *On Humour*. London and New York: Routledge.

Culler, Jonathan. 1981. 'Story and Discourse in the Analysis of Narrative', in *The Pursuit of Signs: Semiotics, Literature, Deconstruction*. London: Routledge and Kegan Paul.

Culler, Jonathan. 1983. *On Deconstruction: Theory and Criticism After Structuralism*. London: Routledge and Kegan Paul.

Culler, Jonathan, ed. 1988a. *On Puns: The Foundation of Letters*. Oxford: Basil Blackwell.

Culler, Jonathan. 1988b. 'Political Criticism: Confronting Religion', in *Framing the Sign: Criticism and Its Institutions*. Oxford: Basil Blackwell.

Culler, Jonathan. 1997. *Literary Theory: A Very Short Introduction*. Oxford: Oxford University Press.

Cupitt, Don. 1997. *After God: The Future of Religion*. London: Weidenfield and Nicolson.

Currie, Mark, ed. 1995. *Metafiction*. London: Longman.

Currie, Mark. 1998. *Postmodern Narrative Theory*. Basingstoke: Macmillan.

Curti, Lidia. 1998. *Female Stories, Female Bodies: Narrative, Identity and Representation*. London: Macmillan.

Darwin, Charles. 1866. *On the Origin of the Species By Means of Natural Selection, Or, The Preservation of Favoured Races in the Struggle for Life*, 4th edn, London: Murray.

Davies, Tony. 1997. *Humanism*. London: Routledge.

Day, Gary. 1996. *Re-Reading F.R. Leavis: Culture and Literary Criticism*. Basingstoke: Macmillan.

Dean, Carolyn J. 1992. *The Self and Its Pleasures: Bataille, Lacan, and the History of the Decentered Subject*. Ithaca: Cornell University Press.

Decker, James M. 2004. *Ideology*. Basingstoke: Palgrave Macmillan.

Deleuze, Gilles. 1986. *Cinema 1: The Movement-Image*, trans. Hugh Tomlinson and Barbara Habberjam. London: Athlone Press.

Deleuze, Gilles. 1989. *Cinema 2: The Time-Image*, trans. Hugh Tomlinson and Robert Galeta. London: Athlone Press.

Deleuze, Gilles. 1998. 'Literature and Life', 'He Stuttered' and 'The Exhausted', in *Essays Critical and Clinical*, trans. Daniel W. Smith and Michael A. Greco. London: Verso.

Deleuze, Gilles. 2000. 'The Brain Is the Screen: An Interview with Gilles Deleuze' [1986], trans. Marie Therese Guirgis, in *The Brain Is the Screen: Deleuze and the Philosophy of Cinema*, ed. Gregory Flaxman. Minneapolis: University of Minnesota Press.

Deleuze, Gilles and Félix Guattari. 1983. *Anti-Oedipus: Capitalism and Schizophrenia*, trans. Robert Hurley *et al*. Minneapolis: University of Minnesota Press.

Deleuze, Gilles and Félix Guattari. 1986. *Kafka: Toward a Minor Literature*, trans. Dana Polan. Minneapolis: University of Minnesota Press.

de Man, Paul. 1979. *Allegories of Reading: Figural Language in Rousseau, Nietzsche, Rilke, and Proust*. New Haven: Yale University Press.

de Man, Paul. 1983. *Blindness and Insight: Essays in the Rhetoric of Contemporary Criticism*, 2nd edn. London: Methuen.

de Man, Paul. 1984. *The Rhetoric of Romanticism*. New York: Columbia University Press.

De Man, Paul. 1986. *The Resistance to Theory*. Minneapolis: University of Minnesota Press.

Derrick, Scott S. 1997. *Monumental Anxieties: Homoerotic Desire and Feminine Influence in Nineteenth-Century U.S. Literature.* New Brunswick: Rutgers University Press.

Derrida, Jacques. 1976. *Of Grammatology,* trans. Gayatri Chakravorty Spivak. Baltimore: The Johns Hopkins University Press.

Derrida, Jacques. 1978. 'Force and Signification', in *Writing and Difference,* trans. Alan Bass. London: Routledge and Kegan Paul.

Derrida, Jacques. 1979. 'Living On', trans. James Hulbert, in *Deconstruction and Criticism,* eds Harold Bloom *et al.* New York: Seabury Press.

Derrida, Jacques. 1982. 'White Mythology', in *Margins of Philosophy,* trans. Alan Bass. Chicago: University of Chicago Press.

Derrida, Jacques. 1983. 'The Principle of Reason: The University in the Eyes of Its Pupils', trans. Catherine Porter and Edward P. Morris, in *Diacritics,* vol. 13, no. 3: 3–20.

Derrida, Jacques. 1984. 'No Apocalypse, Not Now (full speed ahead, seven missiles, seven missives)', trans. Catherine Porter and Philip Lewis, *Diacritics,* vol. 14, no. 3: 20–31.

Derrida, Jacques. 1985a. 'Des Tours de Babel', trans. Joseph F. Graham, in *Difference in Translation,* ed. Graham. Ithaca: Cornell University Press.

Derrida, Jacques. 1985b. *The Ear of the Other: Otobiography, Transference, Translation. Texts and Discussions with Jacques Derrida,* trans. Peggy Kamuf. New York: Schocken Books.

Derrida, Jacques. 1986a. *Mémoires: for Paul de Man,* trans. Cecile Lindsay, Jonathan Culler and Eduardo Cadava. New York: Columbia University Press.

Derrida, Jacques. 1986b. 'Fors: The Anglish Words of Nicolas Abraham and Maria Torok', trans. Barbara Johnson, in Nicolas Abraham and Maria Torok, *The Wolf Man's Magic Word: A Cryptonymy,* trans. Nicholas Rand. Minneapolis: University of Minnesota Press.

Derrida, Jacques. 1988. 'Afterword: Toward an Ethic of Discussion', trans. Samuel Weber, in *Limited Inc.* Evanston: Northwestern University Press.

Derrida, Jacques. 1989. 'The Ghost Dance: An Interview with Jacques Derrida', trans. Jean-Luc Svobada, in *Public,* no. 2: 60–73.

Derrida, Jacques. 1992a. *Acts of Literature,* ed. Derek Attridge. London: Routledge.

Derrida, Jacques. 1992b. 'Passions: "An Oblique Offering"', trans. David Wood, in *Derrida: A Critical Reader,* ed. David Wood. Oxford: Basil Blackwell.

Derrida, Jacques. 1992c. 'Of an Apocalyptic Tone Newly Adopted in Philosophy', trans. John P. Leavey, Jr, in *Derrida and Negative Theology,* eds Harold Coward and Toby Foshay. Albany, New York: State University of New York Press.

Derrida, Jacques. 1994. *Spectres of Marx: The State of the Debt, the Work of Mourning, and the New International,* trans. Peggy Kamuf. New York: Routledge.

Derrida, Jacques. 1995. *Archive Fever: A Freudian Impression,* trans. Eric Prenowitz. Chicago: Chicago University Press.

Derrida, Jacques. 1998. *Monolingualism of the Other; or, The Prosthesis of Origin,* trans. Patrick Mensah. Stanford: Stanford University Press.

Derrida, Jacques. 2000. *Demeure: Fiction and Testimony*, trans. Elizabeth Rottenberg. Stanford: Stanford University Press.

Derrida, Jacques. 2002a. 'The University Without Condition', in *Without Alibi*, ed., trans., and with an Introduction by Peggy Kamuf. Stanford: Stanford University Press.

Derrida, Jacques. 2002b. *Acts of Religion*, ed. Gil Anidjar. London and New York: Routledge.

Derrida, Jacques and Maurizio Ferraris. 2001. *A Taste for the Secret*, trans. Giacomo Donis. Cambridge: Polity Press.

Derrida, Jacques and Gianni Vattimo, eds. 1998. *Religion*. Cambridge: Polity.

Descartes, René. 1977. *Discourse on Method and the Meditations*, trans. F.E. Sutcliffe. Harmondsworth: Penguin.

de Vries, Hent. 1999. *Philosophy and the Turn to Religion*. Baltimore: Johns Hopkins University Press.

Docherty, Thomas. 1983. *Reading (Absent) Character: Towards a Theory of Characterization in Fiction*. Oxford: Oxford University Press.

Docherty, Thomas, ed. 1993. *Postmodernism: A Reader*, 2nd edn. Hemel Hempstead: Harvester Wheatsheaf.

Dolar, Mladen. 1991. ' "I Shall Be with You on Your Wedding-night": Lacan and the Uncanny', *October*, vol. 58.

Dolar, Mladen. 1996. 'The Object Voice', in *Gaze and Voice as Love Objects*, eds Renata Salecl and Slavoj Žižek. Durham: Duke University Press.

Dollimore, Jonathan. 1989. *Radical Tragedy: Religion, Ideology and Power in the Drama of Shakespeare and his Contemporaries*. Hemel Hempstead: Harvester Wheatsheaf.

Dollimore, Jonathan. 1991. *Sexual Dissidence: Augustine to Wilde, Freud to Foucault*. Oxford: Clarendon Press.

Dollimore, Jonathan. 1998. *Death, Desire and Loss in Western Culture*. London: Penguin.

Dollimore, Jonathan. 2001. *Sex, Literature and Censorship*. Cambridge: Polity.

Dollimore, Jonathan and Alan Sinfield, eds. 1994. *Political Shakespeare: New Essays in Cultural Materialism*, 2nd edn. Manchester: Manchester University Press.

Donaldson, Ian, ed. 1988. *Ben Jonson: A Critical Edition of the Major Works*. Oxford: Oxford University Press.

Drakakis, John, ed. 1992. *Shakespearean Tragedy*. London: Longman.

Drakakis, John and Naomi Liebler, eds. 1998. *Tragedy*. London: Longman.

Drolet, Michael. 2003. *The Postmodernism Reader*. London: Routledge.

During, Simon. 1992. *Foucault and Literature: Towards a Genealogy of Writing*. London: Routledge.

Eagleton, Terry. 1976. *Marxism and Literary Criticism*. London: Routledge.

Eagleton, Terry. 1990. *The Ideology of the Aesthetic*. Oxford: Blackwell.

Eagleton, Terry. 1991. *Ideology: An Introduction*. London: Verso.

Eagleton, Terry, ed. 1994. *Ideology*. London: Longman.

Eagleton, Terry. 1996. *Literary Theory: An Introduction*, 2nd edn. Oxford: Basil Blackwell.

Eagleton, Terry. 2003. *Sweet Violence: The Idea of the Tragic*. Oxford: Blackwell.

Eco, Umberto. 1979. 'The Poetics of the Open Work', in *The Role of the Reader: Explorations in the Semiotics of Texts*. Bloomington: Indiana University Press.

Eco, Umberto. 1992. 'Postmodernism, Irony, the Enjoyable', in *Modernism/Postmodernism*, ed. Peter Brooker. London: Longman.

Eco, Umberto. 1993. 'The City of Robots', in *Postmodernism: A Reader*, ed. Thomas Docherty. Hemel Hempstead: Harvester Wheatsheaf.

Edmundson, Mark. 1990. *Towards Reading Freud: Self-Creation in Milton, Wordsworth, Emerson and Sigmund Freud*. Princeton: Princeton University Press.

Elam, Diane. 1992. *Romancing the Postmodern*. London: Routledge.

Eliot, T.S. 1975b. *Selected Prose of T.S. Eliot*, ed. Frank Kermode. London: Faber and Faber.

Ellmann, Maud, ed. 1994. *Psychoanalytic Literary Criticism*. London: Longman.

Empson, William. 1953. *Seven Types of Ambiguity*, 3rd edn. London: Chatto and Windus.

Empson, William. 1965. *Milton's God*. London: Chatto and Windus.

Esterhammer, Angela. 2000. *The Romantic Performative: Language and Action in British and German Romanticism*. Stanford: Stanford University Press.

Fanon, Frantz. 1967. *The Wretched of the Earth*, trans. Constance Farrington. Harmondsworth: Penguin.

Felman, Shoshana. 1983. *The Literary Speech Act: Don Juan with J.L. Austin, or Seduction in Two Languages*, trans. Catherine Porter. Ithaca: Cornell University Press.

Felman, Shoshana. 1987. *Jacques Lacan and the Adventure of Insight: Psychoanalysis in Contemporary Culture*. Cambridge, Mass.: Harvard University Press.

Felman, Shoshana. 1993. *What Does a Woman Want? Reading and Sexual Difference*. Baltimore: The Johns Hopkins University Press.

Felman, Shoshana and Dori Laub. 1992. *Testimony: Crises of Witnessing in Literature, Psychoanalysis and History*. New York: Routledge.

Felshi, Rita. 2003. *Literature After Feminism*. Chicago: Chicago University Press.

Fetterley, Judith. 1978. *The Resisting Reader: A Feminist Approach to American Fiction*. Bloomington: Indiana University Press.

Fineman, Joel. 1991. *The Subjectivity Effect in Western Literary Tradition: Essays Toward the Release of Shakespeare's Will*. Cambridge, Mass.: MIT Press.

Fink, Bruce. 1996. 'Reading Hamlet with Lacan', in Willy Apollon and Richard Feldstein, eds, *Lacan, Politics, Aesthetics*. Albany, NY: State University of New York Press.

Fish, Stanley. 1980. *Is There A Text in This Class? The Authority of Interpretive Communities*. Cambridge, Mass.: Harvard University Press.

Forrester, John. 1990. *The Seductions of Psychoanalysis: Freud, Lacan and Derrida*. Cambridge: Cambridge University Press.

Forster, E.M. 1976. *Aspects of the Novel*. Harmondsworth: Penguin.

Foster, Jeanette H. 1958. *Sex Variant Women in Literature: A Historical and Quantitative Survey*. London: Frederick Muller.

Foucault, Michel. 1970. *The Order of Things: An Archeology of the Human Sciences*. New York: Random House.

Foucault, Michel. 1979. 'What Is an Author?' in *Textual Strategies: Perspectives in Post-Structuralist Criticism*, ed. Josué V. Harari. London: Methuen.

Foucault, Michel. 1980a. 'The History of Sexuality: Interview', trans. Geoff Bennington, in *Oxford Literary Review*, vol. 4, no. 2: 3–14.

Foucault, Michel. 1980b. Introduction to *Herculine Barbin: Being the Recently Discovered Memoirs of a Nineteenth-Century French Hermaphrodite*, trans. Richard McDougall. New York: Pantheon Books.

Foucault, Michel. 1981. *The History of Sexuality: An Introduction*, trans. Robert Hurley. Harmondsworth: Penguin.

Foucault, Michel. 1983. 'The Subject and Power', in *Michel Foucault: Beyond Structuralism and Hermeneutics*, eds Hubert L. Dreyfus and Paul Rabinow. Chicago: University of Chicago Press.

Foucault, Michel. 1985. *The Use of Pleasure* (*The History of Sexuality*, vol. 2). Harmondsworth: Penguin.

Fowler, Roger. 1986. *Linguistic Criticism*. Oxford: Oxford University Press.

Freud, Sigmund. 1957a. 'The Antithetical Meaning of Primal Words' (1910), in *The Standard Edition of the Complete Psychological Works of Sigmund Freud*, vol. XI, trans. James Strachey. London: Hogarth.

Freud, Sigmund. 1957b. 'Findings, Ideas, Problems', in *The Standard Edition of the Complete Psychological Works of Sigmund Freud*, vol. XXIII, trans. James Strachey. London: Hogarth.

Freud, Sigmund. 1976. *Jokes and their Relation to the Unconscious* (1905), in *Pelican Freud Library*, vol. 6, trans. James Strachey. Harmondsworth: Penguin.

Freud, Sigmund. 1977. *On Sexuality: Three Essays on the Theory of Sexuality* (1905), in *Pelican Freud Library*, vol. 7, trans. James Strachey. Harmondsworth: Penguin.

Freud, Sigmund. 1985a. 'Thoughts for the Times on War and Death' (1915), in *Pelican Freud Library*, vol. 12, trans. James Strachey. Harmondsworth: Penguin.

Freud, Sigmund. 1985b. 'The "Uncanny"' (1919), in *Pelican Freud Library*, vol. 14, trans. James Strachey. Harmondsworth: Penguin.

Freud, Sigmund. 1985c. 'A Seventeenth-Century Demonological Neurosis' (1923), in *Pelican Freud Library*, vol. 14, trans. James Strachey. Harmondsworth: Penguin.

Freud, Sigmund. 1985d. 'Humour' (1927), in *Pelican Freud Library*, vol. 14, trans. James Strachey. Harmondsworth: Penguin.

Freud, Sigmund. 1985e. 'Civilization and Its Discontents' (1930), in *Pelican Freud Library*, vol. 12, trans. James Strachey. Harmondsworth: Penguin.

Freud, Sigmund. 1985f. 'Creative Writers and Day-Dreaming', in *Pelican Freud Library*, vol. 14, trans. James Strachey. Harmondsworth: Penguin.

Freud, Sigmund. 1985g. 'Leonardo da Vinci and a Memory of his Childhood', in *Pelican Freud Library*, vol. 14, trans. James Strachey. Harmondsworth: Penguin.

Freud, Sigmund. 1985h. 'Psychopathic Characters on the Stage', in *Pelican Freud Library*, vol. 14, trans. James Strachey. Harmondsworth: Penguin.

Freud, Sigmund. 1986. 'Psychoanalysis' (1923) and 'The Resistances to Psycho-analysis' (1925), in *Pelican Freud Library*, vol. 15, trans. James Strachey. Harmondsworth: Penguin.

Freud, Sigmund. 2003. *The Uncanny*, trans. David McLintock, with an Introduction by Hugh Haughton. London: Penguin.

Freund, Elizabeth. 1987. *The Return of the Reader: Reader-Response Criticism*. London: Methuen.

Fuss, Diana. 1995. *Identification Papers*. New York: Routledge.

Fuss, Diana, ed. 1996. *Human, All Too Human*. New York: Routledge.

Fussell, Paul. 1975. *The Great War and Modern Memory*. Oxford: Oxford University Press.

Gallagher, Catherine and Stephen Greenblatt. 2000. *Practising New Historicism*. Chicago: University of Chicago Press.

Gates, Henry Louis, Jr, ed. 1984. *Black Literature and Literary Theory*. London: Methuen.

Gates, Henry Louis, Jr, ed. 1986. *'Race', Writing, and Difference*. Chicago: University of Chicago Press.

Gates, Henry Louis, Jr, 1988. *The Signifying Monkey: A Theory of Afro-American Literary Criticism*. Oxford: Oxford University Press.

Gates, Henry Louis, Jr, 1992. *Loose Canons: Notes on the Culture Wars*. New York: Oxford University Press.

Gee, Henry. 1996. 'How Humans Behaved Before they Behaved like Humans'. *London Review of Books* 18: 21 (31 October): 36–8.

Genette, Gérard. 1986. *Narrative Discourse: An Essay in Method*, trans. Jane E. Lewin. Oxford: Basil Blackwell.

Genette, Gérard. 1987. *Seuils*. Paris: Seuil.

Gerstner, David A. and Janet Staiger, eds. 2003. *Authorship and Film*. New York: Routledge.

Gibson, Andrew. 1996. *Towards a Postmodern Theory of Narrative*. Edinburgh: Edinburgh University Press.

Gilbert, Sandra M. and Susan Gubar. 1979. *The Madwoman in the Attic: The Woman Writer and the Nineteenth-Century Literary Imagination*. New Haven: Yale University Press.

Girard, René. 1965. *Deceit, Desire, and the Novel: Self and Other in Literary Structure*, trans. Yvonne Freccero. Baltimore: The Johns Hopkins University Press.

Glover, David and Cora Kaplan. 2000. *Genders*. London: Routledge.

Glut, D.F. 1984. *The Frankenstein Catalogue*. Jefferson N.C.: McFarland.

Goldberg, David Theo. 2002. *The Racial State*. Oxford: Blackwell.

Graham, Elaine L. 2002. *Representations of the Post/Human: Monsters, Aliens and Others in Popular Culture*. Manchester: Manchester University Press.

Gray, Frances. 1994. *Women and Laughter*. London: Macmillan.

Gray, John. 2002. *Straw Dogs: Thoughts on Humans and Other Animals*. London: Granta Books.

Green, André. 1979. *The Tragic Effect: The Oedipus Complex in Tragedy*, trans. Alan Sheridan. Cambridge: Cambridge University Press.

Greenblatt, Stephen. 1988. *Shakespearean Negotiations: The Circulation of Social Energy in Renaissance England*. Oxford: Clarendon Press.

Greenblatt, Stephen. 1990a. 'Toward a Poetics of Culture', in *Learning to Curse: Essays in Early Modern Culture*. London: Routledge.

Greenblatt, Stephen. 1990b. 'Culture', in *Critical Terms for Literary Study*, eds Frank Lentricchia and Thomas McLaughlin. Chicago: University of Chicago Press.

Greenblatt, Stephen. 1991. *Marvelous Possessions: The Wonder of the New World*. Oxford: Clarendon Press.

Griffiths, Eric. 1989. *The Printed Voice of Victorian Poetry*. Oxford: Clarendon Press.

Gubar, Susan. 2003. *Poetry After Auschwitz: Remembering What One Never Knew*. Bloomington: Indiana University Press.

Guillory, John. 1993. *Cultural Capital: The Problem of Literary Canon Formation*. Chicago: Chicago University Press.

Hall, Donald E. 2003. *Queer Theories*. Basingstoke: Palgrave Macmillan.

Halperin, David. 1990. *One Hundred Years of Homosexuality and Other Essays on Greek Love*. New York: Routledge.

Halperin, David. 2002. *How to Do the History of Homosexuality*. Chicago: University of Chicago Press.

Hamilton, Paul. 1996. *Historicism*. London: Routledge.

Harari, Josué V. 1979. 'Critical Factions/Critical Fictions', in *Textual Strategies: Perspectives in Post-Structuralist Criticism*, ed. Josué V. Harari. London: Methuen.

Harraway, Donna. 1985. 'A Cyborg Manifesto: Science, Technology, and Socialist-Feminism in the Late Twentieth Century', reprinted in Badmington, ed., *Posthumanism*.

Harrison, Nicholas. 2003. *Postcolonial Criticism: History, Theory and the Work of Fiction*. Cambridge: Polity Press.

Hartman, Geoffrey H. 1981. 'Words and Wounds', in *Saving the Text: Literature/Derrida/Philosophy*. Baltimore: The Johns Hopkins University Press.

Hartman, Geoffrey. 2002. *Scars of the Spirit: The Struggle Against Inauthenticity*. New York: Palgrave Macmillan.

Hassan, Ihab. 1989. 'Beyond Postmodernism? Theory, Sense, and Pragmatism', in *Making Sense: The Role of the Reader in Contemporary American Fiction*, ed. Gerard Hoffmann. München: Wilhelm Fink.

Hawkes, David. 1996. *Ideology*. London: Routledge.

Hawkes, Terence. 1972. *Metaphor*. London: Methuen.

Hazlitt, William. 1910. 'On Shakespeare and Milton', in *Lectures on the English Poets and The Spirit of the Age*. London: Dent.

Heffernan, James A.W. 1993. *Museum of Words: The Poetics of Ekphrasis from Homer to Ashbery*. Chicago: University of Chicago Press.

Heidegger, Martin. 1967. *What Is A Thing?* trans. W.B. Barton, Jr and Vera Deutsch. Chicago: Henry Regnery.

Heidegger, Martin. 1977. 'The Word of Nietzsche: "God Is Dead" ', in *The Question Concerning Technology and Other Essays*, trans. William Lovitt. New York: Harper Torchbooks.

Hemingway, Ernest. 2000. 'Ernest Hemingway: An Interview', in *The Norton Anthology of Short Fiction*. New York: Norton.

Henderson, Mae Gwendolyn. 1993. 'Speaking in Tongues: Dialogics, Dialectics and the Black Woman Writer's Literary, Tradition', in *Colonial Discourse and Post-Colonial Theory: A Reader*, eds Patrick Williams and Laura Chrisman. Hemel Hempstead: Harvester Wheatsheaf.

Hertz, Neil. 1979. 'Freud and the Sandman', in *Textual Strategies: Perspectives in Post-Structuralist Criticism*, ed. Josué V. Harari. London: Methuen.

Hirst, Paul and Penny Woolley. 1982. *Social Relations and Human Attributes*. London: Tavistock.

Hobbes, Thomas. 1840. *The English Works of Thomas Hobbes*, ed. Sir William Molesworth, vol. IV. London: John Bohn.

Holland, Norman N. 1980. 'Unity Identity Text Self', in *Reader-Response Criticism: From Formalism to Post-Structuralism*, ed. Jane P. Tompkins, Baltimore: The Johns Hopkins University Press.

Hollander, John. 1985. *Vision and Resonance: Two Senses of Poetic Form*, 2nd edn. New Haven: Yale University Press.

Homans, Margaret. 1994. 'Feminist Fictions and Feminist Theories of Narrative', in *Narrative* 2: 3–16.

Hough, Graham. 1967. *The Romantic Poets*, 3rd edn. London: Hutchinson.

Hurley, Kelly. 1996. *The Gothic Body: Sexuality, Materialism, and Degeneration at the Fin de Siecle*. Cambridge: Cambridge University Press.

Hutcheon, Linda. 1988. *A Poetics of Postmodernism: History, Theory, Fiction*. London: Routledge.

Hutcheon, Linda. 1989. *The Politics of Postmodernism*. London: Routledge.

Hynes, Samuel. 1990. *A War Imagined: The First World War and English Culture*. London: Bodley Head.

Irigaray, Luce. 1977. 'Women's Exile', in *Ideology and Consciousness*, no. 1: 62–76.

Irigaray, Luce. 1985. 'This Sex Which Is Not One', in *This Sex Which Is Not One*, trans. Catherine Porter and Carolyn Burke. Ithaca: Cornell University Press.

Iser, Wolfgang. 1995. 'Interaction Between Text and Reader', in *Readers and Reading*, ed. Andrew Bennett. London: Longman.

Irwin, William. 1999. *Intentionalist Interpretation: A Philosophical Explanation and Defense*. Westport, Connecticut: Greenwood Press.

Irwin, William, ed. 2002. *The Death and Resurrection of the Author?* Westport, Connecticut: Greenwood Press.

Jacobus, Mary. 1986. *Reading Woman: Essays in Feminist Criticism*. London: Methuen.

Jakobson, Roman. 1960. 'Closing Statement: Linguistics and Poetics', in *Style in Language*, ed. Thomas A. Sebeok. Cambridge, Mass.: MIT.

James, Henry. 1986. *The Art of Criticism: Henry James on the Theory and Practice of Fiction*, eds William Veeder and Susan M. Griffin. Chicago: University of Chicago Press.

Jameson, Fredric. 1988. 'The Politics of Theory: Ideological Positions in the Postmodernism Debate', in David Lodge, ed., *Modern Literary Theory*. London: Longman.

Jameson, Fredric. 1992. 'Postmodernism and Consumer Society', in *Modernism/Postmodernism*, ed. Peter Brooker. London: Longman.

Jameson, Fredric. 1993. 'Postmodernism, or the Cultural Logic of Late Capitalism', in *Postmodernism: A Reader*, ed. Thomas Docherty. Hemel Hempstead: Harvester Wheatsheaf.

Jay, Martin. 1993. *The Denigration of Vision in Twentieth-Century French Thought*. Berkeley: University of California Press.

Jencks, Charles. 1993. 'The Emergent Rules', in *Postmodernism: A Reader*, ed. Thomas Docherty. Hemel Hempstead: Harvester Wheatsheaf.

Johnson, Samuel. 1969. *Dr Johnson on Shakespeare*, ed. W.K. Wimsatt. Harmondsworth: Penguin.

Jolly, Roslyn. 1993. *Henry James: History, Narrative, Fiction*. Oxford: Clarendon.

Jones, Ernest. 1953–7. *Sigmund Freud: Life and Work*. London: Hogarth.

Judovitz, Dalia. 1988. *Subjectivity and Representation in Descartes: The Origins of Modernity*. Cambridge: Cambridge University Press.

Kant, Immanuel. 1988. *The Critique of Judgement*, trans. James Creed Meredith. Oxford: Clarendon Press.

Kermode, Frank. 1967. *The Sense of an Ending: Studies in the Theory of Fiction*. Oxford: Oxford University Press.

Kermode, Frank. 1975. *The Classic*. London: Faber and Faber.

Kermode, Frank. 1979. *The Genesis of Secrecy: On the Interpretation of Narrative*. Cambridge, Mass.: Harvard University Press.

Kermode, Frank. 1983. 'Secrets and Narrative Sequence', in *Essays on Fiction 1971–82*. London: Routledge and Kegan Paul.

Kittler, Friedrich. 1997. 'Romanticism – Psychoanalysis – Film: A History of the Double', in *Literature, Media, Information Systems*, ed. John Johnston. Amsterdam: G + B Arts International.

Knight, Stephen. 1980. *Form and Ideology in Detective Fiction*. London: Macmillan.

Knopp, Sherron E. 1992. ' "If I saw you would you kiss me?": Sapphism and the Subversiveness of Virginia Woolf's *Orlando*', in *Sexual Sameness: Textual*

Differences in Lesbian and Gay Writing, ed. Joseph Bristow. London: Routledge.

Koestler, Arthur. 1964. *The Act of Creation*. London: Hutchinson.

Kramnick, Jonathan Brody. 1998. *Making the English Canon: Print-capitalism and the Cultural Past, 1700–1770*. Cambridge: Cambridge University Press.

Krieger, Murray. 1992. *Ekphrasis: The Illusion of the Natural Sign*. Baltimore: The Johns Hopkins University Press.

Kristeva, Julia. 1986. 'Word, Dialogue and Novel', in *The Kristeva Reader*, ed. Toril Moi. Oxford: Basil Blackwell.

Kristeva, Julia. 1991. *Strangers to Ourselves*, trans. Leon C. Roudiez. Hemel Hempstead: Harvester Wheatsheaf.

Lacan, Jacques. 1977a. *Écrits: A Selection*, trans. Alan Sheridan. London: Tavistock.

Lacan, Jacques. 1977b. 'Desire and the Interpretation of Desire in *Hamlet*', trans. James Hulbert, *Yale French Studies*, no. 55/56. *Literature and Psychoanalysis. The Question of Reading: Otherwise*, ed. Shoshana Felman.

Lakoff, George and Mark Johnson. 1980. *Metaphors We Live By*. Chicago: University of Chicago Press.

Lane, Christopher. 1995. *The Ruling Passion: British Colonial Allegory and the Paradox of Homosexual Desire*. Durham: Duke University Press.

Leavis, F.R. 1948. *The Great Tradition*. London: Chatto and Windus.

Leavis, F.R. 1972. *Revaluation: Tradition and Development in English Poetry*. Harmondsworth: Penguin.

Leavis, F.R. and Denys Thompson. 1964. *Culture and Environment: The Training of Critical Awareness*. London: Chatto and Windus.

Lecercle, Jean-Jacques. 1990. *The Violence of Language*. London: Routledge.

Lentricchia, Frank and Andrew DuBois. 2003. *Close Reading: The Reader*. Durham NC: Duke University Press.

Levi, Primo. 1987. *If This Is A Man* and *The Truce*, trans. Stuart Woolf. London: Abacus.

Levi, Primo. 1989. *The Drowned and the Saved*, trans. Raymond Rosenthal. New York: Vintage.

Loomba, Ania. 1998. *Colonialism/Postcolonialism*. London: Routledge.

Lyotard, Jean-François. 1984. *The Postmodern Condition: A Report on Knowledge*, trans. Geoff Bennington and Brian Massumi. Manchester: Manchester University Press.

Lyotard, Jean-François. 1992. 'Answering the Question: What is Postmodernism?' in *Modernism/Postmodernism*, ed. Peter Brooker. London: Longman.

Lyotard, Jean-François. 1997. *Postmodern Fables*, trans. Georges van den Abbeele. Minneapolis: University of Minnesota Press.

MacCabe, Colin. 2003. 'On Impurity: the Dialectics of Cinema and Literature', in *Literature and Visual Technologies: Writing After Cinema*, ed. Julian Murphet and Lydia Rainford. Basingstoke: Palgrave Macmillan.

Macherey, Pierre. 1978. *A Theory of Literary Production*, trans. Geoffrey Wall. London: Routledge and Kegan Paul.

Machor, James L., ed. 1993. *Readers in History: Nineteenth-Century American Literature and the Contexts of Response*. Baltimore: The Johns Hopkins University Press.

Mahony, Patrick J. 1987. *Freud as a Writer*. Expanded Edition. New Haven: Yale University Press.

Mahood, M.M. 1957. *Shakespeare's Wordplay*. London: Methuen.

Manguel, Alberto. 1997. *A History of Reading*. London: HarperCollins.

Mansfield, Katherine. 1930. *Novels and Novelists*, ed. Middleton Murry. London: Constable.

Marriott, David. 2000. *On Black Men*. Edinburgh: University of Edinburgh Press.

Martin, Wallace. 1986. *Recent Theories of Narrative*. Ithaca: Cornell University Press.

Marx, Karl. 1976. *The German Ideology*, in Karl Marx and Frederick Engels, *Collected Works*, vol. 5. London: Lawrence and Wishart.

McGann, Jerome J. 1985. *The Beauty of Inflections: Literary Investigations in Historical Method and Theory*. Oxford: Clarendon.

McQuillan, Martin, ed. 2000. *The Narrative Reader*. London: Routledge.

Melville, Stephen. 1986. *Philosophy Beside Itself: On Deconstruction and Modernism*. Minneapolis: University of Minnesota Press.

Melville, Stephen and Bill Readings, eds. 1995. *Vision and Textuality*. Basingstoke: Macmillan.

Meltzer, Françoise. 1994. *Hot Property: The Stakes and Claims of Literary Originality*. Chicago: University of Chicago Press.

Miller, D.A. 1981. *Narrative and its Discontents: Problems of Closure in the Traditional Novel*. New Jersey: Princeton University Press.

Miller, D.A. 1989. ' "Cage aux folles": Sensation and Gender in Wilkie Collins's *The Woman in White*', in *Speaking of Gender*, ed. E. Showalter. London: Routledge.

Miller, J. Hillis. 1963. *The Disappearance of God: Five Nineteenth-Century Writers*. Cambridge, Mass.: Belknap Press.

Miller, J. Hillis. 1980. 'The Figure in the Carpet', in *Poetics Today* 1, 3: 107–18.

Miller, J. Hillis. 1982. '*Wuthering Heights*: Repetition and the "Uncanny" ', in *Fiction and Repetition: Seven English Novels*. Oxford: Basil Blackwell.

Miller, J. Hillis. 1987. *The Ethics of Reading: Kant, de Man, Eliot, Trollope, James, and Benjamin*. New York: Columbia University Press.

Miller, J. Hillis. 1990. 'Narrative', in *Critical Term for Literary Study*, eds Frank Lentricchia and Thomas McLaughlin. Chicago: University of Chicago Press.

Miller, J. Hillis. 1991. 'Thomas Hardy, Jacques Derrida, and the "Dislocation of Souls" ', in *Tropes, Parables, Performatives: Essays in Twentieth-Century Literature*. Hemel Hempstead: Harvester Wheatsheaf.

Miller, J. Hillis. 1992. *Ariadne's Thread: Story Lines*. New Haven: Yale University Press.

Miller, J. Hillis. 1994. 'Derrida's Topographies', in *South Atlantic Review*, 59, 1: 1–25.

Miller, J. Hillis. 2000. 'Deconstruction and a Poem', in *Deconstructions: A User's Guide*, ed. Nicholas Royle. Basingstoke: Palgrave.

Miller, J. Hillis. 2001. *Speech Acts in Literature*. Stanford: Stanford University Press.

Millett, Kate. 1969. *Sexual Politics*. London: Rupert Hart-Davis.

Mills, Sara, ed. 1994. *Gendering the Reader*. Hemel Hempstead: Harvester Wheatsheaf.

Mitchell, W.J.T. 1986. *Iconology: Image, Text, Ideology*. Chicago: University of Chicago Press.

Mitchell, W.J.T. 1994. *Picture Theory: Essays on Verbal and Visual Representation*. Chicago: University of Chicago Press.

Moi, Toril. 1985. *Sexual/Textual Politics: Feminist Literary Theory*. London: Routledge.

Montag, Warren. 2003. *Louis Althusser*. Basingstoke: Palgrave Macmillan.

Morrison, Toni. 1993. *Playing in the Dark: Whiteness and the Literary Imagination*. London: Picador.

Mulhern, Francis, ed. 1992. *Contemporary Marxist Literary Criticism*. London: Longman.

Münsterberg, Hugo. 1916. *The Photoplay: A Psychological Study*. New York: Appleton.

Munt, Sally, ed. 1992. *New Lesbian Criticism: Literary and Cultural Readings*. Hemel Hempstead: Harvester Wheatsheaf.

Murphet, Julian and Lydia Rainford. 2003. 'Introduction', *Literature and Visual Technologies: Writing After Cinema*, eds. Murphet and Rainford. Basingstoke: Palgrave Macmillan.

Nancy, Jean-Luc. 1987. 'Wild Laughter in the Throat of Death', in *Modern Language Notes*, vol. 102, no. 4: 719–36.

Nancy, Jean-Luc. 1993. 'Laughter, Presence', in *The Birth to Presence*, trans. Brian Holmes *et al*. Stanford: Stanford University Press.

Nero, Brian. 2003. *Race*. Basingstoke: Palgrave Macmillan.

Nicholls, Peter. 1996. 'The Belated Postmodern: History, Phantoms and Toni Morrison', in Sue Vice, ed., *Psychoanalytic Criticism: A Reader*. Oxford: Polity.

Nietzsche, Friedrich. 1968. *The Will to Power*, trans. Walter Kaufmann and R.J. Hollingdale. New York: Vintage.

Nietzsche, Friedrich. 1980. 'On Truth and Lie in an Extra-Moral Sense', in *The Portable Nietzsche*, ed. Walter Kaufmann. New York: Random.

Nietzsche, Friedrich. 1989. *Beyond Good and Evil: Prelude to a Philosophy of the Future*, trans. Walter Kaufmann. New York: Vintage.

Nietzsche, Friedrich. 2003. *Twilight of the Idols* and *The Anti-Christ*, trans. R.J. Hollingdale. London: Penguin.

Nuttall, A.D. 1992. *Openings: Narrative Beginnings from the Epic to the Novel*. Oxford: Clarendon Press.

Nuttall, A.D. 1996. *Why Does Tragedy Give Pleasure?* Oxford: Oxford University Press.

Orr, Mary. 2003. *Intertextuality: Debates and Contexts*. Oxford: Polity.

Partridge, Eric. 2001. *Shakespeare's Bawdy*. London and New York: Routledge.

Pask, Kevin. 1996. *The Emergence of the English Author: Scripting the Life in Early Modern England*. Cambridge: Cambridge University Press.

Patterson, Annabel. 1990. 'Intention', in *Critical Terms for Literary Study*, eds Frank Lentricchia and Thomas McLaughlin. Chicago: Chicago University Press.

Phelan, James, ed. 1989. *Reading Narrative: Form, Ethics, Ideology*. Columbus: Ohio State University Press.

Pinker, Steven. 1995. *The Language Instinct: The New Science of Language and Mind*. London: Penguin.

Pittock, Malcolm. 2001. 'The War Poetry of Wilfred Owen: A Dissenting Reappraisal', in *The Literature of the Great War Reconsidered: Beyond Modern Memory* ed. Patrick J. Quinn and Steven Trout. Basingstoke: Palgrave.

Plato. 1961. *The Collected Dialogues of Plato, Including the Letters*, eds Edith Hamilton and Huntington Cairns. New Jersey: Princeton University Press.

Price, Martin. 1983. *Forms of Life: Character and Moral Imagination in the Novel*. New Haven: Yale University Press.

Procter, James, ed. 2000. *Writing Black Britain 1948–1998: An Interdisciplinary Anthology*. Manchester: Manchester University Press.

Procter, James. 2003. *Dwelling Places: Postwar Black British Writing*. Manchester: Manchester University Press.

Punter, David. 1996. *The Literature of Terror*, 2nd edn, 2 vols. London: Longman.

Punter, David and Glennis Byron. 2003. *The Gothic*. Oxford: Blackwell.

Quinn, Arthur. 1993. *Figures of Speech: 60 ways to turn a phrase*. California: Hermagoras Press.

Rabaté, Jean-Michel. 1996. *The Ghosts of Modernity*. Gainesville: Florida University Press.

Rabaté, Jean-Michel. 2001. *Jacques Lacan*. Basingstoke: Palgrave Macmillan.

Rashkin, Esther. 1992. *Family Secrets and the Psychoanalysis of Narrative*. Princeton, NJ: Princeton University Press.

Raven, James, Helen Small and Naomi Tadmor, eds. 1995. *The Practice and Representation of Reading in England*. Cambridge: Cambridge University Press.

Readings, Bill and Bennet Schaber, eds. 1993. *Postmodernism Across the Ages*. Syracuse, New York: Syracuse University Press.

Regan, Stephen, ed. 1992. *The Politics of Pleasure: Aesthetics and Cultural Theory*. Buckingham: Open University Press.

Rich, Adrienne. 1986. 'Compulsory Heterosexuality and Lesbian Existence', in *Blood, Bread, and Poetry: Selected Prose, 1979–1985*. London: Virago.

Ricks, Christopher. 1984. 'William Wordsworth 1: "A pure organic pleasure from the lines"', in *The Force of Poetry*. Oxford: Clarendon Press.

Ricks, Christopher. 2002. *Allusion to the Poets*. Oxford: Oxford University Press.

Ricoeur, Paul. 1978. *The Rule of Metaphor: Multi-Disciplinary Studies of the Creation of Meaning in Language*, trans. Robert Czerny. London: Routledge and Kegan Paul.

Ridley, Matt. 1994. *The Red Queen: Sex and the Evolution of Human Nature.* London: Penguin.

Riley, Denise. 1988. *'Am I That Name?': Feminism and the Category of 'Women' in History.* Basingstoke: Macmillan.

Rimmon-Kenan, Shlomith. 2002. *Narrative Fiction*, 2nd edn. London and New York: Routledge.

Rogin, Michael. 1994. 'Sucking Up'. *London Review of Books*, 16, 9 (12 May): 26.

Ronell, Avital. 1989. *The Telephone Book: Technology, Schizophrenia, Electric Speech.* Lincoln: Nebraska University Press.

Rorty, Amélie Oksenberg, ed. 2001. *The Many Faces of Evil: Historical Perspectives.* London and New York: Routledge.

Rose Jacqueline. 1993. *Why War?* Oxford: Blackwell.

Rose, Jacqueline. 1996. *States of Fantasy.* Oxford: Clarendon Press.

Rose, Mark. 1993. *Authors and Owners: The Invention of Copyright.* Cambridge, Mass.: Harvard University Press.

Ross, Thomas W. 1972. *Chaucer's Bawdy.* New York: Dutton.

Ross, Trevor. 1998. *The Making of the English Literary Canon: From the Middle Ages to the Late Eighteenth Century.* Montreal: McGill-Queens University Press.

Royle, Nicholas. 1991. *Telepathy and Literature: Essays on the Reading Mind.* Oxford: Basil Blackwell.

Royle, Nicholas. 2003. *The Uncanny.* Manchester and New York: Manchester University Press/Routledge.

Rushdie, Salman. 1990. *Is Nothing Sacred?* Cambridge: Granta.

Russell, Bertrand. 1968. *The Autobiography of Bertrand Russell*, 3 vols. London: George Allen and Unwin.

Ryan, Kiernan, ed. 1996. *New Historicism and Cultural Materialism: A Reader.* London: Arnold.

Sacks, Oliver. 1991. *Seeing Voices: A Journey into the World of the Deaf.* London: Picador.

Said, Edward W. 1975. *Beginnings: Intention and Method.* New York: Basic Books.

Said, Edward W. 1978. *Orientalism.* London: Routledge and Kegan Paul.

Said, Edward W. 1983. *The World, the Text, and the Critic.* London: Faber and Faber.

Said, Edward W. 1993. *Culture and Imperialism.* London: Chatto and Windus.

Saussure, Ferdinand de. 1974. *Course in General Linguistics*, ed. Charles Bally and Albert Sechehayne, trans. Wade Baskin, with an introduction by Jonathan Culler. London: Fontana.

Schwartz, Daniel R. 1999. *Imagining the Holocaust.* Basingstoke: Macmillan.

Schwartz, Hillel. 1996. *The Culture of the Copy: Striking Likenesses, Unreasonable Facsimiles.* New York: Zone Books.

Sedgwick, Eve Kosofsky. 1985. *Between Men: English Literature and Male Homosocial Desire*. New York: Columbia University Press.

Sedgwick, Eve Kosofsky. 1991. *Epistemology of the Closet*. Hemel Hempstead: Harvester Wheatsheaf.

Sedgwick, Eve Kosofsky. 1994. *Tendencies*. London: Routledge.

Sedgwick, Eve Kosofsky. 2003. *Touching Feeling: Affect, Pedagogy, Performativity*. Durham: Duke University Press.

Shklovsky, Viktor. 1965. 'Art as Technique', in *Russian Formalist Criticism: Four Essays*, eds Lee T. Lemon and Marion J. Reis. Lincoln: University of Nebraska Press.

Showalter, Elaine. 1977. *A Literature of Their Own: British Women Novelists from Brontë to Lessing*. New Jersey: Princeton University Press.

Showalter, Elaine, ed. 1989. *Speaking of Gender*. London: Routledge.

Showalter, Elaine. 1991. *Sexual Anarchy: Gender and Culture at the Fin de Siècle*. London: Virago.

Showalter, Elaine. 1993. 'On Hysterical Narrative', in *Narrative*, 1, 1: 24–35.

Sinfield, Alan. 1994. *Cultural Politics – Queer Reading*. London: Routledge.

Sinfield, Alan. 1994. *The Wilde Century: Effeminacy, Oscar Wilde and the Queer Moment*. London. Cassell.

Smith, Adam. 1986. *The Wealth of Nations*, Books I–III, ed. Andrew Skinner. Harmondsworth: Penguin.

Smith, Angela, ed. and introd. 1997. *Wide Sargasso Sea*. Harmondsworth: Penguin.

Smith, Barbara Herrnstein. 1968. *Poetic Closure: A Study of How Poems End*. Chicago: University of Chicago Press.

Smith, Barbara Herrnstein. 1981. 'Narrative Versions, Narrative Theories', in *On Narrative*, ed. W.J.T. Mitchell. Chicago: University of Chicago Press.

Smith, Barbara Herrnstein. 1988. *Contingencies of Value: Alternative Perspectives for Critical Theory*. Cambridge, Mass.: Harvard University Press.

Smith, Bruce R. 1994. *Homosexual Desire in Shakespeare's England: A Cultural Poetics*. Chicago: University of Chicago Press.

Smith, Grahame. 2003. *Dickens and the Dream of Cinema*. Manchester: Manchester University Press.

Spargo, Tamsin, ed. 2000. *Reading the Past: Literature and History*. Basingstoke: Palgrave.

Spivak, Gayatri Chakravorty. 1987. *In Other Worlds: Essays in Cultural Politics*. London: Routledge.

Steiner, George. 1961. *The Death of Tragedy*. London: Faber.

Stevens, Wallace. 1951. *The Necessary Angel: Essays on Reality and the Imagination*. New York: Alfred A. Knopf.

Stewart, Garrett. 1984. *Death Sentences: Styles of Dying in British Fiction*. Cambridge, Mass.: Harvard University Press.

Stewart, Garrett. 1990. *Reading Voices: Literature and the Phonotext*. Berkeley: University of California Press.

Still, Judith and Michael Worton, eds. 1990. *Intertextuality: Theories and Practices*. Manchester: Manchester University Press.

Suleiman, Susan R. and Inge Crosman, eds. 1980. *The Reader in the Text: Essays on Audience and Interpretation*. New Jersey: Princeton University Press.

Sword, Helen. 2001. *Ghostwriting Modernism*. Ithaca: Cornell University Press.

Sypher, Wylie, ed. 1956. *Comedy*. New York: Doubleday.

Tatum, James. 2003. *The Mourner's Song: War and Remembrance from the Iliad to Vietnam*. Chicago: University of Chicago Press.

Taylor, Charles. 1989. *Sources of the Self: The Making of Modern Identity*. Cambridge: Cambridge University Press.

Thieme, John. 2001. *Postcolonial Con-texts: Writing Back to the Canon*. London: Continuum.

Thomas, Keith. 1971. *Religion and the Decline of Magic: Studies in Popular Beliefs in Sixteenth and Seventeenth Century England*. London: Weidenfield and Nicolson.

Todd, Jane Marie. 1986. 'The Veiled Woman in Freud's *Das Unheimliche*', in *Signs* 2/3: 519–28.

Todd, Janet. 1988. *Feminist Literary History: A Defence*. Cambridge: Polity Press.

Todorov, Tzvetan. 1981. *Introduction to Poetics*, trans. Richard Howard, Minneapolis: University of Minnesota Press.

Todorov, Tzvetan. 1993. *On Human Diversity*. Cambridge, Mass.: Harvard University Press.

Touval, Yonatan. 1997. 'Colonial Queer Something', in *Queer Forster*, eds Robert K. Martin and George Piggford. Chicago: University of Chicago Press.

Veeser, H. Aram, ed. 1989. *The New Historicism*. New York: Routledge.

Veeser, H. Aram, ed. 1994. *The New Historicism Reader*. New York: Routledge.

Veyne, Paul. 1988. *Did the Greeks Believe in their Myths? An Essay on the Constitutive Imagination*, trans. Paula Wissing. Chicago: University of Chicago Press.

Vickers, Brian, ed. 1981. *Shakespeare: The Critical Heritage, Volume 6, 1774–1801*. London: Routledge and Kegan Paul.

Walder, Dennis. 1998. *Post-Colonial Literatures in English: History, Language, Theory*. Oxford: Blackwell.

Waller, Marguerite. 1987. 'Academic Tootsie: The Denial of Difference and the Difference It Makes', in *Diacritics*, vol. 17, no. 1: 2–20.

Ward, Graham. 1996. *Theology and Contemporary Critical Theory*. London: Macmillan.

Warhol, Robyn R. and Diane Price Herndl, eds. 1997. *Feminisms: An Anthology of Literary Theory and Criticism*, revised edn. London: Macmillan.

Weber, Samuel. 1973. 'The Sideshow, or: Remarks on a Canny Moment', in *Modern Language Notes*, 88: 1102–33.

Weber, Samuel. 1987. 'Laughing in the Meanwhile', in *Modern Language Notes*, vol. 102, no. 4: 691–706.

Weber, Samuel. 1992. *The Return to Freud: Jacques Lacan and the Dislocations of Psychoanalysis*. Cambridge: Cambridge University Press.

Weber, Samuel. 2000. 'Uncanny Thinking', in *The Legend of Freud*, Expanded Edition. Stanford: Stanford University Press.

Weeks, Jeffrey. 1998. 'Introduction to Guy Hocquengham's *Homosexual Desire*', in *Literary Theory: An Anthology*, eds Julie Rivkin and Michael Ryan. Oxford: Blackwell.

Wellek, René. 1963. 'Literary Theory, Criticism, and History', in *Concepts of Criticism*. New Haven: Yale University Press.

Wesling, Donald and Tadeusz Slawek. 1995. *Literary Voice: The Calling of Jonah*. Albany, NY: State University of New York Press.

Wexman, Virginia Wright, ed. 2003. *Film and Authorship*. New Brunswick: Rutgers University Press.

White, Hayden. 1978. *Tropics of Discourse: Essays in Cultural Criticism*. Baltimore: The Johns Hopkins University Press.

White, Susan. 1991. 'Allegory and Referentiality: *Vertigo* and Feminist Criticism', *Modern Language Notes*, vol. 106.

Whiteside, Anna and Michael Issacharoff, eds. 1987. *On Referring in Literature*. Bloomington: Indiana University Press.

Williams, Linda Ruth. 1995. *Critical Desire: Psychoanalysis and the Literary Subject*. London: Edward Arnold.

Williams, Patrick and Laura Chrisman, eds. 1993. *Colonial Discourse and Post-Colonial Theory: A Reader*. Hemel Hempstead: Harvester Wheatsheaf.

Williams, Raymond. 1969. *Modern Tragedy*. London: Chatto and Windus.

Williams, Raymond. 1976. *Keywords: A Vocabulary of Culture and Society*. London: Fontana.

Williams, Raymond. 1992. *The Long Revolution*. London: Hogarth.

Wilson, Richard and Richard Dutton, eds. 1992. *New Historicism and Renaissance Drama*. London: Longman.

Wimsatt Jr, W.K. and Monroe C. Beardsley. 1995. 'The Intentional Fallacy', in *Authorship From Plato to the Postmodern: A Reader*, ed. Seán Burke. Edinburgh: Edinburgh University Press.

Winters, Yvor. 1957. 'The Audible Reading of Poetry', in *The Function of Criticism: Problems and Exercises*, 2nd edn. Denver: Alan Swallow.

Wittgenstein, Ludwig. 1984. *Philosophical Investigations*. Oxford: Blackwell.

Wolfreys, Julian. 2002. *Victorian Hauntings: Spectrality, Gothic, the Uncanny and Literature*. Basingstoke: Palgrave.

Wood, Marcus. 2002. *Slavery, Empathy and Pornography*. Oxford: Oxford University Press.

Wood, Sarah, ed. 1995. *Home and Family*. Special issue of *Angelaki*, 2: 1.

Woolf, Virginia. 1942. *The Death of the Moth and Other Essays*. London: Hogarth Press.

Woolf, Virginia. 1988. 'Henry James's Ghost Stories', in *The Essays of Virginia Woolf*, vol. 3, 1919–1924, ed. Andrew McNeillie. New York: Harcourt Brace Jovanovich.

Wright, Elizabeth. 1998. *Psychoanalytic Criticism: A Reappraisal*, 2nd edn. Cambridge: Polity.

Young, Robert. 1981. 'Introduction', in *Untying the Text: A Post-Structuralist Reader*, ed. Robert Young. London: Routledge and Kegan Paul.

Young, Robert. 1990. *White Mythologies: Writing History and the West*. London: Routledge.

Young, Robert. 1991a. 'Poems That Read Themselves', *Tropismes* 5: 233–61.

Young, Robert, ed. 1991b. *Neocolonialism*. Special issue of *Oxford Literary Review*, 13.

Young, Robert. 1995. *Colonial Desire: Hybridity in Theory, Culture and Race*. London: Routledge.

Young, Robert. 1996. *Torn Halves: Political Conflict in Literary and Cultural Theory*. Manchester: Manchester University Press.

Young, Robert. 1999. 'Freud's Secret: *The Interpretation of Dreams* was a gothic novel', in *Sigmund Freud's The Interpretation of Dreams: New interdisciplinary essays*, ed. Laura Marcus. Manchester: Manchester University Press.

Young, Robert. 2000. *Postcolonialism: A History*. Oxford: Blackwell.

Zipes, Jack. 1988. *Fairy Tales and the Art of Subversion: The Classical Genre for Children and the Process of Civilization*. London: Methuen.

Žižek, Slavoj. 1991a. *Looking Awry: An Introduction to Jacques Lacan through Popular Culture*. Cambridge, Mass: MIT Press.

Žižek, Slavoj. 1991b. *For They Know Not What They Do: Enjoyment as a Political Factor*. London: Verso.

Index